THOMSON

WADSWORTH

Publisher: *Clark Baxter*
Executive Editor: *David Tatom*
Development Editor: *Drake Bush*
Assistant Editor: *Rebecca Green*
Editorial Assistant: *Reena Thomas*
Technology Project Manager: *Michelle Vardeman*
Marketing Manager: *Janise Fry*
Marketing Assistant: *Tara Pierson*
Advertising Project Manager: *Stacey Purviance*
Project Manager, Editorial Production: *Trudy Brown*

Art Director: *Maria Epes*
Print/Media Buyer: *Doreen Suruki*
Permissions Editor: *Kiely Sexton*
Production Service: *Mary Deeg, Buuji, Inc.*
Photo Researcher: *Sue C. Howard*
Copy Editor: *Linda Ireland, Buuji, Inc.*
Cover Designer: *Brian Salisbury*
Cover Image: *Brian Salisbury*
Compositor: *Buuji, Inc.*
Text and Cover Printer: *Quebecor World/ Kingsport*

Printed in the United States of America
1 2 3 4 5 6 7 08 07 06 05 04

For more information about our products, contact us at:
Thomson Learning Academic Resource Center
1-800-423-0563

For permission to use material from this text, or product, submit a request online at
http://www.thomsonrights.com
Any additional questions about permissions can be submitted by email to
thomsonrights@thomson.com.

Library of Congress Control Number:
2004104730

ISBN 0-534-55343-5

Thomson Wadsworth
10 Davis Drive
Belmont, CA 94002-3098
USA

Asia
Thomson Learning
5 Shenton Way #01-01
UIC Building
Singapore 068808

Australia/New Zealand
Thomson Learning
102 Dodds Street
Southbank, Victoria 3006
Australia

Canada
Nelson
1120 Birchmount Road
Toronto, Ontario M1K 5G4
Canada

Europe/Middle East/Africa
Thomson Learning
High Holborn House
50/51 Bedford Row
London WC1R 4LR
United Kingdom

Latin America
Thomson Learning
Seneca, 53
Colonia Polanco
11560 Mexico D.F.
Mexico

Spain/Portugal
Paraninfo
Calle Magallanes, 25
28015 Madrid, Spain

D1514973

Public Administration in the New Century

A Concise Introduction

JEFFREY D. GREENE
University of Montana

THOMSON

WADSWORTH

Australia • Canada • Mexico • Singapore • Spain
United Kingdom • United States

To my Mother and Father

*Like my previous publishing endeavors,
without their support, encouragement, and insistence,
this book might not have been written.*

Contents

Preface

Public Administration in the New Century: A Concise Introduction stems from years of teaching public administration and public policy. The original purpose was to fulfill the need for a concise, introductory textbook for master's of public administration (MPA) students who lack background in public administration and political science. Students in MPA programs come from many diverse backgrounds and disciplines. Although many MPA programs are housed in political science departments, students often have little background in public policy analysis, public budgeting, or general political concepts. Over the years students have asked for a short book that includes the essentials of public administration. Although many excellent textbooks exist, most are large, comprehensive books. Thus, the goal was to write a simple, fairly concise, and readable book that covers the basics of public administration.

This book is written at a level that is appropriate for both undergraduate and graduate students. Public administration is a broad, interdisciplinary field of study, and large, comprehensive books tend to cover the material impressively. The great difficulty in writing Public Administration in the New Century: A Concise Introduction was to determine what to include and exclude, which was not a simple task considering the breadth and scope of public administration as a practical field and as an academic discipline.

The book contains nine chapters. Many subjects that often receive an entire chapter in a full-length, comprehensive text are merged into appropriate chapters. Chapter 1 provides an introduction that poses the initial question found in most public administration textbooks: What is public administration? This chapter provides an overview of the numerous factors that affect public management, including the context or environment in which public administration functions and some basics about the American political system. Chapter 2 looks at the development of public administration as a discipline in the United States and contains short biographies of some major contributors to the discipline. Chapter 3 is dedicated to the concept of bureaucracy. Chapter 4 examines the fundamental concepts of organizational theory and management. Chapter 5 covers the basics of personnel administration, including the impact of unions and organized labor in the public sector. Chapter 6 examines public budgeting and finance. It includes a history of budgeting in the United States and discussion of the politics of public budgeting. Chapter 7 focuses on public policy, including policy analysis. Chapter 8 examines a variety of issues relating to government performance, including measuring public sector productivity, privatization, and the reinventing government movement. The last chapter examines ethics and public administration.

Another goal in writing this text was to provide a "realistic" presentation of public administration. Throughout the book comparisons are made between public and private management. The purpose of this comparison stems from a commonly held myth about the superiority of the private sector. Public management is often compared to private business, which is both useful and necessary. However, a myth exists in our society that good managers and employees tend to find jobs in the private sector, leaving less qualified individuals to manage public agencies. Although this is a myth, public administration is not without its problems, many of which are addressed in this book.

The book contains two recurring themes: (1) the comparison of public to private management, and (2) how politics constrains managing in the public sector. It was written during turbulent times in the United States. The aftermath of terrorist attacks, a new series of corporate scandals, and a stagnant economy raised many issues about the role of government and public administration in society. These concerns are reflected in this book.

The world of public management is an exciting field that employs more than 19 million people in the United States. Public administration affects all our lives by providing critical services that range from fire protection to national defense. Government and its agencies tackle many problems and help shape the future, hopefully providing better communities and a better society. I hope that you enjoy reading *Public Administration in the New Century: A Concise Introduction*.

ACKNOWLEDGMENTS

Before we begin our journey into the world of public administration, a number of people deserve credit for their assistance with *Public Administration in the New Century: A Concise Introduction*. Writing a book is a difficult endeavor, and along the way one becomes indebted to those who help. Special thanks should be extended to Clark Baxter of Thomson Wadsworth, who originally approved the project; to David Tatom, the political science editor at Wadsworth; and to Heather Hogan, the developmental director at Wadsworth. A very special thanks is extended to Drake Bush who served as the editor of the book. Everyone at Wadsworth assisted in every way possible, at every stage of production, to make *Public Administration in the New Century: A Concise Introduction* a better book. It was a pleasure to work with David Tatom, Drake Bush, and the production staff at Wadsworth on this project. I am very grateful for their support throughout the process. I also thank Mary Deeg at Buuji, Inc. for her expertise and guidance through the production process.

In addition, I would like to thank the following reviewers: Brian Cherry, Northern Michigan University, and Douglas Ihrke, University of Wisconsin–Milwaukee.

I also thank John Sheagren, a graduate student in the MPA program at the University of Montana at the time, who read the early drafts of the manuscript. His input was vital in helping to create a concise, readable book. Finally, I would like to thank the MPA students at the University of Montana who encouraged me to write this book.

Jeffrey D. Greene

1

Understanding Public Administration

The Accomplishing Side of Government

> The true test of good government is its aptitude
> and tendency to produce good administration.
>
> ALEXANDER HAMILTON

The tragic events of September 11, 2001, made American public administration very visible and illustrated the importance of government. Early
on that Tuesday morning, several teams of Arab terrorists hijacked four
large commercial jetliners and crashed three of the planes into landmark buildings. Two of the jetliners hit the World Trade Center in New York City and one
crashed into the Pentagon. The fourth plane never reached its intended target
and crashed in a rural area of Pennsylvania. September 11, 2001, marked the
worst terrorist act ever committed on American soil and Americans were
shocked and angry. The agencies of government immediately came to the forefront from all levels of government. New York City emergency crews (firefighters, police officers, and other emergency service workers) arrived at the
crumbling Twin Towers—the icon for capitalism for the western world. Many
public workers died trying to save people attempting to escape the collapse of
the towers, adding to the more than 3,000 who died on that morning. Federal,
state, and local agencies of government coordinated their efforts to handle the
disaster. President George W. Bush declared a war on terrorism, and within a

few months the Taliban government in Afghanistan that harbored many of the terrorists believed to be responsible for the attack had fallen.

Americans expected their government to act, and it did. The agencies of government, such as the Federal Emergency Management Agency (FEMA), the Federal Bureau of Investigation (FBI), the National Guard, the Department of Defense (DOD), the Department of Transportation (DOT), and the agencies of New York City rose to the occasion and managed the aftermath of the events of September 11. For the first time in history, surveillance aircraft manned with multinational crews from NATO (the North Atlantic Treaty Organization created to defend Europe in the Cold War) were used to patrol American airspace. American fighter jets patrolled airspace over New York and Washington, DC, and commercial passenger travel was completely shut down for several days. Even a new federal agency was quickly created, the Office of Homeland Security,[1] to handle terrorism and improve communication among federal, state, and local agencies. Although the war on terrorism continues, the importance of the agencies of government was clearly illustrated. From rescue and cleanup operations in New York City to military strikes in Afghanistan and enhanced airport security measures, public administration became highly visible and received nearly 24-hour coverage on major news channels like the Cable News Network (CNN). The events of September 11, 2001, were horrible, but imagine how bad the attacks would have been without government and public agencies in place to deal with the disaster.

Despite the obvious presence of government and public administration, most Americans remain relatively untutored about government agencies until they need them. Public administration handles most of the nation's disasters ranging from hurricanes to airline crashes, and more recently the threat of terrorism. Events such as the war with Iraq and natural disasters like Hurricane Isabel are very visible and attract a great deal of media attention. But government also handles many less visible tasks such as regulating meat processors, public health matters that include sanitation and vaccinations, essential services such as sewers and water provision in the nation's cities, and maintaining public highways and public education. From national defense to delivering the mail, the work of government is immense and essential.

WHAT IS PUBLIC ADMINISTRATION?

Public administration has been called the accomplishing side of government.[2] Often simply referred to as "the bureaucracy," government agencies handle a varied array of services that range from national defense to police and fire protection. It is sometimes difficult to describe public administration because of the breadth of the activities handled by public agencies, and because often we are not conscious of how public administration is involved with our everyday lives. Simply stated, public administration is the management of government agencies. We seem to have an easier time grasping the idea of "*business administration*," which is the management of business enterprises. Business enterprises are organizations that exist for an economic purpose (to make money) and the management of these organizations is *business administration*. Managing businesses involves many complexities, such as finances, marketing, production, sales, and the like, but their purpose is clear. From boards of directors who oversee corporations to the line workers who assemble products, the concept of business administration seems easy to understand for most people. Moreover, we often have a positive image of business administration. After all, most people can relate to the products that are produced such as DVD players, televisions, computers, and automobiles. The names of many businesses, such as Sony, Dell, General Electric, and Toyota, are household words for most Americans.

But public administration has a different image, and many of the services provided by government are either poorly understood, less visible, or have a "negative image." It is more difficult to relate to the Department of Commerce or Department of the Interior than it is to Microsoft, Coca-Cola, or Ford Motor Company. Microsoft is well known for its famous Windows operating systems for computers. Most people are familiar with the line of cars that automobile makers produce because most Americans own cars, whether they own a Ford Explorer, a Honda Accord, or a Cadillac. Everyone can relate to the famous soft drink company Coca-Cola and its competitors. Corporations usually produce products or services. Banks handle our checking accounts and credit cards, and loan us money. Automobile manufacturers produce cars and trucks. But what does the Department of the Interior produce? Does it manage the nation's forests or the national parks? What does the Department of Commerce handle?[3] Clearly, the Department of Commerce has something to do with commerce, but precisely what does it do? Box 1.1 contains the mission statement for the Department of Commerce. Did you know that the weather report we hear every day is made possible because of the Department of Commerce? The Department of Commerce handles many other things as well, such as maintaining important statistics and conducting the census. Some agencies, such as the Internal Revenue Service (IRS), are better known; everyone must file taxes. Other agencies, such as the Environmental Protection Agency (EPA) or the Federal Bureau of Investigation (FBI), are also well known to most Americans. The EPA is designated to protecting the environment, and the FBI hunts down dangerous criminals and, more recently, has made terrorism a top priority.[4] But the comparison between public administration, managing Superfund cleanups, or collecting taxes that pay for national defense does not seem to be parallel to the activities of business administration, which includes building products like automobiles or personal computers. Although everyone knows that a city's fire department puts out fires, most of us will never have to call the fire department. For many of us, this makes public administration seem more distant, unless one is involved with organizations that deal with agencies on an ongoing basis. Perhaps America's love for the marketplace makes business administration easier to describe and grasp. We are very aware that we are driving a Ford Explorer or a Chevy Blazer, but we are less aware about the highways and bridges that are necessary for us to use our cars. We are well aware of the presence of the local police, but most of us have little direct contact with

---

BOX 1.1   Do You Know What the Department of Commerce Does and How It Affects You?

**Mission Statement for the
U.S. Department of Commerce**
The Department of Commerce
promotes job creation, economic
growth, sustainable development and
improved living standards for all
Americans by working in partnership
with business, universities,
communities and workers to:

1. Build for the future and promote
   U.S. competitiveness in the global
   marketplace by strengthening and
   safeguarding the nation's economic
   infrastructure.
2. Keep America competitive with
   cutting-edge science and
   technology and an unrivaled
   information base.
3. Provide effective management and
   stewardship of the nation's
   resources and assets to ensure
   sustainable economic opportunities.

The Commerce Department touches
the daily lives of Americans in many
ways—it makes possible the weather
reports heard every morning; it

facilitates technology that Americans
use in the workplace and home every
day; it supports the development,
gathering and transmitting of
information essential to competitive
business; it makes possible the
diversity of companies and goods
found in America's (and the world's)
marketplaces; it supports
environmental and economic health
for the communities in which
Americans live and it conducts the
constitutionally mandated decennial
census which is the basis of
representative democracy.

NOTE: The Department of Commerce was created
in 1903 as the U.S. Department of Commerce and
Labor. In 1913, the department was split into two
separate cabinet-level departments: the
Department of Commerce and the Department of
Labor. The Department of Commerce includes
many functions and departments, such as the
Weather Bureau (since 1940) and the Patent Office
(since 1904).

SOURCE: U.S. Department of Commerce (2002).

---

them. Moreover, the decisions made by large corporations can have a more visible impact on citizens than those made by many agencies of government. For example, the price that large oil companies, such as Exxon, pay for crude oil has significant consequences on interest rates, banking, local economies, and even the global economy. Although average citizens pay little attention to the price of a barrel of crude oil, they can see the impact in the amount they pay for gasoline and other oil-related products, which affects their disposable income. Although it is often difficult to see or touch, public administration plays a major role in deciding important questions in our society. Public administration is actually everywhere, and our fate as a nation and as individuals depends on complicated networks of a vast bureaucratic system that, although largely unseen, is central to our individual and collective lives.[5] (See Box 1.2 for a sample of some of the questions that involve public agencies.)

Public administration is the management of government agencies.[6] But the roots of public administration are based in *law* rather than *economics,* which is not the case for business administration.[7] For example, the U.S. Constitution

---

BOX 1.2   Questions That Involve Public Administration

- What is the quality of the air that we breathe?
- How safe are our neighborhoods and city streets?
- Is the water we drink safe?
- Are highways planned and maintained properly?
- Will there be parks, playgrounds, and recreational facilities for our leisure time?
- How well will the next generation be educated?
- Do our senior citizens, the poor, and the unemployed receive adequate benefits?
- Are our communities well designed for living?
- Will a letter that we mail be delivered promptly?
- Where should we concentrate society's research development resources: on space exploration or the human body?

- Is the nation's nuclear arsenal controlled and managed properly?
- Are the fish in the lakes and streams of the nation safe to eat?
- How safe are our work environments?
- Are doctors, nurses, and hospitals capable of healing the sick?
- Is the hairstylist certified to perform work for his or her customers?
- Can we be sure that the house we purchase and live in is well constructed?
- Is our money safe in the local bank?
- Is the nation adequately prepared to deal with terrorists?
- Are the commercial airliners maintained properly and safe to fly?

SOURCE: Adapted from Richard Stillman, *The American Bureaucracy: The Core of Modern Government*, 2nd ed. (Chicago: Nelson-Hall, 1996), p. 3.

---

empowers the main institutions of the federal government. Section 8 of the Constitution grants Congress the power to lay and collect taxes. The Sixteenth Amendment, which was ratified in 1913, goes further and specifically allows for a national income tax. Under this power, Congress enacts laws that define who will be taxed, the amount they must pay, and the general guidelines for allowable deductions. To carry out these laws, Congress created the Internal Revenue Service (IRS) to handle the details of collecting taxes. The duties of the IRS include making procedures, writing detailed rules, and handling the paperwork. Legislatures usually write general laws and empower agencies to work out the details needed to implement laws. This allows agencies a great deal of discretion (referred to as *bureaucratic discretion*) in formulating policies. The role of the IRS is critical because it collects taxes that pay for vital programs and services, such as Social Security and Medicare. Similar examples can be found for every government agency. These agencies are created to administer and implement public law; and law is critical for public administration. Five types of law affect public administration: constitutional, legislative, executive, administrative, and judicial.

Constitutional law establishes the legal functions of government. The U.S. Constitution created the Congress, the presidency, and the Supreme Court. Because the United States has a *federal* system—a system in which power is shared among the various levels of government—each of the 50 state governments also has its own constitution that establishes state institutions (state legislatures, governors' offices, and state courts) and authorizes states to create local governments. In addition to establishing the powers of the institutions of government, constitutional law also specifies the rights of citizens and other governments.

Legislative law is the type of law that is most commonly recognized by most people. Legislative law refers to the laws that are approved by legislative bodies such as Congress and the state legislatures. Under the federal and state constitutions, legislatures are empowered to pass laws, such as the Civil Rights Act of 1964. This law made it illegal to discriminate on the basis of race, sex, national origin, and a host of other attributes. To implement and administer this law, Congress created the Equal Employment Opportunity Commission (EEOC). Before the EEOC or any agency can be established and implement law, enabling legislation must be passed that creates the agency and grants it power. Legislatures monitor the behavior of agencies through the enabling legislation and appropriations (the money given to agencies each year to operate). The budget of an agency is critical because it sets limits on expenditures. Agencies lobby legislatures for funding and other resources, and often try to expand their authority. Typically, legislatures appropriate the total amount of money that an agency is authorized to spend and specify the programs in which funds must be spent. Thus, the legislature can make agencies more or less powerful through their "power of the purse." Legislatures can also affect the way agencies behave and limit bureaucratic discretion by passing other legislation that requires agencies to hold public hearings and get input from the public before implementing a policy.[8]

Executive orders are another type of law that affects public administration. The government's chief executive, the president or the governor, issues executive orders. Within the constraints that have been imposed by the legislature, executive orders can greatly affect the administrative behavior of agencies. Executive orders are commonly issued by presidents and can have a tremendous impact on public administration. In 1965, President Johnson issued Executive Order 11246, which directed all companies with federal contracts to provide equal opportunity in employment in their hiring and promotion practices. This executive order affected thousands of government contractors that employed more than 26 million workers or about one-fourth of the nation's workforce at the time. Executive orders can have a significant impact on the internal operation of agencies. This was the case in 1962 with Executive Order 10987, which authorized collective bargaining within federal agencies. Federal-state relations are often rearranged by executive orders. In 1987, President Reagan issued Executive Order 12612. This order set limits on the ability of federal agencies to preempt state law and allowed maximum flexibility for states to manage their own affairs. The order was issued during a time when many responsibilities were being devolved from the federal government to the states.

Administrative regulations[9] *(administrative law)* involve another type of law that influences public administration.[10] Resolutions are promulgated because Congress or state legislatures often delegate enforcement of legislation to the administrative agencies of the executive branch of government. Administrative regulations are rules written by the agencies that carry the force of law. For example, the original Clean Air Act of 1963 provided support for air pollution research and assisted the states in developing their own pollution control agencies. The Clean Air Act of 1970 went much further in regulating air pollution. It required the Environmental Protection Agency (EPA) to establish national air quality standards and emission limits, and required the states to develop implementation plans. Later amendments phased out or regulated many other sources of toxic and hazardous air pollutants. The EPA was delegated authority to implement and enforce the law, including many regulations that it had developed within the agency. In 1971, the power of the EPA was tested in Birmingham, Alabama.[11] The EPA, charged with setting and enforcing standards and guidelines for air quality, actually overstepped state and local agencies and shut the city's polluters down for more than 30 hours until the air quality improved. At the time, this created quite an intergovernmental crisis.[12]

The tendency for legislatures to delegate authority to administrative agencies can blur the distinction between politics and administration. Over the years, delegating authority to agencies has resulted in a growth of agencies that exercise a combination of judicial, legislative, and administrative power.[13] An old debate in the discipline of public administration involves separating politics from administration (this is referred to as the politics–administration dichotomy and will be discussed in greater detail in Chapter 2). The original idea was that administrative agencies were supposed to *implement* the law, not make the law. However, for decades the tendency has been to grant increasing authority to agencies. In many cases, agencies implement law that is written and developed within their agencies to achieve the objectives established by legislatures. This has led many to argue that politics cannot be separated from administration. Legislatures grant less discretion to agencies in criminal law than in civil law, but in many states motor vehicle agencies can automatically suspend the licenses of drivers who refuse to submit to blood alcohol tests after being arrested for driving under the influence of alcohol.[14] Legislatures can grant agencies wide discretion in making additional rules and procedures, such as adjudicating cases by taking driver's licenses from drivers who either refuse to take a blood alcohol test or fail the test. In most states, legislatures set the tolerable limits for blood alcohol readings.[15]

Federal administrative agencies fall under the Administrative Procedures Act,[16] which sets guidelines that agencies must follow in making and administering rules. Rulings by most agencies (with a few exceptions) are subject to judicial review by the courts. States tend to follow the national model. But the important point involves the mixing of powers. Agencies often mix *quasi-judicial* and *quasi-legislative* powers (which does not seem to follow the principle of separation of powers). Clearly, this mixes politics and administration. In

Chapter 2, we will see that one school of thought in the discipline of public administration holds that politics cannot be removed from administration and that public administration should be thought of as administration-as-politics. The school of thought is called the New Public Administration.

Judicial law is the last type of law that affects public administration. The courts hear real cases to form this type of law. The decisions reached by courts can cause internal or external changes for agencies, or simply uphold a ruling or practice by an agency. For example, several issues that were ultimately resolved by the U.S. Supreme Court in *Miranda v. Arizona*,[17] forced law enforcement officers to read those being arrested a set of basic rights. Today, almost everyone is familiar with the *Miranda* requirements: the right to remain silent, and if that right is waived, statements made may be used in a court of law; the right to attorney; and so on. Fortunately, most of us are familiar with the idea of a person being *Mirandized* because of television rather than actually being arrested. But *Miranda* and other cases have greatly affected law enforcement in the United States by adding a host of procedures and requirements to the operating practices of various agencies.

Personnel matters often are taken to court, as we will see in the chapter on personnel administration. In *Griggs v. Duke Power*,[18] the U.S. Supreme Court held that intelligence tests could not be used in promotion practices unless they could be shown to be job-related because the tests had an adverse impact on minorities. Although this case involved a public utility, the idea of using testing that was job-related affected both public agencies and private businesses. In many cases, the courts uphold the practices of agencies. In *Personnel Administrator of Massachusetts v. Feeney*,[19] the U.S. Supreme Court found that a state law requiring that veterans who pass the civil service test be given hiring preference over non-veterans was legal. Although women challenged the case because men with lower scores were being hired instead of women, the Court upheld the practice. Some state constitutions, including the Montana State Constitution, contain preferences for veterans. It is clear that laws have an enormous impact on public administration; but unlike private businesses, which are based on *economics,* the roots of public administration are embedded in *public law.*

POLITICS, POWER, AND AUTHORITY

The world of public management involves politics, power, and authority. Politics can be defined many ways, but political scientist Harold Lasswell[20] has provided the simplest definition. Politics is simply about "who gets what, when, and how." Politics involves the struggle for control of society's public institutions and the use and allocation of scarce resources; the struggle over which public policies should be implemented (e.g., whether there should be more or less regulation over business practices such as the banking industry); and the clash over the direction in which society should move—whether we want a smaller, more limited national government that allows for greater individual freedom and flexibility for state and local governments, or a large, active federal government that seeks to make society more equitable and protects the rights of minorities and those with fewer advantages. But all of these matters ultimately can be viewed within the framework of the question: "Who gets what, when, and how?"

Public administration involves power, which is the ability to influence and control others. Public agencies are empowered by law to implement and administer public policies, and often to make public policies. For example, the Internal Revenue Service (IRS) is empowered to administer most federal income tax matters, including tax collection. The IRS has the authority—the right to use power—to collect taxes. If individuals do not pay their taxes, the IRS has the power to collect the taxes using every legal means available, which often involves prosecution in federal court. And their record of winning in court has been rather impressive over the years.

THE CONTEXT OF PUBLIC ADMINISTRATION AND AN OVERVIEW OF THE AMERICAN POLITICAL SYSTEM

Decisions about who gets power and authority are made in the political arena, and public administration is a part of the arena. Because public agencies get their funds and mandates from political institutions such as legislatures, they cannot operate without the influence of politics. The operations of public agencies are influenced by most of the elements of the American political system.

Public administration has many aspects aside from public law, such as federalism, interest groups, political parties, political culture, ideology, and other realities of the American political system. Public administration does not function in a vacuum. It is part of a complex system of social, political, and economic factors that reflect our society and culture. The influences that affect American public administration can be divided into two large categories: environmental factors and political factors.

VALUES ABOUT GOVERNMENT AND PUBLIC ADMINISTRATION

Values are perceptional filters through which we see the world. They are the underlying beliefs that people have concerning many aspects of society including politics, economics, government, and public administration. Values tell us what is "right" and what is "wrong." They are a set of preferences and prejudices that defines the world for each of us. With regard to public administration, values are the "beliefs and sentiments that people have concerning the nature of public administration, its purpose, and the expected behavior of public agencies toward citizens."[21] Although values will be discussed in greater detail in the chapter on ethics, two converse sets of values have influenced the public's attitude toward public agencies and administrators. They may be thought of as the "*cynical* view versus the *positive* view about government."[22] Additionally, a third view emerges between the cynical and positive views—an approach that is called the *rational* view.

The cynical view holds that government and public administration are necessary evils. Although government is needed to perform certain critical tasks (such as national defense), those holding this view believe that government does more harm than good. Moreover, government usually oppresses the majority for the benefit of the few, namely, the wealthy and privileged. Cynics believe that all politicians are basically the same, crooked and corrupt. Politicians only care about themselves and getting elected. In fact, there is some reputable academic support for this point. David Mayhew's classic book, *Congress: The Electoral Connection,* suggests that the first goal of Congress is to get reelected and that Congress structures itself to facilitate reelection of its members.[23] Even if politicians are voted out of office, the cynic sees those who replace them as being the same. The bureaucracy is equally as mistrusted and believed to base its decisions on politics in the worst sense of the term. For those who hold this pessimistic view of government, politics can be summed up with the old adage, "the one with the gold makes the rules." Cynics can find many examples that illustrate how administrative rules support the wealthy and powerful, such as tougher penalties for burglary than for white-collar crimes and more lucrative tax breaks for the wealthy than for the rest of society. They also point to corporate scandals. For example, what penalty was imposed by government for those responsible for the failure of Enron, which was the largest corporate failure in American history and which cost workers their jobs and retirement plans? Despite a little soft stepping and showmanship, the penalties were rather light in the eyes of the cynic.[24] A poor person can rob a bank and get life in prison, but executives can steal millions and get slapped on the wrist—and they get to keep the money. The idea that the bureaucracy serves the greater good or the public interest is nothing more than talk, in the view of the cynics. Protecting the environment, helping the poor, promoting equity, and creating a more civil society is just fluff. After all, programs like affirmative action have less impact on the powerful and wealthy. It is the blue- and white-collar middle classes that are hit the hardest by affirmative action programs. Even in foreign policy, the cynic sees loans made by our government to Asian governments when the Asian markets collapsed in the 1990s as just a way to ensure that American banks do not lose money. In the end, the cynic believes, the wealthy and powerful always win, and government ensures that they do.

Proponents of the cynical view see those working in the agencies of government as incompetent bureaucrats who look after their own self-interest at the expense of the public's interest. This results in a growing bureaucracy that makes decisions that are not in the best interest of most citizens but, rather, help the powerful and the bureaucrats themselves. Moreover, the bureaucracy is wasteful and inefficient. In recent years, even politicians have made careers out of viewing government and the bureaucracy as "the problem" rather than "the solution" to the nation's woes. This was the case with Ronald Reagan who was elected to the presidency as a Washington outsider and was a leading critic of the federal government, including the bureaucracy. Even Washington insiders like the former Senate majority leader Bob Dole have criticized the bureaucracy. During the national health care debate in the early 1990s, Dole likened the nationalized health care proposal proposed by the Clinton administration to using the postal service as a model. This does little to help the reputation of public management or those who work in public agencies. The bottom line of the cynical view is that government cannot be trusted. The roots of the cynical view in the United States probably go back to the mistrust of centralized government that was so prominent during the colonial era.

A completely opposite position has a positive view of government and public administration. In this view, although government sometimes does restrict some individual freedoms, government protects citizens and communities from conditions that are beyond their control, such as environmental pollution. Recently in Libby, Montana, the federal government intervened to help remedy the effects of years of mining pollution by the W. R. Grace Company that left many in the town seriously ill.[25] Private companies would not clean up or help those harmed by pollution if government (the EPA and the U.S. Department of Justice in this case) did not intervene. In this positive view of government, the large size of the American population and the complexity of society limits individual participation in administrative decisions and public policy, but interested citizens can participate through elections and interest groups. Public administrators are not the self-serving, incompetent bureaucrats described in the cynical view; rather, they are honest, intelligent professionals who serve the public interest. Moreover, government improves the quality of society through well-planned programs that gradually make changes that have a positive impact on people's lives. This view holds that government is not nearly as inefficient as commonly believed. In fact, government programs are more efficient and more equitable at bringing about positive social change than the marketplace.[26] This view is founded on the belief that a large, active government can have a positive impact on society by bringing needed changes and solving many problems that would be left unsolved or inadequately addressed by the private sector. This view is associated with the orthodox school of Public Administration, which will be discussed in Chapter 2. The bottom line of this position is that government is necessary and performs numerous functions that are needed in modern society. Public administration consists of the agencies of government that were created by democratic institutions to help govern society. Thus, public administration is also legitimate.[27]

Finally, there is a third approach that is neither cynical nor positive. The *rational approach* (which is based largely in a theory known as public choice that will be discussed in greater detail in Chapter 8) holds that government and public administration is neither good nor bad. Government and other actors in the process are driven by self-interest, just like in the marketplace. Individuals and groups weigh the intervention of government into a policy issue. Government intervenes when those with sufficient power apply pressure for intervention. Because powerful individuals and organizations possess a disproportionate amount of political resources (the resources that agencies need to survive such as money, information, and political support), they are more likely to participate in the process and influence public policy than average citizens. This can result in a policy that benefits the few at the expense of the general public who do not have a concentrated or organized interest in the policy matter. But the policy will be opposed if others who also have a concentrated interest organize an opposing interest group, which often occurs. Because competing groups with conflicting goals influence public administrators, who also have their own sets of values and perceptions, policy will typically vary in rationality. In this context, the term *rationality* refers to a policy that is sensible, has clear objectives, and employs methods that are capable of resolving the issue. Policy will be efficiently determined and effectively implemented in cases where interest groups agree on the policy's objectives and methods. Policy will be inefficiently determined and ineffectively executed when interest groups disagree on the policy's objectives and methods. In the rational view, public administrators are no more honest or selfish than anyone else, although they are, like everyone else, driven by self-interest. The behavior of public administrators in regard to public policy is affected by the degree of organizational agreement that exists on the policy's objectives and the methods involved, and by the administrators' own sets of values and perceptions.[28] The characteristics of these three views are summarized in Table 1.1.[29]

ENVIRONMENTAL CONDITIONS

Social conditions play a major role in the type of legislation passed by Congress and state legislatures, and therefore they influence public agencies. The mood of the nation during the Watergate Era (the early 1970s) had a tremendous impact on the types of legislation enacted by Congress. For example, the Watergate scandal led to a number of sweeping campaign reforms. The scandal involved a group of burglars breaking into the Democratic headquarters in the Watergate Complex during the 1972 Richard Nixon–George McGovern presidential race and the subsequent cover-up by the Nixon administration. The election reforms included public financing of presidential campaigns, greater disclosure of the sources of campaign funds, limits placed on the amount that an individual or organization could give to campaigns and parties, and the creation of political action committees (PACs). Abuse of presidential power led to limiting the power of the president to send military forces into conflict, something that Congress granted President Johnson during the Vietnam War and later rescinded.[30] Additionally, because of abuses involving the impoundment of appropriated funds during the Nixon administrations, Congress changed the budgetary process to take back more control over the federal budget and to place conditions on the ability of a president to impound funds. *Impoundment* is the power of the president to withhold money allocated by Congress. The assassination of President John F. Kennedy and Martin Luther King's march in Washington to the Lincoln Memorial (where his "I had a dream" speech was given) reflected the mood of the times and were partly responsible for the pas-

Table 1.1 Values about Public Administration

	MODELS OF PUBLIC ADMINISTRATION		
Characteristics	Cynical Model	Ideal or Positive Model	Rational Model
Nature of government	Bad, corrupt, and self-serving	Good, serves the public good, and brings positive changes to society	Neutral
Nature of public agencies	Protect the interests of the rich and powerful rather than the general public	Protect all persons from circumstances that are beyond their control. Implement public law to make a better society for all citizens	Achieve common goals more easily than can be done individually
How public agencies gold *make decisions*	"Those with the make the rules"	Equal opportunity for access and participation in decisions	Power is based on the control of resources
Characteristics of public administrators	Selfish, shortsighted, and dishonest	Honest, intelligent, and dedicated	Average: influenced by their own values and goals, and pressures from those around them
How we know if the decisions are "good" or if policies are working	Continued protection of the influential and powerful (the elites of society)	Liberty and justice for all if society continues to make progress toward greater equity and fairness	Continued legitimacy to collect the taxes needed to perform government services and implement policies

SOURCE: Adapted from Donald Klingner, *Public Administration: A Management Approach* (Boston: Houghton Mifflin, 1983), p. 10.

sage of the 1964 Civil Rights Act. The Cold War era was characterized by a fear of a war with the former Soviet Union and the spread of communism around the world. The Central Intelligence Agency (CIA) was allowed wide flexibility to operate during the Cold War, including arranging assassinations. But following the abuse of executive power during the 1960s and 1970s, the practice was formally banned. Following the terrorist attacks on the World Trade Center and the Pentagon in 2001, state-sponsored assassination was once again allowed. This type of switch in policy illustrates how the "mood of the times" influences what government actions are considered acceptable.

Economic conditions, considered as an environmental factor, affect public administration. The late 1970s are remembered for the horrible state of the American economy. The oil embargo of the early 1970s caused many economic changes in the United States and the western world. During the Carter administration, economists developed a new term: *stagflation*. High interest rates, high inflation, high unemployment, and an overall stagnant economy characterized this period. In public administration, agencies were forced to deal with "cutback management" and "retrenchment." During most of the 1980s and throughout the 1990s, economic conditions improved. Wall Street soared and the economy boomed. A prosperous economy provides higher tax revenues, which means more money for agencies and the activities of government. Conversely, recessions cause decreased revenue while boosting costs of such things as welfare and unemployment benefits, which often results in budget deficits. Like any organization, when funding is cut, the organization functions differently. An agency has more difficulty obtaining its objectives if adequate funding is not available. For example, if a city cuts its sanitation inspection budget and does not have enough inspectors (or the workload increases so inspections are less thorough), public safety may be compromised. Cutting the staff of a regulatory agency can backfire. For example, during the 1980s, the Reagan administration sought to reduce federal involvement in many areas, particularly in the regulations imposed on businesses. Many believe that the reduced regulation led to the savings and loan bank scandal in the mid-1980s that cost billions of dollars to resolve and landed Charles Keating in jail.[31]

Public administration and the economy are related. With passage of the Employment Act of 1946, the federal government accepted responsibility for managing the economy. Today, we take the government's role in the economy as a given. Many federal agencies are involved in the national economy, including the Bureau of Economic Analysis and the Federal Reserve. We expect government to understand economic trends and manage the economy to increase prosperity. Both major political parties are in agreement on the goal of economic prosperity, but they often disagree on how to achieve it. (The economy, monetary policy, taxation, and agencies that are responsible for managing the economy, will receive much more attention in the chapter on public budgeting.) For now it is adequate to note that the economy, government, and public agencies are intertwined in the goal of "growing" the economy to bring greater prosperity for Americans.

Other environmental factors affect the world of public administration. Today we live in the information and technological age. Changes in technology have revolutionized the world in which we live. The Industrial Revolution has long faded, but it changed the world forever. It brought about major changes through innovations that allowed production of all types of goods and made products more affordable. It also was a financial revolution, as new methods of financing were discovered. Just think about the technological changes that have occurred over the past 100 years, such as the telephone, the automobile, the airplane, and the television. The telephone has changed the way we communicate; the automobile has changed the way we move from place to place; the airline industry has made it possible for us to move all over the world; and television has changed the way we entertain ourselves and stay informed. During the past 20 years, we have seen the rise of cable news networks like CNN, Fox, and CNBC and public service networks like CSPAN. Today Americans can watch news as it happens. Television has also changed politics, which in turn has changed other elements of our political system, including public agencies. The electronic media, particularly television, have made agencies more visible. Fifty years ago people did not see the Federal Aviation Administration clean up airline crashes or see the horror stories that have been broadcast about some of the practices employed by the Internal Revenue Service. When J. Edgar Hoover and the FBI hunted down bank robbers in the 1930s, the world was not watching on CNN. But when the Bureau of Alcohol, Tobacco, and Firearms (ATF) got into a shooting match in Ruby Ridge, Idaho, with white separatist Randy Weaver in 1992, the nation was watching. The higher visibility has contributed to more accountability.[32] Additional oversight was imposed on the IRS after many of its practices were disclosed, and congressional hearings were held on the practices of the ATF after the Ruby Ridge incident. The Rodney King arrest was caught on videotape and broadcast on television for the world to see. The incident led to the Los Angeles riots in 1991,[33] which brought political changes to Los Angeles and more accountability for the Los Angeles Police Department.

Sometimes "technology" can backfire in the world of government and for politicians. During the Watergate scandal, it was revealed that President Nixon had taped many of his conversations in the Oval Office, and a legal struggle ensued to get control of the tapes.[34] The tapes provided hard evidence that Nixon was involved in covering up the Watergate incident. Nixon's denial of any responsibility for the Watergate burglary weakened his office's executive authority and ultimately led to his resignation. He is the only president in our history to resign from office, which was also broadcast live on television. The pace of changes in technology in recent years is remarkable. Most students reading this book cannot remember a world without cable and satellite television, VCRs and DVD players, CD-ROMs, the Internet, cell phones, and computers—but most of these items have been introduced to the mass market only within the last 25 years.

How does technology affect public administration? Not only do public agencies use computers, cell phones, videotapes, the Internet, and the like, but often they must regulate new technologies in such a way that technology will continue to advance while the public will be protected. For example, the growth of the commercial airline industry created the need for someone to ensure safety in light of all the additional air traffic. Thus, we have air traffic controllers who monitor the skies and clear aircraft for landing at airports. All major airports in the nation are publicly owned and most are publicly managed. The United States has had a long history of preferring private ownership with government regulation and oversight. For example, most public utilities (electric and gas, water systems, etc.) are investor-owned entities that operate under heavy government regulation. Many of the nations of Europe have taken the exact opposite approach; in some countries, state-owned businesses are common. What about privacy issues regarding your cell phone? Can something you say on your cell phone be held against you in a court of law without a legal wiretap? Can you view whatever you like on the Internet? Is using your credit card to make purchases on the Internet safe? Should the Internet be regulated? Actually, Congress imposed a moratorium on taxing the Internet, and to date regulations have been minimal. This is one of the few modern technologies that has not fallen under the regulatory hand of government, at least at this point in time.[35]

Computers have revolutionized the way modern society works. We can now store and retrieve data and perform calculations that were an arduous task less than 20 years ago. Like the effect on the private sector, many new technologies have helped enhance the work of government. One can now use the Internet to access data from the Census Bureau or read U.S. Supreme Court decisions, without waiting days or weeks for the printed versions to arrive in the mail, and can even pay your taxes online. *E-government,* the idea of making government accessible online, has grown tremendously over the past few years. Without a doubt, this has already changed the way government and its administrative agencies operate. The marvels of contemporary technology have changed the way we live and the way we do business. Government business can now be conducted with teleconferencing, cell phones, and the Internet. Materials that once had to be mailed from coast to coast or to other parts of the world are now posted on Web sites. Projects can be completed using the Internet through collaboration between different units of agencies and even between different agencies. What once took weeks or months to do can now take days, or in many cases can be handled instantly, thanks to advances in telecommunications.

Technology, however, also creates many new problems for government and public agencies. While France generates most of its electricity from nuclear power, the United States slowed down its nuclear growth many years ago to a near standstill. Forty years ago, it was believed that nuclear energy would be the wave of the future, but the near meltdown of the Three Mile Island nuclear plant (located in Pennsylvania) illustrates the precarious relationship that exists between technology and energy policy. The Industrial Age relied heavily on the use of oil and coal (fossil fuels). The oil shortages of the early 1970s created political and economic problems, and made the nation rethink its energy policy. Nuclear energy is one solution that is more efficient than damming up rivers to build hydroelectric plants, but there are consequences. The U.S. Department of Energy encouraged the development of nuclear plants for many years, but local residents have been unwilling to have nuclear plants built in their backyards. The Three Mile Island experience caused fears in the public about the safety of nuclear power plants. The Chernobyl incident (where nuclear waste leaked into the atmosphere in 1985 in the former Soviet Union) did little to help apprehensive feelings in the United States. The problem with nuclear power plants involves storing the nuclear waste (called spent rods), which remains active for thousands of years. Until new methods are perfected for recycling or more safely storing nuclear waste, most Americans will likely maintain their NIMBY (*not in my backyard*) attitude about nuclear energy. What does this mean for public administration? America wants and needs electricity to operate. How does government go about providing adequate power without destroying the environment, and how does it ensure that power is provided at a price that people and industries can afford? During the oil embargo of the early 1970s by the Arab oil cartel, OPEC

(Organization of Petroleum Exporting Countries), the federal government imposed price limits that backfired and exacerbated the oil shortage. Americans were used to having cheap power and cheap gasoline. But by imposing limits on the price that oil companies could charge, the flow of oil further slowed and Americans waited in long lines for a few dollars worth of gas. Many economists have argued that if government had not altered the market price, the cost of gasoline would have been even more expensive, but there would not have been shortages. After the price controls were removed, the cost of gasoline adjusted to the market price and there was no longer a shortage, although gasoline would be more expensive than in the past.

Environmental conditions like the ones discussed here have an effect on public administration and public policy. Public agencies are influenced by environmental conditions, but they also influence those conditions. Environmental conditions have an impact on both internal and external aspects of agencies. Social conditions, such as the antiwar sentiments of the 1960s and 1970s, which ultimately affected public opinion and diminished public support, made fighting the war in Vietnam difficult to continue. The fact that the number of senior citizens will mushroom as Baby Boomers begin retiring in the near future places enormous pressure on government and its agencies to rethink health care policy and prepare for a new era. Social conditions clearly affect public administration, as we turn to the agencies of government to cope with the realities of the times. As the population grows older, the demands placed on government and public administration in areas of domestic public policy will change. Public administration must work within the social fabric of the times. Currently, that includes responding to new issues such as terrorism and changing to meet the demands of an aging population. In the last century, the agencies of government adapted to an ever-changing environment to fight world wars, battle the Cold War, regulate an expanding economy, and deal with social changes like the civil rights movement and the challenges of a society filled with 76.8 million Baby Boomers.[36] Social, technological, and other environmental factors are constantly changing, and public administration both reacts to and contributes to those changes.

POLITICAL FACTORS THAT AFFECT PUBLIC ADMINISTRATION

Another set of important factors that affect public administration are found in the political system. Although all elements of the American political system have an impact on public administration, several are of critical importance. Public administration is also a part of the political system. Political conditions include the political structure of the system itself, such as federalism and separation of powers. Interest groups play a significant role in formulating public policy and the decisions made by public agencies. There are various types of political conditions that include the institutions of government, political culture, public opinion, and ideology. Several unique characteristics of our political system are the following.[37]

- *Popular consent* is the idea that governments draw their powers from the governed.

- *Popular sovereignty* is the right of the majority to govern themselves.

- *Majority rule* holds that only those policies that collectively garner the consent of a majority of citizens will become law.

- *Individualism* is the value and focus placed on individuals in our democracy and culture. Individualism holds that the primary function of government is to enable the individual to achieve his or her highest level of development. This makes the interests of the individual as important or more important than those of the state.

- *Equality* is the idea that everyone is equal under the law.

- *Personal liberty* usually refers to individual freedoms. It initially referred to freedom from government interference; today it includes demands for freedom to engage in a variety of practices free from governmental discrimination.

- *Federalism* refers to a political system in which power is shared among the various levels of government—in the case of the United States, the federal government and the states. Local governments are created by their states.

- *Separation of powers* refers to the splitting of power between the legislative, executive, and judicial branches of government. This creates an intricate system of checks and balances.

- *Pluralism* is a political model in which political power and resources are scattered so widely in our diverse democracy that no single group or individual can dominate or monopolize any substantial area of policy.

- *Interest groups* are a critical component of pluralism. An interest group is a collection of individuals organized to express attitudes or positions held in common in an effort to influence public policy.

- *Political culture* is a set of values, attitudes, and beliefs that people hold about how political and economic life should be carried out.

- *Capitalism* is considered to be an extension of individualism. Capitalism is an economic system that favors private control of business with minimal government interference and regulation in private industry.

- *Ideology* refers to a specific course of action that people want government to take. Most of the population adheres to one of the four dominant ideologies in the United States: liberal, conservative, libertarian, or populist. The clash of ideologies helps to shape public policies in the political arena.

- *The Constitution* is the ultimate written law of the land. It establishes the institutions of government and their powers, and specifies a wide range of civil liberties for citizens. The American political system is based on written law, all of which stems from the Constitution.

- *Rule of law* is closely related to the Constitution. Rule of law is the idea that we are governed by laws that are created in a democratic process rather than by the whims of kings or those in power. We elect officials, such as presidents, mayors, city council members, and members of Congress, as our representatives; they make and implement the law. As citizens, we obey the laws and abide by the rulings of courts and other administrative agencies. The rule of law allows due process and the right to appeal decisions. If a majority of citizens are unhappy with a law, democracy provides various ways to change it.

FEDERALISM, INTERGOVERNMENTAL RELATIONS, AND SEPARATION OF POWERS

The American political system is a federal system. Federalism is a political system in which power is shared among the various levels of government.[38] This creates a complex web of intergovernmental relations (IGR) among the different levels of government. There are horizontal and vertical dimensions of federalism and intergovernmental relations. The horizontal dimension affects interjurisdictional matters among governments and agencies within the same sphere, such as law enforcement cooperation between a city police department and the county sheriff's department. The vertical element is illustrated when law enforcement agencies from various levels of government—federal, state, and local—work together to solve crimes. Sometimes intergovernmental conflict occurs when the levels of government or agencies either clash or fail to cooperate. Interstate compacts, which are allowed in the U.S. Constitution, are formed to manage regional problems and illustrate both the vertical and horizontal dimensions of federalism. They often involve the creation of intergovernmental agencies or commissions. For example, the Delaware River Basin Commission was created to manage flood control and conflicts over the use of water from rivers in the Delaware River basin area. It is a compact among four states (Delaware, New Jersey, New York, and Pennsylvania) and the federal government. In the United States, constitutionally, power is shared between the federal government and the states. Local governments are created by the states. Each level of government performs three basic functions: legislative, executive, and judicial. Public administration consists of the functions performed by the three levels of government. At each level, the chief executive officer is assisted by administrative agencies to implement the law and carry on the functions of government. The three separate branches share power, and the founding fathers designed the system to separate power in order to create a system of checks and balances. The system of checks and balances ensures that no single branch can dominate decision making. Legislatures enact laws, and presidents and governors have veto power over laws enacted by the legislative branch. Even after a law has passed through the legislative and executive branches, it can be challenged and repealed in court. In some states, laws can be enacted or overturned by citizens using an initiative process (a method that places proposed laws on ballots to be approved or rejected by citizens).

This system of checks and balances between the executive, legislative, and judicial branches of government is called separation of powers. The president and members of Congress are elected separately and serve terms of different lengths. Moreover, each branch has powers that are independent from those of the other branches of government. The founding fathers were fearful of a concentration of power in any single branch, which was clearly stated by James Madison in *Federalist 10*. One of the most famous statements from the *Federalist Papers* comes from *Federalist 51:* "[I]f men were angels, no government would be necessary." *Federalist 51* recognizes that one must grant the government enough power to govern but also must force it to control itself. The idea of separation of powers, which fragments power, was the founding fathers' solution that would keep abuse of power in check.[39] Over time, power began to become more concentrated in the executive branch, which houses most of the administrative agencies of government. As society became more complex and urbanized, new agencies were added and old agencies enlarged to handle an expanding array of problems and demands.

Federalism has been in a constant state of change since the U.S. Constitution was signed in 1787. Prior to ratification of the Constitution, the former colonies operated under the Articles of Confederation, which was a confederacy with power residing in the members of the new nation—the states. Under the Articles of Confederation, the nation nearly failed because the national government was so weak; it did not even have the power to tax. Bickering between the states over a variety of issues led to abandoning the Articles for a new constitution that granted greater powers to the national government. After the Constitution was ratified, many years were spent trying to establish the legitimacy of the new nation. During this period, the nation struggled with the appropriate balance between federal and state power. After a series of landmark Supreme Court cases—such as *Marbury v. Madison*[40] (established the concept of judicial review), *McCulloch v. Maryland*[41] (established that the U.S. Constitution contained implied powers), and *Gibbons v. Ogden*[42] (allowed federal intervention into economic areas that involved interstate commerce)—the legitimacy of the federal government was established, but the nation operated under dual federalism for more than 100 years. Dual federalism split power between the federal government and the states, leaving each division with its own sphere of separate authority and responsibilities. This model of federalism, often described as "layer-cake" federalism, lasted until the mid-1930s. During this period, the nation grew rapidly due to the Industrial Revolution, massive immigration, and westward expansion. Also, the states' rights issue that was supposed to have been settled by the Civil War remained an issue throughout the civil rights movement. Public administration endured the spoils and patronage system, and in 1883, the Pendleton Act authorized the federal civil service, which slowly began the process of creating a professional public service.

From the late 1930s until 1960, cooperative federalism dominated. In this model, the federal government and the states cooperated with each other and were more intermingled than in other eras. During this time, the New Deal programs of Franklin Roosevelt were implemented, and the nation battled the Great Depression and fought World War II. Also during this era the idea of "super government" emerged. More and more agencies were added, and there was a tendency toward a greater federal role in society, although the role was limited to providing technical assistance rather than control. Executive power would continue to increase with the Executive Office of the President and a growing bureaucracy to fight the ongoing Cold War and to deal with the realities of living in the "atomic age."

By the early 1960s federalism shifted again, resulting in an even greater tendency toward centralization of power. Creative federalism sought a more active federal role to achieve social responsibilities. National priorities took precedence in the fight against poverty, crime, injustice, and racism; environmental concerns; urban renewal; education; and the advancement of civil rights. States became conduits for federal programs, and money flowed into the states and localities to support the attainment of national goals. The main tool by which money was passed into the states was grants-in-aid, which came with strings attached and mandates. This allowed the federal government to control the programs and achieve national objectives. President Johnson's Great Society programs were ambitious, but the nation was also engaged in the Vietnam War. It was a time of great social change and clashes between values. During this period, power shifted from the states to Washington. The role of the states and local governments was to implement programs under federal control. The role of public administration further increased, as agencies were responsible for implementing the Great Society programs.

Since the early 1970s, the United States has had several versions of "new federalism." Beginning with Richard Nixon, the process of devolution (returning power to the states) has continued for more than 30 years. The shift began with the 1972 State and Local Fiscal Assistance Act (or General Revenue Sharing Act). This law provided the mechanism for restoring balance among the federal, state, and local governments that was lost under creative federalism. The key difference between the new federalism and creative federalism was that now states and local governments were given control over the resources provided by the federal government through the idea of "revenue sharing." Revenue sharing allowed much more flexibility for the states and their local governments because there were fewer strings (or mandates) attached to the funds. The idea was that states and localities could better determine their needs than the federal government. In the 1980s, President Reagan continued the new federalism but accelerated the pace of devolution and cut funding for many programs, which caused critics to coin the phrase "fend-for-yourself federalism." Over the years, state and local governments had become more dependent on federal aid. The Reagan administration severely cut state and local aid during the 1980s and completely stopped general revenue sharing in 1986. During the 1990s, the flow of funding into the states increased under

President Clinton. However, federal revenue for the states has never returned to the levels of state and local budgets in the late 1970s. Currently, federal revenue comprises about 18 percent of all state and local spending. Some have argued that during the 1990s the nation experienced a return to the idea of "cooperative federalism," but most scholars still consider the new federalism (or some form of it) to be in effect. Figure 1.1 illustrates the three levels of government.

PLURALISM AND INTEREST GROUPS

The idea of pluralism affects public administration in terms of forming and implementing public policies. The theory of pluralism holds that power is group-based (i.e., resides in interest groups). Proponents of this theory claim that because America has multiple access points, each group has equal opportunity (though not necessarily equal ability) to compete with other groups for power and resources. Political scientist Robert Dahl made the theory of pluralism famous in his classic book entitled *Who Governs?* The theory holds that several important inherent characteristics of the American political system give special importance to the role of interest groups.[43]

- Contemporary government is so complex that individuals must join groups to participate in politics. Thus, power becomes defined as an attribute of individuals in relationship with each other in the process of decision making. Decision making here refers to passing specific policies and laws that are advantageous to individuals or groups and founded in self-interest (e.g., tax breaks for business owners) or based in ideology (e.g., reducing or increasing welfare benefits for the poor). The point is that individuals participate through groups in the political process to influence outcomes, and the access points to the decision-making process include public agencies.

- These power relationships are very fluid; that is, they are formed for a particular decision, and after the decision is made, they dissolve and are replaced by a different set of power relationships when the next decision is made.

- There is no permanent distinction between elites and masses. Individuals who participate in decision making at one time are not necessarily involved in the next decision. Individuals move in and out of the ranks of decision making simply by becoming active or inactive in politics.

- Multiple centers of power exist within a community, and no single interest group totally dominates all decisions or is totally dominated by another interest group.

- Competition exists between various interests so that public policy is the result of bargaining and negotiation among competing interest groups.

Interest groups are groups of individuals and organizational representatives who have a stake in a particular public policy or set of policies. Interest groups

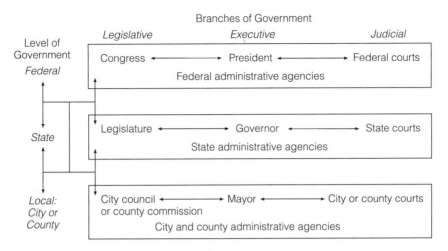

FIGURE 1.1 Levels of Government and Functions

SOURCE: Adapted from Donald Klingner, *Public Administration: A Management Approach* (Boston: Houghton Mifflin, 1983), p. 6.

come in many forms and represent virtually every special interest that one can imagine.[44] Interest groups lobby the access points of government, including public agencies, to influence public policy. The impact of interest groups on public policy has important implications for public administration and the political system. Since many agencies serve or develop clienteles (the people or groups that benefit from an agency's existence), iron triangles can form between the legislature, agencies, and interest groups. Since most agencies also make public policy, interest groups can have tremendous influence on agencies as well as the legislature. For example, the Department of Agriculture provides many benefits for the agricultural industries and farmers. Interest groups from this sector exert pressure on both the Department of Agriculture and Congress to continue or increase various types of benefits. The cozy relationships that develop and influence public policy are illustrated in the diagram of iron triangles (see Figure 1.2).

Some agencies are responsible for regulating industries. For example, among other responsibilities, the Food and Drug Administration (FDA) must approve new drugs produced by pharmaceutical firms before they can be sold in the marketplace. If cozy relationships develop between the FDA and pharmaceutical firms, new drugs may be approved that help the sales of a corporation but turn out to be unsafe for patients. *Bureaucratic capture* occurs when an agency becomes "captured" by the industry that it is supposed to regulate, or by the clientele that it is supposed to serve. This phenomenon will be examined more closely in the chapter on public policy. The term *iron triangle* suggests that the three-way relationship is effective at controlling the public policy outcomes, but some have suggested that the process is more fluid and involves more actors. For example, some think "issue networks" more accurately describe the policy-making process.[45] While the iron triangle suggests a small identifiable circle of participants, the concept of issue networks suggests that

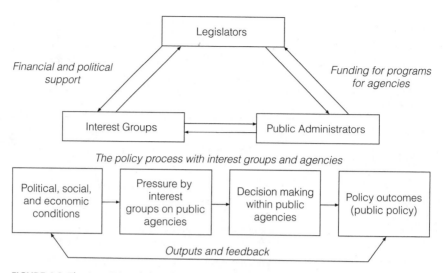

FIGURE 1.2 The Iron Triangle Model and Policy Process

SOURCE: Adapted from Donald Klingner, *Public Administration: A Management Approach* (Boston: Houghton Mifflin, 1983), p. 15.

the participants are largely shifting, fluid, and often anonymous. Issue networks will be discussed in more detail in the chapter on public policy.

POLITICAL CULTURE

Public administration is also affected by political culture. The roots of the cynical and positive views of government described earlier illustrate how some people may feel about government, but those attitudes are part of a larger phenomenon. The patterned set of attitudes, beliefs, and expectations that describe how people believe political and economic life should be carried out is called political culture. *Political culture* is a way of perceiving or interpreting politics. Note that political culture has a strong normative element—that is, it is about how politics "ought to be" or "should be" carried out. Everyone is influenced by the political culture in which they were raised. Political culture is not the same as *ideology*, which will be discussed later. Ideology involves a specific course of action that government should take, such as the direction of policy or action on specific issues. Political culture has more to do with general attitudes and beliefs about political and economic life, such as the belief that some political behavior is acceptable or unacceptable. For example, in some areas of the nation, the direct initiative (a way that citizens can place an issue directly on the ballot without the approval of the legislature in order to change or make a new law) is perfectly acceptable, while in other parts of the nation the idea of initiative is ludicrous and unacceptable. (The use of initiatives is common in the West and nearly absent in the South.) Political culture also involves the way economic life should be carried out. In some parts of the country, legalized gambling is not a big issue, but in other parts of the nation, the political culture views gambling as a sure way to ruin society. Daniel Elazar described the basic political cultures found in the United States.[46] Although at some level, there is a national political culture, the basic cultures found in the United States are: moralistic, individualistic, and traditionalistic.

The moralistic political culture emphasizes the commonwealth or common good conception of politics. Politics is considered to be an activity that seeks to improve society. In other words, politics is viewed as a noble enterprise in which those in power try to promote the public good in terms of honesty, unselfishness, and commitment to the public welfare. Those holding office are expected to maintain high moral standards of conduct. The idea of "moral" often is influenced by religion in the South but associated with "civic duty" elsewhere in the nation. Moralistic political cultures are found throughout the nation in the New England states, parts of the South (such as parts of Virginia, North Carolina, and Tennessee), and in states in the West, including California, Washington, Oregon, and parts of Montana.

The individualistic political culture views politics as just another business that exists in a marketplace. In this model, government exists for strictly utilitarian ends to handle the functions demanded by the citizens it was created to serve. In other words, government should be limited to those activities that people want it to perform. States where this is the dominant political culture are characterized by less concern for issues, limited participation, ambivalence toward the bureaucracy, and corruption in government. Politics is viewed as just another business and a means by which people can improve their socioeconomic positions. Some corruption is expected; it is just the nature of politics. The main concerns revolve around functionality; that is, the street lights must burn, the highways and traffic signals have to work, and the garbage must be collected. Government is measured on how well it responds to the demands of those it serves and how well public operations are performed. Government is viewed as a source of favors rather than a means to achieve a great society based on the commonwealth ideals found in moralistic culture. Examples of states where this culture is dominant are Illinois and Indiana. Most Midwestern states have some elements of the individualistic culture, particularly those settled by German immigrants.[47]

The third primary culture is called traditionalistic. It is characterized by an "elitist" vision of politics and views the function of government as being limited to preservation of the existing order or status quo. This view holds that a hierarchy exists and seeks to limit real political power to a small, self-perpetuating group drawn from the established elite. In states where this culture dominates, the general public views most issues to be of little importance, and there is a lack of citizen participation. There is an antibureaucratic attitude, and political parties are viewed as being a source of favors or patronage. These areas tend to be conservative with regard to public policy. The traditional political culture is found mainly in the Deep South where the landed gentry settled and established plantations.[48]

Although the United States does have a national political culture[49] that includes fairly commonly held feelings about liberty, equality, democracy, and civic duty, there are regional variations across the nation. Implementation of public policies, such as civil rights or environmental regulations, can vary greatly around the nation because of the way the policies are regarded by the public. Describing the task of desegregating schools in the South as "difficult" is an understatement. School boards and state and local agencies were not always cooperative, despite orders from the federal courts. In the late 1950s, President Eisenhower had to send the military to Little Rock, Arkansas, to force desegregation in a Little Rock high school.[50] Imposing air quality standards on Birmingham, Alabama, in the 1970s was not well received by state and local officials. In fact, one journalist likened it to the EPA's Little Rock case.[51] These cultures provide a set of contextual inducements and constraints on public policy in the states and, therefore, affect the public agencies that implement and administer the policies. Recent waves of immigrants from Asia, Africa, and Latin America have also tried to integrate their cultures into the mainstream of American life. Political culture is not a stationary concept; it is constantly mixing and blending. For example, the migration of people from the northeast into the South has changed the culture of the "New South," for lack of a better term. The South is part of the Sunbelt, which has experienced rapid population growth over the past few decades. Filled with new industries and retirees, the dynamics have changed. Although the change is gradual, cultures mix over time. Regional and geographic differences are considered to be less important than they once were in politics. As Figure 1.3 suggests, however, there is still a great deal of variation between different areas of the nation.[52]

IDEOLOGY

The role that government plays in society is influenced by the specific courses of action that people believe government should pursue. Ideology plays a significant role in the American political system and affects public administration in many ways. Ideology is often involved when people split into different corners of the political arena, take sides on issues, and clash over "what government should do." It also splits us into liberal versus conservative camps. Liberals tend to support redistributive policies, government services, active government, progressive taxes, and activities that maximize participation. On the other hand, conservatives tend to favor distributive policies, minimal government services, regressive taxes, weaker government, and limited citizen participation. Liberals and conservatives clash over fundamental public policy and the role of government. Should we spend more money on the military or for increased aid for the poor? Do we want to regulate the Internet or leave it alone? Do we want to try to rehabilitate those convicted of crimes or just "lock them up"? Should abortion be a protected right or should the states be able to decide that issue? Such questions test one's ideological tendencies.

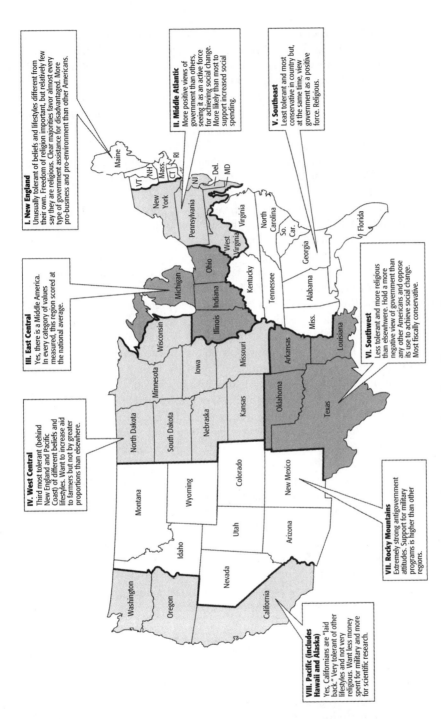

I. New England
Unusually tolerant of beliefs and lifestyles different from their own. Freedom of religion important, but relatively few say they are religious. Clear majorities favor almost every type of government assistance for disadvantaged. More pro-business and pro-environment than other Americans.

II. Middle Atlantic
More positive views of government than others, seeing it as an active force for achieving social change. More likely than most to support increased social spending.

V. Southeast
Least tolerant and most conservative in country but, at the same time, view government as a positive force. Religious.

III. East Central
Yes, there is a Middle America. In every category of values measured, this region scored at the national average.

IV. West Central
Third most tolerant (behind New England and Pacific Coast) of different beliefs and lifestyles. Want to increase aid to farmers but not by greater proportions than elsewhere.

VI. Southwest
Less tolerant and more religious than elsewhere. Hold a more negative view of government than any other Americans and oppose its use to achieve social change. Most fiscally conservative.

VII. Rocky Mountains
Extremely strong antigovernment attitudes. Support for military programs is higher than other regions.

VIII. Pacific (includes Hawaii and Alaska)
Yes, Californians are "laid back." Very tolerant of other lifestyles and not very religious. Want less money spent for military and more for scientific research.

FIGURE 1.3 Map of the United States with Regional Opinions about Government

SOURCE: Grover Starling, *Managing the Public Sector,* 6th ed. (Belmont, CA: Wadsworth, 1993), p. 150.

Most of us are rather moderate in our political positions.[53] But those who are active in the political arena are atypical compared to the average citizen. Those who run political parties, such as the Republican National Committee (RNC) and the Democratic National Committee (DNC), and those involved with political campaigns tend to be far more conservative or liberal than most of us. They are referred to as political activists or elites. They are better informed, closer to the issues, and more committed to the process than the average citizen. Political parties have a tremendous impact on public administration because they seek to gain control of America's political institutions, such as the presidency, legislatures, and the courts, to carry out their party platforms. (A party platform is a group's agenda, which specifies the direction for public policy.) Once in office, parties can shape public policy, control funding for agencies, and provide direction through executive orders and staffing the high-level offices of the administrative branch with those friendly toward the party's agenda. This is tempered by the presence of civil service and professional government employees who work under administrations controlled by different political parties. Power in some agencies dwindled during the Reagan administration because President Reagan's agenda was to get government off the backs of businesses. Agencies like the EPA, the Occupational Safety and Health Administration (OSHA), and the Equal Employment Opportunity Commission (EEOC) were viewed less favorably and could not administer their duties with the same level of "zeal" as in the past. During the Clinton administrations, the power of these agencies was increased.

Citizens' expectations of government vary greatly. In socialist countries like Sweden and Denmark, citizens expect a much wider range of services and government activities than in more capitalistic nations like the United States. Government in Sweden does more and citizens expect more of their government than is the case in America. Government is expected to be a "positive government" in the sense that it is supposed to play a more active and initiating role than the one we expect our government to play in the United States. In fact, this comparison illustrates the major ideological splits in America. Most of us would view the socialist governments of Sweden and Denmark as being too intrusive in matters in which government has no business being involved, but many Americans also believe that our government is too intrusive. For example, health care in socialist countries is provided by or through the government. Although we may be heading in that direction at some point in the future, aside from Medicare (health insurance for our senior citizens) and Medicaid (health care for the poor), health care is predominantly provided through the private and nonprofit sectors in America.

Although the trend for several generations was greater government involvement in services and activities, public sentiment has shifted several times. In the 1960s, public administration responded to an ideological shift to undertake massive new social programs with intensity and determination. But by the 1980s, the orientation had changed dramatically. The guiding doctrine became the idea that throwing money at social problems had only failed. Each generation uses the language and issues of its time to examine the proper role of government. We have seen several shifts in the United States, ranging from a government that is restrained and cautious about intruding into the private sector's capability or jeopardizing individual freedoms, to an activist government that extends control to provide for the common good. Public administrators caught in political mood swings often see the spirit of laws change while the letter of the law remains the same. For example, there were no changes in the antitrust laws that got Microsoft into hot water during the Clinton administration, but the election of George Bush in 2000 saw government literally back off from the desire to split the software giant. Nothing had changed except those now in power had a different ideology. Civil service was originally advocated as a reform to increase productivity in government administration and end the spoils system and patronage. Since reforms were based on the merit principle, it allowed better professionalization of government administration. More recently, the same reforms have been viewed as obstacles to organizational productivity and a hindrance to equitable hiring in government. Federal regulation of certain industries was once viewed as a way of protecting the public interest, but later viewed as a way to shield powerful industries from a more competitive market when the regulated industries gained too much influence over the very agencies that were supposed to regulate them.[54]

Ideology is an important factor, but the roots of the major ideologies in America come from an earlier version of *liberalism* associated with John Locke[55] and other political thinkers of the 17th century. Locke provided the fundamental set of beliefs that shaped our government: that we are born free and created equal; that we have the right to pursue our own happiness; and that we have a right to own private property. These and other basic beliefs are reflected in our *Declaration of Independence*. The ideals of 17th-century liberalism included several fundamental characteristics that are still very much a part of our political system and that have had a major impact on public administration, including the concepts of capitalism and individual freedoms (or liberties).

CAPITALISM

Capitalism is considered to be an economic extension of individualism. Most Americans adhere to the belief that capitalism is a good thing because it provides many material items that make us more comfortable, and it allows the majority of us to maintain a reasonably good standard of living. Capitalism is an economic system in which the means of production and distribution are privately or corporately owned and development is proportionate to the accumulation and reinvestment of profits gained in a free market.[56] The basis of capitalism usually assumes the superiority of free markets over government-controlled economies. Americans love the marketplace. We are a nation of consumers; we love to buy things and love the choice of products available in the marketplace. Capitalism can generate a great deal of wealth for individuals, at least for those who own the means of production. It made the industrialists (often called robber barons) of the 19th century—like John D. Rockefeller (in the oil industry), Cornelius Vanderbilt (in the shipping industry and later in railroads), Andrew Carnegie (in the steel industry), and many others—very rich. More recently, capitalism made it possible for Microsoft founder Bill Gates to become the wealthiest person in the nation. Michael Dell, who dropped out of the University of Texas to start Dell Computers, was the wealthiest person in the nation under the age of 40. In 2002, his wealth was $16.5 billion and he was 37 years old.[57] This would not be possible in a socialist society like Denmark where taxation makes it virtually impossible to accumulate large amounts of wealth. Most of the wealth in America is produced in the private sector.

A basic belief in the merits of capitalism is widely accepted by virtually all Americans. How does capitalism work? The characteristics of the competitive marketplace are relatively simple. Market theory is based on an idealized model in which firms seek to maximize profits, are small relative to their industries, and where no restrictions exist to prevent firms from entering or exiting any industry. This occurs in an economy that is relatively unregulated by government. Although firms seek to maximize profits, their ability to inflate prices is guarded by competition. Consumers are well informed (referred to as perfect information by economists) and have defined preferences about alternative goods and services (the idea of preference orderings used by economists). The consumer is supreme in the competitive market. Competition forces efficiency in the market because firms must compete against similar firms for customers. Efficiency is also guarded by the ability of businesses to enter or exit markets.[58] If firms make unusually high profits, new firms will enter the market until profits return to a normal level. Price in the market is based on a combination of production cost, supply, and demand. The efficient use of resources, which is guarded by the inherent incentives in the market, provides capitalism with supremacy over other models. Market theory is generally associated with *private goods,* the types of goods that are easy to exclude others from using. (This is in contrast to *public goods,* such as street lighting and the national defense, which are goods that are difficult to exclude others from using.) Outcomes in the market are judged by efficiency, which refers to lowering the costs of production to gain a competitive advantage over a firm's competition.[59] Thus, consumers get good products at fair prices and firms make enough money from selling their products to justify their efforts. This is the essence of free market theory. In the real world, market configurations can range from perfect competition to monopolies, but it is the idealized model to which all other models are compared. When we think of capitalism, we tend to think of the competition associated with free markets. But in the real world, markets are not nearly "free," and numerous conditions that are well known to economists and social scientists can cause markets to fail.

Many myths exist about capitalism in America. We have never had truly free markets in the United States as described by Adam Smith in *The Wealth of Nations* (1776). In a free market economy, an "invisible hand" (the term used by Adam Smith) regulates prices, wages, product mix, and so on, and consumers sort out the differences between good and bad products. Economists have considered our economy to be best described as a "mixed economy" rather than the *laissez-faire* capitalism described by Smith.[60] We often believe many of the myths because we have a propensity toward the ideals of capitalism and pay less attention to the role of government in our capitalistic system. For most of us, it is the results of capitalism that affect us—employment and a better material life. Although we may hope to become wealthier, the part of capitalism that so many of us admire involves the product and service choices that are available to us in the marketplace, and the ability to buy goods and services because we have jobs. It is wonderful to go into a grocery store and have so many brands of products available on the shelves, or to see the choices we have when we want to buy home electronics at a store like Best Buy or Circuit City. For almost any purchase, whether it is a new car or a new computer, Americans have choice. The freedom to choose between competing products brings vitality to the marketplace.

It is true that our economy contains a large degree of individualism, but it is important to realize two points. Although we have competition and choice in the marketplace, government has been involved in the economy since the nation was founded. Government has a lot to say about what goes on in the marketplace, such as whether a product is safe, whether automobiles must have seat belts, and whether the meat we buy in grocery stores is safe to eat. The second point involves what is often described as "corporate capitalism." Large national and multinational corporations dominate our society. Economists have long recognized that there is a tendency for oligarchies to develop in markets (domination by the few or the best). Think about the number of airlines you can name—or the number of automobile manufacturers and national hotel chains. Also, think of the investment that would be required to start an airline. The investment would be colossal, and government would be involved. The small firm described in Adam Smith's classical economics does not dominate our economic system.[61] Although entrepreneurialism still exists (and there will always be room for crafty businesspeople to find a niche to exploit and start small businesses), large corporations dominate the system.[62] Most goods and services are produced in the private sector, but markets cannot provide everything. For example, all nations require protection from other nations. The amount of money that should be spent on national defense is determined in the political arena, since citizens disagree on how much defense the nation needs.

Capitalism is important for public administration and creates some interesting dilemmas that will be discussed in later chapters. By definition, public bureaucracies are monopolies, which runs counter to the principles of free markets. Moreover, a number of public agencies are involved with promoting business, some with regulating businesses, and others with managing the economic environment in which businesses function. It is fair to state that business and government need each other, but the "rules of the game" are not made in the boardrooms of corporations. Businesses come to Washington (and to state capitols like Sacramento, Albany, and Tallahassee) to try to get advantageous legislation for their industries. Capitalism is more complex than the idealized model, but it is part of American culture and ideology.[63] But capitalism often conflicts with public administration. Some argue that businesses do not want "good government" because an efficient government encroaches on businesses' freedom by serving as a countervailing force.[64] Those holding this view see government as the only check on business practices that harm society. The tension comes from the fact that government has a regulatory role in the economy and a moral obligation to enforce fairness.

Business and government are not always in conflict, however, even when it comes to regulation. In many cases involving deregulation, the regulated industries are the strongest opponents to deregulation. For example, when the airline industry was being deregulated in the 1970s, the airlines opposed being deregulated. Increased competition would mean that some airlines would fail, and some did. Contrary to popular belief, businesses prefer not having any serious competition. When airlines were regulated, the firms operated in a stable, predictable market that made profits more secure. Similar cases can be found with other industries that were deregulated. Moreover, when things get tough, the loud talk about "getting government off the backs of business" turns into lobbying for favorable legislation and even bailouts. During the 1980s, the federal government made loan guarantees to save America's third largest automobile maker, Chrysler. Economist John Kenneth Galbraith has argued that we cannot afford to let our large industries go broke.[65] We depend on them for many things, including the jobs they create, their products, and the tax that they (and their employees) pay. Capitalism is a part of the American way of life, and while government and business often are at odds on many issues, government needs business for economic growth and stability, and businesses need government to maintain the money supply, oversee the workings of our financial markets, help keep the game fair, and help create a stable society with many opportunities for business. Moreover, the government purchases billions of dollars of goods and services from the private sector each year. Thus, another myth about capitalism in the United States is that government and businesses are natural adversaries. In reality, a great deal of cooperation takes place between government and industry.

The private sector cannot handle all of the nation's needs. Government plays a critical role in the economy. Government agencies are needed for risky enterprises. Although plenty of corporations are willing to take risks to make money, when the risks are too high, corporations often back out and leave the venture for government unless the venture can be handled as a public–private partnership (which shares the risks). Private companies build and maintain private roads (toll roads), but they would not build and maintain the nation's interstate highway system. This venture began during the 1950s (during the Cold War) and at the time was justified largely as being needed for national defense. Today, we see the impact of the interstate system to be greater on industries such as trucking, travel, and the automobile industry than on national defense. The cost for building this large system of superhighways was colossal; no corporation would put up the amount of capital needed for such a project. And aside from the physical cost of construction, acquiring the land on which to build the interstate highway system would have been practically impossible for corporations. The taxing power of government can cover the heavy risks that must be borne for such projects as interstate highway systems, space exploration, airports, and missile systems for national defense. Although the private sector does invest tremendous sums of money in the economy, large national undertakings with high risks and requiring large amounts of investment are usually left for government.

Government and its agencies are also needed because of a host of areas in which markets simply fail.[66] Market failure occurs in several areas, but one type is known as natural monopolies. Most natural monopolies involve some type of utility service, such as provision of water and sewerage, electricity, natural gas, or cable television. An old example illustrates what can occur when the competitive market tries to handle a service that is a natural monopoly. During the 1700s, the British government experimented with private provision of water in London. The experiment was a disaster. To install their pipes, water companies were constantly digging up the streets, and the firms were not making enough money to justify their efforts. As many as three or four different water companies serviced some streets. Ultimately, the firms formed cartels, and the price of water became more costly than it was under public provision.[67] Thus, the free market approach failed. Natural monopolies exist in areas where it is more economical for a single provider to deliver a service than having open competition. The equipment, access, and supplies needed to provide most utilities cannot be competitively provided in these areas by competing firms. Thus, government intervenes and regulates a single provider. Natural monopolies remain until technology makes it possible to have competition. For example, the telecommunications industry was considered to be a natural monopoly until technology changed. Today we have competition in this area, and the cost of long distance telephone charges has dropped significantly. In other areas considered to be natural monopolies, such as cable television, technology has recently changed. Cable companies, which still tend to operate as franchises in most areas, now have intense competition from satellite companies that do not require the same infrastructure (namely, cables buried in the streets or fastened to telephone poles). But natural monopolies in some areas, such as water and sewerage, are not likely to change because there is little probability that changes in technology for pumping water into our cities will occur. In cases involving natural monopolies, government either produces the service itself, such as creating a municipal water authority, or allows a nongovernmental organization to provide the service, which is heavily regulated by government.[68]

Capitalism remains, but we live in a world characterized by *big corporations* and *big government*. Peter Drucker argued that American society was dominated by the business world at the beginning of the 20th century, but times have changed. It is not that business is any less important or smaller; in fact, the business world is much larger today than in the past. What is different is that 100 years ago, most modestly educated people could name the heads of America's big businesses (John D. Rockefeller, Andrew Carnegie, and the other great founders of big businesses), while today hardly anyone can name the CEOs of General Motors Corporation, Ford Motor Company, or General Electric. The general public recognizes only Bill Gates and a few celebrity CEOs, such as Lee

Iacocca (who saved Chrysler Corporation from bankruptcy during the 1980s with the help of the federal government). Drucker argues that this is because government has become larger and more important and because corporations, though now larger, are also bureaucracies.[69] Corporations, capitalism, and icons like Wall Street remain, but those who run giant corporations are as unknown in the minds of Americans as the bureaucrats who run government bureaus. This point by Drucker illustrates how large public and private bureaucracies dominate modern society.[70]

INDIVIDUAL RIGHTS AND LIBERTIES

In the United States we are guaranteed certain freedoms. These freedoms are specified in the U.S. Constitution and the Bill of Rights. Those who work in public administration share these ideas as much as other Americans. These rights form a part of the context of public organizations. For example, the United States allows its press the most freedom of any press in the world. Public organizations must operate under "sunshine rules" (meaning in the open or in public view) for the most part. One might liken managing public agencies to managing in a "fishbowl."[71] The idea of openness and sunshine laws is a unique characteristic of American public administration and distinguishes it from the rest of the world. Unlike management in the private sector, management in the public sector is much more constrained, partly because the decisions made by agencies are more open to public scrutiny.

Many rights are afforded U.S. citizens, such as protection from unwarranted seizures of property by the state. The takings clause of the Fifth Amendment of the U.S. Constitution forbids government to take private property without justly compensating the owner. In a California case, the California Coastal Commission granted a permit to the property owners to replace a small bungalow on their beachfront lot with a larger house upon the condition that they would allow the public an easement to pass across their beach, which was located between two public beaches. The County Superior Court granted the appellants a writ of administrative mandamus and directed that the permit condition be struck; however, the state court of appeals reversed, ruling that imposition of the condition did not violate the takings clause of the Fifth Amendment, as incorporated against the states by the Fourteenth Amendment. The case went all the way to the U.S. Supreme Court. The Court ruled in favor of the landowners and reversed the holding that the takings clause had been violated.[72] Thus, we are afforded extensive hearings and rights of appeal in the administrative process so that the state cannot easily trample our rights. This adds "red tape" to public administration, but it also allows us a voice and rights that few are afforded in other parts of the world.

The list of rights, such as freedom of speech, press, and religion, are basic to all of us but form a critical part of the context in which public administration functions. Additionally, public organizations must deal with a related matter, majority versus individual rights. This is one of the long-standing conflicts in our society. We believe in the idea that the majority should rule, but we also recognize that minorities should have certain rights and protections. The problem is not that our political culture does not believe in minority rights; the problem lies in determining which rights minorities should have and in what matters the majority should rule. This has been a basic conflict for some time. In no area has this been more controversial than in efforts to reduce the effects of past discrimination, such as affirmative action programs. (Affirmative action will be discussed in detail in the chapter on personnel administration.) Do attempts to remedy past discrimination amount to legalizing discrimination against members of society who are not members of protected groups (as defined by law)? The aftermath of the terrorist attacks on the World Trade Center and the Pentagon caused a great deal of hostility toward Arab Americans living in the United States, which in some cases resulted in physical attacks. Despite these incidents, most Americans are comfortable with the idea of protecting the rights of minorities. After all, we are a nation of immigrants.

Since ideology is concerned with the particular course of action government should pursue, it affects public administration. Conservatives want government to get out of the marketplace; liberals want government to take a stronger role in regulating the activities of businesses. Shifts in ideology coupled with economic and social conditions of the times have caused several shifts to occur in the past century. During the 1930s, President Franklin Roosevelt tried to combat the Great Depression with his New Deal programs. This marked a major shift from the past and the beginning of the idea of "super government," as well as the beginning of modern liberalism in the United States. The idea was that government and its agencies were needed to solve economic and social problems that were too large for the states to handle by themselves. President Lyndon Johnson further advanced the idea of big government trying to resolve problems in the 1960s with his Great Society programs. By the 1980s, Ronald Reagan was elected partly on the idea that government had exacerbated many of the nation's social and economic problems. This antigovernment position marked a decisive shift toward more conservative values and the idea of smaller, more efficient government that overall would be less intrusive into the lives of citizens and in the marketplace. During the Johnson administration, public agencies mushroomed as government was expected to do more for society; but during the conservative Reagan administrations, the orders changed, causing a shift in the power and expectations of federal agencies. Thus, who is in power makes a difference in the work of public administration, and this is directly tied to ideology. Table 1.2 illustrates how a shift from a liberal ideology to a conservative ideology affected the behavior of public agencies in the 1980s. Much of the work that government performs is not affected by shifts in power because some matters involve general administration functions, and in some areas, such as with the issues of veterans' benefits and agricultural policy, both major political parties are in agreement about the direction policies should take. Regardless of who is in power, public administration is important because it implements public law, and those in power need the agencies to administer public policy.

**Table 1.2 How Ideological Shifts Changed the Behavior
of Federal Public Administration during the 1980s—
The Supply-Side Era**

	Supply Side (1980s)	Demand Side (pre-1980s)
Size of Bureaucracy	Sharply reduced	Expanded to meet public and special interest needs
Federal Role	Sharply restricted	Feds take lead in most policy areas
Regulation of Business	As much deregulation as possible	Strong public sector role in private sector on behalf of consumers and citizens
Source of Policy Direction	Top-down—from chief executive with centralized controls	Bottom-up—from legislative and special interest groups
Operational Emphasis	Operating functions with "bottom-line results"	Emphasis on staff functions (planning, policy analysis, etc.) and critical of business practices
Key Personnel Staff	Reliance on temporary appointees drawn from business or "new right" supply-siders	Career professionals committed to the public interest and application of expertise to public problems
Agency Policy Development and Management Approach	Tolerant of risk taking, entrepreneurship, and contracting out for public services	Emphasis on consensus building, conciliation, and "muddling through" coupled with professionalism, planning, analysis, and evaluation
Political/Administrative Relationships	Sharp split in roles of political policy-making careerist administrators	Cooperative relationships between appointees and careerists
Reliance on Ideology for Governance of Bureaucracy	Heavy reliance on supply-side theory and economic methodology	Little or none—pragmatic orientation most often used

SOURCE: Adapted from Richard Stillman, *The American Bureaucracy* (Chicago: Nelson-Hall, 1987), pp. 259–260.

HOW LARGE IS THE PUBLIC SECTOR?

One curiosity for most students of public administration is found in a simple question: How large is the public sector? There are many ways to measure the size of the public sector: budgets, assets, number of employees, percentage of governmental spending in the total gross domestic product (GDP), and the like. Regardless of how one measures the size of the governmental sector, the work of government is immense. The U.S. federal government is the largest business on earth by almost any measurement one uses. (Larger bureaucracies are found in Russia, China, and India in terms of number of employees.)[73] It employs roughly 3 million civilian workers and has an annual budget of more than $2 trillion. In the United States, there are more than 87,000 governments with fixed assets that exceed $5 trillion (the private sector's fixed assets exceed

$22 trillion). Currently, more than 19 million public workers are directly employed by government, handling a variety of tasks. This excludes some 3 million people who are paid by government contracts and roughly 3 million more people in the armed services. Table 1.3 illustrates the size of the workforce, excluding contract employees and the military. Additionally, about one out of every six jobs in the United States is a government job. Federal employment has remained relatively stable since World War II, but the number of employees working at the state and local level has continued to increase. In 1950, state and local governments employed about 6 million people. Today, more than 16 million people work at the state and local level.

Another way to measure the size of the public sector is by the amount of money that government spends. Table 1.4 shows how much U.S. government spending has grown since the early 1900s. The size and scope of the public sector has grown dramatically, largely due to the expansion of government services. The effect of government spending in the economy is enormous, constituting about one-third of the total GDP since the late 1950s.

Government spending is not equal at all levels of government. Table 1.5 illustrates the pattern in government spending since the Great Depression. Today, the federal government accounts for two-thirds of all government spending. The 2003 federal budget was $2.3 trillion, and expenditures at the state and local level now exceed $1.7 annually. (Government spending will be covered in greater detail in the chapter on public budgeting.)

The debate over the proper size and scope of the public sector is a longstanding argument. Many view the increases in government spending as an intrusion into the economy, while others see it as necessary for handling society's complex social and economic problems. Governments borrow a lot of

Table 1.3 Number of Governments and Public Employees in the United States

Type of Government	Number of Units	Number of Employees	Percent of Total Public Employment
Federal	1	2,895,000	15%
State	50	4,719,000	24%
Local	87,453	11,906,000	61%
Counties	3,043		
Municipalities	19,372		
Towns	16,629		
School Districts	13,726		
Special Districts	34,683		
TOTAL	**87,504**	**19,521,000**	**100%**

NOTE: There are also 358 tribal governments that are usually not included in the total number of governments found in the United States.

SOURCE: U.S. Census Bureau, *Government Finances 1998–99.*

Table 1.4 Total Government Spending, 1902–2000

Year	Total Expenditures (in dollars)	Expenditures per per Capita (in dollars)	Percentage of GNP/GDP
1902	$1,660	$20	8%
1913	3,215	33	13
1927	11,220	94	21
1932	12,437	100	21
1938	17,675	135	21
1940	20,417	154	20
1946	79,707	561	38
1952	99,847	646	29
1958	134,931	784	30
1964	196,431	1,034	30
1970	332,985	1,643	34
1976	626,115	2,926	36
1980	932,000	4,115	34
1990	2,279,000	8,921	39
1995	2,820,000	11,630	38
2000	2,772,500	9,658	28

NOTE: The early budget expenditures are shown as a percentage of gross national product (GNP) whereas later budgets are reflected as a percentage of gross domestic product (GDP).

SOURCE: U.S. Census Bureau, *Government Finances 1998–99,* and *Statistical Abstract of the United States Online 2002* at http://www.census.gov/statab/www/.

Table 1.5 Federal, State, and Local Spending Compared, 1929–1998

Year	Federal	State	Local
1929	17%	23%	60%
1939	47%	23%	30%
1960	64%	17%	19%
1998	66%	18%	16%

NOTE: The data reflect the percentage of total government spending.

SOURCE: U.S. Census Bureau, *Government Finances 1998–99.*

money, and some feel that when the government borrows money, it "crowds out" investors in the marketplace (who presumably could put the money to better use). This is as much of an ideological debate as it is an economic debate. One thing is for certain: Government and public administration is a large business. Problems emerge when attempts are made to gauge the size of the public or private sectors. Government has become so deeply involved with society that it is difficult to discern what to count as public, private, or quasi-public.[74] Statistical data fail to reflect the actual size and influence of government. For example, the political campaign process is clearly governmental in that large amounts of money are expended to elect people to office, but virtually none of this is recorded. In other cases, the size of government is understated when activities require very little money and few government employees and yet have a great impact on society. For example, how important is the Federal Reserve System? Relative to agencies like the Department of Defense, it is rather small, but it has a critical impact on the economy. This is especially true of regulatory agencies that control such matters as interstate commerce or occupational safety. One must not be misled by figures; the size of government and the public sector is hard to measure, and its size is probably very much understated.[75] Even the number of employees does not accurately indicate the size of government, since thousands of jobs are created by government contracts.[76]

The size and scope of government have clearly grown significantly since the Great Depression. When the nation was young and mainly agricultural, there was less need for services that we take for granted today. The Industrial Revolution and massive immigration of the 19th century made the nation more urbanized. Historically, the private sector provided many of the services that were later taken over by government. Rapid growth, urbanization, demographic shifts, and shifts in ideology placed more pressure on government to provide an array of services that were unnecessary in an earlier, simpler era. During the 20th century, the United States gained superpower status as a nation with interests and commitments that are global. The debate over the appropriate size and scope of government between liberals and conservatives has more to do with "degree and direction" than with whether or not government is needed.

We live in an era characterized by big government, big bureaucracy, and large corporations and nonprofit organizations. We depend on them to carry on our way of life, and our dependence on large organizations is not likely to change in the foreseeable future. Although many examples that illustrate why we need government agencies exist, the point should be clear: Public administration is needed to perform many tasks, from keeping statistics on the population and business activity, to staffing our international embassies and managing the nation's foreign affairs. Moreover, public administration functions in a complex environment that is constantly changing and evolving. We expect government and its agencies to provide services, and we expect them to be responsive and accountable for their actions. Agencies are affected by social, political, and economic changes and by ideological shifts. They also help shape changes in our society. Public agencies are an integral part of our lives, whether we realize it or not.

SUMMARY

Public administration does not function in a vacuum. It is affected by most of the elements of the American system of government. This chapter has briefly presented some of the contextual factors that affect public administration in the United States, including federalism and separation of powers, attitudes, values, interest groups, and ideology. Unlike private corporations, which are driven by economics, public administration is rooted in public law, and this chapter has presented the basic types of law that affect public management. Modern society depends on government and its agencies to perform an array of critical tasks that range from putting out fires and looking after foreign affairs, to ensuring that the nation is defended.

This chapter also took a brief look at the size of the public sector. Although the public sector is very large, trying to gauge its importance by examining data on employment and spending can be misleading. Government is necessary for modern society, and its importance in maintaining our way of life and standard of living cannot be overstated. Public administration is everywhere in our society, whether we realize it or not.

NOTES

1. On June 7, 2002, President Bush proposed a new Department of Homeland Security with a $37.4 billion budget. The department would be a cabinet-level department organized into four broad divisions, plus the Secret Service and an office for coordination with state, local, and private sector efforts. In November 2002, Congress formally approved making Homeland Security the 15th cabinet-level department.

2. Describing public administration as the "accomplishing side of government" should be credited to Grover Starling, *Managing the Public Sector,* 5th ed. (Fort Worth, TX: Harcourt Brace, 1998), p. 1. His quote also appears in Richard Stillman II, *Public Administration: Concepts and Cases,* 7th ed. (Boston: Houghton Mifflin, 2000), p. 3.

3. Handling the national park system is one of the many duties of the Department of Interior. The forest service is part of the Department of Agriculture.

4. The roles of agencies often change over time. The FBI was the subject of a great deal of criticism some months after the terrorist attacks of September 11 when it was disclosed that the agency had information that terrorists were training in flight schools in the United States. FBI director, Robert Mueller even said that the agency had information that may have revealed the terrorists' plot. In a press conference in May 2002, Mueller talked about reorganizing the agency to focus its efforts on terrorism, which was the major threat at hand. Like other agencies, the FBI's role has changed with the times. Early in the history of the FBI, the agency focused its efforts on bringing dangerous criminals to justice. During the Cold War, it focused on communist threats, and today it is focusing on the activities of terrorism. See Michelle Mittelstadt (*Dallas Morning News*), "Changes Afoot at FBI," *The Missoulian,* p. A-1, May 30, 2002.

5. See Richard Stillman II, *The American Bureaucracy: The Core of Modern Government,* 2nd ed. (Chicago: Nelson-Hall, 1996), p. 3.

6. Although no uniform definition of public administration has ever been accepted universally, all the definitions share some fundamental similarities. For our purposes, *administration* refers to the management of the affairs of government through its main institutions. The *bureaucracy* is the departments and agencies of government, which are managed by appointed and elected officials.

7. It has been argued that management in the public sector can be viewed from three perspectives, all of which bear pressure on public managers simultaneously. These perspectives are managerial, political, and legalistic, and all three are embedded in our political culture. See Alan Rosenbloom, *Public Administration: Understanding Management, Politics, and Law*

in the Public Sector, 4th ed. (New York: McGraw-Hill, 1998), Chapter 1.

8 During the Cold War Era, the National Aeronautics and Space Agency (NASA) was created with its primary purpose to reach the moon before our rivals in the former Soviet Union achieved this goal. NASA is better known today for space exploration and launching space shuttles, but its original purpose, which it achieved, was to put a man on the moon. After reaching its goal in the late 1960s, NASA has had to struggle to get funding. This leads one to believe that agencies should not ever fully attain their goals, or at least never have a goal that is as specific as reaching the moon.

9. Administrative law is typically defined as the branch of the law dealing with government agencies (*Merriam-Webster's Dictionary of Law,* 1996). Kenneth F. Warren provides a more in-depth definition: "[A]dministrative law deals with (1) the ways in which power is transferred from legislative bodies to administrative agencies; (2) how administrative agencies use power; and, (3) how actions taken by administrative agencies are reviewed by the courts. More specifically, administrative law is concerned with the legal developments which have so dramatically increased the powers and scope of the administrative branch." Kenneth F. Warren, *Administrative Law in the Political System,* 3rd ed. (Upper Saddle River, NJ: Prentice-Hall, 1997), p. 23.

10. See George Berkley and John Rouse, *The Craft of Public Administration,* 7th ed. (New York: Brown and Benchmark, 1997), Chapter 11.

11. See Patrick Sloyan, "The Day They Shut Down Birmingham," in Richard Stillman II, Ed., *Public Administration: Concepts and Cases,* 3rd ed. (Boston: Houghton Mifflin, 1984), pp. 156–165.

12. Ibid.

13. See Donald Klingner, *Public Administra-tion: A Management Approach* (Boston: Houghton Mifflin, 1983), p. 17.

14. Ibid.

15. The legal drinking age in all 50 states is 21 years of age. All 50 states passed "safe roads acts" in response to pressures from grassroots interest groups like Mothers Against Drunk Drivers (MADD) and in response to pressure from the federal government, which passed the Uniform Drinking Age Act in 1984. If a state did not cooperate, the federal government could withhold that state's federal highway funds. By the end of the 1980s, states had imposed much stricter drinking and driving laws. This federal policy was based on research evidence following the lowering of the drinking age in 29 states to 18, to match the age at which people obtained voting rights. This was followed by significantly more alcohol-related crashes among young drivers, with some states reporting a 30 percent rise among new drivers. Later analysis of the effects on road fatalities of various policy strategies attributed a 5–6 percent cut to the higher drinking age introduced in 1984.

16. The Administrative Procedures Act of 1946 (APA) was passed by Congress to tell agencies how to make rules and decisions. The act has been amended many times over the years and brings some standardization to administrative practices and procedures. Aside from definitions and rules, it also contains the Freedom of Information Act and Privacy Act of 1974, which establishes policies about the availability of information to the public and about privacy. Rule-making provisions describe the procedures that agencies must follow when making rules, which includes time allocated for public comment on proposed rules. Due process is also guaranteed to those who have a case adjudicated by the government, and the actions of agencies are subject to judicial review. The APA covers the whole federal structure with the exception of the Congress and the courts.

17. *Miranda v. Arizona,* 384 U.S. 436 (1966).

18. *Griggs v. Duke Power,* 401 U.S. 424 (1971).

19. *Personnel Administrator of Massachusetts v. Feeney,* 442 U.S. 256 (1979).

20. Harold Lasswell, *Who Gets What, When, and How?* (New York: Meridian Books, 1958).

21. Donald Klingner, *Public Administration: A Management Approach,* p. 7.

22. See Richard Stillman II, *The American Bureaucracy: The Core of Modern Government,* Chapter 1.

23. See David Mayhew, *Congress: The Electoral Connection* (New Haven, CT: Yale University Press, 1986). Mayhew's book is a classic in the literature on Congress. The essence of his book is that self-interest drives Congress. Another account that illustrates the cynical view is found in Philip M. Stern's, *The Best Congress Money Can Buy* (New York: Pantheon Books, 1988). In this classic book, Stern examines the effect of the campaign reforms that occurred after the Watergate scandal in the early 1970s, namely, the creation of political action committees (PACs). The book suggests that public policy is bought and sold in the halls of Congress and that campaign finance reforms have had little effect.

24. The scandals involving Enron, WorldCom, and Arthur Andersen did result in some corporate responsibility legislation being enacted in 2002. The Sarbanes-Oxley Act established a five-member board, called the Public Company Accounting Oversight Board, to oversee corporate activity.

25. Associated Press, "U.S. Justice Files against Grace over Spinoff Funds," *The Missoulian,* p. B-1, May 28, 2002. In a similar vein to the famous Enron case, W. R. Grace and Company was accused by the U.S. Department of Justice of hiding assets before it declared bankruptcy over the cleanup in Libby, Montana. The dispute in Libby, Montana, involved a vermiculite mine that operated for many years, leaving many workers ill with asbestos-related health problems. As of May 2002, more than 325,000 asbestos injury claims had been filed against W. R. Grace and Company.

26. This position is described thoroughly by Frederick Moser, *Democracy and the Public Service,* 2nd ed. (New York: Oxford University Press, 1982).

27. For accounts of why government and public administration are needed, see Charles Goodsell, *The Case for Bureaucracy:*

A Public Administration Polemic, 3rd ed. (Chatham, NJ: Chatham House, 1994), and George Downs and Patrick Larkey, *The Search for Government Efficiency: From Hubris to Helplessness* (Philadelphia: Temple University Press, 1986).

28. The rational view is described by Vincent Ostrom and Elinor Ostrom, "Public Choice: A Different Approach to the Study of Public Administration," *Public Administration Review 31,* No. 2 (March–April, 1971), pp. 203–216. Additionally, public choice theory is described in greater detail in Vincent Ostrom, "Some Developments in the Study of Market Choice, Public Choice, and Institutional Choice," in Jack Rabin, W. Bartley Hildreth, and Gerald Miller, Eds., *The Handbook of Public Administration* (New York: Marcel Dekker, 1989), pp. 861–882.

29. This section relies heavily on the descriptions provided by Donald Klingner. Full credit is given to Donald Klingner, who does an excellent job of articulating these positions in *Public Administration: A Management Approach,* pp. 7–11.

30. The Gulf of Tonkin Resolution involved an incident where North Vietnamese forces fired on American warships in 1964. The law gave the president broad powers that were used to escalate the war. A decade later public support for the war diminished and Congress rescinded these powers in the War Powers Act in 1974.

31. The way Congress opted to handle the bailout is unique. The problem with the savings and loan scandal was caused by the lack of enough bank examiners to handle regulation. In 1984, the head of the agency that regulated savings and loan banks requested 750 additional examiners. The request for additional bank examiners was rejected by the Office of Management and Budget (located in the Executive Office of the President) because the Reagan administration's policy was to free businesses from regulation. Moreover, the agency was told to further reduce the number of bank examiners. The agency responsible for regulation was simply too small and too understaffed to handle the bailout, which was complicated. Congress

opted not to use public administration to handle the largest financial debacle in the nation's history at the time. New legislation, the 1989 Financial Institutions Reform Recovery and Enforcement Act, created a board to oversee the savings and loan bailout. The actual work was handled by the Resolution Trust Corporation (RTC), which was managed by the Federal Depositors Insurance Corporation (FDIC). The FDIC is funded by a tax on Federal Home Loan Banks that are privately owned, which is handled by another organization, the Resolution Funding Corporation (REFCORP). Neither the RTC nor REFCORP have any employees. The work was accomplished by employees of the privately owned Federal Home Loan Banks. See David Schuman and Dick W. Olufs III, *Public Administration in the United States,* 2nd ed. (Lexington, MA: D. C. Heath, 1993), p. 33. It should also be noted that the recent Enron scandal, where the company hid debts in off-book organizations to enhance the value of its stock, is the largest business failure in U.S. history to date. This scandal also involved public administration, namely, the Securities and Exchange Commission (SEC), which regulates the stock and securities industry.

32. ATF agents wounded Randy Weaver and killed his wife, Vicki, in a shootout at the couple's cabin in Ruby Ridge in 1992. A day earlier, Weaver's armed 14-year-old son was killed in a gun battle with a U.S. marshal, who also died. The incident led to congressional hearings and the threat that some ATF officers would be prosecuted. All charges were ultimately dropped.

33. Officers stopped Rodney King for speeding on March 3, 1991, and police beat him repeatedly, delivering multiple baton blows and six kicks, inflicting skull fractures and brain and kidney damage. The entire beating was captured on amateur videotape and broadcast by the news media on television. The incident led to the worst riots in Los Angeles since the Watts riots in the 1960s. Four Los Angeles Police officers were charged with assault with a deadly weapon and excessive use of force. They were acquitted of state charges in April of 1992.

34. The U.S. Supreme Court case involving the White House tapes is *United States v. Nixon,* 418 U.S. 683 (1974). The Supreme Court ruled that "executive privilege" is not absolute and does not allow a president to refuse to turn over evidence that is needed in a criminal trial. The use of the term *technology* in regard to taping devices may seem dated to most readers, but such an activity was not possible 100 years ago.

35. In November 2001, President George W. Bush signed the Internet Tax Non-Discrimination Act. This law extended through November 1, 2003, the moratorium on new, special, and discriminatory Internet taxes. The original law was enacted in 1998. Congress enacted the original moratorium to give the Internet an opportunity to get established before being subjected to taxation. Many state governments are seeking to repeal the law so they can tax various transactions related to the Internet. Currently, states are limited to the catalog rule for taxing sales: If a store selling something on the Internet also has a store in the state, the state can tax the Internet sales, but if there is no store in the state, the state cannot tax the sales). The law also forbids other taxes related to the Internet.

36. Many titles have been given to various generations. The term *Baby Boomers* refers to that generation born between 1946 and 1964. The 50 million babies born in the late 1960s through the mid-1970s are sometimes called Generation X. They are the children of the early Baby Boomers, those born immediately following World War II. The title of Generation Y is given to those born between 1976 and 1990. Some distinct differences exist between these three generations. For discussions about the impact of the different generations on American society, see William Strauss and Neil Howe, *Generations: The History of America's Future* (New York: William Morrow, 1991); Susan MacManus, *Young v. Old: Generational Combat in the 21st Century* (Boulder, CO: Westview Press, 1995); and Fernando Torres-Gil, *The New Aging Politics and Generational Change in America* (New York: Auburn House, 1992).

37. The basic characteristics listed here draw from those included in Karen O'Connor and Larry Sabato, *American Government: Continuity and Change,* 2000 ed. (New York: Longman, 2001), Chapter 1, and David Schumann and Dick Olufs III, *Public Administration in the United States,* 2nd ed. (Lexington, MA: D. C. Heath, 1993), Chapter 2.

38. For an excellent history of federalism maintained by the federal government, visit http://usinfo.state.gov/usa/infousa /facts/crsrepor/federal.htm.

39. James Madison, John Jay, and Alexander Hamilton, *The Federalist Papers* (New York: Bantam Classic Books, 1989).

40. *Marbury v. Madison,* 5 U.S. (1 Cranch.) 137 (1803).

41. *McCulloch v. Maryland,* 17 U.S. (4 Wheat.) 316 (1819).

42. *Gibbons v. Ogden,* 22 U.S. (9 Wheat.) 1 (1824).

43. These points appear in James Lester and Joseph Stewart, *Public Policy: An Evolutionary Approach,* 2nd ed. (Belmont, CA: Wadsworth/Thompson, 2000), pp. 13–14.

44. There are seven types of interest groups. *Occupational and professional:* Includes the National Education Association (NEA), which represents the interests of professional educators (particularly public schoolteachers); the American Medical Association (AMA), which represents the interests of the medical profession (specifically physicians); and unions that represent organized labor, such as the AFL–CIO and Teamsters. *Economic interests:* Includes organizations representing utilities and businesses, such as the National Restaurant Association (NRA) and the American Hotel and Motel Association (AHMA), which promote the interests of the lodging, hospitality, and food and beverage industry, as well as associations that represent banking and finance and various types of manufacturing industries. *Personal characteristics:* Includes groups such as the National Organization for Women (NOW) and the National Association for the Advancement of Colored Persons (NAACP). *Ideological:* Includes many high-profile groups such as the National Rifle Association (NRA), a powerful interest group that seeks to protect the rights of gun owners and opposes legislation that requires registration, and the American Civil Liberties Union (ACLU), which promotes the right to free speech. Also included are organizations associated with the Christian Coalition, the John Birch Society, and the Moral Majority. *Environmental:* Includes groups like Green Peace, The Wilderness Society, and the Sierra Club. *Public interest:* Includes grassroots organizations like Mothers Against Drunk Driving (MADD) and the Nader Organization. These groups are truly concerned with public interest matters at the national, state, and local levels. *Government:* One of the most powerful lobbies in Washington is the intergovernmental lobby, comprised of various organizations that represent the interests of governments, including the League of Cities, the International City/County Management Association, and the National Conference of State Legislatures. See James Q. Wilson and John DiIulio, *American Government: Institutions and Policies* (Boston: Houghton Mifflin, 2002), Chapter 9.

45. For a good discussion about the concept of issue networks, see Hugh Heclo, "Issue Networks and the Executive Establishment," in Richard Stillman II, Ed., *Public Administration: Concepts and Cases,* 6th ed. (Boston: Houghton Mifflin, 1996), pp. 409–418.

46. Daniel Elazar, *American Federalism: A View from the States* (New York: Thomas Crowell, 1972).

47. Given the "mixing" that has occurred over time, pure versions of these cultures no longer exist for entire states. There are tendencies, such as the South being traditionalistic, but these cultures are most identifiable by examining smaller geographic areas, such as the Chicago area (individualistic) or New Orleans and the surrounding area (traditionalistic). Also, bear in mind that over time these cultures have likely become mixed due to migration, such as migration of people

from the Northeast to the Southeast and other Sunbelt states. These cultures also are likely to change as immigrants from Asia and other parts of the world come to the United States.

48. See James Lester and Joseph Stewart, *Public Policy: An Evolutionary Approach,* pp. 12–13. The predominant political cultures were brought to America in various waves of immigration during the past two centuries. They originated in northern and western Europe and were brought with the Puritans and the English, French, Germans, and Scandinavians. The cultures persist to this day and affect the kinds of policies that are adopted in states.

49. Many political scientists believe that the United States does have a national political culture that includes at least four major elements that the majority of people have common feelings about, regardless of geographic region. *Liberty* is synonymous with freedom, which may be thought of as the right to do whatever you please as long as it does not hurt someone else or infringe on someone else's rights. *Equality* is a belief based on the ideal that everyone should have an equal vote, equality under the law, and equal access to opportunity. Note that equal access of opportunity is not the same as equality of results. Most people believe in the ideals of *democracy,* particularly that government officials should be held accountable to the people. The element of *civic duty* holds that people should take civic duties, community affairs, and so on seriously.

50. During Eisenhower's second term, desegregation became one of the primary issues on the national agenda. Although personally unenthusiastic about desegregation, Eisenhower sent federal troops to Little Rock, Arkansas, to enforce a court-ordered school desegregation decision. His administration supported the civil rights legislation that passed Congress in 1957 and 1960, and he prohibited discriminatory practices in the District of Columbia and in federal facilities such as navy yards and hospitals.

51. Patrick Sloyan, "The Day They Shut Birmingham Down," *The Washington Monthly* (May 1972), pp. 41–51.

52. Political culture tends to be associated with states or regions but may vary even with states. For example, the southern coastal area of South Carolina tends to have a very traditionalistic political culture, but the upper region of the state has a very moralistic political culture.

53. James Lester and Joseph Stewart, *Public Policy: An Evolutionary Approach,* pp. 14–15.

54. Allan Lerner and John Wanat, *Public Administration: A Realistic Reinterpretation of Contemporary Public Management* (Englewood Cliffs, NJ: Prentice-Hall, 1992), pp 4–5.

55. The most influential work by John Locke is the *Second Treatise of Government* (there were two treatises on government, but the second deals with the liberal state). In this work, Locke describes the fundamental principles of the liberal state. He believed that the liberal state evolved from a near perfect state of nature and that people's greed became the chief defect that fouled up the perfect state of nature. See John Locke, *Two Treatises of Government* (New York: Cambridge University Press, 1963). Conversely, another great philosopher, Thomas Hobbes, believed that the state of nature is less perfect than indicated in Locke's theory. Hobbes saw life in the state as nasty, harsh, and short. The liberal state had to be created to bring order to chaos. For Hobbes, a good government allows the maximum amount of freedom for people while maintaining enough control to maintain order. People surrender their freedom to the state. For Locke, the individual mattered most: People have basic rights that cannot be taken away, and people have created government to protect those rights. Is America more like the state described by Locke or by Hobbes? This subject has been debated for many years. Although most of us prefer the description provided by Locke, many believe that in reality our society has many of the elements described by Hobbes in his classic book, *Leviathan.* For a thorough discussion about liberalism in America, see Louis Hartz, *The Liberal Tradition in America* (New York: Harcourt, Brace, 1955).

56. This definition is widely accepted. *The American Heritage Dictionary of the English Language,* 3rd ed. (Boston: Houghton Mifflin, 1992).

57. This information came from *Fortune Magazine Online* at http://www.fortune.com/lists/40under40/snap_1.html.

58. In market theory, the goal is to reach a state of perfect efficiency known as Pareto optimality. This state exists when resources are allocated in such a way that no one's position can be improved without a loss to someone else. In other words, this may be thought of as a state of equilibrium where any movement comes at the expense of another firm.

59. See Charles Wolf, *Markets or Governments: Choosing between Imperfect Alternatives* (Cambridge, MA: MIT Press, 1988).

60. Capitalism evolved as a revolt against mercantile systems (state-controlled economies).

61. Interestingly, in the 1700s, Adam Smith warned us about corporate ownership. He did not like such ventures because if management were separated from ownership, it would be less likely to look after the best interests of the firm. Smith recognized that stockholders and management are severed in this arrangement, which he felt was a very unwise way to organize a business. For an interesting discussion about Smith's dislike for "combina-tions" and corporate organization, see John Kenneth Galbraith, *The Age of Uncertainty* (Boston: Houghton Mifflin, 1977), p. 26.

62. For a good discussion of the origins of capitalism, see Karl Polanyi, *The Great Transformation* (Boston: Beacon Press, 1957). There has been an ongoing debate over the importance of economic concentration in the United States; see John Kenneth Galbraith's classic book, *The New Industrial State* (Boston: Houghton Mifflin, 1967), and James Barber, *The American Corporation: Its Power, Its Money, Its Politics* (London: MacGibbon and Kee, 1970). Also, for many years Thomas Dye has been publishing a book entitled *Who's Running America?* The book has gone through many editions and been updated many times. See Thomas Dye, *Who's Running America?* (Boston: Duxbury Press, 1976).

63. For excellent discussions about capitalism in the United States, see William Simon, *A Time for Truth* (New York: McGraw-Hill, 1978); George Gilder, *Wealth and Poverty* (New York: Basic Books); and Jude Wanniski, *The Way the World Works* (New York: Simon and Schuster, 1983).

64. Marshall Dimock, "The Restorative Qualities of Citizenship," *Public Administration Review 50* (January–February, 1990), pp. 21–25.

65. John Kenneth Galbraith, *The Age of Uncertainty,* Chapter 9.

66. Many types of market failure go beyond the scope of this book. Natural monopolies are used here simply as an example. For an excellent discussion about market failures, see Charles Wolf, *Markets or Governments: Choosing between Imperfect Alternatives.* Also see Jeffrey Greene, *Cities and Privatization: Prospects for the New Century* (Upper Saddle River, NJ: Prentice-Hall, 2002), Chapter 1.

67. Steve Hanke and Stephen J. K. Walter, "Privatizing Waterworks," in Steve Hanke, Ed., *Prospects for Privatization* (New York: Academy of Political Science, 1982), pp. 104–113.

68. In the case of water utilities, there are about 54,000 water systems in the United States; 22,600 of the systems are government owned and operated. Most water systems in the nation are operated by public utility organizations (technically called investor-owned public utilities). This information is available from the American Water Works Association at http://www.awwa.org.

69. Ownership (stockholders) is separated from management in corporations.

70. Peter Drucker describes how capitalism and the world of business have changed in *People and Performance: The Best of Peter Drucker on Management* (New York: Harper & Row, 1977), Chapter 1.

71. Graham T. Allison, "Public and Private Management: Are They Fundamentally Alike in All Unimportant Respects?" in Richard Stillman II, Ed., *Public*

Administration: Concepts and Cases, 4th ed. (Boston: Houghton Mifflin, 1988), pp. 283–298.

72. *Nollan v. California Coastal Commission,* 483 U.S. 825 (1987).

73. Richard Stillman II, *The American Bureaucracy: The Core of Modern Government,* p. 10.

74. Barry Bozeman made this point very clear in his book *All Organizations Are Public* (San Francisco: Jossey-Bass, 1987).

75. Robert D. Lee, Jr., and Ronald W. Johnson, *Public Budgeting Systems,* 4th ed. (Gaithersburg, MD: Aspen, 1994), p. 23.

76. Robert D. Lee, Jr., *Public Personnel Systems* (Rockville, MD: Aspen, 1987), p. 8.

2

Studying Public Administration

An Overview of the Discipline

It is the object of administrative study to discover, first,
what government can properly and successfully do, and secondly,
how it can do these proper things with the utmost possible efficiency
and at the least possible cost either of money or of energy.

WOODROW WILSON

THE STUDY OF PUBLIC ADMINISTRATION

Why do we study public administration? As indicated in Chapter 1, government and public agencies play a pivotal role in modern society. They essentially
"manage" the affairs of the state and implement a wide variety of policies that
affect virtually everyone in society. From establishing speed limits to promoting
research and development at universities, government and its agencies are
everywhere. But is the primary quest for public administration *efficiency?*[1] Or is
it *effectiveness* in achieving stated objectives? Or is it *responsiveness* to the needs of
society? Or is the purpose of public administration to advance *social equity* in
American society? Over the years, public administration has been all of these
things and more.

The study of public administration has gone through many phases and is still evolving. Public administration is both a practice (or profession) and an academic discipline. The practice involves the work of the 19 million people who are employed in government agencies at the federal, state, and local levels. The academic discipline involves studying the activities that take place in public agencies, mainly by professors and other researchers. Public administration is a multidisciplinary field that involves other academic areas, including political science and management. Throughout its history in the United States, there have been close links between the practice of public administration and the academic discipline. This is reflected in the discipline's leading journal entitled *Public Administration Review (PAR)*, which regularly contains articles authored by practitioners. As in all academic fields, it is impossible to understand public administration in the present without having some knowledge about the past and how the field developed. Public administration has a rich past. The study of public administration is concerned with understanding the complexities of public agencies. This includes understanding the environment in which public agencies function, how they function, what they do, and why they do it. By assembling a body of knowledge and working closely with those in the practical field, it is believed that the efforts of the discipline will help create better government, better public agencies, and therefore a better society. The body of knowledge is acquired through rigorous research involving methodologies that range from simple observations to complex econometric models. Public administration is a social science because it studies social phenomena and human behavior. The field of inquiry is broad and complex, just like the world in which public agencies exist.

Public administration also trains future public administrators in master's of public administration programs (an MPA is comparable to the master's of business administration, or MBA, degree offered by business schools) and provides continuing education and training for midcareer employees through executive institutes and doctor of public administration (DPA) programs. Both the MPA and DPA degrees are geared toward the practitioner, while PhD programs in public administration are research-oriented. The training includes courses in numerous areas of management, organizational theory and behavior, personnel administration, budgeting and financial management, public policy, program evaluation, and administrative law. The academic discipline helps shape the practice, and the practice also shapes the discipline as those in the discipline respond to changes in the practical field. The world of public administration is constantly evolving, and the discipline does more than observe and study the practical field. The close involvement with the practice of public administration makes the discipline unique and rich because it helps those in the discipline relate to the everyday world of public management.

THE DISCIPLINE OF PUBLIC
ADMINISTRATION: A BRIEF OVERVIEW

Public administration and the bureaucracy date back many centuries, but the discipline of public administration is not that old. In the United States, we attribute the beginning of public administration as a field of study to Woodrow Wilson's article "The Study of Administration," which was published in 1887. The discipline, born in political science, may be thought of as an "unwanted child." This still is the case for many public administration programs that are housed within political science departments. Since the beginning of American public administration, a tension has existed between "PA types" and regular political scientists.[2] This is largely due to the focus of public administration, which views organizations and the behavior of bureaucrats in an entirely different way from political science. Originally, public administration was a welcome addition to political science (during the early 1900s). Public administration focused on administering public bureaucracies, and the field did rather well at developing an impressive amount of knowledge. But that soon changed as public administration forged its own reputation, developed its own professional associations and journals, and pursued its own interests. Nonetheless, the tension remains. Although born within political science, for the most part, public administration has never been completely comfortable with political science as its academic home, and there has always been a desire to break away and form separate schools. Many public administration programs have broken away, but public administration is still very linked to political science. For many political scientists, public administration was something less than, and an adjunct to, the mother discipline. "PA types" sometimes have been viewed as being interested in such things as counting manhole covers and animal control in cities. To some political scientists, this is hardly comparable to studying the diplomacy between nations and the other great endeavors of political science. The discipline of political science, however, has had its own problems unrelated to public administration; for many years, political science fought the reputation of being a junior member of the social sciences.

The development of public administration as an academic discipline has been described as *locus* versus *focus,* and the past 100 years or so have been termed "a century in quandary" by Nicholas Henry. *Locus* refers to "where" the field is, and *focus* refers to "what" the field studies.[3] Like most social sciences, public administration eventually saw a dispute develop over "how" the field should study whatever it is supposed to study. Nicholas Henry separates the development of the discipline into a series of paradigms[4] that help us to briefly walk through the stages of development of the "unwanted child of political science."[5] The major paradigms gave birth to several major schools of thought: the *classical school* (the early period), *the behaviorists* (the empirical period that sought to study actual behavior), and the *administration-as-politics school* (the New Public Administration era). More recently, a *refounding movement* has emerged (the era of reinventing government, privatization, and public choice theory) that challenges the primary school, the orthodox school of public administration.[6] (See Box 2.1, which appears later in this chapter, for a comparison of the assumptions and underpinnings of these various schools of thought).

CLASSICAL PERIOD: THE POLITICS-ADMINISTRATION DICHOTOMY AND THE PRINCIPLES OF PUBLIC ADMINISTRATION (1900–1940)

Major Points of the Classical School

- The idea of bringing competence to governmental administration.
- Politics can be separated from administration.
- A generic view of administration. Administration is administration.
- A strong belief in the efficacy of science. A science of administration is possible; scientific principles of administration can be discovered and then applied to administrative settings.
- The techniques of business administration are applicable to public organizations.
- People are segmentally involved with their work.
- A mechanistic view of people and the world.
- Money is the primary motivator for workers.
- The purpose of administration is to implement public law.
- A strong commitment to democracy (the Reform Era).

Wilson's essay, "The Study of Administration," reflected the basic philosophy held by public administration during the classical period and is considered to be the first truly theoretical literature on American public administration. Wilson wrote during a time of widespread corruption in government as the progressive movement sought to clean up government using several techniques. His article suggested that there was a distinction between political functions and administering agencies. Partisan politics was blamed for many of the problems during this era, so it is not surprising that the early writers would want to separate politics from administration. Wilson and many reformers sought to bring competence to government through science, while other reformers wanted to change structures of government to limit the power of political parties. The era might also be summed up as two models fighting for control of American democracy: *rule by factions,* which reflected the desires of political machines that dominated urban politics, versus a *public interest* model, which reflected the aspirations of reformers. If the structure could be changed (primary elections, city manager form of government, at-large elections, etc.) and competent administration put in place, government and democracy would work better. The primary goal was to establish neutrally competent professional administration.

The politics–administration dichotomy is conceptually simple. Politics involves the activities that have to do with formulating policies for the state, and administration is the execution of those policies. In other words, policies are formulated in the democratic processes of government institutions, such as Congress, and then given to the executive branch and its agencies of government for implementation. Wilson believed that administration should be concerned with the detailed and systematic execution of law and that there was little difference between business and public administration. Early reformers believed that government should and could become more businesslike in its operations. Administration was believed to be administration. The central idea of separating politics from administration was that politics—the struggle with ideology, vision, debate over the direction of policy, and the ultimate passing of public law—should take place in legislatures and political arenas. Once policies were created and enacted into laws, and had passed judicial scrutiny if challenged, government agencies were only supposed to implement them. Mixing politics and administration made administrative activities less efficient and effective. The agencies of government were not considered to be part of the political arena. Political parties had used the agencies for political purposes on a regular basis, particularly for providing patronage jobs for those loyal to the party. Civil service reform was one remedy. The ideal behind civil service reform was to insulate government workers from political interference so they could perform their jobs and bring expertise to government service. Thus, the politics–administration distinction was based on the belief that politicians decide if a road should be built, and then turn to engineers to build the road. Influenced partly by other developments of the era, namely Frederick Taylor's scientific management,[7] the classical school held that there could be only "one right way" to build a road. Politicians determined policies, and then turned to "administrative engineers" to implement them.[8]

The mode of the times was characterized by reformism, particularly at the local level. This helped create a very close relationship between the discipline of public administration and the practical field. The New York Bureau of Municipal Research (founded in 1906 to promote better management of local government) created the nation's first school of public administration in 1911. The school was called the Training School for Public Service. Political scientist Charles Beard was the school's first director. In 1924, the program was moved to Syracuse University, making it the first program associated with a university—the Maxwell School of Citizenship and Public Affairs.[9] In 1926, Leonard White published the first textbook entirely devoted to public administration, which echoed the separation of administration from politics. In short, the guiding paradigms of this era were that politics should not be mixed with management and that management can be studied scientifically. This implied that a science of administration was possible because administration was "value-free."[10] The early years of public administration were dominated by these ideas.

During the 1920s, public administration was emerging as its own distinct field within political science. The discipline of public administration taught different courses than political science, such as organization theory, budgeting, and personnel management.

The second phase of the classical period focused on the principles of good administration by centering on managerial expertise. Because of its knowledge of management, industry and government both utilized those from the academic field of public administration. Administration was administration, whether the organization was in the public or private sector. Thus, the principles were thought to be universal. After all, the goal of science was to discover the laws of the universe; the goals for a science of administration were to discover the principles (perhaps the closest thing to laws in the minds of the classic school) to enhance our understanding, apply them, and make more efficient administrative organizations. The idea that administration is administration came to be known as the *public-private dichotomy.* That is, the principles of good administration are the same whether one is administering a bank or a city. Wilson believed that the field of administration was the field of business. But the focus of public administration during this period was more on upper management, organizational charts, and executives, while business administration had given much more attention to the lower end of the organization, namely, the assembly line. Taylor's scientific management was not as concerned with the higher levels of organizations. His focus was on how to make line workers (or production) more efficient. It was the responsibility of management to discover the "one best way of doing something" and to then teach it to the workers. Taylor's work was aimed at finding the most efficient physical movements that would minimize worker fatigue and, therefore, enhance productivity. Additionally, the classical era was dominated by a particular vision of the world and people. It believed that people were only segmentally involved with their work, which led to the idea that money was the primary motivator. Also, the classical school had a very mechanistic view of the world: if one could understand how the parts worked, they could be manipulated. The purpose of Elton Mayo's famous Hawthorne studies, which were conducted at a Western Electric plant near Chicago in 1927, was to examine the relationships between workers, work environment, and productivity. Although he set out to perform a "typical" scientific management inquiry, Mayo's remarkable findings ignited the human relations movement (he discovered the importance of the informal group) and laid the early seeds for the behaviorist movement that would come later.[11] Also during this time period, German sociologist Max Weber defined the bureaucratic form of organization, and Mary Parker Follett offered a management philosophy based on individual motivation and group problem solving, which would later lead to the more modern idea of participatory management.[12]

In 1937, Luther Gulick and Lyndall Urwick published a report for President Roosevelt's Committee on Administrative Science that contained the famous acronym POSDCORB. The *Papers on the Science of Administration* turned out to be one of the most influential publications ever on the "principles" of administration. The acronym represented seven points that helped in understanding the work performed by administrators. POSDCORB stands for planning, organizing, staffing, directing, coordinating, reporting, and budgeting (the CO are used together for coordinating). These principles greatly affected the discipline and continue to be discussed in public administration textbooks today. The principles had a normative element, like most of the work of this time period. That is, good administration *should* use the principles to be more efficient. Public administration, as an academic field of inquiry, would run into problems with political science over the desire to establish separate schools of public administration.[13] In 1939, the American Society for Public Administration (ASPA) was established. It became the leading professional association of public administration practitioners and scholars. ASPA publishes the leading journal, *Public Administration Review (PAR)*. ASPA was formed in part as a response to the tensions between those teaching public administration and those in the discipline of political science. People in public administration generally felt that people in political science did not adequately understand or nurture the needs of those who were interested in improving the performance of public organizations.[14] One of the central goals of ASPA, which remains to this day, is to promote professionalism in public administration. Professionalism is typically tied to education and training. This requires close ties to universities to maintain an educational experience with a curriculum that properly prepares those seeking to enter a profession. The 1930s is when the "rise of the administrative state" began.[15] The response to the complexities of the Great Depression and later World War II brought more government and more public administration. Despite its growth and rise in prestige, the classical school of public administration would face an internal conceptual challenge that eventually caused the discipline to abandon many of its ideas.

BEHAVIORIST PERIOD (1940–1970): PUBLIC ADMINISTRATION AS POLITICAL SCIENCE (1950–1970) AND AS MANAGEMENT (1956–1970)

Major Points of the Behaviorist Period

- Dispute that public administration has discovered principles of administration.
- Advocating the study of real behavior.
- A logical-positivist view of science.
- Belief that values can be separated from facts (fact-value dichotomy).
- Concern is aimed at organization and structure to make better organizations.
- Descriptive more than prescriptive.
- American Society for Public Administration (ASPA) founded in 1939.

- Herbert Simon offers a new "twin" paradigm for public administration.
- Public administration returns to political science, still as the unwanted child.
- One division of public administration focuses on management.
- Debate over the public-private dichotomy continues.
- Anthony Downs applies economic principles to predict behavior in bureaus and bureaucrats. This was the forerunner to public choice theory.
- The subfields of comparative and developmental administration are tried.

Chester Barnard published *The Functions of the Executive* in 1938.[16] Barnard viewed organizations differently from the way they were viewed by the classical school. He saw them as cooperative systems in which the functions of executives were to balance the needs of the organization with the needs of the individual, and to establish more effective communication. The guiding doctrine viewed organizations as closed systems with workers only segmentally involved. This book greatly influenced Herbert Simon. In *Administrative Behavior,* Simon argued that for every "principle of administration" there was a counterprinciple, which rendered the classical principles useless even for teaching people about management.[17] How could something be a principle of administration if there was always a counterprinciple? Simon went further by showing that limits exist on the ability of human organizations to process and handle information. He realized that decision makers needed to make "rational decisions," but argued that it was incorrect to assume that all of the alternatives available to decision makers were known along with the consequences. Simon did not believe that decision makers waded through all of the alternatives, evaluated their advantages and disadvantages, and then chose the "best" alternative. Instead, he believed that those making decisions chose the alternative that "satisficed" the problem from their point of view. This idea was the core of Simon's theory of "bounded rationality"—the idea that people (and managers) are rational decision makers within limits. His ideas were a sharp contrast to the principles advocated by the classical literature; and his work essentially ended the classical period's idea of "principles of administration" once and for all, and made the study of administration a truly modern social science.[18]

The "behavioral revolution" had arrived. The focus of the behaviorists was simple; they studied "real" behavior with the individual often being the basic unit of analysis. The approach was multidisciplinary, called for rigorous use of the scientific method, and was descriptive in nature. The principal concern was with organization structure and management. Behaviorists sought to modify the hierarchical structure and appeal to a broad range of human needs to more effectively motivate workers in the organization. The classical schools tended to be normative in both political science and public administration. For example, the classical school in political science tended to study institutions, such as Congress, by examining their functions and legal obligations, and evaluated institutions based on whether they performed their legal duties. The behaviorists were less concerned with normative dimensions than was the classical school. They wanted to study how a bill "really" becomes law by examining members of Congress and other actors in the policy process. In public administration, the classical school often evaluated administration in the same fashion. That is, good administration *should* be doing certain things, such as organizing, planning, and the like. The classical approach had focused on executive decision making, had a top-down orientation, taught the virtues of span of control, urged specialization, and demanded centralization. The behaviorist approach called for a wider span of control, decentralization, an employee-oriented mode of supervision, and later participatory decision making. The behaviorists wanted to know what managers really do, and they made some interesting discoveries that will be discussed in Chapter 4. Whether it is the behavior of managers, formulation of public policy, or sexual behavior,[19] behaviorists, regardless of their academic discipline, wanted to know *how* and *why* something functioned. To the behaviorist, the central questions revolved around understanding and explaining the realities of the organization and life inside the organization. In the discipline of public administration, that meant examining bureaucracies from a very different perspective than in the past to understand how and why organizations function as they do.

Following the work of Simon and others, public administration went in several different directions. The discipline had in many respects lost its academic *locus.* Some returned to political science—the mother discipline. Many, even those who had remained friendly toward public administration, believed that it might evaporate as a discipline.[20] It was a period of struggle as public administration sorted out what it would become next. This was a time of soul searching for the discipline, with some opting for the behavior mode and others trying to find a niche within political science. It was a difficult time. In the late 1960s, public administration was no longer included as an organizing category for the American Political Science Association's annual conferences (this meant that there were no panels on public administration at the conferences), and few public administration articles were published in the major political science journals. Political science was changing, too. David Easton's *The Political System: An Inquiry into the State of Political Science* was an influential book that gave political science more clout. Easton, borrowing from the biological sciences,[21] applied the idea of a "systems model" to political analysis.[22] Easton is credited with popularizing the idea that "politics is a system." Anthony Downs further strengthened the stature of political science with *An Economic Theory of Democracy* in 1957, which brought economic analysis into the discipline.[23] For public administration, new hope emerged with the promising new subfields of comparative and developmental administration. Like comparative politics, comparative administration focused on administration in other countries, and developmental administration focused on administration in the third world. The problem with the comparative and development focuses was that American public administration was very much "culture-bound" to the ideals of American democracy and maintained a practitioner orientation.[24] Those studying comparative administration tried to break away from this problem by focusing more on theory-building, while American public administration has always maintained its "practitioners' orientation." By the 1970s, courses in comparative and developmental administration were in many curricula, but were typically not required as MPA courses. For the most part, the subfields of comparative and developmental administration turned out to be a disappointment for the field of public administration.[25]

During this same era, roughly 1956 until 1970, another group focused on "public administration as management." Schools of business administration and management were growing in the nation at the time and helped make this alternative to the political science focus possible. Management concentrated on many of the same areas of interest as public administration. Many of the courses were already included in MPA curriculums, such as organization theory, behavior, planning, decision making, management science, human resource management, information systems, budgeting, auditing, and productivity. For this group, management was management regardless of where it was applied. In 1956, *Administrative Science Quarterly* was founded with the idea that the public-business distinction was false. Thus, the public-private dichotomy was alive and well at the time, and the orientation was toward a generic management theory. But debate soon emerged regarding whether public and private management were truly the same. For many years, public administration tried to explain what *public* in the term *public administration* meant. The issues raised that caused public and private organizations to be compared included the following questions.[26]

- What is an organization's proper role toward its external environment?
- Can the similarities between public and private organizations be understood by examining the parts or only by looking at the organization as a whole?
- Are the similarities and differences of equal importance?
- Should the proof (or evidence) of the existence of similarities and differences be based on case experiences or on dominant patterns found in the entire population of organizations?

Not surprisingly, two perspectives quickly emerged. Analysts who believed that public and private organizations are similar held that both types of organizations seek to achieve *instrumental goals*. That is, goals are goals. Those who felt that there is a difference between public and private organizations believed that the goals of public organizations are *social in nature*. Analysts who believed public and private organizations are similar believed that understanding is based on examining the *parts*, whereas those who felt that public and private organizations are distinctly different believed one has to examine the *organization as a whole*. Those who felt that organizations are generic saw the similarities and differences weighted equally, while those who believed that public and private organizations are different felt that they are similar in all unimportant aspects. The two perspectives also disagree on the basis of evidence to be used, with those who believe public and private management to be similar preferring case studies and experience, and those who see distinct differences preferring to examine patterns found in the universe of all organizations.[27] The bottom line was that the public-private dichotomy remained unsettled. Figure 2.1 illustrates some of the major differences between public and private organizations.

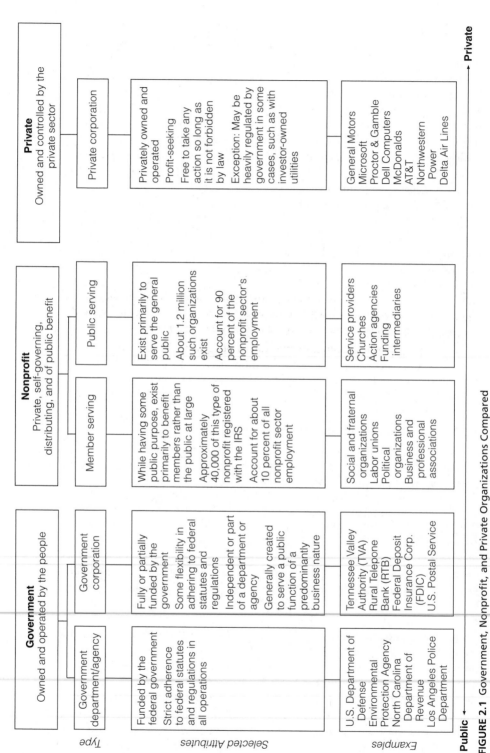

FIGURE 2.1 Government, Nonprofit, and Private Organizations Compared

SOURCE: Adapted from Grover Starling, *Managing the Public Sector*, 6th ed. (Fort Worth, TX: Harcourt, 2002), p. 10.

The debate over differences and similarities produced a lot of literature, including Graham T. Allison's famous article "Public and Private Management: Are They Fundamentally Alike in all Unimportant Respects?"[28] Allison's article, which is still required reading today in many public administration programs, brought to light at least eight critical differences between public and private management.[29] The article was written in the 1980s, which illustrates that the public-private dichotomy was still an issue at that time.

- In the public sector, managers have relatively short time horizons. The budget process and political pressure are mainly responsible for the short-term focus.

- Leadership does not last long in public organizations. Appointees who occupy the highest positions average 18 months of service in office. Thus, the relatively quick turnover of leadership affects public bureaus.

- Performance measures are often vague or arbitrary in public service. There is no inherent standard for measuring the rate of return or overall effect for most public services. Moreover, there is no profit motive.

- Public managers have less discretion over personnel matters. Hiring, firing, promotions, salary, and discipline issues are constrained by legislation, and there are conflicts between appointed and career positions.

- Public programs must often pursue values of equity, fairness, and negotiated consensus, rather than the more narrow goals of efficiency and competitive performance.

- Government officials operate under more scrutiny from the public, which expects public officials to act with more fairness, responsibility, accountability, and honesty than managers in the private sector. The mass media pays much closer attention to the operations and decisions of public agencies than it does to those of private corporations.

- Public managers typically have much less authority over the organization and over those who may influence a policy area. They must resort to persuasion and build political coalitions in order to enact policies.

- Public officials are more often subject to scrutiny and direction from outside institutions such as courts and legislatures.

More will be said about public versus private management in later chapters, but this illustrates that the public-private dichotomy still had the attention of scholars. Despite years of discussion and debate, the public-private dichotomy remains.

During this period, management scholars published many significant articles and books that greatly influenced public administration, including Douglas McGregor's concept of Theory X and Y, Victor Vroom's work on the "process" of motivation, Robert Blake and Jane Mouton's "managerial grid," and Chris Argyris's work on an open-system theory of organizations.[30] The contributions made by management scholars during this period were impressive and were founded in the behaviorist school of thought.

THE NEW PUBLIC ADMINISTRATION
(1968–1980s)

Major Point

- The "new public administration" emerges with a 1960s radical view of the times. It stresses organizational humanism, policy advocacy, participatory bureaucracy, representative bureaucracy, and clientele advocacy. Its goal is to use the power of the bureaucracy to remedy many of society's ills and injustices; it is concerned more with equity than efficiency.

One of the most notable developments in the late 1960s was the development of a new school of thought that came to be known as the "new public administration." This perspective represented a radical departure for the discipline. The focus was not on studying the efficiency or effectiveness of public organizations. Reflecting the mood of the times, this new school was very normative in nature and very activist. The new public administration was very moral and eager to bring about change. It sought to use public agencies to advance the needs of clienteles and to use the power of the bureaucracy to remedy the social problems of the times. This school of thought stressed organizational humanism and rejected the "rationality" of the behavioral school. Cost-benefit analyses, efficiency, and organizational design were not the tools of the new public administration. In fact, they rejected the idea of cost-benefit analyses, as failing to serve human needs and develop the right types of policies, at least as defined by their school. A conference held at Syracuse University in 1968 with Dwight Waldo and a group of young public administrationists produced, *Toward a New Public Administration* (published in 1971), which remains the premiere work in this area. The "New PA" would have a lasting impact on public administration, although it did not become the mainstream focus of American public administration. Perhaps its greatest impact was to force the issue of equity into the public administration arena. Prior to this time, the focus remained on creating efficient and effective organizations.

This era also saw a rise in professionalism for the practitioner and the founding of the National Academy of Public Administration in 1967. A wealth of literature was produced including Anthony Downs with, *Inside Bureaucracy,* which applied the principles of economics to organizations (the forerunner of public choice theory). Aaron Wildavsky published his famous, *Politics of the Budgetary Process,* which would put incrementalism into the mainstream of public budgeting. In 1969, management scholar Peter Drucker, famous for management by objectives earlier, wrote a book, *The Age of Discontinuity,* that would challenge government to govern and let the private sector produce society's goods and services. This was the forerunner to the privatization movement that would become prominent in the 1980s. Of course, public administration had a long history of producing great literature, which continues to this day.[31]

PUBLIC ADMINISTRATION AS PUBLIC ADMINISTRATION (1970–) AND THE REFOUNDING PERIOD (1980–)

Major Points

- Public administration moves into a new age and sees itself as "public administration."

- The National Association of Schools of Public Affairs and Administration (NASPAA) is founded and becomes the accrediting body for master's of public administration programs. Professionalism and standards are established that give public administration programs greater prestige and greater quality.

- The discipline matures and houses a diversity of ideas, all seeking to improve some aspect of public organizations or society.

- Many MPA programs leave political science departments or are created in areas outside of political science.

- The orthodox school of public administration (the dominant school of thought in the discipline at this stage) is challenged. Challenges come from public choice theory, the privatization movement, and the reinventing government movement.

- Efficiency must be balanced with other competing goals, such as public accountability and equity.

The National Association of Schools of Public Affairs and Administration (NASPAA) was founded in 1970.[32] The foundation of NASPAA may be viewed as a rise in confidence in the field of public administration and an act of succession.[33] In 1983, NASPAA became the formal accrediting body for master's of public administration programs nationwide. The accreditation brings with it greater prestige for the MPA programs and enables the programs to attract better faculty and students. Surveys conducted by NASPAA indicate that the succession from the discipline of political science is real. Table 2.1 indicates that most public administration programs are no longer housed within political science departments. MPA programs have increased over the past 30 years, along with the number of students. The curriculums have been improved, which has helped to produce a better-educated and better-trained group of new, young professionals for the practical field. Although many programs are not accredited by NASPAA, namely smaller programs, the presence of this organization has helped to raise the level of MPA programs across the nation. For years there was a debate over the appropriate academic home for public administration. Although the debate is not entirely settled, public administration appears to have been split in several different ways, with some programs remaining in political science and others forming their own separate schools.

Table 2.1 Where Master of Public Administration (PA) Programs Are Located for Selected Years

Organizational Pattern	1973	1977	1981	1985	1991	1995
Separate professional schools	25%	21%	17%	14%	13%	16%
Separate departments in large units	23%	31%	33%	34%	38%	35%
PA programs combined with another professional school (such as business administration)	17%	8%	10%	15%	9%	5%
PA programs within political science departments	36%	40%	39%	31%	36%	33%
Unclassified organization*	0	0	1%	6%	6%	10%
	N = 101	N = 156	N = 192	N = 193	N = 222	N = 232

*Unclassified organization typically includes interdisciplinary programs and institutes that are not attached to specific academic departments or schools.

SOURCE: Adapted from Nicholas Henry, *Public Administration and Public Affairs*, 7th ed. (Upper Saddle River, NJ: Prentice-Hall, 1999), p. 47.

Today, as mentioned earlier, more programs are separate than are housed within political science departments.

Public administration has been well established since the 1970s. By that time, it had its own professional associations, accreditation, and professional journals; and it had developed a rich body of literature that was multidisciplinary, scientific, and theoretical. Yet, it had also been true to its commitment to maintain a "practitioner orientation." Since the 1970s, MPA programs have become increasingly popular. The discipline houses a diversity of ideas and several schools of thought, but the synthesis of all that the years have created is called the orthodox, or mainstream, school of public administration. The orthodox school adheres to the basic elements of public administration. Combining the best of what public administration as a discipline has offered over the years is how the orthodox school was created. Generally, this school believes that democracy is realistically achievable only if power is concentrated so that it can be held accountable. Otherwise, responsibility blends into the social surround.[34] Public administration tends to accept the institutions that have emerged to govern and seeks to make them more efficient and effective.[35] The orthodox school is concerned with institutional continuity and public accountability. Government must be concerned with efficiency, but must also accommodate equity and other concerns that are important to society.[36] The orthodox school emphasizes that public institutions are the principal vehicles for expressing common and public concerns. Strong public institutions are necessary to govern. Moreover, this school believes that public agencies do serve the public interest—a concept that is included in ASPA's Code of Ethics.[37] The orthodox school of public administration believes that privatization is based on the erroneous assumption that the public and private sectors are fundamentally alike and both subject to the same set of incentives and disincentives. Public administration claims the public sector cannot be fairly compared to private business. Governments function in a political environment, whereas private firms exist in a competitive-economic milieu.[38] In short, the orthodox school has a strong commitment to democracy, government, and its institutions. Moreover, the goals of public administration are to acquire knowledge, train future public administrators, and create strong, stable, and effective organizations to help govern society.

During the late 1980s and through the present day, public administration has received new challenges from public choice theory (from economics), the privatization movement, and the reinventing government movement. During the late 1970s, a movement began to question the efficiency of government relative to the private sector. Government was viewed as inefficient by design because it was a monopoly. In 1971, Vincent and Elinor Ostrom published an article, "Public Choice: A Different Approach to the Study of Public Administration," in the *Public Administration Review*.[39] The article, published in public administration's most prestigious journal, was the first of many publications that challenged the way public bureaucracies operate. A wave of literature hit public administration from the new public choice school throughout the 1970s and 1980s. Applying the techniques and theories of microeconomics, public choice theorists believed that the behavior of public bureaucrats was normal. Like everyone else, they are motivated by self-interest. In the marketplace, self-interest is fine because it is checked by market mechanisms. But in public agencies it leads to a variety of pathological problems that result in a bloated, expensive, and inefficient government. Scholars such as James Buchanan, Gordon Tullock, and Vincent Ostrom made this theory very popular in the 1980s. Concurrently, the privatization movement was launched when E. S. Savas[40] discovered that public garbage collection was significantly more costly than private collection. A wave of efficiency studies that covered virtually every conceivable service seemed to confirm that the private sector could produce the same services as the public sector at significantly lower costs. Thus, the push came to privatize services that could be handled by the private sector. Savas's work emerged during a fiscally stressed time (the late 1970s), and by the end of the 1980s, the term *privatization* was widely known and recognized by public administration, although it had many critics. In 1992, David Osborne and Ted Gaebler wrote a book, *Reinventing Government,*[41] in which they challenged the basic way government worked. In short, government had become so complicated that "process" and too much "accountability" made accomplishing anything next to impossible. This posed a new challenge for public administration. Many in public administration fought the ideas, but efficiency was once again at the forefront of the discipline. Some have referred to this latest era as the "refounding" period because of the many challenges to the existing nature of government bureaucracy.[42] (Privatization, public

BOX 2.1 The Development of Public Administration as a Discipline: An Overview of the Four Major Periods

The ideological premises have varied during different periods.

I. Classical Approach (Late 1880s–1940s)

1. *Politics-administration dichotomy:* Believed that politics could be removed.
2. *Generic management orientation:* Believed that public and private management were similar—the public-private dichotomy.
3. *Mechanistic view of humans and the world:* Believed that behavior could be manipulated through incentives and rewards.
4. *Science of administration:* Held a strong belief in the potential of science.
5. *Centralization:* Believed in centralization of the organization.
6. *Commitment to democracy and the public interest.*
7. *Legalistic and prescriptive:* Believed in a legal approach and held a prescriptive orientation.
8. *Major figures:* Frederick Taylor (scientific management); Max Weber (concept of bureaucracy); Chester Barnard (authority); Luther Gulick (wrote extensively about the role of administration in government); Mary Parker Follett (opposed the general assumptions of Taylor's scientific management).

Major goal was efficiency and the belief that science could be used to discover the principles of administration and to build efficient organizations. This shool also had a strong commitment to democracy and was primarily normative. Lasting contributions: Birth of the field of public administration and creation of key organizations and publications like the American Society of Public Administration (ASPA) and the *Public Administration Review (PAR).*

II. Behaviorist Approach (Late 1940s–1970s)

1. *Studies actual behavior* (rather than using a normative approach): The concern is with *what* managers do and *why* they do what they do, rather than focusing on what managers *should* do. The goal is to learn about real behavior in order to better understand public management.
2. *Generic management:* Believes that public and private management are similar.
3. *Logical-positivist outlook:* Believes that social science should attempt to emulate the hard sciences; believes strongly in the virtues of the scientific method.
4. *Fact-value dichotomy:* Originally believed that facts could be separated from values, but this was a problematic idea from the outset that has since been abandoned to a large degree.
5. *Concern for organizational structure and management.*
6. *Descriptive rather than prescriptive:* The primary goal is to *describe* the realities of management and organizations.
7. *Literature-enriched:* This era produced many great advances in understanding organization, such as Theory X and Y, processes of motivation, systems analysis, and cost-benefit analysis studies based in "rationalism."
8. *Major figures:* Douglas McGregor (Theory X and Theory Y); Herbert Simon (bounded rationality); Elton Mayo (Hawthorne studies, although they were conducted earlier); Aaron Wildavsky (public budgeting); Anthony Downs (*Inside Bureaucracy* examines the internal dynamics of government bureaucracies).

The behaviorists' goal is to understand organizations so that better, more efficient organizations can be constructed. The study of "real" behavior and rationalism are at the core of this school of thought. Lasting contributions: Rich infusion of social sciences. Behaviorism is still widely used.

III. Administration-as-Politics (New Public Administration, 1960s–1980s)

1. *Stresses organizational humanism:* A countermovement against the rationalism associated with organizations.
2. *Policy advocacy:* Believes that bureaucrats have an obligation to be policy advocates.
3. *Participatory bureaucracy:* Believes that members of the organization should participate in decisions.
4. *Representative bureaucracy:* The idea that the composition of organizations should reflect the makeup of society in terms of race, ethnicity, and so on.
5. *Clientele representation:* Believes that government bureaucracies must look after their clienteles to the degree of advocacy.
6. *Orthodox school of PA:* The school within PA that holds that government institutions, including the bureaucracy, are the principal vehicles for governing. This school sees a positive role for government in society.
7. *Politics-administration dichotomy:* Believes that administration cannot and should not be separated from politics.
8. *Major figures:* George Frederickson (who helped to develop the idea of the New PA); Dwight Waldo (the prolific PA writer and commentator who helped with the

New PA but is in the orthodox school of public administration).

The principal goals of the New Public Administration are equity, process, accountability, and policy advocacy. The New Public Administration represented a countermovement against the ideals of the behaviorist movement. This school is epitomized by the value changes that occurred during the 1960s, which were embraced by the New Public Administration school of thought. The *orthodox school of public administration* is not the "New PA." It consists of "mainstream" public administration that represents the best developments in the discipline over time. Major figures in the orthodox school are: Richard Stillman (one of the leading spokespersons of this school); Harry Hatry (also a major spokesperson for the orthodox school of PA), and earlier, Frederick Moser—all of whom demonstrate a strong commitment to the values of public service and the idea that strong, competent government agencies are necessary to govern.

IV. The Refounding Period (Currently Developing, Late 1980s–)

1. *Public-private dichotomy:* Holds that public and private sectors have differences but also similarities. Government can learn from the private sector.
2. *Politics-administration dichotomy:* Politics complicates management but cannot be separated from it.
3. *Reinventing government:* Osborne and Gaebler are credited with the concept, which seeks to make government work more efficiently.
4. *Results orientation rather than process orientation:* Seeks to balance efficiency with other

(continued)

BOX 2.1   *continued*

concerns but seeks a lower-cost government. The notion of "doing more with less."

5. *Performance measures:* Seeks to make government more efficient and accountable while minimizing the use of privatization.

6. *Public choice school:* Questions the ability of public bureaucracies to look at anything other than self-interest of the agencies, which is based on the idea that bureaucrats are driven by self-interest. Major figures associated with public choice include Vincent Ostrom, James Buchanan, and Gordon Tullock.

7. *Privatization:* Increasing the use of the private sector in producing and delivering services. The major figure associated with privatization is E. S. Savas.

8. *Major figures:* David Osborne and Ted Gaebler *(Reinventing Government);* John Dilulio (has written extensively about the idea of reinventing government); and Peter Drucker (perhaps the most significant management author of the late 20th century).

The goal of the Refounding Period (also called the Era of Reinvention) is efficiency, although efficiency is balanced with other concerns. The Refounding Period also represents a countermovement against the New Public Administration, ranging from incremental changes to radical reforms. Among the largest complaints of this new school of thought is that government, under the New PA paradigm, sacrificed efficiency for equity and process. It also challenges the mainstream, orthodox school of public administration that adheres to the values of public service. Lasting contributions: fundamental rethinking about the field and the legitimacy of public administration.

---

choice, and reinventing government will be discussed in greater detail in Chapter 8.)

Despite the recent challenges, public administration has remained intact by incorporating many of the challenges into the discipline. Privatization turned out to be more than a passing fad, but public administration incorporated it into the field by viewing it as another tool of management. Moreover, after nearly a 30-year debate, recent studies have found that the pace at which privatization was being adopted has slowed, and use of privatization may have been overstated.[43] Public employees still provide most public services, and in some instances, privatized services are being returned to government.[44] Public choice theory was largely rejected and never took hold with mainstream public administrationists. The reinventing government movement was more palatable because it simply tried to enhance the performance of public organizations with modifications rather than radical changes. Regardless of the many challenges over the years, public administration is now an established discipline with a rich history and continues to advance professionalism and the pursuit of knowledge about public organizations.

SOME PEOPLE TO KNOW: GREAT CONTRIBUTORS TO PUBLIC ADMINISTRATION

"Top ten" lists are popular these days. You see them on David Letterman's *The Late Show,* and they appear in many places on the Internet. It would be difficult to get those who study public administration to agree on a "top ten" list of the greatest contributors to the field. The figures included here, actually a list of twelve, have all contributed to our understanding of public administration, organizations, and politics. There have been many great contributors to the discipline of public administration, including many who were actually not in the field of public administration.[45] This section offers a selection of people with which students of public administration should have some familiarity. It is not suggested that these are the "most important" figures or the "top ten," although many would make anyone's listing of the great contributors to the field. They are not ranked in an order of importance but are presented based on time periods, with each time period being represented. In the following chapters, the people noted here will join many other great contributors. Actually, this list might better be coined "twelve important people who have contributed to the discipline of public administration." This section provides a brief summary and a photograph of each person.

Woodrow Wilson (1856–1924): Founder of American Public Administration, and Much More

Woodrow Wilson, a reform-minded professor at the time, set the tone for the classical period of public administration with "The Study of Administration" (published in the *Political Science Quarterly* in 1887). Publication of this article is considered to be the beginning of American public administration. In the article, Wilson articulated a view that legitimate authority to make policy should be limited to elected public officials, courts, and political appointees—not civil servants. This is the main point of the dichotomy between politics and administration. Wilson would go on to be pres-

© CORBIS

ident of Princeton University, governor of New Jersey, and later the nation's 28th president. Wilson was a talented academic and had both a law degree and a PhD in history. His work was widely published and read. His classic on Congress, *Congressional Government,* earned him his PhD from Johns Hopkins University. The Reform Movement coincided with Wilson's time in academics and his political career. Wilson helped bring about many reforms as governor of New Jersey. While serving as the nation's president, he continued to usher in reforms, such as the Federal Reserve System, the Clayton Antitrust Act, and the Federal Trade Commission.

Frederick Taylor (1856–1915): Scientific Management

Born into a wealthy Philadelphia family, Taylor disappointed his parents when he went to work in a metal products factory. He was appalled at the factory's inefficiency and the practice of its skilled workers purposely working slowly. This inspired Taylor to propose solutions that he believed would solve productivity problems. By studying the time it took each worker to complete a step, and by rearranging equipment, Taylor believed he could discover what an average worker could produce under optimum conditions. He believed that promising higher wages would create an incentive for workers to exceed this "average" level. Thus, scientific management was born. *Principles of Scientific Management,* published in 1911, would help make Taylor one of the most influential figures from the industrial age. Although scientific management no longer dominates the literature, we can thank Taylor for making us so aware of time, productivity, and efficiency, all of which are still concerns in modern organizational life.

Max Weber (1864–1920): The Concept of Bureaucracy

Max Weber was born into a tense and difficult family in Erfurt, Germany. His mother was a religious humanitarian, and his father was a strict and harsh authoritarian. By all accounts, Weber had a difficult early life, disliked authority, got in trouble with his teachers at school for not always showing proper respect, and lived at home until he was 29. He was also hospitalized several times for psychological problems. But he would leave a lasting impact on the world and become a highly respected professor and scholar during his lifetime. Sociology in Germany in the late 19th and early 20th centuries was dominated by the "father of sociology"—Max Weber. He was first to intellectually articulate the concept of bureaucracy, which earned his place in the literature of many disciplines including public administration. Weber believed that bureaucracy was the most rational method known to administer modern societies, and he articulated the organizational characteristics of bureaucracies with impressive detail. He also differentiated between three types of authority in terms of legitimacy: traditional, charismatic, and legal-rational. In each of these cases, the basic question he addressed was: On what basis do those in authority have the right to give orders to their followers? Weber believed that the legal-rational model was the ideal type for modern societies.

Mary Parker Follett (1868–1933):
A Thinker Ahead of Her Time

Follett was born into an affluent Quaker family in Quincy, Massachusetts. She was educated at the Thayer Academy but had to take on a significant role within the family in her teens when her father died. In 1892 she entered the Society for the Collegiate Instruction of Women in Cambridge, Massachusetts (later Radcliffe College) where she graduated in 1898 in economics, government, law, and philosophy. Mary Parker Follett was "a thinker well ahead of her time." She is known for her pioneering work on management. She approached organizations as group networks rather than as hierarchical structures, and attended to the influence of human relations within the group. In terms of current debates around management, this perspective is hardly revolutionary, but it was radical at the time and stood well outside of the mainstream. Moreover, Follett rejected the whole notion of scientific management. In 1930, she developed a management model based on individual motivation and group problem solving—the forerunner to participatory management. In *The New State,* she argued that group organization and local networks provide the key to democratic advance. She believed that the study of democracy had focused too much on the study of institutions when it should have been based on how people behave together.

Elton Mayo (1880–1949): The Hawthorne Studies and
the Human Relations Movement

George Elton Mayo was born in Australia. His father was an engineer, and several generations of his family had been prominent in the fields of medicine and law. After trying his hand at several fields of study, including medicine, he completed his education in psychology and philosophy at the University of Adelaide in 1907. Mayo moved to the United States in 1922 and become an associate professor at Harvard in 1926. The following year, he and a team of associates began conducting the famous Hawthorne studies, which took five years to complete. These studies were actually called the *Western Electric Researches.* In 1933, Mayo published *The Human Problems of an Industrial Civilization,* which was the preliminary report of the Hawthorne studies. The Hawthorne studies were the genesis of the thought behind the human relations school of management. In his career, Mayo highlighted the importance of communication between management and workers, and identified the now-accepted notion that work satisfaction lay more in recognition, security, and sense of belonging than in monetary rewards. Elton Mayo, the short, bald, chain-smoking man who was filled with such an incredible amount of energy and spirit, greatly affected the study of organizations forever.

Chester Barnard (1886–1961): Organizations as Systems of Exchange

Born into a family of modest means in Malden, Massachusetts, Chester Barnard completed three years of study in economics at Harvard (he never finished the degree) before beginning a long and impressive career. He joined American Telephone and Telegraph as a statistics clerk, and in 1927 became the president of New Jersey Bell. During his lifetime, he published 37 articles and one book, *Functions of the Executive*. This book would be his most important contribution to understanding organizations. His work provided thoughtful insights about organizational life. *Functions of the Executive* remains one of the most widely cited books in the literature on management. His work impressed one person in particular at the time who went on to lead a revolution in the field of public administration—Herbert Simon. Barnard believed that organizations were made up of individual humans with individual motivations. He also believed that large organizations contain smaller, less formal groupings whose goals need to be harnessed to those of the whole for organizations to be effective. Barnard, who wrote extensively on the idea of authority, held that authority only exists insofar as people are willing to accept it, and he developed his "zone of indifference," which is included in Chapter 4. Barnard gave us a more realistic insight to what really goes on in formal organizations. Because of his work, new subfields in organization thought, such as decision making and communication theory, were created.

Herbert Simon (1916–2001): The Idea of Bounded Rationality

Few people have had more impact on the discipline of public administration and decision making than Herbert Simon. More than any one person, he shaped the agenda of public administration since 1937 and made it a behavioral social science. Simon was born in Milwaukee, Wisconsin, and received his PhD in political science with a specialization in public administration from the University of Chicago in 1943. The breadth of his work was enormous. He mainly taught in schools of industrial management during his career, but he won a Nobel Prize in economics. He involved himself in many areas, including computer science and psychology, and helped to lay the foundation for artificial intelligence (computers that "think"). His articles have appeared in journals from every field of the social sciences except anthropology. Heavily influenced by the work of Chester Barnard, Simon revolutionized the discipline of public administration by disputing that "principles of management" had been discovered. In his article entitled "Proverbs of Administration" and in his book *Administrative Behavior,* he essentially laid to rest any remaining thoughts about the classical principles of administration. They simply were not true. Simon is most remembered for his idea of

© Bettmann/CORBIS

"bounded rationality"—the idea that people can only be rational decision makers within limits. In Simon's view, people who behave rationally are not "optimizing" anything at all (the idea of optimizing or maximizing was once incorporated into economic theory); they simply are making decisions based on what their environment tells them they can and cannot do. People do not strive for the best decision; they look for what is possible within the bounds of their given situation. That is, they "satisfice," which means they search for actions that are "good enough" rather than the optimal ones. Thus, Simon took *economic man* from economics and made the concept more realistic as *administrative man.* This was his legacy for more than 50 years.

Dwight Waldo (1913–2000): The Statesman
with Eclectic Views about Public Administration

Waldo is remembered more for his observations about the contributions of others than for his own contributions to the field. His commentary of the discipline was insightful, and no one was more supportive or critical of public administration than Waldo. He was born and raised on a hog farm in DeWitt, Nebraska (pop. 500). Waldo earned his PhD in political science from Yale University in 1942. His dissertation was later published as *The Administrative State: A Study of the Political Theory of Public Administration.* Waldo declined to take a teaching position during the middle of World War

Institute of Governmental Studies, University of California, Berkeley

II. He worked in Washington as a price analyst in the Office of Price Administration and later as an analyst in the Bureau of the Budget until 1946. He then accepted a teaching position at the University of California at Berkeley. Waldo became more and more interested in public administration and began to critique many aspects of the field. His commentary generated many articles and a number of books. The theme of most of his work related to history. He later moved to the Maxwell School of Citizenship and Public Affairs at Syracuse University, where he remained until he retired in 1979. In addition to his insightful commentary and critiques, Waldo gathered a group of young students for a conference at Syracuse in 1968, which ignited a new school of thought called the "New Public Administration." Anyone seeking insights into the discipline should read his work.

Peter Drucker (1909–): Management by
Objectives, and Much More

Peter Drucker is probably the most famous man-agement author of our times. His influence on management in both the private and public sectors has been enormous. Born in Vienna and educated as a lawyer, he is probably the world's best-known management consultant. He has written 29 books that have been translated into most of the world's languages (there are currently more than 5 million copies in print). He is perhaps best known for the idea of management by objectives (MBO), which became very popular during the early 1970s. According to Drucker, organizational design must follow organizational purpose. That is, we cannot properly design an organiza-tion until we clearly understand its goals. Drucker has written on virtually every known managerial and organizational phenomenon. He has been at this for more than a half century, yet he is considered to be one of the "youngest" thinkers in America because he always looks toward the future. Moreover, he has made management aware of itself and its problems. Drucker has long been asso-ciated with the Claremont Graduate University in California where the gradu-ate school of management bears his name. Additionally, his organization has a foundation for nonprofit management at http://www.drucker.org.

Peter F. Drucker

Aaron Wildavsky (1930–1993): Budgetary Politics
and Incrementalism

When one thinks about public budgeting, one thinks about Aaron Wildavsky. Born in New York City in a family of Russian Jewish immigrants, Wildavsky became a household name in the fields of public administration and political science. He earned his PhD from Yale University, and with the exception of a short time at Oberlin College, he spent the rest of his life at the University of California at Berkeley. The American Political Science Association (ASPA) created an award in honor of his contributions, the "Aaron Wildavsky Enduring Contribution Award." Wildavsky's name

Richard and Rhoda Goldman School of Public Policy, University of California, Berkeley

was synonymous with public budgeting. In 1961, he wrote an article titled "The Political Implications of Budgetary Reform," in which he developed the concept of budgetary incrementalism and its political nature. That is, governmental budgeting tends to use last year's budget to determine the size of the next year's budget, and the process of passing a budget is not a rational process so much as it is a "political" one. This led to his classic book, *The Politics of the Budgetary Process* (1964), which became standard reading for public budgeting classes. He wrote and co-authored many books during his career, including *Speaking Truth to Power: The Art and Craft of Policy Analysis* (1979), *How to Limit Government Spending* (1980), *The Beleaguered Presidency* (1991), and *Planning Budgeting in Poor Countries* (1993) with Naomi Caiden (this book won an award from the American Society for Public Administration). Wildavsky researched and studied budgeting for more than 40 years and was considered to be the world's leading expert on the budgetary process both inside and outside of academic institutions.

E. S. Savas (1931–): Privatization Is the Key to Better Government

Born in New York City and educated at the University of Chicago and Columbia University (PhD in 1960), Emanuel S. Savas brought the idea of privatization to center stage more than 30 years ago. While working for Mayor Lindsey in New York City in the late 1960s, Savas discovered several peculiar things about public versus private provision of services. The most important discovery was that the private sector was significantly cheaper than publicly operated departments. He also found that public departments did not really know how much it cost to perform tasks such as collecting garbage or removing snow from streets. His early inquiries sparked an interest that would last throughout his career. Savas provided the empirical evidence to start the "great privatization debate" that lasted for many years in public administration and economics. Although he was not the only person involved in the debate (plenty of economists, including the public choice school, joined him), his empirical and theoretical work was groundbreaking. He became the leading figure associated with the virtues of "privatizing the public sector." E. S. Savas is considered to be a pioneer in privatization research. As of this writing, he has authored 10 books and more than 129 articles. Among his most famous books is *Privatization: The Key to Better Government* (1987), which has been published in 13 foreign editions. Savas never attributed the lower efficiency typically found in public operations to bad managers or bad employees; he attributed the lower efficiency to the nature of "monopolies," which have no competition.

Professor E. S. Savas

David Osborne and Ted Gaebler:
Reinventing Government

During the early 1990s, a new wave of reform hit public administration. It was called "reinventing government." Largely influenced by Peter Drucker in *The Age of Discontinuity* (1969), the privatization movement, and books like *In Search of Excellence* from the early 1980s, David Osborne (top photo) and Ted Gaebler (bottom photo) started a new movement that focused on making government work better by getting rid of "red tape" and other obstacles. They called for a "results orientation" that could revitalize public organizations and for the use of public-private partnerships. Their book is filled not with theoretical ideas but with real examples of how government can be improved and of how the "reinventing government" scheme has worked for real governments. What gave their book credibility was that both were involved in the real world of government. David Osborne was a consultant for state and local governments, and Ted Gaebler was the former city manager of Visalia, California, and Vandalia, Ohio. *Reinventing Government: How Entrepreneurial Spirit is Transforming the Public Sector* was published in 1992 and was an extremely popular and influential book. It even led the Clinton administration to embrace the idea, study its use at the federal level, and create a famous report entitled "The Gore Report on Reinventing Government." Osborne and Gaebler are credited with making the idea of "reinventing government" a household word in the public sector. David Osborne is associated with the Public Strategies Group, a consulting firm that helps governments improve their performance (http://www.psgrp.com). Ted Gaebler is currently the county administrator of Nevada County, California. Both Osborne and Gaebler have published many other books, including *Positive Outcomes: Raising the Bar on Government Reinvention* (1999) by Ted Gaebler and others, and *Banishing Bureaucracy* (1997) by David Osborne and Peter Plastrik.

Public Strategies Group

Ted Gaebler

SUMMARY

This chapter has presented an overview of the history of the development of public administration as an academic discipline. Public administration was born into political science and quickly became an "unwanted child." The discipline has spent much of its history searching for its own identity and an appropriate academic home. The discipline has gone through many stages of development: Beginning with the classical period, the discipline was then revolutionized by the behaviorial school and Herbert Simon, but ultimately matured into its own discipline with its own journals, conferences, and professional associations. Although still largely connected to political science, public administration is a diverse, multidisciplinary field of study that continues to maintain a largely practitioner-based orientation. Over the years, public administration did break away from political science to form its own curriculums that are tailored to studying administration in a different way from traditional political science. The focus of public administration is the administrative apparatus of government at all levels and over time. It has developed creditable standards of excellence by developing its own accreditation organization. And, throughout the history of the discipline, public administration scholars and researchers have developed an impressive body of literature and continue to advance our state of knowledge about many dimensions of public organizations.

NOTES

1. The concepts of efficiency, effectiveness, and responsiveness will be discussed in greater detail in Chapter 4. For our purposes here, efficiency simply means using the least amount of resources possible, such as time, money, and personnel, to adequately handle the job. Effectiveness is simply goal attainment. Responsiveness refers to "responding" to the needs of citizens or clientele groups.

2. Political scientists use the term "PA types" to describe those who teach public administration. At times, it carries a negative connotation.

3. The idea of locus versus focus is credited to Robert Golembiewski, *Public Administration as a Developing Discipline: Part I: Perspectives on the Past and Present* (New York: Marcel Dekker, 1977).

4. This chapter relies heavily on the excellent description of the development of the discipline of public administration provided by Nicholas Henry, which he organizes into five major paradigms in *Public Administration and Public Affairs,* 7th ed. (Upper Saddle River, NJ: Prentice-Hall, 1999), Chapter 2. Also see Dwight Waldo, *The Enterprise of Public Administration: A Summary View* (Novato, CA: Chandler and Sharpe, 1979), and Richard Stillman II, *Preface to Public Administration: A*

Search for Themes and Direction (New York: St. Martin, 1991).

5. For the full account, see Nicholas Henry, *Public Administration and Public Affairs,* Chapter 2.

6. Everyone in the discipline of public administration may not accept the "refounding era" as a distinct era. The developments during this period may be viewed as just a challenge or series of issues that occurred. In fact, many of the challenges, such as privitization, have simply been incorporated into the discipline. However, it is the author's opinion that the "refounding period" is real and distinct. Privtiza-tion, public choice theory, and the idea of reinventing government have posed challenges to the orthodox school of public administration. The orthodox school is the primary school of thought currently; the term refers to the mainstream public administra-tionists who adhere to the primary values of the discipline that have been synthesized over the years.

7. Frederick W. Taylor, *The Principles of Scientific Management* (New York: Harper Brothers, 1911).

8. Two major groups in the classical period stand out. One was the scientific

management movement, led by Frederick Taylor's ideas, and the other was the "departmentalists." The latter group focused on the formal organization, and its tool was the organizational chart. Addressing problems, for the departmentalists, involved identifying the tasks necessary to accomplish organizational objectives and then grouping and coordinating employees in such a way as to maximize organizational efficiency. Familiar concepts were chain of command, span of control, line-staff functions, and the like. The primary mechanism for control and coordination was hierarchy. The coupling of these two areas was based in a mechanistic view of human beings, which holds that behavior can be predicted, that humans are segmentally involved with work, and that behavior can be manipulated using incentives and rewards. See Brian Fry, *Mastering Public Administration: From Max Weber to Dwight Waldo* (Chatham, NJ: Chatham House, 1989).

9. Ibid, p. 23. The New York Bureau of Municipal Research's Training School for Public Service was founded with $250,000 donated by Ms. E. H. Harriman. Ms. Harriman had tried to get the school established at a university but was turned down by Harvard, Yale, and Columbia. See Luther Gulick, "George Maxwell Had a Dream," in Frederick Moser, Ed., *American Public Administration: Past, Present, and Future* (Syracuse, NY: Maxwell School of Citizenship and Public Affairs and the National Associations of Schools of Public Administration, 1975).

10. Ibid, p. 24.

11. Elton Mayo, *The Human Problems with an Industrial Civilization* (New York: Macmillan, 1933; reprinted by the Division of Research, Harvard Business School, 1946).

12. Frederick W. Taylor, *The Principles of Scientific Management;* Mary Parker Follett, *The New State* (New York: Longman, Green, 1923), and *Creative Experience* (New York: Longman, Green, 1924).

13. The Public Administration Clearing House held a conference at Princeton University in 1935 and the report generated from that conference illustrated the tensions between public administration and political science. Years earlier, political science had accepted public administration as a new subfield, but now it rejected the idea that separate and distinct schools of public administration should be established. There has always been a tension between public administration and political science that continues to this day.

14. This idea comes from Dwight Waldo, one of the leading statesmen in the discipline of public administraton, and is included in Nicholas Henry's detailed account of the development of public administration as a discipline. See Nicholas Henry, *Public Administration and Public Affairs,* 6th ed., p. 25. For Waldo's comments, see Dwight Waldo, "Introduction: Trends and Issues in Education for Public Administration," in Guthrie Birkhead and James Carroll, Eds., *Education for Public Service: 1979* (Syracuse, NY: Maxwell School of Citizenship and Public Affairs, 1979), p. 15.

15. Dwight Waldo, *The Administrative State: A Study of the Political Theory of American Public Administration* (New York: Ronald Press, 1948); Fritz Morstein Marx, *The Administrative State: An Introduction to Bureaucracy* (Chicago: University of Chicago Press, 1957); James Q. Wilson, "The Rise of the Bureaucratic State," *The Public Interest 41* (Fall 1975), pp. 77–103.

16. See Chester Barnard, *The Functions of the Executive* (Cambridge, MA: Harvard University Press, 1968).

17. See Herbert Simon, *Administrative Behavior* (New York: Macmillan, 1957).

18. In 1978, Simon was awarded a Nobel Prize for his work.

19. The Kinsey Institute at Indiana University made an international reputation for itself by studying sexual behavior following the same principles of inquiry found in all of the behavioral sciences. Their Web site is http://www.indiana.edu/~kinsey.

20. Nicholas Henry, *Public Administration and Public Affairs,* p. 35.

21. General systems theory has its origins in biology. In the early 1920s, K. Ludwig von Bertalanffy broke from the popular emphasis on the cell to examining organs in their relationship to one another. Other

prominent researchers that used systems theory early on were physiologist Ralph W. Gerard and economist Kenneth E. Boulding. See Ludwig von Bertalanffy, "General Systems Theory: A New Approach to the Unity of Science," *Human Biology 23* (1951), pp. 303–361; Anatol Rapoport, *Strategy and Consciences* (New York: Harper & Row, 1964); and Kenneth Boulding, "General Systems Theory: The Skeleton of Science," *Management Science 2* (1956), p. 198. Also see Robert D. Lee and Ronald W. Johnson, *Public Budgeting Systems,* 4th ed. (Gaithersburg, MD: Aspen, 1989), Chapter 5. Norbert Weiner is credited with bringing systems theory to organization theory and management in his book *Cybernetics* (Cambridge, MA: MIT Press, 1948).

22. David Easton, *The Political System: An Inquiry into the State of Political Science* (New York: Knopf, 1953).

23. Anthony Downs, *An Economic Theory of Democracy* (New York: Harper & Row, 1957). Public administration published some excellent classic literature during this era, such as Charles Lindblom's classic article, "The Science of Muddling Through," that built on the idea of bounded rationality. Charles Lindblom, "The Science of Muddling Through," *Public Administration Review 19* (Spring 1959), pp. 79–88. The era also produced a popular book that greatly affected the work of business management, William H. Whyte's *The Organization Man* (New York: Simon & Schuster, 1956). This book, considered to be a classic in its field, essentially described "the corporate man or the IBM man" at the time.

24. Nicolas Henry, *Public Administration and Public Affairs,* p. 37.

25. Ibid, pp. 37–38.

26. James Perry and Kenneth Kraemer, "Part Three: Is Public Management Similar or Different from Private Management?" in James Perry and Kenneth Kraemer, Eds., *Public Management: Public and Private Perspective* (Palo Alto, CA: Mayfield, 1983), p. 56.

27. This information is included in Nicholas Henry, *Public Administration and Public Affairs,* 6th ed., in Table 2.1, p. 37.

28. Graham T. Allison, "Public and Private Management: Are They Fundamentally Alike in all Unimportant Respects?" in James Perry and Kenneth Kraemer, Eds., *Public Management: Public and Private Perspectives* (Palo Alto, CA: Mayfield, 1983), pp. 72–92. Wallace Sayre is the person who said, "Public and private management are fundamentally alike in all unimportant aspects."

29. Ibid.

30. Douglas McGregor, *The Human Side of Enterprise* (New York: McGraw-Hill, 1960); Chris Argyris, *Integrating the Individual and the Organization* (New York: Wiley, 1964); Robert Blake and Jane Mouton, *The Managerial Grid* (Houston, TX: Gulf, 1964); Victor Vroom, *Work and Motivation* (New York: Wiley, 1964).

31. The literature listed here is only intended to serve as a sample. This overview is not intended to be a literature review of the discipline.

32. An excellent history of NASPAA is included on their Web site at http://www.naspaa.org.

33. Nicholas Henry, *Public Administration and Public Affairs,* p. 45.

34. Dwight Waldo, *The Enterprise of Public Administration* (Novato, CA: Chandler and Sharp, 1980), p. 110.

35. Louise White, "Public Management in a Pluralistic Arena", *Public Administration Review 49* (November/December 1989), p. 524.

36. Richard Stillman, "Ostrom on the Federalists Revisited," *Public Administration Review 49* (January/February 1987), p. 83.

37. No clear definition of *public interest* exists that is agreed upon by scholars. Although the term is commonly used, it is also controversial due to the lack of an accepted definition. For our purposes here, the public interest refers to actions that place the interest of the public (or society as a whole) above individual interests. However, determining what this truly means has always been problematic. The concept of the public interest will be discussed in Chapter 8.

38. George Downs and Patrick Larkey, *The Search for Government Efficiency: From*

Hubris to Helplessness (Philadelphia, PA: Temple University Press, 1986).

39. Vincent Ostrom and Elinor Ostrom, "Public Choice: A Different Approach to the Study of Public Administration," *Public Administration Review 31* (March/April, 1971), pp. 203–216.

40. Savas has written a number of books on privatization, but his classic book is *Privatization: The Key to Better Government* (Chatham, NJ: Chatham House Press, 1987).

41. David Osborne and Ted Gaebler, *Reinventing Government* (New York: Addison Wesley, 1992).

42. Richard Stillman II, *Public Administration: Concepts and Cases,* 7th ed.

43. Mildred Warner and Amir Hefetz, "Privatization and the Market Role of Local Government: Small Growth in Contracting Underscores Dominance of Service Provision by Public Employees" (Washington, DC: Economic Policy Institute, 2001). This study was produced at Cornell University for the Economic Policy Institute. It is available at http://epinet.org or at http://www.cce.cornell.edu/restructuring.

44. Ibid., p. 14.

45. The reason for this section is that many students have requested such material. The author assumes responsibility for making the selection of those included in this sample list of great contributors to public administration. Many other great contributors could have been mentioned, and most of the individuals omitted here will be mentioned later in the book.

3

Bureaucracy

You will find that the State is the kind of organization,
which, though it does big things badly, does small things badly, too.

JOHN KENNETH GALBRAITH

BUREAUCRACY: THE PART OF
GOVERNMENT WE LOVE TO HATE

The bureaucracy is often criticized and is the subject of many jokes. Most
Americans do not think of bureaucracies in a positive light. We have had too
many experiences of being shuffled from desk to desk and transferred all over
the organization on the telephone when we are trying to get an answer to what
we believe is a simple question. When asked about bureaucracy, most people
respond that it means "problems over silly rules" and a lot of "red tape."[1] The
term *bureaucracy* typically refers to the agencies of government, but as we will
see later in this chapter, bureaucracy is also a "form of organization" found in
both the public and private sectors. *(Bureaucracy as an organization refers to assembling various elements of labor and expertise in a way that enables complex tasks to be
accomplished)*[2] Our experiences dealing with large organizations, whether large
corporations or government, are often similar. But bureaucracies play a vital
role in our lives. They provide police protection, put out fires, regulate land use,
educate children, and maintain our highway system. They also propose new

laws and ordinances, write budgets, and implement public policies. Private corporations are also bureaucracies by definition, and they build automobiles and televisions, handle our personal banking, provide insurance for our homes and personal health, and provide air transportation, all of which make our lives in the modern world more pleasant.[3]

Public bureaucracies are our main concern here, and their reputation is typically worse than that of private organizations. Public bureaucracies are often thought of as offices staffed with mindless *bureaucrats* (another word with negative connotations in our society that refers to the people working in public agencies) who are overpaid, unresponsive, inefficient, impersonal, and often arrogant. Bureaucrats are also considered to be dangerous because they are an independent force in government. They operate with little control from either elected officials or voters. They have been insulated by civil service regulations, which were originally implemented to protect them from political forces under the belief that neutral competence was a worthy value. They are also accused of elitism because they tend to serve the needs of the upper classes while, for the most part, ignoring the needs of the poor and disadvantaged.

The bureaucracy is often portrayed as the problem with government—the reason that government does not seem to be able to accomplish much. Some consider public agencies to be inept, and examples are readily available. About six months after the tragic terrorist attacks of September 11, 2001, it was disclosed that the Immigration Service had just approved visas for two of the highjackers who died in the World Trade Center crashes.[4] Americans and the families of victims of the terrorist attacks were appalled, and rightfully so. How could the same government that was tracking down terrorists have an agency approving their visas long after they had died, especially in light of all the publicity that included the terrorists' photographs being displayed all over the media? In another example, a Chicago cancer patient applied for Medicare. She received a letter indicating that she was not eligible since she had died more than a year earlier. In an equally bizarre case, a citizen in Prince William County, Virginia, received a legal notice about his overdue taxes. The notice stated that if the bill were not paid promptly, the county would take legal action. The amount due was one cent.

Government decisions do not always seem to make a lot of sense. During the mid-1980s, the state of Pennsylvania was paying around $500,000 each year to the Pittsburgh and Lake Erie Railroad, which was used for about 250 passengers each day. At this price, the state could have bought each rider a new car every three years. And, the federal government continues to operate Amtrak (the federally owned passenger rail service) despite the fact that it loses more than one billion dollars each year.[5] Tales of agencies paying $600 for toilet seats or more than $7,000 for coffee makers do little to help the image of government or public bureaucracies regardless of how the costs are justified.[6] Of course, such examples do not accurately reflect the work or general performance of government as a whole. The same government capable of such things also fights wars, provides national defense, helps to eradicate diseases, assists in managing the economy, provides the infrastructure needed for a modern society that is constantly changing, and promotes and nurtures many needed social changes.[7] There are a lot of myths associated with the bureaucracy (see Box 3.1 for a sample), but some of the criticism of public agencies is justified.

All modern societies are "administered" societies. Large organizations dominate the social landscape, and to function effectively in modern society, we must deal with these organizations as a customer, citizen, client, or a member. Whether the state of Florida, IBM, Ford Motor Company, Exxon, or the Internal Revenue Service, large organizations (both public and private) clutter our lives. Knowing how large organizations work, what strengths and weakness they have, and what motivates them gives us some tools that help us survive in a world filled with "bureaucracies." Despite their bad reputation among average citizens, knowing how large organizations work can enable us to get done the things we need to get accomplished.

THE CONCEPT OF BUREAUCRACY

Bureaucracy is the administrative part of government. It consists of all executive offices and the roughly 19 million people who work in these offices in the United States at all levels of government. Bureaucracies predate the United States; all of the great European powers had bureaucracies.[8] At the federal level, bureaucracy consists of a set of complex, hierarchical departments, agencies, and commissions, and their staffs that were created to help presidents carry out their duty to implement and enforce the law.[9] All of the states have created similar systems to help the governor, and each local government has its administrative apparatus as well. Bureaucracy also is a form of organization, and understanding its nature is helpful to anyone who has to deal with a public agency, or a large private corporation for that matter.

Max Weber was the first to articulate and define the nature of bureaucracies in the early part of the 20th century (more will be said about his work in Chapter 4). Weber believed that bureaucracies were rational and necessary to organize modern societies because of the complexity of society itself. His "legal-rational ideal-type" is the one with which most of us are familiar because most large organizations fall into this category. Weber believed that bureaucracies tend to have certain characteristics, including:

- *Hierarchical structure.* This is the formal organizational structure illustrated in organizational charts. It simply means that there is a top and a bottom to the organization, with some type of executive leadership at the top overseeing various specialized departments. In Weber's view, the organization should be shaped like a pyramid. However, organizations can be "tall" or "flat." Tall organizations have a lot of departments and supervisors between the top and the lower levels of the organization. Flat structures have fewer supervisors and middle management between the executives and the rank-and-file areas of the organization.

BOX 3.1 Myths and Realities about the Bureaucracy

Myth #1: Bureaucracy Is the Problem with Government

Bureaucracy is widely criticized on television and radio, in books, and by presidents, the press, the public, and academics. Almost everyone likes to take a shot at bureaucracy. It is blamed for a variety of social ills from causing nothing but "red tape" to failing to cure cancer. In the words of Charles Goodsell, "Bureaucracy stands for a splendid hate object."

In reality, the bureaucracy is the core of any modern government. It is here that the bulk of the work of government gets done—"where the rubber meets the road," so to speak. Public bureaucracies educate more than 4 million public school children every day, pay out more than 3 million unemployment checks every week, deliver around 5 million Social Security checks every week, maintain around 400,000 miles of interstate highway (and another 4 million miles of public roads), run more than 170 veterans hospitals, run 144 embassies around the world, put astronauts into space, provide about 4 percent of the population with welfare assistance, handle more than 166 billion letters

and packages each year, register and license more than 14 million automobiles and trucks, and fund more than one-third of all the research conducted in the nation. Whether this work is done efficiently or wisely is open for debate, but nevertheless, public bureaucracies carry out most of the work of government. Therefore, bureaucracy is *not* the problem with government—rather, it makes government and a modern society possible. It is true that bureaucracy has two sides: It creates both problems and possibilities for change, in the same way that government governs in both good and bad ways.

Myth #2: Government Bureaucracy Is Too Large and Monolithic

Much of the criticism about public bureaucracy involves size—the bureaucracy is overwhelming and too large. Statistics are frequently produced to illustrate the size of government, showing the U.S. government to be the nation's largest employer, the consumer of one-quarter of the gross national product, and the fourth largest bureaucracy on

---

- *A chain of command.* Stated simply, chain of command refers to the fact that everyone has a boss or a supervisor.
- *Division of labor and specialization of labor.* A bureaucracy divides labor into specialized units. For example, universities typically break their work into a lot of divisions, such as administration, various colleges and schools that have broad areas of expert knowledge, and then into academic departments. Within the academic departments, even professors have specialized areas of expertise. The biological sciences, for example, are not grouped with the social sciences or the maintenance department. It would not be possible to carry out higher education without the various services and tasks handled by administrative departments, such as the registrar's office, housing, accounting, and the like.

earth (coming in behind Russia, China, and India in number of employees). The bureaucracy spends more than a trillion dollars annually. These figures are reasonably accurate, but present only part of the picture.

In reality, the American bureaucracy is not one massive organization but numerous smaller units. There are more than 86,000 bureaucracies in the nation, and most are located at the local level. With regard to employ-ment, one out of every six jobs is a government job. Thus, most people do not work for the government. The federal government employs roughly 2.6 million workers (and nearly the same amount in the military), but the workers are scattered through more than 45,000 units of government at the federal level, and only about 330,000 work in Washington, DC. Most are scattered throughout the nation in regional or local offices.

Myth #3: Bureaucrats Are All Alike
The typical bureaucrat is often described as a green-eye-shaded underachiever or nonachiever, but evidence suggests that there is no "typical bureaucrat." Bureaucrats perform many jobs, and so there are many varieties of public employees. More than 9,000 federal job categories describe such tasks as drug enforcement, flying space shuttles, and delivering mail. People engaged in these activities are far from being "lamebrains." More than 36 percent of all government employees (federal, state, and local) work at professional occupations (by comparison, only 12 percent of private sector workers are classified as professionals). At the federal level, two-thirds of govern-ment workers are in "professional" occupations. For example, the U.S. Department of Health and Human Services employs 4,000 biologists, chemists, and physicists; 2,000 mathematicians, statisticians, and engineers; 17,000 medical doctors and health care specialists; 5,000 public health officers; and 30,000 legal claims or benefits personnel. As Frederick Mosher once noted, public service is increasingly becoming a "professional state."

SOURCE: Richard Stillman, *The American Bureaucracy: The Core of Modern Government*, 2nd ed. (Chicago: Nelson-Hall, 1996), Chapter 1.

- *Routine behavior that follows standardized procedures.* Bureaucracies assemble expertise by definition, but they carry out their duties following established, routine procedures. For example, at a university, registration procedures are standardized along with the rules for dropping or adding classes. And although rules and procedures may be modified or upgraded due to technology or policy changes, they are implemented the same way year after year. Over time, colleges and universities have gotten better at handling the complexities of providing higher education and training.

- *Promotion based on demonstrated performance.* Promotion should be based on individual performance rather than on the whims of a supervisor. People who perform their jobs well should not be discriminated against, since the purpose of the organization is to perform a variety of complex tasks. As we will see in the chapter on personnel administration, public organizations typically have well-developed procedures to handle this function, such as job descriptions, performance appraisal procedures, and other standardized techniques. The idea that one should be promoted based on performance is the centerpiece of the concept of a merit system.

- *A goal orientation that emphasizes the efficient and effective attainment of the organization's goals.* Organizations exist for a purpose, whether it is managing the parks and recreation resources of a city, collecting taxes for the federal government, or manufacturing and selling automobiles. Organizations must configure themselves in such a way and utilize their available resources (material and human capital) so that they achieve their goals in an efficient and effective manner. Organizations are complex social entities, and the dynamics involve formal and informal dimensions. (Chapter 4 deals more thoroughly with organization theory.)

- *Productivity, whereby all work and actions are evaluated according to established rules, and control of employees according to specific rules and procedures (standard operating practices) that are supposed to be applied impersonally to everyone.* Productivity—that is, the output of work—is geared to established, clearly stated expectations and guidelines. Moreover, in bureaucracies, everyone is supposed to be treated in accordance with established, standard operating procedures. This helps build stability and continuity for the organization and its workers, and it enhances productivity.

The bureaucracy contains additional features and complexities that will be discussed later, but almost anyone who has worked for any type of large organization, such as a grocery store chain, a fast-food chain, or Wal-Mart, already recognizes that these characteristics apply to all large organizations—or at least that they are supposed to apply. Organizational theory and the ideal-type described previously are sometimes a little different from the way organizations function in the real world, as we shall see in Chapter 4.

GROWTH OF THE FEDERAL BUREAUCRACY:
A BRIEF HISTORY

Today the executive branch of the federal government has approximately 2.6 million employees.[10] Often called the "fourth branch" of government because of its power, bureaucracies are plentiful and very powerful. But conditions have changed a lot since 1789. The American bureaucracy has gone through three distinct stages referred to as the Jefferson, Hamilton, and Madison models (illustrated in Table 3.1). For the first 150 years, the United States did not have a bureaucracy in the contemporary sense of the word. Today we think about bureaucracy as complex, highly organized and specialized organizations that function as the administrative apparatus of the nation. The Founding Fathers, however, were silent about the administrative mechanisms of the new nation.

Table 3.1 Political-Bureaucratic Relations—Three Distinct Stages

Attribute	Jefferson Model 19th Century	Hamilton Model Late 19th, Early 20th Centuries	Madison Model Post–World War II Era
Socioeconomic setting	Largely rural, stable, isolationist	Predominantly nation-building	Mature welfare state with global responsibilities
Political authority basis	Homogenous community life	Rapid social, political, and economic change	Interest groups, liberalism, scientific, changes, and international responsibilities
Bureaucratic duties	Limited	Expanding	Diverse
Generalist/specialist personnel	Generalists	Growth of professional and specialist staffs	Mixed generalist and specialized personnel
Fiscal controls	Sharp limits imposed by the legislature	Increased executive control and authority through executive budgets	Mixed controls depending upon agency and policy area
Organizational autonomy and dependency	Highly dependent upon the legislature	Increasing autonomy	Mixed organizational autonomy and dependence on the legislature
Use of external or internal controls	Primarily external controls based on laws	Greater reliance on internal controls based upon public professions and their norms	Highly complex mix of both external and internal controls
Ideological basis of political-bureaucratic relationship	"The best government governs the least"	Dominated by the politics-administration dichotomy	Dominated by interest group liberalism

NOTE: From time to time there have been swings back to the older ideals. For example, during the 1960s and 1970s, there were attempts to return to a Jefferson model largely due to the Vietnam War, Watergate, civil unrest, and the general mood of the times. Richard Stillman provides an excellent discussion about these three models in his book (see Source note).

SOURCE: Adapted from Richard Stillman, *The American Bureaucracy: The Core of Modern Government,* 2nd ed. (Chicago: Nelson-Hall, 1996), p. 379.

During George Washington's presidency, there were only three departments, and all three had existed under the Articles of Confederation—the departments of Foreign Affairs, War, and Treasury. The original departments were small and had limited duties. For example, the Foreign Affairs Department had only nine employees, and the War Department had 80 civilian employees in 1801 and commanded a few thousand soldiers.[11] The Treasury Department was the only department with any significant duties, which included collecting taxes, managing the debt, and operating the national bank. There were only a total of 3,000 appointed civilian officials at the end of the Federalist period, and only 95,000 in 1881.[12]

Congress had determined, by a very close vote, that the administrative agencies would be subordinate to the president (the vote was actually a tie and was broken by Vice President John Adams in the Senate). The heads of the departments were called secretaries and had to be approved by the Senate but could be removed by the president, which is still the case today. Among the largest growth areas during this period was the Post Office, which had to expand to meet the demands of a growing nation. In fact, the Post Office explains most of the growth in the size of the national government up until the Civil War. Personnel in the executive branch increased from 4,887 to 36,672 (an eightfold increase), but 86 percent of this can be attributed to the growth of the Post Office Department.[13] The Post Office was pulled from the jurisdiction of the Treasury Department and made a cabinet-level department in 1829 under President Andrew Jackson This change was made to aid the president with patronage rewards to give away, such as appointments and mail-carrying contracts.

Between 1816 and the Civil War (1861), new departments were slowly but steadily created. President Lincoln created the Department of Agriculture during the Civil War to help provide food to carry on the war. However, it did not receive cabinet-level status from Congress until 1889. After the Civil War, the pace of government expansion increased, but often the newly created jobs were used for patronage (jobs, favors, or other benefits that are given to friends and political allies for their support). During this era, the system operated as a "spoils system," which is a system where government employees are fired if their party loses the election and replaced with workers from the winning party. Senator William Marcy of New York is credited with the famous phrase "To the victor belongs the spoils." During this same era, reformers began to call for the establishment of a more professional civil service. Passage of the Pendleton Act in 1883 established the federal civil service, but it only covered a small portion of workers (about 10 percent), and presidents used the Pendleton Act to "lock in" their people into protected jobs as more workers were covered over the years. The Pendleton Act established open, competitive exams and a bipartisan three-member Civil Service Commission (the Civil Service Commission functioned until 1978 when the system was revised). Although reformers were trying to "clean up" government in the 1880s, the Pendleton Act was not passed until an angry job seeker assassinated President Garfield in 1881. Slowly, more employees were covered, and a professional civil service began to emerge that replaced the spoils system with a merit system. (This is discussed in greater detail in the chapter on personnel administration.)

The bureaucracy continued to grow along with the nation. During the late 1880s, Congress began efforts to regulate the economy, which marked a significant shift from service to regulation. The first regulatory agency was the Interstate Commerce Commission (ICC), created in 1887. It was an *independent regulatory commission* that was outside the major executive departments. In the case of independent regulatory commissions, the president appoints members who hold their positions for fixed periods of time and who, for all practical purposes, cannot be removed by the president (unless they fail to uphold their oath of office, which is rare). The ICC was created to combat widespread price fixing (especially in the area of railroads) and other unfair business practices that occurred after the Civil War. President Theodore Roosevelt persuaded Congress to create the Department of Commerce and Labor in 1903 to oversee employer-employee relations. President Roosevelt was a Progressive who supported the idea of more economic regulation. Roosevelt was shocked at the conditions in factories, mines, and shops across the nation. He felt that labor conditions were intolerable because of the long hours, poor wages, dangerous working conditions, and the fact that businesses refused to recognize an employee's right to join a labor union. The late 1880s and early part of the 1900s was the era of the "robber barons." Industries had grown so large, wealthy, and powerful that they were able to bully workers with little resistance.

President Woodrow Wilson was also a reformer and brought many more changes to the federal level. He convinced Congress to split the Department of Commerce and Labor into two departments in 1913. Wilson did not believe it was possible for one organization to look after the interests of business and labor, particularly at a time when the nation was becoming heavily industrialized. In 1914, Congress created another independent regulatory commission, the Federal Trade Commission (FTC). The FTC's function was to protect small businesses and the general public from unfair competition, which mainly came from the big businesses. The size of government was greatly affected by ratification of the Sixteenth Amendment in 1913, which authorized a federal income tax. The income tax provided the federal government with one of its greatest powers—money that could be used to expand government activities. From the late 1800s through the 1920s, businesses engaged in a tug-of-war with government and the Progressives. The business establishment was not willing to just lie down and accept the desires of the reform movement that was trying to clean up government and many industries. By the 1920s, the reform movement was in full swing, and many changes were being implemented at the local level that would find their way into the federal sphere. Reformers called for professional management to bring greater competence to government and end the corruption associated with partisan politics.

The size and scope of the federal government changed greatly during the Great Depression when the rise of the "bureaucratic state" truly began. Franklin D. Roosevelt (FDR) sought to revitalize the economy by creating a multitude of new agencies to regulate business practices and other aspects of the economy. The proper role of government in the public's eyes had changed due to economic hardship, and most people welcomed Roosevelt's far-reaching proposals, which came to be called the New Deal. With the New Deal programs, the size and scope of government mushroomed. There was no longer a "hands-off" approach to managing the economy or *laissez-faire* capitalism. Government got involved in many aspects of economic life largely due to the necessity of relieving human suffering caused by the economy. During Roosevelt's first three months in office, Congress approved every new regulatory measure that was proposed by the president. The National Industrial Recovery Act was an unprecedented effort to regulate industry. To ensure that market prices were maintained, Congress approved the Agricultural Adjustment Act—a bill that regulated prices and production of agricultural products. The Federal Deposit Insurance Corporation (FDIC) was created to insure bank deposits, and the Federal Securities Act gave the FTC the authority to supervise and regulate stocks and bonds. The Securities Exchange Act of 1934 created the Securities and Exchange Commission (SEC), which actually oversees the trading of stocks and bonds. Joseph Kennedy, the father of future President John F. Kennedy, was the first chairperson of the SEC.[14] These laws were designed to restore investor confidence in the economy by providing more structure and government oversight. Many of Roosevelt's programs were initially blocked by the Supreme Court, which adhered to the idea of *laissez-faire* capitalism. It was not until Roosevelt threatened to pack the Court with additional justices (the Constitution does not specify the number of justices that can sit on the Supreme Court) that the Court began to reverse its decisions in favor of the New Deal legislation. Once the New Deal programs were declared constitutional, many new agencies and commissions were formed. Among the many laws implemented was the National Labor Relations Act of 1935 (NLRA). This legislation recognized organized labor and established procedures for arbitration. Moreover, most of the nation's basic welfare programs were initiated during this period and that meant more agencies to administer the programs. The idea of "super government" was now part of the American landscape.

The size of government continued to expand during and after World War II. During the war, the federal government employed nearly 4 million civilian employees (the war involved over 16 million military personnel). Taxes were increased to pay for the war, and after the war, tax rates never did drop back to prewar levels. The tax increase provided money with which to continue government expansion, partly to fight the Cold War and to move into new areas domestically. Although federal civilian employment dropped, the number of government programs and agencies continued to grow. The G.I. Bill provided loans for veterans, and the Veteran's Housing Authority made loans available for veterans to buy homes. With each new agency, the government became more and more involved with citizens' lives and the economy.

The aftermath of World War II also created what President Eisenhower called the "military-industrial complex." It is comprised of the Department of Defense and a maze of defense-related industries. World War II created the need for weapons, and the Cold War created the need to continue to advance the nation's weapons systems and equipment. Although the military has downsized several times, it has constantly upgraded its technology. For example, today's military is much smaller than it was 40 years ago and has fewer ships and aircraft, but it has more firepower than ever. Nonetheless, the military establishment remains a well-entrenched bureau that illustrates the nature of the "bureaucratic state." The resources that it commands are still immense, despite downsizing, and its importance is paramount to modern society.

Soon after World War II, the civil rights movement began, and by the 1960s President Lyndon Johnson initiated his Great Society programs. This was the most ambitious era of growth since FDR's New Deal programs. The Great Society, as it was called, created another wave of growth in the American bureaucracy and expanded the government's involvement in social and economic affairs. Business regulation was now firmly in place, and various forms of social regulation increased significantly in the 1960s. In 1964, the Equal Employment Opportunity Commission (EEOC) was created. During the 1960s, two new cabinet-level departments were added: the departments of Transportation (DOT) and Housing and Urban Development (HUD). Government expansion continued with more departments, programs, and agencies being added until the 1980s. In 1970, the Post Office was removed as a cabinet department and became a government corporation. The 1970s would see a new department created to deal with the nation's energy problems (the Department of Energy was created in 1977 during the Carter administration) and two additional departments that were part of a major reorganization, the Department of Health and Human Services and the Department of Education. During this period, government began to focus on the environment and a variety of consumer safety issues, each bringing with it more bureaucracy. Most of the expansion of government corresponds to major crises of some sort, such as war, social problems, or economic hardship. During times of crisis, Congress appears more prone to listen to the president and respond to some urgent need by creating another bureaucracy. For example, during the 1960s and 1970s, departments and agencies were added to deal with crime, urban problems, poverty, the environment, and racism. In 2002, in an effort to combat terrorism, the government made the Office of Homeland Security a cabinet-level department. This was the largest single reorganization of the federal bureaucracy since the creation of the Department of Defense after World War II.

Despite the efforts to downsize the federal government since the 1980s, the federal bureaucracy is still there and well entrenched. Once an agency is established and receives funding, it is very difficult to abolish it. Considering the number of agencies that might have been abolished, few federal agencies actually have been abolished. However, there are some cases. For example, the Civil Aeronautics Board (CAB), which regulated airline routes and fares, was an agency that was dissolved. Once the airline industry was deregulated, there was no need for the CAB. It was formally dissolved in 1984.[15] Some agencies continue long after their purpose has passed. For example, the Rural Electrification Administration (REA), located within the Department of

Agriculture, was created in the 1930s to bring electric power and telephone service in rural areas, particularly in the South. Yet it continued to function until 1994 when, for all practical purposes, all households had electricity. In 1994 Congress finally eliminated the REA as an agency but "transferred" many of its responsibilities to the newly created Rural Utilities Service (RUS).[16] Today the federal bureaucracy is comprised of roughly 2,000 departments, agencies, and commissions.[17]

ADMINISTRATIVE STRUCTURE
OF THE FEDERAL GOVERNMENT

The U.S. federal government is the largest "business" on earth with 2.6 million civilian employees and an annual budget of about $2.5 trillion. Like all large organizations, the government is a complex web of departments, agencies, and commissions. Figure 3.1 is an organizational chart that illustrates the overall organization of the federal government. Figure 3.2 is an organizational chart of the executive branch, which is by far the largest of the three branches of the federal government. A multitude of advisory resources including the Executive Office of the President, which was created by Franklin D. Roosevelt in 1939, the 15 cabinet-level departments, and thousands of advisory boards assist the president. The Executive Office of the President (EOP) is comprised of the president's most trusted advisors. It consists of several agencies that were created to help coordinate the work of other agencies, such as the Office of Management and Budget (OMB) that handles preparation of the executive budget proposal. Typically, those in the EOP have closer access to the president than cabinet secretaries. The closest advisors in the inner circle are sometimes called the "kitchen cabinet," a slang term used to describe people who have easy access to the president and, more importantly, are very trusted by the president. The EOP includes a number of offices such as the White House Office, National Security Council, Council of Economic Advisors, Domestic Policy Staff, Office of Science and Technology, and the Office of Administration. (It includes other offices as well; see Figure 3.2). The most recently created department is the Department of Homeland Security, which was created by George W. Bush in 2002.

About 333,000 federal workers actually work in Washington; the rest work in field offices scattered throughout the nation. For administrative purposes and to improve service, the nation is divided into regions, with major federal agencies having offices in each region. (The number of domestic regions is typically 10 but can vary among agencies.) Figure 3.3 illustrates the domestic regional network used by many federal agencies.[18] Like all bureaucratic organizations, the government is divided into specific areas of expertise to handle highly specialized functions, such as the Occupational Safety and Health Administration (OSHA), which handles matters related to occupational safety, the State Department, which handles foreign affairs, and so on. Agencies fall into four

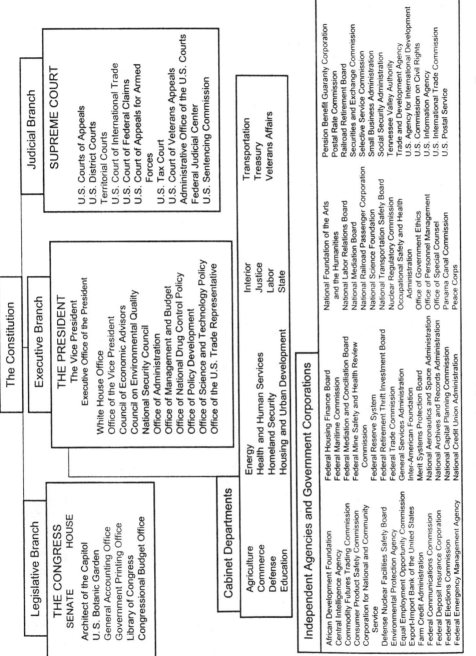

FIGURE 3.1 Organizational Chart for the U.S. Federal Government

SOURCE: U. S. Government, *United States Government Manual* (Washington, DC: Author, 2002). The chart has been updated to reflect Homeland Security.

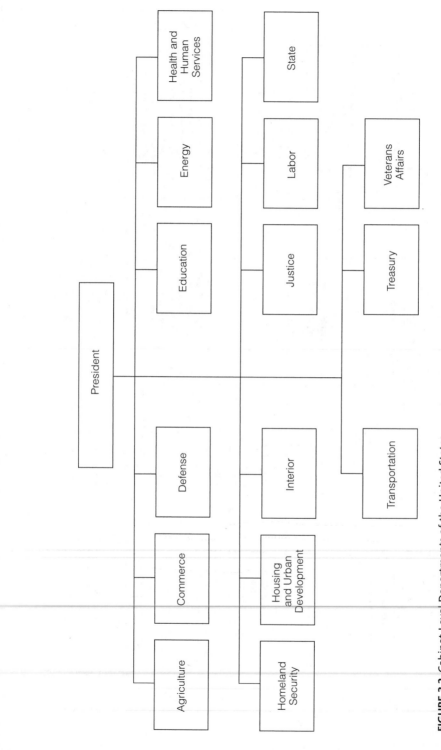

FIGURE 3.2 Cabinet-Level Departments of the United States

NOTE: The 15 cabinet departments are shown in alphabetical order. The heads of cabinet departments report directly to the president.

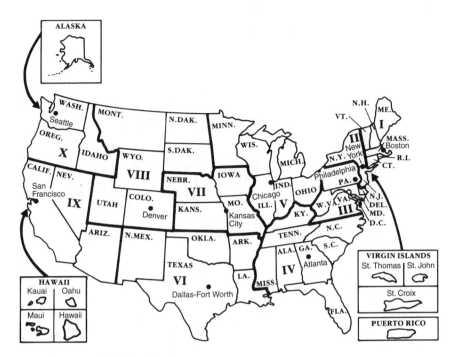

FIGURE 3.3 Sample Federal Regions

SOURCE: Offiice of the Federal Register, National Archives and Records Service, General Services Administration *United States Government Manual, 1980–1981* (Washington, DC: U.S. Government Printing Offiice, May 1, 1980) p. 984.

categories: cabinet departments, government corporations, independent agencies, and regulatory commissions. Table 3.2 lists the cabinet departments, their budgets, and the number of employees.

Cabinet Departments

Currently, there are 15 cabinet-level departments, which are shown in Table 3.2. These departments are directly under the president. The heads of these departments are called secretaries, except for the head of the Justice Department, who is the Attorney General. An undersecretary or deputy secretary, and a host of assistant secretaries that manage specific agencies within the larger department, assist the head of each department. Departments are divided into many agencies, bureaus, offices, and sections. Because the cabinet-level departments administer policy for the entire nation in their specialized areas, they often have offices located throughout the nation, usually by region, with local offices under the regional offices. The cabinet-level departments employ about 60 percent of all federal workers. Departments vary in size and in prestige. All cover broad areas of responsibility. Departments are often organized to nurture and promote the interests of their clienteles (i.e., those "customers" who utilize the services of the agency). Such agencies are called clientele agencies. An example is the Department of Agriculture, whose agencies' work

Table 3.2 The Executive Departments of the U.S. Government

Department	Year Created	Number of Employees*	Total Budget* (in million dollars)	Principal Duties	Major Subagencies
State	1789	22,900	5,261	Develops foreign policy Negotiates treaties Protects citizens abroad	Foreign Service Passport Agency Bureau of Consular Affairs Bureau of Diplomatic Security
Treasury	1789	146,00	387,222	Pays federal bills Collects taxes Mints coins and prints currency Supervises national banks	Internal Revenue Service Bureau of Alcohol, Tobacco and Firearms (ATF) Secret Service† U.S. Mint Customs Service†
Interior	1849	67,600	7,937	Supervises federal lands and parks Runs federal power plants Supervises Indian Affairs	National Park Service U.S. Fish and Wildlife Service Bureau of Indian Affairs Bureau of Land Management
Justice	1789, 1870	119,800	15,474	Gives legal advice to the president Enforces federal laws Supervises federal prisons	Federal Bureau of Investigation Drug Enforcement Administration Bureau of Prisons Immigration and Naturalization Service
Agriculture	1889	99,000	55,015	Assists farmers and ranchers Conducts agriculture research Protects forests from fires and diseases Inspects meats, poultry, and egg products Promotes nutrition	Food Safety and Inspection Service Forest Service Agriculture Research Service Federal Crop Insurance Corporation Farmers Home Administration
Commerce	1903, 1913	38,300	4,065	Conducts U.S. census Monitors weather Grants patents Protects U.S. business	Bureau of the Census Bureau of Economic Analysis Patent and Trademark Office Minority Business Development Agency
Labor	1903, 1913	16,700	32,125	Administers federal labor laws Promotes the interest of workers	Occupational Safety and Health Administration Bureau of Labor Statistics Employment Standards Administration Office of Labor Management Standards

Department	Year			Function	Agencies
Defense	1789, 1798, 1947	731,000	251,385	Manages armed forces / Operates military bases / Civil defense	National Guard / National Security Agency / Joint Chiefs of Staff / Departments of Army, Navy, and Air Force
Housing and Urban Development	1965	10,400	30,950	Housing needs / Develops and rebuilds urban communities / Promotes urban improvements, such as streets and parks	Community Planning and Development / Government National Mortgage Association / Fair Housing and Equal Opportunity
Transportation	1967	64,900	40,465	Improves mass transportation / Develops and administers highways, railroads, and aviation / Offshore maritime safety	Federal Aviation Administration / Federal Highway Administration / National Highway Safety Administration / U.S. Coast Guard‡ / Federal Transit Administration
Energy Management	1977	17,100	14,366	Conserves energy resources / Conducts research and development	Office of Civilian Radiation Waste / Office of Nuclear Energy / Energy Information Administration
Health and Human Services	1953, 1979	58,500	359,106	Promotes public health / Enforces pure food and drug laws / Conducts research	Food and Drug Administration / Public Health Service / Health Care Planning Administration
Education	1953, 1979	4,600	30,474	Coordinates federal education policies / Administers aid to education / Promotes educational research	Office of Education and Rehabilitation Services / Office of Elementary and Secondary Education / Office of Postsecondary Education / Office of Vocational and Adult Education
Veterans Affairs	1988	206,000	43,074	Promotes the welfare of veterans of the U.S. armed forces	Veterans Health Administration / Veterans Benefits Administration / National Cemetery System
Homeland Security	2003	170,000	37,450	Intelligence clearing house designed to protect the United States from terrorist attacks. The department merged 22 existing agencies but does not include the FBI or CIA.	Immigration and Naturalization / U.S. Coast Guard / Customs Service / Border Patrol / Federal Emergency Management Agency / Secret Service / Transportation Security Administration

*The budget and employee data are from fiiscal year 1998 except for Homeland Security, which is an estimated budget for 2005.
‡Now a part of Homeland Security; there are other agencies that have also been merged into Homeland Security, such as the border inspection and part of the animal and plant health inspection service.

SOURCE: Adapted from Michael Lemay, Public Administration: Clashing Values in the Administration of Public Policy (Belmont, CA: Wadsworth/Thomson Learning, 2002), pp. 16–17.

benefits farmers and the agricultural industry through its Extension Service, which has offices scattered throughout farming areas to help farmers. The departments of Labor, Veteran's Affairs, and many others have agencies that appeal to clientele groups. Clientele agencies are directed by law to foster and promote the interests of specific groups, and these groups form powerful lobbies that apply pressure to Congress to keep the benefits coming.

Not all departments are clientele agencies. For example, the mission of the Department of Defense (DOD) is not to foster and promote the interests of military contractors, but contractors and the states and communities in which their plants are located benefit greatly from working with the DOD. The DOD, one of the better-entrenched bureaucracies (often called the military establishment or military-industrial complex), has close dealings with defense-related industries and provides contracts worth billions of dollars each year to maintain the military's weapons and equipment needs. The awarding of a contract to a large company like Rockwell or Boeing can have a major impact on a local area where the firm has factories that build aircraft, tanks, or other military equipment. Like other groups, contractors form powerful lobbies that apply pressure to Congress to keep the contracts coming for projects that help the nation, their companies, and their local communities.

Government Corporations

Government corporations are actually public businesses created by Congress to perform functions that could be provided by private firms. They exhibit some of the characteristics of public agencies and of private corporations. They are formed when government elects to engage in activities that are primarily commercial in nature for reasons that should serve the public interest. Unlike public agencies and commissions, most government corporations are expected to be economically self-sustaining. Bipartisan boards of directors usually control government corporations. Some of the most familiar government corporations are the U.S. Postal Service Corporation, the Federal Deposit Insurance Corporation (FDIC), Amtrak, and the Tennessee Valley Authority (TVA). Some government corporations, like COMSAT (the Communications Satellite Corporation) were even allowed to issue stock and make profits. COMSAT was incorporated in 1962 by Congress to establish a commercial system of international communications using satellites. Congress selected this route because no private corporation at the time could afford to start up such a corporation. It was government-sponsored but financed by issuing public stocks. In 1999, COMSAT merged with Lockheed Martin. Unlike most government corporations, COMSAT was a publicly held organization similar to most any corporation (with the exception that it was originally sponsored by the federal government).[19] In other cases, Congress stepped in when industries began to fail. For example, once passenger rail systems were no longer profitable, Congress created Amtrak to ensure that passenger service by train would continue.[20] Table 3.3 shows some of the government corporations that are operating today.

Table 3.3 Selected Government Corporations

Agency	Created	Staff	Principal Function
Tennessee Valley Authority (TVA)	1933	14,510	Operates river-flood control system system of dams. Generates and sells power.
Federal Deposit Insurance Corporation (FDIC)	1933	8,265	Insures individual bank deposits up to a specified amount. Oversees business activities of member banks.
National Railroad Passenger Corporation (Amtrak)	1970	23,000	Provides national and intercity rail passenger network. Controls approximately 23,000 miles of track and more than 500 terminal stations.
U.S. Postal Service	1970*	853,298	Delivers mail throughout the United States and territories. Is the largest government corporation.

*Created in 1789 as part of the Offiice of Postmaster General, located in te Department of the Treasury. During Andrew Jackson's presidency, it became a cabinet-level department. In 1970, the U.S. Postal Service became a government corporation.

SOURCE: U.S. Government, *United States Statistical Abstract* (Washington, DC: Author, 1998); U.S. Government, *United States Government Manual*, (Washington, DC: Author, 1997–1998).

Independent Executive Agencies

Independent agencies are called that because they are outside of the cabinet departments. They are called "independent" because they are supposed to be immune from influence by the president and Congress. Most have a narrow function to perform, such as the Environmental Protection Agency or the National Aeronautics and Space Administration. Sometimes political pressure can elevate an independent agency to a cabinet-level department, such as was the case with Veteran's Affairs. The expanding national focus on the environment has led many to call for the Environmental Protection Agency to be given cabinet-level status. Even President Bush stated that he would like to see the EPA have cabinet-level status. There are many independent executive agencies. Some of the more important ones are shown in Figures 3.1 (see p. 91). Table 3.4 contains a small selection of independent executive agencies.

Independent Regulatory Commissions

Independent regulatory commissions are agencies created by Congress to exist outside the major influences of cabinet-level departments to regulate a specific activity. Due to the complexity of economic issues, Congress wanted to have agencies that could develop expertise and provide continuity of policy. It was beyond the ability of Congress or the courts to handle these matters, and neither had the time nor the expertise to deal with complex economic-related issues. Examples of independent regulatory commissions include the Securities and Exchange Commission, the National Labor Relations Board, the Federal

Table 3.4 Selected Independent Agencies

Agency	Created	Staff	Principal Function
General Services Administration (GSA)	1949	944	Centralized purchasing agent for the federal government. Manages government properties and acts as the federal government's business agent.
National Science Foundation (NSF)	1950	13,729	Promotes scientific research. Provides grants to schools, colleges, and universities for research and scientific instruction programs.
National Aeronautics and Space Administration (NASA)	1958	21,996	Operates U.S. space exploration programs. Builds, tests, and operates space vehicles. Its original mission was putting a man on the moon, which it did in 1968.
Environmental Protection Agency (EPA)	1970	6,164	Charged with operating programs that reduce air and water pollution. Enforces environmental laws.

SOURCE: U.S. Government, *United States Statistical Abstract* (Washington, DC: Author, 1998); U.S. Government, *United States Government Manual* (Washington, DC: Author 1997–1998).

Reserve Board, and the Federal Communications Commission. All of these regulatory areas require the assistance of "experts." Thus, it is not uncommon for some of the nation's most respected experts in the specific fields to serve on the boards or commissions, such as Alan Greenspan, the chairperson of the Federal Reserve Board. Older regulatory boards and commissions tended to focus on a specific industry or area, such as the Securities and Exchange Commission (1934) and the Interstate Commerce Commission (1887). The boards of older regulatory agencies are relatively independent from partisan pressure. Most are operated by boards comprised of five to seven members who are nominated by the president and confirmed by the Senate for staggered terms to increase the chances for having bipartisan boards. The members of independent regulatory agencies cannot be easily removed.[21] Newer regulatory commissions (those created since the 1960s) have tended to focus more on how business practices or working conditions relate to health and safety, such as the Occupational Safety and Health Administration (OSHA). A single administrator, who can be removed by the president, typically administers the newer regulatory agencies. Table 3.5 shows some selected independent regulatory agencies—both some older and some newer agencies.

ADMINISTRATIVE STRUCTURE OF STATE
GOVERNMENTS: AN OVERVIEW

The organization of state bureaucracies is similar to that of federal bureaucracies, with a few notable exceptions. All states have the same three divisions of government—the legislature, judiciary, and the executive branches. Most of the

Table 3.5 Selected Independent Regulatory Agencies

Agency	Created	Staff	Principal Function
Federal Reserve (FED)	1913	1,760	Sets policy for interest rates and controls money supply.
Federal Trade Commission (FTC)	1914	965	Regulates unfair business practices, prevents monopolies from forming in the economy, and protects consumers' rights.
Securities and Exchange Commission (SEC)	1934	2,861	Regulates stock and securities exchanges, and all companies that sell stocks and bonds to the public.
Equal Employment Opportunity Commission (EEOC)	1964	2,631	Works to stop discrimination on the basis of race, religion, national origin, age, and disability. Examines claims of discrimination in the workplace.
Federal Elections Commission (FEC)	1974	300	Supervises elections to ensure compliance with federal election law.

NOTE: Employment data are from 1997.

SOURCE: U.S. Government, *United States Statistical Abstract* (Washington, DC: Author 1998); U.S. Government, *United States Government Manual* (Washington, DC: Author, 1997–1998).

bureaucracies of state governments are located in the executive branch, and their duty is also to help implement the law, perform regulatory functions, and the like. Most states have a cabinet system in the executive branch, but many states also have "long ballots." That is, some of the heads of large state agencies are elected to office rather than being appointed. In these cases, the governor does not have equivalent power to the president. All governors now have veto power, but most governors have limited appointment and removal power relative to the president. In about half the states, the governor and lieutenant government run together on a ticket, but the other half can elect members of different parties to those offices. Long ballots are fairly common, and independent agencies and commissions are often more independent than at the national level. This greatly fragments power in the executive branch in many states. Additionally, the equivalent to the Office of Management of Budget (OMB) at the state level (state budget offices) typically do not have the same degree of centralization and coordination powers of the OMB. State legislatures usually do not have an equivalent level of staff and expertise to predict and forecast revenues and expenditures, as does the federal level. Of course, there are exceptions. Large states like California and New York have more resources and professionalized legislatures and governments than most states. For example, California can rank with many nations because of its size and complexity, and it takes a professional government to administer a state of its size. A few states have very elaborate and well-organized budgetary systems. South Carolina, for example, has what is called the Budget and Control Board that centralizes and manages the state's budget and finances. Moreover, many state legislatures are still part-time assemblies by law. It is common for legislatures to meet for a very short annual session, or every other year (a biennial system) for a short session.

For example, Montana's legislature meets every other year for a 90-day session. Part-time legislatures are very dependent on the agencies of state government because of their short legislative sessions. Fortunately, the quality of state administration has improved impressively during the past 30 years. Today, state bureaucracies have high-quality personnel, more resources, and better salaries than in the past.[22] The maze of agencies in the states can be very complex, and the states employ about the same amount of workers as the federal government—20 percent of all government employees.[23]

ADMINISTRATIVE STRUCTURE OF LOCAL GOVERNMENTS: AN OVERVIEW

The administrative structure found at the local level varies greatly and includes counties, cities, towns, and many types of special-purpose districts, including school boards, water authorities, ports authorities, and fire districts. Local governments have no independent powers. They only have those powers granted by their states. They are "creatures of their states." State sizes vary greatly. North Carolina, the twenty-ninth state in geographic size, has 100 counties, whereas Montana, the third largest state geographically, has only 56 counties. (Most western states also have much larger counties than states in the East.) Some states, such as New Jersey, are heavily populated, while others, mainly found in parts of the West, are more sparsely populated. This greatly affects local governments because some large rural states, like Wyoming and Montana, do not have any large cities, at least by Eastern standards. The size and complexity of local governments are also diverse. Large cities, such as New York City, have governments that are as large and complex as some state governments. There are also a lot of local governments—more than 86,000 of them. Most of the government workforce (60 percent) is employed at the local level (the largest single group is schoolteachers). Although many variations in institutional structures are found at the local level, four primary types of local government structures exist: the commission form, weak mayor, strong mayor, and council-manager.

The *commission* form is found mainly at the county level and in some small cities or towns, and in most special-purpose districts. Commissioners are elected at large—that is, they represent the whole district. Once elected, the commissioners appoint one of the members as the chairperson. This type of government is very decentralized, with each commissioner controlling certain functions or departments. The chair has little, if any, central authority. The *weak mayor* form is basically a system characterized by weak executive authority. It is the equivalent to state systems where the governor's powers are weak due to long ballots, independent boards and commissions, and a strong legislature. In cities with the weak mayor form of structure, the mayor is usually more of a figurehead, and most of the executive power resides in elected commissions that administer departments and approve budgets. In many cases, the mayor is appointed by the city council. The *strong mayor* system distributes power between the chief executive officers and the legislature (or city council). An elected mayor has centralized authority to propose budgets, appoint department heads, and coordinate programs. The city council's authority to approve budgets provides a check on the mayor's powers. Mayors have more power under this arrangement than in any other type of local government structure. Under the *council-manager* form of government, an elected city council or commission appoints a professional city manager to function as the chief executive officer. The city manager works at the discretion of the council or commission, but has power to hire department heads. Cities that use this form often have a mayor appointed by the council who acts as a figurehead but who has little administrative power. This form of government was the type advanced by reformers and Progressives early in the 20th century to bring professional administration to local government. City managers are typically trained in public administration, and their specialty is managing municipalities.[24]

GETTING BUREAUCRACIES
TO WORK TOGETHER:
INTERGOVERNMENTAL RELATIONS

One of the strengths of the federal system is that it allows various levels of government to work together while at the same time allowing greater flexibility to state and local governments. Under federalism, the nation is not straightjacketed into a single policy in every policy matter that exists. Policies that are needed in large urban areas may not work well in rural areas. State and local governments typically have a lot of latitude to develop policies that are suitable for their environment in most (but not all) matters. The relationships between the various levels of government are characterized by shared responsibilities. *Intergovernmental relations* (IGR) is a convenient term that is used to describe the relationships that exist between the federal, state, and local levels of government. It encompasses a broad range of activities that may be coordinated, uncoordinated, or antagonistic.

There is a great deal of cooperation among the various levels of government, but there is also conflict. Local governments have long been responsible for operating public schools in most states. Most government employees (out of all 19 million government employees) are either schoolteachers or school administrators. There has been a trend during the past 20 years for local schools to receive more assistance from their states and the federal Department of Education. The states and the Department of Education have assisted by making broad policies and by providing grants and other financial assistance for specific programs such as curriculum development and special needs programs for students with disabilities. One of the inherent problems with federal grants is that they usually involve compliance requirements, which often creates tensions. The Department of Education coordinates grants with 50 state departments of education. Local schools often resent the pressures that are imposed to meet certain conditions in order to receive the assistance, and sometimes view the requirements as interference rather than assistance. If the school system approves of a program, it is likely to support it and comply with the requirements. Conversely, some programs create problems within the community. For example, teaching sex education in the public schools created tensions in some communities because it clashed with community values. Some parents felt that sex education was mishandled and was an intrusion on family matters. The situation was exacerbated when communities felt that the federal government was imposing sex education in their local schools.

Achieving racial balance in public schools was controversial for many years. The federal government imposed this laudable goal, and while most people associate it with desegregation in the South, some of the most notable conflicts occurred in other regions. For example, in the 1980s, a Kansas City school district sued the state and surrounding school districts for maintaining what they believed were segregated school systems. For several years, a district court judge assumed a large degree of control over planning for the school district, including ordering the creation of magnet schools. The judge went so far as to determine who should pay for the changes—75 percent of the costs were to be paid by the state and 25 percent by the local school district. In 1987, it became clear that the local school district could not pay its share because the state constitution limited local taxes. The only way to increase taxes was by a two-thirds vote by citizens for a new tax levy, so the judge ordered that the levy be placed on the ballot. However, the voters did not cooperate. They were already paying more per student than neighboring school districts. The judge then ordered that taxes be increased (nearly doubled) to pay for the desegregation plan. The tax bill on a $75,000 home at the time was about $1,500 per year. With the court-ordered tax increase, the tax bill on the same home became $3,000 per year. In response, voters and the state sued the federal government. Three years later the case reached the U.S. Supreme Court, which ruled that the U.S. District Court judge could not directly tax the citizens but that the court could order a local government body to levy the taxes to remedy a constitutional violation. The judge ordered that taxes be raised for the district and neighboring school districts, and over time the tax rate actually increased more than the court had originally ordered before the lawsuit. This case, *Missouri v. Jenkins,* illustrates how IGR plays out in our system of federalism.[25]

Overlapping jurisdictions sometimes cause problems. The question that usually arises in conflicts is: Who is in charge?[26] In most instances, we begin with the premise of national supremacy. Whenever a conflict arises and there is a direct conflict with a federal law or policy, the supremacy clause of the U.S. Constitution usually trumps state law or local ordinances. For example, during the 1980s a conflict arose regarding whether local governments had to pay overtime to workers involved in "essential" services. In *Garcia v. San Antonio Metropolitan Transit Authority* (1985), transit workers in San Antonio, Texas, were asked to work split shifts to accommodate the peak loads at rush hour. This caused long breaks between shifts and very long days for the workers. Workers believed that federal rules required overtime pay for such circumstances and sued the city. The city disagreed, claiming the workers were involved in an essential service that was historically provided by local governments and therefore outside of federal control. In 1976, the U.S. Supreme Court had accepted the rationale provided by the city in *National League of Cities v. Usery,* but this time the Court reversed the ruling and held that no state or local activity was outside of federal control.[27] Thus, state and local governments must abide by the Fair Labor Standards Act and pay overtime to workers.

Students often ask how the legal drinking age was raised to 21 in all fifty states. The answer comes from another intergovernmental conflict. The federal government wanted the drinking age raised, but some states did not cooperate. Congress passed a law penalizing states that did not increase the drinking age by withholding their federal highway funds. Thus, Congress used its spending power to control state behavior. The conflict ended up before the U.S. Supreme Court in *South Dakota v. Dole.* South Dakota sued, claiming that the Twenty-First Amendment gives states the right to regulate all matters concerning alcohol. Since the Constitution clearly gave this power to the states, South Dakota argued that the federal government could not circumvent this provision by withholding federal highway funds. The Supreme Court agreed with South Dakota that states have the right to regulate matters pertaining to alcohol, but ruled that Congress had acted legally through its spending power, which is granted in Article I, Section 8, of the U.S. Constitution. Under federalism, states do not have to accept federal money if they do not like the mandates that are attached. Over time, states and local governments became dependent on federal revenues. The dependency allowed them to keep taxes lower than would have otherwise been possible, to offer an array of programs, and to undertake construction of many new facilities.

It is up to state and local administrators to apply for grants—the federal government does not force a jurisdiction to take grants, although pressure may be applied. Thus, grants have limitations regarding coordination and control if the state or local governments view them as more of a burden than an asset to the community. The increase in federal grants began slowly in the 1960s and mushroomed in the 1970s, and these programs have remained popular. Federal funds currently account for about 24 percent of all state and local government revenues (the percentage was higher in the 1970s). The focus of grants has also changed over the years. During the 1950s, in light of the Cold War, grants were aimed at military preparedness, which was the original purpose of the interstate highway system. In the 1960s, the focus changed to social purposes, such as job training, education, and urban problems (e.g., crime and rebuilding the nation's inner cites). In the 1970s, the focus shifted toward housing, energy, and other social programs. And in the 1980s, the grants slowed considerably and many responsibilities were shifted back to the states. During the Clinton administration and thus far in the Bush administration, grants are flowing again into the states, but not at the pace found during the 1970s. Currently, there are more than 600 federal programs, and most involve IGR.

TAKING A CLOSER
LOOK AT BUREAUCRACY

The only thing that saves us from the bureaucracy is inefficiency.
An efficient bureaucracy is the greatest threat to liberty.

EUGENE MCCARTHY

Bureaucracies are not nearly as inefficient as commonly believed. In fact, their very design makes it possible for them to complete very complex tasks that otherwise would be impossible. Granted, there are problems with efficiency that will be discussed later in this book, but bureaucracies build automobiles, television sets, and computers in the private sector. In the public sector, they perform a varied array of tasks like monitoring the weather and delivering many services, such as public education.

Bureaucracy is often thought of as an organizational chart[28] with someone at the top, departments scattered through the middle, and other departments at the bottom. Most organizations have an organizational chart to illustrate their chain of command. Chain of command refers to everyone having a supervisor or a boss. Figure 3.1 (see. p. 91) illustrates the general organizational chart for the U.S. government. Each department contains many offices and employees, and each office has its own organizational chart that is not shown in the figure. The power of a bureaucracy comes from its ability to organize itself in such a way that very complex tasks can be performed.

To illustrate how bureaucracies perform complex tasks, we will shift our focus from organizations like the Department of Defense and the Environmental Protection Agency to an organization with which all students are familiar—a university. Public universities are government organizations, but all colleges and universities, public or private, are bureaucracies. Public colleges and universities are part of public administration because they are agencies of government. The purpose of a college or university is education, training, and research. Colleges and universities are institutions where students come to earn degrees and gain training that will help them pursue careers. Universities produce biologists, chemists, actors, teachers, journalists, physicians, lawyers, architects, dentists, and economists, to name only a few of the professions. This is part of the business of higher education. Universities also conduct research of every imaginable type, which generates books, articles, and reports so that our knowledge about the things we study continues to increase. Of course, universities do many other things, but the primary focus is supposed to be maintaining an institution of higher learning. The university accomplishes its mission by using a bureaucratic structure. It organizes itself to provide classes and to maintain grounds and recreational facilities, classrooms, libraries, parking lots, dormitories, and the like. Like all bureaucracies, the university requires a lot of people. Some department has to handle registration for classes. Some department has to operate the library. Another department has to provide food service, and so on. Moreover, someone has to teach classes. By asking yourself the following questions, you can "see" the bureaucracy at your own college or university:

- Who heads your college or university?
- Who assists this person in managing the organization?
- What departments do you find in the central administration?
- In which division is the department of political science located?
- In which division or college is the department of biological sciences located?
- In which department are public administration classes taught?
- How do you get enrolled as a full-time student at your college or university?
- How do you register and pay for classes?
- Which department or office helps you get a dormitory room?
- How is food service handled and how do you get a meal ticket?
- What is needed to check books out of the library?
- How do you get authorization to park your car on campus?
- How do you drop or add a class after the semester begins?
- Where do you go if your student loan or financial aid gets fouled up?

This list could go on and on, but the point is, most students learn during their time at a university "how to get things done." They also become socialized or indoctrinated into the workings of bureaucracy. All the rules and regulations that govern a university are made using bureaucratic procedures.

But is there any other way to organize a university? Is there any other way to organize a corporation? To date, we know of no method by which to organize large institutions other than the bureaucratic system. There are different varieties of bureaucracy, and we know a lot about the nature of them, but most of the alternatives that are suggested are simply modifications to bureaucracy. The alternatives to bureaucracy that do exist are inadequate in a modern complex society. How does one feed 290 million people? How does one go from Los Angeles to Atlanta to attend a meeting? Large food corporations that buy and process food and then distribute it to grocery stores and restaurants are bureaucracies. If you need to fly to Atlanta to attend a meeting, the trip is made possible by a bureaucracy. If you stay in a hotel while attending the meeting, a bureaucracy provides your accommodations and food. Whether public or private, bureaucracies are part of our daily lives, and they are all organized on the same principles.

Figure 3.4 is an organizational chart for a university. It is predicated on the same principles as the organizational chart used by Delta Air Lines, Hilton Hotels, and large grocery chains like Safeway. The head of the university is

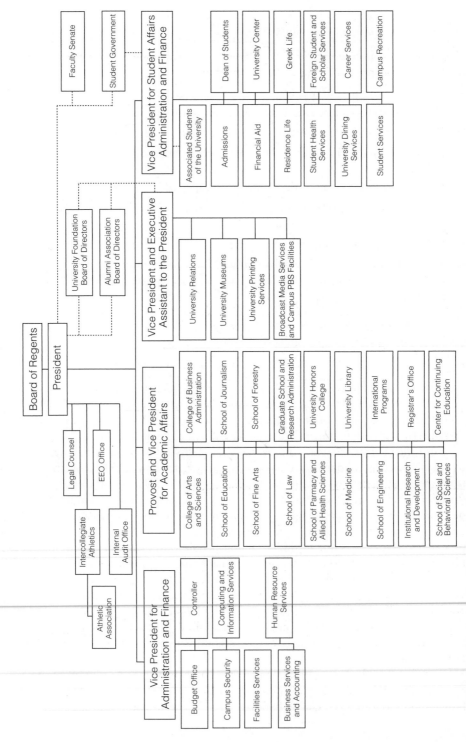

FIGURE 3.4 Sample University Organizational Chart

NOTE: This is an example of a typical organizational structure of a university.

the president (called a chancellor in some schools), who is assisted by a staff and a number of officials who handle finances, legal matters, and academics. The president is responsible for setting goals and maintaining a vision for the institution. The provost is typically the next in line and is responsible for running the day-to-day operations of the university. A staff that includes an associate and an assistant provost assists the provost. Universities are divided into colleges and schools that are headed by deans, who also have staffs to help them manage their areas. Academic departments, like political science or public administration, are located in this area. For example, political science is usually housed in a college of arts and sciences or in a college of social and behavioral sciences. But it takes a lot of administrative offices to make a university work. Thus, there is a human resource office (a staff function) to handle benefits and insurance, an accounting department to handle purchasing and pay bills, and a maintenance department to maintain the buildings and grounds. And there are many academic departments that teach specific subjects to students (a line function).[29] As illustrated in Figure 3.4, a university has many departments. Moreover, the larger the university, the more complex the organizational chart. A university is a complex social organization comprised of administrators, staff, faculty, and students (and, of course, physical structures).

Bureaucracies are often criticized for proliferating (growing). Tasks that once could be performed by only a few people eventually require much larger staffs, more directors, more money, and additional resources. The resources that public bureaucracies rely on do not come from selling goods and services to the public. Funding is secured through the budgetary process. Critics see this as unnecessary growth. But all organizations have a tendency to grow if they can. Businesses expand to gain more market share, and the work of government also increases. Critics argue that in the private sector, businesses can only grow if they generate enough sales in the marketplace to pay for the growth. When it comes to the public sector, critics claim that government is overproducing services to advance agencies' powers and build empires. (This criticism is discussed in greater detail in Chapter 8.)[30] Thus, some argue that government grows unnecessarily because there is no connection between the source of the funds that pay for government to operate and the work that an agency performs. In the private sector, the link is the price charged for goods or services, and customers choose whether to buy whatever a firm has to offer. This link is missing in government because the revenues come from taxes, and not from sales that must be generated in the marketplace. So government is criticized for creating a large, cumbersome, inefficient bureaucracy that continues to grow, overproduce services, and not look after the public's interest. The idea of "proliferation" is illustrated in Box 3.2 (New Element "Administratium" Discovered). Box 3.3 contains some cynical quotations and some of the "principles" that many associate with the bureaucracy.

BOX 3.2 New Element "Administratium" Discovered

A major research institution has recently announced the discovery of the heaviest element yet known to science. This new element has been tentatively named "Administratium."

Administratium has 1 neutron, 12 assistant neutrons, 75 deputy neutrons, and 111 assistant deputy neutrons, giving it an atomic mass of 199. These 199 particles are held together by a force called morons that are surrounded by vast quantities of lepton-like particles called peons.

Since Administratium has no electrons, it is inert. However, it can be detected as it impedes every reaction with which it comes into contact. A minute amount of Administratium causes one reaction to take over 4 days to complete, when it would normally take less than a second.

Administratium has a normal half-life of 3 years; it does not decay, but instead undergoes a reorganization, in which a portion of the assistant neutrons and deputy neutrons and assistant deputy neutrons exchange places. In fact, Administrium's mass will actually increase over time, since each reorganization causes some morons to become neutrons forming isodopes.

This characteristic of moron-promotion leads some scientists to speculate that Administratium is formed whenever morons reach a certain quantity in concentration. This hypothetical quantity is referred to as "Critical Morass."

Scientists paid little attention to Administratium for many years. They were well aware of its existence, but were surprised to find it to be the heaviest element yet discovered. How does one recognize Administratium? You will know it when you see it.

Anonymous

SOURCE: The public bureaucracy has always been the subject of many jokes. Most of the jokes satirize bureaucracies and bureaucrats. This "joke" was received at a state agency (a state university) via e-mail. The author is unknown.

ANATOMY OF BUREAUCRACY:
AN ORGANIZATIONAL CHART
OR SPHERE OF COOPERATION

Organizations can take two major forms that are reflected in the way their organizational charts are designed—tall or flat. Tall and flat organizations come in degrees—that is, degrees of being tall or flat. The university shown in Figure 3.4 is a relatively tall organization. Figure 3.5 (See p. 110) illustrates that the Department of Commerce has a relatively "flat" organizational chart. In fact, the secretary is shown to the side of the organization. Tall organizations tend to centralize power, whereas flat organizations decentralize authority as much as possible. The popular image of business as having a tyrant as a CEO, who pigeonholes power and commands all activities from the top floor of a tall skyscraper, is largely a myth. Many large corporations are relatively flat, with power very decentralized. For example, Philips and Hewlett Packard both have been used to illustrate highly decentralized organizations.

BOX 3.3   Some Principles Associated with Bureaucracy

Acheson's Rule: A memorandum is written not to inform the reader but to protect the writer.

Boren's Laws: When in doubt, mumble. When in trouble, delegate. When in charge, ponder.

Chapman's Rules of Committees: (1) Never arrive on time, or you will be stamped a beginner. (2) Don't say anything until the meeting is half over; this stamps you as being wise. (3) Be as vague as possible; this prevents irritating others. (4) When in doubt, suggest that a subcommittee be appointed.

Parkinson's Rule of Committees: A committee will spend as much time as necessary to perpetuate itself, exclusive of its reason for existence.

Murphy's Law: If anything can go wrong, it will.

O'Toole's Corollary to Murphy's Law: Murphy was an optimist.

Meskimen's Law: There is never time to do something right, but there is always time to do it over.

Parkinson's First Law: Work expands to fill the amount of available time for its completion.

Parkinson's Second Law: Expenditures rise to meet income.

The Peter Principle: In every hierarchy, each individual rises to his or her own level of incompetence, and then remains there. Thus, every position is filled with an incompetent person.

Smith's Principle: Never do anything for the first time.

Robertson's Rule: The more directives you issue to solve a problem, the worse it gets.

SOURCE: Adapted from James Q. Wilson and John Dilulio, *American Government*, 7th ed. (Boston: Houghton Mifflin, 2002), p. 42

Do organizational charts truly reflect how bureaucracies really work? Are they an accurate image? Years ago economist John Kenneth Galbraith presented a very different image to which many multinational corporations (such as the electronic conglomerate Philips[31]) conform.[32] The bureaucracy may be more accurately pictured as a "sphere" than as a tall or flat organizational chart. Even earlier, Galbraith put forward a phenomenon he termed the "technostructure." He believed that the multinational corporation, which is by any account a very large bureaucracy, had long replaced the classical firm in economics. Large organizations get their power by being able to assemble many areas of expertise to perform very complex tasks. Bureaucracies bring together administrators, architects, engineers, health care specialists, attorneys, and workers into a single organization. The power comes from being able to coordinate all of the expertise in a way that accomplishes the organization's goals, which includes maintaining a "human" organization.[33] Galbraith believed that the modern corporation is not managed by a powerful individual, but by a committee. The committee is comprised of high-level managers, and specialists such as lawyers, accountants, and engineers form the technostructure. The CEO or president is largely a figurehead, according to Galbraith. Moreover, in the case of corporations, boards of

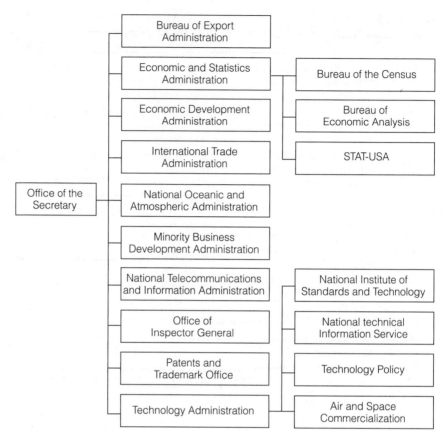

FIGURE 3.5 U.S. Department of Commerce Organizational Chart

SOURCE: U.S. Department of Commerce.

directors are more fluff than substance. They are comprised of people who typically know little about the actual workings of the firm. Stockholders own corporations, but management runs businesses pretty much as it sees fit, having been separated from ownership long ago.

Is it possible that the same is true for large public organizations? Is a large federal bureau operated by a "technostructure" (a committee comprised of managers, staff, and advisors—i.e., technocrats) or by the secretary who is appointed by the president and who wields great power? The secretaries of federal bureaus tend to hold policy preferences that are consistent with those of the president. The largest difference between large corporations and federal bureaus relates to *politics* and *economics*[34] rather than *organization*. Government bureaus are in place to implement policy. Political fortunes change quickly in Washington, and with the changes come appointments and removals of the members at the highest levels of the technostructure. In bureaus that perform routine tasks, it makes little difference which political party resides in the White House. But for some of the better-known bureaus, a new technostructure replaces the old one, and new policy directions are often pursued. For example, during the Clinton administration, the attorney general's office pursued the breakup of Microsoft and aggressively sought to punish the tobacco industry. With the election of George Bush, the foes of Microsoft and the foes of the tobacco industry found deaf ears in the new administration. Bush's attorney general, John Ashcroft, sought a quick settlement with Microsoft and no longer pursued the tobacco industry with any meaningful vigor. The Bush administration had new policies to pursue, which is a significant difference between corporations and government bureaus, especially agencies that can bring about policy changes. Government bureaus are either in the business of public policy or handling routine matters, such as processing Medicare paperwork or issuing retirement checks. The technostructure and its committees handle much of modern management in both the private and public sectors. At lower levels of government bureaus, workers continue from one administration to another.

Figure 3.6 illustrates the idea of an organization constructed as a circle rather than as a tall or flat organization, as in the traditional organizational chart. Advisors, committees, and high-level staff who make decisions and set policies are located in the center of the circle. The visualization provided in Figure 3.6 requires one to imagine the various levels (or spheres) in the circles "turning" as interaction occurs between the various departments and levels of the organization. Ideally, this would be a three-dimensional animated drawing that is dynamic and moving with each level and functional area represented by different colors. The organization is still a hierarchy; the line workers and staff are located in the outer areas of the circle, and the powerful members of the technostructure are in the center. Galbraith argues, however, that the relationships between departments and units in the sphere are not as static or orderly as an organizational chart suggests. Rather, the departments communicate, interact, and work with each other to get things done. This is what truly gives a bureaucracy its power—the ability to have a diversity of expertise interact.[35]

As we will see in Chapter 4, communication and interaction are not always perfect in organizations. Although it may be argued that the circle diagram just represents another way to draw an organizational chart, this technostructure may provide a more dynamic description of modern public bureaucracies and large corporations than traditional organizational charts. This is not to suggest that organizations do not have leaders or leadership. The point is, some organizations are so large and complex that it takes a team of experts to manage them.[36] Even though the organizational chart remains the principal way to illustrate the structure of organizations, the idea of organizations being of "circular design" or a "sphere" is conceptual food for thought. Some economists and corporations, like the multinational giant Philips, have recognized the circular model for years. It is plausible that the organization of our public bureaucracies fits into the same sort of mold.

CEO or head

Technostructure directors

Excutive departments

Second level departments

Third level of departments and offices

Field offices, staff, and workers

FIGURE 3.6 The Technostructure: Another Way of Looking at Large Organizations

SOURCE: John Kenneth Galbraith, *The Age of Uncertainty* (Boston: Houghton Miffllin, 1977), pp. 257–279

INSIDE BUREAUCRACY

What kinds of people work in public bureaucracies? Are they just like us, or do they have certain discernible characteristics? For that matter, do they differ from the people who work at large corporations? More importantly, what types of officials administer public bureaucracies?[37] In 1966, Anthony Downs published an insightful book titled *Inside Bureaucracy.*[38] Downs attempted to illustrate a variety of the characteristics of bureaucracies, including the characteristics of the people who work in them.[39] He differentiated between bureaus and corporations, since the value of corporations is evaluated outside the firm. Thus, Downs saw a difference between public and private bureaucracies.[40] According to Downs, those who run public bureaucracies fall into five "ideal–types" of bureaucrats, which he acknowledged to be an oversimplification.[41] But his concept of ideal-types of bureaucrats is useful because anyone who has ever worked in or dealt with government bureaus regularly can recognize people who show the characteristics of Downs's ideal-types. They are labeled: *climbers, advocates, zealots, statesmen,* and *conservers.* The names tend to suggest certain behaviors that appeal to common sense. The basic classification that separates these people is their motives. There are two types of self-interested officials and three types of mixed-motive officials. Of course, these ideal-types also apply to employees who are not yet officials.[42]

Self-Interested Officials

Climbers are bureaucrats motivated solely by the desire to maximize their own personal power, income, and status. They tend to be the rising stars who will take whatever action is needed to advance their own goals. Once they have reached the highest point they can achieve in a bureau, they tend to jump ship to another bureau to continue to advance their careers and self-interest. Purely self-interested officials are motivated almost entirely by goals that benefit themselves rather than their bureaus, the public interest, or society as a whole. Because they can adapt to changing environments and do well regardless of the objective standard employed, one may think of them with the saying "the road upward" because promotion and success is what drives them. Climbers are found at the lowest levels of the organization partly because new recruits tend to have greater ambitions, since their careers are just beginning.[43]

Conservers regard convenience and security as paramount to their self-interest. In contrast to climbers, conservers seek merely to retain the amount of power, income, and prestige that they already have. They tend to protect the status quo and resist change. They also tend to be very "rule-oriented" because they use rules and regulations to resist change. Thus, conservers may be described as "holding on to what you've got." Some personality types are born conservers, but in organizations climbers can become conservers when they no longer believe that they can advance their careers further. Conservers are more prominent in the middle levels of bureaus. Those who have reached the peaks of their careers and middle-aged people who have lost their youthful energy are more likely to be conservers.

Mixed-Motive Officials

Zealots are loyal to relatively narrow policies or concepts, such as the development of certain military arms (missile defense systems, nuclear submarines, etc.). They seek power both for its own sake and to advance the policies to which they are fanatically loyal—so called *sacred policies.* Zealots are so committed to their causes that they will pursue their goals even when faced with overwhelming odds against winning. Zealots are very optimistic, energetic, and aggressive. They are found in newer agencies and often are the reason that new agencies are created. (New agencies are often "split" from existing agencies.) Zealots may be thought of "men and women on a mission." They are highly focused on a narrow cause, which tends to make them poor general administrators.

Advocates are loyal to a broader set of functions or to a broader organization than zealots. They also seek power because they want to have a significant influence on policies and actions concerning those functions or organizations. Advocates tend to promote the ideals of an agency, such as law enforcement or environmental protection, but in a much broader way than zealots. Advocates are found in all levels of organizations, but are very prone to be involved with newer organizations. They are optimistic and energetic, but they are far more directed than zealots. Thus, they are more likely to listen to their supervisors, peers, and subordinates. Advocates at higher levels of the organization espouse broader policy goals than those at lower levels. They tend to promote everything under their jurisdiction because their focus is on overall performance rather than any one part of the agency. Moreover, maintaining financial support for operations is also based on overall performance. Thus, advocates will advocate their functional area. They are the largest single group of the five idea-types and tend to make good general administrators.

Statesmen are different from any of the other types. They are loyal to society as a whole, and they have a desire to attain the power necessary to have a significant influence on national policies. They are altruistic to a large degree because they are loyal to the "general welfare" and committed to serving the "public interest" as they see it. Thus, statesmen tend to resemble the ideal bureaucrat often described in public administration textbooks because they sincerely do seek to serve a greater public good. Statesmen vary in energy from being lazy to hyperactive. Lazy statesmen promote very broad views but take little action. They are good critics but poor achievers. Statesmen are inclined to be philosophical and academic because their broad views often conflict with their narrow areas of functional responsibility in the organization. They also are less confrontational and seek to reconcile clashes through compromise. Because they are usually loyal to society as a whole (rather than their supervisor or even the agency), they tend to be found at the highest and lowest levels of organizations.

One can imagine that having all five of the "ideal-types" (or even people who approximate these types of individuals) in a bureau could cause tension, and it does. But all of these types are necessary to accomplish certain activities despite the dysfunctional aspects that may occur. One can also see that whichever ideal-type controls an organization would likely affect how the organization behaved. This was one of the major points of Downs's study. Of course, these are only ideal-types, but they help us understand something about the personalities and preferences of some of the people who run public agencies. In reality, people may approximate the ideal-types, but one does not have to look very hard to find individuals in agencies who resemble those described by Downs. This is not to suggest that these types of motive-driven bureaucrats are the only types of personalities found in organizations. Researchers have classified employees into a variety of types based on different criteria, such as the *ambivalent, indifferent,* and *ascendant*.[44] But the ideal-types described by Downs serve as a conceptual framework that allows us to, at least to some degree, categorize five major types of individuals found in public bureaus based heavily on their motives.

LIFE CYCLES OF BUREAUCRACIES

All organizations, whether public or private, go through various stages of development. At some point, a bureau is born and begins what can be termed a "life cycle." The stages of development, maturity, and decline have caught the attention of scholars for many years.[45] The major causes of both growth and decline are rooted to a large extent in the environment in which bureaus operate. As society develops, certain functions grow in prominence and others decline. Bureaus are likely to be more affected by environmental changes than by internal changes. But there is a cumulative effect that occurs because of the interplay between the internal and external dimensions, and turnover in bureaus can be relatively high despite the career nature of public service. The types of bureaucrats that dominate an organization, such as climbers, advocates, or zealots, can have a tremendous effect on operations.

Figure 3.7 is a drawing that illustrates the life cycles of organizations. It generally corresponds to the idea of a "life cycle of bureaus."[46] Organizations are all created at some point, and many believe that the "young" organization is filled with the most *esprit de corps* (organizational energy and vitality by members of the organization). Franklin Roosevelt created many new bureaus for that very reason—older bureaus were too established and set in their ways to tackle new problems with zeal and energy. During the 1960s, President John Kennedy also recognized that creating new agencies was the best way to get energetic organizations (what Peter Drucker termed the *high-spirited organization*).[47] This was partly the reason for the success of the Peace Corps. All organizations are born, grow, mature, and then decline—Figure 3.7 reflects this idea. Bureaucracy has both a positive and a negative side. Because of organization, expertise, energy, and the like, bureaucracies can accomplish a lot of positive things. But over time they tend to lose their organizational zeal and become characterized by all the bad attributes that we associate with bureaucracy—red tape, too many "silly" rules, rules becoming more important than the organization's mission, dysfunctionality, and so on. Eventually, an organization goes into a severe period of decline (also called a period of bewilderment in the diagram).

The model in Figure 3.7 can apply to both public and private organizations. In the public sector, an agency may be reorganized, lose much of its funding, and become impotent. It may even be dissolved (although this is rare). In the private sector, an organization that moves into the final stages will likely either go bankrupt or be sold. This process occurs for many reasons, including changing social and economic conditions, but most likely the process is inevitable. The question that is raised is: How do we keep organizations in the more positive areas of the process? It is possible that with good management, leadership, and a redefined vision and mission, a public organization can reverse the process and move back into a positive zone, or stay longer in the positive areas illustrated in Figure 3.7. However, some agencies simply run their course. For example, when airlines were deregulated, there was no reason for an agency to set fares and routes for the airline industry. Thus, the Civil Aeronautics Board (CAB) was dissolved during the 1980s. If

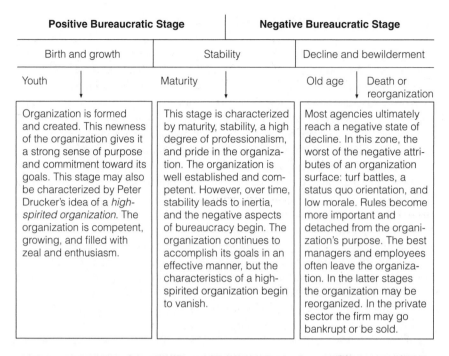

Positive Bureaucratic Stage		Negative Bureaucratic Stage
Birth and growth	Stability	Decline and bewilderment
Youth	Maturity	Old age Death or reorganization
Organization is formed and created. This newness of the organization gives it a strong sense of purpose and commitment toward its goals. This stage may also be characterized by Peter Drucker's idea of a *high-spirited organization*. The organization is competent, growing, and filled with zeal and enthusiasm.	This stage is characterized by maturity, stability, a high degree of professionalism, and pride in the organization. The organization is well established and competent. However, over time, stability leads to inertia, and the negative aspects of bureaucracy begin. The organization continues to accomplish its goals in an effective manner, but the characteristics of a high-spirited organization begin to vanish.	Most agencies ultimately reach a negative state of decline. In this zone, the worst of the negative attributes of an organization surface: turf battles, a status quo orientation, and low morale. Rules become more important and detached from the organization's purpose. The best managers and employees often leave the organization. In the latter stages the organization may be reorganized. In the private sector the firm may go bankrupt or be sold.

FIGURE 3.7 The Life Cycle of Organizations

the political environment changed radically and we no longer wanted the federal government to protect the environment, the EPA would quickly move into the bewildered stage and probably be dissolved (although this is not a likely scenario).

Agencies go through periods of rise and decline, just like corporations. In the private sector, corporations are well aware of their products' life spans and constantly reevaluate the market and plan for changes and potential diversification to ensure the long-term survival of their firms. In the public sector, there is an old bureaucratic joke that says, "never fully accomplish your agency's mission or you may be out of business." In a sense, this happened to NASA, which runs the nation's space program, once it reached the moon. Despite all the wonders of modern technology that NASA has provided, such as solar calculators and the like, NASA has had trouble securing appropriate funding for many years. The urgency of reaching the moon before the former Soviet Union did has passed, and members of Congress do not see any shortage of technology given the rise of the high-tech computer industry and related industries. NASA's budget has not increased much during the past 15 years, and yet it continues to function, though at a more subdued level than 30 years ago, and continues to accomplish impressive things.[48]

SUMMARY

This chapter has examined the growth of the federal bureaucracy and its general organizational structure. The bureaucracy in the United States had humble beginnings and grew slowly. Several waves of growth and changes made America an "administered society" with a highly developed, professional bureaucracy. Although intergovernmental relations among agencies at the federal, state, and local levels usually work smoothly, conflicts do arise and often must be settled by the courts.

The organizational chart is typically used to illustrate the structure of organizations. Organizations can be designed to be "tall," with power and authority more centralized, or "flat" with power and authority more decentralized. Additionally, some have offered alternatives to the traditional and static organizational chart—the idea of a sphere of cooperation.

The greatest power that a bureaucracy possesses is its expertise and the ability to coordinate its resources, which in turn determines the organization's effectiveness. Bureaus contain a number of "ideal-types" of bureaucrats who can greatly affect the performance of an agency. Bureaus also develop over time. They go through a life cycle that begins with the creation of the organization and continues through several stages. They may ultimately be dissolved or reorganized if, over time, their usefulness diminishes. However, unlike the private sector, where the penalty for poor organizational performance is bankruptcy, public organizations continue to operate for as long as they can secure funding and resources from the legislature.

NOTES

1. One of the better books ever written about this subject is Barry Bozeman, *Bureaucracy and Red Tape* (Upper Saddle River, NJ: Prentice-Hall, 2000). Bozeman's book examines many of the criticisms and pathologies associated with modern bureaucracy in an evenhanded manner. Also, Charles Goodsell wrote one of the better books defending the need for public bureaucracies, *The Case for Bureaucracy: A Public Administration Polemic,* 3rd ed. (Chatham, NJ: Chatham House, 1994).

2. One of the best books available that articulates how bureaucracies actually work is James Q. Wilson's, *Bureaucracy: What Government Agencies Do and Why They Do It* (New York: Basic Books, 1989). This book is considered to be standard reading in many MPA programs.

3. Francis E. Rourke, *Bureaucratic Power in National Politics,* 2nd ed. (Boston: Little, Brown, 1972).

4. This was an embarrassing event for those working in immigration services. How could they approve two of the highjackers six months after the event when the highjackers themselves, whose names had been posted all over the news media, were deceased? Most Americans simply wrote this off as clear illustration of the incompetence of the public bureaucracy.

5. Chris Suellentrop, "Amtrak: The Little Engine That Couldn't," Slate.com (June 26, 2002). This article can be viewed online at http://slate.msn.com/default .aspx?id=2067378 or by going to

Slate.com and searching for the title or identification number, 2067378.

6. These examples are real and are often blamed on cumbersome and restrictive procurement rules that limit what agencies can do and place ridiculous specifications for purchases.

7. For many examples of this nature, see George Downs and Patrick Larkey, *The Search for Government Efficiency: From Hubris to Helplessness* (Pittsburgh, PA: University of Pittsburgh Press, 1986). Note that the theme of this book is that government is not as poorly managed as commonly believed, and that private businesses are not as well managed as the myth of private sector superiority leads us to believe.

8. See Richard Stillman II, *The American Bureaucracy: The Core of Modern Government*, 2nd ed. (Chicago: Nelson Hall, 1996), Chapters 1 and 2, for an excellent discussion about the development of American bureaucracies.

9. Karen O'Connor and Larry Sabato in *American Government: Continuity and Change*, 2000 Election Update ed. (New York: Longman, 2001), p. 304.

10. The Internet gateway to access the federal Web site is http://www.firstgov .com.

11. James Q. Wilson, "The Rise of the Bureaucratic State," in Richard Stillman II, *Public Administration: Concepts and Cases*, 3rd ed. (Boston: Houghton Mifflin, 1984), pp. 56–57. Wilson's original article was published in *The Public Interest 41* (Fall 1975), pp. 77–103.

12. Ibid.

13. Ibid, p. 59.

14. The Web site for the Securities and Exchange Commission is http://www .sec.gov.

15. The CAB was originally established in 1938. The CAB's authority to handle consumer complaints against airlines was transferred to the Department of Transportation.

16. Congress created the agency as part of the Rural Electrification Act of 1936. Critics were arguing that there was no longer a need for this agency. In 1994, Congress eliminated the REA and the Rural Development Administration

(RDA), both housed in the Department of Agriculture, but they created a new agency, the Rural Utilities Service (RUS), which continues to handle rural water and sewerage, electricity, telecommunication, and other utility projects. The purpose of the new agency is similar to that of the old, but the new agency helps rural areas maintain their system and bring in new technologies. Thus, for all practical purposes, the original agency still exists under a new name with a modified mission and purpose. The Web site for the RUS is http://www.usda.gov/rus.

17. Experts disagree over the exact number of agencies, bureaus, offices, and commissions that comprise the federal government. See David Nachmias and David Rosenbloom, *Bureaucratic Government: U.S.A.* (New York: St. Martin Press, 1980).

18. The regional breakdowns shown here are not used by all agencies. The specific regions, usually illustrated by maps, can be found on the Web site of most agencies or in the *United States Government Manual* for all agencies. The United States Government Manual can be viewed online at http://www.access.gpo.gov/nara/nara001 .html.

19. See Lloyd D. Musoff, *Uncle Sam's Private, Profitseeking Corporations: Comsat, Fannie Mae, Amtrak, and Conrail* (New York: Free Press, 1982).

20. Ibid.

21. The Supreme Court ruled in 1935 that Congress intended for independent regulatory agencies to be independent panels of experts that would be as insulated as possible from partisan politics. See *Humphrey's Executor v. United States*, 295 U.S. 602 (1935).

22. Frederick Mosher argues that because of the rise in professions and specializations used in government, the public service is becoming a very "professional state." See Frederick Moser, *Democracy and the Public Service*, 2nd ed. (New York: Oxford University Press, 1982), Chapter 5.

23. Ann Bowman and Richard Kearney, *State and Local Government*, 5th ed. (Boston: Houghton Mifflin, 2002), Chapters 6 and 7.

24. Ibid, Chapters 8 and 10.

25. *Missouri v. Jenkins,* 110 S. Ct. 1651 (1990). The Tenth Amendment of the U.S. Constitution reserves powers for the states. However, the Supreme Court does not always rule consistently, even in areas of education. In *United States v. Lopez,* the Supreme Court ruled that Congress had overstepped its authority with the Gun Free Zone Act of 1990, which made it illegal to carry a firearm within 1,000 feet of a school. Following a wave of school shootings, Congress wanted to help make schools safer. In this case, Lopez was arrested for bringing a gun to a school in San Antonio, Texas. See *United States v. Lopez,* 115 S. Ct. 1424 (1995).

26. Because of the overlap and complexities of management, some scholars have argued that there is another concept that is overlaid on intergovernmental relations—intergovernmental management (IGM). Intergovernmental relations can be viewed as a picket fence with each level of government represented in most policy areas, at least to some degree. IGM refers to the activities of program professionals (subordinates of the generalist administrators) who specialize in policy areas and the details of management and implementation. See Deil Wright, *Understanding Intergovernmental Relations,* 2nd ed. (Monterey, CA: Brooks-Cole, 1982).

27. Both cases involved the Fair Labor Standards Act that was amended in 1974 to extend the act's minimum wage and maximum hour provisions to almost all employees of states and their political subdivisions. The Supreme Court ruled in favor of the city's argument in *National League of Cities v. Usery,* 426 U.S. 833 (1976), which was overruled in *Garcia v. San Antonio Metropolitan Transit Authority,* 469 U.S. 528, 572 (1985).

28. Organizational charts were popular in the classical period of public administra-tion. In his famous "Proverbs of Administ-ration" (discussed in Chapter 2), Herbert Simon not only offered a counterprinciple but also found contra-dictory principles in the principles themselves. He noted that the traditional administrative doctrine called for a narrow "span of control" (the principle that a manager could only supervise a limited number of employees to maintain effective communication). This principle tended to create "tall" organi-zational charts because managers could only supervise a limited number of employees. But the traditional literature also argued that if organizations were to maximize effective communi-cation, they should minimize the number of hierarchical layers. Thus, they also argued for a "flat" organizational structure. The discussion of tall versus flat organiza-tions has been around for a long time. See Herbert Simon, *Administrative Behavior* (New York: Macmillan, 1957).

29. In Chapter 4, more distinctions will be made about the types of departments or functions that are found in organizations, namely, line and staff. In the example of a university, a personnel department is a staff function, and the academic departments, like biology and public administration, are line functions. Typically, line functions are directly involved with the production of a product. If one interprets teaching as delivering the product, then departments and faculty are performing a line function. The idea is easier to illustrate in industries where actual products, like DVD players and computers, are produced. Those involved with assembling computers are in a line function, and those in the human resource and sales offices perform staff functions.

30. In Chapters 7 and 8, the arguments presented by public choice theorists are examined in more detail.

31. The multinational corporation Philips displays a model in its headquarters that illustrates the conceptualization of the organization being a sphere, not a static chart. It is more difficult to illustrate on paper than it is with a physical model on display. The corporation Royal Philips Electronics is based in the Netherlands. It is ninth of the world's Fortune 500 companies. The Philips office is located in Eindhoven, the Netherlands, http://www .philips.com.

32. John Kenneth Galbraith, *The Age of Uncertainty* (Boston: Houghton Mifflin, 1977). This book was made into an interesting PBS television series that is available from the Public Broadcasting

System. Galbraith does not provide a graphics image of the technostructure in his books, but does articulate it clearly. He did use a sophisticated graphic design in the PBS series "The Big Corporation" that was similar to the one shown in Figure 3.6.

33. We will see in Chapter 4 that many modern management experts, such as Peter Drucker, argue that the modern organization must first be a human organization to survive. The classical model of the firm as a profit-maximizing organization has largely been abandoned by most in the field.

34. Economics here refers to the pursuit of profit in a competitive environment, and politics refers to implementing the policies dictated by the party in power through organizations that are monopolies.

35. The organizational chart can be easily modified to show informal lines of communication and interaction, but the conceptualization of "moving parts" in the circle or sphere gives a more dynamic description of large organizations, and one that is potentially more accurate.

36. Galbraith first articulated the idea of a technostructure in his classic book *The New Industrial State* (Boston: Houghton Mifflin, 1967). In his PBS series, Galbraith again described and illustrated the idea of the technostructure.

37. The term *types* refers to the kinds of officials that work in public bureaucracies, including their personalities, tendencies, predispositions, and the like.

38. Anthony Downs, *Inside Bureaucracy* (Prospect Heights, IL: Waveland Press, 1994). The Rand Corporation published the original book in 1966.

39. Downs tested a series of hypotheses based on the idea that the types of bureaucrats who dominate and run bureaus affect the behavior and performance of the bureaus. For the most part, his hypotheses were confirmed.

40. Downs was very prominent in bringing economic analysis to political science and public administration. The difference between public and private bureaucracies has more to do with measuring their performance and value than basic structure. It is also possible that some, if not all, of his five ideal-types of bureaucrats do not correspond to some "ideal-types" of employees found in businesses. One can also find climbers, conservers, advocates, and the like in private organizations.

41. Anthony Downs, *Inside Bureaucracy,* pp. 88–89.

42. All of the descriptions of the ideal-types are credited to Anthony Downs. Although some of the descriptions have been paraphrased, they come from Downs's, *Inside Bureaucracy,* pp. 88–90.

43. Downs goes into considerable detail describing each of his ideal-types. For example, (1) climbers seek to increase their prestige and aggrandize in ways that face the least resistance. They will try to acquire specific functions that are not performed by anyone else in the bureau. Thus, they have a strong tendency to create new functions for their bureaus. (2) If they cannot successfully create new functions, they will capture (or take) functions performed by persons whose power to resist is limited. This means that the climber's selection of functional areas is influenced just as much by power considerations as by any logical linkage with the climber's present role. (3) Climbers have a strong tendency *not* to economize unless they can use at least some of the savings to finance an expansion of their own functions. If the savings are returned to the appropriations agency, this might reduce the next year's appropriations. Thus, the climber will not economize operations. (4) Climbers will jump to another bureau if they believe they can increase their prestige and power. The presence of opportunities for a climber to "jump" to another agency weakens the control the current agency has over them. Downs articulates and explores these and many other attributes about each of his ideal-types.

44. Descriptions of other ideal-types, such as ambivalents, indifferents, and ascendants, come from Robert Presthus, *The Organizational Society* (New York: Alfred Knopf, 1962). Other so-called types have been described by other researchers. Presthus's categories of employees were based more on their attitudes toward work and their careers than the ideal-types described by Downs. Ascendants are similar

to "climbers." They are interested in getting ahead in their careers and are willing to do the work necessary to succeed. Ambivalents are interested in the work, but not in advancing their careers to reach the higher echelons of the organizations. Indifferent people are, as the name suggests, not interested in much more than drawing their paychecks.

45. Anthony Downs, *Inside Bureaucracy,* Chapter 2. This chapter contains an excellent discussion about the stages of development and decline of public bureaucracies.

46. Ibid.

47. Peter Drucker, *People and Performance: The Best of Peter Drucker on Management* (New York: Harper & Row, 1977).

48. Barry Bozeman argues that we can view and study bureaucracies in two ways: normatively and empirically. If we go the normative route, we focus on the values that bureaucracy should serve and the discrepancies between these values and actual behavior. The empirical method makes no judgments about the values and goals of bureaucracy, but attempts to identify the elements of bureaucracy to determine what bureaucracy "is." In other words, the empirical view tries to explain bureaucratic behavior without making judgments about the behavior itself. These two approaches exist side-by-side in the study of public administration because the social sciences tend to have methodological pluralism—that is, they use various methods of inquiry aside from the empirical (or scientific) approach. See Barry Bozeman, *Bureaucracy and Red Tape,* Chapter 1.

4

Fundamentals of
Organizational Theory
and Management

Organizations are complex, goal-seeking units. In addition to the penultimate task of realizing goals, they must undertake two related tasks if they are to survive: they must maintain the internal system and coordinate the "human side," and they must adapt to and shape the external environment.

WARREN BENNIS

THE STUDY OF ORGANIZATIONS

Organizations are one of the principal focuses of public administration. After all, the organization provides the structure in which public administration works. In a sense, the context of public administration may be the organization itself.[1] Organizations are systems of consciously coordinated activities that are carried out by people (members of the organization) to achieve specific ends. All organizations, even relatively simplistic ones, contain at least a rudimentary division of labor with some degree of specialization among members. As organizations grow and become more complex, the degree of specialization among activities generally becomes greater, and the need for better coordination increases. The relationship between size, complexity, specialization, and the need for coordination is extremely important for public agencies.[2]

Organizational theory studies virtually everything that is associated with organizations. It is a large field of study that includes examining organizational design, motivation, organizational culture, managerial styles, group behavior, leadership, and communication. Concepts and practices like management by objectives (MBO), transactional analysis, quality circles, job enrichment, and organizational development are all a part of organizational theory.[3] The goal of organizational theory is to enhance our understanding of organizations and organizational life and, hopefully, discover ways to improve organizations. The essential question posed in studying organizations is: How do they work? This chapter provides an overview of some of the major aspects of organizational theory and some of the basic elements of management.

Large organizations are complex configurations comprised of people, rules and regulations, structures, materials, equipment, and expertise. All of these elements are important, but management, people, and organizational design have received the most attention. There are a number of approaches (or models) that can be used to study public organizations. Three of the more significant models may be thought of as *political, organizational,* and *humanistic* approaches.[4] A model is a set of assumptions specifying characteristics that the observer believes to be important, and these assumptions affect what the observer sees and studies. A model is a template or conceptual framework that seeks to represent something in the real world. The three primary models (there are subsets of each) focus on three very different aspects of organizations and allow us to view organizations from different perspectives.

POLITICAL APPROACHES

Political models are rooted in political science. They actually go back to James Madison, who was one of the designers of the American system of government. Madison was one of the authors of *The Federalist Papers,* a series of 85 essays that described how America's system of government should work. Not only did *The Federalist Papers* help get the U.S. Constitution ratified, they also provided a rough blueprint about the new political system. Approaches to public administration that are derived from political science share common links to the work of James Madison.[5] These approaches focus on the structures and functions of government agencies and the public policy-making process. Two politically oriented models are still widely used today. They are the structures/functions model and the public policy model.

Models that examine *structures and functions* define public organizations in a way similar to describing the anatomy of the human body or the mechanical configuration of an automobile. These models diagram the formal legal powers and relationships among organizations. The emphasis is on the formal organization, its procedures, and legal structures. This model sees organizations as a system of components that perform a variety of functions and activities, which includes the behavior of administrators and agencies. The problem with this approach is that it fails to adequately describe the behavior that occurs within agencies and seldom focuses on *how* agencies are managed. Moreover, policy outcomes are viewed simply as the result of interaction within the formal institutions of government. This approach maps out the legal, procedural, and structural arrangements found in public organizations, which is something that we need to know to understand public agencies. Many of these arrangements and the legal foundations that authorize organizations at the federal level can be found in the *United States Government Manual*.[6]

Another approach that comes from political science is the *public policy* model. As the name suggests, the focus is on the complexities and dynamics of the public policy process. This includes the agencies, decision makers, and players who are involved in making public policy. The process develops because of conflicts between competing interest groups who have different values and objectives. Interest groups seek to influence outcomes in the process by using money, votes, and resources to gain access to decision makers. The effectiveness of interest groups is based on their success in attaining advantageous policy outcomes. The success of agencies is based on their ability to meet the needs of the interest groups that support them and to handle the problems that result when clashes among competing interest groups occur. This model is primarily found in public policy analysis, which is the subject of a later chapter. Studying organizations from this perspective utilizes the behavioral method (described in Chapter 2). It is typically a rigorous form of inquiry that provides great insight into the real workings of the public policy process and how agencies behave in the process. However, it reveals very little about managerial dimensions of organizations or other aspects of organizational life. The institutions are usually taken as a given, since the focus is on interaction between interest groups, people, agencies, and other institutions of government.

Political approaches are interesting and useful. They define the organizational, procedural, and legal structure of political institutions and agencies. They also enhance our understanding about the behavior of the institutions, groups, and people involved in the policy-making process.

ORGANIZATIONAL APPROACHES

Organization-based approaches are considered to be the true beginning of organizational theory in the managerial sense of the term. These approaches were the first to shed light on many of the realities of organizations and organizational life. Organizational models are multidisciplinary, involving many disciplines outside of political science and public administration. The basics of organization theory begin with two very influential figures: Max Weber (1864–1920) and Frederick Taylor (1856–1915).[7] Neither of these men were the first to write about or study organizations or management, but their work provided the impetus to a rapid expansion of our knowledge. Weber had the least impact on practitioners at the time; his impact was much greater on academicians. In the modern world, Weber's description of bureaucracy still helps to shape the way that most of us view large organizations. One must bear in mind that his descriptions were about an "ideal-type" or "model" bureaucracy. He was the first to clearly describe the concept of bureaucracy (some of his characteristics of bureaucracy are included in Chapter 2). He described an organization that he knew was not fully achievable. It was a model that reflected the fundamental elements of efficient and effective organizations that he saw developing in Germany in the 19th century. His model was superior to all previous methods of administration. For Weber, the bureaucracy was the only way that modern societies could organize themselves. Modern societies were simply too complex to be administered without bureaucracy. Actually, Weber described three ideal models (they were based on *traditional, charismatic,* and *legal-rational* models of authority), but only his *legal-rational* model is truly applicable to modern society.

For Weber, bureaucracy was simply an organization that had certain characteristics and was organized in a rational way. Weber described a *hierarchical structure* arranged like a pyramid, with each position responsible to the one above it. Labor is divided *(division of labor),* and specialized duties are assigned to each position. The organization is governed by *rules;* thus, decision making is based on the application of standardized rules that apply equally to everyone and are designed to accomplish organizational goals. The bureaucracy is *impersonal;* officials make decisions according to the responsibilities assigned to their positions. *Authority* is vested in positions rather than in a person. Thus, both those who exercise authority and those over whom it is exercised accept its legitimacy. Selection and promotion are based on *merit* using objective standards. Weber's legal-rational organization created rationality and order, and enabled government to accomplish large, complex tasks. Many characteristics were included in his descriptions of what he referred to as the *legal-rational* model. The following points sum up other elements of Weberian bureaucracy:[8]

- Fixed and official jurisdiction, ordered by rules and administrative law
- Regular activities distributed in a fixed manner
- Authority by directives according to fixed rules
- Rights and duties of administrators prescribed by law
- Principles of official hierarchy with levels of graded authority, which establishes superior-subordinate relations
- Management based on written documents that are maintained in files
- Separation of public from private lives of officials
- Administration as a full-time job requiring expertise and specialized training
- Positions held for life, free from political and personal considerations, which confers independence
- Management follows specific, learned rules that are transferred from one official to the next
- Regular compensation, fixed salary, as a function of rank
- Hierarchical career ranks with fixed conditions of promotion, and promotion based on examinations or seniority

Weber believed that the rationally organized bureaucracy was the most efficient form of administration. Despite his articulate descriptions of an effective bureaucracy, he also foresaw problems. He noted that once bureaucracy is established, it is among those social structures that are the most difficult to destroy.[9] As bureaucracy grows and becomes more powerful, it turns on the very society that created it and attempts to reorder society into categories of stability and rationality.[10] In other words, over time, society itself becomes bureaucratic because it becomes more socialized into thinking and behaving more "bureaucratically." Whether this is true or not is subject to debate because later in the 20th century (during the 1960s and 1970s) there was a revolt against the cold and impersonal ways of bureaucracies, whether public or private. But the revolt, mainly carried out by America's youth, did not seriously damage bureaucracy. It did contribute to many social changes that affected organizations, such as the creation of the New Public Administration school in the discipline of public administration (discussed in Chapter 2), and it was the impetus for changes in businesses, first in academic studies and later in the real world.[11] Weber once noted that he did not look forward to a world comprised of little people holding onto little jobs in hopes of getting a bigger one. Weber made many criticisms about the very organization about which he so skillfully articulated.[12] Although some of his observations have turned out to be incorrect, Weber's bureaucracy remains the beginning point for studying large organizations.

Frederick Taylor studied another dimension of organizations, namely, the part that is directly involved with production. All organizations have two primary types of behavior: the collective behavior of the organization as a whole that is reflected in its output, and the internal behavior of its members. For many years, the focus in studying business organizations was on finding the right methods to get workers to be more productive, and therefore achieve greater output. This world fascinated Taylor. Workers were thought to be lazy and only segmentally involved with their work. The primary motivator was assumed to be money, and management's job was to use science to find the best way to perform tasks and then train the workers to follow these procedures. The formula was rather simple: Science directs, money motivates, and workers will produce. This was the guiding doctrine in the world of business administration, and it was provided by the principles of Frederick Taylor's scientific management.[13]

Taylor was a controversial figure even during his own time. The ideas espoused in his scientific management principles aroused distrust and suspicion among workers who feared the potential of exploitation. During the 1920s, efficiency experts with stopwatches symbolized everything that clerical and blue-collar workers feared the most from the dehumanizing effects of scientific management. Workers were viewed as "cogs in the wheel" to be managed by the "carrot and the stick." It should come as no surprise that the American labor movement was strongest in industries where mass production and scientific management techniques were widely used.[14] Of course, management was friendly to Taylor's ideas that promised increased worker productivity, but when Taylor's ideas were applied to government workers, public outcry led to congressional investigations.[15] Taylor's organization was viewed as a "closed system" that focused on production and efficiency. The emphasis was at the lower levels of the organization because that was where products were produced.[16]

Taylor also had a number of principles associated with his theory. Little attention was paid to the idea that organizations could be "open systems" that are affected by an array of external factors, although much later, when systems theory was introduced, it became obvious that neither businesses nor public organizations are closed systems.[17] (Systems theory is discussed later in this section.) Although Taylor is best remembered for trying to find the "one best way" of performing a given task, his position contained four main principles that delineated what he saw as management's duties and responsibilities in teaching workers the right way to perform a task. Note that the fourth principle, in the following list of Taylor's principles of scientific management, actually suggests splitting the work between management and workers to build true cooperation:[18]

1. Deliberate gathering of knowledge by means of *time and motion studies* (conducting studies to find the best way to perform tasks)

2. Scientific *selection* of workers, and then their progressive *development* (selecting the best workers and properly training them)

3. Bringing together this science and the trained worker by offering some *incentive* to the worker (offering money to motivate workers, although Taylor believed money was an adequate incentive)

4. Complete *redivision* of the work of the establishment to bring about democracy and cooperation between the management and the worker (cooperation with workers by having management perform part of the work previously performed by workers). If management is to teach workers the "one best way" to do something, they must know how to do it themselves. Taylor predicted that because of this sharing of work, labor strikes would not occur if scientific management were properly used. (Apparently this idea was not widely adopted by industries at the time.)

Although Taylor's ideas may seem dated, they are still very influential in modern management and thought.[19] With respect to the study of businesses, time and motion studies are still done, and the idea of trying to find the most efficient way to produce goods and services is still very much alive and well in the new century.[20]

In the world of public organizations, the focus was different. Those who studied public agencies were more concerned with executive management. The emphasis was on finding the right "principles of administration" and applying them to public bureaus. Great attention was given to the organizational chart and ways to enhance efficiency. It was believed that better designs would improve coordination and communication, and therefore, efficiency. For many years, a plethora of principles of administration were the guiding doctrine for those who studied public administration, with activities such as planning, organizing, staffing, directing, coordinating, reporting, and budgeting (POSD-CORB) receiving a considerable amount of attention. In its day, Luther

Gulick's "Notes on the Theory of Organization," which gave us the acronym POSDCORB, was extremely influential.[21] The focus of "administrative science," as this branch of organizational theory was sometimes called,[22] emphasized positions in organizations more so than people. Coupled with an array of other concepts, like chain of command (the idea that a defined line of authority exists), span of control (the idea that a manager can effectively supervise only a certain number of subordinates), and line/staff positions (line positions are directly involved with producing something while staff positions play a supportive role), the classic public administrationists thought they were making progress in discovering the principles of administration. Like business administration, public administration had a lot of faith in science to provide the principles and procedures needed to create more efficient organizations. Many believed that a science of administration was possible—that administration could be similar to biology, physics, and other established sciences.[23]

Using science to learn about organizations proved to be useful and revealed much about organizations, but the hope that science would reveal a universal set of "principles of administration" was never fulfilled. In time, the aspiration to discover "principles" was abandoned, along with the idea that politics can be separated from administration in public organizations, largely due to critics who argued that the "principles" were either too inflexible to apply to every situation or too vague to be helpful in specific situations.

The strongest criticism came from Herbert Simon[24] who dismissed the idea of using the principles as guiding wisdom because he saw the principles as being mutually contradictory. For example, at the same time that they called for tall organizations to ensure that the chain of command was followed and that proper authority was maintained because everyone would know exactly who to report to, the principles also called to limit the levels of hierarchy to ensure that communication did not get distorted flowing through the chain of command, which suggests that the organization be as flat as possible. How can an organization be both tall and flat? Perhaps the idea was to create a tall organization, but not so tall as to create too many levels of hierarchy to ensure that communication not be distorted. This sounds reasonable, but how do we know when an organization is too tall or not tall enough? As Simon and others argued, the principles are often simply too vague to have meaningful application. Whatever the rationale, Simon literally went principle by principle and showed that a counterprinciple existed for virtually every one of the tenets of administrative science, at least as it was defined at the time.[25]

One articulate critic predates Simon by many years. Mary Parker Follett (1868–1933) was one of the leading critics of scientific management and the ideals of the principles of administration long before it became popular to criticize them.[26] Follett was born many years before her time, and it would be decades before her insight was fully appreciated. Her work was not appreciated at the time because she was so far outside of the accepted paradigm. It has been said that she wrote too late because scientific management was already accepted, and she was too early because the problems with scientific management had not yet been revealed.[27] From the outset, Follett adamantly opposed the entire doctrine of scientific management. The basic assumptions of scientific management rested on the belief that gathering data and utilizing the scientific method would lead to the discovery of the one best way to perform a given task. This view assumed that a fact was constant over time; that a fact today was the same fact yesterday, and would still be a fact tomorrow. At the time, science was searching for laws similar to the law of gravity and the other scientific laws that had been discovered in every imaginable field of endeavor. Science had made great progress in many fields, especially in the hard sciences such as physics. But such a static notion of the social world was something that Follett could not accept. Follett essentially argued for what the scientific community today recognizes as *relativism,* and she also argued for a form of participatory management. Today she is considered to be among the greatest of the early public administration thinkers. Her basic positions may be summed up as follows:

- The value of every fact depends on its position in the whole world process and is bound by its multitudinous relations.

- Facts must be understood as the whole situation, considering whatever sentiments, beliefs, and ideals enter into it.

- The world and its [social] organizations are not frozen; they are always changing and evolving.

- The idea of experts with a limited scope or perspective is suspect, since one becomes an expert not by being a specialist in a small area but by applying insights into the relationship of the specialty to the whole. (Thus, she was suspicious of some of Weber's ideas, and particularly the idea of experts.)

- Process is important in ensuring that administration is public. Dynamic organizations utilize the dynamics of the human spirit rather than mechanization.

Most of the principles of administration at the time emphasized the position rather than the person—so, in short, Follett argued for organizational humanism before it had been studied.

Mary Parker Follett's positions were the antithesis of both Taylor's scientific management and many of the tenets of classic public administrationists at the time. The paradigm of the time focused on chain of command, span of control, line positions being superior in power to staff positions, and the like, but these were simply not what Follett saw as the most important elements of organizations. For Follett, the organization itself was a static structure, regardless of the design. It was the human element that made organizations dynamic. Mary Parker Follett's work and vision goes much further than what is presented here. Her ideas were daring, and her insight was ahead of the era in which she lived.[28]

Thus far, the early elements of organizational theory appear to have mainly produced disappointments. Max Weber described bureaucracy, but his model falls short of describing the real organizations in which we work. Frederick Taylor spent a career extolling the virtues of scientific management, but much of his work has been dismissed and hardly seems applicable to most government agencies. The early public administrationists spent their energies trying to use science to discover the "principles of administration" and to figure out how to remove politics from administration, but their efforts where abandoned once these goals were shown to be unrealistic and unattainable. Organizational approaches would not go away, but they would change drastically.

The next wave of organizational approaches rejected the administrative science idea that organizations were closed systems. Viewing an organization as a system, whether it is a closed or open system, involves conceptualizing the components of the organization as a set of interrelated parts. Closed-system models focus on the organization, its internal structures, internal dynamics, and decision-making processes with little regard to the external environment. These models recognize the existence of the world outside of the organization, but it is management's responsibility to control external environmental factors to limit their impact on the organization. Open-system models assume that the external environment influences the organization. Because organizations depend on resources from outside the organization, open-system approaches emphasized the relationship between the organization and its larger environment. These models recognized that organizations alter their structure, functions, and output in response to laws, interest groups, changing conditions, and values that are accepted by the larger society.[29]

Systems theory emphasizes the interactive and interrelated set of elements that affects the organization, usually conceptualized as inputs entering the system, the processing of the inputs and making decisions, which generate outputs, with feedback affecting newer inputs back into the system. This process is continuous; thus an organization is constantly undergoing change.[30] The basic systems model is illustrated in Figure 4.1. Weber's model of bureaucracy is technically an open system; systems theory would develop much later. In the late 1940s and 1950s, there was a wave of bringing systems theory into the social sciences, an idea that was borrowed from biology. Norbert Weiner presented the idea of an organization as an adaptive system in 1948.[31] In 1953, David Easton brought systems theory into political science, and henceforth politics was viewed as a system.[32] In 1960, John Pfiffner and Frank Sherwood popularized the idea of systems theory in organizational theory.[33] The concept took hold and has remained the most popular way to view organizations.[34]

The idea of viewing organizations, both public and private, as systems has greatly changed the way we see the agencies of government and large corporations. For example, a public university interacts with the community on an ongoing basis. It is, first of all, a member of the community; it is involved with civic matters in the community, its employees and administration live in the community, and it contracts services with the local community. It is unrealistic to believe that the community does not affect the university or that the presence of the university does not affect the community. The university also must adapt its internal workings to requirements imposed by both the state and federal governments. For example, if the receipt of federal grants comes with conditions that require modification to the physical structures or internal procedures, the uni-

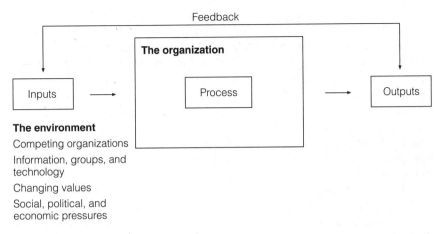

FIGURE 4.1 The Organization as a System

SOURCE: Adapted from Peter Schoderbek, *Management Systems,* 3rd ed. (Plano, TX: Business Publications, 1985), p. 204.

versity must comply. Laws are often passed that require even structural changes to buildings. When Congress passed the American Disabilities Act of 1990, many universities had to install elevators in old buildings to accommodate people with physical disabilities. By the early 1990s, most states had responded to a variety of pressures and banned smoking in public buildings, which forced state universities and other agencies to comply. Many local governments passed ordinances that also banned smoking in private businesses. Civil rights legislation altered the hiring, promotion, and other personnel practices of both private businesses and public agencies. Over time, values change in society and these work their way into the operation of all organizations. Of course, the degree to which an organization is "open" varies. For example, the Department of Defense and the Central Intelligence Agency are less open than the U.S. Forest Service, mostly for national security reasons. But the idea that the external environment affects organizations is something that we take for granted today.

Organizations are dynamic entities that are affected by both external and internal factors. Agencies and businesses do not operate in vacuums. In the real social world, things are less articulate than the models of system theory drawn up by academicians. Organizations are not created by nature; they are social institutions created by people. Most phenomena in the social world are highly imperfect, constantly changing, and a bit messy. Regardless of how we define or conceptualize organizations, they are structures that are managed by and employ people to perform tasks aimed at achieving some established goal, whether it is maintaining the nation's defense, managing foreign affairs, or designing and producing software at Microsoft. Some researchers felt that existing models and theories failed to adequately explain how organizations really worked. Thus, another perspective was needed—the *humanistic approaches* that focus on the people who work in organizations.

HUMANISTIC APPROACHES

By the 1940s organizational theory was changing. The humanistic approaches, which included a major subfield called organizational psychology, provided new insight by focusing on the individuals who work in organizations. Humanism examined the effect that organizational conditions have on people. The new focus included taking a careful look at such things as decision making, leadership, motivation, and reward systems. Much of the focus of humanism is on the individual (or small groups of individuals) and organizational conditions. The humanistic approach did not become popular until the 1940s, but it actually began during the 1920s in an experiment that came to be called the Hawthorne studies.

In 1927, Elton Mayo (1880–1949) and his student assistant, F. J. Roethlisberger, conducted a five-year study that was supposed to reveal how changes in environmental workplace conditions affected worker productivity. The study took place at a Western Electric relay assembly plant in Chicago. Mayo and Roethlisberger conducted many experiments. Perhaps the most famous are the ones that attempted to show the effect of illumination on worker productivity. One study involved a group of female workers assembling telephone relays. Mayo kept changing the work environment, but no matter how the work environment was changed, productivity kept increasing. More lighting, less lighting, longer rest breaks, and shorter rest breaks seemed to have no impact. The experiments appeared to meet all of the expectations of the scientific method. Careful records were kept, and the experiments were conducted simultaneously in a test room and a control room, with each change introduced one at a time while all other conditions remained constant. The test resulted in people working whole-heartedly as a team. Western Electric officials initiated an interview program to try to discover what could have been overlooked. By their standards, the experiment had failed, since changes in the work environment did not have the anticipated effect. Mayo and his team did not find the "one best set of environmental work conditions" that maximized productivity. Instead, they discovered that the workers were responding to the attention they were getting rather than the work conditions. This is now referred to as the *Hawthorne effect*. The second discovery was that informal social structures (the informal group) had a strong effect on work groups—the physical conditions were of secondary importance. Mayo found that the groups imposed pressure on their members to achieve production levels, as opposed to workers responding to levels set for them by management. The workers viewed themselves as a group and represented themselves in that way to management.

The Hawthorne studies are considered to be a major breakthrough in organizational theory. The breakthrough in management thinking had nothing to do with worker efficiency as it relates to the physical work environment; it had to do with worker efficiency related to their *attitude toward work*.[35] These studies revealed information that we take for granted today, but what was discovered had not yet been conceptualized at that time.[36] Moreover, the Hawthorne studies shifted the focus from the organization to individuals and earned Mayo the title of "father of human relations." The Hawthorne studies ignited the human relations movement, partly because the results led some to believe that a happy worker would be a productive worker.[37] This is, of course, not necessarily true.

The belief that productivity is influenced by employees' reactions to organizational conditions created several new waves of research. Organizational psychologists focused on the causes of job satisfaction. Organizational humanists, like Chris Argyris and Douglas McGregor, tried to figure out how organizations could be managed and structured to balance the need for productivity with individual job satisfaction. Argyris contributed much to our understanding of the individual and the organization, including observations about some basic inconsistencies between the growth trends of the healthy personality and the requirements of formal organizations.[38] The emphasis of the organizational humanists was on developing techniques for leadership, conflict resolution, and decision making that recognized the importance of expanding employee participation in the organization. Also, Abraham Maslow developed his influential *needs theory of motivation* to illustrate that humans have needs that must be fulfilled (Maslow's needs theory will be discussed later in this chapter.)

The concept of roles was often used to explain the relationship between the individual and the organization. Roles are simply a set of expected behaviors that people holding certain positions in the organization are supposed to perform. We learn how to fulfill the roles we play in organizations because the expectations are communicated to us from supervisors and other employees. The expectations are also affected by our own preferences and values. In the real world, conflicts often arise because the expectations of supervisors and coworkers differ from our own ability to perform and our preferences. For example, suppose that you are hired by a county to conduct sanitation inspections of health care facilities. Your supervisor informs you, after you are hired, that you are expected to conduct 20 inspections per week, but you feel that only 10 inspections can be conducted properly. In time, a conflict over the supervisor's expected productivity and your professional standards may emerge. Role conflicts can be simple or extremely complex because they can involve personalities, professional standards, personal growth aspirations, organizational expectations, and the like. Roles are important for several reasons. Most people select careers and jobs that they hope will fulfill their own personal and professional needs, and most people do need the income from their jobs to sustain themselves. Roles are the way that labor is divided in organizations, and there is constant communication between supervisors and employees about the expectations of their roles. Roles are also the way that organizations control the behavior of employees. If an employee fails to fulfill expectations, supervisors can punish the employee, even to the point of dismissal.[39]

Among the more popular developments was Douglas McGregor's (1928–1964) concept of Theory X and Y. McGregor's Theory Y model created an alternative to the assumptions of Taylor's scientific management. McGregor presented two opposite ways to view workers and, therefore, two different managerial models. The basic assumptions for Theory X were as follows:

- Management is responsible for organizing the elements of productive enterprise (money, material, equipment, and people) in the interest of an economic end.

- Management is responsible for directing people's efforts, motivating them, controlling their actions, and modifying their behavior to fit the needs of the organization. People are not capable of self-control or self-direction. In the absence of order, chaos will prevail.

- People will be passive and even resist the organization's needs unless management persuades, punishes, rewards, and controls the activities of workers. External forces, such as fear or money and other rewards, motivate people. The behavior of workers can be modified by using incentives and disincentives. Thus, the "carrot-and-stick" approach to supervision works because people respond to incentives and disincentives.

McGregor believed that management had caused these assumptions to appear to be true by the conditions they had created in organizations. Years of adhering to the doctrines of Taylor's scientific management had created organizations where humans were treated as commodities rather than dynamic resources. He offered an alternative called Theory Y that had a different set of basic assumptions, as follows:

- Management is responsible for organizing the elements of the enterprise in the interest of economic ends. (This is the same assumption used in Theory X.)

- People are not passive by nature or resistant to organizational needs. They have become so as a result of their experiences in organizations that were created by management, not by nature. Management is responsible for creating this problem.

- The motivation, potential for development, capacity for assuming responsibility, and readiness to direct behavior toward organizational goals are all present in people. Management is responsible for making it possible for people to recognize and develop these human characteristics for themselves.

- Management's essential task is to arrange organizational conditions and methods of operation so that people can achieve their own goals best by directing their own efforts toward organizational objectives. (This is the idea of letting people develop careers that satisfy their personal objectives and at the same time help the organization achieve its goals.)

McGregor blamed management for not developing conditions that would satisfy the human need for development and building an *esprit de corps* that would enable both the organization and its employees to attain their goals.

McGregor's idea seems common today because most of us pursue what we view as our own personal and professional goals through organizations, while simultaneously helping the organizations in which we work achieve larger organizational goals. McGregor had a positive view of people and their capabilities.

He believed that people are capable of self-control and self-direction and that they can motivate themselves if the environment is conducive to that. The problem rests in management's mentality and the way organizations have been constructed and designed in the past. He did not believe that the carrot-and-stick approach to supervision worked in all organizations. The more complex and professional the organization, the less likely these assumptions would be valid.

Granted, McGregor's Theory X and Theory Y are models that represent two opposite views of organizations and people. It is likely that reality falls somewhere in between. All workers are not capable of self-direction, self-control, and self-motivation. Taken literally, Theory X appears to describe a sweatshop mill during the Industrial Revolution, but this is misleading. One may view Theory X and Theory Y as representing a highly authoritative organization with a strict chain of command versus a more participatory organization. Whether it is possible for most organizations to follow the doctrine of Theory Y is subject to debate, but it is unlikely that it could apply to all organizations. There are examples of large organizations that are considered to be Theory Y firms, such as the computer giant Hewlett Packard. However, most discussions with military personnel confirm that the armed forces do not subscribe to the principles of Theory Y. An old adage in the military says, "We protect democracy; we don't practice it." The military may be an extreme example, but it illustrates that Theory Y is not for everyone.

Theory X and Y are best viewed on a continuum, with Theory X on one end and Theory Y on the other, and with middle ground between them. Perhaps Theory Y was most significant in that it provided an alternative view of workers that was radically different from the ideals of scientific management— one that was in the new tradition of the organizational humanists. Theory Y was the impetus for Theory Z, which was articulated by William Ochi in the early 1980s. Theory Z entailed quality circles, employee participation, and job enrichment.[40] Ochi believed that productivity is improved by greater communication, feedback, and worker involvement in self-managed work teams.[41] Ochi and others stressed the idea of self-managed work teams, which was indeed a radical shift from Frederick Taylor's ideas. Today, Theory X and Theory Y are often used as models to represent the hard (Theory X) versus soft (Theory Y) styles of management.

Organizational humanism has advantages over the other approaches by providing much deeper insight into the core of organizational life. Its focus on the needs of individuals rather than on an abstract political system or the mechanistic diagrams of organizational theorists provides insight about what might be done to improve the relationships between employees and organizations. One obvious criticism is that organizational humanism focuses so much on the needs of employees that it deemphasizes efficiency and productivity in organizations. One is left with the idea that a "happy worker who is fulfilling his or her personal growth needs" is also a productive worker, and therefore organizational efficiency and effectiveness will improve. This is the same erroneous conclusion drawn by the human relations movement after the Hawthorne studies. A happy worker is not necessarily a productive worker, and a less-than-happy worker is not necessarily an unproductive worker. Organizational humanists tend to have a very positive view of humans and their capacities, and many skeptics are still not convinced about the validity of these ideas. Taken together, however, the three approaches tell us a great deal about organizations, the legal relationships between public organizations, how the conceptualizations apply to the real world, and the needs and relationships that exist within organizations. Most agree that no universal principles exist to be uncovered, but each theory gives us a better understanding of the complexities of organizations and the people who work in them.

MODELS OF DECISION MAKING:
AN OVERVIEW

One of the most important dimensions of organizations is decision making. Making decisions is at the center of public administration, and few areas have received more attention. How decisions are made, by what standards, at what cost, and for whose benefit are questions of continuing interest. At times, the decisions made by bureaucracies can be very controversial. For example, the handling of the Cuban Missile Crisis by President Kennedy in the early 1960s amounted to a showdown between the United States and the former Soviet Union, and the possibility of war was a very real scenario at the time. Fortunately, the stakes are not usually this high in most decisions made by bureaucracies.

Before examining some of the models of decision making, we should note that there are two major types of decisions involving organizations—organizational decisions, which are reflected in the output or policies that are generated, and internal decisions that affect day-to-day operations within the organization. Organizational decisions may be thought of in terms of the political model. For example, an organizational decision is illustrated when the Federal Aviation Administration (FAA) decides to tighten or loosen its rules on airline safety inspections because of political or economic pressures. The same applies to regulating banks and industries that are polluting the environment. During the 1980s, the decision by the Reagan administration to "look the other way" in regulating savings and loan banks led to an expensive financial bailout. Failing to adequately check the accounting practices of businesses trading stock on Wall Street partly contributed to the scandals involving Enron and WorldCom. These scandals led to calls for additional oversight of the accounting industry, since one of the nation's largest and most respected accounting firms was involved. President Bush signed a law in 2002, the Sarbanes-Oxley Act, that created a five-member national oversight board.[42] The decisions made by public bureaucracies, especially regulatory agencies, are often affected by policy mandates from the administration that occupies the White House. The Reagan administration made it clear that it wanted to reduce regulation of businesses. Decisions are affected by many other factors, including rulings by the courts, societal values, economic conditions, and the values of the people involved in decision-making processes.

Internal decisions are those that managers and administrators make on a regular basis in the daily course of their work. These decisions may not affect major policy matters that go beyond the organization.[43] Routine decisions have to be made on an ongoing basis and occur often enough that an established set of guidelines can often be used. Routine decisions are illustrated by what FAA safety inspectors do when they find violations by a major airline. If policies or standard practices are in place, their decisions are guided by policy. A routine decision may also be something as seemingly mundane as an employee asking to change vacation to a time that is typically not convenient for the organization. Most organizations have established procedures for handling this type of request, but someone still must make a decision and say yes or no. Managers are concerned with internal decisions that affect the daily operations. But the decisions that affect the external environment, such as decisions to reduce regulation of businesses that are polluting the environment or to allow the building of a highway that will run through a wilderness section of a state, are the types of decisions that capture the attention of the public and interest groups.

Regardless of the type of decision, models of decision making provide frameworks to illustrate how individuals and groups make decisions in organizations. The two major decision-making models are the *rational* and the *incremental* models. The rational model is based on economic models of decision making.[44] These models assume that decision makers are consciously rational. Being rational in this context refers primarily to goal-directed behavior. Rational models are concerned with such things as efficiency (maximizing the output in relation to a specified input) and *assume that by behaving rationally, a decision maker will try to get the most output from the least amount of input of resources.* Embodied in this idea are cost-benefit principles. Cost-benefit criteria are used to evaluate whether the benefits that will be gained in the alternatives being considered will justify the costs. One assumes that if the costs are greater than the benefits, the decision is not rational and should not be pursued. Thus, rational models seek to help people make the most "rational" decisions possible. To accomplish this, decision makers are supposed to define the goals that are to be achieved, select ways to achieve the goals, evaluate each alternative solution thoroughly by assessing the costs and benefits of each alternative, and then select the best alternative.[45] If this method is followed, decision makers will make rational decisions.

Since the rational model comes from economics, several concepts are included. The term *utility* refers to a measurement of satisfaction. In the case of decision making, utility is a numerical value that indicates how well a particular alternative satisfies the goals or expectations for resolving the problem. Some models also incorporate the idea of self-interest. Economic theory suggests that people (and decision makers) pursue courses of action that satisfy their own self-interest. The idea of self-interest complicates this model because various motivations come to play. Are decision makers trying to resolve a problem in a way that is in the public's interest or in their own self-interest?

Rational choice theory is addressed in detail in Chapter 8. The rational model is often cited as the "ideal" way to make decisions, especially those involving major public policies. Specifically, the model breaks decision making down into several phases:[46]

1. Establish a complete set of operational goals with relative weights allocated in different degrees to which each may be achieved.

2. Establish a complete inventory of other values and resources with other weights.

3. Prepare a complete set of the alternative decisions that will resolve the problem.

4. Prepare a complete set of valid predictions of the cost and benefits of each alternative, including the extent to which each alternative will achieve the various operational goals, consume resources, and realize or impair other values.

5. Calculate the net expectations for each alternative by multiplying the probability of each benefit and cost for each alternative by the utility of each, and calculate the net benefit (or cost) in utility units.

6. Compare the net expectations and identify the alternative (or alternatives if two or more are equally as good) with the highest net expectations.[47]

Stated more simply, the rational model (sometimes called the *rational-comprehensive* model) merely means defining one's goals, analyzing the available alternatives, and selecting the alternative that best meets the goals.

The *problem-solving* model is similar to the rational-comprehensive model except that one begins by defining the problem that must be resolved (rather than the goals that one is trying to achieve). This means one thoroughly examines the dynamics of the problem before proceeding. Decision makers then follow similar procedures except that the process may be less mathematical. The problem-solving model is not grounded entirely in economic theory, so some of the assumptions (particularly, the pursuit of self-interest) are absent. In making decisions using the problem-solving model, one simply defines the problem, examines and assesses the advantages and disadvantages of alternatives, and then selects the alternative that seems to be the best solution.

Either of these models would be an ideal way to solve problems or make decisions, but unfortunately, many problems are associated with the rational models. The models assume that the decision maker (a person or a group) has the time to undertake the procedures just described; that the decision maker understands the problem that must be resolved, has a clear goal that can be articulated, and has a set of alternatives that can be evaluated; and that there is ultimately a *best* decision that can be reached.[48] Such an idea is unrealistic at best. Variations of these models are more reasonable. Perhaps in making major decisions, for example, an agency could use something that approximates the *problem-solving* model, recognizing that it is always impossible to gather all the reasonable alternatives and fully evaluate the effects of each one, since there are always unintended consequences that are overlooked or simply cannot be known at the time. Economists have added uncertainty to the rational model, but it is still inadequate.

The inadequacies of the rational-comprehensive model led Herbert Simon to develop his idea of "bounded rationality." Simon compared "economic man" to "administrative man" and determined that the idea of a maximizing decision maker was simply unrealistic. Economists later added various other strategies, such as the idea that decision makers may try to minimize an outcome or the effects associated with an outcome, rather than always trying to maximize an outcome. Simon argued that because of time constraints and incomplete data, decision makers only seek to "satisfice" when selecting alternatives for their decisions. That is, rather than evaluating all the possibilities, they simply search until they find a solution that satisfices their needs. They will stop searching for potential solutions once they reach this point. A decision is then made, and administrators will not expend any more time on this particular problem.[49] This does not mean that decision makers do not make rational decisions; it means that their rationality is limited because of environmental restrictions and their own ability to process and handle information. Thus, decisions are rational (they are made with the idea that they will achieve desired goals), but are a limited rather than a comprehensive form of rationality.

The idea of "bounded rationality" greatly influenced the study of decision making. Charles Lindblom's famous article entitled "The Science of Muddling Through" was a logical extension of Simon's idea.[50] Lindblom evaluated the rational model against the incremental model and argued that decisions are made incrementally. *Incrementalism* holds that decisions are produced by a series of limited successive comparisons with a relatively narrow range of alternatives. It uses the status quo rather than abstract goals as its reference point for making decisions. The idea that policies and organizational decisions are made incrementally provided insight into how policies and changes evolve and seemed to fit better with organizational and political realities. One may think of the incremental model as building on decisions of the past. For example, as we will see in the chapters on budgeting and public policy, the political and organizational realities make rational decision making nearly impossible in the real world. In developing public budgets, decision makers tend to use the budget from the previous year as the basis for the next year's budget.[51] Policy makers must have a reference point or base, so they use the last year's budget as the base and focus the debate on incremental increases or decreases in the budget. The same is typically true for decisions on most public policies. Once a program is in place and operating, decision makers are far more prone to work with it and make incremental changes rather than eliminate the program and start over. This is what happened when President Bill Clinton tried to revolutionize the health care system in the early 1990s. The changes were too radical and involved too much change too quickly, which does not fit well into the way that our political system works. New programs tend to be phased in and often are spin-offs from other programs. Moreover, the Clinton proposal stepped on the toes of many well-entrenched interest groups. Thus, the proposal failed.

The merits of the economic-based models have been debated and compared to political realities, which includes the idea of *political* rationality.[52] The debate has led to the introduction of some interesting new conceptualizations like *groupthink* and the *garbage can* model of organizational choice. Groupthink is a condition that can inflict a group decision-making process by affecting the dynamics of the group to agree with and support flawed decisions. It can affect groups such as committees or the president's closest advisory group. Groupthink occurs when some members of a group seek unanimity in lieu of realistically appraising alternative courses of action that would produce a better decision. Usually, an informal group leader promotes one preferred course of action and uses various methods to gain the support of other members.[53]

Irving Janis developed a set of case studies to illustrate major decisions in which groupthink was present and another set of cases where groupthink was not a factor. Groupthink may be thought of as what can occur when a committee or advisory group has to make a decision but does not appropriately examine alternatives because someone in the group takes action to get everyone to go along, often just to please the head of the committee or group, such as the president of a nation or a large corporation. A person who seeks to push an alternative under consideration can alter the group's dynamics because of the pressure to conform. The evidence suggests that individuals who are usually strong-willed and independent thinkers can be influenced to go along with very bad decisions or recommendations. Janis's book examined such incidents as the decision to invade Cuba in the Bay of Pigs, the Cuban Missile Crisis, the decision to go beyond the 38th Parallel in Korea, parts of the Vietnam war, and Watergate. In some cases, groupthink was present, and in other cases groupthink was not a factor. Janis tried to isolate the conditions in which groupthink occurs. In the case of the Bay of Pigs, President Kennedy's advisors overlooked critical information and provided poor advice because certain members of the group wanted the Bay of Pigs invasion to proceed and convinced other members to go along. The Bay of Pigs was a disaster. During the Cuban Missile Crisis, President Kennedy was well aware of the previous failure and better controlled the dynamics of the group and the information. The Cuban Missile Crisis stands as a classic in successful political decision making.[54]

Citing a case in contrast, it has been well documented that President Johnson's in-group of advisors tried to silence all members who expressed doubts about the Vietnam War. Social pressures were applied to "domesticate" the members and bring them back in line with the mindset of the group. Dissent within certain limitations was allowed, but it was not to go outside of the advisory group. In effect, the group that Johnson assembled sought to support his commitment to the war, although there were plenty of members in the group who would have been outspoken dissenters had some group leaders not successfully silenced them. Groupthink is not a process that decision makers can use to make decisions. Rather, it is a phenomenon that can take hold in a group and distort the decision-making process. Thus, understanding the concept of groupthink can help decision makers be aware of the pitfalls that can occur if a group becomes so cohesive that it insulates itself from reality and fails to objectively consider alternatives before making recommendations or decisions.

The garbage can theory suggests an alternative perspective about the nature of decision making that centers on ambiguity. It does not provide a process or model that managers can use to make decisions, but does provide a larger understanding of the processes that may exist in large organizations. It is one of the most interesting models advanced and contains an entirely different perspective from traditional ideas about decision making. The garbage can model holds that decision processes in organizations are filled with ambiguity. Ambiguity refers to organizations having goals that are unclear or vague, technologies that are not well understood, histories that are difficult to interpret, and participants who wander in and out of the decision-making processes.[55]

The researchers who examined this idea termed organizations with these characteristics "organized anarchies." Such organizations have several characteristics.[56] *Preferences and goals are poorly defined and understood*. Members of the organization do not define their preferences about policies and goals with any degree of precision. In cases where the goals are well defined, the goals often conflict with other organizational goals. The organization has no real coherent structure; it is just a loose collection of ideas. *Technologies also are poorly understood*. Not understanding the technologies of the organization means that members of the organization really do not understand what the organization does.

Universities were used to illustrate organized anarchies. In the case of a university, do faculty members understand how the financial aid office, the registrar's office, and other administrative offices really work? Of course, the same can be said in the other direction: Administrative officers may not understand how academic departments work. The lack of understanding about what goes on in other departments or divisions means that members are only familiar with the technologies in their particular unit or department and do not understand the technologies outside of their small part of the larger organization. The collective effect of this characteristic is that no one fully understands the organization. *Participation in decision making is fragmented and inconsistent*. Participants drift in and out of the decision-making process. For example, sometimes members attend critical meetings, and other times they do not. This adds to the ambiguity of the decision-making process and does not facilitate making coherent, rational decisions because the participants in the decision processes are not constant; they vary from one meeting to the next. *Four separate decision-making streams* are used (problems, solutions, participants, and choice opportunities). None of these streams are connected; thus, decision making is not coherent, logical, or rational. Each stream, operating independently, may play a part in decisions that are believed to be in the best interest of the organization, but often are contradictory to decisions made elsewhere in the organization. From time to time, the streams do connect, and when they do, the result can be a major decision. This is the ideal place and opportunity to make decisions. The connection of the four streams is what gives the model its name—the *garbage can* model.

Decisions, therefore, are the function of a mixture of problems, solutions, participants, and resources with changing participants. The streams do not remain connected. When they connect again at some point, the participants, problems, solutions, and the like will be different. Thus, an entirely new decision will be made that may have no bearing or relationship to the decisions reached previously. The authors who developed this model liken organizations to collections of choices looking for problems, issues looking for decisions, solutions looking for issues to resolve, and decision makers looking for work.

The thrust of this model is that an organization may appear to be organized, but a closer look reveals that it is fragmented and dysfunctional, with all of its elements in the wrong order. Solutions should not be in search of problems to solve; it should be the other way around. Since the four streams operate independently, the best description is organized anarchy. Thus, the structure of organized anarchies is a flow of four streams and their associated processes throughout the organization. Decisions rely on the occasional coupling of the four streams in the *garbage can,* which is left largely to chance.

The implications of this model are interesting because it helps explain why organizations filled with intelligent people, expertise, talent, technologies, opportunities, and resources can be so dysfunctional, lose sight of the organization's purpose, pursue conflicting goals, and make questionable decisions. As organizations grow and become complex, they need greater coordination to function effectively. Because of their size, it is easy for organizations to become more like the garbage can design. Many decisions have to be made in large organizations that are highly decentralized.[57] Power is not concentrated but dispersed throughout the organization. Over time, various units become relatively autonomous from other units. The goal or goals of the organization become less clear because of the multitude of functions the organization performs. Moreover, the mission and goals may become mutually contradictory. Although universities were used to illustrate organized anarchies (and universities are often considered to be unique organizations), the model certainly has application to large governmental bureaus and other types of organizations. The implications of the model raise a number of questions. First of all, how do organized anarchies develop? That is, do they start out as organized anarchies, or do they become this way over time? How are decisions made in most organizations? Is there a central executive group of decision makers who make most important decisions, like the *technostructure* described in Chapter 3, or are decisions delegated to lower units throughout the organization? If decisions are delegated, to whom are they delegated, and what are the long-term consequences of having important decisions made throughout a large organization at a variety of levels? That is, what occurs over a long period of time if units increasingly become more autonomous? Is it possible that over time, the primary decision-making *stream* of a coherent organization can break into *streams* that become separated? The long-term effect of greater autonomy, growth, complexity of operations, diversity of operations, and the like may result in organizations becoming organized anarchies if coordination cannot be maintained.[58]

Thus, we have several very different ideas about decision making. Are decisions reached through the rational process described by economists that produces decisions in which the benefits are maximized and the costs are minimized? Or are decisions made through incremental changes based on very limited comparison that satisfice what is needed at the time? When decision makers try to solve problems, do they go through a rational-comprehensive process? Or do they search for the best solution they can find that will resolve the problem at hand under the limitations of time and other resources? Are many organizations actually "organized anarchies"? Are the decisions made by committees often influenced by groupthink? Although incrementalism has prevailed as the most accepted description of political and organizational reality, ideas like groupthink and the garbage can model help to enlighten us about the realities of decision making. Models based in the rational-comprehensive or the incremental traditions provide frameworks that help us better understand how decisions are made. Many techniques, such as "decision trees," have been developed in areas of management science that can be used to help decision makers. Sometimes decision makers may use techniques that resemble models based on a rational approach to aid them in making their decisions. But in the world of public administration, the idea of incrementalism remains the most accepted description, since it appears to best fit the real world of politics and public management.[59]

NATURE OF MANAGERIAL WORK

Management in the public sector is more constrained[60] and complicated than in the private sector. This is because public managers must deal with many restrictions that are less prevalent or absent in the world of private management. Public sector managers must deal with public laws that specify what they can and cannot do, civil service restrictions, and public employee unions. Public sector managers also must deal with many intangibles because often they are involved in public services that are not analogous to producing a product in the private sector. The most perplexing problem is usually politics. Whether it is dealing with the wishes of Congress, the president, a state legislature, or a city council, the managers of public agencies face a complicated world of complex political dynamics. What was desirable during the administration of one governor does not always carry over into the next administration. The survival of an agency depends on funding secured through a political process rather than on measured sales. The lack of the profit motive makes it more difficult to quantify performance and effectiveness. (Performance standards are discussed in detail in Chapter 8.)

On a basic level, the work of managers is the same—management is getting work accomplished through (or with) other people. This is not an easy task. The nature of managerial work is similar for public and private managers. The manager's activities have been characterized as varied and fragmented. The vast majority of tasks are of brief duration. A great variety of activities are performed but with no consistent pattern or sequence. The trivial tasks are mixed with the consequential, so that managers must shift their focus quickly and frequently.[61] All managers perform the same basic tasks and activities that we once referred to as POSDCORB (planning, organizing, staffing, directing, coordinating, reporting, and budgeting). POSDCORB is the acronym provided by Luther Gulick to represent the set of activities that was ultimately rejected as the "principles of administration." This is because these activities are not principles; they are fundamental *activities* that are performed by all managers. The activities are not limited to POSDCORB; the list is actually much longer. Managers must also motivate, train, build employee morale, build teams, monitor performance, mentor employees, and communicate, to name only a few of the other activities.

Two schools of thought exist in the study of management—the *normative* and *descriptive* schools. The normative, as the name suggests, deals with what managers should or ought to do. This is an old approach that still carries great weight. Early social science was based on normative methods, and management textbooks are often still built around these concepts. Henri Fayol is credited with providing the "principles of management" during the 19th century. (Box 4.1 lists Fayol's basic principles of management.) The normative approach defines management as the process of getting the job done. Management effectiveness is said to increase when organizational activities are efficiently planned, organized, coordinated, and controlled. *Planning* includes such activities as deciding the objectives of an organization and determining the means of achieving the objectives. *Organizing* includes grouping organizational activities in some logical fashion, structuring relationships among group members, and defining various relationships among work groups or units. *Coordinating* involves the process of motivating, leading, and communicating with employees for the purpose of achieving organization goals. (Motivation is finding the right incentives to satisfy workers' needs and make workers more productive. *Leadership* entails the manager's ability to influence behavior, and *communication* is the transmission of information within the organization.) *Controlling* is the process of seeing whether organizational goals are being achieved. This process involves establishing performance standards, measuring actual performance, comparing actual performance against the standards, and taking corrective action to ensure that performance standards are maintained. There is no questioning the fact that managers perform these tasks, but merely knowing the functions of management is an inadequate description of what managers do.

The descriptive school also focuses on activities that managers perform, but the behavioral method is emphasized. The descriptive school is less concerned with what managers *should* do and more concerned with what managers *actually do*. Researchers have identified four categories of activities that managers perform: personal, interactional, administrative, and technical.[62]

1. *Personal activities.* These are truly personal matters that are generally not job-related, such as calling your banker or broker, or buying a car while you are at work. Also included is managing one's own time. Personal matters are considered important, as it is now recognized that too often careers have destroyed personal lives. The common wisdom today is that management must try to achieve a balanced approach that allows managers to meet the demands of their work and their personal lives. For example, it is believed that managers should take time off and take vacations, which helps to reduce burnout and many other problems.[63]

BOX 4.1   Henri Fayol's Principles of Management

Fayol provided the following principles of organization. He called them *principles of management*.

Specialization of labor: Encourages continuous improvement in skills and the development of improvements in methods.

Authority: The right to give orders and the power to exact obedience.

Discipline: No slacking, bending of rules.

Unity of command: Each employee has one and only one boss.

Unity of direction: A single mind generates a single plan and all play their part in that plan.

Subordination of individual interests: When at work, only work-related things should be pursued or thought about.

Remuneration: Employees receive fair payment for services.

Centralization: Consolidation of management functions. Decisions are made from the top.

Scalar chain (line of authority): Formal chain of command running from top to bottom of the organization, like a military system.

Order: All materials and personnel have a prescribed place, and they must remain there.

Equity: Equality of treatment (but not necessarily identical treatment).

Personnel tenure: Limited turnover of personnel. Lifetime employment for good workers.

Initiative: Thinking out a plan and doing what it takes to make it happen.

Esprit de corps: Harmony, cohesion among personnel.

SOURCE: Henry Fayol, *General and Industrial Management,* translated by Constance Storrs (London: Pitman, 1949).

---

2. *Interactional activities.* Research suggests that most of a manager's time (80 percent) is spent interacting with people (with peers, superiors, or subordinates; on the telephone; or attending meetings). This helps to explain why communication skills are critical for a manager to be effective.[64]

3. *Administrative activities.* Research suggests that a small amount of a manager's total time is spent processing paperwork, budgeting, monitoring policies, and on other noninteractional work. This finding has surprised many because research also indicates that managers typically believe too much of their time is spent on administrative activities.[65]

4. *Technical activities.* This refers to truly "technical" work. As managers move up the career ladder, less of their time is spent on technical work. First-line supervisors spend a lot of time with technical matters and hands–on activities, middle managers spend less time on technical matters, while executives spend very little, if any, of their time working on technical matters.[66]

The typical manager is a very busy person. One study found that in a typical day, a first-line manager[67] was engaged in 583 activities.[68] Another study of executives found that executives engaged in 50 distinct activities each day.[69] A study of federal executives found that dealing with people outside the organization occupied 20 to 30 percent of managers' time. Receiving and reviewing information for internal matters took about 55 to 60 percent of their time.[70] A study of middle to lower managers found that 25 percent of their time was spent directly supervising employees, 28 percent on a variety of interpersonal matters, 22 percent on handling materials and equipment of the workplace, 5 percent on planning, and 20 percent in meetings.[71]

Managers' jobs usually involve a *hectic pace* because of the volume of work and time constraints. Most studies have found that managing is largely a verbal activity. Managers rely heavily on *oral communication* and prefer oral to written communication. There is a *reactive nature* to managerial work. Although a general consensus exists that proactive planning is better than being in a reactive mode, the realities of the workplace force managers to be "reactive" (to constantly "put out fires"). Managers cannot always be proactive for several reasons. Many managers do not like planning, partly because it requires time, and managers often feel they do not have enough time. Plenty of managers are convinced that the best-laid plans seldom turn out as planned. There are also *political realities* associated with managerial work. Politics is a reality of organizational life. Politics is everywhere in all types of organizations, whether public or private. Here we are referring to "organizational politics" rather than the larger political influences that come from the political system. The political influences of the political system further complicate life for public managers. Politics affects such things as networking, relationships, and career objectives. Managers have to be aware of the larger political arena, as well as the political dynamics and realities of their organizations, if they are public managers.[72]

What types of skills do managers need to perform such a diversity of tasks? Researchers have identified a number of categories of skills that effective managers need.[73] These skills generally correlate with the activities that managers perform. Four major categories of skills are interactional, conceptual, administrative, and technical.[74] Box 4.2 includes each of these skills with some specific examples of how managers use them.

There is a difference between *ability* (the knowledge and skills one currently possesses) and *capability* (the capacity to learn new skills and attain expanded knowledge). Skills can be learned and developed, but everyone has strengths and weaknesses. The skills needed to be an "ideal" manager are simply too varied for everyone to master them. The degree to which a manager must have adept skills in these categories varies with the level of the organization in which they work. Some managers must have a lot of technical skill in their area of expertise, whereas others need more administrative skills. For example, the director of computer services for a university would likely be well versed in computers and would also need administrative skills, while the dean of a large division of a university would need fewer technical skills but far more administrative skills because of the size and complexity of the academic division.

BOX 4.2 Management Skills

Interactional Skills

These include interpersonal, communication, leadership, motivation, group process, and conflict resolution skills. These skills are needed to:

- Create and maintain a network of personal contacts inside and outside the organization
- Effectively communicate with others
- Develop effective work groups
- Handle interpersonal and group conflicts
- Lead and motivate employees to perform
- Promote a sense of fairness and equity in reward systems
- Establish and maintain a work environment that is conducive to productivity

Conceptual Skills

These include analytical, decision-making, and organizational skills. These skills are needed to:

- Collect and analyze information about the internal and external environments
- Understand the meanings of "environmental changes"

- Reflect these meanings in designing jobs and structure
- Make appropriate (and effective) managerial decisions
- Bring about necessary organizational changes

Administrative Skills

These include the basic functions associated with the normative approach: planning, organizing, coordinating, and controlling. These skills involve abilities needed to:

- Develop and follow plans, policies, and procedures effectively
- Process paperwork in a timely and orderly manner
- Manage expenditures within a budget

Technical Skills

These skills involve the ability to use the knowledge, tools, experiences, and techniques of a specific discipline such as chemistry, engineering, law, or psychology to solve technical problems.

SOURCE: Kae Chung and Leon Megginson, *Organizational Behavior: Developing Managerial Skills* (New York: Harper & Row, 1981), pp. 21–22.

Generally, the higher one goes into executive management, less emphasis is placed on technical skills and greater emphasis on administrative skills. The one skill that generally applies to all levels of management is communication. A manager must be able to communicate to be effective.

Managers have to wear many different hats because they must play a variety of roles, which helps to illustrate the complexities of modern management. Managers must serve as *directors* to determine what needs to be accomplished in their department. They must be *producers*, which involves not only motivating others but also maintaining their own level of motivation. Managers also must be *coordinators*; they must maintain the structure and flow of work. And they must be *facilitators* in order to foster teamwork and manage interpersonal conflicts that inevitably arise in organizational settings. They must be *monitors*, which entails reviewing information and analyzing performance to ensure that the proper output of the department is maintained. They also should be *mentors* and be well versed in coaching employees and providing opportunities for individuals to development their careers. Managers must be *innovators*. In this role, they are active in facilitating organizational change and adapting to new policies and procedures. And finally, managers must serve as *brokers,* which is necessary for acquiring resources. Each role requires special skills that pull managers in a variety of directions, but all these skills are necessary for managers to be effective in their jobs, regardless of whether they are in public agencies or private corporations. We ask a lot of managers: We ask them to perform a variety of tasks that require an array of skills if they are to function in the very complex world of public management.[75] Box 4.3 illustrates the skills that are associated with these managerial roles.

BOX 4.3   Managerial Roles and Associated Skills

Managerial Roles	*Associated Skills*
Director Focusing self and others on what needs to be accomplished.	**Strategic and tactical planning:** assessing external opportunities and constraints, determining strategies for accomplishing the organization's mission, setting specific objectives for each unit, and indicating how those objectives will be accomplished. **Delegating:** assigning responsibilities to others, clarifying expectations, providing support, and holding them accountable for desired results.
Producer Motivating self and others to accomplish stated goals.	**Time and stress management:** reducing personal stress by, among other things, establishing priorities and using one's time efficiently. **Motivating:** using goal-setting techniques and reward systems to motivate self and others to achieve desired results.
Coordinator Maintaining the structure and flow of work systems.	**Operational planning:** determining how to use financial, physical, and human resources to achieve unit goals and objectives. **Organizing skills:** designing jobs and work flows, and orchestrating work operations, to facilitate task accomplishment.
Monitor Reviewing information and analyzing performance data to ensure results are being achieved.	**Written communication:** expressing ideas in writing in a clear, succinct, and organized manner. **Critical-thinking/Problem-solving skills:** using concepts and theories to discover or interpret underlying patterns, and reasoning a problem through before making a decision. **Oversight skills:** measuring performance and evaluating outcomes to determine whether operational plans are being achieved as intended.

MANAGERIAL STYLES

All managers have managerial styles. These styles can run the gamut of possibilities because they tend to be hybrids of management models that are modified to fit the manager's personality. Many factors contribute to a management style, including personality, values, and organizational culture. Standard models have been developed by organizational behaviorists. Theory X and Theory Y, discussed earlier, represent two management styles—the hard-nosed approach versus the soft-nosed approach. The hard versus soft approach is a good beginning for understanding management styles. Figure 4.2 illustrates how Theory X and Theory Y would look on a continuum, and the methods of communication

Facilitator Fostering teamwork and managing interpersonal conflict.	**Team-building skills:** establishing group cohesiveness and trust and leading groups in achieving collective tasks. **Conflict management:** addressing the sources of interpersonal conflicts, mediating disputes, and handling disturbances. **Participative decision making:** involving employees in making decisions affecting their work units.
Mentor Coaching employees and providing opportunities for individual development.	**Interpersonal skills:** relating to and communicating with others effectively by taking into account their needs, feelings, and capabilities. **Developing others:** enabling employees to reach their full potential by coaching, counseling, evaluating, and training. **Creative thinking:** developing new insights and innovative solutions to improve performance.
Innovator Facilitating organizational adaptation and change.	**Adaptability/flexibility:** modifying personal behaviors and strategies in different situations and under changing circumstances to achieve organizational objectives. **Managing change:** designing and implementing planned changes to enable the organization to accomplish its mission more effectively.
Broker Maintaining external legitimacy, acquiring resources, and brokering change.	**Oral presentation skills:** expressing ideas or conveying information effectively to others in individual or group situations. **Political/negotiating skills:** building coalitions and negotiating with external actors to protect and promote the interests of the organization or organizational unit.

SOURCE: Adapted partly from Robert Quinn, S. R. Faerman, M. P. Thompson, and M. R. McGrath, *Becoming a Master Manager: A Competency Based Framework*, 2nd ed. (New York: Wiley, 1996).

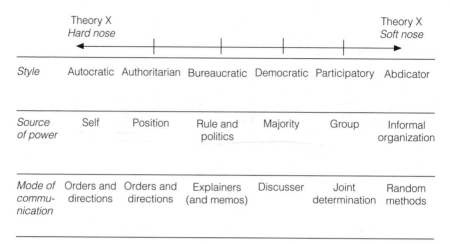

Theory X Hard nose					Theory X Soft nose
Style	Autocratic	Authoritarian	Bureaucratic	Democratic	Participatory	Abdicator
Source of power	Self	Position	Rule and politics	Majority	Group	Informal organization
Mode of commu- nication	Orders and directions	Orders and directions	Explainers (and memos)	Discusser	Joint determination	Random methods

FIGURE 4.2 Hard versus Soft Management Styles

SOURCE: Clark C. Caskey, "Developing a Leadership Style," *Supervision* (April 1964). It should be noted that Caskey used the term "no nose" instead of "soft nose" for Theory Y.

that managers working with each approach would use.[76] Theory X and Theory Y provide an interesting reference point for describing some managers, but management style is more complex than what is implied by the hard-nosed and soft-nosed distinction.

One of the most popular models of management style is called the managerial grid.[77] It was developed during the 1960s and provides a range of management styles based on two important factors: concern for workers and concern for production (see Figure 4.3). It visualizes five pure types of management styles: the country club manager, the sweatshop manager, the impoverished manager, the administrative manager, and the team manager. Each of these styles is based on the emphasis that managers place on their concern for production and employees. The ideal type, according to management scholars, is the team manager (the 9,9 score in the grid). This type of manager has a high concern for both the work and the employees. This person is able to build *esprit de corps* and involve everyone in the work, probably in the mode of the *high-spirited organization* described by Peter Drucker (an organization where the culture causes almost all employees to take pride in their work and be highly motivated). The "normal" manager is the administrative manager, who has an equal degree of concern for the work and employees (the 5,5 score on the grid). Each of these managerial styles represents a tendency that managers may exhibit. For example, the manager who has a great concern for production but little concern for employees is primarily concerned with getting the work out regardless of the cost to employees. The country club manager wants employees to be happy—at the expense of productivity, if necessary. This type of manager is likely to be more concerned with being liked by employees than with production. The impoverished manager is typically someone who has lost interest, who has been demoted, or who, for whatever reason, is on the way out of the

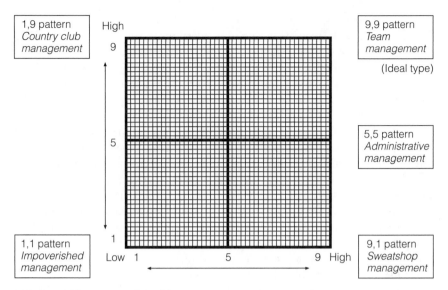

FIGURE 4.3 The Managerial Grid

SOURCE: Adapted from Robert Blake and Jane Mouton, *The New Managerial Grid* (Houston, TX: Gulf, 1978), p. 11.

organization. This type of manager has no concern for either getting anything done or the needs of employees. Without a doubt, such a manager would not last long in most organizations. All of these types of managerial styles represent pure models that probably do not exist in the real world, but tendencies toward these models do exist. Many other ways have been used to describe managerial styles, such as *laissez faire* (hiring competent people, and then taking a hands-off approach to supervision), *authoritative* (the hard-nosed approach), and the like. Some managers tend to be good at delegating work in a proper way, while others are *hands-on managers* who spend too much time doing things that should be delegated. The point is, managerial styles vary, as do leadership styles.

LEADERSHIP

Leadership is closely associated with management. The term *leadership* is used loosely in our society. We hear about leadership all our lives, but the concept is poorly defined in the everyday world. What is leadership? What makes an effective leader? Are great leaders born, or can leadership skills be learned and developed? What are the differences between a manager and a leader? In organizational settings, leadership is typically defined as the process of influencing other people toward accomplishing group or organizational tasks. This is a rather simplistic definition, although it is widely accepted. Leadership is considered to be a tool of management, which suggests that it can be learned, but all managers are not leaders and all leaders are not managers. A member of a work group may have no authority whatsoever but may in fact be an influential leader in the group. While skills may be polished, leadership usually implies something greater to most of us above and beyond influencing workers to achieve organizational goals. Leadership is often thought of as something intangible, a special quality that some people seem to possess. With a slight change in wording from the organizational definition, we can say that *leadership is the ability to lead, influence, and inspire others.*

When we think of great leaders, we often think of presidents or heads of state—people who have led a whole nation. In many respects, this may be the ultimate test for a great leader. A nation is a complex entity to operate. The president or head of state must assemble a team of advisors, fill cabinet positions, establish policy goals, and make progress toward attaining those goals. Most importantly, leaders provide direction and vision for an entire nation and, in some cases, the world. Leaders are held responsible and accountable for things that are often beyond their control, and they are judged on how well they handle the stream of problems that occur while they are in office, which may range from natural disasters and economic crises to international conflicts. Effective leadership is particularly obvious during times of crisis. Winston Churchill led Great Britain through its darkest hours during World War II. Franklin Roosevelt led the United States through the Great Depression and most of World War II. Both Churchill and Roosevelt are considered to have been "great leaders." What separated these men from others? Some argue that leaders rise to the occasion, become great leaders, and then their time passes and they slip from this role. This is exactly what happened in the case of Winston Churchill who led Great Britain commendably during World War II, but then was tossed out of office once the war was over. Perhaps his time had passed.

During the past 75 years, the United States has had 12 presidents. Their leadership styles and effectiveness as leaders have varied. Franklin Roosevelt was truly a charismatic leader. His "fireside chats" helped American through some of it darkest times. He led America through most of World War II and dealt with the worst economic depression in the nation's history. He was able to slowly change the mood of the nation and deal with many of the nation's domestic and international problems. Moreover, he was able to assemble an effective team, created the Executive Office of the President, and managed the nation effectively. Lyndon Johnson was by all accounts an effective leader in Congress prior to becoming president. He was able to push through legislation that seemed impossible at the time, including early civil rights legislation. As president, he continued his record of getting legislation passed. His Great Society programs were the most ambitious legislative effort since Roosevelt's New Deal programs of the 1930s. He ushered in social change like the 1964 Civil Rights Act, which remains the primary set of civil rights laws. But Johnson got bogged down with the war in Vietnam, which ultimately caused him not to seek reelection. Jimmy Carter, a former governor of Georgia, was perhaps the most intelligent individual to serve as president in modern times. He was a nuclear engineer by training. Moreover, he was a very decent and honest individual. He changed the perception of the "imperial presidency" that had evolved over the years. In many ways, he tried to present himself in a more informal fashion than his recent predecessors. But he was an ineffective president because he was too technical in nature and too much of a hands-on manager to get much accomplished. Carter inherited the energy crisis, an economy in perhaps the worst shape of any since the Great Depression, and had to deal with the Iranian hostage crisis. He did not deal effectively with any of these crises. His presidency was considered to be, by and large, a disaster. Ronald Reagan, called the "great communicator," inherited everything that had plagued the Carter administration. But Reagan possessed many of the skills of Roosevelt and changed the mood of the nation in the early 1980s. The economy improved, the power and pride of the military were restored, and he maintained a high approval rating throughout his years in office. He delegated work to others and used his skills in communication to talk to the public. The nation's confidence increased, the economy grew, and despite his share of scandals, he left as a very popular president.

All the presidents mentioned here accomplished some very impressive things during their time in the White House, but they are remembered for their overall performance.[78] Granted, the descriptions provided are brief and oversimplified, but these presidents were leaders, and they displayed varying degrees of "effective" leadership. It is beyond the scope of this book to evaluate the effectiveness of presidents, but something can be said about their leadership styles. Some were excellent at selecting staff and advisors and utilizing these resources to the fullest. Some became too bogged down with the details of policy and even daily affairs because of their inability to delegate and their lack of understanding of the way Washington worked. Some were outstanding communicators who could motivate, rally the nation, and send a message of confidence across America. Some were better politicians than others, but all were leaders by definition. The task each faced was greater than the task of a CEO of the largest corporations. Heads of state must deal with economies, administration, foreign affairs, national security issues, and crises of various types. They also must have a vision and provide direction for their nation. What makes some presidents effective leaders while others are less effective? These questions regarding presidents and other political leaders are of great interest to political scientists, but the traits displayed by these leaders are the same traits, characteristics, and skills applicable for leaders in organizations such as the Department of Commerce, Microsoft, General Motors, and in the organizations where we work. Can whatever it is that makes a person a leader occur on a smaller scale? One does not have to be Gandhi, Winston Churchill, or some other well-respected world leader to display leadership. *Leadership* is the ability to create and maintain the process of influencing other people for the purpose of achieving goals.[79] But what qualities and attributes are necessary to lead, influence, and inspire others to achieve goals? This dynamic of leadership often seems to be intangible.

Researchers have extensively examined the idea of leadership and have identified a number of common traits or characteristics that most leaders seem to possess. *Leaders have followers.* Not all managers are leaders. Managers have

others to supervise, but if their subordinates are not willing to accept and follow the supervisory authority, the managers are not leaders. Subordinates may
comply out of fear, but such compliance is not a response to leadership. This is
partly why varying degrees of leadership have been shown in presidents, chief
executive officers, and others who have held prominent positions. Being president of a large corporation, the head of a large federal bureau, or president of
the United States allows a person to demonstrate leadership by making the
organization work effectively; but many fail at this task because they lack the
leadership skills needed in the particular position or because, some might argue,
they were not well matched for their organization. It is possible for someone to
be an effective leader in one organization but be ineffective in another. For
example, a person may be very effective at leading the Peace Corps but may be
ineffective as head of the Department of Labor. This was the case with Sergeant
Shriver in the 1960s. By the same token, all leaders are not managers. Some
leaders may have followers but may not have the formal authority to manage.
For example, informal leaders in a work group who have no formal authority
whatsoever can be very influential in the work group. *Leaders have emotional
appeal.* Managers are expected to be rational decision makers and problem
solvers. They are expected to use their analytical minds in the process of establishing and achieving organizational goals. But they are also expected to be
charismatic people with vision who can alter the mood of their subordinates
and raise their hopes and expectations. That is, if they are leaders, they can lead
and inspire those who work for them.

Trait Theory

Most leadership theories prior to the 1950s were concerned with identifying
the personal traits of successful leaders. Researchers searched for the psychological, emotional, intellectual, and motivational characteristics that were associated with successful people. Some refer to these studies as the *Great Man*
approach because great leaders were often examined, such as presidents and
great business leaders. Extensive lists were compiled of traits, but no universal
list was ever found that is applicable to all situations. The traits that typically
have appeared in lists include a strong desire for task accomplishment, persistent
pursuit of goals, creativity and intelligence used to solve problems, a self-assured
personality, and the ability to influence other people. There are also several *skills*
that great leaders appear to possess. Great leaders appear to be clever, conceptually skilled, creative, diplomatic and tactful, good speakers, knowledgeable about
group tasks, organized, persuasive, socially skilled, and decisive.

Trait theorists usually focused on success rather than failure, but a few studies have examined the traits of unsuccessful managers or leaders. The limited
research that has been conducted has associated unsuccessful managers with
traits such as poor temperament and procrastination. Also, some attitudinal factors seem to be associated with poor management and leadership, such as being
overly concerned with morale, lacking of a sense of proportion, and over-
managing (i.e., the inability to delegate).[80]

After years of extensive research, it is fair to conclude that good leaders probably do have certain traits and characteristics, but simply listing those traits provides an incomplete description of leadership. Listing such traits, such as being decisive, commanding, having a sense of presence, and the like, has failed to answer many obvious questions. We know that leadership is not a universal quality. Some people simply are not leaders, and some people who seem to have some of the fundamental qualities of leadership have no desire to take on leadership roles. Moreover, a person who is a proven leader in one situation may fail in another. For example, being an effective governor of a state does not ensure that one will be a good president for the entire nation. Likewise, being an effective leader in one corporation or agency of government does not ensure that one will be effective in another agency. This was illustrated in the case of the Peace Corps. During the 1960s, Sargent Shriver (a member of the Kennedy family by marriage) headed the Peace Corps and was extremely effective. Later he was appointed secretary of the Department of Labor and was much less successful.[81] Some believe he was well matched for the Peace Corps but a poor match for the Department of Labor. The Peace Corps was a new organization filled with energy and mission. The Department of Labor was an established, well-entrenched, cabinet-level department that had all of the characteristics of an "old bureaucracy." The idea of matching people with positions in which their personalities and leadership styles might be most effective was one area that caught the attention of behaviorists.

Behavioral Theories of Leadership

Behavioral-based studies examined leadership behavior from an entirely different perspective. The focus of these studies was on the relationship between leader behavior and employee reaction and task accomplishment. Rather than focus on what effective leaders are, behavioral researchers sought to find out what leaders actually do. Two very famous sets of studies were conducted by two major universities.

Ohio State University Studies

The Ohio State University (OSU) studies on leadership began shortly after World War II and originally concentrated on military organizations. The intention was to identify the major dimensions of leadership and to examine the effects of leadership behavior on employee satisfaction and performance. The researchers developed a list of leadership behaviors (instruction, communication, production emphasis, task assignment, evaluation, fraternization, consultation, fair treatment, and so forth). The OSU group identified *consideration* and *initiating structure* as two major dimensions of leadership. Consideration refers to leadership behavior that can be characterized by the respect, trust, supportiveness, and concern a leader has for employees. Initiating structure refers to leadership behavior that defines and organizes group tasks, assigns the tasks to employees, and supervises their activities. The studies found that initiating structure was positively related to employee performance but was also associated with such negative consequences as absenteeism and grievances. Consideration was positively related to low absenteeism and grievances but was negatively or neutrally related to performance. When both consideration and structure were high, both productivity and satisfaction tended to be high.[82]

University of Michigan Studies

About the same time that the OSU studies were being conducted, another group of researchers at the University of Michigan were examining leadership styles associated with high-performing and low-performing groups. Researchers identified two leadership styles that were similar to those used in the OSU studies. They called the styles *production-centered* and *employee-centered*. The production-centered leader closely supervises employees to ensure that tasks are being performed according to specified procedures. This type of leader uses formal authority to influence behavior and achieve performance. The employee-centered leader uses general supervision, delegation, and supportiveness to supervise employees. This kind of leader exhibits concern for employee' personal growth and task achievement.

The studies failed to find any consistent relationship between the use of one leadership style and managerial effectiveness. The studies found that effectiveness and leadership style varied among industries. For example, production-centered leadership was effective in less structured job situations, such as railroad track crews where supervisors provide technical and operational instructions. Production-centered leadership was found to be dysfunctional in highly structured situations, such as insurance clerks where the employees needed less detailed supervision. In a study conducted later, University of Michigan researchers found that both production-centered and employee-centered leaders were able to increase productivity in clerical tasks situations but found that satisfaction was higher in employee-centered work groups. This study was used to argue that employee-centered leadership was more effective than production-centered leadership.[83]

Contingency Theory of Leadership

Fred Fielder argued that the leadership is a function of the leader's characteristics and situational factors.[84] Effectiveness increases when these two factors are well matched. The characteristics of leaders in management situations vary. Some place emphasis on getting the job done (task-oriented); others place the emphasis on getting along with people (relationship-oriented). Relationship-oriented leaders are concerned with doing a good job, but they are more concerned with maintaining good interpersonal relationships. Their self-esteem depends largely on how other people relate to them. Their sensitivity to others helps make them very effective at applying participative leader behavior. Task-oriented leaders are concerned with getting the job done. Their self-esteem is driven by accomplishment of tangible goals. They want to assemble a group of people that can produce results. When things are under control, they often pay more attention to the needs of employees. Fiedler's theory assumed leaders are predisposed toward a particular leadership style, either the task orientation or the relationship orientation. Fiedler believed that leaders who described the characteristics of their least preferred coworker (LPC) in positive terms were relations-motivated; those who described the LPC in negative terms were task-motivated.

There are other major determinants of contingency leadership. *Leader-member relations* refer to the degree to which leaders maintain good relations with subordinates and the degree to which subordinates are willing to comply. *Task structure* involves the degree to which the task is well defined and standardized, or ambiguous and vague. The situation is believed to be favorable to the leader when tasks are well structured and workers know what has to be done. *Position power* categorizes the formal power of the leader. This involves the extent to which the position enables the leader to gain compliance from subordinates. Position power includes formal authority and the power to grant rewards. The more position power leaders have, the more favorable the situation.

The contingency theory predicts that task-oriented leaders will perform better in high- and low-control situations and that relationship-oriented leaders perform best in moderate-control situations. In high-control situations, task-oriented leaders are most comfortable because they have control and are driven to accomplish tasks. High-control situations are very structured, and employees are generally well trained to perform tasks. Fielder believed that relationship-oriented leaders would not find these situations challenging because their interpersonal skills would not be as useful. Relationship-oriented leaders like to use their interpersonal skills to resolve issues and problems. Low-control situations should also be a good match for task-oriented leaders because they can provide workers with the direction and structure needed to perform and accomplish goals. In moderate-control situations, relationship-oriented leaders perform best because they are able to accomplish the goals using their interpersonal skills. Relationship-oriented leaders are sensitive to the needs of others and encourage employees to participate to help solve problems; task-oriented leaders are so concerned with accomplishing goals that they often ignore the needs of other members. It is easy to understand why certain types of leaders would be good matches in some situations, but it is less clear for other situations that involve the relationship orientation. Figure 4.4 shows the classifications for situations and matches based on the major dimensions of contingency theory. The idea that a task-oriented leader would match well in both highly structured and unstructured situations is clear. The leader is well suited for either maintaining or creating structure. What is less clear is whether the relationship-oriented leader would be a good fit for some of the situations where the leader-member relations are poor. The task-orientated leader is less concerned with being liked by subordinates, while relationship-oriented leaders have more difficulty being effective in situations if they are disliked.[85]

Fielder did not believe that it was easy to select leaders that were good matches for the organization or that training designed to change the leader's behavior was effective. He adamantly argued that the situation must be altered

	Situation is favorable for leader ⟷						Situation is not favorable for leader
Leader-member relations	Good	Good	Good	Good	Poor	Poor	Poor	Poor
Task structure	Structured	Structured	Unstructured	Unstructured	Structured	Structured	Unstructured	Unstructured
Position power	Strong	Weak	Strong	Weak	Strong	Weak	Strong	Weak
Recommended leadership orientation	Task-oriented			Relationship-oriented				Task-oriented

FIGURE 4.4 Contingency Theory of Leadership: Situational Factors and Appropriate Leadership Orientation

SOURCE: Adapted from Joseph Champoux, *Organizational Behavior: Essentials Tenets for a New Millennium* (Mason, OH: South-Western, 2000), p. 224.

to fit the leader's predisposition. The value of contingency theory rests in its attention to the fact that leadership style and situations are not always compatible. Despite its limitations conceptually, contingency theory helps explain why some leaders and are a good fit in some organizations but fit poorly into other organizations (like the case of Sargent Shriver with the Peace Corps and Department of Labor mentioned earlier).

Path-Goal Theory of Leadership

Robert House developed the path-goal theory of leadership, which explains how and why certain leadership behaviors are more effective than others in various situations.[86] It also specifies situational conditions under which each style can be used effectively. The origin of path-goal theory is in the expectancy theory of motivation, which is described in greater detail in the section on motivation later in this chapter. Expectancy theory specifies a path that will achieve goal attainment. The theory holds that people make choices based on how they perceive the valence of rewards, the performance-reward instrumentality, and the effort-performance expectancy. That is, individuals will be motivated to perform tasks if they perceive that their efforts can result in task accomplishment (expectancy), their performance leads to certain rewards (instrumentality), and the rewards can satisfy their needs (valence).

Path-goal theory holds that leaders can influence behavior by helping to clarify for employees the path to goal attainment. The term *path-goal* is used because the theory focuses on how a leader influences employees' perceptions of valence, instrumentality, and expectancy. A manager can become a path-goal leader by matching rewards to employee needs, matching rewards to performance, and matching jobs to people. Thus, path-goal theory views motivating employees to be the same as leading them. However, it goes further by trying to explain why certain leadership behaviors are more effective than others in specific types of situations. Leadership behaviors can be directive, supportive, participative, or achievement-oriented. Directive leadership behavior clarifies performance expectations and helps employees or work groups see what must be accomplished, when it must be accomplished, and how it is to be accomplished. Supportive leadership behavior focuses on the humanistic side and includes concern for subordinates as people and assisting them to satisfy their needs. Supportive leaders are open, friendly, and approachable. Participative leadership behavior includes consulting with employees and seriously considering their ideas before making decisions. This helps empower employees and makes them actively involved in decision making. Achievement-oriented leadership behavior emphasizes the idea of excellence and high standards in performance. This leadership behavior instills confidence in employees' abilities to achieve to reach both goals.

The path-goal model also presents two sets of contingency factors: personal factors and work environment factors. Personal factors are subordinates' perceptions about their abilities, their perceptions about the source of control (called locus of control) over what happens to them, and their perceptions about the people in positions of authority (called authoritarianism). Work environment factors include tasks, the nature of the system of authority in the organization, and the primary work group. Figure 4.5 illustrates the basic structure of the path-goal model. The path-goal model helps us understand why different leadership behaviors are necessary depending on the nature of the work group and the organization. Thus, a leader has several options to select based on the situation. The model has been amended to include additional leadership behaviors that focus on social interaction, path-goal clarification, political action needed to increase the group's power, and the leader's charismatic behavior.[87]

Additional Ideas about Leadership

Although leadership has been studied extensively, no consensus exists on predicting who will be a successful leader. Leadership still contains some intangible elements. This has led to several theories that break from the traditional behaviorist mode. For example, one alternative theory focuses on *leadership mystique*.[88] This conceptualization sees three major dimensions to leadership: *a sense of mission, a capacity for power,* and *a will to survive and to persevere*. Sense of mission is a vision about the future state of the organization and is something more than a written, strategic plan developed by a committee. The result is something that drives the leader to excel to create and realize the dream. The quest to achieve the dream or goal drives the leader emphatically. This idea could help explain why leaders sometimes rise to the occasion and then fade after the mission is complete. Leaders also have a capacity for power. That is, a leader has the ability to get and use power effectively to pursue the mission. Pursuing something with such intensity forces the successful leader to have a strong will to survive and to persevere over adversity. Under the leadership mystique model, leaders have the ability to go against all odds to achieve their goals.

During the 1970s, a new wave of theories based on charisma emerged. One such theory is transformational leadership. The model incorporates one of the most intangible qualities of all, namely, charisma. Charisma is the most important element of transformational leadership. Charisma tends to give a leader power, as well as high levels of self-confidence and self-esteem. Transformational leaders use their charisma to lead, but recognize variations in skills and abilities, and encourage growth for subordinates. Thus, these leaders have good interpersonal skills that are used to counsel and assist employees in a very personalized manner. This dimension is referred to as *individualized consideration* in the model. Another dimension is called intellectual stimulation, which refers to the leader's ability to build awareness of problems and solutions. Transformational leaders, as the name suggests, are able to lead and inspire by stimulating subordinates, and they have the ability to make work, goals, and achieving exciting. They instill high standards and a will to achieve in their subordinates, and they often change the organization's culture. Empirical research shows positive relationships between transformational leadership and organization performance.[89] Research suggests that charismatic

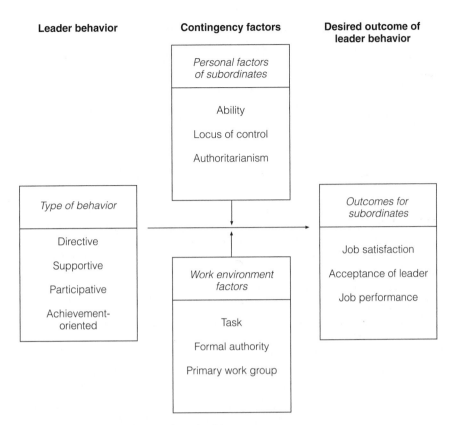

FIGURE 4.5 Path-Goal Theory of Leadership

SOURCE: Adapted from Joseph Champoux, *Organizational Behavior: Essentials Tenets for a New Millennium* (Mason, OH: South-Western, 2000), p. 226.

leaders seem to emerge during periods of crisis. Considerable research has been conducted on the effect of charisma, and most of the findings have been positive. Charismatic leaders are able to attract followers who energetically help pursue the leader's vision. Charismatic leaders can inspire their subordinates to extraordinary levels of performance. How does a person learn to be charismatic? It is probably a skill that cannot be learned. However, charismatic people do not fit in all situations. They, too, have circumstances and situations that are better for their abilities and talents. As noted earlier, charismatic leaders often appear during times of crisis. Perhaps such a leader has the right qualities, the right personality, and the right vision for that particular situation. Winston Churchill was considered to be a "back bench scribbler" in Parliament, and yet he rose to the occasion and led Great Britain through World War II. But being charismatic can sometimes cause these leaders to clash with other personality types, such as another leader who also possesses similar abilities.

Leadership clearly is an important element of management, whether a manager is managing a public agency, a corporation, or a nation. Perhaps our perceptual processes help us to recognize leadership. That is, "we know one when we see one." This idea may seem facetious, but empirical research is heading in that direction. Researchers have examined how people compare behaviors they associate with leadership with observations of leaders. Thus, recent inquiries are trying to learn more about why we recognize leaders when we see them.[90]

THEORIES OF MOTIVATION

Motivation is one of the most critical aspects of management. *Motivation can be defined (in the managerial context) as trying to find the proper incentives that satisfy workers' needs and cause them to work toward achieving organizational goals.* In order to understand motivation, we need to understand human behavior. Behavior is believed to be goal-oriented. That is, behavior is generally directed to achieve some goal, whether it is a personal goal or a professional goal within an organizational context. In organizations, we cannot ignore individual behavior.

As discussed earlier, organizations are now viewed as systems. They are sociological/technical systems composed of individuals, groups, tasks, technology, and management controls. To understand these systems, we must examine the relationships among the interrelated components and their impact on human behavior and organizational performance. The survival of organizations depends on being able to satisfy both individual and organizational goals. This includes satisfying organizational goals, such as productivity (task functions), and the individual goals of employees (maintenance functions). People join organizations for a variety of reasons. Most people depend on the organizations for their economic livelihood and to satisfy some of their social and psychological needs. Organizations are composed of human and nonhuman components: individuals, groups, tasks, technology, and management control systems. Individuals are the members of organizations; social groups are small groups of people who interact closely with each other inside organizations; tasks are work-related activities performed by members; technology is information, expertise, and equipment that require skills and knowledge to create and/or operate; and management controls are various systems designed to influence the behavior of organizational members. In such a complex system, how can we motivate workers? To understand motivation in organizations, we must first have some understanding of human behavior.

Behavior is very complex, but it is believed that there are two primary components: motives and goals. Motives are often defined as wants, needs, drives, or impulses within an individual. Motives are thought of as describing the "why" element of behavior, and they vary in strength. An employee may want more money and a promotion to enhance prestige and a personal ego. In order to achieve this, the employee must establish some set of goals. Goals are the "things" (rewards or something a person is trying to achieve) toward which motives are directed. There are two categories of theories about motivation. One is based on fulfilling individual needs or determining the factors that motivate people to work, and the other is directed at understanding the behavioral "process" of motivation. We may think of these as *content theories* and *process theories*.

Content Theories of Motivation

People have a multitude of needs, and satisfying those needs is our lifetime objective. Studying needs is important because it helps to explain the internal causes of behavior. Needs refer to internal stimuli that can cause a person to act. Needs are not full explanations of human behavior or motivation, but needs theory is important for managers to understand because in order to manage, direct, and coordinate human behavior in organizations, we need to be able to predict human behavior, at least to some degree. In order to predict behavior, we must understand the causal relationships. And in order to comprehend these relationships, we must do sufficient and meaningful research to generate hypotheses that can be tested under controlled conditions. This, of course, provides empirical findings for managers in the field.

There are different "types" of human needs. Abraham Maslow (1908–1970) made the theory popular many years ago. His hierarchy of needs is still widely used. Maslow believed that five types of needs exist that must be satisfied sequentially. Physiological needs (the lowest level) are basic needs such as food, water, shelter, health, and the like. Safety or security needs ensure that one has a next meal, a place to live, and a sense of stability. Social needs include companionship, affection, and friendship. Self-esteem needs involve such things as recognition, status, and other rewards and achievements that satisfy one's ego. Self-actualization (the highest level) entails a higher level of growth and advancement both personally and professionally, and can involve internal growth. Once a person has reached the highest level, the lower-level needs have all been fulfilled; there is, then, the freedom to strive for additional growth and satisfaction. Figure 4.6 shows Maslow's model. The diagram also includes some general and organizational factors that can be associated with each level. Notice that the diagram is like a series of steps. Maslow associated the energy that results through self-actualization, the highest level on the psychological health scale, with benefits to the organization.[91]

Lower-level needs are easier to satisfy than higher-order needs. Higher-order needs are more important to managers than lower-level needs. According to Maslow, our society has satisfied about 85 percent of existence needs, 70 percent of safety needs, 50 percent of socialization needs, 40 percent of self-esteem needs, and only about 10 percent of self-actualization needs. (There is little empirical evidence to support Maslow's assertion.) Some, like Maslow, argue that existence needs are relatively well satisfied in our society. Most people have satisfied these basic needs, and even for the disadvantaged, there are numerous programs in place to ensure that most people have at least some security (such as minimum wage, Social Security, workers' compensation, unemployment, etc.).[92] Relatedness needs have become more important in organizations in

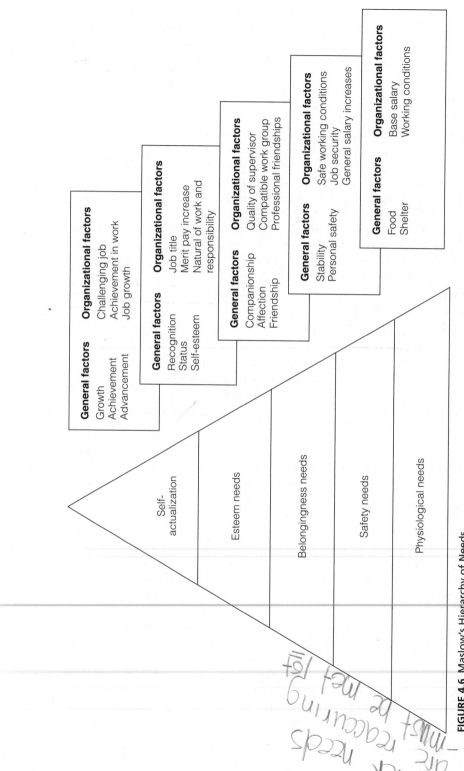

General factors
Growth
Achievement
Advancement

Organizational factors
Challenging job
Achievement in work
Job growth

General factors
Recognition
Status
Self-esteem

Organizational factors
Job title
Merit pay increase
Natural of work and
responsibility

General factors
Companionship
Affection
Friendship

Organizational factors
Quality of supervisor
Compatible work group
Professional friendships

General factors
Stability
Personal safety

Organizational factors
Safe working conditions
Job security
General salary increases

General factors
Food
Shelter

Organizational factors
Base salary
Working conditions

Self-
actualization

Esteem needs

Belongingness needs

Safety needs

Physiological needs

FIGURE 4.6 Maslow's Hierarchy of Needs

SOURCE: Adapted from John Ivancevich, Andrew Szilogyi, Jr., and Marc Wallace, Jr., *Organizational Behavior and Performance* (Santa Monica, CA: Goodyear, 1977), p. 105.

- lower needs
  - must be met for
  - are reoccurring

recent years, and people have become more concerned with "quality of life" issues in their organizations. This has added another dimension to management and has occurred concurrently with our society becoming more legalistic and impersonal. Moreover, in a highly mobile society, it is difficult to develop deep and stable relationships in organizations.[93] Satisfying the highest order of needs, growth-related needs, is difficult. In order to be concerned with higher-order needs, people must be reasonably well satisfied with their lower-order needs. Most importantly, self-actualization is poorly defined in terms of the organization. Despite Maslow's claim that productivity will increase because of self-actualization, it cannot be assumed that self-actualization and organizational productivity always complement each other. By the time people reach the point of self-actualization, they may be less interested in the affairs of the organization and motivated to pursue some other type of interest that is unrelated to the organization.[94]

Maslow believed that people have this series of work motivations and that this is what causes them to do what they do at work. But his model is very simplistic, perhaps too simplistic to describe the complexities that motivate us to work. It is, however, a very good place to start and makes for interesting discussions. Maslow's model has been criticized for placing the needs in an order that is consistent with the culture of the western world. Moreover, his hierarchy of needs assumes that a person cannot go to the next level until the lower level has been satisfied. That is, two sets of needs cannot be in play at the same time.

Clayton Alderfer got around this problem by classifying the same set of needs into existence, relatedness, and growth needs (ERG theory).[95] Unlike Maslow, Alderfer did not see the needs necessarily as a hierarchy. Thus, the pursuit of two sets of needs may be operating simultaneously. Chris Argyris also was a major proponent of the idea of self-actualization and argued that people develop along seven continua,[96] which can be regarded as motivators. According to Argyris, people tend to develop from:

1. Passivity to activity
2. Dependence to independence
3. Behaving in a few ways to many ways
4. Shallow to deep interests
5. Having a short time perspective to a longer one
6. Subordinates to equals and superordinates
7. Lack of awareness of self to control of self

Like Maslow's and Alderfer's theories, Argyris's theory suggests that these tendencies are inherent in people. Thus, organizations should recognize these needs and attempt to assist employees to develop accordingly rather than presenting obstacles to their development.[97] But the problem with Argyris's theory is much the same as that with all needs-based theories of motivation. These models are a simplistic description of motivation based solely on the desire of individuals to fulfill categories of human needs, and organizations are supposed to structure themselves in a way that helps satisfy these needs. Organizations will gain the energy that comes from psychologically well-developed people. This will, in turn, contribute to organizational productivity.

Frederick Herzberg offered a two-factor theory that examines hygiene factors and motivators. His model looked at things that he believed motivated people rather than categories of needs. According to Herzberg, one set of factors is a motivator only in the negative sense. If these factors are not adequately met, they produce job dissatisfaction. Once these factors (called hygiene factors) are satisfied, they become neutral. Hygiene factors typically include salary. Herzberg's research found that when a person is being paid an adequate salary, pay becomes a hygiene factor. This was an interesting finding because the guiding wisdom for many years was that pay was a primary motivator. The evidence is clear that people work for reasons other than to earn money, but very few people would continue to work if they were not being paid. Whether money is a major motivator is probably dependent upon the individual's situation. Herzberg's hygiene factors included pay, company policy and administration, working conditions, peer relationships, competency of one's supervisor, benefits, and job security. Motivators included achievement, recognition, responsibility, advancement, interesting work, and pay. Notice that "pay" appears in both categories.[98]

All of the content theories suggest that employees should be encouraged to develop themselves through meaningful work situations. Modern management has come to believe that people are more motivated for intrinsic reasons than for extrinsic reasons. For example, a highly motivated worker in a pharmaceutical firm may be working extremely hard because of a personal commitment to something associated with the work (like finding a cure for a disease that has affected a member of the worker's family) and less because of the wages. The same worker, because of his or her commitment, may not be as influenced by the salary as long as the worker perceives it as adequate. This is exactly Herzberg's main point. Without doubt, intrinsic reasons are intangible motivators that are beyond the grasp of management. While organizations can offer extrinsic rewards, they can do little about intrinsic rewards other than trying to create an environment that is conducive for employees to fulfill this dimension of their needs. The content theories suggest that intrinsic motivators (meaningful work, responsibility, etc.) are more effective than extrinsic motivators (money, benefits, and other tangible benefits).

How do we know what people want from their jobs? How do organizations go about satisfying needs if, in fact, needs are the key to motivation? Motivation is complicated by the fact that people differ in the way they satisfy needs. Some people are aggressive, and others are restrained. Personality encompasses a set of traits that are usually manifested in the ways that people satisfy their needs. In the organizational context, personality is the dynamics within the individual (psycho-physical systems) that determine an individual's unique adjustments to the environment. One's personality determines how one will react in a given situation. Personality is a very complex concept. It involves traits, values, prejudices, and preferences. We sometimes think of people simplistically as "Type A" or "Type B" personalities. A "Type A" personality is an extro-

[handwritten margin notes: "Explain volunteering?", "Must satisfy intrinsic as much as extrinsic"]

vert who is full of restless energy, whereas "Type B" refers to the more laid-back, relaxed, and easygoing person. Psychologists use several dimensions to categorize personality types—extraversion, introversion, and neuroticism (emotionality). Box 4.4 illustrates four types of personalities that are derived from these traits or tendencies.

In organizations, we have all of these types of people, which makes it difficult to try to satisfy individual needs. How does an organization satisfy the needs of a work group comprised of introverts, extroverts, and the full range of personality types? Without a doubt, it is a challenging task. Needs vary, personalities vary, and organizations must somehow remain productive. Many argue that we have gone too far in trying to satisfy needs and in assuming that satisfying needs is the key to increased productivity. After all, we typically choose our jobs and decide whether to stay or change jobs. There is little doubt that if our needs are not met at work, we probably will be less satisfied than if we find our work fulfilling. But some people do not want their needs fulfilled at work, probably because their needs cannot be fulfilled there. They would rather be at home doing something they enjoy, such as a hobby. For these people, work is an economic necessity, but it does not mean that they enjoy it or can be forced to enjoy it. What is clear is organizations are limited in how well they can satisfy individual needs.

Process Theories of Motivation

Process theories are less concerned with the substantive things that motivate us to work and more concerned with the process and means by which we are motivated to act. Most process theories are based in psychology and the many theories of behavior that have been developed over the years. A few of the most popular ones will be discussed here. Stimulus–response theories assume that a stimulus causes some given behavior. One of the best-known stimulus–response examples is Pavlov's experiment in which dogs were conditioned to salivate at the sound of a bell. This experiment illustrated that behavior can be conditioned. Some psychologists have conceptualized the person as part of an environment in a similar way to how an atom is part of its environment. This is known as field theory, which contains the idea of *expectancy*. The emphasis is placed on the forces within the environment that stimulate a person to act. Unlike the stimulus–response models, field theory uses a cognitive model that sees the individual as a thinking organism. People will act in accordance with what they expect to happen. Stimulus–response models emphasize past experiences, but expectancy theory focuses on the future, recognizing that the individual has choices in the environment.

Expectancy was combined with instrumentality in Victor Vroom's V-I-E (valence-instrumentality-expectancy) theory. This turned out to be one of the most influential theories ever developed in organizational theory. Vroom's conceptualization was that a person questions the likelihood *(expectancy)* that a certain behavior or course of action will produce a desired outcome. The behavior is considered to be an *instrument* to attain a desired outcome. The concept of *valence* refers to how strongly a person wants a desired outcome to occur. That

BOX 4.4   Personality Types Found in Organizations

Adjusted extroverts can be described as adaptable, assertive, carefree, easygoing, gregarious, sociable, stable, warm, and so forth. These characteristics enable them to better satisfy their needs in an interaction-oriented society like ours. Since they can easily socialize and maintain personal contacts, they are able to draw on the resources of other people to help satisfy their own needs. A problem with this type may be that it is not a favorable combination for task performances requiring concentration and persistence, such as scholastic achievement, scientific research, or precision workmanship.

Anxious extroverts are often called neurotic extroverts because they are high on both extroversion and anxiety. Their traits can be described as aggressive, excitable, hyperactive, impulsive, restless, tense, touchy, and so forth. Because of these traits they may act prematurely to gratify their own needs. They may satisfy their needs in an inappropriate manner. They may get what they want but often at the expense of other people. A high level of anxiety is generally disruptive of performance.

Adjusted introverts are introverted and have a low level of anxiety. Their traits can be described as calm, composed, controlled, gentle, relaxed, even-tempered, meek, passive, stable, and considerate. They are usually able to maintain satisfactory interpersonal relationships with others. They are also likely to prefer job situations that provide peace and stability. The main problem with this type of person is a lack of motivation to achieve high goals.

Anxious introverts are introverted and have a high level of anxiety. Their traits can be described as aloof, anxious, cold, fearful, reserved, shy, unstable, moody, sober, and so on. As children, these people were usually very shy. Evidence suggests that most people overcome their shyness, but it remains a problem for many people. Because of this trait, these people are less likely to be successful at creating and maintaining interpersonal contacts. Thus, they prefer jobs requiring fewer interpersonal contacts. The redeeming feature of these people is that their traits can help them develop the capacity to be self-sufficient. Sine they are relatively unsuccessful in drawing on the resources of other people, they have to learn to be self-sufficient to meet their own needs. Introverts with moderate levels of anxiety can be highly productive at jobs requiring concentration, persistence, and hard work.

SOURCE: Kae Chung and Leon Megginson, *Organizational Behavior: Developing Managerial Skills* (New York: Harper & Row, 1981), pp. 67–68.

is, how much "value" does a person place on achieving a desired result? Mathematical weights are attached to valences that range from −1 to +1, with zero meaning that an individual is indifferent to the outcome. Expectancy theory stressed probabilities. See Figure 4.7 for an example of how expectancy theory operates. In this example, an individual may want a promotion for several reasons that include professional growth, status, and economics. The person has two choices in attempting to achieve this goal: The person can simply work hard, or the person can use office politics to achieve the desired outcome—the promotion. The individual believes that getting the promotion will fulfill the needs shown on the right side of the model (see Figure 4.7). The individual is guided largely by the amount of effort required to achieve the goal of getting the promotion. Thus, in this example, weights can be attached and the course of action mapped (see Figure 4.7). In this case, the value is higher for using politics to achieve the desired outcome. V-I-E theory has been very popular and helps explain the process that we might use when selecting courses of behavior to achieve a goal. Of course, we do not sit around placing numbers ranging from −1 to +1 on paper, but we do attach mental weights to alternatives (this is what the mathematical numbers represent). If we do not believe that a certain behavior will produce a desired result, we are unlikely to pursue it. Figure 4.7 has been simplified to contain only two behavior choices, but most situations contain a number of choices, not just hard work or the office politics route. Because motivation is complex, multiple behavioral options may be available for achieving desired goals.

Does V-I-E theory properly explain the process of motivation in the workplace? Probably not, but it does provide an interesting conceptual model that helps explain part of the process, and it has been incorporated into several leadership models. The theory has been criticized because of some obvious limitations; for example, it does not take into account "time." How much time we will have to spend to achieve a goal can serve as an incentive or disincentive. For example, if you want a graduate degree in public administration (the MPA degree that typically takes two years to complete as a full-time student), but the master's degree in political science with an emphasis in public administration in the same department takes only one year to complete, would you seriously consider the political science degree over the MPA because of the factor of time? If the amount of time is doubled for the MPA degree, the amount of money you would have to spend for the degree would also increase. The point is, *time* is a consideration because it affects a lot of variables in our level of motivation and in selecting goals. Time is also a factor in how long we can maintain our level of motivation. Most of us have difficulty sustaining a high level of motivation over an extended period of time. Also, this theory of motivation does not take into account how our values were acquired in the past, and yet our values influence our decisions about the rewards that we find desirable. The most serious problem associated with all expectancy theories is the reliance on hedonism—the idea that individuals seek to maximize pleasure or minimize

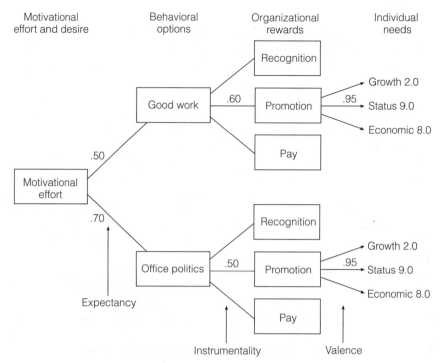

Motivation = Expectancy 3 Instrumentality 3 Valence (V-I-E)
Motivation (good work) = .50 × .60 × .95 × 9.0 = 2.56
Motivation (politics) = .70 × .50 × .95 × 9.0 = 2.94

FIGURE 4.7 Expectancy-Based Theory of Motivation

SOURCE: Adapted from Kae Chung and Leon Megginson, *Organizational Behavior: Developing Managerial Skills* (New York: Harper & Row, 1981), p. 142. V-I-E theory was developed by Victor Vroom, *Work and Motivation* (New York: Wiley, 1964).

pain. The idea of hedonism is deterministic because it suggests that people are always motivated by a desire for pleasure. This cannot be true because we often do things that are not pleasant to do. Moreover, we may seek results that provide rewards without trying to maximize the rewards. This is the idea of "satisficing," which is the same idea advanced by Herbert Simon in his "bounded rationality" model of decision making.

Another process theory involves the idea of equity. This theory contends that an individual compares the effort and rewards of the job in relation to the effort and rewards of others in comparable positions. It focuses on workers' perceptions of whether they are receiving equal pay for equal work. Changes in behavior are motivated by perceived inequities. The perception of being underpaid may cause workers to decrease the quality and quantity of their performance. Equity theory appears to explain why some people might adjust their performance when they see inequities in the workplace. But others have argued that people select behaviors that are consistent with their perceptions of themselves, and that people with high self-esteem will be compelled to perform well, while low performance would be inconsistent with high self-esteem.

Many process theories have been developed in an attempt to explain human behavior.[99] The thrust of understanding motivation as a process involves perceptions, attitudes, and responses to environmental conditions. What makes us respond or act the way we do in organizational settings? As employees, we work in complex environments and must deal with people with varying personalities on an ongoing basis. We also are faced with various rewards, incentives, and disincentives that affect our behavior. Organizations face a dilemma in trying to figure out how to motivate employees. The guiding doctrine suggests that the best motivator comes from within the worker in the form of intrinsic rewards, but organizations can do little to provide such rewards. Public organizations must remain productive to accomplish the work they are mandated to perform by law.

The relationship between the work environment and motivation, which began with Frederick Taylor and Elton Mayo, continues to this day. Many ideas such as ergonomics (designing physical work environments to better fit the worker), job enrichment (redesigning jobs to make them more interesting and challenging), job enlargement (cross-training and allowing workers to expand their jobs), and flextime (letting workers have greater control of their schedules) have been tried in attempts to improve conditions in the workplace. In many ways, motivation remains as elusive as ever, despite the amount of knowledge about it that has been acquired. Are we motivated by money, prestige, advancement, autonomy, or power? Even if research tells us what motivates "most" people, it is still difficult to implement theories because of the variation in people and in organizational dynamics. The field of motivation and management has been largely characterized by fads.[100] Many of these fads, like the "one-minute manager" and "management by objectives," have been in one year and out the next.[101]

One of the largest problems with motivational theories, it has been argued, is that they overlook the role of labor unions and disregard the great variation among individuals. People come in many shapes and sizes, and they are not all motivated by a quest for self-actualization or a particular group of hygiene factors discovered by researchers. Many years ago, Robert Presthus suggested that people fall into three very large categories that represent a great deal of variation: upward mobiles, indifferents, and ambivalents.[102] These groups have three very different views of the workplace that range from a motivation to succeed to the routine receipt of a paycheck. The latter group may perform adequately at work but might care more about their hobbies than getting promoted. They might even prefer to stay home with their hobbies if they did not need the income from work. This, however, does not necessarily mean that they are poor employees; they are just there to do the job and get out. The real world is filled with people who will not respond to the latest motivation techniques and fads. For example, many professors have absolutely no desire whatsoever to be the chair of their departments, while others actively seek to become chair and even to move on to a higher administrative level, such as dean or provost. In addition, employees do bring their problems to work, and these problems are as varied as life itself. They may include financial stress, the death of family members, health and relationship problems, divorce, and substance abuse problems. Burnout is common in many professions. Burnout occurs for many reasons, including too much stress at work or home, and trying to balance the pressures of work with the demands of raising a family. The dynamics of life are simply too complex for a "one-size-fits-all" motivational theory, and peoples' needs are too diverse for organizations to be able to satisfy them. The motivational theories and techniques developed thus far are useful in that they have expanded our knowledge, but one point appears to be clear: There is no single magical formula for motivating workers.[103]

ORGANIZATIONAL CULTURE

Organizational culture is a phenomenon found in all organizations. Cultures vary greatly from one organization to the next, even if the organizations perform essentially the same functions. During the 1950s, William Whyte wrote the best seller *The Organization Man,* which essentially described the corporate organizational culture that characterized so many firms in the 1950s.[104] Whyte articulated what one had to be in order to fit into the organizational cultures of big firms of that era (such as International Business Machines, or IBM). Ideal corporate employees were those who could conform to the norms of the culture, be good citizens, and perform their duties. One developed a special commitment, a sense of dedication, to the firm. Whyte portrayed organizations as providing workers with a sense of belonging and commitment to the social ethic of the organization rather than to an ethos based on individualism—thus the term *organization man,* to describe a person who is committed and dedicated to the organization. It was implied that if one served the firm well, the firm would take care of you with retirement benefits, health insurance, paid vacations, and the like. This was a lifetime commitment, although this unwritten *social contract* only worked in one direction. No provision was made for the unlikely event that the firm failed to take care of its committed employees. Responsibility was placed on individuals to conform and to prove themselves to the firm. Of course, the culture described by Whyte did not last. Since the 1950s, the length of time that people stay with organizations has decreased (although the tendency to stay with the organization has been greater in government, partly due to civil service), and the idea of building lasting loyalty to a firm or any organization has waned. There was a time when people stayed with organizations for their entire working lives, particularly in the days when factories and mills employed so many people. There are many reasons for the change, including the failure of firms to properly take care of employees. There are too many real-life examples of people spending their entire careers with firms and being forced to retire at age 52, after their most productive years have passed. This is what is called *being put out to pasture.* Our society has gone through a number of social revolts against conformity and the "cog-in-the-wheel" view of people in organizations. Since World War II, we have become a very mobile society. People no longer live and work within a short radius of where they were raised. There are more opportunities today for a variety of careers than in the past, and people simply do not hold the same degree of loyalty toward organizations. Moreover, individualism is a deeply embedded part of our culture. Although Whyte's *organization man* has faded away and society and organizations have changed over the years, organizational culture remains a real phenomenon.

Organizational culture can be thought of as the predominant value system of an organization.[105] Organizational culture has been described as a set of values, norms, rites, rituals, ceremonies, ideologies, formal and informal rules, and even heroes in the history of an organization that shape the organization's social and internal working environment.[106] It identifies those things that new employees need to learn to be accepted and to fit into the organization. It includes the standards, expectations, and rules (written and unwritten) that all members are expected to willingly accept and follow. Even today, as Whyte's *The Organization Man* suggested, organizational culture requires some degree of conformity. It is also comprised of slogans, emblems, and symbols that represent the organization. These help to provide an identity for the organization. Most of us are very familiar with famous corporate symbols, such as the emblem attached to Ford Motor Company's automobiles, the trade symbol used by Microsoft, and the famous golden arches used at McDonald's fast-food restaurants. These logos are more than just a marketing tool; they represent the firm and make it distinct from other organizations. For whatever reason, perhaps due to marketing and television, we are more familiar with the symbols of corporations than with those of our public agencies. [107]

Where do cultures come from and how do they develop? The content of an organization's culture develops over time in response to adapting to its external environment and building internal coordinating systems. Over time, a history develops along with traditions and patterns of behavior. For example, corporations like General Motors and public agencies like the Department of Treasury and the U.S. Postal Service have endured for some time. Like all organizations, each has its own distinct organizational culture. Organizational cultures also have subcultures, which grow in the subdivisions, regional offices, departments, and units of organizations. Different occupational groups within organizations also have their subcultures. For example, in hospitals, different subcultures exist for medical doctors, nurses, various types of staff, and administrators. After individuals join organizations, they move deeper into the culture and ultimately, assuming they are compatible and stay with the organization, become insiders. It is well established that an organization's culture affects the behavior of its members. Since we are not all compatible with all organizational cultures, most of us try to find organizations where we are comfortable.

Organizational cultures have both formal and informal aspects that are partly a function of the management philosophy promoted by the executive leadership. Some organizations, such as Microsoft, have relatively informal organizational cultures that promote creativity, casual dress, informality, and a lucrative reward system. Organizational cultures can be strong or weak. This is represented in the degree to which management actively ensures that the desired culture is maintained and promoted. Organizational culture involves many social and philosophical elements, but it is also a statement about the way a firm does business or a public agency conducts its affairs. It defines "how we do things here," which can help instill a sense of pride for those who work for the organization and cause employees to be more supportive of organizational goals.[108] Since management philosophies can change, so can organizational cultures. Organizations must constantly be adapting to the external environment, and as they adapt, changes occur that can modify the organizational culture.[109]

ORGANIZATIONS FOR THE FUTURE

Since the 1960s, many articles have been written about how organizations should be modified to make them more effective. In 1966, Warren Bennis wrote an article that questioned how well bureaucracy could serve the future.[110] He was critical of bureaucracy, although like Max Weber, he recognized that large organizations were necessary for societies to govern and manage their affairs, and for businesses to produce the products needed by society. Bureaucratic organizations have many flaws and problems. Although the list of flaws is extensive, some of the major categories cited by Bennis are:

- Bureaucracy does not adequately allow for personal growth and the development of mature personalities.
- It promotes conformity and groupthink.
- It does not adequately take into account the "informal organization" and the emergent and unanticipated problems associated with the informal organization.
- Its systems of controls and authority are hopelessly outdated.
- It does not possess adequate means for resolving differences and conflicts between ranks and, most particularly, between functional groups.
- Communication and innovative ideas are thwarted or distorted due to hierarchical divisions.
- The full human resources of bureaucracy are not utilized due to mistrust and fear of reprisal.
- Bureaucracy cannot assimilate the influx of new technology and scientists entering the organization.
- It modifies the personality structures such that people become and reflect the dull, gray, conditioned "organization man."

Bennis was critical of bureaucracy but offered ideas about how organizations of the future would look if they were to effectively serve society. Bureaucracy in the Weberian tradition, in his view, would have to be modified. His observations are worth noting here because they provide some insight into the future.

Moreover, since his comments were made nearly 40 years ago, we can reflect on the development of bureaucracy since the 1960s by examining them.

Bennis believed that the *environment* of organizations would be shifting more profoundly, causing relative uncertainty. There would be greater interpenetration of legal and economic factors, causing imperfect, oligopolitistic competition for businesses and more partnerships between government and business as businesses, such as Telstar, undertake large expensive projects. The environment would be characterized by interdependence instead of competition, and larger rather than smaller organizations would dominate the landscape. The *aggregate population characteristics* would cause significant changes in the workforce. People would be more educated; most people would live in urban areas and be more mobile in their jobs due to the lower costs and ease of transportation. Continuing education would become prevalent for colleges and universities to provide a well-trained workforce. *Work-related values* would change due to the increased levels of education and mobility. Bennis believed that people would tend to: (1) be more rational, be more intellectually committed, and rely more heavily on forms of social influence that correspond to their value system; (2) rely more heavily on temporary neighbors and workmates for companionship; and (3) require more involvement, participation, and autonomy in their pattern of work. The *tasks and goals of organizations* would become more technical, complicated, and unprogrammed. Tasks would rely far more on intellectual power and higher cognitive processes than on muscle power. Goals would become more differentiated and complicated, and productivity would be more difficult to measure than during the manufacturing era. *Organizational structure* would experience some significant changes. He believed that organizations would become more adaptive, rapidly changing systems that would more and more be regarded as temporary. Organizations would be organized around problems-to-be-solved rather than rational procedural structures that were described by Weber. The problems would be solved by relative groups of strangers with diverse professional skills who collaborate on projects. Coordination of diverse projects would require that "articulating points" or "linking pins" positions be created. These positions would be new jobs that would require personnel who can speak the languages associated with a diversity of research areas and who can relay and mediate between various project groups. The groups and projects would be connected on organic rather than mechanical lines; and leaders would emerge and adapt to the problems, allowing leadership and influence to be handled by those who seem most able to solve problems rather than being based programmed role expectations. People would be differentiated, not according to rank or roles, but according to skills and training. Bennis believed that temporary systems of diverse specialists solving problems coordinated organically through articulating points would gradually replace the practice of bureaucracy in the traditional sense of the concept. He referred to these new organizations as *organic-adaptive structures*. He also believed that organizational goals and the goals of individuals would coincide more frequently because individuals would identify the organizations' goal of problem solving with their profession.

Bennis also believed that the growth of professions would increase in the next century. Jobs would become more absorbing and interesting because of the increased rise in the professions. Bennis saw traditional bureaucracy as creating a surplus of repression to harness "muscle" to perform and administer tasks in an environment that failed to stimulate workers. He saw the organic-adaptive structures as *structures of freedom* that would permit expression of play and imagination and exploit the new pleasure of work. Neither the organization nor the *organization man* described by William Whyte during the 1950s would characterize organizations in the new century. Bennis did not see his predictions as utopian. He realized that problem solving is not always pleasant and that any work environment has its downside. But it was, in his view, the trend that would characterize organizations in the future, since the old bureaucratic structures would be inadequate to cope with the future.

Whether Bennis was fully correct in his predictions is debatable, but there is little doubt that the world and bureaucracies have changed. The rise of professions, the emergence of the information age, the development of a better-educated workforce than at any time in the nation's history, the interdependence of our social and economic system with the global economy, and nearly a century of arguments by researchers stating that effective organizations need to be *human* organizations have had a huge effect on bureaucracies. The degree to which organizations have changed is more difficult to measure.

By the 1980s, a new generation of researchers were engaged in trying to find out what kinds of organizations seem to perform the best. Thomas Peters and Robert Waterman's *In Search of Excellence* was one of the most influential and popular books published during the 1980s.[111] Peters and Waterman looked for what they defined as the "best-run" companies in the United States and found several consistent characteristics. The "best-run" firms: (1) had a bias for action, that is, a preference for doing something other than sending a question through cycles of analyses and committee reports; (2) stayed close to their customers, learning about their preferences and catering to their needs; (3) exhibited autonomy and entrepreneurship by breaking the corporation into small companies and encouraging them to think independently; (4) were able to find productivity through people, creating for all employees the awareness that their best efforts are essential and that they will share in the rewards of the company's success; (5) were hands-on and value-driven; (6) stuck to the core areas that they knew best; (7) had simple forms, lean staff, few administrative layers, and fewer people in the upper levels of the organization; and (8) were able to maintain a simultaneous loose-tight posture that helped foster a climate (organizational culture) in which there was dedication to the central values of the company. *In Search of Excellence* was a trend-setting book in the private sector. In short, executives stayed in touch with the firm's essential business and did not let the pitfalls of bureaucratic structure keep them from losing sight of the purpose of the firm. But the world of public administration is filled with public policy, legal constraints, and political relationships; and unfortunately, there has not been much research in organization theory about the complexities of the political realities and organizational form in the public sector.

In the early 1990s, David Osborne and Ted Gaebler published *Reinventing Government*,[112] which is perhaps the public sector equivalent of *In Search of Excellence*. *Reinventing Government* ignited new interest in the public sector. Although the idea of "reinventing government" will be discussed more thoroughly in Chapter 8, the thrust was that government needed to become more *results-oriented* rather than *process-oriented*. Osborne and Gaebler believed that there was too much red tape, too many restrictions, and too many cumbersome rules to manage effectively. They were well aware of the political realities, but they were primarily interested in advancing the idea of changing the mindset toward achieving results. They offered many examples of how governments around the nation were working better because of developing strategies that were aimed toward results while working with the complexities of public bureaucracy. The ideas associated with *Reinventing Government* helped to spark a reexamination of the way government agencies work. However, the idea of reinventing government does not address all of the political and legal realities of the public sector or how to balance the goals of efficiency, effectiveness, responsiveness, and accountability (goals that often conflict with each other). It also does not really tell us how to design organizations other than providing us with the results-orientation strategy. *Reinventing Government* was another trend-setting book that remains with us today. The follow-up book, titled *Banishing Bureaucracy* and authored by David Osborne and Peter Plastrik, provided stronger views on modifying bureaucracy to make it work better.[113]

Warren Bennis illustrated that there are new ways to think about designing organizations, and Osborne and Gaebler provided some new ideas about management. David Harmon provided some organizational ideas for the public sector that are similar to those advanced by Bennis (see Box 4.5.) Regardless of how we shape or modify it, bureaucracy remains a reality of the private and public sectors. To design better organizations, we need to understand what is wrong with current structures. While there is no real alternative to bureaucracy, there are ways that internal structures can be modified to make them more effective. The ideas advanced by Warren Bennis nearly 40 years ago provide some possibilities. But public bureaucracies are characterized by inertia; thus, they are slow to change. The public sector is also constrained by many factors and political realities.

One point must be noted here. Organizations are not created by nature; people create them. Society was not created by nature either. One possibility is that the development and even the direction of organizations may be more difficult to control than we think. Because we do not understand all of the cause-effect relationships in society, we create organizations without fully understanding how they will fit with, react to, and adapt to changing conditions in the social environment. That is, their growth and development may have an *organic* dimension that is partly beyond our control. This is not to suggest that organizations take on some type of life of their own, but our efforts to make organizations more effective are exacerbated by the complexities of society, changing economic factors, values, and new issues coupled with

---

BOX 4.5　Thinking about Designing Organizations Differently

The basic organizational chart with its hierarchical structure is based on simple assumptions about how people fit into organizations. New organizational forms are based on new assumptions. Some organizational theorists, like Warren Bennis, predict that future organizations will be in a constant flux, changing form as judgments and forces emerge from interactions among members that are not based on traditional hierarchical interactions. It is hard to visualize such arrangements because they do not fit neatly into our traditional view of the organizational chart. One theorist includes the following points in his view of the way new organizations should be designed.*

1. The primary focus or unit of analysis is the face-to-face encounters between people, rather than the group or the system.
2. People are by nature active rather than passive, and social rather than atomistic. This means they must have a measure of autonomy in determining their actions, and their actions must correspond to their context.
3. The active social nature of people means considerable attention is directed to the subjective meanings people attach to their actions and those of others. These everyday meanings are the basis of knowledge in the organization.
4. The selection of organizational decision rules is the most impor-

tant aspect of determining structure. A structure that takes account of the active social nature of people relies on negotiated meanings arrived at by consensus rather than by hierarchy, bargaining, voting, and contract.
5. Consensual organizations require that each actor bear moral responsibility for his or her actions. The institution and its actions cannot be viewed apart from the intersubjective processes people use to define and take action. The legitimacy of organization actions must be established and sustained in face-to-face encounters between people.

This type of organization is virtually impossible to put on a chart, but in many ways it fits in with important ideas we have about public administration. It focuses on people doing things like delivering services. It tries to look at actions in a practical way. Moreover, it provides more room for individual citizens to collectively talk about what organizations do and how they do it. It tries to make a very "public" sense of public administration. At the moment, such an organization does not exist.

*Michael Harmon, *Action Theory for Public Administration* (New York: Longman, 1981).

SOURCE: Adapted from David Schuman and Dick Olufs, *Public Administration in the United States*, 2nd ed. (Lexington, MA: D. C. Heath, 1993), pp. 146–147.

---

decision-making processes that do not always result in appropriate choices. Sometimes we implement changes designed to fix a problem with organizations, and the changes create unintended consequences and new problems. In the new century, we are still searching for better ways to design organizations and make them work more effectively.

SUMMARY

This chapter has provided an overview of some of the fundamental elements of organizational theory and management. Organizations are complex systems comprised of people, materials, technologies, and processes that exist in complex environments. Organizations are not natural; they are created and designed by people. Thus, they are social institutions. There are three primary approaches for examining organizations: political, organizational, and humanistic. Each of these approaches has inherent assumptions about organizations, and each studies dimensions, that are different from the others. Max Weber first defined the concept of bureaucracy, and his legal-rational model is the basis for all bureaucracies in the modern world. His ideas have been modified many times over the years as people have searched for ways to create better, more effective, more humanistic entities. Henri Fayol gave us the basic principles of management, such as planning, organizing, controlling, and the like. Frederick Taylor advanced his principles of scientific management early in the 20th century, the basic idea of which was that there is "one best way" to perform any task, and it is management's responsibility to use science to discover the best method.

Decision making is a fundamental part of organizations, whether the decisions are routine or involve major changes in policy that may affect the whole society. Decision-making models range from those based in the rational-comprehensive tradition to incrementalism. Managers are involved in a wide range of work that includes performing many tasks that require many skills. Moreover, they have management styles that can be hard-nosed, soft-nosed, or balance the concern for productivity against concern for workers. Leadership is closely tied to management styles but contains some intangible factors that are difficult to adequately describe. Many theories of leadership have been advanced. It is believed that managers can polish their leadership skills within certain limits, but some qualities or attributes found in the most effective leaders, such as charisma, are impossible to learn or develop.

Motivation theories come in two primary forms. Content theories focus on human needs and on how organizations can satisfy employees' needs to enhance organizational productivity. Content theories also look at specific motivators, such as money, prestige, and advancement, and try to find the "right mix" of incentives to motivate workers. However, it is commonly believed that people are best motivated by intrinsic rewards, which are nearly impossible for organizations to provide. Process theories focus only on the "process" and associated behaviors involved with motivation. A number of process theories have been advanced over the years, but the most popular models involve some aspect of expectancy theory. All organizations have organizational cultures, which can have a great impact on organizational performance and continuity. The most common way to maintain a strong organizational culture is by using tradition to maintain the set of values that affects everyone in the organization. Organizational cultures sometimes must be modified to stay aligned with the external environment. This chapter also examined a few prospects about future organizations by looking at predictions made by several well-known organizational theorists.

The study of organizations leads us to one conclusion. Just as many management fads have come and gone, organizational theory also has been characterized by many passing fads. Sometimes it is difficult to separate the fads from real theoretical and empirical knowledge. The fact that we have greatly expanded and enhanced our knowledge about organizations is not in question, but we have yet to develop an adequate model for creating new organizations that is truly effective and satisfies most of the conditions discussed in this chapter.

NOTES

1. Lerner and Wanat have argued that the context of public administration is largely the organization itself. They do no suggest that the organization is a closed system, but that if one wants to understand public administration, one must understand the dynamics of the organization we call bureaucracy. See Allan Lerner and John Wanat, *Public Administration: A Realistic Reinterpretation of Contemporary Public Management* (Englewood Cliffs, NJ: Prentice-Hall, 1992), Chapter 2.

2. Anthony Downs, *Inside Bureaucracy* (Prospect Heights, IL: Waveland Press, 1994), p. 24. Chester Barnard provides one of the most thorough and insightful descriptions of organizations in *The Functions of the Executive* (Cambridge, MA: Harvard University Press, 1958).

3. Many concepts and areas of organizational theory will not be covered in this book, since the field of study is very large. Peter Drucker made the concept of management by objectives (MBO) popular in the 1950s. See Peter Drucker, *The Practice of Management* (New York: Harper & Brothers, 1954). Although now there are many versions of MBO, it originated in industries like General Motors and the du Pont Company after World War I. Drucker and Douglas McGregor both pushed the idea, and at the end of the 1960s, it was commonly used in private industry and government. The basics of MBO are simple. The idea is to manage for results. Typically, MBO has a short-term and a long-term component. The basic idea is to set attainable goals, establish measurable standards, and evaluate how well a person,

department, or organization is achieving the desired goals. In its more modern version, it allows for employee input and usually sets goals for 12-month periods.

Groupthink is a concept developed by Irving Janis that explains how members of a group will tend to accept the group's position even though they believe the decision is wrong. Groupthink often involves pressures from members of the group to force other members to comply. One of Janis's case studies involved the Bay of Pigs and how groupthink led President Kennedy to accept poor advice because his advisors were pressured by other members of the advisory group to go along with questionable advice. The decision was a disaster in the case of the Bay of Pigs, and President Kennedy made changes in the way he was advised in the future. Janis also uses the Cuban Missile Crisis to illustrate a situation in which groupthink did not occur because of what was learned from the experience with the Bay of Pigs. Groupthink is discussed later in this chapter.

Eric Berne developed transactional analysis (TA) in popular books entitled *The Games People Play* (New York: Grove Press, 1964) and *The Structure of Organizations and Groups* (New York: Grove Press, 1963). Berne essentially translated Freudian psychology into a group framework and developed a communication technique which conceptualized that everyone can behave as an adult, child, or parent at different times (Freud's idea of the id, ego, and super ego). Recognizing how they are reacting or behaving helps people realize the manner of their communication. For example, when acting like a parent, we tend to be in a protective, conservative mode. The adult is the rational mature mode, and the child is the immature, self-centered mode.

Organizational development (OD) is defined as the process of increasing the ability of organizations to do what they are mandated to do—perform work. The idea is that organizations should never stop developing, and long-range plans are studied to ensure that organizations continue to make improvements in all areas. Many people are associated with this idea, including Warren Bennis, *Organizational Development: Its Nature, Origins, and Prospects* (Reading, MA: Addison-Wesley, 1969).

Quality circles are a participatory method designed to improve quality that was made popular by William Ochi, *Theory Z* (Reading, MA: Addison-Wesley, 1981). The basis of quality circles comes from Douglas McGregor's popular Theory X and Y, which is discussed in this chapter. Job enlargement and job enrichment are discussed in Chapter 5. These concepts simply refer to expanding the tasks and responsibilities associated with a job to make it more interesting and fulfilling for the employee. See Kenneth Alexander, "On Work and Authority: Issue on Job Enlargement, Job Enrichment, Worker Participation, and Shared Authority," *American Journal of Economics and Sociology* 34 (1975), pp. 43–54.

4. The idea of including political, organizational, and humanistic approaches here is credited to the work of Donald Klingner, *Public Administration: A Management Approach* (Boston: Houghton Mifflin, 1983), Chapter 3.

5. Donald Klingner, *Public Administration: A Management Approach,* p. 43.

6. Due to the marvels of modern technology, the *United States Government Manual* can be viewed online at http://www.access.gpo.gov/nara/browse-gm-00.html.

7. Henry Fayol is often included here as well. Fayol is considered to be the founder of the normative view of management, which includes the ideas of planning, coordinating, controlling, and the like.

8. Barry Bozeman, *Bureaucracy and Red Tape* (Upper Saddle River, NJ: Prentice-Hall, 2000), pp. 17–18. Bozeman includes more than the points noted here.

9. Several books make this point. See Dwight Waldo, *The Administrative State* (New York: Ronald, 1948); Jacques Ellul, *The Technological Society* (New York: Vintage, 1964), and Hannah Arendt, *The Human Condition* (Chicago: University of Chicago Press, 1958).

10. This point is made by David Shuman and Dick Olufs III in *Public Administration in the United States,* 2nd ed. (Lexington, MA: D. C. Heath, 1993), p. 101.

11. The revolt was part of a larger wave of social unrest during the 1960s and 1970s. Many people felt that bureaucracies, both public and private, were too impersonal and dehumanized the individual. Some wanted more input into the processes used by bureaucracies (course evaluations at universities became very common during this period). In the world of business, academics began to redefine the social contract that included businesses. The new social contract called for businesses to be more socially responsible, whereas in the past, their sole objective was supposed to be to make money. Management scholars like Peter Drucker argued that business enterprises had to first be human organizations, recognize their responsibilities to the society in which they existed, and seek to make reasonable profits rather than to maximize profits. Management scholars during this time were operating under ideas and principles that were much newer than those espoused by Taylor and that included participatory and team management concepts and a view of the organization as a system that is affected by an array of external influences.

12. Weber was well aware of the potential conflict between bureaucracy and politics. He believed that a fully developed bureaucracy was overpowering and that the politician ends up in the position of a "dilettante" standing opposite to the "expert." Weber argued that bureaucracies would try to increase the superiority of the professionally informed by keeping their knowledge discrete. That is, the bureaucracy's information would be a

significant source of power. Weber saw an ongoing tension between politics and bureaucracy, since each operates according to a different dynamic. Bureaucracy is rational, but politics is passionate and imprecise. Bureaucrats are permanent, while politicians are temporary. Bureaucrats operate from a set of defined and rational rules, while the politicians respond to ever-changing pressures in the political environment. For Weber, this would be an ongoing problem for the modern world. See Hans Gerth and C. Wright Mills, Eds., *From Max Weber: Essays in Sociology* (New York: Oxford University Press, 1956), particularly "Politics as a Vocation."

13. Frederick W. Taylor, *Principles of Scientific Management* (New York: W. W. Norton, 1967). The original book was published in 1911.

14. Louis Boone and Donald Bowen, Eds., *The Great Writings in Management and Organizational Behavior* (Tulsa, OK: PennWell, 1980), pp. 2–3.

15. Ibid.

16. Henri Fayol (1841–1925) is considered to be the French equivalent to Taylor. He was employed by a mining firm in France and ultimately became the firm's managing director. But unlike Taylor, who focused on the shop and assembly lines, Fayol viewed management from the boards of directors down. Taylor's focus was on planning, organizing, and supervising work at the lowest levels of an organization, while Fayol's work dealt with planning and forecasting for the entire firm, developing organizational and control systems, and achieving better coordination at all levels of the organization. He also was the first to emphasize the idea of a universality of management and to stress the need for teaching management in colleges and universities. See Henri Fayol, *General and Industrial Management,* translated by Constance Storrs (London: Pitman, 1949).

17. Systems theory would not be introduced for organizations until the late 1940s by Norbert Weiner in his classic book *Cybernetics* (Cambridge, MA: MIT Press, 1948). In the early 1950s, David Easton wrote about politics as a system in *The Political System: An Inquiry into the State of Political Science* (New York: Alfred A.

Knopf, 1953). In 1960, John Pfiffner and Frank Sherwood brought systems theory to mainstream of organization studies in their book *Administrative Organizations* (Englewood Cliffs, NJ: Prentice-Hall, 1960).

18. Frederick W. Taylor, "The Principles of Scientific Management," in Louis Boone and Donald Bowen, Eds., *The Great Writings in Management and Organizational Behavior,* pp. 45–46.

19. Many of Taylor's ideas continue to influence modern management. Time and motion studies, time management, efforts to enhance efficiency, and focus on the production process are still very much a part of contemporary organizations, particularly business enterprises.

20. Some of Taylor's work was widely criticized and subject of a scandal. For example, there is some evidence that Taylor may have fabricated some of his findings using a "fudge factor." Also, one of his famous stories about how he taught a laborer named Schmidt to increase his productivity sevenfold in loading pig-iron may have been false. And he may have used the work of an associate, Morris Cooke, without his permission in his famous book *The Principles of Scientific Management.* Whatever shortcomings he may have exhibited in integrity, his work remains very famous and influential. See Louis Boone and Donald Bowen, *The Great Writings in Management and Organizational Behavior* (Tulsa, OK: PennWell, 1980), p. 3. The pig-iron story is included in David Schuman and Dick Olufs III, *Public Administration in the United States,* 2nd ed. (Lexington, MA: D. C. Heath, 1993), pp. 108–109.

21. Luther Gulick's "Notes on a Theory of Organization" is included in Luther Gulick and Lyndell Urwick, Eds., *Papers on the Science of Administration* (New York: Institute of Public Administration, 1937).

22. Administrative science originated in the early 1900s with the work of Frederick Taylor, who is credited with fathering the science of industrial engineering with his principles of scientific management. Those who studied private industry and those who studied public organizations believed

that a science of administration was possible.

23. At the time, the idea of a science of administration included discovering the principles of management and administration. Today, one can argue that a science of administration does exist, but it is a social science that studies administration to enhance our understanding about organizations and management of them. There is no thought that the equivalent of laws of administration exist. Moreover, studying organizations is a multidisciplinary endeavor that involves many disciplines including business administration, public administration, psychology, and many other fields.

24. Herbert Simon, "Proverbs of Administration," *Public Administration Review 6* (Winter 1946), pp. 53–67.

25. Herbert Simon, *Administrative Behavior* (New York: Macmillan, 1957).

26. For more about Follett's ideas, see Mary Parker Follett, *Creative Experience* (New York: Longman, Green, 1924), and *The New State* (New York: Longman, Green, 1923). A number of Web sites are dedicated to Follett. Two of the better ones are located at http://www.onepine.demon.co.uk/pfollett.htm and http://www.infed.org/thinkers/et-foll.htm.

27. David Schuman and Dick Olufs III, *Public Administration in the United States,* pp. 113–116.

28. Ibid.

29. Donald Klingner, *Public Administration: A Management Approach,* p. 46.

30. The merging of both open and closed systems is called *contingency theory.* The focus is on the interactive relationships with the external environment and the internal structures of the organization regarding decision making. One of the major roles for administrators and organizational leaders is to make good decisions under conditions of uncertainty, which is the way the real world usually works. Contingency theory holds that decisions made within the organization must take into account the contextual situation that may be related to every decision. See James March and Herbert

Simon, *Organizations* (New York: Wiley, 1958), and James Thompson, Organizations in Action (New York: McGraw-Hill, 1967).

31. Norbert Weiner, *Cybernetics* (Cambridge, MA: MIT Press, 1948).

32. David Easton, *The Political System: An Inquiry into the State of Political Science* (New York: Knopf, 1953).

33. John Pfiffner and Frank Sherwood, *Administrative Organizations* (Englewood Cliffs, NJ: Prentice-Hall, 1960).

34. Studying organizations as systems allows virtually every dimension of an agency to be examined. Daniel Katz and Robert Kahn envisioned an organization in terms of how energy is brought into the organization, how it is used and transformed while it is there, and how much is produced in the form of goods and services. This is viewed in the framework of inputs, processing, and outputs. The idea of energy flow, energy exchange, and energy transformation enables one to determine if the organization is working efficiently and effectively. They also developed the idea of the roles associated with positions in organizations, which is very important to understanding organizational humanism. See Daniel Katz and Robert Kahn, *The Social Psychology of Organizations,* 2nd ed. (New York: Wiley, 1978).

35. For a good discussion about the impact of the Hawthorne studies on management practices, see Lawrence Steinmetz and H Ralph Todd, Jr., *First-Line Management: Approaching Supervision Effectively,* 3rd ed. (Plano, TX: Business Publications, 1983), pp. 10–13.

36. David Schuman and Dick Olufs III, *Public Administration in the United States,* pp. 113–116.

37. See Elton Mayo, *The Human Problems with an Industrial Civilization* (New York: Macmillan, 1933; reprinted by the Division of Research, Harvard Business School, 1946). Also see Elton Mayo, "Hawthorne and the Western Electric Company," in Richard Stillman II, Ed., *Public Administration: Concepts and Cases,* 3rd ed. (Boston: Houghton Mifflin, 1983), pp. 171–180.

38. Chris Argyris, "The Individual and Organization: Some Problems of Mutual Adjustment," *Administrative Science Quarterly 2* (June 1957), pp. 1–24. Also see Chris Argyris, *Personality and Organization* (New York: Harper Collins, 1958), and *Integrating the Individual and the Organization* (New York: Wiley, 1964). Later, Argyris focused a great deal on learning in the organization in *Overcoming Organizational Defenses: Facilitating Organizational Learning* (New York: Allyn & Bacon, 1990).

39. The idea of roles is discussed at length in Daniel Katz and Robert Kahn, *The Social Psychology of Organizations*. Also, Donald Klingner provides a good overview of roles and organizational humanism in *Public Administration: A Management Approach,* p. 50.

40. William Ochi, "Going from A to Z: Thirteen Steps to a Theory Z Organization," *Management Review* (May 1981), pp. 8–16.

41. William Ochi, *Theory Z* (New York: Avon Books, 1982). Theory Z was an attempt to translate the successful Japanese style of management for American managers. During the time that Theory Z became popular, American industry was trying to improve itself. The aftermath of the oil embargo, mismanagement, and economic recessions had left some of America's largest industries in poor condition. Quality circles and total quality management principles, which were actually developed in the United States but were used by the Japanese, became very popular and helped many American industries recover. For example, W. Edward Deming developed the idea of total quality management (TQM) during the 1950s, but it was rejected by industries such as Ford Motor Company and General Motors. In the 1980s, Ford Motor Company and many other major industrial firms in the United States embraced Deming's idea.

42. The actual law, signed on July 30, 2002, is the Public Company Accounting Reform and Investor Protection Act.

43. James March and Herbert Simon, *Organizations* (New York: Wiley, 1958). Herbert Simon and James March referred to the types of decisions made in organizations as routine and nonroutine.

44. The basis of this model comes from a theory known as rational choice in the discipline of economics. Rational choice theory is discussed in detail in Chapter 8. It is the basis of public choice theory. For our purposes here, rational choice assumes that all behavior can be reduced to the behavior of individuals. Individuals, called rational actors, seek to satisfy their own self-interest. The term for measuring satisfaction is *utility*. Rational actors are self-serving egotists who are driven to make rational decisions that maximize their utility. *Rationality* is not defined in the psychological sense of the word, but as taking action that satisfies an individual's selfish wants, desires, needs, and goals. Thus, people are compelled to make the "best" decision that satisfies their wants and needs within a particular set of circumstances that typically involve making decisions under uncertainty. The theory includes preference orderings, perfect or near perfect information on which to base decisions, and the idea that rational actors respond to incentives and disincentives that affect their behavior. The rational–comprehensive model is an extension of this theory. When used in organizational settings, it helps a person (or decision maker) plot out the logical courses of action (alternatives) that are available. The theory has been modified many times but still assumes that those making decisions are also rational actors. If this is not true, the theoretical grounds of rational choice theory are called into question.

45. George Gordon and Michael Milakovich, *Public Administration in America,* 5th ed. (New York: St. Martin's Press, 1995), pp. 174–175. Gordon and Milakovich provide an excellent assessment of the models of decision making used in public administration in Chapter 6.

46. Thomas Lynch, *Public Budgeting in America,* 4th ed. (Englewood Cliffs, NJ: Prentice-Hall, 1996), p. 19.

47. Ibid.

48. George Gordon and Michael Milakovich, *Public Administration in America,* pp. 174–176.

49. Herbert Simon, *Administrative Behavior* (New York: Macmillan, 1957).

50. Charles Lindblom, "The Science of Muddling Through," *Public Administration Review 19* (Spring 1959), pp. 79–88.

51. Aaron Wildavsky, *The Politics of the Budgetary Process,* 4th ed. (Boston: Little, Brown, 1984).

52. Aaron Wildavsky, who argued that political leaders incur exchange costs when they need support from others, advanced this idea. By supporting some legislation and policies, political leaders antagonize others, which is the concept of hostility costs. Wildavsky goes on to name a number of costs that are incurred in the political process, such as reelection costs and reputation costs. His ideas are interesting and challenged the belief by economists that an economic measure of rationality is sufficient. Wildavsky's concept of additional costs suggests that there are other dimensions to *political rationality* that are not sufficiently covered by the traditional term *rationality* as used by economists. See Aaron Wildavsky, *The Politics of the Budgetary Process,* 2nd ed. (Boston: Little, Brown, 1974), pp. 189–194.

53. This description comes from George Gordon and Michael Milakovich, *Public Administrating in America,* p. 508. The idea of groupthink was developed by Irving Janis, *Groupthink,* 2nd ed. (Boston: Houghton Mifflin, 1982).

54. Graham T. Allison, *Essence of Decision: Explaining the Cuban Missile Crisis* (Boston: Little, Brown, 1971).

55. George Gordon and Michael Milakovich, *Public Administration in America,* p. 199. The original article in which the garbage can model was developed is Michael Cohen, James March, and Johan Olsen, "A Garbage Can Model of Organizational Choice," *Administrative Science Quarterly 17* (March 1972), pp. 1–25. The researchers used universities to illustrate organized anarchies, but the model appears to fit government equally as well.

56. Nicholas Henry, *Public Administration and Public Affairs,* 7th ed. (Upper Saddle River, NJ: Prentice-Hall, 1999), pp. 89–91.

57. It is presumed that a highly structured and centralized organization with strong leadership, direction, sense of mission, and clearly defined goals cannot be described as organized anarchy by definition.

58. The garbage can model does not argue that *all* organizations are organized anarchies or that organizations cannot be coherent structures. The point appears to be that some organizations become organized anarchies if the decision-making mechanisms become detached and coordination fails. Large universities are excellent examples because they are very diverse, autonomous organizations that perform many diverse tasks and have ambiguous goals, and many goals within the organization may conflict. For example, the goals of providing education and training and of conducting research can be conflicting goals.

59. The literature on decision making is extensive and goes far beyond what is presented in this book. For an excellent review of decision making as it relates to public administration, see George Gordon and Michael Milakovich, *Public Administration in America,* Chapter 6. Also see Anthony Downs, *An Economic Theory of Democracy* (New York: Harper & Row, 1957); David Braybrooke and Charles Lindblom, *A Strategy of Decision* (London: Collier-Macmillan, 1963); Herbert Simon, *Administrative Behavior,* 3rd ed. (New York: Free Press, 1976); Anthony Downs, *Inside Bureaucracy* (Boston: Little, Brown, 1967); Irving Janis, *Groupthink,* 2nd ed. (Boston: Houghton Mifflin, 1982); and Allan Lerner, *The Politics of Decision Making: Strategy, Cooperation, and Conflict* (Beverly Hills, CA: Sage, 1976).

60. See Allan Lerner and John Wanat, *Public Administration: A Realistic Reinterpretation of Contemporary Public Management.*

61. Henry Mintzberg, *The Nature of Managerial Work* (New York: Harper & Row, 1973), p. 171.

62. Kae Chung and Leon Megginson, *Organizational Behavior: Developing Managerial Skills* (New York: Harper & Row, 1981), Chapter 1.

63. Ibid.

64. Ibid.

65. Ibid.

66. Ibid.

67. A first-line manager is usually considered to be a foreperson or a low-level supervisor who is near an area of production. In the public sector, an example would be a supervisor over the processing of payroll checks. An example in the private sector would be a foreperson over a particular area of assembly line.

68. R. H. Guest, "Of Time and the Foreman," *Personnel* (May 1956), pp. 478–486.

69. Henry Mintzberg, *The Nature of Managerial Work,* pp. 31–35.

70. Herbert Kaufman, *The Administrative Behavior of Federal Bureau Chiefs* (Washington, DC: Brookings Institute, 1981), p. 87.

71. John Jackson and Timothy Keaveny, *Successful Supervision* (Englewood Cliffs, NJ: Prentice-Hall, 1980), p. 9.

72. Kae Chung and Leon Megginson, *Organizational Behavior: Developing Managerial Skills,* pp. 18–21.

73. M. W. McCall, "Leaders and Leadership: Of Substance and Shadow," in J. R. Hackman, E. E. Lawler, and L .W. Porter, Eds., *Perspectives on Behavior in Organizations* (New York: McGraw-Hill, 1977), pp. 375–386.

74. This section relies heavily on the work of Kae Chung and Leon Megginson, *Organizational Behavior: Developing Managerial Skills,* Chapter 1.

75. Robert Quinn, S. R. Faerman, M. P. Thompson, and M. R. McGrath, *Becoming a Master Manager: A Competency Based Framework,* 2nd ed. (New York: Wiley, 1996).

76. Clark Caskey, who used the term *nosecator* as an indicator of a manager's supervisory style, developed this idea. Caskey's diagram appears in Lawrence Steinmetz and H. Ralph Todd, *First-Line Management: Approaching Supervision Effectively,* p. 145. The original source is Clark Caskey, "Developing a Leadership Style," *Supervision* (April 1964).

77. Robert Blake and Jane Mouton, *The Managerial Grid* (Houston, TX: Gulf, 1964).

78. George Edwards, III, and Stephen Wayne, *Presidential Leadership: Politics and Policy Making* (New York: St. Martin's Press, 1990); Erwin Hargrove, *Presidential Leadership: Personality and Political Style* (New York: Macmillan, 1966); James MacGregor Burns, *Leadership* (New York: Harper & Row, 1978); James MacGregor Burns, *The Power to Lead: The Crisis of the American Presidency* (New York: Simon & Schuster, 1984); Richard Neustadt, *Presidential Power and the Modern Presidents: The Politics of Leadership from Roosevelt to Reagan* (New York: Free Press, 1990).

79. The terms *management* and *managership* often arise in the study of leadership. *Management* is a process of planning, organizing, coordinating, and controlling the activities of others to accomplish organizational goals. *Managership* is the authority to carry out these management functions.

80. R. M Stogdill and A. E. Coons, *Leadership Behavior: Its Description and Measurement* (Columbus, OH: Bureau of Business Research, Ohio State University, 1957); E. A. Fleishman, E. F. Harris, and H. E. Burtt, *Leadership and Supervision in Industry* (Columbus, OH: Bureau of Business Research, Ohio State University, 1955).

81. Francis Rourke, *Bureaucracy, Politics, and Public Policy,* 3rd ed. (Boston: Little, Brown, 1984), pp. 106–109.

82. Joseph Champoux, *Organizational Behavior: Essential Tenets for a New Millennium* (Mason, OH: South-Western, 2000), pp. 222–223.

83. Rensis Likert, *New Patterns of Management* (New York: McGraw-Hill, 1961), and *The Human Organization: Its Management and Value* (New York: McGraw-Hill, 1967).

84. Fred Fielder, *A Theory of Leadership Effectiveness* (New York: McGraw-Hill, 1967).

85. Joseph Champoux, *Organizational Behavior: Essential Tenets for a New Millennium,* p. 224.

86. Robert House, "A Path-Goal Theory of Leadership Effectiveness," *Administrative Science Quarterly 16* (1971), pp. 321–338.

87. Robert House, "Path-Goal Theory of Leadership: Lessons, Legacy and a Reformulated Theory," *The Leadership Quarterly 7,* (1996), pp. 323–352.

88. E. E. Jennings, *An Anatomy of Leadership* (New York: Harper & Row, 1960). Also see E. E. Jennings, "On Rediscovering the Leaders," in J. W. McGuire, Ed., *Contemporary Management Issues and Viewpoints* (Englewood Cliffs, NJ: Prentice-Hall, 1974), pp. 390–396.

89. B. M. Bass, *Leadership and Performance beyond Expectations* (New York: Free Press, 1985). Also see B. M. Bass, "From Transactional to Transformational Leadership: Learning to Share the Vision," *Organizational Dynamics 18* (1990), pp. 19–31. J. M. Burns is credited with developing the idea of transformational leadership; see *Leadership* (New York: Harper & Row, 1978).

90. R. Lord, R. Foti, and C. DeVader, "A Test of Leadership Categorization Theory: Internal Structure, Information Processing and Leadership Perceptions," *Organizational Behavior and Human Performance 34* (1984), pp. 343–378.

91. Abraham Maslow, "A Theory of Human Motivation," *Psychological Review 50* (1943), pp. 370–396.

92. Kae Chung and Leon Megginson, *Organizational Behavior: Developing Managerial Skills,* pp. 62–63.

93. Ibid.

94. Ibid.

95. Clayton Alderfer, *Existence, Relatedness, and Growth: Human Needs in Organizational Settings* (New York: Free Press, 1972).

96. Chris Argyris, *Personality and Organization: The Conflict Between System and the Individual,* p. 50.

97. Robert Lee, Jr., *Public Personnel Systems,* 2nd ed. (Rockville, MD: Aspen, 1987), pp. 282–283.

98. Frederick Herzberg, Bernard Mausner, and Barbara Snyderman, *The Motivation to Work* (New York: Wiley, 1964). Also see Herbert Simon "Organizational Man: Rational or Self-Actualizing," *Public Administration Review 33* (1973), pp. 346–353.

99. For an excellent presentation and discussion of theories of motivation as they apply to public administration, see Robert Lee, Jr., *Public Personnel Systems,* Chapters 11 and 12.

100. Robert Lee, Jr., *Public Personnel Systems,* p. 319.

101. Paul Hershey and Kenneth Blanchard made the idea of the "one-minute manager" popular during the 1980s. See Paul Hershey and Kenneth Blanchard, *Management of Organizational Behavior: Utilizing Human Resources,* 6th ed. (Englewood Cliffs, NJ: Prentice-Hall, 1993).

102. Robert Presthus, *The Organizational Society* (New York: Alfred Knopf, 1962).

103. Robert Lee, Jr., provides a very articulate critique of the shortcomings of motivation theories in *Public Personnel Systems,* pp. 319–322. Although his critique is far more detailed, many of the ideas used here are taken from his summary.

104. William Whyte, *The Organization Man* (New York: Simon & Schuster, 1956). Much of the book is available online at http://www.english.upenn.edu/~afilreis/50s/whyte-main.html.

105. Grover Starling, *Managing the Public Sector* (Belmont, CA: Wadsworth, 1993), p. 468.

106. Joseph Champoux provides an excellent summary of organizational culture in *Organizational Behavior: The Tenets for a New Millennium,* Chapter 4. Also see M. Alverson and P. O. Berg, *Corporate Culture and Organizational Symbolism* (Hawthorne, NY: Walter de Gruyter, 1992); Edgar Schein, *Organizational Culture and Leadership* (San Francisco: Jossey-Bass, 1992); T. E. Deal and A. A. Kennedy, *Corporate Cultures: The Rites and Rituals of Corporate Life* (Reading, MA: Addison-Wesley, 1982); Scott Cook and Dvora Yanow, "Culture and Organizational Learning," in Jay Shafritz and J. Steven Ott, Eds., *Classics of Organization Theory,* 5th ed. (Fort Worth, TX: Harcourt, 2001), pp. 400–413; Harrison Trice and Janice Beyer, "Changing Organizational Cultures," in Jay Shafritz and J. Steven Ott, Eds., *Classics of Organization Theory,* pp. 414–424.

107. There are a few exceptions regarding public agencies and organizations. For example, the culture of the U.S. Marine Corps has endured longer than that of any of America's great corporations. Some of the traditions extend back to 1775, and these traditions are used to strengthen the organization's culture. We are familiar with their public slogans—they are looking for a few good people, the proud, and that special person who will carry on the tradition of the Corps. The internal organizational culture of the Marines has been studied. They define themselves as the elite force of infantry that is highly disciplined, trained, and reliable. The Marine Corps has carved out a specialized niche that separates them from the other armed forces and has maintained it for a very long time by using traditions. Their motto is *Semper Fidelis* (Always Faithful). This example appears in Grover Starling, *Managing the Public Sector,* pp. 469–471. The original source for the example of the Marine Corps is R. Bonds, *The U.S. War Machine: An Encyclopedia of American Military Equipment and Strategy* (New York: Crown, 1983).

108. Grover Starling, *Managing the Public Sector,* p. 471.

109. Sometimes organizational cultures are not well aligned with the external environment, a concept known as *culture gap.* This was the case with the Los Angeles Police Department (LAPD). The culture emphasized crime control over crime prevention and a paramilitaristic approach to police work. Hard-nosed police work was rewarded and encouraged. After the Los Angeles riots that followed the Rodney King incident in 1991, the LAPD was forced to try to modify its organizational culture. See Grover Starling, *Managing the Public Sector,* p. 470.

110. Warren Bennis, "Organizational Developments and the Fate of Bureaucracy," *Industrial Management Review* (Spring 1966), pp. 41–55. For an interesting article about the survival needs of organizations, see Peter Drucker, "Business Objectives and Survival Needs: Notes on a Discipline of Business Enterprise," *Journal of Business 31* (April 1958), pp. 81–90.

111. Thomas Peters and Robert Waterman, *In Search of Excellence: Lessons from America's Best-Run Companies* (New York: Warner Books, 1988).

112. David Osborne and Ted Gaebler, *Reinventing Government: How the Entrepreneurial Spirit Is Transforming the Public Sector* (New York: Addison-Wesley, 1989).

113. David Osborne and Peter Plastrik, *Banishing Bureaucracy: Five Strategies for Reinventing Government* (New York: Addison-Wesley, 1997).

5

Basics of
Public Personnel
Administration

The citizens of today in every developed country are typically employees.
They work for one of the institutions. They look to the institutions
for their livelihood. They look to the institutions for their opportunities.
They look to the institutions for access to status and function in society,
as well as for personal fulfillment and achievement. . . .
Our society has become an employee society.

PETER DRUCKER

Public personnel administration is one of the core areas of public administration. It has a long and rich history and has gone through many
stages of development. Public personnel administration is involved with
virtually everything that relates to employment systems in the workplace,
including many social issues such as affirmative action, sexual harassment,
and other forms of discrimination. The field includes some detailed "nuts-
and-bolts" functions like using procedures for hiring employees, designing
tests, and ensuring that the workforce is well trained. This chapter provides
an overview of some of the fundamentals of public personnel administration.

As Peter Drucker noted many years ago, the United States is an "employee
society."[1] Virtually everyone works for an organization, often a rather large
one. The role of personnel administration, sometimes called human resource
management, has grown tremendously since the 1930s as public and private
organizations have come to realize that people are more than just commodi-

ties. The purpose of public personnel administration is to attract, hire, train, and maintain a productive, satisfied workforce. Personnel departments perform many roles such as examining job descriptions, creating classification systems, handling benefits, and many other functions. They do not provide any services directly to the public. They are *staff* departments (rather than *line* departments) that serve the larger organization. This role is the same in both the public and private sectors, but there are some distinct differences that affect public personnel administration.[2] Most of the differences are related to the nature of public versus private organizations.

DIFFERENCES BETWEEN PUBLIC AND PRIVATE PERSONNEL ADMINISTRATION

The *lack of a profit motive* is the most obvious difference between public and private sector organizations, and this greatly affects the way that personnel are used. The mission of businesses is to earn a profit, and one of the main ways this is done is by hiring only those people who are needed and organizing them in a way that promotes efficiency. Businesses must earn a profit to exist; few public sector organizations generate the funds that sustain their operations. The public sector typically provides collective goods or services—commonly referred to as public goods. In the private sector, it is easier to dismiss employees who do not perform. Government does not have the same incentive to keep labor costs low.

Related to the lack of a profit motive is the fact that *government agencies lack competition.* The public sector is monopolistic; there really is not any true competition. This affects many aspects of management and personnel administration. Citizens, for all practical purposes, do not have a choice about their service provider for police and fire protection or water and sewerage. Aside from complaining, the only choice citizens dissatisfied with the quality of water have in their jurisdiction is to move out of the district. People who are unhappy with the service at a private firm, such as Best Buy or Circuit City, have many other options because these firms have competition. Businesses have an incentive to try to satisfy customers. If they fail over a period of time, they will lose their customers to other firms. If this occurs too often, they may go out of business. And this is not uncommon in the marketplace. Businesses also attempt to keep operating costs low to remain competitive in the marketplace. There is no such incentive in the public sector due to the lack of competition. Moreover, if labor costs and other operating expenses rise, government can raise taxes. Corporations must either raise prices or find internal ways of reducing expenses.

In the private sector, labor costs are considered to be the most controllable of all expenses. When forecasts are missed, layoffs often occur. For example, when the powerful computer technology firm Intel missed its forecast during 2002, more than 4,000 employees were laid off. No such equivalent exists in the public sector. While layoffs do occur, they are minimized because of civil service protections and the power of public employee unions. The monopolistic nature of government is often criticized, but it also provides stability for society, albeit imperfect at times. Fortunes shift and change rapidly in the marketplace, but government must continue to exist. Bankruptcies are rare in government but occur regularly in the marketplace, sometimes even in larger firms.[3] Several corporate giants recently filed for bankruptcy, including Enron, W. R. Grace, and WorldCom. Enron was the largest corporate failure in American history at the time and wreaked havoc on the market. It failed primarily due to fraud that was hidden in its accounting practices. The Enron case triggered Congress to pass a new law to deal with corporate fraud, the first of its kind in our nation's history. The old, well-established firm of W. R. Grace filed for bankruptcy after being held responsible for years of pollution in Libby, Montana. Telecommunications giant WorldCom filed for bankruptcy after being caught in an accounting scandal that destroyed its access to capital.

The public sector is more labor-intensive than the private sector. The term *labor-intensive* refers to requiring a high degree of manual labor to achieve an output of some good or service. Government typically provides services rather than products. Many private sector corporations produce products that can be handled by machines. If it becomes cheaper to use machines rather than employees, private businesses will buy machines. In services areas where machines can be used, the private sector is faster in converting operations to machines than the public sector. Government often requires that a person handle the service. For example, the U.S. Postal Service has used sorting machines for years, but someone literally has to bring the mail to your house. It is hard to turn caseloads in social services over to machines; people must handle them. There are limits on the ability to use machines to replace firefighters, teachers, and police officers. However, the public sector is almost always the last to use new technologies. It lags behind in most every area that can increase efficiency of operations. This is partly to due to inertia in public bureaucracies and partly due to the success of public employee unions in protecting jobs.

Managers in the private sector have greater freedom over personnel matters. A corporation has flexibility in how it hires and fires people. Notwithstanding certain laws that have been imposed by government, such as occupational safety, unemployment compensation, equal employment opportunity, and labor relations, private managers are free to handle most personnel matters as they see fit. Public administrators are bound by red tape and complicated rules that guide personnel decisions. Although government does impose many rules that affect personnel matters in the private sector, the rules set by civil service and public employee unions are usually more rigid. *Authority is less structured in the public sector.* In a private corporation, an employee usually has little doubt about who is in charge or how the chain of command works. In government, authority is more confusing because of the executive and legislative powers. Legislatures make laws, provide funding, and impose rules, but the executive branch also imposes rules and standards. Moreover, the executive branch consists of elected and appointed officials. In theory, there should not be any real conflict. The legislature is supposed to make laws, fund agencies, and let the executive branch execute the law. But in reality, there is more confusion largely because of the dependency of funding. Agencies must maintain good ties with the legislature to ensure that funding continues. The lines of authority are mixed and often conflicting. This should not be the case if Weberian bureaucracy is followed, but reality and theory are often very different.

Amateurs often serve as the heads of public agencies. Private firms are typically led by more experienced executives who will stay with the organization much longer than the heads and high-ranking officials stay in the public sector. The heads of agencies are often selected because of their policy views and ties to the chief executive. Thus, partisan politics is often at the core of their selection; their managerial skills are secondary. In the private sector, managers are usually picked because of their knowledge and technical skills. They are selected because executives believe they can get the job done. This does not mean that the heads of agencies are bad managers, but the criteria used for selection are different. In fact, the heads of agencies and government bureaus often come directly from the private sector. For example, the comptroller general, David M. Walker (the head of the Government Accounting Office), was a former partner in the accounting giant, Arthur Andersen LLP.[4]

Government also uses its personnel systems for multiple purposes. In the private sector, employees are hired for the sole purpose of making products or delivering services, which is directed toward an economic end—making money. Employees in the public sector are hired to perform tasks and deliver services, but the system is also designed to accommodate other functions. For example, government jobs are often used to reward the politically faithful. Patronage has always been a part of government employment. Government employment is also used to reward special categories of people, such as military veterans. Government employment is sometimes used to stimulate the economy. Hiring people during hard economic times makes the personnel system either part of the economic system or a disguised form of welfare, depending on one's point of view. Government personnel systems may be used to achieve socially desirable goals, such as hiring people with physical disabilities. At one time there was a quota system used in the Washington, DC, area that limited the number of people who could be hired from each state. The intention was to make the federal bureaucracy more representative of the population. This practice was stopped in 1978.

Some similarities do exist between the public and private sector personnel systems. Both the public and private sectors employ millions of workers (the total workforce is about 140 million).[5] There are many very small governments in the nation that employ only a few people, just like there are very small businesses that are family owned and operated. There are also giant bureaus like the Department of Defense just like there are giant corporations like General Motors that employ thousands of workers. There is also a great diversity of jobs in each sector. Government employment includes most of the professions (lawyers, physicians, dentists, engineers, and the like). The range of employment includes nuclear scientists, janitors, chemists, clerical workers, and managers. The same is true for the private sector.

Both public and private sector employment has grown tremendously over the years. In the private sector, employment increased because of industrialization and because women entered the workforce in great numbers after World War II. "Rosie the Riveter" never went back to being a housewife after the war was over. The workforce has grown to about 140 million people, and most work in the private sector. Since the Founding Period, federal employment has slowly grown over time, but the fastest period of growth occurred between the Great Depression and World War II. In the early 1930s there were roughly 600,000 federal employees, but by the end of World War II the federal government employed more than 4 million people. The figure quickly dropped to 3 million immediately following the war. The federal budget also has continued to grow. In 1947, the federal budget was $35 billion; the 2003 budget was more than $2.3 trillion. But federal employment has remained relatively stable since the end of World War II (between 2 and 3 million workers since 1950). State and local employment has continued to grow, and surpassed federal employment long ago. State and local governments currently employ roughly 19 million workers. In 1947, local governments employed about 3 million workers; now they employ more than 11 million workers (or 61 percent of the total public workforce). Most of these employees are schoolteachers (about 40 percent). Today, about one out of every six jobs is a government job, but the federal government remains the nation's largest single employer, currently employing around 3 million workers.

EVOLUTION OF PUBLIC EMPLOYMENT IN THE UNITED STATES

From the Gentleman's Administrations of Colonial Elites, through Spoils and Patronage, to the Merit System

Public personnel administration has gone through an evolutionary process in the way that it staffs the offices of government.[6] During the Founding Period, there were very few government agencies and few employees. Those who worked for government were typically selected using a "fitness of character" standard. That is, those who were well educated, had good reputations, and were persons of character were selected for government service. The concept of "fitness of character" had no relationship to technical competence in the modern sense of the term. This was basically an administrative aristocracy. By George Washington's second term, political parties had truly emerged. George Washington and John Adams tended to appoint people from the colonial elite, but most of these people happened to be Federalists (the political party of Washington and Adams). Nepotism was common; appointees were often related to one another. But the average citizen was simply not of suitable "fitness of character" for many government positions. About two-thirds of the highest appointments went to those from the gentry, merchant, and professional classes.[7] When Thomas Jefferson was elected in 1800, he sought to bring balance to the composition by using his appointment power to grant jobs to anti-Federalists. He is sometimes called the *father of patronage* for his efforts. However, both the Federalist and anti-Federalists were usually colonial elites, and they ran the administrative apparatus that existed at the time. Although it may have been a "gentleman's administration," both Adams and Jefferson made plenty of new appointments and tossed out many of the previous administration's appointees. They had no problem relieving those who might not be supportive of their administration.[8] Thus, they were political gentleman, and the seeds of patronage were sown early in the nation's history. Government was very small; the largest department was the post office. America was an agrarian economy, and life, by modern standards, was relatively simple. This era, which lasted from 1789 until 1829, is sometimes called the *guardian period*.

The *spoils and patronage era* (1829–1883) is usually associated with the presidency of Andrew Jackson. The term *spoils system* is attributed to a comment made by Senator William Marcy of New York. Marcy coined the phrase, "to the victor belong the spoils of the enemy." Jackson actually did not remove and appoint people much differently from the way his predecessors did. What Jackson did do differently was transfer the bureaucracy from the gentleman's class to political parties. The rule of the gentleman's class ended during Jackson's administration, and patronage became the norm. He is also credited with allowing the public service to become a corrupt system filled with bribes and graft. Those who followed Jackson would make more blatant use of the spoils system and patronage. The Jacksonian era was also characterized by the democratization of America. Voting requirements, such as property ownership and poll taxes, were removed, and the size of the electorate and the public's interest in politics greatly increased. In 1824, there were 356,000 voters (27 percent of the total electorate), but sixteen years later, 2.4 million persons voted (80 percent of the electorate).[9] It was also during this period that the strength of political parties increased tremendously. In fact, this era was the "golden years" for political parties. Mass voting required strong party organization to win elections. Much of the population could not read, so party workers had to disseminate information. This was a very labor-intensive process and created great numbers of people who would seek government jobs if their party won the election.

Political patronage had advantages and disadvantages. Because government was still relatively simple, high levels of expertise were not needed for most government jobs. Political patronage provided a government bureaucracy that was loyal and responsive to the president (or the mayor or governor, since the same phenomenon was occurring at the state and local level). Patronage also spawned a route for upward mobility for the lower classes, particularly at the municipal level where political machines depended heavily on the poorer classes and immigrants to remain in power. The middle and upper classes were moving to the outlying areas of cities to escape the graft and corruption of political machines. Patronage also created enormous inefficiency due to high turnover and featherbedding (the practice of hiring more people than needed), and it provided no protection for workers who wanted to stay out of politics. Government workers were often expected to contribute part of their paycheck to the party. Patronage also hindered career development, since workers were generally removed if their party lost the election. Thus, it was difficult to develop a stable, professional administration with continuity from one administration to the next.

Some attempted to reform the patronage system. In 1853, Congress passed an amendment to an appropriations bill that required examinations for selecting clerical workers. The law was often abused, but it did establish the use of examinations in the federal civil service. In 1871 Congress passed another amendment to an appropriations bill that gave the president power to establish rules for personnel administration. Ulysses Grant used this new authority to appoint a civil service commission that drafted rules that would have greatly reduced patronage, but Congress would not fund the new system.[10] Reform efforts continued, but reform would not come until President James Garfield was assassinated by an angry job-seeker in 1881. By this time, many reformers believed that experts, rather than political hacks, should run the agencies of government.

Reform finally came in 1883 when Congress passed the Pendleton Act, which was signed into law by President Chester Arthur. The official title was "A Bill to Regulate and Improve the Civil Service of the United States." It was named after Senator George Pendleton, a Democrat from Ohio. The new law included competitive exams, protection from dismissal for political reasons, protection from political coercion, and the establishment of a bipartisan Civil Service Commission that would oversee the system. The Office of Personnel Management and the Merit Systems Protection Board replaced the Civil Service Commission in 1978. Although only 10 percent of federal workers were covered under the new law (mainly clerical workers in Washington and employees at large post offices), it marked the true beginning of reform. Some states followed by passing their own versions of the Pendleton Act (New York in 1883 and Massachusetts in 1884), but most states did nothing. The British civil service system had been influential in creating the new law, but the American version had some different aspects. Like the British system, civil service examinations were competitive, and the intent was to have a neutral civil service free from partisan pressure. But the American system used "practical exams" and allowed lateral entry into the system. The British used intelligence tests and forced everyone to start at the lowest grade. Also, there were no ties to higher education in American civil service. The British had strong ties between universities and their civil services. Upgrading the education requirements of the federal bureaucracy would not take place until the 1930s. The new civil service system did not establish an administrative class; political executives occupied the upper echelon. But the Pendleton Act introduced the idea of the *merit principle* into the civil service system. The merit principle holds that civil service employees should be hired, retained, and promoted based on their technical competence and performance rather than on the political whims of those in power. From 1883 until the present day, the American civil service system has operated under the merit principle.

The reform movement involved other issues besides civil service reform (it was only one part of the larger reform movement), and much of the focus was at the local level. Partisan politics had created widespread corruption, especially at the state and local levels. Scandals were commonplace. Lucrative contracts were awarded to favored businesses. Much of the corruption was tolerated until budget surpluses became deficits in the very late 1800s. Reformers blamed partisan politics; they called for reforms that would limit the power of political parties and would create competent, professional government. Many reforms were advocated and implemented during the late 1800s and early 1900s. With great assistance from reform-minded presidents like Theodore Roosevelt and Woodrow Wilson, the reform movement at the local level sought to clean up the corruption and graft associated with the partisan practices of political machines. There were several types of reformers. Some sought to clean up government by bringing in better people. Others sought to use science to clean up government by implementing systems and principles that worked. The reforms included many structural reforms such as the council-manager form of government, line item budgets, shorter ballots (electing fewer public officials), primaries, at-large elections to break up the ward system that machine bosses used to control cities, and nonpartisan elections. At the state level, more power was granted to governors who were also allowed longer terms in office, greater appointment power, and succession. Reformers revised state constitutions and limited the length of legislative sessions in many states. The leaders of the reform movement were not everyday citizens. They were lawyers, editors, clergymen, academicians, and businesspeople.

Forces other than the reformers helped to end the spoils system and political patronage, as practiced in the 1800s. The new civil service system was slowly expanded to include more workers, and presidents used their power to "freeze in" or "lock in" their party's workers by issuing executive orders before they left office. Congress also played this game by using legislation to "blanket in" political appointees from the ruling political party. These self-interested political maneuvers on the part of presidents and Congress to protect their party's workers had the long-term effect of slowly ending *old-style* patronage by protecting existing jobs. Civil service rules regulated how new workers would be selected and limited the influence of parties on existing workers. There was also an attempt to separate politics from administration to bring *neutral competence* to administration at all levels of government. Although advocated at the turn of the 20th century and partly implemented by President Theodore Roosevelt's Civil Service Rule I in 1907, the Hatch Act,[11] originally passed in 1939, further insulated workers from politics by restricting government workers from participating in the political process.[12] The Hatch Act would later be loosened to allow greater participation, but at the time (and for many years) it effectively insulated government workers.[13] (See Box 5.1 for the current guidelines of the Hatch Act.) Unions also contributed to the demise of patronage. To protect their members, unions opposed dismissals for political reasons.

BOX 5.1 The Federal Hatch Act

The Hatch Act restricts the political activity of executive branch employees of the federal government, the District of Columbia government, and certain state and local agencies. In 1993, Congress passed legislation that substantially amended the Hatch Act, allowing most federal and Washington, DC, employees to engage in many types of political activity.

With the 1993 amendments, most federal and Washington, DC, government employees are now permitted to take an active part in political management or in political campaigns. But these employees are still subject to certain restrictions (see below). However, some federal agencies and categories of employees continue to be prohibited from engaging in partisan political activity.

Federal Hatch Act Do's
Federal employees *can*—

- be candidates for public office in nonpartisan elections
- register and vote as they choose
- assist in voter registration drives
- express opinions about candidates and issues
- contribute money to political organizations
- attend political fundraising functions
- attend and be active at political rallies and meetings
- join and be an active member of a political party or club

- sign nominating petitions
- campaign for or against referendum questions, constitutional amendments, and municipal ordinances
- campaign for or against candidates in partisan elections
- make campaign speeches for candidates in partisan elections
- distribute campaign literature in partisan elections
- hold office in political clubs or parties

Federal Hatch Act Don'ts
Federal employees *cannot*—

- use official authority or influence to interfere with an election
- solicit or discourage political activity of anyone with business before their agency
- solicit or receive political contributions (may be done in certain limited situations by federal labor or other employee organizations)
- be candidates for public office in partisan elections
- engage in political activity while:
  - on duty
  - in a government office
  - wearing an official uniform
  - using a government vehicle
- wear partisan political buttons on duty

SOURCE: U.S. Office of Special Counsel Web site, http://www.osc.gov.

The economy also helped to bring an end to patronage. The economy was growing rapidly with better paying jobs than those available in the public sector. This made public sector jobs less attractive. The nature of many government jobs also changed. As political machines slowly faded, government had to pick up the gap in social services and deal with the increased regulation of business. Thus, government jobs became increasingly more technical and required better trained and educated employees. The turn of the 20th century has also been called the *era of scientific management*. Frederick Taylor's principles affected public personnel management. Scientific management helped widen the scope of the merit system at the federal level and assist in the development of professional government at the local level. Great time and effort were expended in developing new tools of personnel administration, such as job descriptions, position classifications, tests, and productivity measurements. It was only a matter of time until the civil service system extended its coverage. In 1883, only about 10 percent of federal workers were covered, but by 1930, about 80 percent of nonmilitary employees were covered under the civil service system.[14]

Scientific management also strengthened the idea of the politics–administration dichotomy. Given the mess created by partisan politics and political machines, many sought to remove politics from administration. The New York Bureau of Municipal Research was the first of many such bureaus that would spring up in other cities. The bureaus provided a link between scientific management and the public sector. Their staffs developed better job descriptions, productivity measures, training programs, and better practical examinations. Application of the principles of scientific management was aimed at increasing government efficiency, something that had been lacking throughout the history of government service in the United States. The *scientific management period* lasted from 1906 until 1937.[15] This fit well within the context of classical public administration, which also sought to remove politics and enhance efficiency in governmental administration.

By the 1930s, civil service was moving into a new phase characterized by administrative management and the increase of people from professions such as medicine, the sciences, and law.[16] This period lasted roughly from 1937 to 1970. The New Deal programs brought a new view of the role of government. Because of the magnitude of the problems the nation faced due to the Great Depression, many believed that a positive role existed for government to be actively involved in trying to resolve the multitude of problems. *Management* became the new goal of public personnel administration. Efficiency remained the dominant value, but efficiency, it was believed, could be achieved only through effective management. The Brownlow Report was presented to President Franklin Roosevelt in 1937. The report was critical of the Civil Service Commission's past focus on narrowly defined technical and specialized bureaucrats and positions; it emphasized the need for more *generalist* managers. The report also blurred the distinction between politics and administration. People in public service were viewed as having policy and political roles in addition to administrative roles. President Roosevelt issued an executive order that required establishing a professional personnel office in all major agencies. Personnel administration became as much a part of management as budgeting, planning, or the other functions associated with public administration. The thrust of the Brownlow committee's recommendation was to reorganize the executive branch, but Roosevelt's proposals were defeated in Congress by well-entrenched special interests. Roosevelt did manage to make a number of other changes, including creating the Executive Office of the President (EOP).

Efforts for additional reform continued, particularly regarding the relationship between political appointees and career administrators. The history of civil service had focused mostly on positions and grades, with little attention on how political appointees and career bureaucrats interact (aside from efforts to insulate the civil service employees from political abuse). The second Hoover commission (1953) recommended creating a new senior service level. These officials would be politically neutral career types, like those found in most western European nations. Moreover, they would be transferable from agency to agency. Thus, they would be *generalist* administrators. The recommendation was rejected in the late 1950s but was revived and adopted in 1978 as the Senior Executive Service.[17]

During the 1950s, another value was entering into public personnel administration that involved a shift to the professions. Between 1955 and 1970, the number of professionals, such as lawyers, scientists, and physicians, grew tremendously. In 1970, 40 percent of all civil service employees were professionals of some type. This figure has remained around this level for the past 30 years but is predicted to increase in the new century. The merit system had replaced old-style patronage, although the system still allowed political appointees (the newer version of patronage). Since 1970, public personnel administration has been characterized by professional public administration. The idea of building personnel systems around *positions* is no longer present. Today the system is build around the *person*. Since the 1970s, public personnel systems have made politics, administration, and the professions central to the practice of public administration.[18] And, by the late 1980s, 90 percent of all federal workers were covered under a merit system.

The federal civil service has evolved from a gentleman's administration dependent upon the established elites of the Founding Period, through rampant patronage wedded to the spoils system, to a merit-based system that seeks to hire the most qualified workers and provide protection from political coercion. Moreover, the system has changed from one dominated by positions filled with technically competent nonprofessionals to one that is increasingly becoming dominated by the professions. A similar pattern can be found in most state and many local civil service systems. But the merit system was not a panacea. It too would be challenged. The basic principles of merit are shown in Box 5.2. The merit system would come under fire for failing to embody newer values associated with minority and gender representation as well as various forms of discrimination during the 1970s. Other laws were passed over the years that amended the federal civil service to enhance the merit principle, such as the Intergovernmental Personnel Act of 1970 and the Civil Service Reform Act of 1978. The latter act greatly altered the federal personnel system. These two laws were similar in many ways, and both included most of the provisions shown in Box 5.2. Both supported the idea of hiring qualified workers, but the 1978 law added the idea of recruiting from all segments of society. This was designed to increase representation. Both laws supported equal pay for equal work, but the 1978 law emphasized the use of pay as an incentive and recognition for performance. Both laws adhere to the idea of retaining competent workers and dismissing incompetent workers. Nondiscrimination provisions are found in both laws, but the 1978 law extends coverage to marital status, age, and physical

---

BOX 5.2   The Basic Principles of Merit

1. Recruitment should be of qualified individuals from appropriate sources in an endeavor to achieve a workforce that is representative of all segments of society. Selection should be determined solely on the basis of relative ability, knowledge, and skills, after fair and open competition, which ensures that all receive equal opportunity.

2. All employees should receive fair and equitable treatment in all aspects of personnel management without regard to political affiliation, race, color, national origin, sex, marital status, or handicapped condition, and with proper regard for their privacy and constitutional rights.

3. Equal pay should be provided for work of equal value, with appropriate consideration of both national and local rates of pay by employers in the private sector, and appropriate incentives and recognition should be provided for excellence in performance.

4. All employees should maintain high standards of integrity, conduct, and concern for the public interest.

5. The federal workforce should be used efficiently and effectively.

6. Employees should be retained on the basis of the adequacy of their performance; inadequate performance should be corrected, and employees should be separated who cannot or will not improve their performance to meet required standards.

7. Employees should be provided effective education and training when education and training would result in better organizational and individual performance.

8. Employees should be protected against arbitrary, personal favoritism or coercion for partisan political purposes, and prohibited from using their official authority or influence for the purpose of interfering with or affecting the result of an election or a nomination for election.

9. Employees should be protected against reprisal for the lawful disclosure of information that they reasonably believe evidences a violation of any law, rule, or regulation or mismanagement, a gross waste of funds, an abuse of authority, or a substantial and specific danger to public health or safety.

SOURCE: Adapted from Robert Lee, Jr., *Public Personnel Systems,* 2nd ed. (Gaithersburg, MD: Aspen, 1987). The principles listed come from the Civil Service Reform Act of 1978 (P.L. 95-454, 92 Stat. 1111, 1978). These principles apply to the federal civil service.

---

disabilities. Both laws are opposed to partisan influence on merit employees. The 1978 act included some important new principles that modified the federal practice of merit that should be emphasized.

- *Employees are to have high standards of integrity, conduct, and concern for the public interest.* This was partly a response to the Watergate era.

- *Employees should not be penalized for disclosing information about violations of the law, mismanagement, and abuses of authority.* This was known as the "whistleblower" provision and also was a reflection of the mood during the Watergate era.

■ *Employees are to be used efficiently and effectively.* This provision reflected the growing concern that personnel systems are so filled with red tape that effective administration is difficult, if not impossible, to attain. Personnel administration has been referred to as the "triumph of techniques over purpose"; that is, the techniques and methodologies become more important than accomplishing something.[19]

Despite attempts to modify the federal civil service and accommodate demands from minorities for greater equity, the system remained under fire until the idea of affirmative action was fully embraced and an institutional commitment was made to eradicate discrimination in the workplace. The federal government did embrace these practices through laws and internal policies. Box 5.3 shows the major laws passed by Congress with a brief description of each.

CHALLENGES TO THE MERIT SYSTEM: EQUAL EMPLOYMENT OPPORTUNITY, AFFIRMATIVE ACTION, AND REPRESENTATIVE BUREAUCRACY

The merit principle has been a part of the civil service, in varying degrees, since the passage of the Pendleton Act in 1883. It took more than 100 years to get most federal employees (90 percent) covered by merit systems. The merit system was believed to be a way to eliminate or minimize appointments of political hacks to government positions. Classical personnel administration theory was based heavily on the principles of scientific management and Weberian bureaucratic theory. These ideas worked well for building a personnel system based on technical competence and positions. The goals were to get qualified people who could perform their jobs free of political influence (which the Hatch Act provided), situated in a hierarchical organizational structure. The merit system was well suited for attaining such a system. The merit system was based largely on creating standardized practical tests for positions. But between 1934 and 1982, a standardized, multiple-choice test (the PACE exam) was used to select recent college graduates for employment in a variety of federal agencies. This test, like the standardized SAT tests that students typically take to get admitted into college, measured verbal and mathematical abilities thought to be relevant to administrative and professional positions. These tests were believed to be objective with no biases against minorities. Over time, however, it was found that minorities tended to score lower on the tests than white males.

During the 1960s, classical personnel administration theory began to be criticized. Managers complained that civil service rules protected the "deadwood" in government and hindered good management. The civil rights movement questioned the way that government jobs were allocated. The idea of merit had been defined as expertise, but critics argued that academic degrees and previous education and training often indicated social status and political power as much as ability. Critics believed that minorities had been excluded from educational

BOX 5.3 Major Equal Employment Opportunity Laws

Civil Rights Act of 1866 Guarantees to all persons (i.e., nonwhites and noncitizens) the same rights as "white citizens" (42 U.S.C. § 1981). The Civil Rights Act of 1991 broadened section 1981 and clarifies that racial harassment and discrimination are prohibited in employment and in contracts.

Fourteenth Amendment to the U.S. Constitution (1868) Contains a clause prohibiting states from depriving any person of life, liberty, or property without due process of law and from denying any person the equal protection of the laws.

Civil Rights Act of 1871 Allows citizens to sue local government officials (and individuals) who deprive citizens of any constitutional or federal statutory rights (42 U.S.C. § 1983).

Executive Order 8802 (1941) Issued by President Franklin Roosevelt to prohibit discrimination in the federal civil service and by defense contractors. Established the Fair Employment Practices Committee to investigate and resolve complaints of discrimination.

Equal Pay Act of 1963 Is an amendment to the Fair Labor Standards Act of 1938 that prohibits discrimination in compensation based on gender for work requiring equal skill, effort, and responsibility under similar working conditions.

Civil Rights Act of 1964 (Title VII) Prohibits employers, employment agencies, and labor organizations from discriminating on the basis of race, color, religion, sex, and national origin. It was amended in 1972 to apply to both public and private employers with 15 or more employees. (This remains the centerpiece of all the civil rights legislation.)

Age Discrimination Act of 1967 Prohibits discrimination on the basis of age in hiring, discharge, and terms, conditions, and privileges of employment by employers with 20 or more workers and by unions and employment agencies. It was amended in 1986 to specifically cover individuals 40 years of age and older. The law also applies to state and local governments.

Equal Employment Opportunity Act of 1972 Amended the Civil Rights Act to extend coverage to public sector employers and to provide the Equal Employment Opportunity Commission with enforcement powers.

Rehabilitation Act of 1973 Prohibits the federal government, government contractors, and programs receiving federal financial assistance from discriminating against individuals on the basis of physical or mental handicaps.

Pregnancy Act of 1978 Amended the Civil Rights Act to prohibit employers from discriminating against individuals on the basis of pregnancy, childbirth, or medical conditions related to childbirth.

Americans with Disabilities Act of 1990 Prohibits public and private employers with 15 or more employees from discriminating against individuals with disabilities in employment, and requires employers to make reasonable accommodations.

Civil Rights Act of 1991 Allows individuals to receive punitive and compensatory damages under the Civil Rights Act, Americans with Disabilities Act, and Rehabilitation Act if they can establish "malice and reckless indifference to federally protected rights." It also places the burden on the employer to defend practices that adversely affect individuals in protected categories.

SOURCE: Adapted from David Shuman and Dick Olufs, *Public Administration in the United States,* 2nd ed. (Lexington, MA: D. C. Heath, 1993), pp. 289–290.

opportunities in the past, which locked them into low-paying jobs. Their inability to advance was caused by discrimination more so than by their capability. Merit was not an objective process but a discriminatory procedure that favored white males and allowed them to maintain their political power. The merit system was viewed as a *new form of patronage,* one that protected a class of people rather than a political party. Congress passed a series of laws, but many of the laws were contradictory. The Veterans Preference Act of 1944 provided for preferential treatment of veterans, but most veterans were white males. The Civil Rights Act of 1964 and the Equal Employment Opportunity Act of 1972 forbid discrimination on the basis of race, sex, religion, or national origin, but the Age Discrimination in Employment Act of 1967, which prohibits discrimination for those 40 years of age or older, was viewed as a way to lock in white males, thus further restricting the opportunities for minorities. While many laws seemed to be intended to help minorities, other laws seemed to hinder the progress of minorities. Thus, a new set of values entered into public personnel administration that challenged the merit principle, which many had worked hard to make a reality for more than a century.

The civil rights movement was much broader and attempted to help minorities gain access to many opportunities aside from positions in public service. Segregation in the South was perhaps the largest of the issues at the time, but gaining access to higher education, employment, and better housing were of paramount concern. Originally, the civil rights movement was primarily a movement that involved African Americans, but it soon expanded to include many other groups such as Hispanics, Native Americans, and women. With regard to the civil service and employment opportunities, the central concept became the ideas surrounding affirmative action. *Affirmative action* is defined as a planned, aggressive, coherent, management program designed to promote equal employment opportunity for disadvantaged groups—those who have historically been the victims of discrimination. This was one of the most controversial public policies in the nation's history, and few areas were affected more than public personnel systems. Affirmative action holds that due to past discriminatory practices, certain groups have been left out of the process or have become locked into the lower socioeconomic strata and into lower-paying occupations. It is argued that the "playing field" is neither level nor fair, and that deliberate action by government is needed to make the field level. The goal is to increase opportunities for minorities through positive government action backed by laws. Thus, civil rights require greater governmental action to provide special treatment for certain groups.

Typically, the argument for affirmative action holds that if the playing field were level, all segments of society should be represented by the proportionate amount of minorities. That is, if a state such as Mississippi has an African-American population of 35 percent, then, in theory, African Americans should fill 35 percent of the available positions. Since the contemporary definition of *minority* includes women, the proportion should also be that half of all positions should go to females. Even the most adamant proponents of affirmative action know that such a goal will take time to achieve, since minorities are at a disadvantage and have not had the same levels of education, training, and opportunities as white males. Thus, it is assumed that affirmative action will take some time to accomplish. Through the use of quotas, better education and training, and hard-fought political and legal battles, minorities have made considerable progress in both the public and private sectors, but they still have not reached the desired levels.

Table 5.1 illustrates the composition of women and minorities in federal employment in selected years. The figures shown in the table do not reflect the breakdown by pay scales. (See Table 5.2 and Table 5.3 for a breakdown by pay rank and pay scales for women, blacks, and Hispanics.). Typically, women and minorities are better represented in the lower general service pay scales. For example, in 1970 women comprised 72 percent of all GS-1 through GS-6 jobs (these are the lowest general service grades). By 1980, women comprised 74 percent of the same scales. Ten years later, the figure had risen to 76 percent. In 1989, women only represented 9 percent of the highest general service scales used at that time, GS-16 through GS-18. They represented 17 percent of the next lower scale of jobs, GS-13 through GS-15, in 1989.[20] Thus, the gender gap is rather large when one looks at the types of positions that women hold. This is slowly changing. Proponents of affirmative action argue that aggressive efforts have been made to recruit and promote women.[21]

Although affirmative action has been very controversial, it is now well embedded in personnel policy in both the public and private sectors. The way it is supposed to work is either by setting aside a certain number of positions to try to bring about better racial or gender balance, or by giving an advantage to minority candidates who are qualified for the positions. In some cases, to compensate for imbalance in the racial or gender composition of a workforce, affirmative action hires can be used. In such cases, the job listing clearly indicates that the organization seeks qualified minority candidates, and only minority candidates are considered. Critics of affirmative action have argued that it is nothing more than legalized discrimination and that quotas and other techniques should be illegal on their face value. During the 1980s, President Reagan played down the use of quotas and affirmative action, calling for a "color-blind society." Reagan was able to win a restructuring of the Civil

Table 5.1 Women and Minorities in the Federal Civilian Workforce for Selected Years

Employment Group	1970	1980	1990	2000
Blacks	12%	16%	17%	18%
Hispanics	2%	5%	5%	6%
All women	33%	39%	43%	44%
All men	77%	61%	57%	56%

NOTE: The percentages have been rounded. The figures exclude postal workers.

SOURCE: *The Fact Book: Federal Civilian Workforce Statistics* (Washington, DC: Office of Personnel Management, 2001), and U.S. Bureau of the Census, *Statistical Abstract of the United States* (Washington, DC: U.S. Government Printing Office, various years).

Table 5.2 Full-Time Employment of Blacks and Hispanics in the Federal Government by Rank and Pay System, 1985 and 2000

Pay System	1985 Black	1985 Hispanic	2000 Black	2000 Hispanic
All pay systems	16%	5%	17%	6%
General service and related	73%	68%	80%	86%
Grades 1–4 ($13,870–$24,833)	32%	26%	9%	73%
Grades 5–8 ($21,370–$38,108)	40%	34%	33%	27%
Grades 9–12 ($32,380–$61,040)	24%	33%	27%	32%
Grades 13–15 ($55,937–$100,897)	5%	7%	10%	12%
Total executive senior service pay levels	N/A	N/A	.09%	.04%
Wage pay systems	25%	29%	14%	15%
Other pay systems	1%	3%	4%	6%

NOTE: The pay rates are for 2000; the data exclude postal workers. Percentages have been rounded and may not total 100 percent.

SOURCE: Derived from U.S. Bureau of the Census, *Statistical Abstract of the United States* (Online version, 2001). The 1985 data come from Nicholas Henry, *Public Administration and Public Affairs,* 7th ed. (Upper Saddle River, NJ: Prentice-Hall, 1999), p. 326.

Table 5.3 Full-Time Employment of Women in the Federal Government by Rank and Pay System, 1970, 1980, 1989, and 1998

Pay System	1970	1980	1989	1998
All pay systems	33%	39%	48%	45%
General service and related	40%	45%	49%	50%
Grades 1–4 ($13,870–$24,833)	72%	74%	76%	69%
Grades 5–8 ($21,370–$38,108)	33%	46%	54%	70%
Grades 9–12 ($32,380–$61,040)	10%	19%	33%	44%
Grades 13–15 ($55,937–$100,897)	3%	8%	17%	23%
Grades 16–18 ($69,451–$78,200)	1%	4%	9%	N/A
Other pay systems	46%	36%	40%	44%

NOTE: The pay rates are for 2000 except for GS-16 to GS-18, which are for 1989; all data exclude postal workers.

SOURCE: Derived from U.S. Bureau of the Census, *Statistical Abstract of the United States* (Online version, 2001), and Office of Personnel Management, *Demographic Profile of the Federal Workforce* (Online version, September 2000). The 1970, 1980, and 1989 data come from Nicholas Henry, *Public Administration and Public Affairs,* 7th ed. (Upper Saddle River, NJ: Prentice-Hall, 1999), p. 327.

Rights Commission that now allows the president to appoint four of the eight members and to name the chairperson. Although the commission is an advisory committee, it has tended to downplay quotas since the 1980s.[22]

There has been considerable debate over affirmative action, and some states, such as California, Louisiana, Washington, and Florida, have dropped their affirmative action programs. In 1996, California placed an initiative on the ballot

(Proposition 209) that even caused former President Bill Clinton to visit the state to lobby against the initiative. Californians approved the initiative.[23] Public opinion polls suggest that most Americans do not support affirmative action,[24] but it is still official federal public policy backed by federal laws and many court rulings (though the courts have ruled inconsistently over the years). The performance appraisal systems used at the federal level include supervisors' affirmative action records as part of their appraisal.

Affirmative action has reached a crossroads. Critics argue that the playing field has never been level for anyone and that the contention that the status quo only protects white males is an unfounded argument.[25] Moreover, the status quo may protect the privileged classes, which does not include "all white males." Those harmed most by affirmative action have not been the wealthy and well-educated elite, but the low- and middle-class workers whose jobs are more often affected. Controversial books like George Gilder's *Wealth and Poverty* and Murray and Herrnstein's *The Bell Curve* exacerbated the debate during the late 1980s and 1990s.[26] In 1991, Congress passed another Civil Rights Act to negate some of the Supreme Court's rulings[27] and to make it clear that affirmative action was still federal policy. Many of the battles over affirmative action have been fought in Congress and courtrooms. To date, there is a long legal history dealing with affirmative action and related public personnel matters. Some of the major court cases include the following:

- *Griggs v. Duke Power Company* (1971).[28] The case stemmed from the use by Duke Power (a large utility firm located in North and South Carolina) of high school diplomas as a minimum educational qualification and their use of intelligence tests in their process for promotion and advancement. Black employees argued that the practice had an "adverse impact" on minorities. The U.S. Supreme Court agreed and forbid the use of intelligence tests in hiring and promotion systems. The case validated that testing must be job-related and content valid (meaning that the tests accurately measure skills needed to perform the job).

- *Albemarle Paper Company v. Moody* (1975).[29] The U.S. Supreme Court ruled that back pay could be used as a remedy to compensate for past discrimination. Persons paid less than others because of discrimination can receive financial compensation back to the effective date of the Civil Rights Act of 1964.

- *Regents of the University of California v. Bakke* (1978).[30] This is the most famous "reverse discrimination" case to date. Allan Bakke had been denied admission to the University of California at Davis because of a special program that set aside 16 percent of each entering class for blacks and other minorities. The California Supreme Court agreed with Bakke, but the university appealed to the U.S. Supreme Court, which upheld the ruling with a five-to-four vote and ordered that Bakke be admitted. Admittedly, there was no clear-cut policy that emerged from the case about the use of quotas, and the case was limited to educational admissions. The confusion was not clarified with the recent case involving

a similar situation at the University of Michigan, which was decided in
2003 *(Gratz v. Bollinger)*. This case is presented later in this section.

- *Weber v. Kaiser Aluminum & Steel Corporation & United Steel Workers Union*
  (1979).[31] This case has been called the "blue-collar Bakke" decision. A
  white lab technician named Brian Weber charged that the company and
  the union were discriminating against whites by mandating that a joint
  union and company training program for skilled craft jobs be comprised of
  half whites and half blacks. Weber had been denied entrance into the
  program despite the fact that he had more seniority than some of the
  blacks who were admitted. The U.S. Supreme Court held that companies
  could use race as a factor in hiring and promotion policies. Moreover,
  Title VII of the Civil Rights Act of 1964 was aimed at improving the
  economic status of blacks, and the program helped achieve this goal. The
  Court ruled that a voluntary program in the private sector that gave
  special preference to blacks was not in violation of the Civil Rights Act.

- *Memphis Firefighters Local Union No. 1784 v. Stotts* (1984).[32] This ruling held
  that seniority was a legitimate method to use for layoffs. The case came
  about because blacks argued that the seniority system adversely affected
  minorities, but the U.S. Supreme Court upheld the practice of "last
  hired—first fired" as being acceptable.

- *Johnson v. Transportation Agency, Santa Clara County* (1987).[33] In this case, the
  U.S. Supreme Court ruled that higher test scores, more job experience,
  and the judgment of a personnel examining board could be ignored when
  making a promotion based on sex, even if there was no history of past
  discrimination. The case involved Diane Joyce and Paul Johnson. Both had
  applied for a position of road dispatcher in Santa Clara County, California.
  The examination board recommended Johnson, but the agency's director
  ignored the recommendation and gave the job to Joyce because all of the
  agency's 238 skilled craft workers were men. Johnson sued, but the U.S.
  Supreme Court ruled against him, holding that the agency had rightfully
  and legally based its decision on a multitude of practical factors.

- *Richmond v. Croson* (1989).[34] This case made it more difficult to prove job
  discrimination. The ruling overturned a city of Richmond policy that set
  aside provisions for minority contracts in the city's public works projects.
  The Civil Rights Act of 1991 overruled this decision by reinstating
  affirmative action as federal policy.

- *Hopwood v. Texas* (1996).[35] A group of four white applicants (three men and
  a woman) filed a suit against the University of Texas Law School claiming
  they had been denied admissions despite the fact that their LSAT scores
  were higher than black and Hispanic applicants who were admitted. The
  district court ruled in favor of the university, but a federal appeals court
  ruled in favor of the white applicants, holding that the university had
  violated the students' constitutional rights by using race as a selection
  criterion. The U.S. Supreme Court refused to hear the case.

- *Sharon Taxman v. Board of Education of the Township of Piscataway, NJ* (1996).[36] This case involved reductions in workforce in a public school. The decision revolved around two equally qualified female teachers, with the only different factor being race. One teacher was white and the other black. The school had to lay off one of the teachers and decided to retain the black employee. Taxman, the white teacher, sued. An appellate court ruled that Piscataway's affirmative action policy was unlawful. The Supreme Court granted certiorari but never heard the case. Civil rights groups raised money to settle with Taxman. Many civil rights groups feared that the Supreme Court would use the case to overturn *Bakke*.

- *Gratz v. Bollinger* (2003).[37] Because federal courts were ruling differently around the nation, a great deal of attention focused on this case, which was actually several cases combined. The case involved the University of Michigan undergraduate and the law school's affirmative action admissions policies. In a six to three decision announced on June 23, 2003, the U.S. Supreme Court ruled that the university's point system was too mechanistic and unconstitutional. The policy gave "underrepresented" ethnic groups an automatic 20-point bonus on the 150-point scale used to rank applicants. Applicants needed 100 points to guarantee admission. The ruling was confusing. The Supreme Court struck down the points-based undergraduate system because its use of race was not narrowly tailored to achieve the college's interest in diversity and, therefore, was unconstitutional. It upheld the law school's process because it was narrowly tailored. The Supreme Court justices relied on cases defining the scope of permissible affirmative action in the context of public education and concluded that race (and gender) can under certain narrow circumstances be viewed as a "plus" factor in making individualized decisions as to whom should be admitted to a public university in order to promote educational diversity. The case did not apply to private sector affirmative action programs; the focus was on public universities.[38]

As noted previously, the term *minority* has been expanded to include Hispanics, women, and other minority groups. Gender equity is another new value that has been added to public personnel administration. Based on the same rationale as that used regarding African Americans, women have historically been relegated to lower-paying occupations. Even in the new century, the "glass ceiling" is still in place according to women's advocacy groups. The image of a "glass ceiling" symbolizes how women cannot advance beyond a certain level because of an invisible ceiling constructed by a male-dominated society. Female billionaires, such as Martha Stewart, are not the norm for most women. Most women still earn less than men despite the progress that has been made over the past 30 years. Most of the differences in pay are attributed to the fact that women still tend to hold traditional occupations, like secretary, that historically pay less. In management and professional occupations, however, women have faired better. Both women and other minorities have made very impressive progress in academia, law, and medicine. Universities have been one area where women and minorities have made progress. Female and minority faculty have increased significantly in most academic disciplines. Law is another field where women and minorities have advanced. Proponents of affirmative action argue that universities have been among the most active in trying to attract women and minorities to their faculties and have actively used the principles of affirmative action in their hiring and promotion practices. Many of the lawsuits over the use of quotas to reduce past discrimination have involved universities.

Closely related to affirmative action is the idea of *representative bureaucracy*. This idea emerged during the late 1960s, along with the civil rights movement, and was soon followed by the affirmative action efforts of the 1970s. The idea of representative bureaucracy holds that the public bureaucracy should be representative of the population as a whole. That is, it should proportionally include members from all socioeconomic backgrounds, races, religions, and the like. For all practical purposes, representative bureaucracy is affirmative action applied to the public bureaucracy. Although progress has been made in bringing better balance and representation to civil service at all levels of government, minorities and women remain underrepresented, particularly in the higher echelons of government.

SEXUAL HARASSMENT

Another issue that affects public personnel systems is sexual harassment, which is another form of discrimination. The problem is not new, but the practice is forbidden under the EEOC guidelines. *Sexual harassment* is defined as repeated, unwelcome sexual advances, requests for sexual favors, and other verbal or physical contact of a sexual nature. Sexual harassment has been a difficult area to deal with for many organizations because it can take so many forms, such as sexual compliments from a supervisor to a subordinate, or explicit photographs or jokes in the office. Such activity can create a hostile working environment for an employee who is the victim of harassment. The guiding doctrine is that the workplace should be free of this type of discrimination and that sexually explicit comments and advances are not tolerated. The recipients of sexual harassment in both the public and private sectors are most often women. Surveys of federal employees revealed that 42 percent of women and 15 percent of men claimed to have been sexually harassed.[39] It is believed that most sexual harassment goes unreported.

To deal with sexual harassment, organizations have created policies that make it clear that such activity is forbidden. Some firms in the private sector have gone so far as to forbid dating among employees or to ban management from fraternizing with any subordinate. In the public sector, many universities have adopted policies that forbid faculty from dating students and even faculty of higher rank (full professors) from dating faculty of lower rank (such as assistant professors).[40] Sexual harassment, in its worst form, involves an abuse of power by someone in a position of authority. One of the problems of dealing with sexual harassment is that harassment comes in degrees that are not easily defined. No one disputes that blatant sexual requests or physical contact of a sexual nature from a supervisor to a subordinate is sexual harassment. Most also view it to be management's responsibility to ensure that employees do not subject coworkers to explicitly sexual comments, contact, or advances. No employee should be subjected to this type of behavior.

But throughout society we have a problem defining *what is* and *what is not* sexual harassment. What is unacceptable in one workplace is tolerated in another. What actually constitutes sexual harassment? Is it illegal for a male supervisor to ask a female subordinate for a date? If the person declines and the supervisor does not ask again and does not do anything that harms the employee in any way, has sexual harassment occurred? Is having a sexually explicit calendar hanging on the wall of an automobile garage considered sexual harassment if the garage employs females? What if the female employees at the garage complain about the calendar? The problem is compounded by human nature and the belief that, like the politics-administration dichotomy, we can separate two dimensions of life. Sociologists have long recognized that high school and college friendships often result in marriage or a long-term relationship, but most people meet other people through friends or at work. This in no way justifies any form of sexual harassment. It simply illustrates that the organizations in which we work are also social organizations. The problem is in drawing the acceptable lines of behavior and definitions of what constitutes sexual harassment. The guiding principle of management on this issue is that certain behaviors are unacceptable, and many guidelines have been added to standard operating practice manuals forbidding any form of behavior that might be construed as sexual harassment. The safe approach is simply to separate one's personal life from one's professional life. Some have argued for this same point—that is, they have argued that the only workable rule about romance in the office is that there must be none of it.[41] Unfortunately, this is difficult for many people, which illustrates the need for clarity in policies regarding sexual harassment.

A number of high-profile court cases have involved private firms,[42] but the U.S. Supreme Court made its landmark decision on sexual harassment in 1986 in *Meritor Savings Bank v. Vincent*.[43] The case involved a female teller at a bank (Vincent) who had a male supervisor who by all accounts was a "womanizer." Vincent was repeatedly asked out for dates and, after some time, finally agreed. A sexual affair began that lasted for about two years. After the relationship ended, Vincent claimed that she was subjected to harassment by the supervisor and resigned. Vincent then sued, charging that she had been sexually harassed. The bank argued that Vincent had consented to a sexual affair and therefore was responsible. It was simply a case of a breakup between two people in the office, not sexual harassment. The Supreme Court did not agree with the "consent" defense. The Court ruled that whether Vincent consented or not was not the issue. At issue was whether she was subjected to a hostile work environment and sexually harassed. Not only did the Court uphold the idea that harassment is a form of sexual discrimination, but it also held that harassment is not limited to economic or tangible matters. Victims do not have to show that their pay or job was threatened, but only that a "hostile environment" existed. Moreover, employers can be held liable for the behavior of their employees on the grounds that they either knew or should have known that workers were being sexually harassed.[44] This ruling made it clear that it is management's responsibility to make certain that the work environment is free of sexual harassment.

In 1992, the Court toughened its stance on sexual harassment in *Franklin v. Gwinnett County Public Schools*.[45] The case involved a high school student who was sexually harassed by a teacher. The student sued, claiming that the school should have known that sexual harassment was taking place. Her case was dismissed at the federal trial where the court held that Title IX of the Civil Rights Act does not authorize monetary award for damage. This principle had guided the courts up until that time. The trial decision was upheld by an appellate court, but reversed by the U.S. Supreme Court. This decision paved the way for victims of sexual harassment to sue for monetary damages in federal court. The following year, in *Harris v. Forklift Systems*,[46] the Court ruled that some things that are not offensive to men might be offensive to women. The case dealt with the idea of what constituted a hostile work environment. The Court said that its standard would be whether the work environment would offend a "reasonable woman." These cases remain the federal position on sexual harassment in the workplace.

Overall, society appears to have adjusted reasonably well to the concept of sexual harassment. Both corporate America and government appear to have made progress in training and instilling the idea in workers and managers that sexual harassment is unacceptable. This is likely attributable in part to the fact that the baby boomers are now managers in the workplace and, as a generation, are more supportive of these types of values. Moreover, sexual harassment most often affects women, and the baby boomer generation has been more supportive of women's issues. Sexual harassment has not gone away. Some very high-profile sexual harassment cases have emerged, such as the Tailhook[47] incident that involved the U.S. Navy in 1991. The incident occurred at a convention in Las Vegas, which involved a number of violent, sexual assaults on females. That same year, sexual harassment dominated the Senate Judiciary Committee's hearings on Supreme Court nominee, Clarence Thomas, who was charged with sexually harassing Anita Hill.[48] Unfortunately, it is likely there will be more cases because America has yet to reach a consensus about the relationship between power, romance, and life in organizations. But the principle that sexual harassment will not be tolerated in the workplace is now widely accepted and is a permanent part of public personnel administration.[49]

COMPARABLE WORTH

A few years ago, the concept of comparable worth promised to revolutionize the way that people are paid in the public and private sectors. Comparable worth stemmed from the inequity in pay between men and women that continues to exist despite passage of the Equal Pay Act in 1963. After more than

40 years, men still earn more than women, mainly because women have historically been employed in large occupational groups in which pay is lower, such as secretarial work, teaching, clerical work, social work, and nursing. But comparable worth went much further than trying to equalize pay for doing similar jobs. It sought to pay employees based on what they contribute in work to organizations. This was a radical revision to the way pay scales had rationally been constructed. Market indicators and skill levels determine most pay scales. In the private sector, the market is the main factor used to determine the value of labor. In government, pay scales are usually based on what is paid for comparable positions in the private sector and comparisons of similar positions in the governmental sector. Additionally, regional adjustments are made to pay scales, since the cost of living varies around the nation. Proponents of comparable worth argued that a careful analysis of what workers from these groups actually contribute would show that they are grossly underpaid when compared to occupations that are dominated by men, such as truck drivers, carpenters, plumbers, and the like. Studies at the federal level found that women in the General Schedule system earned about 60 percent of what men earned. In real dollars, this amounts to women earning about $18,000 while men earn $30,000.[50]

The issue of comparable worth attracted national attention in 1983 in the state of Washington. The American Federation of State, County, and Municipal Employees (AFSCME), a large public employees union associated with the AFL-CIO, sued the state over equity on grounds of sex discrimination under Title VII of the Civil Rights Act of 1964. The federal district court ruled that Title VII guaranteed comparable worth, but the appellate court reversed the ruling, holding that the state had a right to base compensation on a competitive labor market.[51] Although the legal battle failed, AFSCME reached an agreement with the state, and a systematic upgrading of salaries was initiated in areas traditionally dominated by women. During the 1980s, there was an effort to require pay equity of all employers, but the Reagan administration did not support the idea. Bear in the mind that the Equal Pay Act of 1963 forbids inequity in pay for comparable jobs, but it does not deal with differences between categories of occupations, such as management positions versus clerical positions. It is illegal for a male professor to be paid more than a female professor when all things are relatively equal. But it is not illegal for a professor, regardless of gender, to be paid more than clerical staff.

Equity in pay between men and women has not been resolved, but comparable worth has never materialized. The concept is included in personnel and public administration textbooks mainly for historical or conceptual reasons. Experts found it to be an unworkable concept, and many argued that the inequities found in the marketplace for women would be resolved in time as women move into higher-paying occupations. For all practical purposes, the idea of comparable worth is now simply a part of the history of personnel administration.

LABOR UNIONS IN THE PUBLIC SECTOR

Public employee unions pose another threat to the idea of merit. Organized labor is a reality in the public sector, which tends to be far more unionized today than the private sector. Labor unions emerged for a legitimate reason; management failed to take care of the needs of its workforce and often treated workers unfairly. In the private sector, firms tended to abuse workers during the height of the era of industrialization. Workers were treated like a commodity. Because of the abuses, organized labor emerged to represent workers. The only power that workers had was the collective power that is created when groups organize. Workers learned that they had the power to stop production if they organized, which creates a lot of headaches for business owners and management. The power and right to "strike" became a reality for large organizations like Ford and General Motors many years ago. Thus, the labor movement, which is now nearly a century old, grew quickly in areas such as mining, the automobile industry, and other heavy industries that required skilled labor. Most of the industries were blue-collar types of businesses. Union membership grew from about 3.5 million in 1935 to about 15 million in 1947.

Legislation passed by Congress helped the labor movement. The Labor Railway Act of 1926 recognized the right of some employees to organize unions. The National Labor Relations Act of 1935 (known as the Wagner Act) recognized the right of most workers to join unions. This law also created the National Labor Relations Board (NLRB), which had the authority to prevent employers from engaging in certain specified unfair labor practices. The Norris-LaGuardia Act of 1936 was a pivotal piece of legislation that prohibited courts from issuing injunctions in most labor disputes. The first major piece of legislation that seemed to be partly antiunion was the Labor Management Relations Act (called the Taft-Hartley Act of 1947). This law weakened union strength by creating a set of strict guidelines that defined unfair labor practices. The Taft-Hartley Act has been amended many times. In 1970, it was amended to include the U.S. Postal Service, colleges and universities, and other organizations. By the 1960s, more than 30 percent of the private workforce was unionized, but by the late 1990s the figure had dropped into single digits. Part of the reason was that management started doing a better job of taking care of employees, but one of the main reasons was the decline of America's heavy industries that employed a lot of blue-collar workers. The nation had moved from an industrial society into the technology and information age, which required a different kind of worker. The heavy industries, like the steel industry, remain heavily unionized, but they are much smaller than in the past and comprise a smaller part of the economy. Unlike most western European nations where unions have remained very strong, the American labor movement continues to decline in the private sector.

We now have a service-based economy. As the number of blue-collar workers declined and the number of white-collar workers increased, unions adjusted as best they could to attract new members from large industries such as the airline and travel industries. They were rather successful in getting flight attendants, mechanics, and airline pilots to form unions. Unions tried to expand the occupations beyond the traditional blue-collar worker to occupations like carpenter, plumber, and electrician, in order to attract groups like airline pilots. In the private sector, success was limited because during the height of the labor movement unions developed an unfavorable reputation that was often linked to organized crime. The growing white-collar society was less prone to join unions largely because of their image and a shift in values. Unions also seemed inconsistent to the idea of merit because the basic philosophy of unions is "one for all and all for one." On face value, this goes against the ideals of merit, which is based on individual performance. The idea of a "brotherhood" of anything does not sit well with American individualism. Unionization tends to follow regional patterns, with the heaviest concentration of organized labor found in the northeast and industrial midwest, and the least in the southeast. This pattern remains today and is greatly affected by the attitudes and political culture of the region. For example, most states in the southeast are "right-to-work" states. This means that a person does not have to join a union as a condition of employment or be held to the conditions of the union contract. Moreover, a person can negotiate an individual contract. This greatly weakens the power of unions. Unions have a right to exist under federal law. In the industrial midwest, many states, including Michigan, are "closed-shop" states. That is, workers must join the union if hired and must abide by collective bargaining agreements. Other states, like Montana (a state with a long history of mining that attracted organized labor) fall in the middle. Such states are called "agency states" and workers do not have to join unions as a condition of employment, but they are bound by collective bargaining agreements and must pay union dues (which are often donated to worthy causes by the union if such an agreement exists in the contract). State laws coupled with a changing workforce that was not receptive to unions have caused organized labor to look beyond its traditional, skilled, blue-collar base for members.[52]

While the private sector has become less unionized, union membership in the public sector continued to grow through the 1970s.[53] Prior to that time, observers predicted that unionization would continue until most public workers belonged to unions.[54] This has yet to occur. About 43 percent of all public employees are covered by collective bargaining agreements.[55] The labor movement in the public sector also began with blue-collar and postal workers but expanded to include most occupational groups. For example, most school-teachers (the largest single group of employees at the state and local level) belong to a union. Many public universities have both staff and faculty unions. In cities and counties across the nation, public employee unions have grown. From general office workers, to postal employees, to air traffic controllers, unions are common in the public sector. After President Kennedy signed Executive Order 10988 in 1962, unionization at the federal level skyrocketed from 8 percent to 57 percent between 1963 and 1973.[56] Unions in the public sector are different from their counterparts in the private sector, mainly due to legal restrictions. The right to strike, the largest single power that a union has, is forbidden by law for most public unions. Despite the inability to legally strike, unions have been very effective at negotiating collective bargaining agreements for government workers. The Civil Service Reform Act of 1978 officially recognized the right of all federal employees to organize and negotiate but did not authorize the right to strike. By 1986, more than half the states had comprehensive collective bargaining laws; 14 other states allowed unionization of some of their employees; 12 states allowed public employees the right to strike, and 9 states had no collective bargaining laws.[57]

Strikes have often backfired in the public sector. One of the most famous collective bargaining fiascos in modern times was the Professional Air Traffic Controllers Organization (PATCO) strike in 1981. PATCO was negotiating a new contract to get more pay, a shorter workweek, more benefits, and earlier retirement. The union argued that the job contained too much stress and that the government did not recognize or understand the magnitude of air traffic controller's responsibilities. Air traffic controllers are responsible for managing air traffic at the nation's airports, which involves managing takeoffs and landings. They claimed that newer technologies were available that would enhance air traffic safety and make their work environment less stressful. The government refused to give in, and in July virtually all of the PATCO members voted to strike. The Reagan administration refused to budge and wanted to set an example for other public employee unions. At the time, median household income was about $25,000 per year, and many air traffic controllers made $55,000. The average citizen did not have a lot of sympathy for the air traffic controllers, who earned far more than most Americans. The Transportation Department ran the air traffic controller system during the strike. Supervisors, former controllers brought back from retirement, and controllers from the military staffed airport towers. President Reagan went on national television and made it clear that the air traffic controllers had broken their contract by striking, which was forbidden under the agreement they had signed. Reagan gave the air traffic controllers 48 hours to return to their posts or they would be fired. About 1,000 workers returned, but most did not take Reagan's threat seriously. PATCO's assets were frozen by a court order, and its leaders were arrested. No other union would back the PATCO strike. The union's activities were found to be illegal, and PATCO was decertified.

The PATCO story set the mood for organized labor during the 1980s. Although unionization remains strong in the public sector, PATCO serves as a reminder of the potential consequences of an illegal strike with government.[58] Unions have learned that public sentiment is important, especially in strikes or slowdowns. Public sentiment has turned on unions over the years. In the case of PATCO, there was little public support for the air traffic controllers. The PATCO strike involved about 10,000 air traffic controllers, but ten years earlier a U.S. Postal Service strike involved more than 60,000 workers.[59] Some point to 1979—the year that had the most strikes by public employee unions, with 538 strikes or work stoppages[60]—as a major turning point regarding public sentiment. One of the many strikes that year occurred in New Orleans where police officers went on strike just before Mardi Gras. This effectively canceled the holiday and cost businesses millions of dollars. Since 1979 strikes have become less common in the public sector.[61] Even in the private sector, major strikes are now rare. This does not mean that the labor movement is over; collective bargaining is a reality of the public sector. Unions have been very successful at raising salaries and improving health benefits, working conditions, and pensions for government workers. Of course, this increases the cost of government operations, which must be paid for with tax revenues. One of the most significant differences between public and private labor-management relations is that in the public sector, the negotiations involve public money.[62]

Collective bargaining is at the heart of unionization.[63] It is through this process that unions secure better wages, benefits, job security, and working conditions for their members.[64] Laws, such as the National Relations Labor Act, control collective bargaining. The basic concepts associated with the process include the following:[65]

- *Unit determination* is the process by which a union is recognized as the exclusive representative of a group of employees in contract negotiations. Units may be *agency-based* or *occupational-based*. Agency units include the entire agency, whereas occupational units include only employees in specific jobs, which may involve more than one agency.

- *Scope of bargaining* refers to the range of issues that are negotiable. In some instances, the scope of bargaining is open, meaning that any issues can be negotiated that either side feel are important. More often, the scope is limited to certain specific issues.

- *Unfair labor practices* refer to behaviors that unions or management may not engage in during the process. Many of these conditions were defined in the Taft-Hartley Act and subsequent amendments to that act. These practices include harassing employees or applying pressures to force them to support or oppose a union. The behaviors apply to both unions and management. Both sides are expected to negotiate in good faith.

- *Contract negotiation* is the process that is used for management and labor to define mutually acceptable agreements over issues that are subject to negotiation. The process is often like a poker game, with both sides bluffing to gain an advantage. Each side typically makes demands that they know are unreasonable, then compromises on each issue. The process involves a lot of wheeling and dealing before it concludes. The contract is often miraculously finalized just before the existing contract expires.

- *Impasse resolutions* are resolutions that occur when management and labor fail to reach an agreement through negotiations on their own. There are three ways to resolve an impasse, assuming that laws allow for these procedures to be used. Mediation involves using a neutral third party to help get the process moving again. Impasses occur because communication has broken down, and a mediator can sometimes reestablish a dialogue between labor and management. Fact finding uses a mediator who listens to arguments from both sides and then issues a public report. The report is not binding, but concern over public disclosure often causes both sides to work out their differences. The last resort is arbitration. Arbitration involves bringing in a neutral party to settle the issues. The two sides agree in advance to abide by the arbitrator's decision. Arbitration is more common in the private sector than in the public sector because public agencies must abide by existing legislation. That is, such things as wages and benefits cannot be as freely negotiated in the public sector because they may require tax increases that can only be passed by the legislature.

■ *Contract administration* refers to the process of following the provisions of the contract once a contract goes into effect. Under federal law, both management and labor are obligated to follow the provisions included in the contract. Virtually all contracts contain grievance and disciplinary procedures to handle circumstances when either side feels the provisions have been violated. Employees file grievances against the agency, while disciplinary actions are implemented against employees who have violated their obligations under the contract.

Each of these areas is extremely complex and requires lawyers to work out the legal details of labor contracts.

Labor-management relations are a significant concern in the world of public management, but too often these relations are viewed as a "we versus them" situation. Some have noted that the focus should be on how the objectives of labor can be balanced against the interests of management and the public so that strikes can be avoided.[66] In the private sector, management has been working for many years to try to break down the "we versus them" mentality that almost surely leads to conflict. While most public employee unions cannot legally strike, they can stop or hinder services using a variety of legal techniques, such as having large numbers of workers call in sick, which essentially creates a work stoppage. This tactic has been called the "Blue Flu" in big-city police departments when things are not going well during contract negotiations. Unions are not likely to disappear. Labor-management relations will remain part of the landscape of public personnel administration and part of the world of public management.

WHAT DO PERSONNEL DEPARTMENTS DO? BASIC FUNCTIONS OF A PUBLIC PERSONNEL SYSTEM

The world of public personnel administration exists in the context described previously. As noted earlier, the purpose of public personnel systems is to attract, hire, train, retain, and maintain a productive workforce. Personnel systems involve, at a minimum, some very basic tasks. They include staffing, classification and compensation systems, training and management development, advancement, disciplinary, and grievance procedures. Figure 5.1 is a diagram illustrating these basic functions. People come from different entry points into

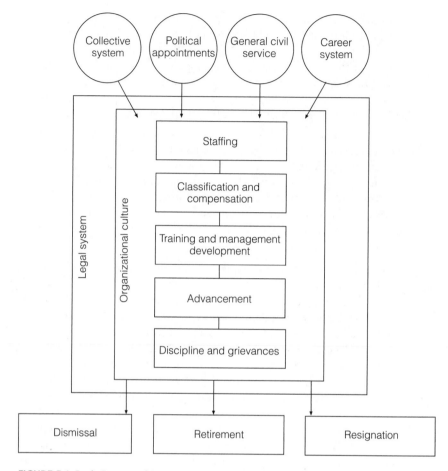

FIGURE 5.1 Basic Personnel System

SOURCE: Adapted from Grover Starling, *Managing the Public Sector,* 4th ed. (Belmont, CA: Wadsworth, 1993), p. 449.

the system.[67] Frederick Mosher identified four sources of entry.[68] Thousands of political appointees enter federal, state, and local personnel systems. At the federal level, the president can appoint nearly 5,000 people to top positions in the executive branch. *Political appointees* range from cabinet-level officials to confidential secretaries. At the federal level, the *general civil service system* is mainly comprised of white-collar workers. Most of these workers are nonprofessionals. The examinations used for filling these positions are practical examinations (not intelligence tests, which are used in the British civil service system). After passing the written test and fulfilling any additional qualifying requirements, the person is placed on a list of eligible candidates.[69] Federal law requires that the agency choose from those who had the highest scores. (Veterans are given special privileges in this process by law.) The focus of civil service is mainly on positions (not the individual) in the traditional manner associated with the principles of Weberian bureaucracy. Most employees enter government service through the civil service. Additionally, there are *career systems* that are outside the general civil service system. Many agencies have developed their own career systems, which usually are comprised of professionals and paraprofessionals. The model career system is often considered to be the military. The military system has been adapted by a number of federal agencies, such as the Federal Bureau of Investigation (FBI) and the Tennessee Valley Authority (TVA). Career systems focus on the *individual* rather than the *position*. The *collective system* is comprised mainly of blue-collar workers whose employment is governed through collective bargaining agreements. As noted earlier, the number of professionals in government has increased greatly and, according to the U.S. Department of Labor, it is likely to increase further in the new century.

Personnel systems perform several basic tasks as illustrated in Figure 5.1. The first task is staffing, which includes the process of recruiting, selecting, and advancing employees based on their ability, knowledge, and skills. Recruitment is a major task for most government agencies, whether the agency is a state university, a city, or the U.S. Postal Service. For example, recruiting faculty at universities usually entails a job listing that clearly states the qualifications, describes the position and includes a deadline for applications to be received, or indicates that the position will remain open until filled. Recruiting faculty at universities does not require testing, but recruiting staff often involves testing. In the case of faculty, an advertisement is usually placed in a national personnel newsletter that has wide circulation across the nation to the appropriate academic field. In the case of a political science department, advertisements are usually placed in the American Political Science Association's national personnel newsletter. Today's technology also allows job listings to be placed on the Internet. According to the U.S. Civil Service Commission, good recruitment includes the following basic guidelines:[70]

- Writing announcements in clear, understandable language
- Advertising in publications that circulate to various segments of the population, and using other media such as radio and television
- Establishing readily accessible job information centers
- Visiting colleges, high schools, and community organizations
- Developing continuing contacts with minority and women's organizations

Selection assumes that distinctions can be made to separate candidates in a fair and objective manner. In the case of recruiting faculty, if a political science department receives 75 applications for a single position, how does it separate the qualified from the less qualified? What criteria does the department use to separate competing candidates? How many candidates will be interviewed? And on what basis will the department ultimately select the single candidate? In cases where written examinations are involved, the examinations must be job-related and valid. That is, a high score on an examination must be shown to be a valid indication of performance on the job.

When examinations are used, the selection criteria is somewhat less subjective than when hiring faculty members at a university. In a typical hiring procedure at a university, once all the applications are received, a review process begins with a set of established criteria. The criteria may include that the candidate will complete his or her PhD by the time the academic year begins, has demonstrated an ability to teach in the required area of expertise, has demonstrated that his or her specialized area is the same as that indicated in the job advertisement, and has a well-planned research agenda. In advance, the faculty would have agreed on what will satisfy these criteria. The process of reviewing the application files then begins. This may be handled by the entire faculty of the department, or by a subcommittee that can include members outside the department. The number is usually reduced to a long list of perhaps 10 or 12 candidates. From that list, a shorter list is compiled, and ultimately the "rule of three" is often used (reducing the list to three people and bringing all three candidates to the university for an interview). The process of reducing 75 candidates to 3 should be as objective as possible. Some candidates simply are not qualified based on the established criteria. It is important to establish minimum "thresholds" that must be met or exceeded. Those who do not meet the thresholds can objectively be removed from the list. Some may not have the appropriate credentials or may be from different areas of expertise within political science.

Reducing the list to an acceptable number of candidates is a process called *certification* in personnel administration. Only a limited number of candidates should be certified according to the merit principle. Reducing the list to a dozen candidates certifies these particular candidates. Usually these candidates receive calls to make sure that they are interested in the position or are still available, and often their references are now checked more thoroughly. Once the final candidates are brought to the campus for an interview, the process becomes more subjective. That is, all of the candidates are supposed to be qualified on paper, and now the decision-making process will be based heavily on their performance at the interview. This allows flexibility for faculty to interact with candidates, ask questions, and observe formal presentations; and it allows candidates to see the university and the local area. After all the candidates have been interviewed, the faculty typically discusses the choices and then votes (often by rank-ordering the candidates), and the candidate with the most votes is offered the job. To complicate matters, sometimes the first choice turns down the job. If this occurs, the job is then offered to the candidate with the second most votes.

A similar procedure often occurs in the search for government employees. The "rule of three" is commonly used and allows managers to meet and interact with candidates before making the final selection. Sometimes people's personalities simply do not mesh well in certain organizations. Other times candidates might not want the job after meeting the people with whom they would be working. This subjective dimension is now considered to be desirable. Training and moving costs are expensive. Moreover, no one is pleased if the new employee and the job do not make a good match. In that case, the employer may have to begin the process again.

The *position classification system* is found at all levels of government. At universities, even professors have position classifications and ranks. Position classification involves identifying the responsibilities of each position in an organization, then grouping the positions according to similarities. A fair compensation system requires an understanding of the duties and responsibilities of all positions. The ideas of equal pay for equal work, constructing effective examinations, and recruiting cannot be achieved without this understanding. Many problems exist with the way that government often handles position classification. Too often the *staff* bureaucrat in the personnel department evaluates the job and the *line* managers must accept that judgment. In private industry, just the opposite is true.[71] In many organizational work situations, position classifications are no longer relevant. For example, in some work arrangements, the environment has become too collegial and too "free form" for rigid position classifications to work well. These situations include college faculties and the military. Some have argued that position classification should be replaced with *rank-in-person* approaches, which use the abilities and expertise of individuals as the basis for making personnel decisions.[72]

Recall from Chapter 4 that Warren Bennis believed that organizations in the new century would be more involved with problem solving than with the duties traditionally performed by functional lines in the traditional bureaucracy. He believed that organizations would become more organic.[73] Those who argue that organizations must be redesigned agree that position classifications are a rather dated way to handle things. But these classifications are still applicable to many traditional government situations and are still used by most governments. Position classifications also involve pay scales, like the GS system used by the federal government. These systems are important but are difficult to create. In the private sector, market-based studies are often used to determine how much a position is worth. In the public sector, many jobs pay less than their private sector counterparts. Ideally, they too are based on some sort of objective criteria, such as surveys of similar positions in the private sector and in other governments. For example, surveys are performed regularly on the salaries of professors nationally and regionally. But state universities do not or often cannot match national or regional averages. The same is true for many positions at all levels of government. For example, those who serve as cabinet heads in the federal government often leave jobs in the private sector that pay considerably more than the top grades of the executive-level pay scales. George W. Bush was the first president to get a $400,000 salary (the annual salary was $200,000 for decades). Almost any top CEO in the nation can more than match that salary, and recall that the U.S. federal government is the largest "business" in the world. For example, Vice President Dick Cheney made $6 million in personal income the year before he became vice president.

Although public service cannot match the private sector for many professional positions, the typical middle-range salaries are more comparable, and the lower-end jobs typically pay more. For example, one fairly consistent finding about privatization of public services is that the private sector typically pays workers less than government workers, has weaker benefits packages, and employs fewer workers to perform the same tasks. This is generally thought to be where most of the savings are found when services are privatized. (This will be discussed in much greater detail in Chapter 8.) Pay scales that are perceived to be fair are critical for maintaining a satisfied workforce. They also must be coupled with competitive benefits packages, such as health insurance and retirement plans.[74] Personnel departments usually handle registering employees for insurance, retirement, and benefits plans.

The pay scales that best illustrate public civil service are those used in the federal system. Most states follow a similar model. Federal jobs in the executive branch come in a variety of grades. The positions range from clerical to cabinet-level personnel. Executive Levels I to V are for cabinet-level members, deputy and assistant secretaries, and other high-ranking officers. Immediately below the executive level is the Senior Executive Service (SES), which was created by the Civil Service Reform Act of 1978.[75] This group consists of a broad range of noncareerists, including advisors, administrative law judges, and scientists. The SES has six basic rankings. Next are the rest of the GS positions, which rank downward from GS-15 to GS-1. (GS is the abbreviation for general schedule.) All GS positions contain 10 grades that determine the actual rank and salary.[76] The rankings also are adjusted for regional variations in the cost of living. For example, as of 2004, the highest GS rank was a GS-15 at the grade of 10. (Table 5.4 contains the GS-1 through GS-15 pay scale for 2004.) The maximum base salary was $113,674, but for employees at this rank living in the Washington, DC, area, the adjusted salary was $130,805 (shown on a separate regional table not included here). Most of these positions involved confidential work or policy making. Confidential workers include clerical employees and chauffeurs. One of the problems facing government in the new century is attracting young, talented people to government service. The GS jobs typically pay 22 to 40 percent less than comparable jobs in the private sector.

Few areas get more attention than *training*. Once hired, all employees require some orientation to the organization and their job. Even universities have an orientation process for newly hired faculty that attempts to acquaint them with the system. Employee handbooks provide written documentation about policies, and job descriptions detail the duties required. Training and development is an ongoing process in most organizations. Technologies are constantly changing and require that employees be trained. For example, the accounting software used by universities is upgraded regularly, and staff members who must work with it on a daily basis often spend hours in training sessions to learn new skills. Training has also become a multibillion dollar business. Private firms and quasi-public organizations offer training in almost every conceivable area, from computer technologies and Web page design, to sensitivity training and supervisory skills. Training programs run the gamut of possibilities. They can be very useful for organizations to help bring about organizational change and to upgrade skills, or they can be a waste of time and money if they

Table 5.4 Federal General Pay Scales and Ranks

SALARY TABLE 2004-GS
INCORPORATING A 2.70% GENERAL INCREASE
Effective January 2004
Annual Rates by Grade and Step

Grade	Step 1	Step 2	Step 3	Step 4	Step 5	Step 6	Step 7	Step 8	Step 9	Step 10	Within-Grade Increase Amounts
GS-1	$15,625	$16,146	$16,666	$17,183	$17,703	$18,009	$18,521	$19,039	$19,060	$19,543	VARIES
2	17,568	17,985	18,567	19,060	19,274	19,841	20,408	20,975	21,542	22,109	VARIES
3	19,168	19,807	20,446	21,085	21,724	22,363	23,002	23,641	24,280	24,919	636
4	21,518	22,235	22,952	23,669	24,386	25,103	25,820	26,537	27,254	27,971	717
5	24,075	24,878	25,681	26,484	27,287	28,090	28,893	29,696	30,499	31,302	803
6	26,836	27,731	28,626	29,521	30,416	31,311	32,206	33,101	33,996	34,891	895
7	29,821	30,815	31,809	32,803	33,797	34,791	35,785	36,779	37,773	38,767	994
8	33,026	34,127	35,228	36,329	37,430	38,531	39,632	40,733	41,834	42,935	1,101
9	36,478	37,694	38,910	40,126	41,342	42,558	43,774	44,990	46,206	47,422	1,216
10	40,171	41,510	42,849	44,188	45,527	46,866	48,205	49,544	50,883	52,222	1,339
11	44,136	45,607	47,078	48,549	50,020	51,491	52,962	54,433	55,904	57,375	1,471
12	52,899	54,662	56,425	58,188	59,951	61,714	63,477	65,240	67,003	68,766	1,763
13	62,905	65,002	67,099	69,196	71,293	73,390	75,487	77,584	79,681	81,778	2,097
14	74,335	76,813	79,291	81,769	84,247	86,725	89,203	91,681	94,159	96,637	2,478
15	87,439	90,354	93,269	96,184	99,099	102,014	104,929	107,844	110,759	113,674	2,915

SOURCE: Office of Personnel Management, http://www.opm.gov.

are nothing more than fads. Since the late 1960s, there have been wave after wave of fads, from the "I'm Ok, You're Ok" sensitivity idea, to a string of motivational-oriented and management skills programs.[77] Despite the faddish nature of some programs, many are useful and can help managers and employees learn many useful skills and acquire new knowledge.

There are many aspects of training and development. The most basic is on-the-job training (OJT) where employees learn the additional skills they need on the job from other employees. This is the most common form of training and is based on the simple idea that skills are passed from one employee to another. Job rotation is another form of training and development. This involves moving employees to other positions that help cross-train them in other areas of the organization. Job rotation has been found to be beneficial for both employees and organizations.[78] Assessment centers are another tool available to organizations. These amount to simulations that realistically replicate real-life scenarios that enable personnel to develop new skills.[79] Typically, assessment centers take place in a simulation laboratory that requires real interaction among participants to solve problems that are played out in scenarios. Most people have seen flight simulators on television that are used to train pilots. These epitomize the idea of training because they are used to assess a pilot's skills in dealing with a wide range of scenarios. Regardless of the form, training is critical for developing new skills or polishing old ones, and for learning new technologies. Training programs can come prepackaged from many reputable organizations, such as the International City/County Management Association (ICMA). The ICMA provides ongoing training, workshops, and seminars for nearly every imaginable aspect of local government. In the modern organization, training workshops are now as common as traditional staff meetings. Training has become a big business in America, and many companies develop programs that are sold to organizations in both the public and private sectors. Training is an integral part of public personnel administration.

Career development is another dimension of personnel systems. Advancement is important to most employees; most people prefer to find careers that are not "dead-end jobs." *Advancement* usually refers to climbing the ladder to higher positions with greater authority and more pay. Most large organizations have developed career tracks that allow those seeking to advance the opportunity to develop their careers. Not everyone wants to climb the so-called ladder of success. Many people are perfectly satisfied to remain in one general area because either they are happy with their jobs or find them challenging and intriguing, or they have interests outside of work and use their jobs only as an economic necessity. Anyone who has ever been a manager understands this reality. Those who use their jobs merely as an economic necessity can be very productive workers and should be rewarded, but they may have no ambitions to move through established career tracks. This is true even for some professions. For example, many professors are perfectly content remaining in academic departments as professors, although once a person reaches the rank of full professor, no further advancement is available inside an academic unit aside from serving as chair or head of a department. For most professors, teaching and research are the most stimulating aspects of their profession; however, some seek to move on to administrative positions in the university.

Most organizations provide new employees with a probation period. People can enter a system from an entry-level position (located at the bottom of the organization) or a lateral position (somewhere above the bottom). Promotion at the state and local levels often involves competitive examinations, but the federal government has avoided this type of system. Promotions often are based on formal performance appraisals that periodically review an employee's job performance. The concept of *management by objectives* (MBO), which was developed by Peter Drucker, allows employees to set objectives with their supervisors. These are used to measure the progress of an employee and can greatly aid the performance appraisal process. The process of performance appraisal must be ongoing. It is unfair to employees and it is a poor management practice to wait until the end of the year to tell employees they are not performing up to par. Performance appraisals are one of the tools of modern personnel administration and management, but they are only as good as the effort that is expended on them. That is, if they are simply a rubber-stamping exercise, they are essentially meaningless. Employees need appropriate feedback to understand where they stand and how they can adjust to improve their performance.

One of the last and least pleasant aspects of personnel systems involves *grievances* and *disciplinary action*. In social organizations, there will inevitably be conflict. Not everyone will be happy with the organization, their supervisors, or their coworkers. The grievance process involves a procedure by which employees can complain about their dissatisfactions. Many complaints involve just listening to employees; others involve filing formal complaints that must be addressed by formal procedures. Most organizations have formal grievance procedures that are also supposed to protect those filing grievances from reprisal. That is, if employees feel that they have been treated unfairly or, in the case of unions, a provision of the contract has been violated, they can file a formal complaint. Most grievance procedures are prescribed by civil service regulations rather than by law. In most cases, the person with a complaint is expected to follow normal administrative channels.

Although students are not university employees, most universities have formal processes for students to file complaints. The system is essentially the same for employees and students. For example, if students are dissatisfied with a professor over some issue, they are expected to first talk to the professor. If that fails, the students should speak to the department chair, and then the dean of the division, the provost's office, and so on. If these avenues fail to resolve the issue, then a formal written complaint should be filed. Most often, the formal process involves filing a complaint by completing a form and talking with someone in the office who handles complaints and grievances. The complaint is then given to a committee that allows both parties to respond in writing and, if necessary, holds a hearing. This is almost always an unpleasant aspect of management in any organization. Most of the time, during the grievance process, the complaint is resolved. If a complaint cannot be resolved within the organization, avenues to resolve complaints outside the organization exist. The last resort is legal action in the courts. Complaints are a reality modern organizations. Although it is impossible to eliminate complaints, it is possible to minimize them by ensuring that fairness is maintained throughout the organization.

Disciplinary action is equally as unpleasant as grievances. When employees perform poorly or fail to follow established procedures, they are subject to reprimand, suspension, demotion, or dismissal. Public managers try to avoid firing employees as long as possible if there is hope that corrective action can resolve whatever problems are involved. In public agencies, disciplinary actions are usually subject to appeal. Often problems in supervision involve personality conflicts, which in turn affect performance. If problems are not resolved, then the larger unit can be adversely affected by higher rates of turnover, reduced motivation, poor morale, poor performance levels, and an increased number of formal grievances. However, management cannot allow poor performance and belligerent employee attitudes to go unchecked, since this also can lead to many problems that will affect overall performance. It is critical that management maintain high and consistent standards that apply equally to all employees. These two unpleasant aspects of public personnel administration are simply realities of the workplace because, in any social setting, there will always be conflict, and there will always be employees who are unhappy and supervisors who use poor judgment.

Public personnel systems are complex but are a core function of modern management. Effective personnel administration increases organizational performance by recruiting, selecting, training, and helping to maintain a satisfied and productive workforce. Personnel systems involve many tasks, such as writing job descriptions, creating and maintaining position classifications, handling certain aspects of pay and benefits systems including insurance and retirement, and dealing with grievances and disciplinary actions. Understanding the complexities of personnel systems is critical for managers. Figure 5.1 (see p. 219) is a simplistic depiction of personnel systems, but it illustrates how employees constantly flow through the system, as well as some of the primary functions performed in modern public personnel management.

SUMMARY

This chapter pointed out some of the key differences between public and private personnel systems. It also covered the major highlights of the evolution of the merit system in the United States and discussed some of the major issues that threaten the principles of merit. As Peter Drucker suggested years ago, we now live in an employee society. Public personnel systems are designed to help people fulfill meaningful goals, earn a living, and accomplish the tasks performed by government. Over the years, we have slowly but constantly shifted the emphasis toward *people* more than the *organization*. The guiding principles of today hold that the dynamic element of organizations is people; the task-oriented sweatshops of Frederick Taylor are now a part of the past in modern societies. Public personnel administration is about people—about creating a well-trained and satisfied workforce that can perform the varied functions needed by society. All organizations must accomplish the functions they are mandated to perform, but in modern society we have learned that people are the key to organizational performance. Public personnel administration provides many of the key tools and support functions to help our public workforce stay productive.

All forms of discrimination threaten the merit principle. If people are not treated fairly, then the whole foundation of merit crumbles. The idea of merit is based on the assumption that the playing field is reasonably balanced and fair. Great progress has been made in reducing discrimination in the workplace, but minority representational problems still exist. The merit principle must be properly administered if it is to have any meaning. But the methods to relieve discrimination also appear to threaten the principles of merit. How can an organization hire the most qualified applicant while at the same time provide special treatment to special groups, whether they are veterans, women, blacks, or Hispanics? This has been one of the most significant challenges for personnel systems. How can the merit principle coexist with organized labor seeking unilateral benefits for all union members? There are no simple answers, but public personnel systems have done reasonably well at handling these conflicting goals and will be likely to continue performing well in the future.

NOTES

1. Peter Drucker described the employee-based society in *People and Performance: The Best of Peter Drucker on Management* (New York: Harper & Row, 1977), Chapter 2.

2. The differences between public and private personnel administration used here come from Robert Lee, Jr., *Public Personnel Systems* (Gaithersburg, MD: Aspen, 1987), Chapter 1.

3. The public sector contains only a few recent examples. During the mid-1970s, New York City technically went bankrupt, and during the early 1990s, Orange County, California, went bankrupt. New York City is the nation's largest city, and Orange County was one of the nation's largest and wealthiest jurisdictions. Both were restored to good financial health and continue to operate.

4. The comptroller general is a nonpartisan, 15-year appointment. The

current comptroller general was appointed in 1998, during the Clinton administration, before Arthur Andersen, one of the world's most respected accounting firms, got caught up in the Enron scandal.

5. This was the latest figure available from the U.S. Census Bureau at the time this book was printed. The figure is from the 2000 census and includes all persons over the age of 16. Figures sometimes vary depending on who is included. This figure is the available workforce, not the number of people actually employed.

6. For a thorough history and analysis of the evolution of public service in the United States, see Robert Lee, Jr., *Public Personnel Systems,* Chapter 2.

7. Nicholas Henry, *Public Administration and Public Affairs,* 7th ed. (Upper Saddle River, NJ: Prentice-Hall, 1999).

8. The first legal conflict over government appointees came as soon as Thomas Jefferson was elected to the presidency in the famous case of *Marbury v. Madison.* The case involved John Adams's midnight appointments of judgeships in the final hours of his presidency to Federalists. Some of the paperwork had not been completed when Jefferson took office. James Madison, the new secretary of state, refused to execute the appointments. The case went directly to the Supreme Court under a provision in the Judiciary Act of 1789. The Chief Justice was John Marshall, an adamant Federalist. Marshall was concerned that Jefferson would ignore the Court's ruling if it ruled in favor of the office seeker, so Marshall crafted a ruling that would greatly enhance the Court's power while ruling in favor of the new administration. The ruling focused on Congress expanding the power of the Supreme Court's original jurisdiction by allowing a *writ of mandamus* to bring a case directly before the Court. The U.S. Constitution provides for no such procedure. The ruling held the provision to be unconstitutional and stuck down part of the Judiciary Act of 1789. This was the first act of Congress to ever be struck down by the Supreme Court. The ruling established the power of *judicial review* (a principle that makes the Supreme Court the main interpreter of the Constitution and allows it to strike down laws passed by Congress, actions of presidents, and state governments). See *Marbury v. Madison,* 5 U.S. (1 Cranch 137) 1803.

9. Robert Lee, Jr., *Public Personnel Systems,* p. 18.

10. Ibid., p. 20.

11. The Hatch Act was passed due to widespread corruption on the part of parties pressuring workers to contribute to political campaigns. Democratic Senator Carl Hatch of New Mexico introduced the bill in 1939 to end political pressure being applied to government workers. Over time, some of the restrictions imposed have been lessened for government workers.

12. Nicholas Henry, *Public Administration and Public Affairs,* p. 283.

13. Grover Starling, *Managing the Public Sector,* 6th ed. (Ft. Worth, TX: Harcourt, 2002), pp. 425–426.

14. Nicholas Henry, *Public Administration and Public Affairs,* pp. 281–283.

15. Ibid., pp. 284–285.

16. Ibid., pp. 285–286. Note that Nicolas Henry breaks this era into several periods.

17. The Civil Service Reform Act of 1978 created the Office of Personnel Management (OPM) and implemented many of the reforms suggested by the second Hoover commission in 1953.

18. Nicholas Henry, *Public Administration and Public Affairs,* p. 286.

19. Robert Lee, Jr., in *Public Personnel Systems,* p. 26, cites the comment about "triumph of technique over purpose." The original source is found in an article by Wallace Sayre, "The Triumph of Technique over Purpose," *Public Administration Review* 8 (1948), pp. 134–137.

20. These figures are included in Table 9.2 of Nicholas Henry's, *Public Administration and Public Affairs,* p. 327.

21. *The Fact Book,* the source of most of the data used in Table 5.1, is available on the Office of Personnel Management's Web site at http://www.opm.gov.

22. Robert Lee, Jr., *Public Personnel Systems,* p. 249.

23. Ann Bowman and Richard Kearney, *State and Local Government,* 5th ed. (Boston: Houghton Mifflin, 2002), Chapter 8. The proposition was approved by a vote of 55 percent to 45 percent.

24. Charlotte Steeh and Maria Krysan, "The Polls—Trends: Affirmative Action and the Public, 1970–1995," *Public Opinion Quarterly 60* (Spring 1996), pp. 144–145. Over the years many polls have been conducted and printed in newspapers such as the *Wall Street Journal, USA Today,* and the *New York Times.* Some of the latest Gallup polls can be found online at http://www.gallup.com (the database is searchable).

25. See Dan Froomkin, "Affirmative Action under Attack" *Washington Post Online* (October 1998). This is a special

series about the challenges facing affirmative action. The series of articles can be viewed online at http://www .washingtonpost.com/wpsrv/politics /special/affirm/affirm.htm.

26. George Gilder, *Wealth and Poverty* (New York: Basic Books, 1981), and Richard Herrnstein and Charles Murray, *The Bell Curve: Intelligence and Class Structure in American Life* (New York: Free Press, 1994).

27. In 1989, the U.S. Supreme Court made a series of rulings (actually five major cases) that made it more difficult to prove discrimination. The cases included *Ward's Cove Packing Company v. Antonio,* which reversed the idea of "disparate impact." Disparate impact referred to an adverse impact on minorities caused by a personnel policy regardless of whether the action was intentional. 490 U.S. 642.

28. *Griggs v. Duke Power Company,* 401 U.S. 424 (1971).

29. *Albemarle Paper Company v. Moody,* 422 U.S. 405 (1975).

30. *Regents of the University of California v. Bakke,* 438 U.S. 265 (1978).

31. *Weber v. Kaiser Aluminum & Steel Corporation & United Steel Workers Union,* 433 U.S. 193 (1978).

32. *Memphis Firefighters Local Union No. 1784 v. Stotts,* 104 S. Ct. 2576 (1984).

33. *Johnson v. Transportation Agency,* Santa Clara County, CA. 480 US 616. (1987).

34. *City of Richmond v. JA Croson Co.,* 488 U.S. 469 (1989).

35. *Hopwood v. Texas,* 78 F.3d 932 (5th Cir. 1990), *cert. denied,* 1996 WL 227009.

36. *Sharon Taxman v. Board of Education of the Township of Piscataway, NJ,* 961 F.3d 395 (3rd Cir. 1996), *cert. granted,* but case was settled out of court. See Linda Greenhouse, "Affirmative Action Settlement: The Overview; Settlement Ends High Court Case on Preferences: Tactical Retreat," *New York Times* (November 22, 1997), p. A-1. The U.S. Supreme Court was set to deal with affirmative action again during the 2002–2003 session. Two cases were scheduled to be heard, both involving the University of Michigan. Many were hoping this would settle the conditions where race can be used as a criterion in college admissions. Neither case had been decided at the time this book was printed.

37. At the time this book went to press, the *U.S. Reports* citation was not available. The citation at the time of the book's printing was *Gratz v. Bollinger,* ___ U.S. ___, 123 S. Ct. 2411, 156 L. Ed. 2d 257 (2003).

38. For an excellent discussion about the case, see Thomas Arn and Deanna Rader's article, "Supreme Court Addresses Use of Race in Admissions," at *Findlaw.com,* http://library.lp.findlaw.com/articles/file /00992/009135/title/Subject/topic/ Labor%20%20Employment%20Law _Employment/filename/laboremploy mentlaw_2_79. This is a four-part discussion about the issue and the case that deals with the implications of the case.

39. Cited in Robert Lee, Jr., *Public Personnel Systems,* p. 238. For the original survey, see Merit Systems Protection Board, *Sexual Harassment in the Federal Workplace: Is It a Problem?* (Washington, DC: Government Printing Office, 1981).

40. The University of Virginia was one of the first to adopt this policy.

41. Cited in David Schuman and Dick Olufs, III, *Public Administration in the United States,* 2nd ed. (Lexington, MA: D. C. Heath 1993), p. 294. The phrase is credited to the anthropologist Margaret Mead.

42. Many cases have been brought against private corporations, including sexual harassment cases involving the popular Atlanta-based restaurant Hooter's. Most of these cases have been won by Hooter's in court, quietly dismissed, or settled out of court. Hooter's is better known for its fight with the EEOC over not hiring males as servers in their restaurants. Hooter's has long maintained that part of its business is built around "sex appeal," and it openly claims not to be a family-oriented restaurant. To date, the EEOC has never completed its investigation.

43. *Meritor Savings Bank v. Vincent,* 106 S. Ct. 2399 (1986).

44. Robert Lee, Jr., *Public Personnel Systems,* p. 238.

45. *Franklin v. Gwinnett County Public Schools,* 503 U.S. 60 (1992).

46. *Harris v. Forklift Systems,* 126 L. Ed. 2d 295 (1993).

47. For more information about the Tailhook incident, which took place at a convention in Las Vegas in 1991, visit http://www.zmag.org/zmag/articles /june94pohl.htm.

48. Anita Hill, now a law professor, was an employee at the EEOC and worked under Clarence Thomas. She accused him of sexually harassing her at the confirmation hearings and presented evidence that was rejected by officials. Thomas was confirmed to the Supreme Court.

49. Sex discrimination includes more than sexual harassment. Discrimination based on sex has also been found in the area of benefits. It is illegal to offer lower benefits to employees based on gender. The first major case was *Frontiero v. Richardson* in 1973. This case dealt with the Air Force providing unequal medical and housing benefits to men and women. Men were automatically granted these benefits, but married women were required to show that they provided more than half the financial support in their marriages. The Supreme Court held that this practice violated the due process clause of the Fifth Amendment. See *Frontiero v. Richardson,* 411 U.S. 677 (1973). Women also made gains with the Pregnancy Discrimination Act of 1978 and the Retirement Equity Act of 1984, which forbid employers to penalize people for taking leaves of absence associated with childbirth, pregnancy, care for a child after birth, and adoption. The laws apply to both men and women who are involved with childbirth, but the Retirement Equity Act does not apply to public employers.

50. The survey was conducted by the General Accounting Office, *Options for Conducting a Pay Equity Study of the Federal Pay and Classification Systems* (Washington, DC: Government Printing Office, 1985), p. 9.

51. *American Federation of State, County, and Municipal Employees v. State of Washington,* 770 F.2d 1401 (1985).

52. For a good history of the labor movement, see J. David Greenstone, *Labor in American Politics* (New York: Alfred Knopf, 1969).

53. For an examination of public employee unionization, see Jack Stieber, *Public Employee Unionism* (Washington, DC: Brookings Institution, 1973).

54. Jim Seroka, "The Determinants of Public Employee Union Growth," *Review of Public Personnel Administration 5* (Spring 1985), pp. 5–20.

55. John Delaney and Raymond Horton, "Managing Relations with Organization Employees," in James Perry, Ed., *Handbook of Public Administration* (San Francisco: Jossey-Bass, 1989), p. 439.

56. Cited in Donald Klingner, *Public Administration: A Management Approach,* p. 257. The original source is *AFL-CIO Manual for Federal Employees,* No. 138 (Washington, DC: AFL-CIO, December 1973), p. 10.

57. David Shuman and Dick Olufs, III, *Public Administration in the United States,* p. 353.

58. Ibid., pp 354–355.

59. Donald Klingner, *Public Administration: A Management Approach,* p. 262.

60. Cited in Nicholas Henry, *Public Administration and Public Affairs,* p. 303. Strikes are illegal for most public employee unions. The term *work stoppage* is used to refer to unions withholding services legally. That is, if negotiations fail a large number of workers will call in sick on the same day to get management's attention. Under most contracts, workers are allowed a certain number of sick days legally. Police departments commonly use this practice. When strikes are legal, workers tend to withhold services when they are most needed, such as schoolteachers striking just before school begins.

61. Ibid.

62. Ibid., pp. 302–303.

63. See Richard Kearney, *Labor Relations in the Public Sector,* 2nd ed. (New York: Marcel Dekker, 1992).

64. Donald Klingner, *Public Administration: A Management Approach,* p. 256.

65. Ibid., pp. 258–263.

66. See Ibid., p. 256.

67. Personnel management can be viewed as a system, which is reflected in Figure 5.1.

68. The four ways to enter government service are used in Grover Starling, *Managing the Public Sector,* 4th ed. (Belmont, CA: Wadsworth, 1993), pp. 448–452. The original source is Frederick Mosher, *Democracy and the Public Service* (New York: Oxford University Press, 1968). The diagram is fully credited to Grover Starling and provides an excellent framework for understanding the process and environment of public personnel systems.

69. Additional qualifications may be required for some positions, such as physical examinations and skill-related requirements. For example, law enforcement often has certain requirements for height for men and women, and firefighters are often required to pass physical tests. Also, background checks are required for some positions, such as law enforcement and areas that involve national security.

70. The Civil Service Commission's recommendations for recruiting are cited in Grover Starling, *Managing the Public Sector,* p. 452.

71. Ibid., p. 456.

72. Ibid., pp. 456–457.

73. Another person who partly agrees with Warren Bennis is Elliott Jacques, who argued for "natural hierarchies and different time frames for modern organizations." See Elliott Jacques, *Work, Creativity, and Social Justice* (New York: International University Press, 1970).

74. Benefits packages, such as health insurance, retirement systems, wellness programs, and the like, are a major part of personnel administration. Most public personnel administration textbooks cover these areas in great detail. See Robert Lee, Jr., *Public Personnel Systems,* Chapter 4; Donald Klingner and John Nalbandian, *Public Personnel Management,* 4th ed. (Upper Saddle River, NJ: Prentice-Hall, 1998), Chapter 2; and Dennis Daley, *Strategic Human Resource Management: People and Performance Management in the Public Sector* (Upper Saddle River, NJ: Prentice-Hall, 2002), Chapter 6.

75. At one time, there were GS-16 through GS-18 positions immediately below the executive level, but these grades are no longer used.

76. GS-16 through GS-18 schedules were formally dropped from the General Schedule effective the first day of the first pay period beginning on or after January 1, 1992. Source: Office of Personnel Management's Web site, http://www.opm.gov.

77. For example, see Thomas Harris, *I'm Ok, You're Ok* (New York: Avon Books, 1973), and Morris E. Massey, *People Puzzle: Understanding Yourself and Others* (Englewood Cliffs, NJ: Prentice-Hall, 1980). Morris Massey is best known for his videos that focus on how values clash in society and the workplace, and how we can better understand ourselves and others by understanding the idea of "value programming." His videos, which deal with the idea that "where you are now is largely determined by where you were when you were being value programmed," have often been used in training programs in both the public and private sectors. Sensitivity training was especially common during the era of racial and generational tensions in the late 1960s and 1970s. Training films, seminars, programs, and books became a very large industry that still thrives today.

78. Herbert Kaufman, *The Forest Ranger: A Study of Administrative Behavior* (Baltimore, MD: Johns Hopkins University Press, 1960).

79. Assessment centers have been used in both the public and private sectors. They may be thought of as "simulations" that allow skills to be developed and assessed. AT&T is well known for having well-developed assessment centers, and the military and the State Department have used simulations in crises for a number of years. Assessment centers are often used to select new managers, but they also can be used to assess and polish skills. The key concept associated with assessment centers is realistic *simulations* where the participant's performance can be assessed.

6

An Overview
of Public Budgeting

A billion here and a billion there, and pretty soon you're talking real money.

EVERETT DIRKSEN
SENATE MINORITY LEADER (1959–1969)[1]

S tudents often yawn when they see the topic of *public budgeting* appear on a
syllabus. For many, this does not seem like the most exciting topic. Yet public budgeting is one of the most critical aspects of public administration and
public policy. Its importance cannot be overemphasized.[2] Public budgeting is
much more than accountants sitting around making entries into the books or
working with spreadsheets on computers.[3] Budget processes and systems are
very diverse and complex, but the core of budgeting is simple. (See Box 6.1.)

A public budget is a document or a plan for how government will spend the public's
money (expenditures) and how it will generate the funds needed (revenues) to pay for
services for the next year.[4] Governments collect revenues, mainly through taxes,
and then spend those revenues on a varied array of services and projects. If they
spend more than the available revenues, they must borrow money to pay for the
deficit.[5] If money is left over, politicians argue over how to use the surplus.
Some may want to use the surplus to fund more programs. Others may want to
pay off debt or give taxpayers a rebate.

The most simplistic way to think about the basic accounting in budgeting is
revenues minus expenditures equal the surplus or deficit. This is a very simple concept, but public budgeting is not a simple process because of politics. Even the

BOX 6.1   Budgeting Made Simple

The process of budgeting is not rocket science. The basics of budgeting are very simple. Budgeting is something that everyone must do, whether we formally construct a budget on paper, use popular accounting software like *Quicken,* or just roughly construct a budget in our minds. Formal budgeting typically uses a year as a time frame, but it can be broken down by the month or even a week.

When we budget, we estimate our approximate income. We usually do not know exactly what our incomes will be for the next year, but we know the approximate amount. We may earn more than we anticipate because of a raise, extra income, changes in the interest we get on our savings accounts or investments, or a change to a different job in which we make more money. Likewise, we may earn less than we anticipated because interest rates may drop or because we took time off from work without pay. But we know the range in which our income is likely to fall. This is called estimating our revenues (or income).

Even the accounting aspect of budgeting is easy to understand. As we earn money and make deposits to our checking accounts, the funds are *credited* to accounts. As we deposit more money, our reserves increase. Each deposit is entered as a credit. When we write checks to pay for things, the amounts are *debited* (charged) to our accounts. This is the simple concept of debits and credits.

By looking at the past year, we know roughly how much we tend to spend at the grocery store each week, how much gasoline we must buy for the car, how much we must pay for insurance for the car, and so on. We may have purchased a new car, in which case part of our income will be spent to make payments on the loan. We may be planning to buy a new computer, television, and compact disc player this year, and we can estimate about what we will pay. We know how much we pay each month for rent (or the mortgage if we bought a house) and how much we pay for utilities such as the telephone, electricity, credit card payments, and the like. Thus, we can estimate most of our expenses. This process is estimating our expenditures (expenses).

Most of us have to live within our means, so we cannot spend more than we earn. If our expenses exceed our income (called a deficit), we must either cut our expenses or borrow money to pay for our expenses. If we spend less than we earn, then we can save the surplus or buy something else. Most families and individuals think of personal budgets in terms of a one-month *cycle* because the accounting systems used by businesses work on a monthly system. That is, our rent is due once per month; our car payments and credit card bills must be paid each month.

This process of budgeting works the same everywhere, in both households and large corporations. Although the process is the same, it becomes much more complex in a large organization like Microsoft or General Electric. The difference in *public budgeting* used by governments lies not in the fundamentals of estimating revenues and expenditures, but in the situation that is created when large sums of public money are collected and organizations seek to have their projects, agencies, and interests funded with "someone else's money." In theory, public budgeting involves collecting money from everyone and using it to pay for the services needed by society. The clash occurs because not everyone agrees on how the money should be spent. The process of determining how the money will be spent is the *politics of budgeting.*

accounting is not always as simple as basic mathematics. Alexander Hamilton noted in *Federalist #30* that in political arithmetic, 2 plus 2 does not always equal 4. This is because of politics. Of course, mathematically 2 plus 2 does equal 4, but Hamilton recognized that when politics is involved, the math is often secondary to *how* the money is spent.

Public budgeting is a highly political process where public policy comes to life.[6] When policy makers and politicians make budgetary decisions, they are making policy decisions, and interest groups appear to make sure that their special interests are accommodated.[7] The process involves who is going to get whatever there is to get from the legislature. If a person wants to know what the nation's commitment is to national defense, finding a cure for cancer, child care, education, and the like, they can find it in the budget. Western societies tend to measure "commitment" in dollars because it costs money to find cures for diseases or to maintain the nation's defense systems. Budgeting is a process where public policies become reality. The budgetary process involves such decisions as the "guns-or-butter" debate. That is, how much will we spend on the nation's defense versus how much will we spend on welfare-related programs? Stated differently, on what basis do we determine to spend \$X on activity A, and \$Y on activity B? This question was raised by V. O. Key in the 1940s, and represents the politics of budgeting because people do not agree how the public's money should be spent.[8]

These are policy questions that must be decided in the budgetary process. The budget is a plan, but it is also a commitment for education programs, highways and transportation projects, and research and development. In short, a public budget is a plan for how the government spends your money; how the government pays for its activities; for government borrowing or repayment of borrowing; something that affects the nation's economy; something that is affected by the nation's economy; and a historical record of government fiscal policy. Budgeting is more than just a document; it is a written record of public policy.[9] This chapter provides an overview of the basics of public budgeting and finance.

DIFFERENT WAYS TO THINK
ABOUT BUDGETING

Public budgets can be seen from at least five different perspectives.[10] *Budgeting is a way to manage the economy.* The major objectives of budget policy involve three very important goals.[11] They include, *allocation of resources* (deciding what will be allocated), *distribution of resources* (this includes redistribution of wealth and equity concerns), and *stabilization of the economy* (efforts to ensure that budget policy promotes economic growth while controlling inflation and unemployment). Each of these goals is important for society as a whole, and the decisions about allocation, equity, and stabilization of the economy are determined in the budgetary process. Fiscal policy greatly influences the economy because it directly affects the collection and expenditure of public money. In theory, public financing holds that citizens must pay for the services needed to maintain society. If everyone pays a small portion, enough revenues will be generated to pay for all the services and activities of government. The 2003 federal budget was $2.13 trillion, the largest federal budget in history at the time. How government spends this money has a direct impact on the economy. For example, during the military buildup of the 1980s, the Reagan administration spent a trillion dollars on defense-related items. This succeeded in restoring the military and at the same time supported a lot of high-tech industries in providing defense equipment, such as F-16 fighter jets, tanks, and weapons. The people who earned money directly from these expenditures took the money and paid mortgages on their homes, bought groceries and new cars, and sent their children to college. The stores in which people spent their money in turn paid employees, purchased goods and services, and so on. This type of spending supported industries and their employees while transforming the military into a smaller, high-tech set of armed forces. Thus, government spending is important for the overall economy.

The tax and spending policy of government can be used to manage the overall economy. British economist John Maynard Keynes argued this point more than 80 years ago.[12] Stated simply, when the economy is booming, government collects more revenue. During times of recession, the economy can be "pumped and primed" by giving tax breaks and incentives to stimulate economic activity. When the economy is performing poorly, government incurs more welfare-related expenses and unemployment benefits. This also can help to stimulate the economy because those receiving benefits spend their money in stores, which has a multiplier effect in the economy. During recessions, government usually spends more than it collects because the economy has stagnated. Government usually operates with deficit spending until the economy recovers. Congress has tried to reduce deficits recently, but past deficits currently have contributed to a national debt of more than $6.9 trillion.[13]

The fiscal policy of government can greatly affect the length of a recession, relieve human suffering during hard economic times, and help the economy to recover. Once the "business cycle" starts moving upward again, the economy begins recovering; and once the recovery is over, government tax collections increase. (The business cycle is well known for its boom-and-bust characteristics.) Economists disagree over the proper role of government to manage fiscal policy. Some believe that monetary policy, which is handled by the Federal Reserve (called the Fed), is the most important element. Monetary policy deals with the supply and cost of money. Some believe that the best way to help the economy is to help businesses that supply goods and services (supply-side theory), while others believe that government spending helps to create a demand by putting cash in people's pocket (demand-side theory), which ultimately helps industries. Although each of these theories has legitimacy, economists have never fully agreed on the "right" approach. What everyone does agree on is that the actions of government are important.

Supply-side theory holds that government should minimize its presence in the economy by keeping taxes low and watching the supply of money. Any intervention on the part of government, which is discouraged, should be to aid producers rather than consumers. (This idea is associated with fiscal conservatives.) Supply-side theory is a contemporary version of classical economics, which is associated with Adam Smith[14] and other classicists like David Ricardo and Jean Baptiste Say. It is sometimes referred to a *laissez-faire* economics, but critics have called it *trickle-down economics* because it favors business and the wealthy. What is left over, according to critics, trickles down to the common person.

Demand-side economics, which is associated with the work of John Maynard Keynes, holds that supply is meaningless if there is no demand. He argued that government must play an active role in the economy during recessions or depressions, and that fiscal policy can be used to manage the economy. Government must intervene to help relieve the suffering of consumers. (This idea is associated with fiscal liberals.)

The monetarists, associated with economist Milton Friedman, believe that neither supply- nor demand-side economic theory is adequate; the key lies with the supply of money. As the economy grows, the supply of money should grow.[15] If the economy shrinks, the supply of money must be reduced. If not, inflation occurs. For centuries a relationship has been recognized between the supply of money and prices.[16] The goal of fiscal policy (and all three of these theories) is to produce a healthy, growing economy with low unemployment and low inflation. The economy affects all of us. It affects the availability of jobs, the interest that we earn on our savings, the interest rates that we pay for car loans, and the amount of money that is deducted from our paychecks. All of this is related back to the federal budget. (More will be said about fiscal policy and economic theory later in this chapter.)

Budgeting is also a way to choose among competing alternative priorities. Do we invest in large-scale nuclear energy projects to ensure that the nation does not have "blackouts" like California experienced a few years ago? Do we build more submarines or increase health care benefits for the nation's senior citizens? Do we help the farmers or do we help cities? Do we fight the war on illegal narcotics or do we build more public transportation light rail systems? Do we spend more money to try to find cures for cancer or do we subsidize tobacco farmers? Do we want socialized medicine so that everyone will have health care or do we want to help those who need insurance and let most people take care of themselves? Do we want to spend more on education or spend the money on foreign aid to enhance our international relationships with other nations? Do we tax the wealthy and reduce the tax burden on the middle class? Budgeting involves choices among competing goals. It also involves a clash of values over how the money should be spent, on which programs and projects, and how the revenue should be raised. Do we expend billions of dollars to build space shuttles and explore space, or do we put that money in Superfund projects to clean up pollution? Clearly, the questions raised here illustrate that budgeting is a political clash over the direction of public policy. These are only a few of the many questions raised during the budgetary process. Budgeting is where ideological clashes occur over what is important and what will be secondary in public policy. Thus, budgeting is a power struggle among competing priorities and interests. This includes the agencies of government that must lobby to ensure that their funding continues. To keep the space program afloat, the agencies must appear before Congress to make their case for funding.

Budgeting is also a way to produce the right mix of programs to balance the needs of the public and private sectors so our economy is productive and individuals are provided for. Our capitalistic-based economy produces losers and winners. It is very productive and provides a high standard of living for most citizens, but many human needs are unmet. Government tends to provide most of the nation's physical infrastructure, such as roads, bridges, and the like. But government also provides services for those who do not prosper under capitalism. By the standards of the nations in the third world, the United States is a wealthy, wasteful nation. But there are still many people in America who are homeless, hungry, and living in poverty.

Budgeting is a way to review and control the agencies of government. As discussed in Chapter 1, both the legislative and executive branches review the behavior and performance of public agencies. The greatest power of Congress is the "power of the purse." Agencies depend on the funding from the legislature to function, and the legislature can hold them accountable for poor performance. Thus, budgeting is a form of control. A few years ago when the tactics of the Internal Revenue Service seemed too aggressive and the media started broadcasting some of the cases, Congress stepped in and formed an advisory board to oversee the IRS's behavior. When the Bureau of Alcohol, Firearms, and Tobacco got into a shooting match in Ruby Ridge, Idaho, Congress held hearings and then Senate Majority Leader Bob Dole threatened to halt funding to the Bureau. Congress has this power. At all levels of government, the legislature has the power to control much of the behavior of public agencies, and its most powerful device is through funding. In a similar vein, budgeting is also a tool of management. Public managers use their budgets to manage their agency. The budget is a financial plan that includes categories of expenditures that are used to carry out activities and implement public policy. Thus, inside organizations the budget is an important management tool.

Budgeting is a form of accounting. A budget is a comprehensive statement about what government did last year and the plan for the next year. It lists all revenues and expenditures, often line by line. It serves as a public statement of government activity in which the activities of government are documented by a complex system of governmental accounting. There are several major formats of budgets, including line-item budgets and performance-based budgets. (Budget formats will be discussed later in this chapter.) Accounting systems keep track of what is spent and how revenues are generated. Accounting is the system of recording, classifying, and reporting financial transactions in an orderly way. Government has its own specialized practices in accounting that typically follow the guidelines suggested by the Government Finance Officers Association (GFOA). Government employs many accountants to keep up with the colossal amount of paperwork generated by government due to the millions of transactions that are recorded. All of the monies generated and all of the expenditures incurred are authorized in the budget. The general budgets of the nation, states, and local governments are based on the proposed budgets of every bureau, department, and agency in the jurisdiction.

A SHORT HISTORY
OF AMERICAN BUDGETING

Public budgeting is a fairly recent development in the United States. Public budgets existed much earlier in Europe (by 1787, England had developed a complete, comprehensive public budget), but they were absent in colonial America in the modern sense of the concept. The Treasury Act of 1789 established the Treasury Department, with Alexander Hamilton as the first secretary. Hamilton argued that it was important to pay the colonial debt to ensure that the new nation remained creditable with other nations in Europe. This turned out to be a wise decision. When the former Soviet Union (U.S.S.R.) was formed in 1917, the new government refused to pay off the debt of the Czar's government. This resulted in the U.S.S.R. being put on the hard currency standard by other developed nations, which lasted until the 1980s. Stated differently, it ruined the Soviet Union's credit rating at the outset with the international community, forcing the U.S.S.R. to pay in hard currency (gold or the equivalent).

Budget preparation was simple during the early days. It amounted to collecting and submitting estimates to Congress via *The Book of Estimates.* There was no executive budget per se. The federal government was small, weak, and limited in its ability to generate revenue. Congress took control of the process and followed a line-item system of budgeting. For more than a century, the federal budget was a legislative-dominated function. Budget reform did not begin at the national level; it began at the local level of government. Budgetary reform came due to the escalating costs of government that were attributed to economic conditions and the waste, graft, and corruption of political machines. By the turn of the 20th century, there was a demand for more centralized and efficient budgeting. Reformers attacked political machines, bossism, corruption, and what they perceived as the decay of traditional American morality. Prior to this time, most governments generated more money than needed. Political bosses did not use formal budgeting, and there was no formal accountability or respectable record-keeping system.

Several types of reformers sought to clean up city and state governments. Progressives wanted to clean up government by making it honest, accountable, moral, and reflective of middle-class values. Their reforms mainly included political remedies such as popular participation, direct democracy reforms (initiatives, recall elections, and referendum), home rule, municipal charter reforms (council-manager and commission forms of government), and the return of honest people to government. A second kind of reformer, sometimes called a municipal research reformer, sought to make government less corrupt and more efficient by using scientific methods. These reformers were responsible for making better systems of accounting and control. They believed that it took much more than honest people to make government work. Their concentration was on tools and techniques rather than on "honesty" or political reforms. They were responsible for creating and implementing cost accounting, uniform reporting systems, centralization, and accrual accounting, a system in which revenues are matched to expenditures during an accounting period to enable more meaningful evaluation.

In 1899, the National Municipal League released a model that would place budget preparation under the mayor. In 1907, the New York Bureau of Municipal Research released a study entitled "Making a Municipal Budget" that became the model used by New York City, and within 20 years, most cities had some similar type of budget. The reform model gave more authority to executives (governors and mayors) and held them accountable for their actions. The reformers worked to eliminate the long ballot and to reduce the number of independent boards and commissions that had sprung up during the Jacksonian era. Ohio, in 1910, became the first state to grant its governor the power to oversee and prepare the state's budget. By 1920, some budget reform had taken place in 44 states, and by 1929, all states had a central budget office. Most reform budgets were *line-item budgets.* Because expenditures are literally listed line by line, these budgets provide a greater ability to see how funds are being spent. Considering the widespread corruption and waste associated with political machines, it is not surprising that reformers wanted to see where the public's money was being spent.

During this same period, changes were beginning to occur at the federal level. President Howard Taft was able to get an appropriation of $100,000 to create a special commission to study the economy and efficiency in government. Frederick Cleveland of the New York Bureau of Municipal Research chaired the committee, which came to be known as the Taft Commission. In 1912, the commission released its report. The report recommended that the executive be placed in control of the budget process, that the presidents assume responsibility for administration, that a bureau of the budget be created, and that the government adopt a uniform classification system. In 1921, Congress passed the Budget and Accounting Act. This act created the Bureau of the Budget (BOB) housed in the Treasury Department and created the Government Accounting Office (GAO). President Warren Harding signed the bill into law. President Woodrow Wilson, the reformer and father of American public administration, had vetoed similar legislation in 1920 because he saw the GAO as a control mechanism of Congress. Wilson believed that the GAO, which had oversight over the executive branch, weakened the president's authority.

Prior to 1921, Congress dominated the federal budget process, but with the passage of the new budget legislation, the budget shifted to the executive branch. In 1939, the Bureau of the Budget was moved to the Executive Office of the President based on a recommendation of the Brownlow Committee's report to reorganize the executive branch. The Bureau of the Budget later became the Office of Management and Budget (OMB). Between 1921 and 1974, the trend was toward increasing executive control over the budgetary process.[17] Thus, the shift was from legislative control to executive control with legislative approval. Congress basically delegated much of its budgetary control to the president, and found that it was better served by letting the president prepare the budget. Congress then examines the budget, makes revisions, and approves it. In 1974, Congress took back some of the control with the Budget and Impoundment Act, which was partly a response to Watergate and President Nixon's impoundment of funds that had been appropriated by Congress. Since 1974, the budget has remained under executive control, but Congress has maintained an active role by creating the Congressional Budget Office (CBO) and new committees to increase its ability to handle the colossal federal budget. This period, from 1974 until the 1990s, has been called the *era of stalemate*.[18] It is possible that a new era has emerged with executive-legislative balance, particularly considering that we have had divided government (having a president from one party and Congress under the control of the other party) for many years.[19]

THE BUDGET CYCLE

The budget cycle is the process in which the budget is planned, prepared, debated, adopted, implemented, and audited. Budget cycles typically contain several distinct but overlapping phases. The budget cycle includes preparation and formulation, legislative review, budget execution, and audit and evaluation phases. The phases are similar at all levels of government, although most local governments systems are usually less complex than the federal government or the states and large cities. Some local governments are very small jurisdictions, and their budget processes are simple. For example, in many New England towns, the budget is often voted on at town hall meetings. However, the federal government and the states have complex, ongoing budgetary processes where billions of dollars will be raised and spent. Figure 6.1 is a diagram of the budgetary process. Some of the phases occur concurrently. The budget process never stops for large governments. Governments cannot wait until a new year begins to prepare the budget. After a budget is implemented, work immediately begins on the next year's budget. Budgets generally follow a fiscal year, which is an accounting cycle. Fiscal years vary, but most governments use July 1 through June 30. The federal government uses a different cycle that runs from October 1 through September 30. Differences in the fiscal years between the federal government and state and local governments alter the time frames. For example, the Montana legislature meets once every other year (called a biennium) and prepares the state's budget for a two-year period. But the state's budget office works year-round, constantly updating estimates and making preparation for the next legislative session.

The first phase is *preparation and policy formulation,* which involves making revenue estimates, gathering expenditure requests from agencies, and dealing

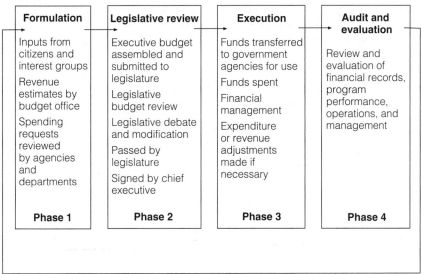

Formulation	**Legislative review**	**Execution**	**Audit and evaluation**
Inputs from citizens and interest groups	Executive budget assembled and submitted to legislature	Funds transferred to government agencies for use	Review and evaluation of financial records, program performance, operations, and management
Revenue estimates by budget office	Legislative budget review	Funds spent	
Spending requests reviewed by agencies and departments	Legislative debate and modification	Financial management	
	Passed by legislature	Expenditure or revenue adjustments made if necessary	
	Signed by chief executive		
Phase 1	**Phase 2**	**Phase 3**	**Phase 4**

FIGURE 6.1 The Budget Process

SOURCE: Adapted from Ann Bowman and Richard Kearney, *State and Local Government,* 5th ed. (Boston: Houghton Mifflin, 2002), p. 212.

with the requests of interest groups. Budget offices, or the OMB at the federal level, gather and assemble the information needed to put together a proposed budget. The information must be analyzed to ensure that the projected revenues will cover anticipated expenditures. Some of the most intense politics of budgeting occurs during this phase because policy is being formulated. Interest groups and the agencies of government converge on the process to get their piece of the pie. Agencies often have their own lobbyists to ensure that they do not lose out. Lobbying is intense and will continue until the budget is passed later in the cycle. Agencies have developed strategies to protect their funding. Some of these are shown in Table 6.1. In most governments, the executive branch prepares the initial budget.

The second phase is *legislative review.* Although the budget is submitted to the legislature, executive-legislative relations continue throughout the process. This phase involves assembling the final budget, holding hearings, listening again to requests from interest groups and agencies, and legislative debate. Lobbyists will continue to apply pressure up until the legislature votes. During this process, the politics of budgeting truly become intense, and the decisions are made regarding how funds will be spent, which projects will be funded, and the level of funding the agencies of government will receive. For example, state universities, which are an agency of state governments, participate in the process to maintain and increase their funding for higher education. Thus, public policy also is finalized in this process. After the debate is over, the budget is approved by the legislature and signed by the chief executive. At this point, the budget has been formally adopted.

Table 6.1 The Budget Game—How to Protect an Agency's Budget

The tactics shown in this table are commonly used by agencies at all levels of government. They are employed to ensure that the agency does not lose funding in the budgetary process.

Rally support for the constituency or clientele	Locate, cultivate, and use clientele groups to further the organization's objectives. Encourage them to offer committee testimony and contact legislative members on the agency's behalf.
Always ask for more than one needs	The more one asks for, the more one usually gets. If an agency does not claim its share of the revenues, some other agency will.
Spend it or lose it	Make sure that all appropriated funds are spent before the fiscal year ends. An end-of-the-year surplus indicates that either the elected officials were too generous with the agency or the agency asked for more than it needed.
Hide new programs behind existing ones	Incrementalism means that existing program commitments are likely to receive continued support. Once a program has a line in the budget, it tends to be left alone. New programs get comprehensive examination. Related to this is the tendency for new programs to begin with low "start-up costs" that are followed by ballooning expenses down the road. This is sometimes called the "camel's nose under the tent" technique (once the nose of the camel is inside the tent, the camel will end up under the tent) and is the same idea as "getting a foot in the door."
A rose by any other name	Conceal unpopular or controversial programs within other program activities and give them more pleasing names. For example, sex education programs might be called "Teaching Values of the Family" or "Programs to Reduce Teenage Pregnancies."
"Let's study it first"	When told to cut or eliminate a program, argue that the consequences would be devastating and should be carefully studied before action is taken.
"Go ahead and just take it all"	When told that the budget must be cut, place the most popular programs on the chopping block. Rely on the constituency to organize opposition. Alternatively, state that all programs are critically important so that elected officials have to determine what gets cut.
A pig in a poke	Place an unneeded item in the budget request that can be given up gracefully while more important programs are protected.
Play one against the other	If the chief executive initiates a budget cut, run quickly to friends in the legislature. Regardless of who is making the cut, go to friends on the other side—legislature versus the chief executive.
Every vein is an artery	Claim that any program cut would undermine effectiveness and that the entire program would have to be abandoned.

SOURCE: Adapted from Ann Bowman and Richard Kearney, *State and Local Government*, 5th ed. (Boston: Houghton Mifflin, 2002), p. 215.

The budget is then *executed* (implemented), and funds become available for agencies to spend in executing public policies. Depending on the government, funds may be earmarked for agencies or transferred (usually quarterly) to agency accounts. This stage also involves making adjustments regarding both revenues and expenditures. Often adjustments are made due to revenue short-falls or unanticipated events.

After the fiscal year ends, the process of *auditing and evaluation* begins. Often auditors have just completed the previous year's evaluations, so auditing and evaluation is an ongoing process. The auditing process involves not only traditional accounting checks and verification, but also evaluation. Evaluation often involves cost-benefit studies and detailed analysis to measure the performance of programs. Cost-benefit analysis can be complex and may involve sophisticated econometric models, but in its simplest form, it evaluates whether the costs of programs and projects exceeded the benefits that were produced. For example, if the federal government spent $20 billion to help build a light rail system and the numbers of passengers who use the system has continued to fall, questions are raised and examined regarding the true benefits of maintaining the system relative to the costs. In many mass urban transportation systems, cost-benefit analyses reveal that it would have been less costly for government to buy every passenger a new car every three years than to spend the money on the rail system. Of course, such evaluations always require qualification. Auditing is conducted to ensure that funds were spent properly and that procedures were followed.

FEDERAL BUDGETARY PROCESS: AN OVERVIEW

Most of what we hear on the news involves the federal budget. Everyone who is interested in public administration should have some idea about the federal budgetary process. Although the budget cycle is essentially the same, the federal process typically has four major phases: formulation, legislative review, budget execution, and audit. Many months of work are involved in planning and analysis, which is part of the *formulation* phase, before the president submits the budget proposal to Congress in January of each year. In the spring of each year, agency programs are evaluated, policy issues are identified, and budget projections are made. In early June, a preliminary budget is given to the president for review. The Office of Management and Budget (OMB) is the key agency in this process. The OMB works with the president and all of the agencies of government to gather the expenditure estimates and policy recommendations. The president also receives estimations of revenues from the Treasury Department. The Council of Economic Advisors, the Treasury Department, and the OMB prepare economic projections jointly. After the various projections are reviewed, the president sets budget and fiscal policy guidelines for the next fiscal year. Guidelines, including expenditure ceilings, are then given to all executive agencies, which prepare their final budget requests during the remainder of the summer. In the fall, final budget requests are sent to the OMB, which reviews them, makes its own recommendations, and submits the final budget to the president for review. Fiscal policy is reviewed again, since changes in the economy are common. All of the agencies use the most recent data from the most recent fiscal year as a reference point (the idea of *incremental budgeting, or using last year's budget as the basis for the next year's budget).* This process consumes the entire fall.

The budget includes two types of spending, mandatory and discretionary. Mandatory spending includes all spending that is made pursuant to laws other than appropriations laws. The fundamental characteristic of mandatory spending is the lack of annual discretion to establish spending levels. Instead, mandatory spending usually involves a binding legal obligation by the federal government to provide funding for an individual, program, or activity. Discretionary spending refers to those programs that are subject to annual funding decisions in the appropriations process. Congress can determine to lower or increase funding by simply reducing or increasing the annual appropriation. Discretionary spending funds most of the actual operations of the federal government. Examples of discretionary spending include funding for the Department of Defense, the Department of Agriculture, the Federal Bureau of Investigation (FBI), the Internal Revenue Service (IRS), and the Environmental Protection Agency (EPA). The most intense part of the politics of budgeting takes place during preparation, but lobbying continues throughout the entire process.

After the president submits the budget to Congress, currently in early February, the process of *legislative review* begins. As noted earlier, between 1921 and 1974, the president dominated the budget process. All of that changed in 1974 with passage of the Congressional Budget and Impoundment Control Act, which altered the process and increased Congress's ability to deal with the budget. The Budget and Impoundment Control Act sought to control the impoundment of funds by presidents and bring more coordination into what was a piecemeal process of putting together a budget.[20] Impoundment occurs when the president refuses to spend money that was appropriated by Congress. Under the new law, the president can still impound funds but only with congressional approval. The new law set spending ceilings and revenue floors for the 13 major federal functions that make up the budget. The federal budget is actually a series of appropriation bills that are coupled together to make up the budget. This turned out to be a significant problem. The law set spending and debt ceilings too low to propose policy during that era. Thus, the effect reduced the importance of the president's budget. The law also established a timetable, which has been modified several times. Table 6.2 contains the timetable for 2002.

In addition, the law created special budget committees in each chamber of Congress to bring more coordination to the process, and established the Congressional Budget Office (CBO), which is Congress's version of the OMB. The CBO's job is to serve as a research office for Congress, which includes preparing an alternative budget based on independent estimates so that members of Congress will not have to rely on the executive branch. Since the mid-1970s, the executive branch has tended to have optimistic projections on the economy, while the CBO has tended to be more conservative. Congress never did very well at following the timetable that it created, which included changing the fiscal year from beginning on July 1 to October 1, and there have been

Table 6.2 Congressional Budgetary Timetable (2002)

Date	Action
5 days before president submits budget	Congressional Budget Office (CBO) sequester preview report
First Monday in February	President's budget submission including Office of Management and Budget (OMB) sequester preview report and adjustments to spending caps
February 15	CBO budget and outlook report
6 weeks after president's budget has been submitted (usually around March 15)	Committees submit views and estimates to the budget committees in each chamber
April 1	Senate Budget Committee reports resolution
April 15	Congress completes budget resolution
May 15	Appropriations bills may be considered in the House even in the absence of a budget resolution
June 10	House Appropriations Committee reports last bill
June 30	House completes action on annual appropriations bills and on reconciliation bill
July 15	President submits midsession review
August 15	CBO sequester update report
August 20	OMB sequester update report with adjustments to caps
October 1	**New fiscal year begins**
10 days after end of session	CBO final sequester report
15 days after end of session	OMB final sequester report and Government Accounting Office (GAO) compliance report

NOTE: The timetable has been altered many times since 1974. This table was being used for the 2003 fiscal budget, which was prepared during 2002.

SOURCE: United States House of Representatives, Budget Committee.

a number of times where the budget debate lasted for months beyond the beginning of the new fiscal year. In these cases, Congress must pass legislation that allows the federal government to continue to operate while the budget is still being worked out. Typically, these special appropriations bills (called *continuing resolutions*) allow government to continue its current service operations. That is, the old budget levels are extended until the new budget is passed and implemented. Congress also failed to follow its own rules. The idea of spending limits and debt ceilings was fine, but Congress just raised the limits if it needed more money. This rendered the spirit of the 1974 reforms moot. More reforms came in the 1980s. The Graham–Rudman–Hollings Act of 1985 attempted to set ceilings and impose automatic cuts (a process called sequestration) if Congress and the president failed to get the budget passed on time. The law also set up targets to achieve a balanced budget by 1991. The Supreme Court struck down some of the provisions of the law.[21]

Congress passed another law in 1987 and met the reductions with the help of creative accounting, but ultimately it was agreed that the targets to reduce the budget deficit were unrealistic. The next law was the Budget Enforcement Act of 1990. This law (called the BEA) was based on revenue increases and spending reductions and was more flexible than the 1985 Budget Reduction Act. Spending limits were specified but could be modified. The BEA created the idea of zero-sum budget making or the idea of pay-as-you-go (PAYGO). This self-imposed system forced Congress to offset any increases in spending by cutting expenditures elsewhere. Unfortunately, this law did not work much better than previous laws and led some members of Congress to call for a balanced budget amendment to the U.S. Constitution to bring fiscal responsibility to the system. The balanced budget amendment failed to pass in Congress. In the new century, Congress is still using the PAYGO system.

Political hardball between the Congress and the president has occurred a number of times over trying to offset spending increases and cutting the budget elsewhere. In 1996, President Bill Clinton refused to sign the Republican budget (Republicans controlled both chambers at that time), which literally shut down part of the government because the Republicans refused to pass a continuing resolution that would have allowed government operations to continue. At odds were two appropriation bills—one that contained provisions for borrowing by the Treasury Department, and another that contained numerous appropriations that President Clinton found unacceptable. He vetoed both bills, and the Republicans refused to pass continuing resolutions. The showdown backfired on Republicans who received the blame for letting the government shut down.

Throughout the 1990s Congress failed to stay within its spending limits, but by fiscal year 1998, largely due to a vibrant economy, the budget actually had a surplus for the first time in decades. Congress also authorized and President Clinton signed a law that would give the president a line-item veto. This historical provision was found to be unconstitutional by the Supreme Court. The era of stalemate has not passed as of this writing, but Congress has shown a little more fiscal responsibility and adopted a pay-as-you-go policy. After the terrorist attacks of September 11, 2001, President Bush enjoyed a more cooperative Congress, but the favorable relationship soon faded. Like all public budgeting, the federal budget epitomizes executive-legislative relations. It is the goal of the president to get the budget approved by Congress without losing too much along the way. After all, the budget is the president's policy agenda for the next fiscal year.

Once the budget is approved, the budgeting is formally *executed*. Law makes budget authority and resources available to the executive branch by means of an appropriation system. The OMB distributes appropriations to each agency, usually quarterly (every three months) or by activities. Expenses cannot be incurred that exceed the apportioned amount. This ensures an efficient and effective way to distribute funds and minimizes additional requests for supplemental funds. During this phase, administrators try to achieve program goals within the constraints of the appropriated funding, but there never seems to be enough money to attain goals. The budget is a finite financial pie, and each agency must operate within these limitations once the budget is executed.

Agencies must plan, manage, and account for their budgets while at the same time implementing whatever public policies they have been mandated to administer. One of the problems cited by critics involves *backdoor spending,* which allows obligations to be incurred without going through the normal appropriations process. Agencies can receive authority to sign contracts for services or even to borrow money that will be repaid later.[22] Congress can authorize off-budget programs, which is also a form of backdoor spending. In 1974 there was an attempt to curb backdoor spending, but the law allowed many exceptions,[23] including a number of very large exceptions such as the Social Security trust fund.

An unusual budgetary phenomenon in the public sector is worth discussing. Amazingly, virtually every agency at every level of government manages to spend every dime every year. In the private sector, managers are often praised for not spending all of their funds (assuming they did not skimp on their services). In some cases, managers and employees get bonuses if they turn in a surplus. However, in the public sector, the phrase is "spend it or lose it." The rationale is that if the agency turns in a surplus this year, next year its funding levels will be cut. Thus, agencies usually go on a year-end spending binge to get rid of all their excess funds. Research has revealed that fourth-quarter obligations at the federal level tend to be much higher than during other quarters of the accounting cycle. (There are some exceptions at the federal level where the money is allowed to carry over.) In practice, some of this money is probably wasted or spent on equipment or items that have been neglected. Some efforts have been made to eliminate this behavior, which is found at all levels of government. One solution could be to just add the surplus back to the agencies' budgets for the next year. But managers feel that this would probably still result in cuts down the road, and budget offices believe that provisions exist for emergency funding and they are not likely to give up control of this power. Another solution is to give managers and/or employees an end-of-the-year bonus, like the practice used by many private companies. The problem with this is twofold. First of all, the public may look at this practice unfavorably. Why should civil servants get a bonus check? Many people would rather have a rebate check sent back to taxpayers or lower taxes. Second, managers may skimp on quality to ensure that they get a bonus. Firms in the private sector have to monitor this behavior. Managers may cut corners where they should not be cutting, which can hurt the firm in the long term. The same is likely true for the public sector. Some state universities have adopted a policy that allows departments to get back a percentage of their surplus. This is a potential solution, but if the percentage is too small, there will not be an incentive to cooperate. For example, if a department in a university only gets back 30 percent of what it has saved (this means the administration keeps 70 percent), the incentive is inadequate. Moreover, this is not money that is generated from sales; it is money taken from the public coffers, and it is supposed to be used wisely.

Good management in the public sector means delivering the service on an accurate budget. If an agency asks for too much money, the excess should be returned to the general fund to be used for other important functions. *(Note*

BOX 6.2 Punishing Efficiency by Robert D. Behn

Like other states, South Carolina has been watching its tax revenues drop. For the past fiscal year, the state had a $133 million deficit. This required South Carolina to withdraw $87 million from its rainy-day fund of $148 million.

From where did South Carolina get the additional $46 million that it needed to cover the $133 million deficit? From state agencies that had saved it.

For a variety of reasons, this move made financial sense. It left South Carolina with $61 million in its rainy-day fund. State Treasurer Grady Patterson told the Columbia newspaper *The State* that he wanted "to avoid going into the general reserve fund because that can affect our Triple A credit rating."

But last year's budget deficit had not come as a complete surprise. South Carolina saw it coming. It knew that tax revenues were not going to match the state's original projections. So the state made a 1 percent across-the-board cut in agency budgets. Moreover, the legislature cut half a billion dollars from the state's fiscal-year 2002 budget, though it recog-

nized that this might cause problems for some departments. So the legislature continued the recent practice that permitted state executives to carry forward into FY 2002 any funds saved from the FY 2001 budget. This let agency managers think about their budgets for FY 2001 and FY 2002 as a single FY 2001–2002 budget.

Some state agencies believed this. They saved their pennies—4.6 billion pennies. The Department of Education saved $10.4 million. The Department of Health and Human Services saved more than $13 million. Now, it turns out, they won't get to keep their savings.

Not that South Carolina responded to its budget shortfall with an approach that is widely different from what other governments do. The standard strategies include across-the-board cuts and the expropriation of any exposed resource. Moreover, these strategies appear to be perfectly reasonable. An across-the-board cut seems only "fair." Everyone must bear the same burden. And if some resources are available, shouldn't they be used to deal with the immediate crisis?

---

that the federal government does not use fund accounting like most states and cities.) Regardless of one's view, the idea of spending sprees at the end of each year is not a solution but is a reality of the public sector. Again, the guiding principle is "spend it or lose it," and there is no adequate incentive to stop this behavior. This practice is not likely to change in the foreseeable future. Box 6.2 illustrates this point.

Like the general budget cycle, the final phase is *auditing*. Agencies are responsible for maintaining their own internal control systems to ensure that funds are spent according to the provisions of the authorizing and appropriating legislation. The OMB reviews programs and ensures that agencies are meeting their objectives. Auditing is simply verifying that all the accounting and other procedures were properly followed. But auditing can also uncover problems. Audits can uncover embezzlement, fraud, and lax accounting systems. The GAO regularly audits and evaluates government programs. Audits have dis-

But what will agency managers in South Carolina learn from these responses to the budget shortfall? From the perspective of the agency executive, the lesson is clear: Don't save money. Don't try to be efficient. Because if you do, you will be punished. The state executives who were smart—you can call them "cynical"—spent every dime.

Nevertheless, some people continue to wonder why the managers of executive branch agencies always spend their budgets down to zero at the end of the fiscal year.

At a congressional hearing several years ago, U.S. Representative Dan Burton reported that as a state senator in Indiana he had overheard an agency head saying, "We have only got what, two months left in the fiscal year. And if we don't spend the money we have got, we are not going to be able to ask for an increase in the next appropriation." This riled Burton: "I would like to figure out some way to give monetary rewards for people in government to come up with ways to streamline and create economies."

Apparently, it had never occurred to state Senator Burton or Congress-man Burton that the first kind of monetary reward that public managers would like for streamlining and creating economies is not to be punished for doing so. A second kind of monetary reward would be to permit the managers to actually keep a portion of the savings and use them to improve other, authorized services.

A quarter of a century ago, Steven Kerr, now the chief learning officer at General Electric, wrote a classic article, "On the Folly of Rewarding A, While Hoping for B." His title captures his point succinctly.

Political leaders—and not just in South Carolina—*hope* that public managers will streamline, create economies, and save money. But they don't *reward* it. Instead, they reward agencies that spend (or hide) every last dime. If political leaders want public managers to save money, they ought to reward very explicitly—and very visibly—agencies that do so.

Punishing efficiency won't create more of it.

SOURCE: From "View," *Governing Magazine Online* (September 3, 2001), http://www.governing.com/view/vu090301.htm. *Used with permission.*

closed that dentists have pulled healthy teeth of poor children to collect Medicaid checks, that employees have embezzled nearly a million dollars by forging signatures, and that the Pentagon paid excessive amounts of money for spare parts.[24] Everyone has heard about those $600 coffee pots (that were essentially Mr. Coffee coffeemakers) and $50 claw hammers that could have been purchased at any hardware store for $15. Audits help to find waste and to ensure that policies are being followed, and they often uncover fraud and corruption. Auditing is a necessary part of the budgetary system.

The federal budgetary process also includes program evaluation, which examines efficiency and effectiveness of government programs. Congress, the GAO, and the OMB each evaluate various programs. This information is used during the next budget cycle to determine whether certain programs are worth continuing. Some of the items in the federal budget are very expensive, particularly items such as space shuttles, ships, bombers, fighter aircraft, and tanks.

These items cost billions of dollars to construct. Also, welfare programs cost a lot of money and are often controversial public policy. Some evaluations have disclosed that very little of the appropriate money actually gets into the hands of the poor. The vast majority of the funds (sometimes 80 percent) go to administrative costs, and the record has been questionable on how effective the programs have been at getting people off the welfare rolls. Some critics claimed that the system was designed to perpetuate dependence for the recipients and to provide jobs for those working in the welfare system, rather than to help people get off of welfare. Many evaluations suggested that many welfare programs were not working, which led Congress to make some significant revisions during the 1990s. The specifics of public policy, including welfare policy, will be discussed in Chapter 7. But evaluating program efficiency and effectiveness has caused many programs to be altered, and this is considered to be a part of the budgetary process because it provides inputs and information that will be used for making future funding decisions. Figure 6.2 illustrates the general budgetary process at the federal level.

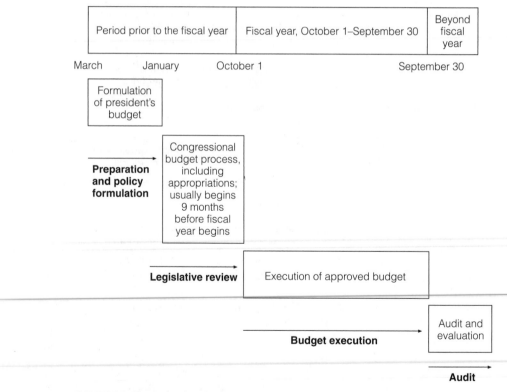

FIGURE 6.2 The Federal Budget Process

SOURCE: Adapted from Grover Starling, *Managing the Public Sector,* 4th ed. (Belmont, CA: Wadsworth, 1993), p. 505.

TYPES OF BUDGETS

Several different types of budget formats are used by governments. The budget document can be constructed in various ways, depending on the desired purpose, such as control, management, planning, or performance. Each type of budget format was designed to accomplish different goals. Each also has distinct advantages and disadvantages. Historically, control or fiscal accountability has been the main purpose of budgeting. *Incrementalism* (using last year's budget as the basis for next year's budget) has dominated the process, and the *line-item budget* has been the typical format. There are two main types of budgets: *operating budgets,* which are in effect for one fiscal year, and *capital budgets,* which include large items such as buildings and expensive equipment.

Line-Item Budgets and Incrementalism

The line-item budget allows control by specifying the amount of funds, line by line in each category, that an agency receives. This system allows for the greatest control because decision makers know in advance how much money has been allocated for each category. Thus, it is easy to follow how the money was spent and what was purchased. This makes it possible to watch every dollar and to ensure that funds are spent for the items listed in the budget. Line-item budgets show exactly where the money goes better than any other format. They provide the best tracking system available. But they do not tell us how effectively the money was spent. In fact, they really do not provide much of an indication about efficiency because we do not know what is being accomplished with the money. That is, they are a great way to track and control money, but they say nothing about whether objectives are being met because they are not tied in any way to stated objectives. Stated differently, line-item budgets do not reveal much about what agencies actually do. Rather than examining objectives, such as reducing the crime rate or increasing the graduation rate in public schools, line-item budgets simply look at last year's budget as the basis for constructing next year's budget. The debate is over incremental increases or decreases in the budget. This process is called *incrementalism* and remains the dominant method used by legislatures.

Incrementalism is popular for several reasons. First of all, it allows for the greatest control over spending. Second, politicians are not usually technical experts, and they approve many aspects of a budget without any expertise in the area. Third, time constraints do not allow for the more arduous process of developing objectives. Typically, once a program is in the budget, it tends to remain there until something occurs to force decision makers to consider eliminating it as a budget line. The hallmarks of incrementalism are *consistency* and *continuity.* The future is an extension of the present, which is a continuation of the past. Long-range commitments are made and honored indefinitely.[25] Aron Wildavsky spent a career studying this process and concluded that incrementalism is the most feasible method for the legislative process.[26]

Performance Budgeting:
Planning-Programming-Budgeting Systems (PPBS)

Line–item budgets were desirable for reformers around the turn of the 20th century because control over how the public's money was spent was of paramount concern. By the 1940s there was a need to use budgeting for more than just control. There was a need to monitor programs more closely and to better manage a much larger, more complex government.[27] The goal was to make programs more effective. The Budget and Accounting Procedures Act of 1950 recommended that the federal government adopt performance budgeting. The idea of performance-based budgets was not a new idea. The New York Bureau of Municipal Research developed the basic idea in 1907. During the 1930s, welfare economics developed many of the ideas that would later be associated with planning-programming-budgeting (PPB). Many techniques of PPB would be developed in operations research and systems analysis at the Rand Corporation during the 1950s. Planning-programming-budgeting was popularized during the 1960s by Robert McNamara (the Secretary of Defense in the Johnson administration), and spread through the whole federal government by President Johnson.[28]

Budgets that focus on management and planning are intended to help move budgeting away from the constraints of line items and incrementalism toward a rational and more flexible process that focuses on results. The focus on planning-programming-budgeting systems (PPBS) is on objectives. The intention is to ensure that money is actually achieving something. Sometimes called program-based budgeting (PBB), those involved in the process set objectives for their agencies and construct budgets that are needed to attain those objectives. The focus is not on line items but on how much funding will be needed to actually reduce crime, patrol and protect the nation's coastline from drug traffickers, or maintain the nation's defense systems. Program-based budgeting systems are a form of performance budgeting and require that an agency set objectives and lay out a financial plan to reach the stated objectives. Planning is critical because it forces an agency to think about the future, identify output measures, and make contingency plans. The key is that there are measurable indictors that will illustrate whether an agency is meeting its objectives.[29]

Program-based budgeting was an effort to bring rationalism into the budget process. But what seemed like a great idea at the time would not last. During the 1960s, the nation was fighting wars on crime, poverty, and Vietnam. Although PPB systems are rational, they are time-consuming and require enormous amounts of paperwork. The idea was largely abandoned by the Nixon administration but was revived at the agency level years later. President Nixon preferred *management by objectives* (MBO), the popular management tool developed by Peter Drucker. Management by objectives involves setting objectives for agencies and requiring regular reports on the progress of achieving the stated objectives. It is less formal and simpler than PBB. Although the Office of

Management and Budget encouraged agencies to use MBO, the practice was short-lived and ceased to exist during President Nixon's tenure in office. Unlike PBB, which was mandated during the Johnson administration, MBO was encouraged rather than required throughout the federal government. Congress was never fully sold on any of the new faddish methods of budgeting. Congress continues to use the basic incremental line-item budget. Program-based budgeting systems were revived at the agency level and continue to be used to this day.

Zero-Based Budgets (ZBB)

Another version of budgeting is *zero-based budgeting (ZBB)*. Zero-based budgeting is a simple idea. Each year agencies must justify their budgets by starting with a "blank sheet" of paper. In theory, the budget is viewed as independent from that for the previous year. It focuses on one fiscal year. Both incremental and PBB budgets usually include five-year projections. Zero-based budgeting is often contrasted to incremental budgeting because it is virtually impossible to construct a budget without looking at that for the previous year, but analysts using ZBB can ignore the data and accomplishments. In incremental budgeting, the previous year's funding levels are the basis for making budget decisions. Zero-based budgeting can also incorporate objectives. Thus, it can be viewed as a type of performance budget. Normally ZBB involves preparing budget proposals and alternate levels of spending grouped into "decision packages." Decision packages are self-contained units for budget choice that contain input and output data with expected levels of performance for each defined level of expenditure.[30] Higher levels of management then examine, rank, and prioritize decision packages. The lowest-ranked packages do not get funded.

The Department of Agriculture used a ZBB approach to create its budget in 1964. The experience was not pleasant. It consumed large amounts of time, required too much documentation, and was therefore quickly abandoned. The problem with ZBB is that one essentially "reinvents the wheel" each year, and the benefits of performing this task usually fail to justify the costs in time and frustration. Peter Pyhrr successfully used ZBB at Texas Instruments. Pyhrr also wrote a book in the early 1970s that popularized the concept and published an influential article in *Harvard Business Review*.[31] President Jimmy Carter, who was the governor of Georgia at the time, read the book and brought Pyhrr to the state to help implement ZBB. President Carter required that ZBB be used at the federal level during his presidency. With the exception of the state of Georgia and during the Carter administration at the federal level, ZBB has been modestly adopted in the public sector. A number of cities use ZBB, as well as several states, including New Jersey, Idaho, Montana, and Illinois. How well ZBB actually works is unclear, but most governments do not use it. There are several different versions of ZBB, but all appear to have similar problems to PBB—too much paperwork, documentation, and the like, and the amount of time expended usually does not justify the effort.

Capital Budgets

Capital budgets are separate budgets for assets that will be used over a longer period of time. They involve special outlays for items such as school buildings, bridges, sewage systems, water systems, and similar items that will last for many years. In contrast, operating budgets usually involve purchasing goods and services that will last for only about a year. For example, while school buildings will be used for many years, office supplies such as pens, paper, staples, and printer cartridges will be used up quickly. Building a sewer treatment plant is a *capital expenditure,* but the chemicals used in the plant are a *current expenditure.*

Although the distinction between items that will be used up in a short time versus items that will be used over time seems clear, problems with classification often occur. A large city may purchase 50 police cars each year because by the end of a year, these cars may be worn out. Are these cars a capital item? Fifty police cruisers cost a lot of money. A large city may use either classification. It may select to use the current budget because the cars must be purchased each year. On the other hand, a small town may buy three or four police cars on its capital budget and use the cars for five years. Governments use arbitrary guidelines to classify many capital and current service items. The size of the government is typically a major factor. Small governments may consider anything that costs over $2,000 to be a capital item, whereas large governments may set a cost of more than $25,000. The general guideline is that anything that will last for a year is classified as a current expenditure regardless of the cost. Small goods that may last for years, such as staplers, desktop computers, or cases of paper, are also classified as current expenditures.

Capital investments are desirable in both the public and private sectors. In private industry, capital investments, such as new equipment, usually help firms become more productive. The public sector invests in many capital projects that are considered to be an investment in the future, such as new schools or making improvements in infrastructure (roads, sewage systems, and water systems) to promote economic development. Spending funds on capital improvements is considered to be more palatable and politically acceptable. All jurisdictions need improvements and maintenance on the infrastructure to handle growth or simply fix old roads, bridges, and the like that have worn out. Most states and municipal governments have capital budgets. The federal government does not make a distinction between capital and current expenditures and does not maintain a separate capital budget.

At the state and local level, capital projects are funded through the sale of general obligation bonds or revenue bonds. Bonds are certificates of debt sold by governments. Those who purchase bonds will eventually recover the amount of the bond plus interest. *General obligation bonds* are paid for with the jurisdiction's general revenues. They are considered to be safer bonds because they are backed by the "full faith and credit" of the government. Government bonds are typically considered to be one of the safest investments available because governments rarely go bankrupt. *Revenue bonds* are paid off with the revenue (or user fees) generated by the project. For example, revenue bonds are typically used to build sports arenas and parking garages. These facilities generate revenue that will be used to pay off the debt.

TAXATION, REVENUES, AND EXPENDITURES

There are two sides of the budget: *revenues* and *expenditures*. Government revenues mainly come from taxes. The justification for taxes is obvious. Government must provide certain essential services, such as national defense, and citizens must pay for it. What is taxed, who is taxed, and how much people must pay have been controversial for a long time. Ben Franklin's famous quote was, "In this world nothing can be said to be certain, except death and taxes."[32] Taxes are unpopular. No one likes to pay them. But they must be collected to pay for the functions of government in order to pay for public goods. There are two types of public goods. They are sometimes called *social wants* and *merit wants*.[33]

Social wants are those needs that must be consumed equally. Those who do not want to pay for these goods (free riders) cannot be excluded from consuming or benefiting from the goods. For example, no one who lives in the United States can be excluded from enjoying the protection of national defense. In this type of traditional public good, the satisfaction of the citizen/consumer is independent of his or her contribution. That is, the *exclusion principle* that applies to private goods does not apply. *Merit wants* are also public goods, but the exclusion principle applies in varying degrees. Examples include welfare benefits, public housing, and school lunches. In these cases, everyone must pay, but most people are excluded from using the specific good or service. The exclusion principle simply is the ability to exclude others from using a good or service. For example, if a person buys a new computer and takes it home, he or she can exclude others from using the computer. The exclusionary principle is easy to apply to private goods.

TAX EQUITY AND TAX EXPENDITURES

Some basic principles and terms are involved with taxation. The concept of *tax equity* has two primary dimensions: vertical equity and horizontal equity. Horizontal equity refers to charging the *same amount* to different taxpayers whose income levels (or ability to pay) is the same. Vertical equity refers to charging *differently* to those with different income levels or ability to pay. This problem arises because people do not earn the same amount of money in the United States. Some people may earn $500,000 per year while others earn $15,000. How does government construct a tax structure that is fair to individuals who run the gamut in terms of their incomes? In reality, government does not achieve true or even approximate equity at any level of government. The distinctions involve manipulating the rates charged to try to achieve equity. Confusion and debate usually emerge regarding the fairest way to levy taxes. The concepts that are involved are regressive versus progressive tax systems. The most regressive taxes are flat taxes, which usually hurt poor citizens because they spend a greater portion of their income on taxed items. Flat taxes, such as sales taxes, charge the same amount to all regardless of their income or ability to pay. If income taxes are constructed as flat proportional structures, then everyone pays the same percentage of their incomes in taxes, but the proportions penalize those with lower incomes. For example, if the income tax were 10 percent for everyone regardless of income, then a person earning $10,000 would pay $1,000 in taxes, leaving $9,000 for all other expenditures. A person earning $100,000 per year would pay more taxes ($10,000), but would have $90,000 left. Critics do not view this as fair. But others argue that the alternative provides a disincentive to earn money and work toward being financially successful. The alternative is a progressive tax structure that takes a larger proportion of a person's income as income increases. That is, the more you earn, the larger the percentage of your income must go for taxes.

Progressive taxes use brackets that attempt to adjust equity by placing a greater burden on those with higher incomes. Federal income tax brackets (and most state income taxes) are progressive. The federal individual income tax brackets for 2001 are shown in Table 6.3. The idea of imposing higher tax rates on people with higher incomes is based on the belief that the tax structure should be based on the "ability to pay." Not everyone agrees, but this is the system that is used. During periods of high inflation, tax brackets can be problematic if incomes are not indexed to account for inflation. *Indexing* involves adjusting income relative to prices. During the 1970s, *bracket creep* occurred because rising prices caused income to increase, which pushed people into higher tax brackets, while losing buying power to inflation. Indexing resolved the problem and is now commonly used.

Other concepts associated with taxation include *tax expenditures,* which are simply revenues that could have been collected, but were deliberately not collected. These include tax exemptions, special exclusions, special credits, and other deductions. *Tax loopholes* are usually not loopholes; they are tax preferences placed there deliberately to give a benefit to certain categories of people. The principle of *benefits received* deals with some services where the burden can be placed on those who use the specific service. The idea of *user fees* epitomizes this concept. The principle cannot be applied to all services in government, but it works for municipal golf courses, parks, and the like. It does not work well for education, which produces positive spillovers for society as a whole.

Tax efficiency refers to a tax that does not appreciably affect the allocation of resources in the private sector, such as consumption and savings, or among competing items for consumption. High taxes on the wealthy, such as *luxury taxes* on high-dollar items like exotic cars or yachts, can have an adverse impact

Table 6.3 Federal Individual Income Tax Brackets for 2001

Bracket #1	15% if one's income was $0 to $27,049 (single) or $45,199 (married couple)
Bracket #2	27.5% from $27,050 (single) or $45,200 (married) to $65,449 (single) or $109,249 (married)
Bracket #3	30.5% if one's income ranged between $65,550/$109,250 and $136,749/$166,449; 35.5% for incomes between $136,750 and $297,349 (single) and $166,500 and $297,350 (married)
Bracket #4	39.1% for all incomes over $297,350 (except married couples filing separately was $148,675 each)

SOURCE: Internal Revenue Service (2000).

because they encourage the wealthy to spend more time on leisure and less time working and earning more income. Luxury taxes, which were tried by Congress in the 1980s, were disastrous and caused some industries to leave the country, such as the yacht industry in South Florida.

Another tax-related concept that is important is *elasticity*. This concept refers to how well taxes give and take with changes in the economy. Some taxes expand with economic expansions and shrink when the economy contracts. Other taxes are inelastic; that is, they are less affected by changes in the economy. This idea is easier to illustrate with products or goods. So-called "sin taxes," which are imposed on products like alcohol and tobacco, seem less affected by changes in economic conditions. *Tax bases* simply refer to the available amount of taxable goods in a jurisdiction (such as the amount of income or land that is subject to taxation). Tax bases vary greatly from one jurisdiction to another. Some states are wealthier, have more industry, and have residents with higher incomes than other jurisdictions do. Some jurisdictions tax more aggressively than others do. The concept of taxing aggressively or less aggressively is called *tax effort*.

A theoretical concept about taxation that is worth noting is known as the *Laffer curve*. This concept is essentially the *law of diminishing returns* applied to taxation. The theory holds that there is an optimal tax rate that will yield the highest amount of taxes, and it is neither the lowest or highest point on the curve. Like the law of diminishing returns, there are two points on the curve that produce the same amount of revenue. Figure 6.3 is an illustration of the Laffer curve. The theory holds that if the tax rate were zero, no taxes would be collected. Likewise, if the tax rate were 100 percent (meaning that the government collected all of the income that people earn), no taxes would be collected because people would have no incentive to work. The theory was developed by economist Arthur Laffer and was widely cited during the Reagan administration. The Laffer curve came to epitomize the idea of supply-side economics embraced during the Reagan era. Applied to taxation, supply-siders argued that the tax rate should be kept low to enhance expansion in the economy. That is,

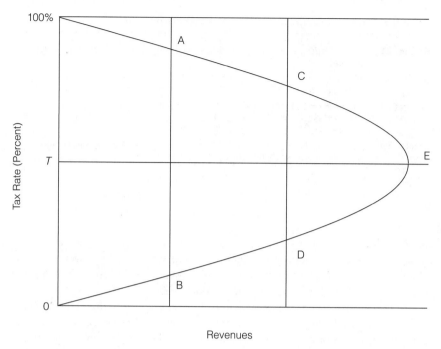

FIGURE 6.3 The Laffer Curve

SOURCE: Adapted from Jude Wanniski, *The Way the World Works,* 2nd ed. (New York: Simon and Schuster, 1983), p. 97. *T* represents the optimum tax rate where the maximum amount of tax revenue can be collected. The theory assumes that if tax rates were 100%, no taxes would be collected. Likewise, the theory assumes that if the tax rate were zero, no taxes would be collected. The theory was developed by economist Arthur Laffer.

when tax rates are low, the economy expands and is more productive than when tax rates are too high.

MAJOR TYPES OF TAXES

Several major types of taxes are used by governments. Each level of government relies on a different type of tax for its primary source of income. The three major methods of taxation impose taxes on *income* (typically progressive income taxes), *wealth* (typically property taxes), and *consumption* (typically general sales taxes).

The individual income tax, which was authorized by the Sixteenth Amendment to the U.S. Constitution, is the main source of tax revenue for the federal government. As shown in Table 6.3, the federal government uses a progressive tax structure. Personal income taxes at the federal level ran from 15 percent to 39.1 percent in 2001. Earlier in the 20th century, there was a 93-percentile bracket, but the progressiveness was gradually dropped. During the

1980s, the Reagan administration lowered the federal income tax brackets. They were raised slightly by President Bush after his famous "read my lip, no new taxes," comment, and were raised again by Bill Clinton. Most states use less progressive structures than the federal government, and most local governments that tax income use flat tax structures.

The income tax structure used at the national level is a *net income tax* rather than *gross income tax*. This means that people are allowed to deduct items and pay their taxes on the net value. The tax is progressive; the more one earns, the more one pays. The principle is based on the "ability to pay." Those who earn more are expected to pay a higher percentage of their income in taxes so those with lower incomes can pay a smaller percentage. During the 1990s, Congress considered a flat tax (roughly 17 percent with few allowable deductions) that would have greatly simplified the federal structure. Taxes would be handled on a postcard. However, special interests defeated the idea. Former House Majority Leader and economist Dick Armey introduced the idea. Indiana Senator Richard Lugar proposed an alternative. His proposal was for a national sales tax. Congress took neither idea very seriously.

Most states tax both personal and corporate income. Wisconsin was the first state to impose a personal income tax in 1911. Forty-three states have some type of income tax. Most are broad-based and vary in degrees of progressiveness. Seven states do not tax personal income (Alaska, Florida, Nevada, South Dakota, Texas, Washington, and Wyoming). Five states do not tax corporate income (Nevada, South Dakota, Texas, Washington, and Wyoming). Fourteen states allow local governments to tax income. The personal income tax accounts for about 25 percent of all state revenue; corporate income taxes account for 6 percent. *Corporate income taxes* are controversial because they are considered to be a *double tax*. That is, corporations pay income taxes (based on net income), and then people holding stocks are taxed on the dividends. Businesses often view this as unfair, since the tax has already been paid before paying dividends. The federal *corporate income tax* is graduated from 15 percent to 35 percent, but for all practical purposes it is relatively flat due to the low dollar amount of new earnings (the first $50,000 is taxed at 15 percent, the next $25,000 is taxed at 25 percent, and the remaining income is taxed at 34 percent until it reaches $10 million, at which point it is taxed at 35 percent).[34]

Sales taxes are consumption taxes. In general, they tax how much of some good or commodity is consumed. Sales taxes are very regressive. They tax everyone equally, but the burden on those with lower incomes is greater. All but five states have a sales tax (Alaska, Delaware, Montana, New Hampshire, and Oregon). The national average for state sales taxes was 5 percent in 2001. Mississippi was the first state to impose a sales tax in 1932. Typically sales tax accounts for about 40 percent of all state revenue. Some states, like Florida, generate more than half their revenue from sales taxes. Many states, like North Carolina, tax virtually all sales (except wholesale transactions or purchases by nonprofit organizations). Most states exclude some sales, such as food and prescription drugs. A few states (such as Hawaii, New Mexico, and South Dakota) expand their taxable base by taxing services. This may be the wave of the future because the service sector continues to be the fastest-growing area of the economy. Sales tax is a primary source of revenue for most states, but total state revenue is comprised of nearly an equal balance between state sales taxes and state income taxes.

Property taxes are tax on personal wealth. In principle, those with more wealth will pay the most. The rationale behind taxing real estate is that local governments must support the property with police, fire, and infrastructure. Property taxes tend to be very regressive. Middle- and lower-income families tend to pay a much larger proportion of their income than wealthier families do. This is because, for the middle class, their home is usually their largest asset. Thus, most of their wealth is being taxed each year. The wealthy tend to have other assets aside from their home. This is the largest source of income for local governments. It is also considered to be an unfair tax, at least according to surveys. States once relied more heavily on property taxes; in the 1940s, property taxes accounted for more than half of all state and local revenue, while today they account for less than 30 percent of tax revenue. States discovered that sales taxes generate much more revenue, and people generally feel that a sales tax is fairer. New Hampshire still collects two-thirds of its revenue from state property taxes, while New Mexico (the lowest) collects 12 percent of its revenue from this source.

Property taxes remain the primary source for local governments. The tax is perceived as unfair by most and is difficult to administer, mainly because of property valuations. No agreement exists over the one best way to valuate property (market value, assessed value, or some other method). Property taxes are calculated using a formula that is based on "mills." A rate of one mill yields $1 for every $1,000 of assessed value. For example, a property rate value of 100 mills applied to a $150,000 property assessed at 20 percent of the market value would yield $3,000. (The formula is *market value* $\times$ *assessment rate* $\times$ *mills* = *yield*. In the example, this would be $150,000 $\times$ .2 $\times$ 100 = $3,000.) Property taxes are the most difficult to administer. Banks have developed systems that guide how much money they will loan on homes, but assessments are not always popular with homeowners. Also, commercial property and land must be assessed. The value of these assets is not constant. Changes in the market, new construction in an area, or someone adding a mobile home park can increase or decrease the value of property. *Circuit breakers* are systems developed to help low-income people and the elderly cope with increased property taxes. Some state and local governments cap the amount of tax one must pay based on income. Others force the property value to be based on purchase price to keep property values from rising too quickly.

There are other taxes and alternative revenue sources for governments, such as *severance taxes*. States that have ample natural resources can collect significant amounts of revenue from this source. Most states have severance taxes, but only a few collect significant amounts. Alaska gets the highest amount from severance taxes, and Wyoming collects 60 percent of its revenue from taxes on coal, oil, and natural gas.

One of the latest and most controversial taxes involves the Internet. The issue of *Internet taxes,* which are a form of sales or excise tax, is prompting new battles in the states. Congress imposed a moratorium on taxing online sales until 2001 (Internet Tax Freedom Act of 1998) because 21 states were levying taxes on Internet access, data downloads, and other services. Internet commerce is one of the fastest-growing areas in the economy, and states want to tap this new source of revenue. Congress blocked the states' efforts under the rationale that the Internet was so new that it needed time to develop. Until Congress passed the Internet Tax Freedom Act in 1998, many states and local governments were imposing taxes.[35] For example, Tacoma, Washington, required Internet service providers (ISPs) to pay a 6 percent gross receipts tax—even ISPs without any employees in Tacoma. Tacoma's law also required everyone who sold a product over the Internet to a Tacoma resident to pay a $72 annual business license fee. Florida had imposed a 7 percent tax on the sale of Internet access, plus an additional 2.5 percent tax on the gross receipts from such sales, and was also allowing cities to impose additional telephone fees on Internet access services.

The Internet Tax Freedom Act was extended in 2001 by Congress through November 1, 2003, and signed by President Bush in 2001. Congress originally wanted to extend the moratorium for five years to 2006. States are battling over how to tax commerce and other services involving the Internet. States argue that they are losing more than $15 billion in revenue each year. This battle is likely to continue. Currently, states can tax sales using the old catalog sales laws, but the U.S. Supreme Court blocked states from taxing beyond this law in a North Dakota case, *Quill v. North Dakota,* on the grounds that taxing a mail-order firm in another state violates the interstate commerce clause. A state can tax Internet sales and catalog sales if a firm operates a store in that state. If the firm does not have a store in that state, Internet sales cannot be taxed.

Taxes are necessary, and governments collect revenue from a variety of sources. The main sources are income, sales, and property taxes. Tables 6.4 and 6.5 show the sources of income and the main categories of expenses for the federal government. Tables 6.6 and 6.7 provide the sources of revenue and expenditures for state and local governments. Table 6.8 provides a listing of tax terminology, which includes the major taxes.

FISCAL POLICY, MONETARY POLICY, AND PUBLIC BUDGETING

As mentioned earlier, fiscal policy is the tax and spending policy of government, and it is one of the primary concerns of the federal budget. The $2.13 trillion spent by the federal government during 2002 has a major impact on the economy.[36] Government spending currently accounts for about one-third of the gross domestic product (GDP). The overall goals of fiscal policy are to manage the economy in such a way that high levels of employment are sustained,

Table 6.4 Total Federal Revenue by Source

Tax Source	Percent of Total Revenue
Individual income tax	48.0 %
Corporate income tax	10.0
Payroll taxes	34.0
Excise taxes	4.0
Other	4.0

SOURCE: Office of Management and Budget, *A Citizen's Guide to the Federal Budget, Budget of the United States Government, Fiscal Year 2001* (Online version), http://www.omb.gov. Receipts in 2001 were $2 trillion.

Table 6.5 Federal Expenditures by Major Category

Expenditure Area	Percent of Total Expenditures
Social Security	23.0%
Nondefense	17.0 *(discretionary)*
Defense	16.0 *(discretionary)*
Medicare	12.0
Interest payments	11.0
Medicaid	7.0
Other entitlements	6.0
Other mandatory	6.0 *(nondiscretionary)*

NOTE: The largest federal program is *Social Security,* which provides monthly benefits to more than 45 million retired workers and their dependents and survivors. *Medicare* covers more than 40 million senior citizens. Medicare was enacted in 1965 and is expected to grow significantly during the new century. *Medicaid,* which provides health care for poor, disabled, and many senior citizens, covers more than 34 million people. The costs of Medicaid are shared with the states. *Other entitlements* provide benefits to people and families with incomes below certain minimum levels. The major programs in this category are Food Stamps, Supplemental Security Income, Child Nutrition, the Earned Income Tax Credit, and veterans' pensions. *Other mandatory* spending consists mainly of federal retirement and insurance programs, unemployment insurance, and payments to farmers. *Interest payments* are made to pay for past deficits and reduce the national debt, which is currently about $6.1 trillion. Federal spending in 2001 was $1.8 trillion and there was a budget surplus of $184 billion, the first budget surplus at the federal level since 1969. It should be noted that some government activity is excluded from the budget and figures shown here. There are some off-budget items, such a debt reduction and activities from government's businesslike operations (the U.S. Postal Service and similar operations). The federal budget for fiscal year 2004 was $2.27 trillion.

SOURCE: Office of Management and Budget, *A Citizen's Guide to the Federal Budget, Budget of the United States Government, Fiscal Year 2001* (Online version), http://www.omb.gov.

prices remain relatively stable, and economic growth continues.[37] Slowdowns in economic growth are a normal part of the business cycle, but more severe slowdowns are called recessions, while extreme slowdowns are called depressions. Fiscal policy typically applies more to the federal government than to state or local governments, but the tax and spending policies of states and local governments also affect their local economies. In 2001, state and local spending accounted for 9 percent of the GDP. Fiscal policy is heavily based in economics and has four primary policy goals:[38]

Table 6.6 Total State Revenue by Source

Tax Source	Percent of Total Revenue
Individual income tax	34.0%
General sales tax	33.0
Other	9.5
Corporate income tax	6.5
Licenses	6.0
Motor fuel taxes	6.0
Alcohol and tobacco taxes	3.0
Property taxes	2.0

SOURCE: Adapted from Ann Bowman and Richard Kearney, *State and Local Government*, 5th ed. (Boston: Houghton Mifflin, 2002), p. 362. The data are from 1998.

Table 6.7 State and Local Spending by Category

Tax Source	Percent of Total Expenditures
Education	36.0%
Public welfare	25.0
Other	17.0
Highways	8.0
Health and hospitals	8.0
Corrections	4.0
Natural resources	2.0

SOURCE: Adapted from Ann Bowman and Richard Kearney, *State and Local Government*, 5th ed. (Boston: Houghton Mifflin, 2002), p. 376. The data are from 2000.

- *Full employment*. Economists view full employment to mean that about 4 percent of the working population is unemployed. During the economic expansion of the 1990s, the unemployment rate dropped below the 4 percent mark. At this rate, the number of people looking for jobs is about the same as the number of available jobs.

- *Price stability*. Inflation causes prices to increase. Inflation can occur under several conditions. One way that it can occur is when too much money is in the economy. If there are too many dollars chasing too few goods, the price of goods rises because the value of the dollar has been devalued. This has occurred often in foreign nations that printed too much money. One of the primary functions of the Federal Reserve is to control the supply of money. Another way that inflation occurs is when the price of some commodity, such as oil, rises significantly. This is what occurred during the Arab oil embargo in the 1970s. Many sectors of the economy are dependent on oil, and when the cost of oil increases, the price of goods that use

Table 6.8 Basic Tax Terminology

Tax Term	Definition
Ad valorem tax	A tax on a percentage of an item's value, such as sales taxes or real estate taxes.
Capital gains tax	A tax on net income from the sale of a capital asset, such as stocks or real estate.
Capital levy	A tax that appropriates part of the assets of individuals or businesses, usually assessed to reduce large debts.
Corporate tax	A tax—federal, state, or local—on the income of corporations.
Custom duties	Taxes collected by government on items imported into, or occasionally exported from, a country. Also called tariffs.
Depletion allowance	Tax credit extended in the United States to owners of exhaustible natural resources, such as minerals, petroleum, and timber.
Double taxation	Application of two taxes on a single item, such as taxation of corporate income and individuals' dividends, both of which are part of corporate income.
Estate tax	Tax on the entire estate of a deceased person, made before the estate is distributed.
Excess profits tax	Tax on profits above a predetermined level, usually applied during a period of war.
Excise tax	Tax on specific items that is usually placed on the manufacturer, such as the tax on tires.
Exemption	The amount and types of income not subject to taxation.
Gift tax	Tax on donated property, designed to prevent avoidance of estate taxes.
Income tax	Tax placed on individual and corporate income.
Inheritance tax	Tax on the portion of an estate received by an individual, usually levied at a progressive rate.
Negative income tax	Tax plan in which people with low incomes receive payments from the government rather than paying taxes.
Sales tax	General tax on the sale price of goods, usually applied at the retail level.
Tax evasion	Avoidance of taxation through illegal means.
Tax loophole	An inconsistency in tax laws that can be either intentional or unintentional. Tax loopholes are usually deliberate tax preferences.
Tax shelter	Financial program used to protect money from taxation using opportunities provided under tax law. Also called a tax preference.
Turnover tax	A levy that taxes items at each step of manufacturing and distribution. This is a general sales tax.
Use tax	Tax on individual use rather than on the sale of an item. Also called a luxury tax.
Value-added tax	Tax on the difference between the value of materials and supplies used by a manufacturer and the value of the finished product.
Withholding tax	Tax, usually progressive, by federal, state, or local governments that is withheld from payments by employers to employees.

oil also rises. There are other reasons for inflation, but when inflation rises significantly, there is a shift in the distribution of real income from those whose incomes are relatively inflexible to those whose incomes are relatively flexible. Thus, inflation tends to hurt people on fixed incomes.

- *Constant economic growth*. One of the major goals of fiscal policy is to tax and spend in such a way as to sustain continued economic growth. As the population increases, it is imperative that economic growth continues. For example, during the early 1980s, the workforce was approximately 115 million. In 2001, the figure was around 140 million. If an economy does not continue to grow but the population continues to increase, not enough jobs are available for the working population. Also, government depends on the economy to generate its revenue. When economies stagnate, tax revenues fall and the government has to borrow money to pay for services. This has another impact in that government borrowing can "crowd out" private borrowing, since both private industry and government borrow from the same sources.

- *Public goods (or collective goods)*. Some activities, goods, and services are public in nature and are produced to serve the society as a whole and the public interest. Public goods are activities, goods, and services such as national defense, police and fire protection, schools, highways, and the like. The difference between public and private goods is found in the ability to restrict consumption. In the case of private goods, which include automobiles, televisions, stereos, and the like, consumption can easily be restricted to those who actually buy the products. When people buy a television and take it home, no one can use it without their permission. However, it is not possible (or, at least, it is more difficult) to restrict the consumption of public goods such as national defense. This provides a rationale for forcing people to pay taxes to pay for the services and reduce the number of free riders (i.e., those who consume the service but do not pay their share of taxes). Everyone benefits from national defense and education, but national defense and education do not come packaged in a box that can be purchased at Wal-Mart. One of the goals of fiscal policy is to ensure that there is an adequate supply of collectively consumed goods.

Fiscal policy assumes that there is a relationship between the total level of spending in an economy and inflation or unemployment. Total spending usually refers to the gross domestic product (GDP), which is the sum of personal consumption, gross private domestic investment, government purchases of goods and services, and net export of goods and services. The ideal unemployment rate is about 4 percent, while an ideal inflation rate is about 3 percent annually. There is disagreement among economists over these figures, but these are the most widely cited figures. Simply stated, in a given year, if the GDP is at the anticipated target level, unemployment is at 4 percent, and inflation is about 3 percent, then the goals of fiscal policy have been achieved.[39] Unfortunately, this is not an easy task to achieve. During the best economic times, we often come close to achieving these goals, but when the economy takes a downturn, either unemployment or inflation rises. During the worst of times, both can rise.

When both unemployment and inflation rise to very high levels, economists refer to this as *stagflation*. Fortunately, this does not occur often because usually there is an inverse relationship between unemployment and inflation.[40] But it has occurred. During the 1970s, the economy stagnated, unemployment escalated, and inflation soared. During the Great Depression, unemployment was 25 percent, the economy literally crashed, and the human suffering that resulted cannot be properly quantified. The grim economic times associated with the Great Depression caused many intellectuals to argue that the old theories of economics needed to be modified. It seemed clear that government had to take a more active role in the economy. Prior to that time, the guiding principles of macroeconomics were founded on the ideas of Adam Smith, which were formulated in the late 1700s. The idea was that the least government is the best government. Part of the reason for the Great Crash of 1929 had to do with the money supply and the lack of fiscal policy.[41] The economy was believed to be largely a self-regulating system, and most believed that the less government fooled with it, the better off everyone would be.

Government can implement fiscal policy and control the supply of money, but economists do not agree on what constitutes the right tax and spending mix. The money supply is controlled through a central bank called the Federal Reserve System (also referred to as the Fed). The Federal Reserve's job is to control the supply of money and credit. It accomplishes this through the use of several tools, including the *open-market operations,* which is a committee called the Federal Reserve Open Market Committee that meets regularly to decide whether to buy or sell government bonds or bills.[42] When government sells bonds or bills, it tightens the money supply because it withdraws money from the system. When it buys bonds, the money supply expands because this feeds money into the system. The Fed also can adjust the discount rate, which is the interest rate the Fed charges member banks for short-term loans. The discount rate affects all other types of interest rates, including the *prime rate* that banks charge preferred customers (mainly large businesses that borrow a lot of money). When the discount rate is increased, it makes the cost of borrowing money more expensive, which discourages people from borrowing money and therefore causes the economy to contract. If the discount rate is decreased, it has the opposite effect and encourages people to borrow money and therefore stimulates the economy.[43] In addition, the Fed can change the *cash reserve ratios* of member banks within certain limits set by Congress. The Fed can tighten the money supply by requiring banks to maintain larger reserves, which makes less money available to be loaned, or it can loosen the cash reserve ratios to make more money available for loans. Although this is a powerful tool, it is seldom used.[44]

The Federal Reserve, which was created in 1913, is now comprised of twelve regional Federal Reserve member banks that are located throughout the twelve regions.[45] Its board is comprised of seven governors, appointed by the president and confirmed by the Senate, including the chairperson. Additionally, on the open market committees, five members from the member banks are included. A committee of nine directors manages each of the twelve regional banks. This committee is comprised of three members from the public sector, three members from the banking industry, and three members from the business community. When the United States was formally taken off the gold standard in 1932, the Fed assumed a greater role in regulating money. In 1971, the United States stopped converting foreign-held dollars into gold. The U.S. monetary system is a paper money system that is technically not backed up by gold. Some consider the Fed to be the most powerful federal agency because of its power over the economy.[46] The control of the supply and, therefore, the value of money is vital to the economy and fiscal policy.

The monetarist school of economics believes that the money supply is the key factor for controlling the economy. Monetarists argue that government spending distorts the activities of the economy because government action is usually reactive. The lag in fiscal policy serves to exacerbate the booms and busts associated with the business cycle. The Keynesians have little faith in the workings of free markets or in the single power of the money supply. A healthy economy is based on the demand for goods and services. This depends on how much money people have to spend. If people spend too much on a given supply of goods, inflation results. If too much money is saved, there will be a reduced demand and recession. In short, Keynesians argue that the role of government is important. It is critical to have a fiscal policy that ensures high levels of demand to keep people working and consuming, and a low interest rate that will keep people from saving too much. Government can regulate these activities by increasing spending, decreasing taxes, and setting interest rates low. Moreover, Keynesians believe that if government does not intervene, the economy will experience extreme periods of boom and bust. The key for Keynesians is an ongoing, healthy economy. If this can be accomplished through budget deficits and public debt, so be it.[47]

Supply-side theory is similar to the classical theory of Adam Smith. According to supply-siders, the economy is best left alone. If government minimized its activity, free markets would work just fine. This school emerged about the time that Ronald Reagan was elected in 1980. Supply-siders blamed too much government intervention for the economic woes of that era. They believed that a return to the basics of free markets would solve most of the problems. The Laffer curve, mentioned earlier, was one of their hallmarks. Supply-siders favored giving tax breaks to businesses. In the classical train of thought, it is most important to give businesses the greater incentive. This translated into many policies during the 1980s, including urban enterprise zones, which became the nation's urban renewal policy for awhile. Enterprise zones gave large tax breaks to those who redeveloped depressed areas in cities. The idea was that capitalism could restore the ghettos of the nation's cities. Although there was some limited success at the state and local level, by and large, enterprise zones failed to produce the anticipated results. Capitalism did not thrive amidst the adversity found in the nation's ghettos.

Fiscal policy is a major debate in the federal budgetary process. Since the 1940s, most Republicans and Democrats have accepted the doctrine associated with Keynesian economics. Although it has never been fully implemented in its purest form, politicians have played with many of the theory's elements. The primary element is that demand is the key to a healthy economy. Gridlock often occurred, however, because Democrats were willing to increase demand by spending, which tended to cause inflation. Republicans were willing to spend less and allow more unemployment to fight inflation. When supply-side theory emerged in the 1980s, it freed Republicans from the gridlock that had existed for many years. Supply-side arguments hold that taxes can be cut, spending can be cut, and this will help stimulate the economy. Thus, the Republicans took the position of getting government off the backs of businesses and letting the market work. The problem with supply-side theory is that it is little more than classical economics rediscovered. These are the same basic theories that were in place when the Great Depression occurred and government waited for equilibrium to return to the economy—something that never occurred. But supply-side theory worked well for President Reagan during the 1980s. The economy improved significantly, taxes were cut, and government regulations were reduced. Deficits also soared and the national debt mushroomed, but the rising debt and budget deficits cannot be blamed entirely on the Republicans or supply-side economics. The problem was that both Democrats and Republicans continued to spend beyond their means.

Fiscal policy and the federal budget are interrelated. Members of Congress, the president, agencies such as the Federal Reserve and the OMB, and various advisory councils are all involved in a process that attempts to construct budgets that satisfy multiple objectives (which are often conflicting), while at the same time formulating fiscal policy. The budgetary process is not a rational process; it is a process that involves consensus and the attempt to satisfy many competing interests. The budget is a critical part of fiscal policy, which affects all of us, and it is an ongoing process that is renewed each and every year.

SUMMARY

This chapter has covered some of the fundamental aspects of government budgeting. The public budgetary process is a political process where legislators, budget analysts, the chief executive, government agencies, and interest groups converge to assemble a plan for the next year that contains the financial commitments necessary for implementing public policy. In the early days of the United States, budgeting was a rather simple process, but due to the growth and complexity of society, it became necessary to develop more rigorous budget and accounting systems. Political machines abused public monies, and reformers responded by implementing a wide range of new systems to bring about control and accountability. Budgeting can use a variety of formats, such as traditional, incremental line-item budgets, and comprehensive budgets that incorporate planning and measurable objectives tied to performance. Many methods have been tried and are still used, but legislatures at all levels of government tend to use the traditional line-item system in which the previous year's budget serves as the base of next year's budget. The debate is over incremental increases or decreases in spending for programs and services.

The federal budget is a significant instrument in the nation's fiscal policy. The way taxes are raised and spent can have a significant impact on the economy. Fiscal policy involves macroeconomic theory, and several competing theories about the role of government in the economy exist. The federal government deliberately intervenes in the economy to achieve aggregate objectives that involve inflation, price control, employment, and continued economic growth. The federal budget has grown to the point that it now accounts for more than $2 trillion each year.

Budgets are a reflection of public policy and the commitment toward achieving certain goals for the nation. In its most basic form, a public budget is a plan that tells us what government will do in the coming year and its plans for subsequent years. It is also a record of the past. Budget policy is an important tool for funding needed programs that are required by society and a tool of fiscal policy for achieving economic prosperity. Different people view public budgeting differently. Economists see budgeting as a way to help manage the economy. Administrators see budgeting as a way to help manage the operations of their agencies. Politicians see public budgeting as way to fund important programs. Accountants see budgeting from the perspective of transactions and record keeping. Public budgeting is about public policy. It costs money to implement and carry out policies such as welfare programs, Social Security benefits for the retired, and the maintenance of national defense. Public budgets are critical for modern societies, and nothing in our society is more political than the budgetary process.

NOTES

1. Researchers have been unable to find a written version of Everett Dirksen's (1896–1969) most famous quotation. Cautioning against treating the federal budget casually, Dirksen observed that the unit of money favored by those seeking to fund programs is a million—later versions had it a billion—dollars. Regardless of whether the amount was millions or billions of dollars, the point is still the same. U.S. Senate Web site, http://www .senate.gov.

2. For an excellent description of the processes of budgeting, see David Nice, *Public Budgeting* (Belmont, CA: Wadsworth/Thomson Learning, 2002).

3. Accounting is the system of recording, classifying, and reporting financial

transactions in an orderly way. Accounting is a significant aspect of public budgeting, but it is not covered in this book. Accounting is a form of record keeping. In the modern world, the most common type of accounting used is called accrual accounting. This system matches expenditures and revenues for a given period, such as a month, a quarter (a three-month period), or a year.

It is beyond the scope of this book to go deeply into accounting, but some basic elements should be noted. All budgeting requires accounting. The basics of accounting involve vouchers, journals, and ledgers. Accounting also involves *balance sheets* that record the value of total assets, liabilities, and equity. Accounting is about entering and maintaining financial transactions. With the exception of the federal government, all governments use *fund systems.* That is, there are a series of funds, such as the general fund, fiduciary funds, and the like. Each fund has its own set of accounts. Accounting involves a simple idea known as a *t-account,* which records credits, debits, and a balance. Accounting also involves cash management, which is the investing of idle funds to make interest for the government, and debt management. Debt management applies to all levels of government. Governments must incur debt to build schools and highways, to expand infrastructure, and the like. Governments usually borrow money by selling various types of bonds, such as general obligations bonds or revenue bonds. The interest incurred with debt must be paid, and financial specialists are required to manage debt. For example, the interest on the federal debt is currently around 11 percent of the annual budget. At the municipal level, a finance officer usually handles the finances for the city. Although it is beyond the scope of this book to cover governmental accounting, the importance of it cannot be overemphasized.

4. Cole Blease Graham, Jr., and Steven Hays, *Managing Public Organizations,* 2nd ed. (Washington, DC: CQ Press, 1993), pp. 213–236.

5. Donald Kettl, *Deficit Politics: The Search for Balance in American Politics,* 2nd ed. (New York: Longman, 2003).

6. For an excellent discussion about the politics of budgeting, see Irene Rubin, *The Politics of Budgeting* (Chatham, NJ: Chatham House, 1997). For the classic book on the subject of politics in the budgetary process, see Aaron Wildavsky and Naomi Caiden, *The New Politics of the Budgetary Process,* 2nd ed. (New York: Harper Collins, 1997). This book is an updated version of Wildavsky's classic book that was published in the 1960s.

7. Dan Axelrod, *A Budget Quartet: Critical Policy and Management Issues* (New York: St. Martin, 1989).

8. V. O. Key, "The Lack of a Budgetary Theory," *American Political Science Review* 34 (1940), pp. 1137–1144.

9. The Office of Management and Budget, the main federal agency with responsibility for preparing the budget, maintains an excellent Web site with the current and previous budgets available. Among the documents is *A Citizen's Guide to the Federal Budget,* which is available online at http://www.omb.gov.

10. The different ways that we can think about budgeting are credited to David Shuman and Dick Olufs, III, *Public Administration in the United States,* 2nd ed. (Lexington, MA: D. C. Heath, 1993), pp. 376–377.

11. These goals are articulated in the classic public finance book by Richard Musgrave, *The Theory of Public Finance: A Study in Political Economy* (New York: McGraw-Hill, 1959), pp. 5–6.

12. John Maynard Keynes, *The General Theory of Employment Interest and Money* (London: Macmillan, 1936).

13. The national debt in 2003 was about $6.9 trillion. For more information about the national debt, see Timothy Penny and Steven Schier, *Payment Due: A Nation in Debt, A Generation in Trouble* (Boulder, CO: Westview, 1996).

14. Adam Smith, *An Inquiry into the Nature and Causes of the Wealth of Nations* (New York: P. F. Collier & Son, 1909). The original book was published in 1776.

15. Milton Friedman, *Capitalism and Federalism* (Chicago: University of Chicago Press, 1972).

16. John Kenneth Galbraith, *The Age of Uncertainty* (Boston: Houghton Mifflin, 1977), p. 194.

17. Donald Kettl, *Deficit Politics: Public Budgeting in Its Intuitional and Historical Context* (New York: Macmillan, 1992), Chapter 6.

18. Ibid.

19. For an excellent history of budgeting, see Robert Lee, Jr., and Ronald Johnson, *Public Budgeting Systems,* 4th ed. (Gaithersburg, MD: Aspen, 1989), Chapter 1.

20. John Marini, *The Politics of Budget Control: Congress, the Presidency, and the Growth of the Administrative State* (Washington, DC: Crane Russak, 1992).

21. David Nice, *Public Budgeting,* Chapters 6 and 11.

22. Ibid., p. 91.

23. Thomas Lynch, *Public Budgeting in America,* 4th ed. (Englewood Cliffs, NJ: Prentice-Hall, 1995), pp. 58–59.

24. Cited in Grover Starling, *Managing the Public Sector,* 4th ed. (Belmont, CA: Wadsworth, 1993), p. 516.

25. Ann Bowman and Richard Kearney, *State and Local Government,* 5th ed. (Boston: Houghton Mifflin, 2002), p. 216.

26. Aaron Wildavsky, *The Politics of the Budgetary Process* (Boston: Little Brown, 1964).

27. David Shuman and Dick Olufs, III, *Public Administration in the United States,* p. 395.

28. Thomas Lynch, *Public Budgeting in America,* pp. 46–47.

29. Ann Bowman and Richard Kearney, *State and Local Government,* p. 217.

30. Thomas Lynch, *Public Budgeting in America,* pp. 50–51.

31. Peter Pyhrr, *Zero-Based Budgeting: A Practical Management Tool for Evaluating Expenses* (New York: Wiley, 1973).

32. Cited in Grover Starling, *Managing the Public Sector,* p. 526.

33. See Robert Lee, Jr., and Ronald Johnson, *Public Budgeting Systems,* Chapters 1 and 2. Also see Thomas Lynch, *Public Budgeting in America,* Chapter 1.

34. This information is available from the Internal Revenue Service. The corporate income tax brackets are also available from Quicken.com, http://www.quicken.com /cms/viewers/article/small_business /42981.

35. Much of the information about the Internet Freedom Act relies on the work posted on Representative Christopher Cox's Web site. Cox, a representative from Orange County, California, was one of the major proponents of the Internet Freedom Act. See http://cox.house.gov.

36. James Gosling, *Politics and the American Economy* (New York: Addison, Wesley, Longman, 2000), Chapter 3.

37. James Gosling, *Politics and the American Economy,* Chapter 2.

38. Thomas Lynch, *Public Budgeting in America,* p. 27.

39. Ibid.

40. Ibid., p. 23. Economists use the Phillips Curve to illustrate the inverse relationship between inflation and unemployment.

41. John Kenneth Galbraith, *The Great Crash, 1929* (Boston: Houghton Mifflin, 1954).

42. Carl Lieberman, *Making Economic Policy* (Englewood Cliffs, NJ: Prentice-Hall, 1991).

43. Thomas Lynch, *Public Budgeting in America,* p. 25.

44. Ibid.

45. The Federal Reserve, the central bank of the United States, was founded by Congress in 1913 to provide the nation with a safer, more flexible, and more stable monetary and financial system. Today the Federal Reserve's duties fall into four general areas: (1) conducting the nation's monetary policy; (2) supervising and regulating banking institutions and protecting the credit rights of consumers; (3) maintaining the stability of the financial system; and (4) providing certain financial services to the U.S. government, the public, financial institutions, and foreign official institutions. The Federal Reserve maintains a Web site that contains more details about its history and operations. The URL is http://www.federalreserve .gov.

46. David Shuman and Dick Olufs, III, *Public Administration in the United States,* pp. 22–23.

47. Ibid., pp. 403–404.

7

Basics of Public Policy

> Public policy is what governments do, why they do it,
> and what difference it makes.
>
> THOMAS DYE

UNDERSTANDING PUBLIC POLICY

There is no area of public administration that is more important than public policy. Public administration is involved in the entire process and is responsible for implementing public policy. Public policy has many definitions, but generally may be thought of as the *programs of action that government deliberately pursues, and whatever government selects not to do.* Government is involved in most every aspect of society to some degree. Programs like affirmative action and veterans' benefits, which are handled by a variety of agencies including the Equal Employment Opportunity Commission, are examples of public policy. Declaring a "war on drugs" to try to stop the flow of illegal narcotics is a public policy that is handled by law enforcement agencies, mainly the Drug Enforcement Agency (DEA) at the federal level. President Bush's decision to send military forces into Afghanistan to take down the Taliban government was a public policy handled by the Department of Defense. And President Bush's ongoing war on terrorism is an example of a public policy that involves a multitude of federal and state agencies, including the Federal Bureau of

Investigation (FBI). The decision to go to war in Iraq epitomizes a very visible public policy.

But public policy also involves government choosing *not* to take action in some areas. The areas include situations where interest groups want government to intervene. For example, at the local level, some citizens and interest groups may want a city to use its zoning powers to restrict certain kinds of businesses from operating in specific areas of the city, such as adult entertainment or bars near churches or schools. For a variety of reasons, the city may opt not to change the zoning restrictions or may simply table the discussion. In a similar vein, many cities refused to deal with the demands made by some interest groups for a "living wage" ordinance.[1] The courts are also involved in making public policy with their decisions. The U.S. Supreme Court routinely decides *not* to hear cases, and most legal scholars consider this to be a decision. The same is true for government in general. Thus, government may opt to "look the other way" on some issues, and this is, in effect, a form of public policy. Nondecisions can be as important as decisions.

Public administrators need to understand the complexities of public policy. Public administration makes policy and is also affected by public policies. Public policy is a very large subfield of political science and a standard area included in the study of public administration. Although largely housed in political science, the study of public policy includes other disciplines such as economics and sociology. Most public policy is *reactive* in nature. That is, policy is formulated as a response to an existing problem rather than being *proactive,* which involves trying to handle issues before they actually arise. Public policy is created in a process that includes formulation, implementation, and evaluation. It is also created in the political arena and typically does not use a rational decision-making process for most issues. This does not mean that experts are not used in the process, but ultimately public policy is determined in a political process. Public policy is everywhere, from something as seemingly mundane as the speed limit posted in your neighborhood to the complexities of our national foreign policy in the Middle East.

There are several different kinds of public policy. Typically, we tend to think of policies as falling into three large categories: *distributive, redistributive,* and *regulatory.* Box 7.1 contains some additional types of policies that are derived from these three basic types. *Distributive policies,* as the name suggests, distribute services to citizens, such as highway policies that benefit all automobile drivers. *Redistributive policies* take from those who have some resource (e.g., money) and redistribute the resource (e.g., redistribute the money to help the poor). These are usually the most controversial types of policies. *Regulatory policies* seek to regulate some type of behavior, such as airline safety, health, sanitation, and safety concerns in hospitals, restaurants, and food processing plants. Policies can also be ideologically *conservative* or *liberal.* Conservatives prefer to have minimal government intervention to bring about social changes, whereas liberals want an active government to force social change. Conservatives generally oppose concentrating power at the national

BOX 7.1   Types of Public Policies

Distributive

Distributive public policies promote private activities that are desirable to society as a whole. These policies are targeted to provide tangible benefits. There appear to be only winners in this process. There is very little visibility or public attention. These activities include grants for scientific research, grants for building airports and roads, and grants for universities. Distributive policies embody the idea of "pork barrel" in Congress because politicians want to send some of the funds to their home states or districts.

Competitive Regulatory

Competitive regulatory policies are aimed at limiting the provision of specific goods and services to only one or a few of several competing distributors. There will be winners and losers, but the winners will be regulated. These policies include granting licenses to airlines, television and radio stations, cable television companies, and electric power producers (and other utility operations). Decisions are delegated to the

bureaucracies, commissions, and the courts.

Protective Regulatory

The purpose of these policies is to protect the public by setting conditions under which private activities may be conducted. Conditions that are believed to be damaging are forbidden; activities that are beneficial are required. These policies require that a sector of society conform to the general law. They are formed in a highly political process involving special interest groups and lobbying efforts. Examples include policies on taxation, advertising practices (such as alcohol and tobacco), unfair business practices, and other regulations that protect the public. Visibility to the public is moderate. Congress and state legislatures make these decisions.

Redistributive

Redistributive policies are intended to manipulate the allocation of wealth and property rights. Visibility is very high, and Congress and courts make the decisions. The decisions are highly

level; they prefer to have power decentralized at the state and local level. Liberals prefer having a strong, active, national government to bring about social equity and to ensure that the law is applied equally throughout the nation. Public policies can also deal with *substantive* problems, such as highway construction and environmental protection, or they can be *procedural* in nature, such as the Administrative Procedures Act of 1946, which mandates the procedures that agencies must use when making rules. Policies can be *symbolic* or *material*, depending on the types of benefits they provide. *Symbolic policies* are simply those honoring an important value, such as proclaiming a national holiday to honor veterans. *Material policies* provide tangible benefits, such as Social Security checks, welfare checks, and Medicare benefits.[2] This chapter covers the fundamental areas of public policy, with special attention given to some of the areas that are most relevant to public administration.[3]

political, ideological, and controversial. The goal is to increase equity in society. When redistributive policies are made, the players tend to be labeled liberals or conservatives. Examples include policies on food stamps, affirmative action programs, welfare benefits, civil rights, and health insurance.

Structural

Structural public policies involve the nation's foreign policy. These policies involve procuring, deploying, and organizing military resources, defense procurements, placement or closing of military bases, and expansion or contraction of the military. Congress makes the decisions in accord with the formal legislative process. The visibility of these policies to the general public is low.

Strategic

Strategic policies assert and implement the basic foreign policy of the nation. Bargaining and debate occur after the policies have been implemented. The president and

federal agencies make decisions. Examples include policies on the sale of armaments and grain, the mix of military forces (e.g., ratio of ground-based missiles to submarine-based missiles), and tariffs imposed on certain countries. These policies are low in visibility to the general public until they are made public; then they may become very controversial.

Crisis

Crisis policies involve short-term responses to immediate threats to national security. Visibility for the general public is typically low. The president and his advisors make the decisions. Examples include policies in response to the crash of a Chinese jet fighter that bumped into an American spy plane off the coast of China in 2001, the Cuban Missile Crisis in the early 1960s, and the Iranian seizure of U.S. hostages in 1979 taken from the U.S. Embassy.

SOURCE: Randall Ripley and Grace Franklin, *Congress, the Bureaucracy, and Public Policy,* 5th ed. (Belmont, CA: Brooks/Cole, 1991), Chapter 1.

THE PUBLIC POLICY PROCESS:
AN OVERVIEW

Many models have been developed to describe the process of making, implementing, and evaluating public policy. The process can be best described with a multistage model. Figure 7.1 contains a widely accepted model that includes the major phases from formulation to policy change or termination.[4] First, a problem presents itself that requires government to consider whether it should intervene. Since most public policy is *reactive*, the existence of a problem or issue usually catches the attention of interest groups and government. For example, the recent scandals involving large corporations like Enron, WorldCom, and ImClone caused the federal government to pass a law that attempts to regulate corporate behavior and accounting practices.[5] However,

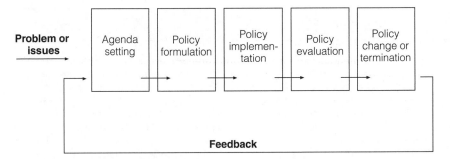

FIGURE 7.1 The Public Policy Process

SOURCE: Adapted from James Lester and Joseph Stewart, Jr., *Public Policy: An Evolutionary Approach* (Belmont, CA: Wadsworth/Thomson Learning, 2000), p. 5.

the mere existence of a problem or issue does not mean that government will necessarily intervene. Many areas of society have problems and issues that remain relatively untouched by government, mainly because government has chosen not to intervene. Reforming the way political campaigns are financed, for example, has been discussed for many years, but to date any campaign finance reform that has been implemented has not been serious enough to make a significant difference in terms of reducing the influence of money or the cost of campaigns. A few years ago the idea of term limits was seriously considered by many states and Congress, but soon faded. Some states did pass term limits for their legislators, but the federal courts ruled that states could not set limits on how long their representatives and senators could serve in Congress.[6] The fading of issues can be attributed to many factors, such as the *attention cycle* that is associated with many policy issues.[7] Many issues capture public attention, but do not remain in the spotlight very long. The real problems remain, but in time, interest in many matters that once seemed critical wanes. This is partly due to the urgency associated with many other issues. Although some issues surface and shed light on serious problems in our society, the attention span for most issues is short. New issues come along and replace them. Thus, the first phase involves getting the issue on the agenda and keeping it there until government takes action. This phase is typically called *agenda setting*.[8]

Agenda Setting

Agenda setting involves various interest groups and government seriously looking at issues, but the issues must get on the political agenda before a policy is created. Most issues never go through the whole cycle shown in Figure 7.1. One can think of something getting on the agenda as placing an issue on the table for discussion. Some issues get help from the media. If an issue gets enough media attention, public awareness is raised and may intensify the efforts of interest groups that have a vested interest in promoting or opposing the issue. Agenda setting is more complex than just getting public discussion about an issue. It involves a system that is comprised of several *streams* that are affected by a variety of environmental and contextual factors. John Kingdon developed one of the most widely accepted agenda-setting models (see Figure 7.2). This model views agenda setting as involving three major streams and being affected by a host of factors. The *problem stream* is concerned with how a problem gets defined. How an issue gets defined is extremely important. For example, the debate over whether sex education should be included in public school curricula may concern only parents who have school-age children. But if the problem is defined more broadly, such as a program to decrease the number of teenage pregnancies and abortions, more members of the community may feel affected and become interested in the issue. For some years, the nation has been fighting a "war on drugs." Defining something as a "war" raises the stakes. But is the problem relating to illegal drugs defined as a criminal problem, a health issue, or a desire to regulate morality? If illegal drug trafficking is viewed as a criminal issue, then the goal is to take action to arrest and jail those involved with the illegal drug trade. If the issue is defined as a health issue, the goals are to work for rehabilitation of drug users and an increase in public awareness of the dangers of drug abuse. If it is defined as a way to regulate morality, the focus is on educating the public about how bad (in a normative sense of the term) the drug problem is and how it damages the moral fabric of the nation. In reality, the drug problem has been defined in many ways, and a variety of policies have been implemented relating to crime, health, and morality. (Illegal drug policy and welfare are used as examples of substantive policy later in this chapter. See Box 7.2, p. 303 and Box 7.3, p. 306.)

The *policy stream* is concerned with the technical plausibility of potential solutions to the problem, and how well the public will accept potential solutions. Considering the many problems found in society, solutions must be feasible and technically possible to implement. For example, it is possible to end all poverty in America, but the cost would bankrupt the nation, and other important problems would have to be ignored. In response to the terrorist attacks on the World Trade Center and the Pentagon, policies were quickly devised to increase airport security and defend the nation from additional attacks. The policies had to be technically possible to implement. For several months, tightened security included bomb walls erected near airport terminals, the presence of military personnel, checking all cars entering airport property, and random searches of passengers. Even a new cabinet-level department was created, Homeland Security. Many debates were involved, including having the federal government take over responsibility for airport security. Long lines and hours of waiting to board planes did not work out very well, and over time, airport security had to be modified after the urgency of the crisis passed. Congress had to deal with questions about how to make flying safer while minimizing the hassle of getting passengers through airports. If flying remained too difficult, many people would stop using the airlines. This task faced by government was not an easy one, but the urgency caused by the crisis forced Congress to act quickly. Fortunately, most policy decisions do not involve crises that threaten the security of the nation.

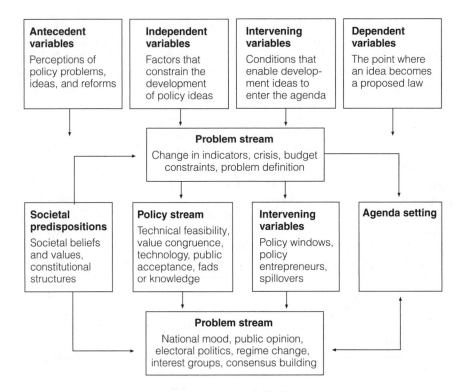

FIGURE 7.2 The Agenda-Setting Process—The Kingdon Model

SOURCE: Adapted from John Kingdon, *Agendas, Alternatives, and Public Policies* (Boston: Little, Brown, 1984).

The *political stream* involves the national mood, public opinion, electoral politics, and a host of other factors that determine whether or not an issue will get on the agenda. A few years ago, the violent clashes between pro-choice and antiabortion groups led Congress to pass laws making it illegal to block an abortion clinic's entrance. After President Reagan was shot in 1983, it seemed that gun control might become a reality, but interest groups collided, and it took years to get a very diluted version of handgun control (called the Brady Bill) passed in Congress. The mood of the nation is not stagnant; it is constantly changing. Public opinion polls and other surveys illustrate that the mood can change a great deal from one decade to the next. During the 1950s, the real threat of war with the former Soviet Union was coupled with rising economic affluence. The 1960s were characterized by social unrest, a war in Vietnam, the civil rights movement, race relations, and continued rising economic affluence. By the 1970s, the energy crisis caused an economic downturn that remained throughout the decade. The 1980s witnessed a shift to more conservative values, the AIDS epidemic, and more favorable policies toward business. The policies that were enacted during these times often mirrored the national mood.

Some view public policy as a cyclical pattern that swings back and forth from liberal to conservative about every 30 years. This thesis sees recurring patterns in public policy that roughly correspond to generations. People's values are formed during a 20- to 25-year cycle when they are young—typically from birth until the early 20s, according to most psychologists.[9] Political attitudes are greatly affected by the predominant ideals and values that are accepted when we come of age. As young people mature, they also begin to hold positions of power and influence, and slowly replace the older generation's political values with those that were emerging when they became politically active. This thesis also holds that the excesses of a liberal generation are corrected by the swing back toward conservatism, which is an ongoing process.[10] Moreover the cyclical thesis holds that American public policy has always been a swing between *private interests* and *public purpose.* This thesis views policy as "values in transition" and is also called the *near-term view* because it tends to occur during 30-year cycles.[11] Additionally, there is a *long-term view* that sees public policy shifts as a zigzag pattern with recurring themes. This view sees public policy as pursuing conservative policies, then reacting to these policies by shifting toward liberalism, and then shifting back to conservative policies again. However, this view does not believe that the liberal versus conservative ideologies are as important as the struggle over who benefits from the policies. The pattern is more erratic than a simple swing back and forth between liberal and conservative and is less tied to generational reactions. Those who hold this view believe that a 30-year period is too short to recognize the pattern; they say it takes about 100 years for the pattern to be recognized.[12]

All three streams can be illustrated with the Watergate scandal in the early 1970s. Following the Watergate scandal, the mood of the nation seemed right for political change (the *political stream*). The scandal revealed corruption and abuse of executive power, which was hardly new to Washington, but the *problem stream* had changed. What was once overlooked or ignored was now an issue or a problem that demanded attention. The *policy stream* led Congress to examine what could be done to clean up the system and hopefully prevent similar scandals from occurring again. A number of new laws were passed that were heralded at the time, but the effectiveness of the policy changes (how well the policy makers achieved their goals) remains questionable. For example, one of the changes involved public financing of presidential elections (but candidates do not have to accept public financing) and the creation of political action committees (PACs). The new laws were supposed to reduce the influence of special interests, force parties and candidates to get smaller contributions (rather than large corporate contributions), and generally clean up the way political campaigns were conducted. Very little of this materialized. First of all, the new election laws were aimed at presidential primaries and elections rather than congressional elections. Congress paid little attention to the way it conducted its own elections. Second, political parties quickly learned how to generate money using the new system and soon were collecting more money than ever. Third, the creation of PACs allowed the same groups, corporations, and labor unions to spend unlimited sums of money on behalf of candidates, even though the law forbid these groups from giving money directly to candidates. Today there is more money in politics than in the past, and the power of interest groups remains about the same. Nonetheless, Watergate was a significant political event that caused changes and intensified pressures in all three of the major streams that affect public policy. The agenda is seldom lacking for issues, but the forces of the problem, policy, and political streams are constantly changing.

Several types of agendas exist. *Systemic agendas* (sometimes called the popular agenda) are those issues that might be subject to action or that are already being acted on by government. This includes the entire universe of potential issues that government might consider. *Institutional agendas* (often referred to as the public agenda) are those issues that are explicitly up for consideration by decision makers, legislatures, or the courts. For example, pressures from Microsoft's competitors, the states, and a favorable administration in Washington nearly led to the breakup of Microsoft during the 1990s. But the mood changed with the election of George W. Bush in 2000, and Microsoft was not split because the breakup was essentially removed from the agenda. Mothers Against Drunk Drivers (MADD) successfully got their issue (to strengthen drunk-driving laws and penalties) onto the institutional agendas of states and Congress in the 1980s. Government action led to safe road acts being passed in most states and caused the legal drinking age to be raised to 21 years of age in all states. This MADD effort, which was one of the most successful in recent years, helped widen awareness of the need to behave responsibly with alcohol. After winning a series of court cases, most of the states and the Clinton administration forced the tobacco settlement to help states regain funds they had spent over the years on tobacco-related illnesses, which produced large sums of money for the states and the trial lawyers. The failure of Enron and other corporate scandals forced issues onto the institutional agenda and caused government to act fairly quickly. Other issues exist that are important but have not yet made it onto the institutional agenda, such as installing infrastructure needed to handle future growth in an urban area. Thus, two agendas exist: one is comprised of issues that will be formally discussed, and another includes issues that are being discussed but are waiting to be placed on the formal agenda.

Several types of issues also exist. *Subject issues,* such as pollution, health care, and business regulation, are broad in nature. These issues are more general, and discussions are often about the aggregate effects. For example, crime, welfare, and education are all subject issues. Issues that involve specific legislation, such as the Comprehensive Environmental Response, Compensation, and Liability Act of 1980 (better known as Superfund), are called *policy issues.* These issues are about subject areas but get very specific and detailed. Issues that relate to a specific project, such as the various issues that surround building a new dam, an airport, or a new military bomber, are called *project issues.* Building a new airport or a mall often causes many clashes among competing interest groups and government. For example, when Denver built its new airport, numerous controversies surfaced. Airports are noisy, cost a lot of money, involve expensive construction contracts, and may damage the environment and quality of life in the area near the facility. Project issues are common at all levels of government but are very visible at the local level. Planning in urban areas is necessary to accommodate future needs. This is one of the areas where governments often try to be proactive. But getting the necessary funding to build sewage systems, water lines, and the like before they are needed is difficult. Often urban governments' policies also turn out to be a reaction to unplanned growth in one part of the city or county. Rebuilding America's downtown areas is an example of a proactive attempt at economic development. Asheville, North Carolina, has attracted millions of dollars in investments for revitalizing its downtown area. The project has taken more than 20 years and has achieved some positive results. But redeveloping downtown areas typically has had only limited success in an era where strip malls are replacing traditional malls that contributed to the original demise of many downtown areas in cities nationwide. Some policy analysts have suggested that cities will redevelop their center areas once it becomes economically feasible to do.[13] For example, when the price of land becomes too expensive, and its availability is scarce, downtown redevelopment seems to work better. The specific projects associated with downtown redevelopment are examples of *project issues*. New issues also emerge—such as building pollution (some buildings have been called "sick buildings" because of the dirty air found in their heating and air conditioning systems), radon, and new health concerns such as the West Nile virus, AIDS, and medical malpractice issues. At one time, all of these were new issues that caught the attention of interest groups and government. There are also cyclical issues, such as budgets that must be dealt with each year, and recurring issues like welfare, public education, and the like that must be examined again because of the failure of previous policy decisions.[14]

Policy Formulation

The second phase of the policy process is called *policy formulation,* or policy adoption. This phase occurs when a law is developed and passed to fix some past problem or to prevent the problem from occurring again in the future. From time to time, laws are passed to prevent a problem that policy makers can see on the horizon, but often these are still in response to a current issue that spurred Congress or a state legislature to act. The five-year moratorium that Congress placed on taxing sales on the Internet was intended to give the Internet a chance to get established before permitting taxes. This debate continues, but for the time being, the tax moratorium remains in effect. During the 1960s, Congress responded to pressures to extend the rights of blacks by passing the Civil Rights Act of 1964. Congress also created the Equal Employment Opportunity Commission to oversee the process of increasing diversity in the workforce, and passed the Voting Rights Act of 1965 to ensure that blacks could vote in the southern states.

Policy formulation involves highly political processes in which interest groups converge to try to get legislation that is advantageous to their groups approved. This phase involves a number of actors or players, including interest groups, Congress or a legislature, the president or a governor, and government agencies. For example, the military is constantly concerned with upgrading the nation's defense systems and weapons, which includes planning for obsolescence of equipment. Thus, the Department of Defense, the president, Congress, interest groups representing defense manufacturers, and groups that oppose building a new weapon system, such as a new jet fighter aircraft, are involved in the process. Why would a group oppose building a new jet fighter? Usually such interest groups believe that the funding needed to build anything can be put to better use, such as feeding the poor or improving the environment. The formulation phase entails all that goes along with getting a piece of legislation passed or a project funded. Most policies are not very visible to the general public. The battles are usually fought among completing interest groups in the legislative process. Lobbying is a critical aspect of policy formulation, and interest groups are actively involved in helping shape public policy.[15] For virtually every issue, alternative policy choices are available. The range of choices to combat poverty includes job training and education, cash payments and negative income taxes for the poor, medical assistance, affordable housing, or some combination of these and other alternatives. The options also include trying to help the poor break the cycle of poverty with various incentives and disincentives. During the Clinton administration, a major welfare reform law was passed that limits the time that a person (with some exceptions) can remain on the welfare rolls.

Policy formulation involves the *iron triangles* (Figure 7.3) that were discussed in Chapter 1. The iron triangle model represents the cozy relationships that can develop between interest groups, agencies, and the legislature in the policy-making process. The term *issue networks* is an alternative way to describe the relationships that develop. (See Figure 7.4.) This configuration is more fluid and temporary than iron triangles. Various interest groups come together to push for a policy, and then move on to another policy. Issue networks are made up of temporary coalitions of interest groups, lobbyists, lawmakers, experts, staff members, and other individual players in the process, who collaborate to shape a particular policy.[16] After the policy is complete, the coalition dissolves and the participants move on to other policies that usually involve different combinations of participants. Unlike the iron triangle model, the issue network model has the participants constantly changing. Even during the crisis that led to heightened airport security, interest groups emerged to have their say in the new systems that were under consideration in Washington. The airlines did not want to install costly doors on the cockpits of jets; the airlines wanted pilots to be authorized to carry handguns. Many pilots were trained in the military and are competent to use weapons. Others wanted armed air marshals on all major flights and all baggage checked for explosives and weapons. The policies that passed were meant to keep armed terrorists from boarding planes and gave the federal government responsibility for airport security. Moreover, all baggage was to be screened, including all checked baggage. Without a doubt, American airports are more secure than in the past, but similar attempts to increase security have been passed by Congress but then lessened over time as interest groups lobbied to reduce the restrictions. For example, after many hijackings in the early 1970s, Congress mandated metal detectors and other security devices.

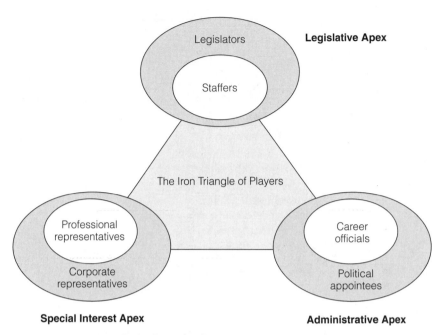

Legislators

Staffers

Legislative Apex

The Iron Triangle of Players

Professional
representatives

Corporate
representatives

Career
officials

Political
appointees

Special Interest Apex

Administrative Apex

FIGURE 7.3 Iron Triangles in the Federal Arena

SOURCE: Adapted from James Lester and Joseph Stewart, Jr., *Public Policy: An Evolutionary Approach,* 2nd ed. (Belmont, CA: Wadsworth/Thomson Learning, 2000), p. 75.

But security was reduced over time due to lobbying and the sense that the crisis had passed. Until the events of September 11, 2001, America had one of the least secure airport systems among developed nations. Technically, it is difficult to secure our airports because of the amount of air traffic in the United States and the cost. The policies that were implemented after September 11, 2001, will likely remain until another crisis occurs, but as the sense of urgency fades, it is very possible that airport security restrictions will be lessened over time.

Policy formulation involves decision making and choices, and the same basic models (the incremental and rational comprehensive models) that are used in public budgeting (described in Chapter 6) are also used in public policy. Public budgeting and public policy are closely related because policies and programs must be funded. Figure 7.5 provides a diagram of how the rational comprehensive model apples to public policy. This model is an ideal way to make decisions but is considered to be unrealistic in most political settings because of the lack of time and other resources. Some notable exceptions exist, however, in the area of public policy. Some agencies are comprised of highly competent experts, such as scientists, economists, or medical specialists. For example, the Centers for Disease Control and Prevention (CDC) are mainly staffed with medical experts and scientists. During the aftermath of the terrorist attacks in 2001, the CDC was faced with determining whether it was feasible to vaccinate the entire nation for smallpox based on a fear that terrorists

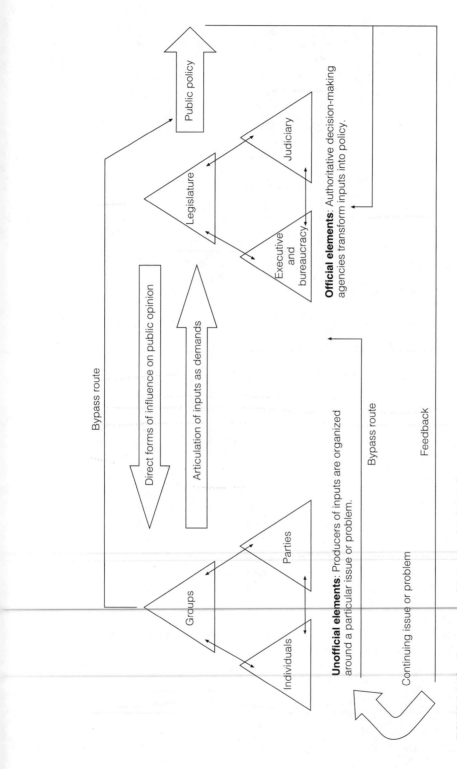

FIGURE 7.4 The Governmental System and Public Policy

SOURCE: Adapted from L. Earl Shaw and John Pierce, *Readings on the American Political System* (Lexington, MA: D. C. Heath, 1970), p. 14.

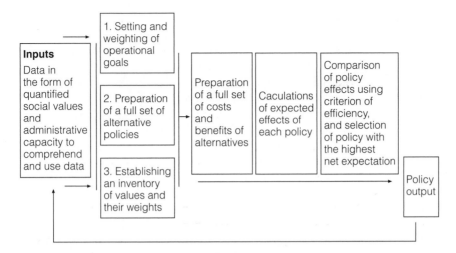

FIGURE 7.5 Rationalist Approach Applied to Public Policy

SOURCE: Adapted from Nicholas Henry, *Public Administration and Public Affairs,* 7th ed. (Upper Saddle River, NJ: Prentice-Hall, 1999), p. 357.

might spread the disease across the nation. Based on the scientific data, the CDC weighed the costs and benefits of a national vaccination program and concluded that vaccinating everyone posed greater risks than dealing with an outbreak of smallpox, if such an outbreak were to occur.[17] This decision was arrived at through a process that approximated the rational comprehensive model. But many policy decisions do not lend themselves to this model, and legislatures seldom use a rational-based model. Policy is formulated in the *political process,* which lends itself more to the incremental model of decision making than to the rational model. The incremental model views policy as a continuation of past government activities, with only small incremental changes made to policies.[18] Incrementalism is a much easier model for decision makers to operate with because it focuses only on incremental changes in past policy. Several key assumptions are made in the incremental model:[19]

- Most decision makers do not have sufficient predictive capabilities to know all of the consequences of each alternative or policy choice.
- Decision makers typically accept the legitimacy of previous or existing policies.
- Sunk costs prevent serious consideration of all policy choices, especially any radical revisions made to existing policy or creation of new policies.
- Incrementalism reduces conflict and is politically expedient.
- The personal characteristics of decision makers are better-suited to the incremental approach. Humans are more often not *value-maximizers* but *satisficers.*

The incremental model is not perfect and has been criticized. For example, it does not explain the efforts at long-range planning that are becoming more common for governments. Urban governments often use long-range planning to accommodate growth and economic development. The military has used long-range planning for many years. And, during the Carter administration in the 1970s, a comprehensive study called Global 2000 was instituted, which examined the relationship between population, resources, and the environment between 1979 and 2000.[20] But planning does not always become policy. Many studies conducted about the threat of terrorism warned about the possibility of terrorist attacks in the United States, but no major policy changes occurred. As noted earlier, most public policy is reactive despite the best efforts at planning and studies that are intended to be proactive. Perhaps the most important criticism of incrementalism is that it fails to explain the dramatic policy shifts that can occur in the political arena. The election of Franklin Roosevelt in the 1930s brought in the idea of large, active government, whereas the election of Ronald Reagan in the 1980s brought about a reversal in many major policy areas. Despite the criticisms and limitations, most observers believe that for the most part, public policy is developed and implemented via small, incremental changes.[21]

Policy Implementation

Policy implementation is what happens once a law is passed. The implementation process consists of a series of governmental decisions and actions that attempt to turn already determined mandates into reality. This process involves the *outputs* of public policy, such as the funding or actual service being delivered. Outputs are not the same as *outcomes,* which are measurable results or changes that can be attributed to a specific policy or set of policies. For example, outcomes involve examining the effectiveness of a policy. After 30 years of affirmative action, how well has it worked to bring about greater diversity in the workplace or society? What effects has it had on race relations? Or, have the billions of dollars that have been spent to reduce poverty actually contributed to a reduction in poverty? Have the many clean air acts that have been passed helped to reduce air pollution? *Outputs* are the policies, resources, and programs; *outcomes* are the results of the programs. Many policies have been mandated by Congress that were intended to clean up and protect the environment, but making these mandates work was largely the responsibility of the Environmental Protection Agency (EPA) and other agencies at the state level. Congress passed the Civil Rights Act of 1964, but its implementation, like most policies, was left to the bureaucracy, which was to iron out the details and make it work. Congress creates the mechanisms for implementation, but how a policy is actually implemented can vary. Legislatures, including the Congress, have a tendency to defer highly controversial decisions to the courts. Making controversial decisions costs votes. Congress never really said that the schools must be desegregated; it was the U.S. Supreme Court that made the policy in *Brown v. Board of Education* in 1954. Thus, once laws are passed, many legal battles are carried out in the courts to sort out the legalities of policy. The Civil

Rights Act has been tested many times and is still being tested in the new century, more than 40 years after the original legislation was passed. Implementation involves writing detailed rules and workable guidelines. This area also involves administrative law that is written by bureaus with enforcement power.

Policy Evaluation

Policy evaluation occurs after a program has been implemented. After a given amount of time, it is possible to examine policies to see whether they have made a difference in the problems they were designed to address. Evaluation involves looking at outcomes. It is concerned with the consequences of public policy. For example, did imposing a national speed limit during the 1970s actually help reduce fuel consumption? Lowering the speed limit did appear to help reduce fatal highway accidents, but downsizing to smaller cars may have done more to reduce the use of gasoline than reducing the speed limit on interstate highways to 55 miles per hour. Evaluating the effectiveness of policies can be tricky. Government can erroneously jump to the wrong conclusion because cause and effect are difficult to demonstrate, especially where social phenomena are involved. Did the safe road acts passed by state legislatures cause the number of accidents related to alcohol to drop—or did that come from a combination of factors, such as greater awareness because of education, a concurrent trend toward more healthy lifestyles, and the like? Did affirmative action cause or just contribute to the increased diversity in the workforce? Was it even a major factor? Other factors possibly could have had more impact than the government program. Furthermore, experience shows that government programs create unintended positive and negative factors that affect a problem. In the case of affirmative action, many other factors have been at play during the past 30 years, including the maturing of the baby boomer generation that is more receptive to the idea of diversity than older generations were. The same can be said about many other policy issues, such as the desire for a cleaner environment. The baby boomer generation is more supportive of environmental laws than previous generations. When evaluating how well a policy or program has worked, analysts must be careful not to make conclusions about cause-effect relationships too quickly because many forces come in play to resolve or alleviate social problems.

Policy evaluation is a significant part of public policy and is needed to modify existing policies to make them work better. It involves careful study of policy to determine whether the intended result has been achieved. Policy evaluation typically involves using carefully constructed research designs (plans that serve as blueprints for investigating research questions) and appropriate tools of analysis such as statistics, surveys, interviews, focus groups, and whatever else is needed to adequately determine whether the policy has worked. For example, a very complex policy evaluation would involve trying to determine if affirmative action has worked and been effective at reaching its goals. The first step is to define what affirmative action was supposed to do. Among other things, affirmative action was supposed to help minorities make advancements in the workforce and society in general. Certain indicators (measurements) may help evaluators determine whether progress has been made in the areas where affirmative action was supposed to have an impact. Several indicators that could be used are educational attainment, advancement and representation in various areas of the workforce, and income levels. Simply looking at data from the 2000 census would be meaningless without a reference point; thus, a research design would want to examine how much change in these and other relevant indicators has occurred over time. This would involve collecting data before affirmative action was implemented and perhaps including data in 10-year intervals, for example, from 1950 through 2000. This would show what the levels of educational attainment and other indicators were before affirmative action and how they changed over a 50-year period. If the indicators reveal that minorities have made progress, it is still not possible to attribute the cause to affirmative action, although it is common to hear such claims. More analysis is needed because many other factors at play during this era likely contributed to any advances, and some factors may have had a negative effect on minority advancement. This is a unique area of policy that has a great impact on public administration and requires special analytical and methodological skills. Measuring how well government performs is examined in Chapter 8.

Policy Change or Termination

The next phase, called *policy change or termination,* involves making adjustments to policies to improve their effectiveness. It involves a reexamination of the entire process to see if changes are needed. If a policy has failed, a determination may be made to modify the policy or terminate it. Conceptually, this is one of the newest areas in the study of public policy (developed during the 1980s).[22] Policies are often revised and modified. For example, during the 1970s, President Nixon brought back daylight savings time and lowered the maximum speed limit to 55 miles per hour to conserve energy. This was the era of the Arab oil embargo when the price of oil skyrocketed and wreaked havoc on the American economy. Daylight savings time is still with us, but the 55-mile-per-hour speed limit was dropped some years ago despite the fact that evidence suggested there were fewer fatal accidents with the lower speed limit. The crisis passed, cars were more efficient, and many citizens and special interests, like the trucking industry, wanted the speed limits raised. Thus, the policy was terminated. Policy termination is less common than policy change, partly because once a program is established, it takes on a life of its own. The agency responsible for the policy usually takes whatever action is necessary to keep the policy alive. There are also sunk costs involved that cannot be recovered. Thus, agencies typically argue that a program should not be abandoned, but simply modified.

Policies are often phased in over time. That is, a law may allow an activity to continue for the present, but then slowly phase it out over a period of time. For example, when it was discovered that freon, the popular coolant used in air conditioners for years, was damaging the ozone, Congress banned its use but allowed the product to be phased out over a long period of time. Freon is still available but is very expensive and has been replaced with a newer, safer coolant. The same idea was used to reduce automobile pollution. Automobile manufacturers were given many years to improve the efficiency of cars and reduce harmful emissions. Policies are sometimes terminated, but more often they are modified or changed. Policies rarely are maintained in the same form as when they were initially adopted. They are constantly evolving and changing.

Policy change can take many forms. It may involve *linear change,* which is simply replacing one policy with another, or modifying the policy. For example, the Jobs Training and Partnership Act (JTPA) simply replaced the older Comprehensive Employment and Training Act (CETA). Policies can be *consolidated* or merged together to form one new policy or program. They also can be *split* to form new, narrower policies. This occurred when the old Atomic Energy Commission was split into the Nuclear Regulatory Commission and the Energy Research and Development Administration in 1974. The reason for the split was due to conflicts between regulatory authority and support functions for nuclear energy that had plagued the Atomic Energy Commission. Some areas of policy are so complex that changes are *nonlinear,* such as changing the New Deal era program (created in the 1930s), Aid for Dependent Children (AFDC), to Temporary Aid for Needy Families (TANF) in the 1990s. In this case, the older program was not just replaced, but an entirely new welfare concept was introduced.

The policy process is complex, and the range of policies is broad—covering topics from fiscal policy to welfare policy. But the process is incomplete without adding conceptual models that help us understand the context in which the process operates. Many models of analysis have been developed to help explain that dimension of public policy.

METHODS FOR STUDYING PUBLIC POLICY

Political scientists and social scientists from other disciplines have developed a variety of models over the years to help enhance our understanding about why and how public policies become reality. This section briefly examines some of the major models and methodologies used to study public policy. Models are different from methodologies. Models provide conceptual frameworks for examining policies, while methodologies involve the philosophies and tools of inquiry. Moreover, studying public policy involves many different types of people who have different goals. The major methodological approaches are the empirical method, the econometric method, and the interpretative or phenomenological method. Unlike the hard sciences, the social sciences have what is called *methodological pluralism*—that is, they use a variety of methodologies. In the hard sciences, the empirical method is the norm, but the social sciences have the three major methodologies just mentioned, as well as a fourth method called critical theory.[23] Although this can cause confusion and professional tensions, many social scientists argue that studying social phenomena does not always lend itself to empirical inquiry, and thus we need alternative methods to enhance our understanding.

Also, studying social phenomena is different from the study of natural sciences because it involves *human behavior.* For example, water boils at a given temperature under normal atmospheric conditions every time. But at what "temperature" does a marriage become a divorce? At what point on some scale does a demonstration become a riot? Gauging social phenomena is more difficult and less precise than gauging phenomena in the natural sciences because human behavior is *reflexive.* That is, humans have the ability to change outcomes in many social settings. For example, economists can make predictions based on their best estimates of hard data about the supply of wheat. Suppose they predict that there will be an oversupply of wheat, which will drive prices down. Farmers who hear this prediction can then plant some other crop, making the prediction false. This is called a *suicidal prediction.* If the farmers had not heard the prediction and responded by changing their patterned behavior, the prediction would have been true.

The opposite of the suicidal prediction is called a *self-fulfilling prophecy.* This involves humans hearing a prediction, believing it, and making it occur through their behavior. What if the news media tells the nation that a certain candidate has won the presidency based on early election returns, and then people in the West opt not to vote because they believe the election is over? People's response to the information (in this case, their not acting) can make the prediction true when otherwise it possibly could have been altered. If a person living in the Southeast goes to a soothsayer and is told she will move to a western state, and the person responds to this prediction by quitting her job and moving to a western state, a self-fulfilling prophecy has occurred. That is, the person was influenced by the prediction and made it come true (or at least this would be the interpretation of most social scientists). Psychologists are well aware of the power of suggestion, which is another way of viewing self-fulfilling prophecies. Suicidal predictions and self-fulfilling prophecies are not part of the natural sciences, but they must be dealt with in the social sciences.[24] Three of the most popular methods for studying public policy are described in the following sections.

Empirical Method

The *empirical method* (also called the *behavioral method*) uses the tools and techniques associated with scientific inquiry to study public policy and other social phenomena. If one understands the basic methods of science, one also understands the goals, reasoning, and tools used by empirical social scientists. The empirical method is rooted in the *logical-positivist* philosophy that sought to discover laws and regularities in nature. Applied to social science, the goal was once to discover the patterns found in the social world. While the hope to discover "laws" was abandoned long ago, the goal has remained to make social science a rigorous discipline that bases its findings on replicable procedures to gain more understanding about the social world. This includes studying the process used to make public policies and the effect of public policies.

Studying public policy using empirical methods means clarifying concepts, gathering hard data, forming and testing hypotheses, using statistical techniques, being descriptive (rather than normative), and developing models that are based on deductive reasoning and supported by data. The behavioral approach, which was described in Chapter 2, holds that inquiries should study real behavior. If given the task of evaluating whether affirmative action has worked, an empirical study would not judge whether the program was "good or bad," but whether it achieved its goals and at what cost. Objectivity is one of the cardinal features of the empirical method. Public policy is viewed as another social phenomenon to examine, and the goals include discovering how the process works, why it works the way it does, and whether the policies have been effective and efficient. The goal of empiricism is to understand and predict rather than to judge something as good or bad. Empiricism often makes prescriptive recommendations that are based on predetermined goals. For example, a study might examine whether capital punishment is more costly than placing convicted criminals in prison for life without the possibility of parole. An empirical evaluation in this example would likely perform a cost–benefit analysis that attempted to measure the costs associated with each alternative. The behavioral revolution began shortly after World War II, and the empirical method is now the most accepted way to conduct research in political science and many other social sciences. However, as noted, other methods are also used to conduct political inquiries.

Interpretative Method

Another methodology involves interpreting politics and policies within their contextual framework. Those who study policies using this approach argue that intuition and contextual understanding are more important for understanding many social phenomena than cold hypotheses, hard data, and quantification of things that, in their view, cannot be quantified. The *interpretative approach* is the antithesis of the empirical method and is sometimes called the *phenomenological, postpositivist,* or *naturalist approach*.[25] This school of thought argues that contextual understanding goes further than the empirical method or the econometric approach in enhancing our understanding by treating each piece of social phenomena as a unique event using ethnographic and other qualitative methods. The model holds that laws and generalizations are not necessary to understand human actions and institutions.

The interpretative method argues that social sciences are different from natural sciences because actions are intentional. That is, actions (like language) have a meaningful or symbolic character. Thus, they must be understood in terms of the intentions of the actors and in the context of the society. While generalizations may be of heuristic value, they are not part of the logical structure of explanation itself. One of the most common methods is the case study approach. The interpretative analysts argue that understanding is more desirable than prediction. This method uses systematic, detached observation and intuition to gain insight into the effects of policies. For example, this method can be employed to study the effect of welfare policies or policies designed to reduce gang violence by examining and interpreting case studies. The interpretative method substitutes the concern for scientific rigor with intuition and immersion in the relevant information about a specific social phenomenon.[26]

Rational Choice Method

The *rational choice method* comes from the discipline of economics and is usually called *public choice* or *political economy* in political science and public administration.[27] The basics of public choice theory assume that politics and policy are based on the actions of individuals who are motivated by self-interest.[28] This means that people will look after their own interests rather than looking after the public interest or being concerned about collective outcomes. Public choice is a simple and parsimonious theory.[29] Its basic principles are easy to understand. The theory assumes that all individuals are *rational actors* (defined by economists as self-serving egotists) who respond to incentives and disincentives to maximize their own self-interest or satisfaction (the term used by economists is *utility*). Thus, rational actors will respond to the cost-laden choices in a way that satisfies their own self-interest. Applied to the public bureaucracy, bureaucrats will behave in a way that is in the public's interest only if it is also in their own self-interest. Serving some greater good (or the public interest) is secondary to serving their self-interest.

Public choice uses the language and tools of microeconomics to examine public policy and policy choices.[30] Economists once assumed that public administrators maximize serving the public interest in the policy process and, thus, will choose the public policies that maximize the public good. By the late 1950s, however, some economists were challenging this idea and argued that those involved in public policy are self-serving egotists just like everyone else.[31] Thus, there are several axioms of public choice. First, political actors, like economic actors, pursue their own self-interest. This behavior is normal and rational according to the theory. The second axiom is referred to as *methodological individualism,* which means that policy makers (or individual decision makers) are the primary unit of analysis. The values of the individual are assumed to be more important than other values, such as collective, organizational, or social values. In other words, the policy actions of an organization can be explained by the actions of individuals in the organization.

Public choice theory is grounded in laissez-faire individualism and free market economics.[32] The theory holds that competitive markets produce goods and services efficiently while public monopolies are inefficient. Inefficiency is viewed as an inherent characteristic of public bureaucracies because of incentive structures that encourage empire building and overproduction of services.[33] Because government agencies are service monopolies, public employees will behave in ways that promote their own interests at the expense of the public's interest in efficiency. Thus, it is believed that the incentive structures of public agencies encourage public personnel to advance their powers, budgets, and agency staffing levels.[34] The theory also explains why government tends to grow. The theory holds that self-interest leads to benign results in the marketplace but creates pathological patterns of behavior in political organizations,[35] mainly in the form of various free-rider and rent-seeker problems.[36] Coalitions of citizens (interest groups) join together seeking special advantages from government. Individuals with concentrated interests in increasing public expenditures literally take a free ride on those with diffuse interests in lower taxes. The iron triangles that develop work against the public at large while serving those with concentrated interests in increasing public expenditures. Public choice theory believes that in the public sector, the citizens (who are members of interest groups) will demand too many services, since increased quantities are not regulated by direct increased costs for those receiving the services.[37] In situations where the public at large is paying to benefit the few, the cost of services to individuals becomes so inexpensive that demand increases. This results in an excessively large demand for services and a bloated, overly expensive, and wasteful government.[38] Thus, government will make too many policies in response to special interests that are not in the best interest of the general public.

Public choice, as a methodology, overlaps with the *rationalist decision-making model*. But the goal is to find the most *rational policy* using *Pareto optimality*.[39] This method assumes an economic state where no one can be made better off without making someone else worse off. Economists recognize that Pareto optimality is virtually impossible to achieve (it is an ideal economic state), but *Pareto improvements* involve making changes that make everyone better off. Pareto improvements involve *trade-offs* (the value being traded and the social costs and benefits incurred in the trade) and *externalities* (desirable or undesirable effects that spill over into other spheres of social actions). Externalities can be positive or negative. For example, pollution is often considered to be a negative externality because it usually is not counted in production costs. If one of the by-products of industrial production is water pollution and someone else—namely, government and taxpayers—must pay for cleanup costs, the externality or spillover is negative. Conversely, education is considered to be a positive externality because it creates positive benefits for society that carry into other spheres of social action. The principles of rational choice are illustrated in Figure 7.6. The diagram uses a hypothetical social value (referred to as Value A) relative to other social values. The indifference curve is the combination of values to which society is indifferent. The value achievement curve contains the optimal combination of values that government can encourage. The point of optimal achievement of Value A and optimal achievement of all other social values is the point of Pareto optimality. Pareto improvements refer to actions that bring society closer to Pareto optimality.

Here is how public choice theory might be applied to a specific policy such as energy conservation and the reduction of air pollution. Automobiles account for 60 percent of the nation's air pollution and about 40 percent of fuel consumption.[40] Some automobiles are very fuel-efficient and generate less air pollutants than others do (such as a Honda Accord versus most sport utility vehicles). Public choice theorists would not argue that laws should be passed banning sport utility vehicles (SUVs), like the Ford Explorer, Jeep Grand Cherokee, and Chevy Blazer, because people should be allowed to own such vehicles, but they would argue that the people who own them should have to

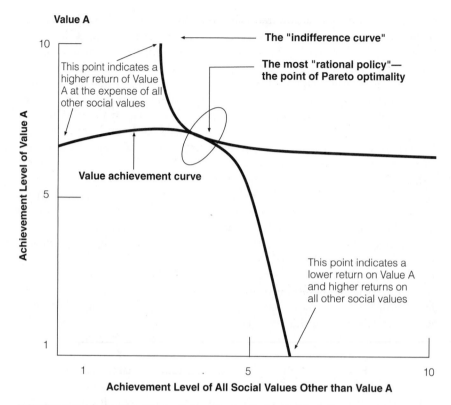

FIGURE 7.6 Public Choice: Pareto Optimality Applied to Public Policy

SOURCE: Nicholas Henry, *Public Administration and Public Affairs,* 7th ed. (Upper Saddle River, NJ: Prentice-Hall, 1999), p. 358.

pay for the costs to society associated with operating them (more fuel consumption and pollution).[41] Under this theory, vehicles that use the least gas and have lower emissions would have the lowest tax, while vehicles that use the most gas and generate the highest emissions allowed by law would have the highest tax. Thus, public choice theorists would turn to the tax structure and impose charges based on fuel consumption and emissions. This would create an incentive for citizens to buy cars that are more fuel-efficient and environmentally friendly, while at the same time allowing individuals the freedom to buy gas-guzzlers if they are willing to pay for the externalities and negative spillovers on society. Public choice theorists would argue that air quality would improve because most people, being rational actors, would not be willing to pay the true costs of driving gas-guzzlers. This example illustrates how several social values come into play with this theory—the freedom to own whatever automobile one prefers (within certain limits), and the goals of a cleaner environment and energy conservation. Public choice theory would argue that the tax system could be used to accommodate all of these values.[42]

Public choice is a parsimonious approach that is based in the selfish, calculating behavior of individuals. Over the past 30 years, public choice theory has gained respect in the area of policy studies, particularly in areas of public finance. Economists, using rational choice models, have been influential in helping to develop a variety of real public policies. For example, fiscal policy, monetary policy, and some welfare policies are based on rational choice theory. The negative income tax developed during the Nixon administration was based on rational choice principles.[43] Table 7.1 compares basic paradigms associated with the empirical, interpretative, and public choice methods.

ADDITIONAL WAYS
TO STUDY PUBLIC POLICY

Additional approaches are used in studying public policy, such as the *historical approach,* which examines history and looks for patterns to help in interpreting policies. This is the method used to develop the zigzag theory and the 30-year recurring pattern thesis discussed earlier. There is also a *normative method* that uses persuasion and selected interpretations of empirical data to make normative arguments. This approach is often closely tied to *ideological approaches* that use various sources of information but interpret them in a way that supports their ideological position. Most public administrators are not policy analysts by training, but they must work with analysts and sometimes conduct research. Thus, public managers must be able to understand some of the basic elements associated with policy analysis. Four major types of policy analysis frequently appear in the everyday world and are very relevant to public administration:[44]

- *Scientific policy analysis.* Analysts using this method search for the causes and consequences of public policies in an objective way rather than undertaking efforts to prescribe policy. Their goal is to *describe* the real world, and they seek to understand cause-and-effect relationships in the social world. They follow the scientific rigor of the empirical methodology and seek to find theories, regularities, and the truth about the impact of public policies. They are social scientists by training and are well trained in the use of sophisticated techniques of analysis. These policy analysts tend to work at universities.

- *Professional policy analysis.* The professional policy analyst studies public policy with the desire to improve it. This group of analysts seeks to apply scientific knowledge to the solution of practical problems, and they believe that, eventually, there will be a true science of public policy. A true public policy science will help decision makers by effectively defining and diagnosing problems, proposing policy alternatives, developing models that will aid policy makers in selecting choices that will achieve desired results, and providing estimates about the feasibility of various policy programs.[45] The analysts trained at policy institutes, such as the Rand Corporation or

Table 7.1 Empirical, Interpretative, and Public Choice Methods Compared

Axioms About	Empirical Paradigm	Interpretative Paradigm	Public Choice Paradigm
The nature of reality	Reality is single, tangible, and fragmentable.	Realities are multiple, constructed, and holistic.	Reality is single, tangible, and fragmentable.
The relationship of the knower to the known	Knower and the known are independent.	Knower to the known is interactive and inseparable.	Knower and the known are independent.
The possibility of generalizations	Time- and context-free generalizations are possible.	Only time- and context-bound statements are possible.	Generalizations are possible. The goal is to find Pareto optimal outcomes.
The possibility of causal linkages	There are real causes, temporally precedent to or simultaneous with their effects.	All entities are in a state of mutual simultaneous shaping, so that it is possible to distinguish causes from effects.	It is possible to establish cause and effect.
The role of values	Inquiry is value-free.	Inquiry is value-bound.	Values are of less concern than in the other methods.
Unit of Analysis	Methodological individualism.	Methodological holism.	Methodological individualism.

NOTE: The rational (public) choice method is less concerned with some of the issues that exist between the empirical and interpretative methods and more concerned with developing mathematically sound models to predict behavior that are based on the assumptions of the theories.

SOURCE: Derived from Yvonna Lincoln and Egon Guba, *Naturalistic Inquiry* (Newbury Park, CA: Sage, 1985), p. 37, and Alexander Rosenberg, *Philosophy of Social Science* (Boulder, CO: Westview Press, 1988), Chapters 1–6.

the Brookings Institute, represent this type of policy analysis. Many similar institutes in the United States as well as international organizations scattered across the world perform this type of analysis. These analysts tend to work in think tanks and policy institutes rather than at universities.

- *Political policy analysis.* Those who study public policy as political analysts are concerned with advocating the "right" policy positions for their ideological group or political party. This method is essentially a normative or ideological approach. Political analysts give credence to certain policy positions while challenging other positions. Political analysts are usually trained in research skills but use those skills along with the rhetoric of their ideological preferences. Political parties or ideological organizations, such as the Heritage Foundation, the Cato Institute, and the Reason Foundation, often employ political analysts who study public policy.

Ideologically speaking, both liberal and conservative organizations are involved in this type of analysis.

■ *Administrative policy analysis.* Administrative policy analysts are typically employed by government agencies and are concerned with achieving efficient and effective policy implementation. They are similar in many respects to the professional analyst and use many of the same scientific-based techniques. They also have most of the same goals as the professional analyst, since they are concerned with improvements in policy in order to achieve sound public policy. The administrative approach is *managerial-based;* that is, it seeks to find better ways to *manage* the implementation of public policy. In the world of public administration, administrative analysts are very common and are found in many, if not most, major governmental agencies. The professional training of administrative analysts is similar to that of professional analysts.

CONCEPTUAL FRAMEWORKS

FOR UNDERSTANDING PUBLIC POLICY:

TWO MODELS OF POLITICS

Understanding public policy often goes directly back to political models. Social models are an abstraction of reality; they are supposed to replicate a part of reality and provide a framework that helps us understand the real world. Good models help explain why things occur as they do and provide a rationale that explains how the real world works. Public administrators work in the real world of politics. Even highly technical and scientific agencies like the National Science Foundation (NSF) and the Centers for Disease Control and Prevention (CDC) are a part of the political system and are affected by politics. Two of the basic models of politics are the elitist and pluralism models. Both have been very influential in understanding politics and public policy, as well as politics in general.

The *elitist model* of politics holds that society is governed by a group of political elites who have a disproportionate amount of political power. The theory dates back to C. Wright Mills and his famous book *The Power Elite.*[46] Those who adhere to this position believe that public policy is a reflection of the desires of a power elite who can push their preferences through the political system. Elites dominate the high positions of government and the corporate sector; thus, they are in position to ensure that policies that are advantageous to them are implemented. These positions include the president and his or her staff, the heads of the major political parties, cabinet-level secretaries, members of Congress, judges, corporate leaders, and the like. For many years, political scientist Thomas Dye has been publishing a book titled *Who's Running America* that describes the elites who hold powerful positions in society.[47] The basic premises of the elitist model include the points shown in Table 7.2.[48]

Table 7.2 Basic Principles of the Elitist Model of Politics

1. American society is divided into those who have political power (the few) and those who do not have political power (the many). Only a small number of people allocate society's resources and make policy; the masses do not decide public policy. Values are determined by elites.

2. Those who govern are not typical of the masses. Elites come from the upper echelons and upper socioeconomic strata of society. They are wealthier, better educated, and have many other social and economic advantages over the average citizen.

3. Nonelites must gradually be integrated into higher positions to avoid revolution or social and political instability. Only nonelites who have accepted the basic values of the elites can be brought into the circles of those who govern.

4. Elites share a basic consensus about the basic values of the social system and are committed to protecting and preserving the system (the status quo). Any changes made to the system must be slow and evolutionary. In the United States, the basics of the elite consensus are for the sanctity of private property, limited government, and individual liberty (freedom).

5. Public policy does not reflect demands made by the masses. Public policy reflects the values of elites, and changes in public policy will be incremental (not revolutionary).

6. Elites are subject to little direct influence from the apathetic masses. The masses are generally poorly informed and can be controlled by the elites, who hold a disproportionate amount of political power. The elites influence the masses far more than the masses influence elites.

7. Public policy is directed from the top downward. Power is concentrated at the top and public policy decisions are made and implemented from the top.

SOURCE: Adapted from James Lester and Joseph Stewart, Jr., *Public Policy: An Evolutionary Approach* (Belmont, CA: Wadsworth/Thomson Learning, 2000), pp. 54–55. The original source of these basic descriptions is credited to Thomas Dye and Harmon Zeigler, *The Irony of Democracy* (Monterey, CA: Brooks/Cole, 1981).

The opposite of the elitist view is the more accepted *pluralistic model*. In this view, power is fragmented and scattered in such a way that it is virtually impossible for a small, identifiable group of elites to control a disproportionate amount of political power. The pluralist model sees competition among interest groups. A power struggle over policy is fought among competing interest groups that seek to get advantageous policies implemented. This model also views the masses as being apathetic and uninformed, but individuals can influence policy by becoming members of interest groups. Robert Dahl defined pluralism as a model in his famous book entitled *Who Governs?*[49] David Truman was one of the pioneers of this theory with his influential book, *The Governmental Process.*[50] Pluralist theory accommodates the idea of elites, but not in the same sense of the term as described in the elitist model. *Elites* may be thought of as *leaders* who hold decision-making positions, but the idea of a ruling class is rejected in the pluralist model. Moreover, leadership is fluid and constantly changing in the pluralist view. Table 7.3 summarizes some of the major principles of the pluralist model.[51]

Table 7.3 Basic Principles of the Pluralist Model of Politics

1. Power is an attribute of individuals in their relationships with other individuals in the process of decision making. Interest groups are the key to understanding American democracy and the public policy process. It is the competition between interest groups in the governmental process that influences public policy.

2. Power relationships are not permanent. They are often formed for a particular decision. After the decision is made, the relationships may disappear and may be replaced by another set of power relationships when the next decision is made. These power relationships involve what we think of today as interest groups.

3. There is no permanent distinction between the elites and masses. Individuals who participate in decision making at one time may not be the same individuals who participate in the next decision at a different time. Individuals move in and out of the ranks of decision makers simply by becoming active or inactive in politics.

4. Leadership is fluid and mobile. Wealth and social status are assets in politics but are only one of many assets that are part of political power. Elites are *elite* only in the sense that they hold leadership positions of power, not because of some superiority of social or ruling class. The term *leader* is a better description than the term *elite* for those who hold temporary positions of political power. Power resides more in the *position* than with the *person*. An aristocracy does not govern America.

5. There are multiple centers and bases of power in society. No single group dominates decision making in all areas.

6. Considerable competition exists between interest groups.

7. Public policy reflects the bargains and compromises reached between competing groups.

SOURCE: Adapted from James Lester and Joseph Stewart, Jr., *Public Policy: An Evolutionary Approach* (Belmont, CA: Wadsworth/Thomson Learning, 2000), pp. 54–55. The original source of these basic descriptions is credited to Thomas Dye and Harmon Zeigler, *The Irony of Democracy* (Monterey, CA: Brooks/Cole, 1981).

These two theories have served as the basis for understanding public policy and politics for many years. Other theories and models besides elitism and pluralism exist, but these two theories have remained important for providing converse conceptual frameworks for building additional models. Both models have been criticized, mainly for being overly simplistic or failing to account for certain anomalies. Regardless of the model used, public policy is about politics and power and those involved in the processes that make authoritative decisions for society.[52] Who makes public policy? The answer varies depending on the model or conceptual framework that is used. If one accepts the elite model, then the ruling class determines public policy. If one accepts the pluralistic model, then public policy is the product of conflict, compromise, and power struggles between interest groups in the governmental process (the policy cycle described earlier). One area in which all models seem to agree is that the average citizen is not included in the process. The mechanisms used by elites, interest groups, and the powerful and affluent are seldom available to the average citizen (or the masses).

WHAT IS THE PUBLIC'S ROLE
IN THE PUBLIC POLICY PROCESS?
EXPERTISE VERSUS DEMOCRACY

Public administration often deals with the idea of citizen participation because laws require allowing public input into certain types of agency decisions. Despite the presence of public hearings and sunshine laws (open meeting laws), the public's voice is not well represented. One of the tensions is the so-called *expertise versus democracy* problem. Part of the public policy process involves public agencies. Bureaus tend to be staffed with experts who possess knowledge about technical matters. But experts can make decisions with little or no input from the general public. And experts often argue that the public's input is not needed in many areas of policy because the public is not qualified to make certain kinds of decisions. For example, experts were warning about the dangers of tobacco, secondhand smoke, and exposure to hazardous chemicals like asbestos long before the public had any idea about these dangers. However, democracy suggests that citizens matter and to leave them out of the process seems, for lack of a better phrase, undemocratic. The problem with bureaucrats in the policy process is that they are insulated; politicians cannot easily fire them, but they can change the policy. Moreover, often their expertise is correct, and politicians rely on their knowledge to make policy in the legislative process. The role of the average citizen seems minimal in the public policy process.

Most theorists and observers seem to concede that the main role for the average citizen is that of voter, and it is believed that the attitudes and opinions of average citizens are reflected in public opinion polls. President Richard Nixon referred to the masses as the "silent majority." He felt that the typical American was different from the special interests and the power players in the political process. He was probably correct. Recall from Chapter 1 that even proponents of government (those who view government in the most positive light) typically hold that mechanisms exist for citizens to influence government (namely, joining interest groups). Many believe that this is an acceptable way for government to respond to inputs and demands of the *public*. The average citizen's main role is to vote, but citizens also are free to join groups that influence policy. Empirical evidence suggests that these are the most common forms of political participation in the United States and in most democracies.

The American political system has many access points where public policy can be influenced and where politicians and policy makers have an open ear to the inputs that are received. But the average citizen plays a minimal role for a variety of reasons. It is believed (and is probably true) that the typical citizen is not very concerned with most areas of public policy. In fact, most areas of public policy are not very visible. Notwithstanding some exceptions that involve local issues, such as public education issues that affect a parent's child or local tax issues, most citizens are more concerned with the activities that occupy their daily lives and either do not have or do not want to take the time to become informed and participate in politics.[53] Stated simply, the average citizen does not care, feels powerless to influence change, or is satisfied enough with the status quo. This is the consensus of the guiding doctrine about the general public. But there have been efforts that date back many years to empower citizens and encourage participation. The primary goal of the League of Women Voters, for example, is to increase participation. Legislation has been passed to make voting easier, such as the motor voter laws that allow people to register to vote when they get their driver's licenses renewed. Many states have gone to great extents to make registration easier. Some states, like Wisconsin, allow voters to register on the same day as the election. Most efforts to increase participation are aimed at voting,[54] but bringing the public into the policy arena means listening to citizens in a meaningful way.

The Kettering Foundation is a public policy research institute that is dedicated to increasing the public's involvement in the policy process. David Mathews, the CEO of the Kettering Foundation, has written extensively about promoting methods that allow the public's voice to be heard.[55] The general position of the Kettering Foundation is that something important can be learned from *public deliberation* about policy issues and that the public's voice deserves to be included in policy formulation. The Kettering Foundation seeks to bring citizens together with decision makers to discuss issues. This typically involves using well-prepared booklets about a policy that have the issue framed with alternative policy choices. The process of deliberation is simply a discussion with a trained moderator who allows everyone's opinion to be heard in an open, but structured, setting. This information is then shared with policy makers, including members of Congress. The results of these deliberations are often inconsistent with public opinion polls because they provide a different type of information (the results of discussions). While public opinion polls can be informative, they are far less thorough and in-depth than face-to-face discussions about issues. The public policy process often requires that public hearings be held to allow people to voice their opinions, but public hearings often produce very little usable information. Even when conducted as carefully as possible, critics charge that they are simply a formality required by law and that the decisions have already been reached. Public hearings can turn into a disaster when people come to gripe and nothing worthwhile is accomplished because most of the participants are on the defensive. Critics argue that the goal of public hearings is to sell decisions that have already been made to the public. The Kettering Foundation[56] promotes public deliberations with the National Issues Forums Institute, Public Agenda, and numerous local organizations nationwide. These forums provide an avenue for the general public to participate (as stakeholders) and influence public policy. According to the Kettering Foundation, the process of deliberation has influenced public policy at the federal, state, and local levels.

But what is the public's role in the policy process? Despite efforts from concerned citizens, political scientists, and civic groups to promote citizen involvement, the empirical evidence suggests that the role of the average citizen is minimal.[57] Moreover, most research suggests that the average citizen is apathetic to politics. This phenomenon has attracted the attention of public choice theorists who argue that special interest groups that are organized and well funded are able to take advantage of the general public and get advantageous legislation and benefits from the public's money. That is, those with a concentrated interest get the public at large to pay for their special privileges because the general public has no real voice in the process (unless they also form interest groups to challenge existing special interests). Regardless of how public administrators choose to handle citizen involvement in policy making, the idea of deliberation is worth examining. Properly framing issues and having a structured, open, and meaningful discussion with participants can be helpful to public administrators and at the same time provide a constructive way for citizens to voice their views. Such a process also allows the public to participate in a meaningful way in the decision making of public agencies.[58]

POLICY ANALYSIS: EXAMPLES
OF SUBSTANTIVE PUBLIC POLICY

One of the most interesting aspects of public policy involves examining real policies. While it is beyond the scope of this book to analyze public policies, Box 7.2 and Box 7.3 include information about two areas of substantive public policies: illegal narcotics policy and welfare policy. These two policy areas illustrate some of the difficulties associated with trying to address societal problems and issues. Both policy summaries come from Public Agenda, a public policy institute that is dedicated to examining a variety of public policy areas and public opinion polls.[59] Each policy summary follows the general format used by the National Issues Forum Institute—the issue is framed, and three alternative policy choices are provided. Also included in each box is some additional commentary about the role of policy analysts who determine how effectively the current policies are working. Both of these policy areas reflect the *professional policy analysis* method described earlier.

SUMMARY

Public policy is one of the most critical areas of public administration. Public administrators are involved in making, implementing, and evaluating public policy. Policy is made in a complex process that involves formulation, implementation, evaluation, and change or termination. The goal of public policy is to resolve societal problems. Public policy is what government does and what government selects to ignore. That is, nondecisions can be as important as decisions about significant issues in society.

Several types of public policy exist: distributive, redistributive, and regulatory. *Distributive policies* "distribute" some good or service, such as Social Security checks or funding to universities for research. *Redistributive policies* (e.g., welfare policy) are more controversial because they take something from

BOX 7.2 Public Policy: Illegal Drugs in America

Overview

Compared with the peak years of the late 1970s, government statistics show that drug use is down in the United States. Over the past several years, use of illicit drugs among adults has been stable, and over the past decade the use of illegal drugs by workers has declined by more than half. Teen drug use has held steady for the past four years after rising sharply in the early 1990s. Teen use of some drugs, such as cocaine and methamphetamine, is down, but use of other drugs like ecstasy has increased, according to the University of Michigan's annual "Monitoring the Future" survey.

Despite the overall decline, most Americans still regard illegal drugs as one of the nation's most serious problems. More than half of the public worries that a family member might become addicted, and seven in ten people say the government is not doing enough to address the problem, despite the fact that in 2001 the federal government spent more than $18 billion dollars fighting the "war on drugs." Public opinion polls reveal that three-quarters of American believe that the nation is losing the "war on drugs." One of the major factors is that a great deal of money is made in illicit narcotics. The lure of easy money makes it appealing and difficult to stop the flow of drugs. Economists have long noted that removing the profitability for the drug trade would remove most of the problem. However, most Americans do not support legalization of drugs.

Getting Tougher with Dealers

Historically, federal and state governments have used two strategies to combat drug use: reducing the supply of illegal drugs and curbing the demand. When most people talk about the "war on drugs," they are thinking about efforts to reduce supply: more aggressive police investigations, tougher sentences for drug users and dealers, greater efforts to intercept drugs before they cross U.S. borders, and supporting antidrug efforts by drug-producing nations. The number of drug offenders in U.S. prisons has risen dramatically over the past two decades, and drug arrests have doubled since 1985.

Reducing demand has often meant drug education programs in schools, public service messages in the media, treatment programs, and drug testing. Despite civil liberties concerns, the courts have generally upheld drug-testing programs for employees and even students involved in extracurricular activities. Also, the federal government is currently in the middle of a five-year, $2 billion antidrug ad campaign.

Critics of the "war on drugs," including an increasing number of law enforcement officials and even a few public officials, such as New Mexico's Governor Gary Johnson (2002), say the campaign hasn't worked, and have called for drug legalization. They argue legalization, like the ending of the Prohibition on alcohol, would undercut drug gangs and allow the nation to focus on drug abuse as a medical problem. Those critics, however, are still a distinct minority.

Marijuana as Medicine?

One area where advocates of legalization have made progress is in the medical use of marijuana. Although the federal government maintains an extremely limited medical marijuana program (so limited that it is down to less than a dozen patients), federal policy for decades has held marijuana to be a dangerous and addictive drug.

In 1996, Californians approved a ballot proposition allowing physicians to prescribe marijuana for specific

(continued)

BOX 7.2 *continued*

illnesses, such as glaucoma, even though federal laws ban its sale and distribution. Other states have followed suit, and similar ballot propositions have passed but been nullified in several other elections. Federal and state officials have fiercely fought to keep the referendums from being implemented, and none have taken full effect. In March 1999, a panel of experts convened by the federal Institute of Medicine found that marijuana does have legitimate medical uses for treating symptoms of cancer and AIDS. While the panel found no evidence that marijuana leads to harder drugs like cocaine, the scientists did warn that marijuana smoke is even more toxic in the long term than tobacco smoke.

Nationwide, two-thirds of the public supports the use of marijuana to ease severe pain. Although most people regard marijuana as a much less dangerous drug than cocaine or heroin, a solid majority opposes general legalization of marijuana, and an even more substantial majority opposes the overall legalization of drugs.

The Public's View

Opinion polls show the public tends to favor a variety of different approaches to the drug problem, mixing liberal and conservative attitudes. There is strong public support for doing everything possible to intercept drug supplies and punish dealers. At a time when the nation's prisons are filled with criminals serving sentences for drug-related crimes, most Americans want even stricter penalties for deal dealers. Most Americans do not support legalization of drugs.

Many people also think permissive messages from parents and the media are one of the main causes of the drug problem. They favor expanded antidrug efforts to discourage use. Expanded drug treatment is favored as well, although this tactic is not as widely supported as stepped-up law enforcement.

Three Perspectives

- One perspective emphasizes strict enforcement of the drug laws, intercepting drug supplies, and doing whatever is necessary to catch and punish drug dealers.
- A second perspective puts its emphasis on cutting demand by preventing drug use and doing everything possible to change tolerant attitudes toward it.
- A third perspective regards drug abuse primarily as a health problem, and favors stepped-up treatment to help users rather than punishing them. Advocates generally favor legalization of some drugs.

---

one group of citizens and give it to another group. Redistributive policies are by far the most controversial public policies and tend to be highly ideological in nature. *Regulatory policies* seek to regulate some activity in society, such as telecommunications, banking practices, or public utilities (electricity and natural gas). The tendency in the United States, unlike many of our European counterparts, is to have private ownership of the means of production and distribution along with government regulation. Many European countries have

The Questions for Policy Analysis

What do we do about illegal drugs? Should we do anything different from what we are doing now? That is, does the current set of policies adequately handle the problems associated with illegal narcotics? Policy analysts must determine whether current public policies are working and at what costs. This includes the consequences of policies, such as filling up the nation's prisons with drug offenders (and the cost), and the effectiveness of treatment and education programs. Most policy areas raise many questions for policy analysis. Are we making progress in the "war on drugs," and why or why not? The debate for decision makers involves what to do next. Much depends on the findings of policy analysis.

The three perspectives may be combined in some form. That is, deal with the *demand* for drugs with treatment and education; go after the sources or *supply* of illegal drugs; and consider whether some drugs should be legalized, which is not popular with most Americans or policy makers. If the use of drugs is dropping, which is supported by empirical evidence, one can argue that it is possible that the nation is on the right course and we should work with existing policies. Ultimately, the questions for policy analysts include:

- What exactly is the drug problem? How has it been defined?
- What are the current policies and are they working effectively?
- What are the exact goals of the nation's illegal drug policy?
- Are we approaching the drug problem correctly?
- Are we making progress in achieving the stated goals?
- Can the current policies be improved, or do we need to alter public policies to make them work more effectively?

Although this policy summary is simplified, it does provide the basics of the issue. What would you do if you were the drug czar of the nation?

Recall that the two drugs that kill more people each year are not included in this policy area: alcohol and tobacco. Both substances are legal. Although there are policies to keep young people from drinking and smoking, these policies are separate from the "war on drugs."

SOURCE: Public Agenda Online (2002). Used with permission. The information has been slightly modified but is fully credited to the work of Public Agenda. For much more information about the illegal drug issue, visit Public Agenda's Web site at http://www.publicagenda.org. Public Agenda is a nonpartisan, nonprofit public opinion research and citizen education organization based in New York City. It was founded in 1975 by social scientist and author Daniel Yankelovich and former Secretary of State Cyrus Vance. Public Agenda offers information on an impressive selection of public issues along with the results of public opinion polls. Their work is also used in National Issue Forums around the nation. Much of this selection appears in the article *Illegal Drugs*, which is available on the Public Agenda Web site.

government-owned industries. Government regulation of such activities as safety, sanitation, and transportation is expected in modern society. Although regulation is also controversial, it is part of the political culture and is generally accepted.

A variety of methodologies are used to study public policy, including the empirical method, the interpretative method, and the rational choice method. The *empirical method* is based on the principles and methods of science, and

BOX 7.3   Public Policy: Poverty and Welfare

Overview

When Congress voted in 1996 to enact sweeping changes in the way the federal government provides public assistance to the poor, the goal—in the words of former President Clinton—was to "end welfare as we know it."

In many respects, that goal has been achieved. The days when someone could receive welfare checks indefinitely are over. The current approach requires many recipients to work for their benefits and also places a five-year time limit on cash assistance. Even the name of welfare changed, from Aid to Families with Dependent Children (AFDC) to Temporary Assistance for Needy Families (TANF).

Since the program went into effect, welfare rolls have been cut in half. Many states report great success in moving people from welfare into jobs. And many studies have demon-strated that working improves the self-esteem of workfare participants and bestows positive benefits on their families. The nation's poverty rate also dropped to 11.3 percent in 2000, its lowest level in 21 years and only slightly higher than the record low of 11.1 percent in 1973.

Some suggest that the economic prosperity of the 1990s played a large role in lowering the poverty rate, creating new jobs for low-income workers and reducing welfare case-loads so dramatically. But while the number of poor Americans has fallen markedly in recent years, those who remain poor have, on average, grown poorer, according to the Center on Budget and Policy Priorities. More than 31 million people live below the poverty line, and more than a third of them are children. It's worth noting that, according to a report by the United Nations Children's Fund, the United States ranks second only to Mexico in the rate of child poverty among the 29 members of the Organization for Economic Development. America's Second Harvest, the nation's largest hunger-relief organization, reports that more people are seeking emergency food aid. It reports that, in 2001, more than 23 million people sought emergency food help, an increase of 2 million over 1997, when the welfare reform law took effect.

Critics say that reform has moved welfare recipients into the ranks of the "working poor," who are employed but cannot earn enough money to lift them out of poverty. Those critics argue that there are insufficient support services—such as child care—to help the working poor remain employed. The Economic Policy Institute reports that, in 1999, nearly half of those who moved from welfare to work were still unable to afford the bare essentials, including food, housing, and medical care. And a recent study of welfare participants by the Manpower Research Develop-ment Corp. suggests that teenagers perform worse at school when their mothers go to work.

Revisiting Reform

With public sentiment so strongly behind the concept of work in exchange for public assistance, it hardly seems likely that the United States will return to welfare as we used to know it. President Bush has proposed toughening the work requirement. Under the president's proposal, the workweek for welfare participants would be increased to 40 hours, from 30, and the percentage of welfare recipients required to work in each state would be increased to 70 percent, from 50 percent. In practice, administration officials say, states typically have about 30 percent of their welfare recipients in jobs because of a provision in the 1996 law that gives them credit for each person moved off their welfare rolls. Bush's proposal calls for the elimination of that loophole, but at the same time the president would allow low-income parents to meet part of their work requirements by participating in organized activities with their children, including the Scouts, sports, and education programs.

President Bush also wants the workfare program to begin putting an emphasis on "healthy marriages." His plan calls for the government to subsidize experimental programs in five or six states that would provide a variety of support services for couples, including counseling. A number of studies have found that two-parent families offer more stability, in addition to higher incomes, and that children of single-parent families are more likely to struggle in school or become involved in crime. But some critics say the administration's efforts to encourage marriage among welfare recipients will prove futile. A study by Cornell University's Community and Rural Development Institute found that three-quarters of all single mothers receiving welfare had already given marriage a try. Even as he touts the benefits of welfare reform, Bush acknowledges: "We ended welfare as we've known it, yet it is not a postpoverty America."

Making the Transition
Workfare critics say the government needs to do more to help welfare parents make a successful transition to work, including providing more funding for such things as child care.

Bush's plan provides no additional funds for child care. The administration has said that states can pay for additional child care and other support services out of the federal block grants they receive to run their welfare programs. The National Governors Association, though, complains that additional money for things like child care would have to come at the expense of other services. The governors also want more flexibility in administering the programs. At a recent meeting, the governors association sent a message to the White House: Just give us the general goals along with the block grants, and we'll work out the specifics based on the individual circumstances in our states. Others suggest there are ways to help the needy other than the federal welfare program, like the Earned Income Tax Credit (EITC), which aims to reduce the tax burden on low-income families with dependent children and to offset the work disincentives associated with welfare. Unlike most other tax credits, EITC is refundable. Studies suggest that former welfare recipients, like the ranks of other low-income families they are joining, are surviving to a large extent on recent expansions of the EITC. But a study by the General Accounting Office, the investigative arm of Congress, found that a third of all low-income people eligible for EITC are not taking advantage of it.

Likewise, it's estimated that as many as 12 million people who are eligible for food stamps are not receiving them. The number of people receiving food stamps dropped more than a quarter between October 1996 and October 2001. Some part of the decline can be attributed to the fact that the 1996 welfare reform law excluded legal immigrants from many federal benefits, such as food stamps. Earlier this year, President Bush proposed restoring food stamp benefits for an estimated 363,000 low-income legal immigrants who have been in the United States at least five years.

(continued)

BOX 7.3 *continued*

And there remain those who say that the best cure for poverty is a job, and that the best solution is an economic policy that fosters vibrant growth. They say, for instance, that the economic expansion of the 1990s did more to create jobs and lift people out of poverty than any other antipoverty program. In fact, during the 1990s, the unemployment rate dropped to its lowest level in three decades.

The Public's View

Surveys show the public strongly supports the concept of requiring able-bodied welfare recipients to work in exchange for benefits, and people generally think the 1996 reform law has worked well. But there are some areas where the public is conflicted about how much the government should be doing for welfare recipients.

Six out of ten people say the welfare reform law is working, according to a 2001 survey conducted by National Public Radio, the Kaiser Family Foundation, and Harvard University's Kennedy School of Government. Yet, the vast majority (73 percent) of those familiar with the welfare reform law agree that people who have left the welfare rolls are still poor, despite having found jobs. Large majorities say they favor additional government aid for the poor, including expanded job-training programs (94 percent), improved public schools in low-income areas (94 percent), increased subsidies for day care (85 percent) and subsidized housing (75 percent), and more tax credits for low-income workers (80 percent).

The public also appears to make a distinction between "the poor" and "welfare recipients." Most Americans say fighting poverty should be a high priority for the government, although

they rate other issues higher. But Americans are also divided on whether welfare recipients really need the assistance: 47 percent say they need the help, and 44 percent say they could get by without it. And while eight in ten Americans say jobs are available for welfare recipients who want to work, many also say those jobs don't pay enough to support a family.

Framing the Issue: Three Perspectives

- One perspective holds that government efforts to reduce poverty have made the problem worse by creating a culture of dependency. The best and most compassionate solution is to phase out most welfare benefits and allow better-equipped communities and private charities to help the poor.
- Another perspective believes that in exchange for public assistance, government is entitled to make demands on recipients. Government programs must firmly guide poor people toward responsible, self-reliant, and productive lives.
- The third perspective acknowledges that a successful antipoverty program has to focus on the needs of the working poor—good education and jobs with livable wages and benefits—and not on their behavior or values.

Some Questions for Policy Analysts

Many questions arise for the policy analyst. What is the gap between the wealthy, poor, and middle class? What is an acceptable standard of living? What is the psychology of poverty? Does it affect people in a way that hurts their ability to become productive citizens and workers? Have welfare programs helped to improve the lives of recipients? Have welfare programs helped to get people off the welfare rolls and into jobs? What is the success rate of getting people jobs? How much of the appropriated funds actually get to the poor? What percent of funds is used up in administrative costs? The role of the policy analyst in this issue involves examining poverty in America over a period of time. For example, an analyst might examine data from the 1930s through 2000 and see how poverty has changed. More importantly, a time series analysis might reveal whether significant changes occurred after major welfare programs were implemented.

Poverty and welfare have been extensively studied. Some of the findings suggest that the gap between the rich and the poor is larger than ever. Some studies suggest that welfare programs have created a dependency on welfare funds that make the cycle of poverty worse because people cannot break out of the system. Studying poverty and welfare has been highly ideological. Conservatives like Milton Friedman, *Tyranny of the Status Quo,* and Edward C. Banfield, *The Unheavenly City Revisited,* have argued that most of the people on welfare are capable of working but that government compounds the problem by giving too many incentives to remain on welfare for as long as possible. Friedman believes that only a small percent of the welfare recipients are truly chronic cases. The United States has a higher percentage of its population in the category of "poor" than any other developed western nation. The figure is at least 10 percent. Of course, being poor in America is different from third world countries, but poverty has not been a major problem for other developed nations. The number is much larger when the so-called

"hidden poor" (or working poor) are included.

The effectiveness of the government's performance on resolving poverty and welfare issues is controversial. Gauging how well government has performed is usually left to policy analysts. For example, conservatives like George Gilder, *Wealth and Poverty,* and Charles Murray, *Losing Ground,* have argued for years that welfare programs have failed. On the other hand, liberals like Michael Harrington, *The Other America,* and Kenneth Auletta, *The Underclass,* argue that the government has a moral obligation to continue its efforts to resolve poverty in America. The liberal position is that government must continue its efforts to help the poor and disadvantaged. Debates over how well welfare programs have worked have produced mixed findings.

NOTE: The references for the books about poverty and welfare noted in this box are: George Gilder, *Wealth and Poverty* (New York: Basic Books, 1981); Charles Murray, *Losing Ground: American Social Policy, 1950–1980* (New York: Basic Books, 1982); Michael Harrington, *The Other America: Poverty in the United States* (New York: Macmillan, 1962); Kenneth Auletta, *The Underclass* (New York: Vintage Books, 1982); Milton Friedman, *Tyranny of the Status Quo* (New York: Basic Books, 1984); and Edward C. Banfield, *The Unheavenly City Revisited* (Boston: Little, Brown, 1974).

SOURCE: Public Agenda Online (2002). Used with permission. The information has been slightly modified but is fully credited to the work of Public Agenda. For much more information about poverty and welfare, visit Public Agenda's Web site at http://www.publicagenda.org. Public Agenda is a nonpartisan, nonprofit public opinion research and citizen education organization based in New York City. It was founded in 1975 by social scientist and author Daniel Yankelovich and former Secretary of State Cyrus Vance. Public Agenda offers information on an impressive selection of public issues along with the results of public opinion polls. Their work is also used in National Issue Forums around the nation. Much of this selection appears in the article *Poverty and Welfare,* which is available on the Public Agenda Web site.

seeks to understand and predict social phenomena. Its foundation is the ideals of the hard sciences, such as biology and physics, but it applies the methods of science to social areas. Studying social phenomena is different from studying the natural sciences, however, because of a concept known as "reflexivity." That is, predictions are more difficult to make because humans have the ability to alter outcomes (known in social methodology as self-fulfilling prophecies and suicidal predictions). Thus, social science has developed other methods that help to deal with this problem. The *interpretative method* is concerned with gaining contextual understanding of social phenomena through systematic inquiry. In this view, situations vary so much that scientific inquiry cannot capture the "context" in which policies exist. The *rational choice* (or *public choice*) *theory* applies the methods, techniques, and assumptions of economics to policy analysis. Rational choice theory views individuals as self-serving egotists who look after their own interests rather than the public interest. Based on this assumption, researchers gain insight into why government behaves as it does and why policies succeed or fail. From the perspective of rational choice, public policy is driven by the self-interested participants who are involved in the process.

There are also several kinds of policy analysts, ranging from those who study policy scientifically in universities, and professional policy analysts working in policy institutes and think tanks who want to improve policy, to ideological and political groups that seek to impose their preferences, and administrative analysts who are interested in improving policy and its implementation through their agencies. The world of public policy is broad and goes far beyond the scope of this book. Public administrators must understand the complexities involved in making, implementing, and evaluating public policies. Public administration is an integral part of the public policy process because agencies often *make* public policy.

NOTES

1. The "living wage" is a mandate requiring that businesses that have contracts with the city pay wages that allow workers to keep up with the standard of living in the area. The wage is usually higher than the federal minimum wage, which is currently about 26 percent lower than during the 1980s when adjusted for inflation. There are several versions of the living wage, with some extending the requirement further than municipal contracts. The New Party has been one of the most adamant supporters of the living wage concept. For information, visit http://www.newparty.org/livwag.

2. See Theodore Lowi, *The End of Liberalism* (New York: W. W. Norton, 1969).

Also see Kenneth Meier, *Politics and Bureaucracy: Policymaking in the Fourth Branch of Government,* 3rd ed. (Belmont, CA: Brooks/Cole, 1993).

3. There are references to public and private goods throughout this book. Public goods are very much a part of public policy. Public goods are good and services where it is difficult to exclude citizens from enjoying the service, such as national defense. Private goods are fairly easy to exclude others from using. Mancur Olson made this distinction relating to public policy in his classic book *The Logic of Collective Action* (Cambridge, MA: Harvard University Press, 1965). Substantive policy analysis is not included in this chapter, since it is beyond the scope of this book,

but it involved examining policies, such as welfare, education, environmental, economic, and similar policies. The purpose of this chapter is simply to cover some of the basic elements of public policy that should be useful for public managers.

4. This model was adapted from James Lester and Joseph Stewart, Jr., *Public Policy: An Evolutionary Approach* (Belmont, CA: Wadsworth/Thomson Learning, 2000), p. 5.

5. Several references have been made to the corporate scandals that characterized the first few years of the new century. Just as a reminder for students, ImClone was the biotech firm whose new cancer drug was rejected by the Food and Drug Administration (FDA), and which got Martha Stewart accused of insider trading.

6. *U.S. Term Limits, Inc. v. Thornton,* 514 U.S. 779 (1995). It is legal for their states to impose term limits for their representatives for state assemblies, but they cannot impose term limits on members of Congress. Term limits was part of the famous Republican *Contract with America in 1996,* but was never approved by Congress.

7. Anthony Downs, "Up and Down with Ecology: The Issue-Attention Cycle," *Public Interest 32* (Summer 1972), pp. 38–50. Downs articulates five stages in the attention cycle. The first stage is the preproblem stage, which is followed by alarmed discovery and euphoric enthusiasm to solve the problem (the second stage). The third stage is the realization that to resolve the problem will entail significant costs. The fourth stage is where public interest in the issue begins to fade, and the final stage is called the postproblem stage where the issue moves into the "twilight realm" and attracts little attention. Not all major issues go through the "attention cycle." Those that do go through these stages are likely to affect a minority, involve a social arrangement that is beneficial to a majority or a powerful minority, and have been previously surrounded by exciting events associated with the problem (e.g., media attention given to an issue like race riots, space shuttle flights, or the like). Also see James Anderson, *Public Policymaking,* 4th ed. (Boston: Houghton Mifflin, 2000), Chapter 3.

8. One of the organizations dedicated to informing the public about public policy and public opinion is the policy analysis institute Public Agenda, located at http://www.publicagenda.org.

9. More will be said about values and ethics in Chapter 9, which included value formation.

10. See Arthur Schlesinger, Jr., "America's Political Cycle Turns Again," *Wall Street Journal,* December 10, 1987, p. 28. Schlesinger predicted that a liberal swing would begin in the 1990s and last until around 2020, when the next major conservative cycle would begin. Also see Arthur Schlesinger, Jr., *The Cycles of American History* (Boston: Houghton Mifflin, 1986).

11. James Lester and Joseph Stewart, Jr., *Public Policy: An Evolutionary Approach,* pp. 23–24.

12. The zigzag or backlash thesis was developed by Edwin Amenta and Theda Skocpol, "Taking Exception: Explaining the Distinctiveness of American Public Policy in the Last Century," in Francis G. Castles, Ed., *The Comparative History of Public Policy* (New York: Oxford University Press, 1989), pp. 292–333. Other more detailed models, such as Paul Sabatier's evolutionary model, view policy changes as an evolutionary pattern because of the interaction between various groups. This model is described in detail in James Lester and Joseph Stewart, Jr., *Public Policy: An Evolutionary Approach,* Chapter 9.

13. This idea was suggested in Edward Banfield's classic book, *The Unheavenly City Revisited* (Prospect Heights, IL: Waveland Press, 1990). Banfield offered the classic conservative arguments on a variety of policy issues.

14. See James Lester and Joseph Stewart, Jr., *Public Policy: An Evolutionary Approach,* pp. 68–69.

15. See James Anderson, *Public Policymaking: An Introduction,* 3rd ed. (Boston: Houghton Mifflin, 1997); Deborah Stone, *Policy Paradox: The Art of Political Decision Making* (New York: W. W. Norton, 1997); V. O. Key, *Politics, Parties, and Pressure Groups* (New York: T. Y. Crowell, 1964); John Kingdon, *Agendas, Alternatives, and Public Policies* (New York: Harper Collins, 1995); Thomas Dye, *Understanding Public Policy,* 9th ed. (Upper Saddle River, NJ: Prentice-

Hall, 1998), Chapter 1; and Randall Ripley and Grace Franklin, *Congress, the Bureaucracy, and Public Policy* (Homewood, IL: Dorsey Press, 1980).

16. For an excellent discussion about issue networks, see Hugh Heclo, "Issue Networks and the Executive Establishment," in Anthony King, Ed., *The New American Political System* (Washington, DC: American Enterprise Institute, 1978), pp. 87–124. Also see James Anderson, *Public Policymaking,* pp. 75–78.

17. The source of this information came from a workshop held at the Kettering Foundation (Dayton, OH) on November 29, 2001. The workshop included specialists from the Centers for Disease Control and Prevention and other government agencies.

18. Among the most famous articles on the idea of incrementalism is Charles Lindblom's "The Science of Muddling Through," *Public Administration Review 19* (1959), pp. 79–88.

19. The assumptions are taken from James Lester and Joseph Stewart, Jr., *Public Policy: An Evolutionary Approach,* p. 93.

20. Ibid.

21. The formulation stage of the policy process can also be viewed as a system. David Easton brought this idea into political science during the 1950s. The system approach views the policy process as interrelated parts where inputs are received, conversion occurs by policy makers, and the output is public policy. The idea works essentially the same as the organizational systems model described in Chapter 4. See David Easton, *A Framework for Political Analysis* (Chicago: University of Chicago Press, 1979).

22. Policy change is a fairly new area of policy studies. Much of the conceptual framework is credited to Paul Sabatier. See Paul Sabatier and Hank Jenkins-Smith, *Policy Change and Learning* (Boulder, CO: Westview Press, 1993).

23. Critical theory is not discussed here, although some political scientists use it to examine policies. It is most often associated with the work of Karl Marx. Stated very briefly, critical theory is very much based in political philosophy. It assumes that something is wrong with the existing order or the status quo. The theory holds that facades blind us and we come to take them for granted and therefore cannot see the truth until we are enlightened. For example, Karl Marx believed that the bourgeois was taking advantage of the workers (proletariat) but did not blame the workers for not being able to see that they could free themselves through a revolution. Often critical theory is revolutionary in nature because it seeks to deconstruct the status quo to free those who are being taken advantage of by the current system. Sometimes Freudian psychology is used to illustrate the principles of critical theory because Freud's idea was that progress could not be made until one becomes aware of one's subconscious (the id, ego, and superego). Once one sees the truth, one can be free. In the contemporary world, most feminist theory is based on critical theory. In its most simplistic form, men have dominated society for centuries, and as soon as women (and men) see the truth, things will change. For an excellent description of critical theory, see Richard Bernstein, *The Restructuring of Social and Political Theory* (Philadelphia, PA: University of Pennsylvania Press, 1978), pp. 171–236.

24. It is beyond the scope of this book to go too deeply into methodology, but public administrators should have some general understanding of the basic methods used by social scientists. For a more thorough description of social science methodology, see Earl Babbie, *The Practice of Social Research,* 7th ed. (Belmont, CA: Wadsworth, 1995), and Janet Johnson and Richard Joslyn, *Political Science Research Methods,* 3rd ed. (Washington, DC: CQ Press, 1995). For more specific methods about policy analysis, see Carl Patton and David Sawicki, *Basic Methods of Policy Analysis and Planning,* 2nd ed. (Englewood Cliffs, NJ: Prentice-Hall, 1993). Also, for an excellent background in public policy analysis, see Robert Heineman, William Bluhm, Steven Peterson, and Edward Kearny, *The World of the Policy Analyst: Rationality, Values, and Politics,* 2nd ed. (Chatham, NJ: Chatham House, 1997). Methodological pluralism is articulated by Paul Roth in *Meaning and Method in the*

Social Sciences: A Case for Methodological Pluralism (Ithica, NY: Cornell University Press, 1987).

25. This approach has a number of different names, but the qualitative nature of the interpretative method is the same. Alexander Rosenberg provides an excellent discussion and comparison of the empirical, interpretative, and rational choice methods in *Philosophy of Social Science* (Boulder, CO: Westview Press, 1988), Chapters 1–6.

26. The interpretative approach has many names, but it involves the concept of *hermeneutics,* which comes from Hermes, the Greek god who frequently spoke in riddles that had to be interpreted by mortals.

27. In this section, *rational choice and public choice* are used synonymously.

28. Anthony Downs was among the first scholars to bring rational choice to political science in *An Economic Theory of Democracy.* His example helps explain why public choice theory has emerged in debates about public policy. Downs was motivated by an anomaly that he noticed in economics, specifically in the field of public finance and welfare economics. In these areas, government action is a key variable, and economists had been successful in using theories based on rational choice to analyze the impact of alternative public policies. Based on their analyses, economists could recommend policies (based on rational choice models) to government decision makers. Downs complained that economists had not succeeded in explaining which policy recommendations government officials would actually follow. Instead, economists were content to indicate which policies *should* be used and to assume that government officials would implement them. Given the assumptions of rational choice, Downs argued that there is no reason to believe that government officials would follow the recommendations of economists. Like other individuals, government officials must be self-serving, rational actors, and it must be assumed that they will make policy as a means of satisfying their own interests; it cannot be assumed that they are a special case and will maximize the public interest. Such an assumption would contradict the underlying theories on which the recommendations themselves were predicated. If government could act in a nonmaximizing manner, the same could be true for others, and the predictions of the whole theory would be called into question. In short, Downs argued that public officials are also rational actors and will follow the recommendations of economists only if those recommendations happen to be in their own interests. By the mid-1960s, public choice theory was well developed and was raising similar questions about the actions of government. With regards to government bureaucracies, rational choice predicts that government will resist efforts to lower costs because officials seek to satisfy their own interests, which include budget maximization, empire building, and protecting the turf of their agency. For a thorough discussion of public choice theory, see Vincent Ostrom, "Some Developments in the Study of Market Choice, Public Choice, and Institutional Choice," in Jack Rabin, W. B. Hildreth, and Gerald Miller, Eds., *The Handbook of Public Administration* (New York: Marcel Dekker, 1989), pp. 861–882. Also see Anthony Downs's classic book on economic theory and democracy, *An Economic Theory of Democracy* (New York: Harper, 1957).

29. Rational choice has developed over a long period of time in economics. Several variations of the theory exist. For a thorough analysis of rational choice, see Alexander Rosenberg, *Philosophy of Social Science,* Chapters 3–6. A classic example of the interpretative theory applied to the study of political science is Richard Fenno's *Home Style: House Members in Their Districts* (Boston: Little, Brown, 1978).

30. Several different schools of public choice study many areas of politics, policy, public finance, voting behavior, and nonmarket decision making. All of the schools use the same models and assumptions, which are also the same as the basic model used in rational choice in economics.

31. The challenge came from a number of scholars, including Anthony Downs, *An Economic Theory of Democracy* (New York: Harper & Row, 1957).

32. William Niskanen, *Bureaucracy and Representative Government* (Chicago: Aldine Atherton, 1971). Also see Thomas Borcherding et al., *Budgets and Bureaucrats* (Durham, NC: Duke University Press, 1977), and Gordon Tullock, *The Politics of Bureaucracy* (Washington, DC: Public Affairs Press, 1965).

33. Robert Bish and Vincent Ostrom, *Understanding Urban Government* (Washington, DC: American Enterprise Institute, 1973).

34. James Buchanan, "Why Does Government Grow?" in *Budgets and Bureaucrats,* pp. 13–14, and Gordon Tullock, "Why Politicians Won't Cut Taxes," *Taxing and Spending* (October/November), 1978, pp. 12–14. Also see E. S. Savas, "Municipal Monopolies versus Competition in Delivering Urban Services," in H. W. Hawley and D. Rogers, Eds., *Improving the Quality of Urban Management* (Beverly Hills, CA: Sage, 1974), pp. 473–500.

35. Milton Friedman, *Tyranny of the Status Quo* (New York: Basic Books, 1984). Also see Dennis Mueller, *Public Choice* (London: Cambridge University Press, 1979).

36. The concept of rents is often associated with government bureaucracy. Rents occur when agents are paid more than the public should have spent for a service. In the public bureaucracy, rents come in the form of fringe benefits, pleasant working conditions, undemanding workloads, and job security. Economists refer to these as "nonpecuniary rents." See Donahue, *The Privatization Decision: Public Ends, Private Means,* pp. 91–94.

37. Irene Rubin, *Running in the Red* (Albany, NY: State University of New York Press, 1982), p. 7.

38. Ibid.

39. Economist Vilfredo Pareto developed the concept of Pareto optimality.

40. Cited in Nicolas Henry, *Public Administration and Public Affairs,* p. 356.

41. This type of tax structure has been used by many states. For example, heavier vehicles cause more wear and tear on roads. Thus, large trucks pay more for their license tags than regular automobiles. For many years the state of Florida charged for license plates based on the weight of the car. For example, a Cadillac cost more than a Honda Accord. The concept is the same as that described in the sports utility example relating to fuel consumption and air pollutants.

42. This section relies heavily on the descriptions provided by Nicholas Henry in *Public Administration and Public Affairs,* pp. 356–361.

43. Milton Friedman, *The Tyranny of the Status Quo* (New York: Basic Books, 1984). For more information about public choice, see James Buchanan and Gordon Tullock, *The Calculus of Consent: Logical Foundations of Constitutional Democracy* (Ann Arbor, MI: University of Michigan Press, 1962). The theory of property rights is also tied closely to public choice. See Garrett Hardin, "Tragedy of the Commons," *Science 162* (December 1968), pp. 1243–1248, and Mancur Olson, *The Logic of Collective Action* (Cambridge, MA: Harvard University Press, 1965). In public administration, Vincent and Elinor Ostrom have been among the most influential public choice scholars. See Vincent Ostrom and Elinor Ostrom, "Public Choice: A Different Approach to Study Public Administration," *Public Administration Review 31* (March/April 1971), pp. 203–216.

44. The types of policy analysts are taken from James Lester and Joseph Stewart, Jr., *Public Policy: An Evolutionary Approach,* pp. 42–44.

45. See Melvin Dubnick and Barbara Barnes, *Thinking about Public Policy* (New York: Wiley, 1983). Also see Donald Paris and Duncan MacRae, *The Logic of Political Inquiry* (New York: Longman, 1983).

46. C. Wright Mills, "The Structure of Power in American Society," *British Journal of Sociology* (May 1958), pp. 29–41. Mills's classic book is *The Power Elite* (New York: Oxford University Press, 1956).

47. Thomas Dye has been publishing this analysis of dominant leadership in the nation since the 1970s. See Thomas Dye, *Who's Running America? The Bush Restoration,* 7th ed. (Upper Saddle River, NJ: Prentice-Hall, 2003). Thomas Dye is also a very widely respected political scientist who studies public policy. See

Thomas Dye, *Understanding Public Policy,* 10th ed. (Upper Saddle River, NJ: Prentice-Hall, 2003). Dye's public policy book provides an excellent integration of models of politics applied to substantive public policy.

48. See Kenneth Prewitt and Alan Stone, *The Ruling Elites: Elite Theory, Power, and American Democracy* (New York: Harper & Row, 1973).

49. Robert Dahl, *Who Governs?* (New Haven, CT: Yale University Press, 1961). Also see Robert Dahl, *Pluralist Democracy in the United States: Conflict and Consent* (Chicago: Rand McNally, 1967), and *Preference to Democratic Theory* (Chicago: University of Chicago Press, 1956).

50. David Truman, *The Governmental Process* (New York: Knopf, 1951).

51. See Robert Dahl, *Polyarchy: Participation and Opposition* (New Haven, CT: Yale University Press, 1971).

52. See Harold Lasswell, *Personality and Power* (New York: W. W. Norton, 1948), and V. O. Key, Jr., *Politics, Parties, and Pressure Groups,* 4th ed. (New York: Thomas Y. Crowell, 1964). Also see Harold Lasswell and Morton Kaplan, *Power and Society* (New Haven: Yale University Press, 1950).

53. One of the classic books on this area is V. O. Key, Jr., *The Responsible Electorate* (Cambridge, MA: The Belknap Press of Harvard University, 1966). Also see Morris Rosenberg, "Some Determinants of Political Apathy," *Public Opinion Quarterly 18* (1954), pp. 349–366.

54. Some states have much higher participation rates than others do. For example, voter turnout tends to be consistently higher in Maine, Minnesota, Wisconsin, and Montana. Voter turnout tends to be lower in the South. Voter turnout tends to be related to poverty; states with large numbers of citizens who are poor seem to have lower turnouts

rates. Political scientists have consistently demonstrated that political participation (of all types) is related to wealth and education. That is, people with high incomes and high levels of education participate at a much higher rate than people with lower incomes and less education. See Ann Bowman and Richard Kearney, *State and Local Government,* 5th ed. (Boston: Houghton Mifflin, 2002), Chapter 4.

55. See David Mathews, *Politics for People: Finding a Responsible Public Voice,* 2nd ed. (Urbana, IL: University of Illinois Press, 1999). Also see David Mathews, "The Public in Practice and Theory," in David Rosenbloom, Deborah Goldman, and Patricia Ingraham, Eds., *Contemporary Public Administration* (New York: McGraw-Hill, 1994), pp. 461–469. The original source of Mathews's article is *Public Administration Review* (March 1984).

56. The Kettering Foundation of Dayton, Ohio, maintains an excellent Web site with links to many organizations that promote public deliberation and citizen involvement in the policy process. The Web site is located at http://www.kettering.org.

57. Elizabeth R. Gerber, Arthur Lupia, Matthew D. McCubbins, and D. Roderick Kiewiet, *Stealing the Initiative: How State Government Responds to Direct Democracy* (Upper Saddle River, NJ: Prentice-Hall, 2001).

58. For more information about the concept of public deliberation and how it can be used in the policy process and by government agencies, visit the National Issues Forums Institute at http://www.nifi.org.

59. Public Agenda is an excellent source of information about current public policies. The institute's Web site is http://www.publicagenda.org.

8

Public Administration and Issues Relating to Government Performance

When Columbus left on his famous voyage, he did not know
where he was going; when he landed, he did not know where he was;
and when he returned, he did not know where he had been.
But he did it all on government money.

ANONYMOUS

GOVERNMENT PERFORMANCE

President Lyndon Johnson once said that if two people agree on everything, you could be sure that only one of them is doing all of the thinking. In the world of politics, there has never been a time when people agreed on everything. This is the nature of both politics and life. In public administration, many contemporary and enduring issues provoke a diversity of opinion and outright disagreement. Gauging government performance is one of those issues. No one fully agrees on the right way to measure what government does. This is partly because government performance cannot be measured solely in economic terms, like profits in the world of business. Rather, measurements often are coupled with goals that are reflected in public policy, which is defined by politics and ideology. Thus, in the discipline of public administration and in the real world of public management, the areas relating to government performance contain some serious controversies.

Measuring government performance entails gauging how well government performs its duties and functions. This includes using both internal measurements, such as productivity of employees, and external measurements, such as deciding if government has reduced the incidence of problems like crime or poverty. Measuring what government does has proven to be an arduous task. At the managerial level, public managers are often viewed as something less than their counterparts in the private sector. In the eyes of critics of government, the *Peter Principle,* the idea that people rise to positions they are not competent to hold and remain there, seems to have been written specifically for government. Of course, the same could be said about the business world; and in the end, this is not true of either the public or private sector. But it is a perception that permeates in our society.[1] Moreover, public perception about government is not helped by the fact that most Americans (two-thirds) believe government is filled with corruption.[2]

The discipline of public administration has addressed several major challenges during the past few decades about government performance. The *privatization debate,*[3] posed a serious challenge in the 1980s. The debate has now lasted for more than 20 years and has yet to be fully resolved. Privatization involves examining the proper balance between the public and private sectors. Proponents of privatization believe that government should spend its time governing and let the private sector produce and deliver most public services. The idea that government should privatize services because it cannot match private sector efficiency did not set well with traditional modes of thought in public administration, such as the orthodox school. In the 1990s, public administration received another challenge from the *reinventing government* movement, which challenged government to remove the red tape and become more results-oriented. Despite suspicions, the traditional school of thought found the idea of reinventing government more palatable because it sought to work with existing government organizations to increase performance. Thus, it was viewed as just another reform movement. Later, ideals of reinventing government would be seriously questioned.

This chapter examines the extent to which we can gauge government performance, the privatization debate, and the reinventing government movement. All of these issues are related to government performance.

GAUGING GOVERNMENT PERFORMANCE:
THE BROAD PERSPECTIVE

The purpose of business is relatively simply to understand. Economist Milton Friedman put it bluntly. The purpose of a business is to make money. Businesses make money by selling goods and services to customers, and society generally benefits from being able to buy automobiles, televisions, computers, food, and the like. There are well-established ways to measure how well businesses perform. If businesses are making money and managing the money in a way that generates profits to be shared with stockholders, then they are performing their function. A number of measures are used to gauge a business's performance, such as return on investment, market share, and customer satisfaction, but all relate to "making money." Productivity (typically defined as the ratio of inputs to outputs) in the private sector also relates to money.[4] In the private sector, companies pay attention to the efficiency of their operations because failure to do so will result in the loss of profits and ultimately cause the firm to go broke.

One of the enduring questions in the public sector is whether government should be managed like a business. This debate goes back to Woodrow Wilson in the classical period of public administration. Wilson, like others during his time, believed that government could and should be managed like a business. Critics have long argued that if government would just manage itself like a business, it would enhance its *efficiency* (spend less money and time to produce comparable levels of service) and *effectiveness* (do a better job of attaining goals). Box 8.1 discusses the concepts of efficiency and effectiveness. But in the public sector, there is no comparable measurement of profit, market share, or return on investment; and the customer in the private sector is not exactly the equivalent of citizens in the public sector.[5] Government performance is much more complex and difficult to measure than the performance of businesses in the private sector, as government operates under a very different set of assumptions.

Because of the differences between the public and private sectors, it seems reasonable to use measures to gauge government performance that are different from those used in business. First of all, government does not produce products, such as washing machines, computers, or automobiles. Government typically provides a broad range of services and cannot quantify unit costs or measure productivity as easily as the private sector. But the private sector also provides services and has little difficulty measuring how well it performs because of the profit motive (making money). Government has developed productivity measurements tailored for the public sector, and the General Accounting Office (GAO) estimated that a 5 percent increase in productivity at the federal level would save $4.5 billion annually.[6] Second, government is left with many of the tasks that the private sector does not want to perform or cannot perform, such as resolving poverty, welfare, and crime issues; administering justice; and taking care of the sewage. Third, government is responsible for regulation and oversight. Although the idea of self-regulation of industries has gained popularity, the only reason that it may work is because of the threat of government regulation. The recent wave of corporate scandals illustrates that private industry does not always succeed at self-regulation. Thus, government must regulate many of the activities of society, including businesses. The nature of these tasks makes managing government agencies different from managing private businesses. Government deals with many public goods, while the private sector deals with private goods. The argument that government is "different" is still very much a part of the government productivity and performance debate. Thus, the public-private dichotomy remains an issue in the new century.

The bottom line for a business is profit. The bottom line for government has been described as *power* and *politics*.[7] All government institutions and

BOX 8.1 The Concepts of Efficiency and Effectiveness

Simply stated, **efficiency** is the ability to produce a product or service in a cost-effective manner. Whether operating a bus system or manufacturing computers, efficiency is being able to provide a service or product at a specified level of quality, at a lower price. For example, if one firm can produce a computer and another firm can produce a computer of equal or better quality for less money, then the second firm is more efficient.

Examples of efficiency are easy to find in the marketplace. Efficiency can be illustrated in what occurred in the personal computer market during the late 1980s and early 1990s. For years personal computers were very costly and International Business Machines (IBM) dominated the market. Other competitors emerged and took advantage of new technologies and processes that lowered the cost of production and the price for consumers. This in turn forced IBM to also reduce the cost of its computers. In short, many of the manufacturers of IBM "clone" computers became more efficient than IBM.

Although the price of a product is determined by a variety of factors aside from efficiency of production, such as supply and demand, price remains the ultimate factor in the marketplace. Companies must do whatever is necessary to keep costs under control. That is, the company must control transportation and shipping costs, materials, and labor to compete with other companies. It must ultimately get its computers into stores like Best Buy and Circuit City at a competitive price.

It is more difficult to force efficiency in the public sector because no true competition exists. With whom does a city compete? Cities can simulate competition or attempt to compare themselves to similar cities, which is often difficult to do. Thus, efficiency in the public sector relies on the self-discipline of government (including political institutions like city councils that control budget appropriations) and the demands of voters, which are usually inadequate and not comparable to the incentives that force efficiency in the marketplace. Moreover, the demands of citizens can contribute to inefficiency rather than efficiency when citizens demand too many services while at the same time resist efforts to raise taxes. Internal measures of efficiency are used in both the private and public sectors, but direct competition *forces* efficiency in competitive markets regardless of how it is measured.

Efficiency is generally defined as a ratio measuring related outputs (the product or service) to inputs (the materials, labor, etc.) used to make the product. In other words, inputs are the resources used to produce a good or service. A municipal refuse collection operation uses inputs such as personnel and equipment (garbage trucks, fuel, etc.) to collect garbage. All of the costs associated with producing the service must be taken into account to determine the actual cost of operations. Outputs are the units of goods or services produced from the inputs. A typical efficiency measurement for refuse collection is cost per household, which is simply the ratio of production costs divided by the total number of households served. For example, if the total cost of collecting residential garbage was $100,000 and 50,000 houses were served, the cost per household would be $2.

Efficiency for government services has been defined as *a relative measure based on previous performance levels or performance levels of other government agencies.* If the cost of performing a given service is lower this year than it was last year, it is

(continued)

BOX 8.1 *continued*

common to assume that efficiency has increased. The lower cost may be attributable to a variety of reasons such as an improved maintenance program that results in less down time for vehicles, using more efficient routes to collect garbage, or the purchase of better equipment that requires fewer employees and uses less fuel. Conversely, increases in costs are considered to indicate deceases in efficiency.

Such comparisons usually require qualification. The tendency to accept increases or decreases in costs as an indication of efficiency is common but can be misleading. Obviously, changes in costs could be attributed to other factors such as crews deliberately taking more time to collect garbage or falsified records. A production system is considered to be more efficient if it has a lower per unit output cost than another system. If the annual cost for collecting garbage is $12 per household in Atlanta and $16 in Orlando during the same year, the difference in relative efficiency may be attributable to an array of factors. These include physical differences between the two cities or in the type of equipment used, labor market differences, variation in the quality of service provided, managerial techniques, pay incentive plans, and accounting practices. If one attempts to compare the efficiency between cities, great care must be taken to ensure that all critical variables are taken into account to develop a meaningful comparison. This is often difficult to do in the public sector because so many factors are involved, including politics. Moreover, as noted earlier, garbage collection is not sold in stores like Wal-Mart. It is easier to compare the output because of the convenience of pricing for items like televisions or lawn mowers.

Efficiency, in both the public and private sectors, takes output as a given

without questioning the output's benefit. Efficiency measurements are only concerned with the manner in which resources are combined into final products. Thus, efficiency is a rather narrow concept that assumes lower cost is desirable when similar goods or services are produced.

Effectiveness is a measurement of *goal attainment*. It is usually expressed as a ratio relating observed output to the desired output for a given time period. It can be thought of as how well established goals are achieved. If a refuse collection operation planned to collect garbage from 50 households per hour but was only able to collect it from 40 households, the operation is 80 percent effective. It is important to note that an operation can be effective without being efficient. If the refuse collection operation planned to collect 50 households' garbage but actually collected 150, it is 300 percent effective but may be achieving these results at three or four times the cost per household of other comparable operations.

The usefulness of measurements of effectiveness greatly depends on establishing meaningful output targets. Government has frequently been criticized for not balancing these two often-competing goals. That is, government can be effective at achieving its goals, such as providing public transportation like buses for its citizens. However, public transportation is often inefficient when buses operate on routes with few passengers, and most public transportation systems require government subsidies to operate. Conversely, the private sector is forced to balance the two concepts in order to survive in the marketplace.

SOURCE: Adapted from Jeffrey D. Greene, *Cities and Privatization: Prospects for the New Century* (Upper Saddle River, NJ: Prentice-Hall, 2002), Chapter 2.

agencies function in the political environment, not the competitive market-place. The system is driven by *politics,* not economics. Economics is a part of the political arena because governments need money to operate, but it is only one part. Politicians must deal with reelection. Even political appointees must keep elections in mind, which means reappointment. Elections are a reality of the political world in a democracy. If the party does not remain in power, political appointees will not be reappointed.[8] Thus, elections and all that goes along with politics affect political appointees. Public managers who are not political appointees must work to expand their budgets and the people they serve. For government managers, larger budgets, more employees, and con-stituencies mean more power and influence. This is an unfortunate reality of the public sector. To achieve personal goals, public managers must cooperate with elected officials and political appointees. Thus, public managers face a different set of incentives, risks, and rewards than private mangers do.

The objectives of government are expressed in public policies. To compli-cate matters further, the environment in which public managers work is filled with public policies that are often inconsistent. These inconsistencies make it difficult for public managers to manage, and even more difficult to gauge per-formance. Government can be thought of as a system of compromises that often produce conflicting policies to satisfy a variety of competing constituents. One does not have to look hard to find inconsistent public policies. For exam-ple, in the early 1990s, President Clinton proposed that the federal government provide universal health coverage for all Americans and increase safety nets for disadvantaged Americans. At the same time, government adopted policies to slow the growth of spending to reduce budget deficits. This latter goal was in conflict with the goals of universal health coverage and increases in welfare spending. President Clinton offered several ways to finance universal health coverage, including raising taxes on tobacco products to cover the costs. Most economists did not believe that raising tobacco taxes was sufficient to pay for the colossal costs of universal health coverage. Effective lobbying efforts by insurance companies and other groups that would be adversely affected ended the goal of universal health coverage. Thus, universal health coverage never became reality; a large amount of effort, money, and other resources were expended, but in the end, very little was accomplished.

Protection of the environment and economic development are two areas that can be used to illustrate how public policies can collide. The federal gov-ernment has implemented many policies to preserve the environment and to protect citizens from risks caused by air and water pollution. At the same time, all levels of government encourage economic development and the creation of jobs. This latter policy can conflict with environmental policies that seek to shut down paper mills, chemical plants, and other polluting industries, resulting in thousands of workers being laid off. This, in turn, causes welfare expenses to increase while depressing the economy. Over the past 40 years, the United States has lost much of its heavy industrial base, such as the steel industry and most of its textile industries. It has even lost the shoe industry to foreign com-petitors. These and other industries have been lost due to the availability of inexpensive labor elsewhere and because "smokestack" industries are considered to be "dirty" industries that pollute the environment. While service industries (e.g., foodservice and retail stores like Wal-Mart) have boomed, they typically pay less than the industries they replaced. Recent generations were the first in American history to expect a decrease in their standard of living. Moreover, the global economy radically changed the nature of competition. While the federal government promotes free (and fair) trade, many businesses have problems competing with government-backed industries like Europe's Airbus (the main international competitor to Boeing). Thus, laudable goals, such as protecting the environment, promoting free trade, and at the same time encouraging economic development have often been in conflict with one another and mutually counterproductive.

Note, however, that people disagree about which goals conflict with one another. For example, many believe it is possible to have economic development and still protect the environment. Recent efforts have concentrated on attracting "clean" industries, and the social contract now expects that products will be produced in an environmentally safe way. While the so-called "dirty" industries have been sent to the Third World, clean industries like computers, pharmaceuticals, and service industries have replaced them in developed nations.[9]

The federal government has implemented many policies to reduce the health risks associated with tobacco use and funds a variety of programs to cure cancer and keep young people from using tobacco products. Tobacco advertising has been banned on television for 30 years, and warning labels were placed on all cigarette packs years ago. This was not an easy fight in Congress because the tobacco industry was (and remains) a relatively strong economic and political force.[10] During the 1990s, the federal government encouraged states to sue tobacco firms, which resulted in a multibillion-dollar settlement to punish tobacco firms and reimburse states for the costs of providing health care over the years. Most state governments have raised taxes on tobacco products to discourage consumption. At the same time, the federal government continues to fund tobacco subsidies to help tobacco farmers who supply tobacco to cigarette manufacturers. Some states (which receive large sums of money from the tobacco settlement each year) continue to invest in tobacco stocks to fund their retirement systems. Many states have not used the tobacco settlement money for health-related matters. The funds have been used for every purpose imaginable. Moreover, tobacco stocks have continued to perform well despite all of the health risks, penalties, and high taxes. The high taxes have brought a greater windfall of revenues for states. In reality, some people are working very hard to find a cure for cancer while other people are working hard to develop and implement programs to reduce the use of tobacco; but, at the same time, still others are working hard to ensure that tobacco, as a commodity, remains plentiful and that prices remain stable through subsidies. All of this activity is firmly based in public policy and funded with government money. How can government effectively reduce the use of tobacco while at the same time subsidizing the raw materials needed by tobacco firms?

Government policies are difficult to evaluate if counterproductive programs exist, and this is often the case. In addition to conflicting public policies, public managers are constrained by many laws that do not apply in the private sector. Decisions in the public sector are often made in public view (sometimes referred to as a fishbowl) and often involve public input. Decisions made by corporations are made in relative privacy. It is fair to conclude that public management is more *constrained* and complicated than management in the private sector. All of these points can affect government performance.

Most major issues are very complex and difficult to measure. National defense, for example, is a very difficult activity to measure. The United States was never attacked by the former Soviet Union during the period (more than 40 years) in which the U.S.S.R. was our most feared adversary. One could take this as evidence that national security worked effectively. However, the level of aggregation is very high, and it takes a significant leap of faith to argue that, since we were never attacked, our national defense was efficient, effective, and well managed. As another example, do we measure the effectiveness of airline safety, which is managed by the Federal Aviation Administration (FAA), on the number of airline crashes that occur during a specified time period? If there are no crashes during a 10-year period, does that mean that airline safety measures were working? Or is it possible we were just lucky? Strict airline safety rules are in place, but the general public does not really know how well the rules are enforced. Commercial airline companies have many incentives for not crashing planes that have little to do with government. An airline company that has too many crashes not only incurs large expenses but also develops a reputation that will cause people to stop using the company. Ultimately, the firm may go out of business. But this is hardly the most desirable reason for striving for safety. Those of us who fly prefer to have some confidence that someone is double-checking the maintenance of the aircraft and taking extra steps to ensure our safety. We expect government to regulate airline safety (and many other aspects of society that affect our health and safety).

When disaster strikes, we turn to government and demand that it take action (the reactive nature of public policy), and often we blame government for not doing enough or not foreseeing the disaster in advance. One prominent scholar recently commented on the difficulties our government faces in preventing terrorist attacks such as that which occurred on September 11, 2001. He noted that prior to September 11, 2001, one FBI agent in Phoenix had observed that a lot of Arabs were taking flying lessons. After the fact, this information seems crucially relevant; but before the fact, it would have been virtually impossible to know whether it was any more relevant than the thousands of other bits of information being reported by other agents. The FBI's failure to foresee what would happen is not a mark of incompetence; rather, it illustrates the difficulty of screening huge amounts of information about uncertain future events in large organizations. With hindsight, we can connect the dots, but it is unlikely that anyone could have connected all the dots prior to September 11.[11] Without a doubt, gauging government performance in situations like this one is difficult.

Public administration has gone through a variety of phases dealing with evaluation of its performance. From 1900 until the 1940s, efficiency was among the primary goals of public administration. Making government more efficient and businesslike was viewed as a way to end the rampant corruption associated with that era. One of the key principles was to make public administration more professional. It was believed that professional managers using the right techniques could increase efficiency while ending corruption. This era was followed by budgetary reforms to control spending. In the 1970s, public administrators tried to enhance the efficiency of public organizations through better managerial techniques. The 1980s were characterized by the privatization movement, which argued that government should increase the role of the private sector to provide public services. Since the private sector is more efficient than government, it was argued, efficiency would increase if government turned over many public services to private firms. In the 1990s, the reinventing government movement was introduced. This movement suggested that government should be more concerned with *results* than *process* to increase efficiency. Public administrators should be empowered with the freedom needed to effectively manage public agencies, which would in turn enhance efficiency and effectiveness. Table 8.1 illustrates the basic phases of reform related to productivity and evaluation since 1900.[12]

GAUGING GOVERNMENT PERFORMANCE:
A CLOSER VIEW

Since the 1970s, all levels of government have paid closer attention to performance and productivity. It was recognized that government had no comprehensive method for evaluating the performance of programs. Congress and state legislatures would appropriate money to solve problems or provide services but usually had no idea whether the programs were achieving their stated goals and objectives. Thus, *public program evaluation* worked its way into the mainstream of government. Program evaluation is similar to policy evaluation, but it is usually conducted by agencies, with reports provided to the appropriate members of the legislature and executive branch. *Public program evaluations are systematic studies and reviews that examine productivity, costs, and effectiveness of government programs.* However, the main concern of most program evaluations is effectiveness, or measuring outcomes and goals.

Program evaluations take many forms but are usually conducted after a program has been functioning for some time. Agencies have found many benefits in conducting evaluations. They provide an indication about whether the program is achieving stated objectives and goals, and they are helpful at budget time when agencies lobby legislatures for money. Program evaluations can be used for a variety of purposes, which include trying to improve programs, justifying the existence of programs, and investigating and auditing programs in order to abolish them, blame them for failure, or change leadership in an agency.[13] The tools and techniques used in program evaluation are similar to those used in policy analysis, but they are applied to a specific program.[14] Program evaluation usually involves developing research designs to perform outcome evaluations that often use cost-benefit analyses.[15] Some of the basic questions raised in a program evaluation include:

Table 8.1 The Evolution of Government Productivity, Evaluation, and Corruption Control

Feature	Efficiency 1900–1940	Budgeting 1940–1970	Management 1970–1980	Privatization 1980–1992	Reinventing Government 1992–Present
Motivation	Good government; more efficient and less corrupt government.	Control of expenses.	Efficiency and effectiveness.	Reduction of deficit, taxes, expenses, and size of government.	Reduction of government expenses, improving efficiency and effectiveness. Making government more flexible by empowering administrators.
Dominant level of government	Local level; federal level by 1930s.	Low involvement by all levels of government.	Federal, state, and local.	Federal.	Local, then federal.
Initiators of productivity movement	Citizens, business people, scholars, and experts.	Budget-oriented public administrators, operations and management specialists.	Elected officials, followed by public administrators and academics.	Citizens and business people, and some academics.	Public administrators, then elected officials.
Initiators of program evaluation techniques	Time and motion studies, Bureau of Municipal Research, New Deal administration.	Great Society administrators, organization development pioneers.	Urban Institute and universities.	Business community, universities, and conservative think tanks.	Public administrators and universities.
Political environment and assumptions	Politics is separate from administration. Efficiency equals better government and less corruption.	Comprehensive efficiency is not explicit as a goal. Budgetary innovations dominate.	Public and private sectors place a high premium on efficiency.	Private sector can improve public sector productivity.	Empowered public administrators can produce an efficient and effective government.
Cultural perspectives on corruption	Corruption results from the misuse of government and pervades government from top to bottom.	Corruption is limited to a few dishonest individuals.	Corruption is a criminal combination of waste, fraud, and abuse that harms taxpayers and citizens.	Corruption is a criminal combination of waste, fraud, and abuse that harms taxpayers and citizens.	Corruption is a criminal combination of waste, fraud, and abuse that harms taxpayers and citizens.
Methods used to control corruption	Isolating politics from administration and making public administration more professional.	Applying the principles of administration in designing organizations and processes used by agencies.	Law enforcement, in the form of new and more restrictive checks, procedures, and investigations of public officials.	Law enforcement, in the form of new and more restrictive checks, procedures, and investigations of public officials.	Law enforcement, in the form of new and more restrictive checks, procedures, and investigations of public officials.

SOURCE: Adapted from Nicholas Henry, *Public Administration and Public Affairs*, 7th ed. (Upper Saddle River, NJ: Prentice-Hall, 1999), p. 195.

- What are the objectives of the program?
- Is the program achieving the objectives?
- What progress has been made during the time the program has been functioning?
- What financial and other costs are being used to achieve the stated goals?
- Are there alternatives or improvements that can be made to make the program work more effectively and efficiently?
- Are there any unintended consequences caused by the program?
- What recommendations can be made to improve performance?

Before a program evaluation can be conducted, performance measures and indicators must be established. Developing measures and indicators is more difficult in the public sector for the reasons stated earlier. Productivity and performance measures have been successful at the local level, which has been attributed to the fact that the types of services provided lend themselves to measurement more easily than those provided by the FBI, the Department of Commerce, the Department of Agriculture, and similar agencies at the federal level. Moreover, the local level has been greatly affected by the privatization debate (discussed later in this chapter), which has served as an impetus for local governments to examine productivity and develop performance measures because it revealed the true costs of producing certain local services. Economists believe that most services provided by local governments are not *public goods* and therefore can be provided by the private sector.[16] At one time, for example, most local governments that collected garbage using in-house departments did not know how much it cost to stop the garbage truck at each house in a residential area, that is, the unit cost per household.[17] Today, most cities are well aware of their unit costs. The private sector uses such information (i.e., the cost per unit of producing or providing a good or service) to find ways to lower costs. But is this appropriate for government? The Federal Aviation Administration (FAA) probably knows how much it costs to conduct an investigation of an airline crash based on averaging the costs incurred over time (which is not the equivalent of determining unit costs for collecting garbage). But should the FAA take action to reduce these costs? Or is it more important to thoroughly investigate accidents and discover the causes of crashes, which might reveal structural problems with certain aircraft? The FAA has found structural problems in some cases, which has forced airlines to make repairs that most likely prevented future crashes and saved lives. How much is this information worth? Clearly, the FAA's service is not comparable to making washing machines on an assembly line in a General Electric plant.

When performance measures are implemented in government, they often lead to what is called *perverse measures*.[18] Perverse measures refer to inaccurate measurements (or poorly constructed indicators) that do not accurately reflect whatever is being measured. They can be found in both government and private industry, but are more common in government. Usually, perverse measurements involve the attempt to quantify something that is not easily quantifiable.

During the Vietnam War, the military measured damage by using an indicator called "body count" (how many of the enemy were killed) to demonstrate its performance and effectiveness in combat. The military has also used many other measures, but those who grew up during the Vietnam War became very familiar with this indicator. The number of casualties is commonly used in war for measurement purposes. This is not a pleasant indicator, but it provides a number that the military can use. There is always a way to quantify most services, but sometimes the method measures the wrong thing. How does a city judge the efficiency and effectiveness of summer youth programs offered in the inner city? Does it count the number of programs it was able to provide with a specified amount of funding and the cost of each program? Does it use the number of people who participated in the programs and the cost per participant? Or is the real measure reflected later in the number of young people who do not end up in the criminal justice system? How does one measure the productivity of the Internal Revenue Service? Is using the amount of fines collected per audit a good measure? Is equating good performance for IRS offices based on the fines they collect an appropriate way to gauge performance? At one time the IRS used this measurement. How does one measure the performance of police officers? Should performance be measured by the number of arrests the police make, or the number of calls to which they respond? What if the police department has established quotas for issuing speeding tickets for each officer who works in a police cruiser? Is basing performance on the number of tickets a police officer issues a good measure or a *perverse measure?*

All of these examples demonstrate that there are ways to gauge productivity and effectiveness in each case, but such measurement is more difficult in the public sector than measuring the efficiency and effectiveness of private corporations. Just because indicators are more difficult to construct, however, does not mean that it is impossible to develop meaningful units of measure. The information in Box 8.1 (see p. 319) illustrates how efficiency measures can be developed for collecting garbage in a city. Law enforcement has been one of the areas in which most cities admit they do not keep track of productivity to the same degree as they do with other services. Surveys indicate that less than a third of cities consistently use productivity measurement in their police departments. Gauging the performance of law enforcement is a difficult area, but the Law Enforcement Assistance Administration (LEAA) has developed indicators for doing so; some of these measurements are included in Table 8.2. Once these measurements are introduced, data can be maintained, which allows performance to be analyzed and compared over time. The measures shown in Table 8.2 are only a sample; many other indicators of police performance exist.[19] The most commonly used indicator that the public sees is the crime rate by types of crimes. This information shows how the rates of crime change from one year to the next. But crime statistics do not measure the daily or annual performance of law enforcement departments, detectives, and officers. More precise measures are needed.

Government has achieved some success at improving public sector productivity, although it has not been spread evenly at all levels of government. Local

Table 8.2 Law Enforcement Productivity Indicators

Intermediate Productivity Measures (Workload/Input)
1. Number of service calls responded to per hour of police officer time, by type of call
2. Number of investigations conducted per hour of police officer time, by type of case
3. Number of arrests per police employee or per $1,000
4. Administrative processing cost per arrest and by type

Final Productivity Measures (Effectiveness/Input)
1. Number of arrests surviving judicial screening per police employee or per $1,000
2. Reduction in reported crime by type per police employee or per $1,000
3. Percentage of households or businesses victimized per police employee or per $1,000
4. Arrests that have survived preliminary screening per police employee or per $1,000
5. Percentage of stolen property recovered per police employee or per $1,000

NOTE: The "per $1,000" provides a unit of cost reflected in terms of each $1,000 appropriated to a department (or unit).

SOURCE: Adapted from George Downs and Patrick Larkey, *The Search for Government Efficiency: From Hubris to Helplessness* (Philadelphia, PA: Temple University Press, 1986), p. 71. The Law Enforcement Assistance Administration (LEAA) developed these indicators.

governments have been successful at developing *performance measures* (the regular collections and reporting of a variety of data about a service that includes information about inputs like money and labor, and outputs such as promptness of delivery of the service). Performance measures provide the data to calculate unit costs, measure satisfaction, and measure the quality and quantity of services. Local governments also have been very effective at developing *workloads* (accepted standards of quantity and quality of tasks that workers or departments must perform) and *benchmarks* (systematic efforts to increase performance using the best techniques and practices available, and making meaningful internal and external comparisons) to increase performance. They have been innovators in developing *citizen satisfaction surveys,* which partially replicate the idea of customer satisfaction data collected by businesses. Since the 1970s, all levels of government have made progress toward creating ways to measure what they do. But governments have not been able to develop and consistently employ performance standards that are comparable to the private sector. Although measures have been developed, the public sector's lack of a simple indicator comparable to profit makes measuring what government does extremely difficult. Part of the reason is because efficiency is not the cardinal virtue of most public organizations. Other equally important and competing goals, such as effectiveness, public accountability, responsiveness, and equity, take attention away from efficiency and productivity. This complicating reality coupled with the lack of a standard measurement that can be equally applied to most government agencies will continue to cause governments to utilize multiple indicators that are relevant to the performance of specific types of government programs and organizations. Many of these measurements, unfortunately, will be perverse measurements because the work of government cannot be universally quantified in terms of profit, return on investment, and the like. Moreover, despite the push toward government efficiency, critics question whether government is truly committed to improving productivity. Many officials view the nature of government work to be so unique and diverse that it cannot be subjected to standardized performance measures.[20]

Many managerial techniques have been employed to try to enhance the quality of government services and improve performance. *Total quality management (TQM)* is a technique that was originally designed by a Bell Laboratories scientist during the 1920s (it was originally called statistical process control). W. Edwards Deming popularized the idea during World War II while helping to convert industrial plants for military production.[21] After the war, most of America's large industries rejected the idea of TQM, but the Japanese adopted it during the 1950s. By the 1980s, American industry was losing to Japan in most markets because of quality control issues. American industry had lost its edge and just could not build reliable products. To rebuild American industry, TQM was finally adopted by many of the nation's major industries. Total quality management is a managerial philosophy, a set of principles, and a series of quantitative techniques that are designed to continuously improve production processes to ensure that customers are satisfied with an organization's products, performance, procedures, and people. During the 1980s and 1990s, *TQM* became one of the buzzwords in public management. Although Deming is credited with popularizing TQM, Joseph Juran, who was sent to Japan to help improve industrial quality, is the individual who defined quality as customer satisfaction and the idea of "getting it right the first time" as the best way to achieve real efficiency.[22]

Although TQM was enthusiastically used (with near religious zeal) throughout American industry during the 1980s and 1990s, government was slow to adopt it. The technique was eventually widely used at all levels of government, but with mixed results. Most government agencies do not follow Deming's *14 Points* (see Box 8.2), but use hybrids that incorporate other techniques.[23] Many have questioned whether TQM is even appropriate for the public sector. After all, it was designed for industry and production lines. One scholar pointed out that the federal government created a series of awards (the original was the Baldrige Award from the Department of Commerce, created in 1987) to reward organizations that were successfully using TQM, but many of the winners have shown deteriorating performance after winning the award. The winners have included General Motors, Xerox, Westinghouse, and the Wallace Company, which filed for bankruptcy.[24] While TQM is considered to have been critical in revitalizing American industry during the 1980s, currently only about one-third of businesses use some form of TQM.[25]

Many argue that TQM is little more than a fad and that it is inappropriate for government. The General Accounting Office reported that more than two-thirds of the federal government's 2,800 offices were using TQM to improve quality, but less than 20 percent of the offices reported any long-term benefits.[26] State governments have used TQM extensively. Surveys revealed

---

BOX 8.2   Deming's 14 Points for Total Quality Management

1 **Create constancy of purpose for improvement of product and service.** Management must change from a preoccupation with the short run to building for the long run. This requires dedication to innovation in all areas to best meet the needs of citizens/clients.

2 **Adopt the new philosophy. Americans have been too tolerant of poor performance and sullen service.** We need a new philosophy in which mistakes and negativism are unacceptable.

3 **Cease dependence on mass inspection.** Inspection is equivalent to planning for defects; it comes too late, and it is ineffective and costly. Instead, processes must be improved.

4 **End the practice of awarding contracts on price tag alone.** Purchasing departments customarily operate on orders to seek the lowest-priced vendor. Frequently, this leads to supplies or services of low quality. Instead, they should seek the best quality and work to achieve it with a single supplier for any one item in a long-term relationship.

5 **Improve constantly and forever the system of operations and service.** Improvement is not a one-time effort. Management and employees are obligated to continually look for ways to reduce waste and improve quality.

6 **Institute modern methods of training on the job.** Too often, employees learn their jobs from other employees who were never trained properly. They are forced to follow unintelligible instructions. They cannot do their jobs because no one tells them how.

7 **Institute modern methods of leadership.** Lower-level managers must be empowered to inform upper management about conditions that need correction; once informed, management must take action. Barriers (such as reserved parking places for top management) that prevent employees from doing their jobs with pride must be removed.

8 **Eliminate fear.** Many employees are afraid to ask questions or to take a position even when they do not understand what the job is or what is right or wrong. People will continue to do things the

---

that nearly three-quarters of the states used TQM programs in a variety of state agencies. Local governments have shown less commitment to the idea. Only a third of cities embraced TQM; 11 percent had a strong commitment, and 22 percent had a "token" commitment.[27] Of 21 major local service functions, only 8 functions were using TQM-based programs.[28] Total quality management is a management philosophy that involves a commitment to fix problems "upstream" (before the fact) rather than "downstream" (after the fact).[29] The appropriateness of TQM in the public sector is subject to debate. A review of Deming's points in Box 8.2 reveals that measures to gauge performance have to be developed to ensure quality, but developing accurate measures for many public sector activities is difficult.[30] Moreover, TQM lends itself to activities that have a sequential nature in producing something, that is,

wrong way or to not do them at all. The economic loss from fear is appalling. It is necessary for better quality and productivity that people feel secure.

9. **Break down barriers between staff areas.** Often staff areas—departments, units, and so on—are competing with each other or have goals that conflict. They do not work as a team so they can solve or foresee problems. Worse, one department's goals may cause trouble for another. Each discipline must stop optimizing its own work, and instead work together as a team for the company as a whole. Multidisciplinary quality control circles can help improve design, service, quality, and costs.

10. **Eliminate slogans, exhortations, numerical goals, and targets for the workforce.** These never helped anybody do a good job. Let people put up their own slogans. Although workers should not be given numerical goals, the organization itself must have a goal: never-ending improvement.

11. **Eliminate work standards and quotas.** Quotas focus on quantity, not quality. They are usually a guarantee of inefficiency and high cost. To hold a job, a person meets quotas at any cost, without regard to damage to the organization.

12. **Remove barriers to pride of workmanship.** People are eager to do a good job and distressed when they cannot. Too often, misguided managers, faulty equipment, and defective materials stand in the way. These barriers must be removed.

13. **Institute a vigorous program of education and training.** Because quality and productivity improvements change the number of people needed in some areas and the jobs required, people must be continually trained and retrained. All training must include basic statistical techniques.

14. **Create a structure in top management that will push every day on the above 13 points.**

SOURCE: Adapted from Grover Starling, *Managing the Public Sector*, 4th ed. (Belmont, CA: Wadsworth, 1993), p. 592. Some points have been slightly modified and paraphrases of Deming's discussions have been added. Used with permission.

to activities such as processing Social Security checks that have a "production-like" dimension. Most government agencies and services do not have this dimension.

Despite the best efforts of reformers and the adoption of innovative techniques like TQM, government remains much less efficient than the private sector at producing services and less effective at developing meaningful ways to measure performance. Efficiency comparisons between government and private organizations performing similar tasks almost always favor the private sector.[31] Thus, during the late 1970s and throughout the 1980s, many argued that government could greatly improve its efficiency by privatizing services. Privatization struck at the core of government inefficiency and ignited a controversial, highly charged debate.

PRIVATIZATION

Few topics have been more controversial or caused more ripples in the discipline of public administration than privatization.[32] Privatization involves increasing the use of the private sector to achieve public goals and provide services. Public administration generally has viewed privatization as a threat. In essence, privatization offers government a way to enhance productivity and efficiency by purchasing goods and services from the private sector. The idea is that if government cannot be efficient, we should let the private sector provide services.

The privatization movement began at the local level where most services are not considered to be public goods. Does it really matter who collects garbage, paves roads, maintains buildings, changes streetlights, or operates city cafeterias? Privatization advocates argued that there was no sensible reason for government to continue to produce services that could be produced more efficiently by private firms. What mattered was that taxpayers would save money; furthermore, privatizing services would free up funds for government to spend on other important projects. But this was taken as a slap in the face to traditional public administration and was viewed as a sure way for public employees to lose their jobs. Not surprisingly, the most adamant critics were public employee unions and liberal academics who viewed privatization as a way to dismantle the state. Moreover, traditional public administration believed that most services were essential services that should be provided by public employees. Critics argued that services such as collecting garbage, providing water and sewage treatment, and providing for the public health should not be devolved to the market or contracted to private vendors who could go broke. Accountability is lost if services are devolved to the market because the market is based on the ability to pay and is not concerned with equity.

Privatization quickly became an intense ideological debate that has lasted several decades. It was the most dominant issue in public administration during the 1980s and early 1990s. It struck at the center of government performance by making *efficiency* the cardinal unit of measurement. Privatization studies exposed the vast differences in cost between public and private organizations performing similar tasks. Economists were able to demonstrate that efficiency was significantly different in the two sectors, and favored private production in most services.[33] Traditional public administration has had a hard time arguing against efficiency. (See Box 8.3 for a discussion of privatization in relation to democracy and capitalism.)

The ideological controversy about privatization has pitted the merits of positive government action and responsibility (the liberal view) against the virtues of capitalism and free markets (the conservative view) as the best means for achieving public goals. Privatization is a very broad concept.[34] It can signify something as large as shrinking the welfare state, or something as narrow as substituting a team of private workers for an all-but-equal team of civil servants to carry out a particular task.[35] Privatization comes in many forms, including

---

BOX 8.3   Democracy, Capitalism, and Privatization

Democracy and capitalism are the larger concepts that are part of the privatization debate. Privatization illustrates part of the interaction that occurs between democracy and capitalism. Democracy creates public institutions to handle the government's business, such as national defense or airline safety, or transportation systems. Capitalism is synonymous with our economy. However, capitalism is more interwoven with government than the prevailing popular myth indicates. Government and capitalism are often portrayed as rivals involved in an ideological tug-of-war—countervailing forces that keep each other in check. But government and capitalism interact on a daily basis to provide services at all levels of government. National defense involves various government institutions and agencies and large private contracts with firms such as Boeing that engineer and develop the machinery of national defense. America has a long history of preferring private ownership with government oversight. Airlines in the

United States are private corporations that fall under numerous public safety regulations. Legislatures appropriate money for highways, city streets, bridges, and subway systems that are usually constructed by private firms.

Democracy establishes the structures and conditions for governing, and capitalism generates wealth in the economy by providing products and services for consumers, including government. Capitalism also provides a taxable base to fund government activities. Democracy needs capitalism to create a healthy, vibrant economy, and capitalism needs democracy to provide structure and stability. But the appropriate size and scope of the public and private sectors was not resolved in the 20th century. Privatization is part of this debate because it threatens a long pattern of government expansion into many aspects of American life, including the economy. This debate continues in the new century.

SOURCE: Adapted from Jeffrey D. Greene, *Cities and Privatization: Prospects for the New Century* (Upper Saddle River, NJ: Prentice-Hall, 2002), p. 27.

---

simple contractual arrangements with private businesses and nonprofit organizations to provide basic services (the most common form used in the United States). The purest version involves getting government completely out of both the *production* and the *delivery* of a wide range of services. In this method, the service is completely devolved to the marketplace. Privatization also encompasses a broad range of activities such as deregulation, tax reduction, voucher systems, and public divestiture of government properties. Privatization is intended to enhance efficiency and reduce government involvement in economic activities.[36] All of the ideas and practices associated with privatization involve increasing private sector participation in areas typically considered public sector responsibilities.

Although there is no single, accepted definition, *privatization may be thought of as the attainment of any public policy goal through the participation of the private sector.*[37] Some examples of privatization include a city contracting with a private company to collect and dispose of residential garbage (contracting), selling a municipal golf course to a private company (divesting or selling off assets), and leasing the local public hospital to a national hospital management corporation. In cases where leases are involved, the government still owns the assets but allows a private firm to operate the facility and keep the profits. At the state level, states may contract with private paving companies to build and maintain highways, or to handle a variety of health and human services. At the national level, examples of privatization include the military contracting with a national food service company to operate all food service on military bases, and the postal service contracting with major airlines to carry mail across the country rather than operating its own planes. All of these examples are forms of privatization that have been commonly used for many years in the United States. From the perspective of government, the motivation for using privatization is to save money.

The ideological underpinnings of privatization are based in the characteristics of a freely functioning market economy.[38] Proponents of free markets believe that a market economy produces many desirable things, such as economic and technological progress, efficient utilization of society's resources, a rising standard of living, a reasonably equitable distribution of wealth, and a society characterized by social mobility and political freedom.[39] In this view, government intervention beyond its minimal functions (those dealing with purely public goods, such as national defense) impairs efficient resource use, impedes economic progress, and inhibits social mobility and political freedom. This perspective is grounded in a theory based on an idealized model of a perfectly competitive market tending toward full employment for the economy as a whole and efficient use of resources by firms and individuals.[40] Privatization proponents believe that government should confine itself to those activities related to governing and let the private sector produce society's goods and services.[41] The 1980s were ripe for the privatization movement. Government had gained the reputation of being unable to convert ideas into reality; it seemed far more concerned with process than with actually accomplishing something. Government was also viewed as expanding too deeply into the economy and the private lives of citizens. In short, government was too big, too inefficient, and wasteful. Privatization became one of the primary policies of the Reagan Revolution and was widely adopted at all levels of government, but with a great deal of resistance. In a philosophical sense, privatization represented the ideals of a countermovement that opposed the expansion of government and sought to redefine the proper balance between the public and private sectors.[42] Some of the advantages associated with privatization are shown in Table 8.3.

Privatization was not a new idea. Government contracting predates the Constitution. In fact, the use of contracting has been extensive throughout the nation's history at all levels of government. Historically, the private sector performed many functions that were eventually taken over by the public sector.[43] As society became more complex because of industrialization, urbanization,

Table 8.3 Some Advantages of Privatization*

Nine Advantages Associated with Privatization

1. Privatization harnesses competitive forces and brings the pressures of the market-place to bear on inefficient producers. It permits better management, free of most of the distracting influences that are characteristic of political organizations.

2. The costs of managerial decisions are felt more closely by the decision makers whose own rewards are often at stake.

3. Competition helps reveal the true costs of production and eliminate waste, since contracts are granted to those offering the highest quality of service at the lowest cost.

4. Economies of scale can be realized through reduction of overhead and start-up costs by spreading supply over a larger area. Private firms often take advantage of economies of scales in service delivery by performing an activity in more than one locality.

5. Increased flexibility can be achieved in the use of personnel and equipment for short-term projects, part-time work, and specialized needs without having to maintain a municipal bureaucracy.

6. The performance of private contractors can serve as a yardstick for comparison of the efficiency and effectiveness of services that are produced in-house. Competition from private firms can spur municipal workers and management to improve productivity.

7. Avoiding public employee unions reduces personnel costs and civil service rules, which tend to escalate the cost of producing services.

8. Personnel costs are reduced by not having to pay for employee benefits packages.

9. If government sells unproductive assets (divestiture), such as golf courses, convention centers, or hospitals, it receives large cash payments, and private firms use the assets more wisely. At a minimum, government should lease these assets to private firms (management contracts).

*This table is not intended to be all-inclusive. There are many other advantages associated with privatization.

SOURCE: Adapted from E. S. Savas, *Privatization: The Key to Better Government* (Chatham, NJ: Chatham House, 1987), p. 112; Ruth DeHoog, *Contracting Out for Human Services* (Albany, NY: State University of New York Press, 1984), pp. 6–8; Stephen Moore, "Privatization in America's Cities: Lessons for Washington," *The Heritage Foundation Backgrounder Number 652* (Washington, DC: The Heritage Foundation, 1988), pp. 2–5; D. Fisk, H. Kiesling, and T. Muller, *Private Provision of Public Services* (Washington, DC: Urban Affairs Institute, 1979), p. 7.

---

and changing social values, government assumed more economic and social responsibilities. The idea of a large and expanding government became the norm as the expectations and demands placed on government mushroomed. For many, government action was viewed as the solution to society's problems. Consequently, government began providing an increasing array of services. Some have suggested that this caused government to become overloaded, which caused excessive public spending and proliferation of the bureaucracy.[44] The case for privatization was built on government inefficiency and poor productivity. Privatization proponents found theoretical support from various schools of economics, such as market theory, public choice theory, and property rights theory. (See Box 8.4 for a brief description and example of property rights theory.) Each of these schools provided convincing arguments about why government should spend its time governing, which it is well suited for,

BOX 8.4   The Case of Two Airlines and Property Rights Theory

One of the most frequently cited examples used to illustrate the performance of privatization is a comparison of the performance of two airlines in Australia. One of the airlines was a government operation and the other a private corporation. Efficiency was compared between the two operations over time, which provided a longitudinal dimension. The government imposed mandates on both airlines in an attempt to ensure equality of operations. The mandates went to considerable length. For example, each airline was required to use similar aircraft and fares were heavily regulated. Despite the severe regulatory restrictions, the relative efficiency of the two airlines was different. Efficiency indicators were 100 percent to 12 times higher for the privately owned airline. This pattern was consistent over a ten-year period. The better efficiency of the private airline was attributed to the characteristics associated with property rights. The comparison of the two airlines has been widely cited to illustrate the virtues of private ownership and to show that private firms can perform at twice the efficiency as publicly managed organizations.

Property rights theory treats the modern package of property rights as one of the various possible configurations. Public institutions represent an alternative property rights arrangement to private ownership. Property rights theory is grounded in the rational choice tradition. The theory explains differences in the behavior of organizations entirely on the basis of the individual incentives created by the structure of property rights. Like public choice, property rights theory assumes that individuals seek to look after their own self-interest. The theory holds that property will be cared for in proportion

to the amount the individual stands to gain from tending it. Conversely, the more diluted property rights become, the less motivated the individual will be to use the property in an efficient manner. Private ownership concentrates rights and rewards whereas public ownership dilutes them. This is often referred to as the *tragedy of the commons* dilemma. For example, most citizens will not pick up trash on a city's sidewalk or in a public park even if they are taxpayers of the jurisdiction, but they will pick trash off their lawns at home. This illustrates the simple idea of diluted property rights. Since property rights are diluted in public ownership, it is argued that public bureaucracies will perform less efficiently than private enterprises. Private businesses have concentrated property rights; therefore, businesses have an incentive to manage their assets efficiently.

NOTE: For thorough discussions about property rights theory, see Louis de Alessi, "Property Rights and Privatization," in *Prospects for Privatization,* Steve Hanke, Ed. (New York: Academy of Political Science, 1987), pp. 24–35; Armen Alchian, "Some Economics of Property Rights," *Politico 30* (1965), pp. 816–829; Brodkin and Young, "Making Sense of Privatization: What Can We Learn from Economic and Political Analysis?" in *Privatization and the Welfare State,* Sheila Kammerman and Alfred Kahn, Eds. (Princeton, NJ: Princeton University, 1988), pp. 121–156; and Harold Demsetz, "Toward a Theory of Property Rights," *American Economic Review 57* (1967), pp. 347–359. Also see Garret Hardin, "The Tragedy of the Commons," *Science 162,* pp. 1245–1248.

SOURCE: Adapted from David Davies, "The Efficiency of Public versus Private Firms: The Case of Australia's Two Airlines," *Journal of Law and Economics 14* (1971), pp. 149–165. The efficiency measures used were tons of freight and mail carried per employee, number of paying passengers per employee, and revenue per employee. The private airline averaged carrying more than twice the amount of freight and mail per employee, the number of paying passengers was 20 percent higher, and the average revenue per employee was $9,627 versus $8,428.

and let the private sector produce and deliver services. The theoretical support was important because it gave advocates of privatization grounding in academic theories.

Market theory has been important in the privatization debate because competitive markets have produced most of the nation's wealth. Moreover, the market is designed to produce goods and services efficiently. Market theory is based on an idealized model in which firms seek to maximize profits, are small relative to their industries, and have no restrictions preventing them from entering or exiting any industry. Although firms seek to maximize profits, their ability to inflate prices is guarded by competition. Consumers are well informed (referred to as perfect information) and have defined preferences about alternative goods and services (the idea of preference orderings). The consumer is supreme in the competitive marketplace. Firms must compete with similar operations for their "market share." Competition is the main factor that forces efficiency in the market. Efficiency is also guarded by business's ability to enter or exit markets.[45] If firms make unusually high profits, new firms will enter the market until profits return to a normal level. Price in the market is based on a combination of production cost, supply, and demand. The efficient use of resources, which is guarded by the inherent incentives in the market, provides the free market with supremacy over other models. In the real world, market configurations vary between near-perfect competition and monopolies, but the free market is the idealized model to which all other models are compared.[46] Outcomes in the market are judged by efficiency, which may be thought of as a contest among various ways of performing a task or producing a service. If the market can provide a service at a lower cost than government, or if it can provide a superior service at the same cost, then the market is considered more efficient.[47] Choice is a key element in market theory because the behavior of firms without competition is similar to that of any monopoly. Market theory sees a variety of choices among competing products as critical to force efficiency in the marketplace. Private firms would like to be monopolies, but competitive markets provide inherent protections against this because other firms will be attracted to and enter the industry in pursuit of profit. The penalty in the marketplace for failing to be efficient is bankruptcy, something that seldom occurs in government.[48]

Government cannot fully simulate a competitive marketplace because governments are monopolies, and monopolies are inherently inefficient due to the lack of competition.[49] The problem with government lies in the nature of government itself. Government is not an economically driven institution where efficiency is necessary for survival; it is a *political* institution designed to *govern*. Financing for public services is secured through a political process that is not directly connected to the actual services being produced. Markets connect the cost of producing something to the income necessary to sustain operations. The connection is provided by the price charged to customers who decide whether to make a purchase. This is not the case with government because the revenues that sustain government activity usually come from taxes, which are considered to be a nonprice source.[50] This makes governmental organizations more likely to use indicators such as budget size to measure performance, and it causes the internal standards and incentive structures to reward personnel for justifying costs rather than reducing them.[51] Thus, the inefficiency of public services is not because of bad commissioners, mayors, managers, or workers but, rather, is a natural consequence of a monopoly system.[52]

Public choice theory (discussed in Chapter 7) was the most influential theory that supported the case for privatization. According to public choice theory, public managers are driven by self-interest, just like private sector managers, but in public monopolies, self-interest leads not to efficiency but to pathological problems that cause inefficiency. Public choice theorists view inefficiency as an inherent characteristic of public bureaucracies because the incentive structures encourage empire building and overproduction of services.[53] Because government agencies are service monopolies, public employees will behave in ways that promote their own interests at the expense of the public's interest in efficiency. Thus, public choice theorists believe that the incentive structures of public agencies encourage public personnel to advance their powers, budgets, and agency staffing levels.[54] As noted in Chapter 7, public choice theory assumes that all individuals are rational actors (defined by economics as self-serving egotists) who respond to incentives and disincentives to maximize their own self-interest or satisfaction (the term used by economists is *utility*). Applied to the public bureaucracy, bureaucrats will behave in a way that is in the public's interest only if it is also in their own self-interest. Serving some greater good is secondary to serving one's self-interest.[55] The powerful impact of this theory on the privatization debate rests in its ability to explain why government cannot be efficient. Public choice theory does not attribute the blame for inefficiency to public managers and public employees who are simply behaving rationally. It attributes the problem of inefficiency in government to the natural characteristics of monopolies that create incentives for public employees and managers to behave in ways that are counterproductive to the goal of efficiency.

The theoretical foundations of privatization are a powerful part of the privatization debate.[56] The thrust of the theories may be summed up as *markets* versus *monopolies*. Market theory and public choice theory both focus on the positive attributes of the competitive marketplace and highlight the inefficiency found in public monopolies.[57] These theoretical arguments set the debate in such a way that, to counter them, someone had to argue that something was more important than efficiency.

THE CASE AGAINST PRIVATIZATION

Critics of privatization had a tough argument to make. Arguing against efficiency was not an easy task. Early in the debate, privatization's critics contested the studies that demonstrated private firms to be more efficient than public operations, usually arguing that the methodologies used in the studies were flawed and that the benefits were overstated. This position was not very effective or convincing. Critics were more effective at pointing out that simple cost comparisons between public and private organizations failed to demonstrate how privatization would perform over time in the real world. This was a legitimate concern. Most of the evidence was based on simple cost comparisons, but over the years longitudinal studies (studies that examine something over a period of time) became more common. But these studies also tended to favor privatization. Critics were the most successful by avoiding the efficiency issue altogether and focusing on other problems with privatization.[58] Thus, the arguments against privatization tended to emphasize issues relating to equity and public accountability. With the exception of contracting out for services, which does not affect accountability or equity because government remains responsible for provision, quality levels, and financing, most forms of privatization fall short in these areas. Public accountability in the marketplace is usually left to government regulation, and equity is typically of little concern, since buying goods and services is based on the ability to pay.

The strongest opposition to privatization came from the orthodox school of public administration in academia and public employee unions in the governmental sector.[59] The orthodox school of public administration believes that democracy can only be achieved if power is concentrated so that it can be held accountable. Otherwise, responsibility blends into the social surround.[60] The orthodox school tends to accept the institutions that have emerged to govern and tries to make them more efficient and effective.[61] The concerns are institutional continuity and accountability. Government must be concerned with more than efficiency. The orthodox school argues that public institutions are the principal vehicles for expressing common and public concerns.

Not only does the orthodox school hold that strong public institutions are necessary to govern, but it also rejects the basic assumptions of public choice theory. The idea that behavior of public managers can be explained by a parsimonious theory that sees all people as self-serving egotists is unrealistic in the orthodox view. Public managers and workers are not viewed as the self-serving, budget-maximizing bureaucrats described in public choice theory. Rather, public administration (which had been promoting professionalism in public services for nearly a century when the privatization debate arose) views public managers as sincere, well-trained professionals committed to professionalism and high standards in the public sector. Moreover, their activities serve the public interest.[62] In the view of the orthodox school of public administration, public choice theory creates an enfeebled, even nonexistent state that may have served 18th-century needs in America, but is not capable of dealing with the awesome tasks faced by the nation in the 21st century.[63] The whole of public choice theory, in the orthodox view, is based on erroneous assumptions about the superiority of competitive markets and private business. If private management is in fact so superior and private businesses so efficient and well managed, why do most new businesses fail? Markets are appropriate arenas for fast-food chains, hotels, and computer manufacturers to compete with each other, but they are not the appropriate arenas for providing essential public services. The recent corporate scandals making headlines are nothing new to American society. During the height of the privatization debate, 115 of the top 500 companies in the United States (23 percent) were either convicted of major crimes or had paid a major civil penalty for serious misbehavior.[64] Critics pointed to the questionable ethics and practices of modern business as a reason to question the appropriateness of using privatization.

The problem of public accountability is seen as a critical issue. Critics of privatization have argued that it is more difficult for the public to hold private firms responsible than elected officials or bureaucrats when problems with services arise.[65] *Sector blurring,* a term that refers to mixing responsibility for the provision of services between the public and private sectors, is viewed as a threat to the accountability of legitimate political institutions.[66] The orthodox school of public administration holds that the general public must have a clear perception of who is responsible for services. Since sector blurring results in distortion by breaking down the division between the public and private sectors, public administration opposes most forms of privatization. They argue that the roots of public administration are embedded in public law (rather than economics and the competitive marketplace), and reject the argument that most public sector functions can be handled by the private sector.[67] The orthodox school of public administration believes that privatization is based on the erroneous assumption that the public and private sectors are fundamentally alike and both subject to the same set of incentives and disincentives.[68] Public administration's position on the public–private dichotomy is that the public sector cannot be compared to private business.

Governments function in a political environment, whereas private firms function in a competitive-economic milieu.[69] Because the objective of private firms is to maximize profits, firms may skimp on service quality. The possibility that a business may be unable to complete a job or adequately provide a service is a major concern. Unlike government, contractors often go bankrupt. This is exactly what happened to a New Jersey city that shut down its own sanitation department and contracted its entire garbage-collecting services to a single firm. The city even donated its garbage-collecting equipment to the contractor. The firm went bankrupt and sold off all of its equipment, including the equipment that had been donated by the city. This created a sanitation nightmare, and the city had to take back control of collecting garbage.[70]

Inadequate competition is another problem. For many services, such as fire protection, few contractors exist.[71] If a city were to privatize its fire department and sell off its equipment, imagine the problems that would result if the firm it contracted with went bankrupt. The city would be vulnerable and accountable. Government simply cannot afford to operate in a state characterized by this type of instability. Public bureaucracy has its own set of problems, but it serves as a protection against the unpredictable fluctuations inherent in the marketplace. Public administration argues that the public and private sectors are fundamentally alike only in the unimportant areas.[72] Businesses are concerned with making money by satisfying market segments of customers. Government must provide public services in an equitable manner and must remain accountable for its actions to the entire public.[73]

The strongest arguments against privatization, especially the contracting out for services, have focused on the possibility of corruption. Critics have argued that the absence of adequate competition might foster relationships between those granting contracts and contractors that are not in the best interest of the general public. This is illustrated in the case of Union City, New Jersey, where many of the city's contracts were awarded to companies that were owned by the mayor.[74] When cozy relationships develop between government and private contractors, monitoring contractors can be neglected, which can lead to high costs and lower-quality services.[75] Critics have argued that those who favor privatization tend to ignore the impressive examples of inefficiency, corruption, and waste in the American experience with defense contracts, construction projects, and health care that have been privately produced with public money.[76] Privatization's opponents view contracts as one of the most common and lucrative sources of corruption in government.[77] Although the abuse has been diminished by public bidding and other techniques designed to improve the integrity of the process, private contractors doing business with governments are still one of the sources of campaign funds and support for politicians.[78]

Displacement of public employees, and especially public employee unions, is another significant concern for critics of privatization. What happens to public workers when they lose their jobs because of privatization? One study estimates that between 1980 and 1987, contracting caused 1.5 million state and local jobs to be transferred to the private sector.[79] Critics argue that displacement of public workers causes expenditures to increase for public assistance, job training, and unemployment compensation. Critics also contend that increases in these expenditures can offset any savings realized through privatization.[80] Pressure from public employee unions has led to a variety of policies that help protect public workers when services are privatized; these are known as "no-layoff" policies.[81] Critics charge that private firms might bid low to be awarded a contract and recoup the initial losses in the future. This practice, known as "lowballing," is a major concern to public employee unions. They argue that this practice causes public employees to lose their jobs while misrepresenting the actual costs to government and taxpayers.[82] Critics also have contested the idea that contracting helps to slow the growth of government. They argue that government's role in society continues to grow even though fewer public employees may be hired to deliver services. Contracting has often been used to circumvent hiring freezes while expanding programs and services. From this perspective, contracting is seen as a facade. It masks the true size and scope of government while serving to maintain a myth of less government.[83] Some have argued that contracting is actually a disguised form of public employment, since thousands of jobs exist because of government contracts.[84] Selling off government assets is even worse because government loses complete control over the service and the assets needed to provide the service.[85]

Critics of privatization also have been able to ground their position in economic theory, mainly the theory of market failure and public goods. Opponents of privatization acknowledge the accomplishments of the market but associate its evolution with a variety of negative consequences, such as macroeconomic instability, microeconomic inefficiency, and social inequity.[86] Thus, the deficiencies of the market require government to intervene to enhance efficiency and social equity.[87] This view is based on an idealized model, but one of an informed, efficient, and humane government that is capable of correcting the deficiencies of the market. Moreover, their ideal model assumes that government possesses the expertise to take action that serves the public interest.[88] The theories of market failure and public goods have been used to justify government provision. These theories are briefly summarized in Box 8.5.

Over time, the debate about privatization became tamer, and privatization came to be viewed as a technique that could be used in appropriate situations. Developing performance measures in public organizations and the reinventing government movement are more palatable for most critics. These ideas are more consistent with the beliefs of the orthodox school of public administration, which tends to accept existing institutions and try to make them more efficient and effective. As the debate slowed and was replaced by the reinventing government movement, which is discussed in the next section, it was revealed that after all of the debate and controversy, public employees still provide most public services. Most levels of government use and continue to use privatization. At the beginning of the debate, surveys found that 80 percent of cities used some form privatization. By the late 1990s, virtually all cities were using privatization in varying degrees. The debate was really over how much the use of privatization should be *expanded*. In the new century, it appears that the orthodox school of public administration has persevered. The privatization movement has slowed, and the guiding doctrine of the public sector remains in the hands of the orthodox school. Public managers need to be aware of the privatization movement and its theoretical foundations. The movement emerged during fiscally stressed times and during a conservative political shift. Public managers will continue to hear about the advantages of the competitive marketplace compared to the inefficiency of government operations throughout their careers. The public-private dichotomy has endured for more than a century in American public administration; thus, it is worth the public administrator's time and effort to become familiar with these arguments, which may surface again during future fiscal crises.

REINVENTING GOVERNMENT

After an intense decade of debate over the virtues and pitfalls of privatization, a shift began to occur in the early 1990s with the publication of *Reinventing Government: How the Entrepreneurial Spirit Is Transforming the Public Sector.*[89] The reinventing government era came about because of a variety of intellectual, political, and fiscal forces. Like so many reform movements, reinventing government was born at the local level. Privatization and public choice theory had forced a discussion about the proper roles of the public and private sectors, and brought efficiency to the forefront of the debate. The problem in the eyes of the

BOX 8.5   Why Do Markets Fail?

Perfect markets do not exist. In the real world, markets are less perfect than the idealized model used in market theory. Market imperfections include "imperfect information," meaning consumers often do not have good information about products or prices. The lack of information affects "preference orderings," which makes it difficult for consumers to make competent decisions about purchases. For example, firms often do not disclose adequate safety information about products. In no area is this more evident than with tobacco products. For years tobacco firms knew that their products were associated with a variety of health risks but never disclosed this information. Tobacco firms even lied to Congress about the addictive quality of nicotine. Government intervention, a few whistle-blowers, and many lawsuits were required to make the companies disclose this information to the general public.

Examples abound where companies have failed to disclose safety information about their products. This was the case with certain Chevy trucks, which had a tendency to explode in certain types of common side-impact collisions due to the location of the fuel tank. General Motors also withheld information about safety issues with its famous rear-engine Corvair (built to compete with Volkswagen's popular Bug) in the early 1960s. (The Corvair case made consumer advocate Ralph Nader famous with his book *Unsafe at Any Speed*.) General Motors was well aware of these problems but never divulged them until they were revealed in lengthy lawsuits. Would sales have been as strong for Chevy trucks if consumers knew that the gas tanks exploded so easily upon a side-impact collision? Would consumers have bought the popular Corvair had they known that it was dangerously

unstable at higher speeds because of poor design?

Cases such as these are common. The point is that in the marketplace, the idea of "perfect information" or even near-perfect information is an erroneous proposition. Economists modified their theory years ago to account for imperfect information, but critics point out that the idea that consumers can make competent decisions in the absence of government oversight is a major flaw in market theory.

Market failure occurs because it is not easy to enter into markets. It is virtually impossible for firms to move from one industry to another because of barriers like large capital investments that are needed to enter an industry. This is evidenced by the tendency for oligarchies (domination by a few large firms) to develop, which makes it difficult for new firms to enter the market. How easy is it to start a new airline? The costs of entering the airline industry are colossal. The major airlines must order billions of dollars worth of jets to upgrade their fleets. It is an understatement to say this serves as a disincentive for new firms to enter the industry. The concept of "increasing returns to scale" refers to costs continuing to decline as production volume increases. This phenomenon provides an advantage for large-scale producers, such as firms like General Electric or General Motors.

Public goods are a form of market failure. Everyone shares these goods simultaneously, and no one can be excluded from sharing the benefits. Generally, it is not possible to stop nonpayers (free riders) from consuming public goods. Examples include sidewalks, street lighting, and national defense. Individuals must be compelled to pay through taxation for

(continued)

BOX 8.5 *continued*

these services, and government must intervene to combat free riders (those who avoid paying yet still enjoy the benefits of public goods).

Market failure occurs because of externalities. Externalities are the spillovers produced by industry and can take the form of benefits or costs. Where business activity produces spillovers, efficiency is distorted because external benefits or costs are excluded from production calculations. When externalities take the form of benefits, too little will be produced. Conversely, when externalities are net costs, too much will be produced. Pollution is a classic example of a negative spillover. Education is an example of an activity that produces a positive spillover. Since the market tends to produce too much pollution and too little education, a rationale exists in these activities for government to intervene to restrict negative effects (regulate pollution) or assume responsibility for production of a service (such as education). According to one critic, such inadequacies in the market will pro-

duce too many cigarettes and too little health care.

Natural monopolies are a form of market failure. Natural monopolies occur in situations where a single firm can provide a service more economically than multiple firms. Examples typically include various types of utilities such as providing electricity or distributing natural gas. Natural monopolies are considered to be temporary until technology enables viable alternatives. For example, the breakup of the Bell System in telecommunications occurred when technology enabled long distance telephone service to be handled more competitively. Since the breakup of the Bell System, consumers have had a choice between several highly competitive firms (such as AT&T and MCI, which recently purchased one of its large competitors, Sprint) for long distance telephone service. Moreover, these companies face competition from new technology industries such as cellular telephone companies like Cell One and Internet providers. Thus, the once natural monopolistic tele-

"reinventing" reformers was that government is so concerned with process, it cannot effectively accomplish its goals. Thus, the movement had a results-orientation that wanted government to loosen some of its cumbersome rules and regulations designed to ensure accountability, and thereby let public managers manage. Public administration had battled with privatization, which was usually viewed as a threat, but the reinventing government movement had a different message. It did not focus on ideological debates about the proper balance between the public and private sectors, and it was not perceived as a way for public employees to lose their jobs or a way to dismantle government. Rather, the reinventing government movement saw the relationship between the public and private sectors as a partnership and sought to free government agencies and managers to perform and accomplish goals. This idea was much more palatable to the orthodox school of public administration because it worked within existing institutions and structures. The goal was simply to make government work better. Moreover, it gave more power and freedom to public

communications industry is no longer considered a natural monopoly. The cable industry has also received new competition from satellite dish companies, such as digital television disks that can be placed in a window. Thus, in time, it is believed that natural monopolies will eventually become part of the competitive marketplace. Until then, natural monopolies remain an aspect of market failure.

The term *market failure* usually is concerned with deviations from competitive equilibrium and Pareto-efficient outcomes. Even perfectly functioning markets can fail to meet socially acceptable standards of equity. One clear feature of capitalism is that it produces winners and losers. That is, some are left out of the wealth generated by capitalism. In welfare economics, distributional equity is a shortcoming of the market. In freely functioning markets, the principal devices that deal with equity are philanthropy and charity. These devices are inadequate for equitable redistribution in the modern world. It

is also acknowledged that trade-offs between efficiency and equity must be determined by a social consensus in the political arena. Since the ability to pay determines who receives services in the market, some groups (namely the disadvantaged and poor) are excluded. This provides justification for government intervention to remedy problems relating to equity.

NOTE: For an excellent discussion about the failures of the market, see John Kenneth Galbraith, *The Age of Uncertainty* (Boston: Houghton Mifflin, 1977), and Charles Wolf, *Markets or Governments: Choosing between Imperfect Alternatives* (Cambridge, MA: MIT Press, 1988). For a simple and interesting discussion about natural monopolies, public goods, and other forms of market failure, see Robert Heilbroner and Lester Thurow, *Economics Explained: Everything You Need to Know about How the Economy Works and Where It's Going,* 4th ed. (New York: Simon and Schuster, 1998), Chapter 13. For a good discussion of the modern economics and its consequences on government, see Peter Drucker, *Post-Capitalist Society* (New York: Harper Collins, 1993). Ralph Nader's book on the dangers of automobiles is *Unsafe at Any Speed: The Designed-in Dangers of the American Automobile* (New York: Grossman, 1972).

SOURCE: Adapted from Jeffrey D. Greene, *Cities and Privatization: Prospects for the New Century* (Upper Saddle River, NJ: Prentice-Hall, 2002), Chapter 1.

managers. This helped make the ideas associated with reinventing government more easily accepted at all levels of government.

Very few of the ideas in the movement were new. Most had been thoroughly covered in the debates surrounding privatization and efforts to improve government performance. But the reinventing government movement highlighted what private managers can do and emphasized why public managers cannot perform with the same degree of freedom. David Osborne and Ted Gaebler articulated the differences in public and private management and made a convincing argument that the public sector could perform better if it focused on results by altering some of its processes. Public choice scholars had emphasized that public monopolies are inherently inefficient by design because of the incentive structures. Public choice theory never said that public managers were any less competent than private managers. Public managers were just responding rationally to the incentives that exist in monopolies. The reinventing government message ignored much of the public choice argument and based its idea on the value of accomplishing something. The message was positive rather than negative. Government could accomplish many things by simply making some alterations in the system. The notion that government could accomplish positive things was even accepted by liberals, who had been among the most adamant opponents of privatization and public choice theory.

Osborne and Gaebler (and others associated with the reinventing government movement) managed to create a collection of ideas and ideals that enjoyed a broad acceptance. Government, bureaucracies, and monopolies could be efficient and effective, accomplish great things, and be entrepreneurial at the same time. Once the message was clearly understood, the reinventing government movement did not face many of the obstacles that privatization had to face a decade earlier. The movement affected all levels of government and even inspired the Clinton administration to establish the National Performance Review, with its stated goal of helping to make the federal government less expensive and more efficient by redesigning, reinventing, and reinvigorating the national government.[90] Vice President Al Gore headed the National Performance Review commission, which was the eleventh reform commission created in the 20th century by the federal government.[91] The report produced by the commission echoed the same values and principles of the reinventing government movement.[92]

The main principles of reinventing government are included in Box 8.6. There were four main categories of reforms.[93]

- *Cut red tape.* The recommendation included streamlining the budget and procurement processes, decentralizing human resources policy, eliminating regulatory overkill, and empowering state and local governments.[94] This idea was the same as that advocated by Osborne and Gaebler. They argued that red tape hindered the public sector and that by eliminating the red tape, which is a process originally implemented to ensure accountability and control, managers could be more effective. The book *Reinventing Government* cites a number of examples of how local governments found ways around red tape that saved the jurisdictions a lot of money in making purchases.[95] But the Government Accounting Office (GAO) made similar recommendations years ago.

- *Put customers (citizens) first.* This included giving citizens a voice and a choice, introducing competition to government service organizations (the idea of managed competition, which was part of the privatization movement and had been used for a number of years by local governments), creating market dynamics, and using market mechanisms to solve problems.[96] These ideas also came directly from the book *Reinventing Government,* which got many of its ideas about "putting the customer first" from *In Search of Excellence,* published in the early 1980s.[97] The idea of "putting customers first" has long been considered a key element to the success of businesses. *In Search of Excellence* found that most successful companies listened to their customers and tailored their products and services to customer needs. Customer satisfaction also was a primary goal of total quality management (discussed earlier in this chapter). But the customer-citizen comparison is not an exact equivalent. Governments serve *populations* and society, and this cannot always be reduced to

BOX 8.6 The Major Points of Reinventing Government

Catalytic Government: Steering Rather than Rowing

Catalytic governments separate *steering,* or providing guidance and direction, from *rowing,* or producing goods and services. Osborne and Gaebler give numerous examples such as contracts, vouchers, grants, and tax incentives.

Community-Owned Government: Empowering Rather than Serving

Community-owned governments push control of services out of the bureaucracy and into the community. Examples show how bringing communities into the picture empowers the people who are the intended recipients of services and results in better performance.

Competitive Government: Injecting Competition into Service Delivery

Osborne and Gaebler believe that improving both the quality and cost-effectiveness of government services can be achieved through competition rather than regulation. Introducing competition does not necessarily mean that a service will be turned over to the private sector; rather, the crucial function of competition is ending government monopolies.

Mission-Driven Government: Transforming Rule-Driven Organization

Mission-driven governments deregulate internally, eliminating many of their internal rules and radically simplifying their administrative systems such as budget, personnel, and procurement. They require each agency to get clear on its mission, and then free managers to find the best way to accomplish that mission, within legal bounds.

Result-Oriented Government: Funding Outcomes, Not Inputs

Result-oriented governments shift accountability from inputs to outputs, or results. They measure the performance and reward agencies, so they often exceed their goals.

Customer-Driven Government: Meeting the Needs of the Customer, Not the Bureaucracy

Customer-driven governments are those that make an effort to perceive the needs of customers and to give customers a choice of producers. They use surveys and focus groups to listen to their customers, and put resources in the customers' hands.

Enterprising Government: Earning Rather than Spending

Enterprising governments stress earning rather than spending money. They charge user fees and impact fees, and use incentives such as enterprise funds, shared earnings, and innovation funds to encourage managers to earn money.

Anticipatory Government: Prevention Rather than Cure

Anticipatory governments seek to prevent problems rather than delivering services to correct them. They redesign budget systems, accounting systems, and reward systems to create the appropriate incentives.

Decentralized Government: From Hierarchy to Participation and Teamwork

Decentralized governments transfer decision-making authority to those individuals and organizations at the bottom of the organizational hierarchy. They restructure organizations, empower employees, and create labor-management partnerships.

Market-Oriented Government: Leveraging Change through the Market

Market-oriented government utilizes market mechanisms instead of administrative programs to provide goods and services to the public. They reinvent themselves through the application of market-oriented incentives.

SOURCE: David Osborne and Ted Gaebler, *Reinventing Government: How the Entrepreneurial Spirit Is Transforming the Public Sector* (New York: Addison-Wesley, 1992).

individual citizens. Moreover, government services must be provided in an equitable manner as defined by law. It is erroneous to believe that citizens can be viewed as consumers of government services that are paid for with their taxes in the same sense that a consumer buys a new car, television set, or DVD player. There are processes in the democratic system that allow citizens to express their views and even remove politicians from office. Politicians do cater to voters and special interests for funding and votes. But government agencies, such as regulatory agencies like the EPA, cannot be consumer-driven in the same way that Ford Motor Company or Dell Computers caters to its customers. How does government make itself consumer-driven in the market sense of the term? Can one imagine the Department of Defense asking Americans (the general public) how they would like national defense delivered? The principal role of the Department of Defense is to ensure that the nation is adequately defended. This entails being ready to protect American interests at home and abroad with military force, and fight wars if necessary.

- *Empower employees to get results.* This recommendation involves decentralizing decision-making power, holding all federal employees accountable for results, giving federal workers the tools needed to do their jobs, enhancing the quality of the workplace and work life for federal employees, forming a labor-management partnership, and exerting leadership.[98] One of the centerpieces of reinventing government was to empower managers and employees and pursue a strong results-orientation. If employees become stakeholders, they will work harder, feel that they are a part of the organization, and work to help the organization accomplish its goals and overall mission. Freeing managers to manage creates accountability problems. Much of the red tape found in governmental institutions was placed there to make government accountable. Public managers were not intended to be free to interpret the law as they saw fit; they are supposed to manage agencies that implement and follow public law. Public managers are involved in the policy process and have discretion (known as bureaucratic discretion). What proponents of reinventing government wanted to do was to give managers enough discretion to effectively manage their agencies.

- *Cut back to the basics.* This recommendation includes phasing out unneeded services and replication, collecting more revenues (by imposing more user fees), investing in greater productivity, and reengineering programs to cut costs.[99] These recommendations echoed the complaints public choice theorists had been making for many years. Public choice theorists had long claimed that government overproduces services and is rampant with replication, waste, and inefficiency. Moreover, they called for the increased use of user fees 30 years earlier. The reasoning behind public choice's advocacy for user fees was that the public at large should not have to pay for the benefits of the few. It is doubtful that those promoting the reinvention of government had public choice theory in mind, but they successfully repackaged many of the public choice ideas with these recommendations. Efficiency issues date back to the classical period in public administration, and since then, many recommendations and techniques have been used to try to enhance efficiency. The thrust of this recommendation was to cut costs and reduce waste, which was hardly a new idea, given that enhancing efficiency was not a new concept.

Virtually all of these recommendations had been made in the past. It was the packaging that was new, coupled with the mood of the times. The National Commission on State and Local Public Service, which was established in 1991 (two years before the National Performance Review commission), made similar recommendations. Some of the ideas associated with reinvention were inspired by studies of businesses conducted more than a decade earlier, which found that the most effective companies were those that are results-oriented.

The results of the reinventing government movement have been felt at all levels of government, but the success of the reforms is subject to debate.[100] Congress passed 36 laws relating to the National Performance Review, including the Government Performance and Results Act of 1993, the Government Management Reform Act of 1994, the Federal Acquisitions Streamlining Act of 1994, the Federal Acquisitions Form Act of 1996, and the Information Technology Management Reform Act of 1993. By 1996, about one-third of the recommendations of the National Performance Review commission had been implemented. This was estimated to have saved $58 billion and to have eliminated 160,000 federal jobs and more than 2,000 field offices. Federal agencies scrapped more than 16,000 pages of regulatory and administrative burdens, which saved about $28 billion. But like many reforms of the past, enthusiasm began to wane. The GAO found that many agencies remained in the planning stage with reinvention efforts. The reinvention reforms seemed to be effective in improving the procurement procedures and some regulatory matters, but budgeting and human resource management were largely untouched.[101]

By the late 1990s, criticisms began to surface about the ideals of reinventing government, particularly from the discipline of public administration. The central idea behind reinventing government was to loosen up the system to enable managers to manage and achieve results (much like the private sector). But when a results-orientation replaces the process-orientation, problems arise regarding accountability and democratic principles. Government is not a private business. Rules, regulations, and procedures are put in place for accountability and to reduce the possibility of corruption. When controls are removed, the possibility of corruption is more likely because of the lack of oversight. It is well established that public administrators are involved in making public policy. Granting them too much freedom above and beyond the discretion they already have raises serious accountability issues. Moreover, once the recommendations were implemented, public employees started losing their jobs. Ultimately, Congress mandated that the federal workforce be cut by 12 percent over a five-year period, which amounted to nearly 273,000 lost jobs. Federal managers became suspicious about the real agenda behind the National Performance Review's recommendations. It became viewed as a job-cutting and downsizing plan to reduce the cost of government. Such efforts hardly helped morale in the public workforce.

The downsizing and job-cutting efforts contributed to removing enthusiasm for reinventing government and provided an incentive to keep "reinvention" in the planning stages at the agency level. It was also quickly relearned that the purpose of most government programs is not aimed at individuals (customers) but at the whole population or subsets of the entire population. For example, environmental protection is not and cannot be consumer-oriented. The goal is to protect the environment for society as a whole. The same is true for most state services. The problems with reinventing government bring us back to the problems stated earlier. Government operates under laws passed in a democratic process, and public administration functions in the political arena. Public administration is not an economically driven institution like private business. Its rules, environment, and purposes are very different. Moreover, it must be held accountable for its actions by the democratic process and by the law. Accountability for private corporations is very different. Their customers and the stockholders, who have the option to stop using their products or to sell their stocks, hold private firms accountable. This is not the way accountability works in the public sector.

Although we are still in the era of reinvention, the zeal once associated with the idea has waned. The movement succeeded in making us think about the importance of results versus the importance of stability. Traditional public administration continues to hold that it is possible to attain important goals through the public bureaucracy, but results cannot come at the expense of accountability or the commitment to democracy. Public managers, in this view, are not supposed to have the same freedoms as private managers. They are bound by law, procedure, and are accountable for their actions. Government does not operate in the competitive marketplace. The reinvention era has not completely run its course, but it appears that the values of the orthodox school of public administration (the traditional public administration school discussed in Chapter 2) are still very much the core of public management in the new century. Reinventing government has influenced public administration, but its impact may have been greatly overstated.[102]

The privatization debate brought the *public-private dichotomy* back to the mainstream, and the reinventing government movement carried it a step further. The essence of reinventing government, once all of the cloaks were removed, was that government could operate similarly to private business with a strong results-orientation. One of the problems with too much of a results-orientation is that the "ends may justify the means." Government is well equipped to establish goals, provide necessary services, and govern. Government, for the most part, does not deal with products; it deals with public policy. Public policy and public goods should be handled through democratic processes rather than market mechanisms. While freeing public managers and increasing their discretion may increase their capacity to achieve results, the costs must also include losing some accountability. Thus, after a century of debate, we are once again arguing over whether government and business can be compared, and whether it is appropriate to operate public agencies in a businesslike fashion.

SUMMARY

This chapter has provided a brief overview of three important areas related to government performance. The idea that government is less efficient than private industry is an issue that is not likely to go away. Comparing government to business has limitations because of the lack of the profit motive in government and the nature of many governmental tasks. There are some activities in government that are similar to tasks in the private sector (those functions that are not public goods), but many activities cannot be transferred and have no equivalent in the private sector. For example, for constitutional reasons, administering justice cannot be handled by the private sector. National defense and the nation's military is not likely to be transferred unless the nation is willing to employ mercenaries to defend the nation. But the private sector is deeply involved in national defense through contracting. It is the private sector that develops and builds military equipment, such as F-16 fighter jets and M-1 tanks. There has always been a public-private partnership between government and private industry in many governmental areas. Moreover, government is responsible for regulatory activities that oversee many aspects of society, including private business.

Measuring government performance is difficult partly because there is no single measure that fits all government organizations. Government is unique in many respects. It is a monopoly, and monopolies have some inherent characteristics that adversely affect efficiency. But efficiency is not the only goal of government. Public accountability and equity issues cannot be ignored. The privatization debate has faded, but privatization was not a fad. It has been a part of the landscape of government since the nation was founded. What has changed is that some activities have been devolved back to the market, and the use of the private sector has been expanded in providing services that were once considered to be exclusively public sector responsibilities. However, it must be emphasized that public employees still provide most public services, despite years of downsizing, cutbacks, and budgetary retrenchment.

The reinventing government movement attempted to make government more results-oriented. The goals included freeing managers to manage in order to enhance efficiency and effectiveness. The movement caused a number of changes during the 1990s, including the National Performance Review, which implemented a variety of changes in certain areas of government. But reinventing government ran into problems because it runs counter to the values of public accountability. After more than a decade of trying to *reinvent government,* the movement appears to be fading and may turn out to be another passing fad, but one that did have an impact. Reinventing government made us think about the values of accomplishing goals quickly and efficiently versus the values of prudent processes designed to enhance accountability. It illustrated how cumbersome government processes could be improved. But perhaps government should not operate in the faster lane of the marketplace. Efficiency is important, and efforts should be made to reduce waste, but efficiency in the political arena has some limitations. Efficiency can be applied to the legislative process.

We could measure the performance of legislatures by the number of bills they pass and the cost. Actually, calculations are made that tell how much it costs to produce a page of public law, but this is not the meter used to gauge the performance of legislatures. There are many times when the process of deliberation used in legislatures appropriately slows and checks the urge to pass laws that should not be passed. In public agencies, it may also be wise to use more prudence when developing policies and administrative laws that will affect society.

The customer-citizen comparison is also important. Businesses focus on their customers and market segments, which is necessary for them to survive in the competitive marketplace. But can government agencies be *citizen-oriented?* Some activities of government can and do focus on clienteles, particular groups, and in some cases citizens. But this must be balanced with the need to be concerned with the general public, or the population as a whole. One of the major criticisms of interest group politics (i.e., pluralism, which is discussed in Chapter 7) is that the voices of special interests are heard and their pressure causes action. That is, special interest groups are able to get preferential treatment in the governmental process. Reinventing government advocated a customer orientation, but citizens may not be the exact equivalent to customers. There is disagreement over whether government can or should be *citizen-oriented* in a similar sense to how private business is customer-oriented.

Criticisms about government waste and inefficiency are not new. Measuring government performance is difficult because performance is viewed through political perceptions rather than economic standards. Whether government is doing a good job in reducing crime, dealing with poverty, or solving other social problems depends on one's political position. Determining whether General Motors had a good year is much easier to quantify.

NOTES

1. For an excellent discussion about government efficiency and government-business comparisons, see George Downs and Patrick Larkey, *The Search for Government Efficiency: From Hubris to Helplessness* (Philadelphia, PA: Temple University Press, 1986).

2. "Confidence in Political Institutions," *Harris Survey* (November 1995), pp. 1–4.

3. Public choice theory was at the center of the privatization debate. It caused many ripples in the discipline, as it challenged some of the basic assumptions about how public agencies perform, decision making in nonmarket situations, and the nature of public finance. The idea that public managers and employees are self-serving individuals never set well with the orthodox school of public administration. Public choice theorists effectively argued that government is inefficient by design because government is a monopoly, and all monopolies, whether public or private, are inefficient because of the lack of competition. Public choice theorists did not argue that public managers were poor managers; they argued that public managers behaved rationally but that behaving rationally in the public sector led to inefficiency because of the incentive structures found in government organizations. Public choice theory is discussed in Chapter 7.

4. *Efficiency* and *productivity* have the same definition. Typically, they refer to the amount of time, labor, money, and materials needed to produce something.

5. Government is frequently compared to private businesses. Meaningful comparisons

are critical. For example, the U.S. Postal Service has been the subject of many jokes because of its perceived lack of efficiency and often blatant incompetence. Citizens often view the post office being staffed with lazy, overpaid workers. Most Americans have had experiences with the post office where packages did not arrive in a reasonable time, postal employees provided poor service, and so on. For example, in the early 1990s, during the debate over nationalizing health care, critics often asked whether we wanted to use the post office as a model to deliver health care. This was intended as satire, but it was very effective because most of us can relate to the post office, and it did not seem like a good model to emulate—even if the comparison was not fair. Most often, the postal service is compared to private companies like United Parcel Service (UPS) and Federal Express, which usually appear to be far more efficient and reliable than the postal service. However, when the U.S. Postal Service is compared to postal services operated by other countries, such as Japan, Germany, or France, one finds that the U.S. Postal Service is very efficient. In fact, studies have shown that the U.S. Postal Service moves more letters and more tons of packages more cost-effectively than any other postal service in the world. See Downs and Larkey, *The Search for Government Efficiency: From Hubris to Helplessness,* p. 17.

6. Cited in Nicholas Henry, *Public Administration and Public Affairs,* 7th ed. (Upper Saddle River, NJ: Prentice-Hall, 1999), p. 194.

7. Lawrence Lesser, *Business, Public Policy, and Society* (Fort Worth, TX: Dryden Press, 2000), p. 81.

8. Ibid.

9. Some argue that the social contract changed as the baby boomer generation came of age. See George Steiner and John Steiner, *Business, Government, and Society: A Managerial Perspective,* 5th ed. (New York: Random House, 1988), Chapters 8, 9, and 10.

10. For an interesting account of the battle in Congress, see Thomas Eagleton, *Issues in Business and Government* (Englewood Cliffs, NJ: Prentice-Hall, 1991), Chapter 3.

Thomas Eagleton was a senator from Missouri for many years and was present during the clash over tobacco that occurred in the 1970s. Also see A. Lee Fritschler and James M. Hoefler, *Smoking and Politics: Public Policy Making and the Federal Bureaucracy,* 5th ed. (Upper Saddle River, NJ: Prentice-Hall, 1996).

11. Anthony Downs made his observations at an address to his 50th class reunion at Carlton College in Northfield, Minnesota, on June 21, 2002. His entire speech is available at http://www.anthonydowns.com.

12. This table is credited to Nicholas Henry, who provides a much more in-depth discussion about the history of reform in increasing government productivity and evaluation in *Public Administration and Public Affairs,* Chapter 7.

13. Ibid., p. 213.

14. It is beyond the scope of this book to examine program evaluation in detail. The literature is extensive and many of the technical tools and techniques used in policy evaluation are also used in program evaluation. An excellent description of how to conduct program evaluation is provided by Ronald Sylvia, Kathleen Sylvia, and Elizabeth Dunn in *Program Planning and Evaluation for the Public Manager,* 2nd ed. (Prospect Heights, IL: Waveland Press, 1997). Also, Nicholas Henry provides an excellent review of the history of program evaluation in *Public Administration and Public Affairs,* Chapter 7.

15. Ronald Sylvia, Kathleen Sylvia, and Elizabeth Dunn, *Program Planning and Evaluation for the Public Manager,* Chapters 5–8.

16. Public goods are goods that are difficult to exclude people from using even if they have not paid for the service, such as streetlights and national defense. Economists tended to agree that most (but not all) services provided by cities and counties were technically not public goods. For example, collecting garbage, providing water and sewerage, paving streets, maintaining traffic lights, landscaping, and the like are not public goods.

17. E. S. Savas found that most cities that collected garbage using in-house depart-

ments did not know the true cost of production. Savas spent much of his career studying city services. See E. S. Savas, *Privatization: The Key to Better Government* (Chatham, NJ: Chatham House, 1987).

18. Harry Hatry is credited with developing the term *perverse measures*. See Harry Hatry, *A Review of Private Approaches for Delivery of Public Services* (Washington, DC: Urban Affairs Institute, 1983).

19. For an analysis of law enforcement indicators, see George Downs and Patrick Larkey, *The Search for Government Efficiency: From Hubris to Helplessness,* pp. 71–73.

20. Paul Epstein, "Get Ready: The Time for Performance Measurement Is Finally Coming," *Public Administration Review 52* (September/October 1992), pp. 513–519. Also see David Ammons, "Overcoming the Inadequacies of Performance Measurement in Local Government: The Case of Libraries and Leisure Services," *Public Administration Review 55* (January/February 1995), pp. 37–47; David Ammons, "Common Barriers to Productivity Improvement in Local Government," *Public Productivity Review 9* (Winter 1985), pp. 293–310. Also see Jonathan West, "City Government Productivity and Civil Service Reforms," *Public Administration Review 10* (Fall 1986), pp. 45–59.

21. The scientist who developed the original idea was Walter A. Shewhart. W. Edwards Deming was born in Iowa and taught physics at Yale University, where he received his PhD. Deming was responsible for revitalizing American industry during the 1980s and was very much in demand as a consultant until his death in 1993.

22. Nicholas Henry, *Public Administration and Public Affairs*, pp. 219–220.

23. See Evan Berman and Jonathan West, "Municipal Commitment to Total Quality Management: A Survey of Recent Progress," *Public Administration Review 55* (January/February 1995), pp. 57–66.

24. Nicholas Henry articulates this point in *Public Administration and Public Affairs,* p. 221. Japan created the Deming Prize in 1951 in honor of W. Edwards Deming. One American firm, Florida Power and Light, won the Deming Prize from Japan but then scrapped the whole idea of TQM after upper management changed.

25. Ibid., p. 219. The original source is a survey conducted by the Massachusetts Institute of Technology (MIT). See "More Quality Than You Think," *Fortune* (April 18, 1994), p. 24.

26. Cited in Nicholas Henry, *Public Administration and Public Affairs,* p. 220.

27. The findings are based on the survey conducted by Evan Berman and Jonathan West, "Municipal Commitment to Total Quality Management: A Survey of Recent Progress," pp. 57–66.

28. Ibid.

29. One of Deming's critical points involved getting it right the first time. After the problem has occurred it is too late because any efficiency gains have been lost.

30. In the public and private sectors, many acronyms are used for TQM. Usually TQM is not the acronym used in the public sector.

31. See Jeffrey Greene, *Cities and Privatization: Prospects for the New Century* (Upper Saddle River, NJ: Prentice-Hall, 2002), Appendix A. Appendix A contains an efficiency comparison between public and private organizations producing similar services. In most services, the public sector is less efficient. Most of these studies were conducted by economists and appeared in reputable academic journals.

32. National Academy of Public Administration, *Privatization: The Challenge to Public Management* (Washington, DC: Author, 1989), p. vii.

33. Many studies have been conducted over the past 30 years that have found private production of an array of services to be more efficient than government production. With only a few exceptions where studies produced inconclusive findings, there is a general consensus that private production is less costly for most services. Some of the major studies include: David Davies, "The Efficiency of Public versus Private Firms: The Case of Australia's Two Airlines," *Journal of Law and Economics 14* (1971), pp. 149–165; Louis de Alessi, "The Economics of the Evidence," *Research in Law and Economics 2* (1980), pp. 1–47; Louis de Alessi, "Managerial Tenure under Private and Government

Ownership in the Electric Power Industry," *Journal of Political Economy 82* (May–June 1974), pp. 645–653; Roger Ahlbrandt, "Efficiency in the Provision of Fire Services," *Public Choice 16* (Fall 1973), pp. 1–15; Leland Neuberg, "Two Issues in the Municipal Ownership of Electric Power Distribution Systems," *Bell Journal of Economics 6* (1977), pp. 303–323; Barbara Stevens, "Scale, Market Structure, and Cost of Refuse Collection," *Review of Economics and Statistics 60* (1977), pp. 438–448; Robert McGuire and Robert Ohnsfelt, "Public versus Private Water Delivery: A Critic Analysis of a Hedonic Cost Approach," *Public Finance Quarterly* (July 1986), pp. 339–350; Barbara Stevens, "Scale, Market Structure, and Cost of Refuse Collection," *Review of Economics and Statistics 60* (1977), pp. 438–448.

One study summarized the findings of 50 empirical studies that compared the relative efficiency between public and private operations. In 40 of the 50 studies, private provision was found to be more efficient. See Thomas Borcherding, Werner Pommerehne, and Fred Schneider, *Comparing the Efficiency of Private and Public Production: The Evidence from Five Countries* (Zurich, Switzerland: Institute for Empirical Research, University of Zurich, 1982).

34. John Donahue, *The Privatization Decision: Public Ends, Private Means* (New York: Basic Books, 1989), p. 5.

35. Ibid., pp. 5–6.

36. See E. S. Savas, *Privatization and Public-Private Partnerships* (New York: Seven Bridges Press, 2000), for a thorough discussion of the various forms of privatization. Also see Savas's classic book, *Privatization: The Key to Better Government* (Chatham, NJ: Chatham House Press, 1987).

37. National Academy of Public Administration, *Privatization: The Challenge to Public Management,* p. vii.

38. Peter Drucker is credited with providing the first comprehensive description of privatization, although he referred to the concept as "reprivatization" in the *Age of Discontinuity.* Robert Poole shortened the term *reprivatization* to *privatization* in 1976. See Robert Poole, Jr.,

Cut Local Taxes without Reducing Essential Services (Santa Barbara, CA: Reason Press, 1976). The Reason Foundation maintains an impressive database of privatization studies at http://www.reason.org.

39. Milton Friedman, *Free to Choose: A Personal Statement* (New York: Harcourt Brace, 1980). Also see Friedman's classic work about free market economies in *Capitalism and Federalism* (Chicago: University of Chicago Press, 1962).

40. Charles Wolf, *Markets or Governments: Choosing Between Imperfect Alternatives* (Cambridge, MA: MIT Press, 1988), p. 2.

41. Peter Drucker, *The Age of Discontinuity* (Boston: Harper & Row, 1969), pp. 233–234.

42. Paul Starr provides one of the best articulations of the case against privatization. See Paul Starr, "The Meaning of Privatization," in Sheila Kammerman and Alfred Kahn, Eds., *Privatization and the Welfare State* (Princeton, NJ: Princeton University, 1988), pp. 124–137. A similar table is included with descriptions and examples in Jeffrey D. Greene, *Cities and Privatization: Prospects for the New Century,* Chapter 1.

43. The services include functions at all levels of government ranging from education and social services to transportation systems. For example, for many years the private sector operated subways, utilities, and many other services in cities. Largely due to the corruption of the political machines that controlled many of the nation's cities and granted favors to the private firms that ran various services, such as transportation systems, services were gradually taken over by the public sector to ensure greater public accountability. See Bernard Ross and Myron Levine, *Urban Politics: Power in Metropolitan America,* 6th ed. (Itasca, IL: Peacock, 2000), Chapters 5, 8, and 15. Also see Dennis Judd and Todd Swanstrom, *City Politics: Private Power and Public Policy* (New York: Harper Collins, 1994), especially Chapters 1 and 2, which discuss the transition from private cities to public, municipal corporations. Part Four of this book contains a detailed discussion about how the private city appears to be returning. For an analysis of New York City's experience with its subway system,

see James Ramsey, "Sell the New York City Subway: Wide-eyed Radicalism or the Only Feasible Solution," in *Prospect for Privatization,* pp. 93–103.

44. See Stuart Butler, *Privatizing the Federal Budget: A Strategy to Eliminate the Deficit* (New York: Universe Books, 1985), and Peter Drucker, *The Age of Discontinuity,* 1969.

45. In market theory, a state of perfect efficiency (Pareto optimality) exists when resources are allocated in is such a way that no one's position can be improved without a loss to someone else. In other words, this may be thought of as a state of equilibrium where any movement comes at the expense of another firm.

46. Economists realize that information is imperfect and that consumer decisions are based on risk, uncertainty, and imperfect information. The ideal model is described to illustrate the ideas associated with perfect markets.

47. Charles Wolf, *Markets or Governments: Choosing Between Imperfect Alternatives,* p. 18.

48. Jeffrey D. Greene, *Cities and Privatization: Prospects for the New Century,* Chapter 1.

49. Efforts have been made to simulate competition using a technique called "managed competition," which has been widely used at the local level. Cities divide their jurisdiction into zones and contract out the zones while allowing their municipal department to participate in the competitive bidding process to provide the service. Typically, the public department is guaranteed certain areas of the city so that public employees will not lose their jobs. This technique has proved to be useful for making publicly managed departments more efficient, partly because the true costs of operations are revealed and they can bid for other zones in the city aside from the areas that have been reserved for their department.

50. Charles Wolf, *Markets or Governments: Choosing Between Imperfect Alternatives,* Chapter 1. Economists do not consider tax revenues to be the equivalent to revenues generated from sales in the private sector.

51. Ibid.

52. See E. S. Savas, *Privatization and Public-Private Partnerships,* Chapter 1.

53. Robert Bish and Vincent Ostrom, *Understanding Urban Government* (Washington, DC: American Enterprise Institute, 1973).

54. James Buchanan, "Why Does Government Grow?" in Thomas Borcherding, Ed., *Budgets and Bureaucrats* (Durham, NC: Duke University Press, 1977), pp. 13–14, and Gordon Tullock, "Why Politicians Won't Cut Taxes," *Taxing and Spending* (October/November), 1978, pp. 12–14. Also see E. S. Savas, "Municipal Monopolies versus Competition in Delivering Urban Services," in H. W. Hawley and D. Rogers, Eds., *Improving the Quality of Urban Management* (Beverly Hills, CA: Sage, 1974), pp. 473–500.

55. Privatization finds support in another economic theory that focuses on government failure. The theory holds that nonmarket failure results from the distinct characteristics of nonmarket supply and demand. As noted in the text, markets link the costs of producing something to the income necessary to sustain operations. This link is provided by the price charged to consumers. This link does not exist in nonmarket activity. In the absence of this link, the value of the output is separated from the cost of production. This results in misallocation of resources and disequilibrium between supply and demand. Nonmarket failure also is linked to the internal operations of government organizations. Because government operations are typically monopolies, adequate incentives are lacking to develop internal standards that are efficient. In private firms, inefficient internal operating practices affect profits. Internalities are the standards that apply within organizations to guide, regulate, and evaluate organizational performance. In market organizations, the internal system must be connected to the external pricing system. In nonmarket organizations, internalities are disconnected with the external purpose of the organization. Nonmarket organizations are likely to use budget size as an indicator of performance due to the political context in which they exist. Performance of personnel is then evaluated

in terms of either expanding the budget or protecting it from cuts. Thus, the incentives within nonmarket organizations are to reward personnel for justifying costs. Charles Wolf has written extensively on this theory. See Charles Wolf, "A Theory of Nonmarket Failure: Framework for Implementation Analysis," *Journal of Law and Economics* (April 1979), pp. 107–140; Charles Wolf, "A Theory of Nonmarket Failures," Public Interest 55 (1979), pp. 114–133; and Charles Wolf, *Markets or Governments: Choosing Between Imperfect Alternatives,* Chapter 1. Also see Francis Bator, "The Anatomy of Market Failure," *Quarterly Journal of Economics 72* (1958), pp. 351–379.

56. Property rights theory was a part of the theoretical framework for privatization. For a complete discussion of property rights theory, see Louis de Alessi, "Property Rights and Privatization," in *Prospects for Privatization,* pp. 24–35; Armen Alchian, "Some Economies of Property Rights," *Politico 30* (1965), pp. 816–829; Brodkin and Young, "Making Sense of Privatization: What Can We Learn from Economic and Political Analysis?" in *Privatization and the Welfare State,* pp. 121–156; and Harold Demsetz, "Toward a Theory of Property Rights," *American Economic Review 57* (1967), pp. 347–359. Also see Garret Hardin, "The Tragedy of the Commons," *Science 162,* pp. 1245–1248.

57. The theme of Charles Wolf's book *Markets or Governments: Choosing Between Imperfect Alternatives* is that the choice between government and market provision is a choice between imperfect alternatives.

58. See Harry Hatry, "Privatization Presents Problems," in Bruce Stinebrickner, Ed., *Annual Editions: State and Local Government,* 5th ed. (Guilford, CT: Dushkin Press, 1989), pp. 220–221.

59. The large public unions have been the most vocal in the debate, in particular the American Federation of Government Workers and the American Federation of State, County, and Municipal Employees. The American Federation of State, County, and Municipal Employees maintains an excellent Web site in opposition to privatization, including case studies about contracting failures and an online version
of the latest edition of *Government for Sale.* The material is linked on their home page at http://www.afscme.org.

60. Dwight Waldo, *The Enterprise of Public Administration* (Novato, CA: Chandler & Sharp, 1980), p. 110.

61. Louise White, "Public Management in a Pluralistic Arena," *Public Administration Review 49* (November/December 1989), p. 524.

62. No clear definition of the public interest exists that is agreed upon by scholars. Over the centuries, there have been categories of definitions. For our purposes here, public interest refers to actions that place the interest of the public (or society as a whole) above individual interests.

63. Richard Stillman, "Ostrom on the Federalists Revisited," *Public Administration Review 49* (January/February 1987), p. 83.

64. Cited in George Steiner and John Steiner, *Business, Government, and Society,* p. 328. The original source is a study conducted by *U.S. News & World Report.*

65. Ira Sharkansky, "Policy Making and Service Delivery on the Margins of Government: The Case of Contractors," *Public Administration Review 40* (March/April 1980), pp. 116–123.

66. Barry Bozeman, *All Organizations Are Public* (San Francisco: Jossey-Bass, 1987); Ronald Moe, "Exploring the Limits of Privatization," *Public Administration Review 47* (November/December 1987), pp. 453–460; Paul Starr, "The Limits of Privatization," in *Prospects for Privatization,* pp. 124–137.

67. Ron Moe, "Exploring the Limits of Privatization," pp. 453–460.

68. Ibid.

69. George Downs and Patrick Larkey, *The Search for Government Efficiency: From Hubris to Helplessness,* Chapters 1 and 2.

70. For many examples of privatization failures, see John Hanrahan, *Government for Sale* (Washington, DC: American Federation of State, County, and Municipal Employees, 1986).

71. There are few private, for-profit fire protection companies in the nation. One

exception is the Rural-Metro, which has served the Scottsdale, Arizona, area for more than 60 years and operates nationwide.

72. Graham T. Allison, "Public and Private Management: Are They Fundamentally Alike in All Unimportant Respects?" in Richard Stillman, Ed., *Public Administration: Concepts and Cases,* 3rd ed. (Boston: Houghton Mifflin, 1983), pp. 453–467.

73. Ted Kolderie, "Two Different Sides of Privatization," *Public Administration Review 46* (July/August 1986), pp. 285–286.

74. Phillip Fixler and Robert Poole, "Status of State and Local Privatization," in Steve Hanke, Ed., *Prospects for Privatization* (New York: The Academy of Political Science, 1987), p. 174. For many other examples of failures in contracting out local services, see John Hanrahan, *Government for Sale: Contracting Out, The New Patronage* (Washington, DC: American Federation of State, County, and Municipal Employees, 1977).

75. Ruth DeHoog, *Contracting Out for Human Services,* p. 12.

76. Paul Starr, "The Limits of Privatization," pp. 124–137.

77. Lyle Fitch, "Increasing the Role of the Private Sector in Providing Public Services," in Willis Hawley and David Rogers, Eds., *Improving The Quality of Urban Management* (Beverly Hills, CA: Sage, 1974), pp. 501–559.

78. This comment is credited to Lyle Fitch, which is cited in DeHoog, *Contracting Out for Human Services,* p. 12.

79. National Council on Employment Policy, *The Long Term Employment Implications of Privatization* (Washington, DC: Dudek, 1989), p. 1.

80. See John Hanrahan, *Government for Sale,* Chapter 1.

81. For example, Los Angeles adopted a formal "no-layoff" policy many years ago. Similar policies have become common in many cities (and even the federal government). In short, a "no-layoff" policy promises that no employee will be laid off due to privatization or contracting. Usually, governments handle this through internal transfers, normal attrition, or voluntary early retirements for those who qualify.

82. See Hanrahan, *Government for Sale,* Chapter 1. Also see American Federation of State, County, and Municipal Employees, *Passing the Bucks: The Contracting Out of Public Services* (Washington, DC: Author, 1983).

83. Elinor Brilliant, "Public or Private: A Model of Ambiguities," *Social Science Review* (September 1973), p. 39.

84. Robert Lee, *Public Personnel Systems,* p. 8.

85. A study by the GAO regarding federal layoffs found that the costs of welfare-related expenditures were offset greatly by the savings realized through federal contracting. The study involved nearly 10,000 workers who lost their jobs at the Department of Defense due to contracting. The GAO study found that the government saved $65 million through contracting and paid out only $200,000 related to the layoffs. See Stephen Moore, "Contracting Out: A Painless Alternative to the Budget Cutter's Knife," in *Prospects for Privatization,* p. 68.

86. See John Kenneth Galbraith, *The Age of Uncertainty* (Boston: Houghton Mifflin, 1977), Chapter 1. Also see John Kenneth Galbraith, *The Affluent Society* (Boston: Houghton Mifflin, 1958), Chapters 1–2.

87. Charles Wolf, *Market or Governments: Choosing Between Imperfect Alternatives,* p. 3.

88. Ibid., p. 3.

89. David Osborne and Ted Gaebler, *Reinventing Government: How the Entrepreneurial Spirit Is Transforming the Public Sector* (New York: Addison-Wesley, 1992).

90. National Performance Review Commission, *From Red Tape to Results: Creating a Government That Works Better and Costs Less* (Washington, DC: U.S. Government Printing Office, 1993), p. 1.

91. There were 10 commissions that preceded the National Performance Review. The reform commissions included Theodore Roosevelt's Keep commission of 1905, the Taft commission of 1912, the Brownlow committee of 1937, the First Hoover commission of 1949 and the Second Hoover commission of 1953, the Volcker commission of 1989, and the Grace commission of 1984. Unlike the

previous commission, which used staffs from the private sector and universities, the National Performance Review employed 250 experienced federal employees from all areas of the federal government. For an excellent analysis of the National Performance Review, see Nicholas Henry, *Public Administration and Public Affairs,* pp. 200–210. In 2003, yet another major commission reported, the Volcker Report. Like many other reports, the second Volcker report, titled "Urgent Business: Revitalizing the Federal Government for the 21st Century," called for major reorganization of the federal government. *PA Times, 26,* No. 2 (February 2003), p. 1.

92. Ibid., p. 200. The four major summary points for the National Performance Review are credited to Nicholas Henry but have been slightly modified with additional comments added to each of the four points.

93. The National Performance Review report contained 280 reforms that required legislation.

94. Nicholas Henry, *Public Administration and Public Affairs,* p. 201.

95. Many of the claims made by reinventing advocates, like Vice President Al Gore, turned out not to be true. For example, many claims were made that the procurement procedures used by the federal government caused taxpayers to pay excessively high prices for items (such as office supplies) that can be purchased for less off the shelves of retail stores, such as office supply stores. Examples were provided, such as the famous $600 Mr.

Coffee. But a journalist who compared office supply prices at Office Depot with the prices paid by the General Services Administration found that the prices paid by government were significantly lower than retail prices. Cited in Nicholas Henry, *Public Administration and Public Affairs,* p. 205. The original source is Tom Shoop, "Price War," *Government Executive* (December 1993), pp. 4–5.

96. Nicholas Henry, *Public Administration and Public Affairs,* p. 201.

97. The equivalent book to David Osborne and Ted Gaebler's *Reinventing Government* for the private sector is *In Search of Excellence: Lessons from America's Best-Run Companies* by Thomas Peters and Robert Waterman (New York: Warner Books, 1988). Although *In Search of Excellence* dealt with private businesses, it had a great deal of impact on public administration and management in the public sector.

98. Nicholas Henry, *Public Administration and Public Affairs,* p. 201.

99. Ibid.

100. Donald Kettl and John DiIulio, Jr., Eds., *Inside the Reinvention Machine: Appraising Government Reform* (Washington, DC: Brookings, 1995).

101. Nicholas Henry, *Public Administration and Public Affairs,* p. 204.

102. See Felice Perlmutter and Ram Cnaan, "Entrepreneurship in the Public Sector: The Horns of a Dilemma," *Public Administration Review 55* (January/February 1995), pp. 29–36.

9

Ethics and Public Administration

To be good is noble. To tell people how to be good is nobler,
and much less trouble.

MARK TWAIN

ETHICS IN GOVERNMENT
AND PUBLIC ADMINISTRATION

In the aftermath of Watergate and the Vietnam War, ethics increasingly became
a core part of public administration. Many public administration programs
added ethics courses to their curricula. The same occurred in schools of business. Prior to that time, philosophy departments taught most classes about
ethics. *Ethics refers to a moral philosophy or a set or moral principles[1]—a set of standards that guide our conduct and help us when we face decisions that involve moral
choices.*

The study of ethics examines what is good and bad, right and wrong, and
just or unjust. In public administration, this involves studying what is right and
wrong, good and bad, and just and unjust in organizations. But it is impossible
to fully understand the importance of ethics without considering how ethics
evolve and how they affect society as a whole.

Often people have two sets of ethical standards that conflict: their personal
code of ethics, and their professional standards. Most believe that, ideally, the

360

two ethical codes should be the same. Why should a person adhere to one set of standards at work and another set of standards elsewhere? The two sets of ethics can collide, however, when organizations expect employees and managers to perform tasks that conflict with their personal standards. Such conflicts can be caused by religious-based beliefs or by personal moral standards that people adamantly and sincerely wish to follow.

Ethics reflect our personal and professional standards, but the underlying concept that gives meaning to ethics is *values*. Values are perceptional filters through which we see the world; they define what we view as *right*. Most values are culture-bound, meaning that ethics that are derived from the values of society and its culture. Thus, ethics and values are connected and are very *normative* in nature. That is, they indicate how one *should* behave in a given situation or under a particular set of circumstances. Ethical codes of conduct exist for most professions, such as medicine, law, academics, and even public administration (the ASPA's Code of Ethics is discussed later in this chapter).[2] These codes of conduct make a statement about what is expected of those who work in the profession, and they set out principles that are to be followed.

In the world of government, the term *ethics* often conjures up references to all of the scandals, misbehavior, bribery, and other illegal and corrupt activities of public officials.[3] Unfortunately, we hear very little about the virtuous behavior of civil servants or public officials. Notable events like Watergate, the "Keating Five" (see Box 9.1), the Iran-Contra affair, and the Whitewater investigation quickly come to mind. The private sector also has been plagued by scandals and corruption. The failure of Enron, insider trading on Wall Street, shady accounting practices by one of the nation's most respected accounting firms, and even scandals in the clergy have done little to help the image of society's institutions. Surveys have consistently shown that most Americans believe that business and government are filled with corruption. But the significance of moral principles in government means much more than reactions against public wrongdoing. Much of what government does involves ethical decisions in public policy (e.g., abortion, euthanasia, capital punishment, legalized gambling, and war). Government is often expected to maintain a higher standard in order to set an example for society, but a long history of corruption and scandals has been counterproductive to this goal.[4] This chapter provides a brief overview of how ethics affects public administration, the workplace, and society.

SOURCES OF VALUES
IN AMERICAN SOCIETY

Ethics are derived from *values*. Values develop as we learn the customs, norms, rules, expectations, manners, and the right and wrong ways of doing things while growing up in society. That is, we are *taught* or we *acquire* the values of society through a very complex socialization process that begins as soon as we are born. Figure 9.1 illustrates this process. Some psychologists refer to it as

---

**BOX 9.1   Whatever Happened to Charles Keating?—
The Case of Lincoln Savings and Loan**

One of the most egregious examples of financial fraud in recent memory involved Lincoln Savings and Loan of Irvine, California, and its owner, Charles H. Keating, Jr. Keating controlled Lincoln through a parent holding company, American Continental Corporation of Phoenix, Arizona. The federal government seized Lincoln in 1989. By the time the government finished cleaning up the mess years later, the cost to American taxpayers had escalated to more than $3 billion—an amount that, according to an official of the Federal Bureau of Investigation, "eclipses the annual losses from all U.S. bank robberies."

Lincoln's owner, Mr. Keating, was found to have defrauded investors out of billions of dollars. He was convicted in 1993 on 77 counts of racketeering, conspiracy, bank fraud, interstate transportation of stolen property, misapplication of funds, and securities fraud. Keating had been active politically, contributing large sums to legislators he thought would keep federal regulators off his back.

Five U.S. senators, who came to be known as the "Keating Five" because of their close association with Mr. Keating, became the subject of a Senate ethics investigation. Following extensive hearings, the "Keating Five" were reprimanded by their Senate colleagues for intervening with regulators on Mr. Keating's behalf after they had accepted campaign contributions from him. Also, the Washington-based law firm that represented Lincoln agreed to pay $41 million to settle charges by federal regulators that it had "knowingly aided and abetted the violation of regulations" by its client.

Mr. Keating was ordered to pay $122.4 million in restitution for defrauding investors and was sentenced to a prison term of twelve years and seven months. Because of the publicity surrounding his case, Keating became known as the "poster boy of the savings and loan crisis." However, after serving four years and nine months of his sentence, Mr. Keating was released in 1996 when his state and federal criminal convictions were overturned on technicalities. In 1999, Charles Keating, 75 years old at the time, entered into a plea agreement with U.S. prosecutors. Under the agreement, he admitted guilt for the first time but did not have to pay a fine or return to prison. Also, the government agreed to dismiss fraud charges against his son.

What type of message does this send to society?

SOURCE: Adapted from Lawrence Lesser, *Business, Public Policy, and Society* (Fort Worth, TX: Dryden Press, 2000), pp. 36–37.

---

value programming because we acquire values from a variety of influences during a roughly 20-year cycle that begins at birth. Value programming has three major phases or stages through which we all pass. The three phases are *imprint, modeling, and socialization.*[5] Technically, all three stages are socialization processes.

During the value programming cycle, our immediate family, religion (or lack of religion), friends of our family, the educational system, the media, work, and college (for those who go to college) provide sources of values. As we work our way through the model shown in Figure 9.1, our world expands and we are influenced by more and more value sources, such as television, peers at school,

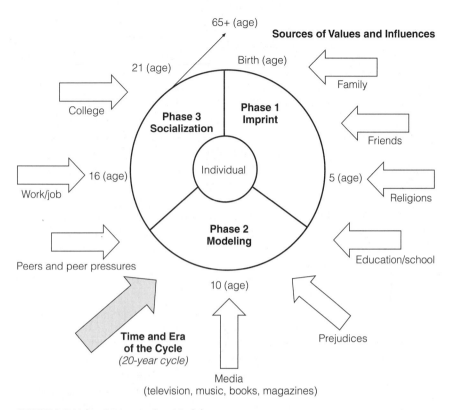

FIGURE 9.1 Value Programming Model

SOURCE: Derived from models included in Morris Massey, *People Puzzle: Understanding Yourself and Others* (Englewood Cliffs, NJ: Prentice-Hall, 1980).

books, movies, and real-life events that we experience. As we move through the stages of this process, the values also become more diverse as we move further away from the influence of our parents and immediate family. Each of the major sources of values teaches us a right way of doing something. The values that are being learned are reinforced through the system by our friends, neighbors, churches, schools, and the like. This is also the period during which our *conscience* is formed—the internal component that assists our moral reasoning.[6] This process occurs with each generation and is heavily influenced by the time period in which we grew up. Times change, and operating values of society are modified.[7]

The value programming process slows as we reach our early twenties when, according to psychologists, our basic system of values has been formed. These values are called "absolute values" or "gut-level values." They are the type of values that tells us how we feel about things such as abortion, the work ethic, marriage, the family, war, politics, and other issues that have a right and wrong component. Although values can be modified, it is virtually impossible to change the effect of 20 or more years of experiences and programming. *Absolute values* are considered to be permanent and only subject to some modification. *Relative values are temporary, faddish values that tend* to be important to us while we are young but fade away as we grow older.

The process of value programming is complicated by several other factors. One is the environmental characteristic of social class stratification (the way people fall into the socioeconomic structure: lower, middle, and upper classes and the lifestyles associated with the various classes). The process is also affected by a variety of demographic factors like race and the region in which we grew up. Growing up in a large urban area like Seattle or New York City is very different from being raised in rural Wyoming or in a rural town in South Carolina. The process is complex, and the sources of values do not always echo identical messages. If they did, we would all be very similar. Families vary greatly, but white-collar (middle-class) families tend to share many of the same values, which affect their children. Blue-collar (working-class) families are also part of the middle class and share many common values about life that are passed along in the process. The same is true of the upper middle class (the professional class), but their values are not identical to those held by the white-collar and blue-collar groups.[8] All three groups have some distinctive values that are passed along to their children.

Society is constantly undergoing change, and the values being conveyed become modified over time from one generation to the next as they are influenced by the events of the contemporary era in which people come of age. For example, the operating values of society today are very different from the values of the founding period in the mid-1700s. Women and people who did not own property could not vote. Moreover, the role of women in society was very different. Today it is perfectly normal for women to hold positions of authority in society's institutions, which represents a substantial shift in values.

After we reach early adulthood, we basically have our set of operating values. We have reference points that help us with issues that we face in life. The model does not suggest that learning stops or that our values cannot be altered to some degree by experiencing significant emotional events. This model, however, is not about individual personalities; it is about value characteristics of generations or groups of people. All the people from a single generation do not turn out exactly the same, but each generation shows a variety of distinct characteristics. At the same time, certain characteristics, norms, and customs are passed along to each generation. For example, the idea of democracy, civic duty, values about political culture, and many other beliefs seem to carry over. This process produces values about individualism and competition that have been around for a number of generations. It teaches us that working hard is good and being lazy is bad, that democracy is good and dictatorships are bad. Understanding this phenomenon helps us see how a diversity of values can exist in society at the same time and how certain values seem to remain (although they may be modified from the views of earlier generations).

In the workplace, we must deal with people from different generations. Understanding the sources of values, beliefs, preferences, and prejudices is important because all of these affect the decisions we make as adults. Moreover, they affect the decisions and attitudes of those with whom we work in organizational settings. It has long been recognized that American public administration is culture-bound because it adheres to values associated with democracy, the Constitution, the Declaration of Independence, and public law. These values cannot be readily transferred into a society such as Iran or China.

Our value system contains some tensions, and these tensions carry over into our ethical codes. For example, corporate and government scandals have been common in our society. Many of these scandals likely relate back to some competing values, such as our quest for success, power, material goods, and pleasure versus other moral values that teach us to be honest, kind, merciful, unselfish, and not materialistic, greedy, or self-centered. Clearly, the religious-based *puritanical* morals are in conflict with the competitive and materialistic values, which hold that one can accomplish and achieve great things if one works hard, and that some of the rewards for working hard are money, material wealth, and power.

More than 40 years ago, Gabriel Almond made a number of observations about values in our society that are related to this point.[9] His observations are worth noting here because they say so much about the American people and the society in which our public organizations exist. Almond believed that the characteristics of America's value orientation consisted of several interrelated traits, which are included in Box 9.2. In short, he believed that the value orientation of Americans tended to be *atomistic* (individualistic) rather than *corporate* (group- or team-oriented), *worldly* (materialistic) rather than *unworldly* (religious or spiritual), *highly mobile* rather than *traditional, compulsive* rather than *relaxed,* and *externally directed* rather than *autonomous* (independent). If these value traits are in fact accurate, then something very important is implied not only about our value system, but also about the ethical norms we will adopt. If our value system teaches us to be individualized, materialistic, competitive and externally directed, these traits will likely be justified in our ethical code.

Ethics reflect our values and justify certain behaviors, but they also may serve to temper excesses in behavior.[10] Ethics in the United States are affected by the tensions between individualism, competition, material success, and religious-based morals that come mainly from Christianity. These values apply to citizens, politicians, public managers, policy makers, and corporate leaders. How can one be competitive, materialistic, and selfish while at the same time incorporating the conflicting values taught by religion? This is a tension that has existed for a long time in our society, and it further complicates our ethical codes of conduct.

PUBLIC ADMINISTRATORS AND ETHICAL ORIENTATIONS: TWO MODELS THAT AFFECT ORGANIZATIONS

The study of ethics has two primary schools of thought that affect organizations. These schools reflect the problem of balancing the tension that can arise between an individual's personal code of ethics and the ethical code imposed by organizations. The *theory of amorality* holds that organizations should be

BOX 9.2 Gabriel Almond: Some Thoughts about the American Competitive Ethic and General Values of the American People

1. General Value Orientation

The degree of atomization in the United States may be greater than in any other developed culture. Americans are primarily concerned with "private" values rather than social, group, political, religious, or moral values. The concern is with private, worldly success.

The attachment of Americans to their private values is characterized by an extreme degree of competitiveness. The American individual and family is in a state of competition with other individuals and families for success and achievement. American culture tends to be atomistic rather than corporate, and the pressure of upward mobility is intense.

Americans view themselves as being in a state of competition with other individuals and families for values that are largely material in character. What Americans seem to want is material evidence of success—money, position, education, and the consumer goods that are in vogue at the moment. While the stress is toward money or what money can buy, the important thing is not the money itself, but the sense of accomplishment or fulfillment that it gives. The sense of accomplishment rests on matching and exceeding the material standard of community and social class. It requires external approval and conformity. Because the stress is on having what others want and on material culture, Americans tend to be caught up in an endless race for constantly changing goals—the newest housing, the latest in automobiles, and the most fashionable in dress and appearance. This love of innovation, improvement, and change tends to be confined to material culture. Attitudes toward human and social relationships seem to be more conservative.

There are certain derivative elements of this general value orientation that deserve further explanation. First, intense individual competitiveness, in which the purpose is to get more of whatever people want, produces diffuse hostile tension and general apprehension and anxiety, which pervades every aspect of the culture including the competing unit, the family. The fear of failure and the apprehension over the hostility that is involved in one's relations with other people produces on the one hand an extraordinary need for affection and reassurance, and on the other, an extraordinary tendency to resort to physiological and spiritual narcosis. In other words, as a consequence of being impelled by cultural pressure toward relationships in which one is aggressively pitted against others, the resulting unease and apprehension is characteristically mitigated by demands for external response, attention, and warmth, or by escapism. Thus an excessive concern with sexuality, an

amoral—that is, they should base decisions on economic concerns that affect the organization. This means that the organization should be placed first when decisions are made. Another dimension involves keeping organizations away from making certain kinds of moral judgments, namely, those that involve religious-based values. In other words, businesses and public organizations may have to deal with things that might be borderline in terms of what some peo-

excessive resort to alcohol, and what is a uniquely American narcosis of the soul—widespread addiction to highly stimulating mass entertainment radio, movies, and the like—provide cultural means for discharging hostility and allaying anxiety.

2. Value Expectations

Americans are optimists as to the ends and improvisers as to means. The riches of the heritage and mobility of the social order have produced a generally euphoric tendency. That is, the expectation is that by hard work and effort people can achieve or approximate their goals. This overt optimism is so compulsive an element of American culture that factors that threaten it, such as failure, old age, and death, are dismissed from the focus of attention and handled in perfunctory ways.

3. Attitudes toward Morality

Several trends exist regarding moral norms. The norms of Christianity still constitute an important theme in American culture. Since these moral standards are in obvious and continual rivalry with the competitive ethic, Americans tend to suffer from ambivalence and conflicts in determining what is "proper." Under normal circumstances this conflict does not appear to have a seriously laming effect. It tends to be disposed of by adding moral coloration to actions that are really motivated by expediency, and an expediential coloration to actions that are motivated by moral and humanitarian values. These tendencies are related to a rather widespread naïve belief in the compatibility of morality and expediency. While this ambivalence is a factor that affects American behavior, there is also a characteristic pendulum-type movement between the two ethics. Thus, if generous actions, motivated by moral and humanitarian considerations, are accepted without gratitude, are misinterpreted, or are unrequited, a "cynical rejection" of humanitarianism may follow, resulting from the humiliation of having been "played for a sucker." To yield to humanitarian impulses in the marketplace or to moderate one's own demands in light of Christian considerations, to give without the expectation of receiving, to suffer injury without retaliation—these are impulses that have a partial validity; but it is dangerous to give way to them, since they dull the edge of competitiveness, confuse, and retard the forward course of action.

SOURCE: Gabriel Almond, *The American People and Foreign Policy* (New York: Praeger, 1960), pp. 48–53. This selection has been edited. The full version included a comparison of the cultures of other nations.

ple consider to be moral. This orientation attempts to get around the tension between personal and organizational values by making the organization amoral. Note that being "amoral" is not the equivalent of being not moral or immoral. Amoral has to do with being *benign*. In the case of public organizations, amorality may be described as "neutral competence." Employees simply perform their jobs based on accepted professional standards.

In the world of business, the amoral position is the norm for most corporations (with some exceptions, such as J. C. Penney's that was built on a highly religious foundation and the company encouraged executives and employees to read the Bible). The amoral orientation also suggests that organizational life and the marketplace are "games" in which a completely different set of rules, standards, and accepted practices exist. But critics charge that government, organizations, and managers cannot hide in "ethical sanctuaries." All professionals such as lawyers, doctors, educators, and public administrators are faced with ethical dilemma and conflicts. The business world and organizational life have been compared to a poker game, but critics have argued that business and government are vital social institutions, and that to compare their activities to a game with more permissive rules trivializes these important institutions.[11]

The *theory of moral unity* holds that it is possible to harmonize high levels of personal ethics with the demands of organizational life. This means that the actions of organizations can be judged by the same ethical standards that are held in society rather than by a special set of more permissive ethical standards. Those who adhere to the theory of moral unity believe that only one standard should exist. According to the moral unity orientation, people in organizations do not act as cogs in wheels in an impersonal machine; they act as individuals and citizens. A strong precedent was established at the Nuremberg trials that tried Nazis for war crimes. Western societies expect members of organizations to follow their own consciences and reject forced implementation of highly unethical practices. In the United States, "whistleblower" laws that protect those who expose misconduct in organizatons have strengthened this ideal. Even the U.S. military has a system that allows soldiers to refuse to follow commands of superiors under certain conditions.

Although the moral unity orientation is more pleasant and palatable for most of us, critics argue that it is unrealistic. The real world does not work that way. It is tough, hard, competitive, and vicious. These critics claim that moral unity makes for interesting discussion, but until human nature changes, organizations must remain amoral. In the world of government and business, sometimes people must do things that are inconsistent with their personal ethics. The real world is not utopia. Decisions have to be made that are unpleasant and, at times, ruin human lives. President Truman made the decision to use the atomic bomb to end the war and save thousands of American lives. Was this decision unethical? Is spying to gain intelligence about our foes unethical? Or is it justified to use intelligence to try to prevent terrorist attacks? Are the practices used to gain intelligence unethical? What practices should we use to gather intelligence? Are government-backed assassinations unethical? By our personal standards, everything about this dimension of the world (spies, secret agents, double agents, informants, payoffs, and the like) is probably unethical. Realists will argue, however, that it is a nasty job that has to be done. This double standard is used to justify the need for two sets of ethical standards.

The idea of moral unity in our ethical code and in the conduct of our institutions is complicated by the realities of the world. The application of personal moral standards is overpowered by the grim reality of a competitive, insensitive world. Moreover, organizations are powerful agencies of control. Most people are not in a financial position to dictate whether they will abide by organizational rules and ethics, or conform to more permissive standards. The tensions between the amoral and moral unity orientations are similar to the tensions between some of our cultural values like competition, success, and materialism versus religious-based morals. The amoral versus moral unity orientations also reflect the debate over whether morals are relative (culture-bound) or whether there are universal morals that apply everywhere.

To complicate matters further, there are *subjective ethics* and *prescriptive ethics*. The principle behind subjective ethics holds that people act impulsively, propelled by a combination of needs and feelings that cannot be understood by others. This makes ethics situational and individual. Moreover, these actions cannot be predicted to occur in other situations because circumstances vary.[12] In organizational settings, situational ethics are useless for developing standards that administrators can use in ambiguous situations. They are only useful for justifying a particular action under a particular set of circumstances that may never occur again. The opposite of subjective ethics is prescriptive ethics, which are absolute behavioral standards. The problem with setting absolute standards is the lack of flexibility for interpretation. Prescriptive ethics tend to be sets of "thou shall not do X, Y, and Z" rules, which are often contradictory, confusing, and vague in a vein that is similar to the "principles of management" used during the classical period of public administration. Subjective ethics are so loose that no standards can be found to apply to others, while prescriptive ethical codes are so rigid that one needs to clarify the standards and determine if there are any exceptions to the rules. Even religious-based morals have troubled theologians for centuries. The world's major religions all contain something that resembles the ten commandments of Christianity. One of the commandments is "Thou shall not kill." Are there exceptions for war and self-defense? Not surprisingly, theologians have developed exceptions and conditions under which actions that appear to break some of the commandments can be justified. This generally applies to all prescriptive ethics and causes them to be confusing and require interpretation. One of the problems with ethics in general is that there are so many from which to choose, and all appear to be subject to interpretation. But we cannot avoid ethics; they are a part of society and life. Aside from cultural influences, other sources also have influenced our ethical codes of conduct.[13]

RELIGION AND PHILOSOPHICAL SYSTEMS

Public administrators can look back over several thousand years of philosophical and religious discussion about ethics. The literature contains a rich source of ethical principles. Religion is one of the oldest sources for ethical conduct. For example, the golden rule and the ten commandments of Christianity provide ethical codes of conduct. All major religions have an equivalent to the golden rule: "Do unto others as you would have them do unto you." Stated differently, a contemporary version of this rule is to treat people in the same manner that you would like to be treated. Many of these religious and philosophical ideas have been incorporated into our ethical system over time. Everyone has heard of the principle that the ends justify the means, which is a modern, looser interpretation of Machiavelli's idea that is often used in the world of business. This is "not exactly" what Machiavelli said, and it is thought to be unethical by many. Cost-benefit analyses embody the idea of utilitarianism. And the idea that private property and private ownership is a good thing dates back to Aristotle's argument, "that which is owned in common by the greatest number has the least care devoted to it."[14] This idea served as the basis of what later became known as the "tragedy of the commons"[15] and has had a lasting impact on western thought and values. Some of the major sources of principles are briefly presented in the following list.

- *The Greeks.* Socrates believed that a higher law existed than human's written law (he called it moral law). He believed that virtue and ethical behavior were associated with wisdom. Plato believed in the theory that absolute justice exists and that it can be discovered through intellectual effort. Plato set up a 50-year program to train rulers and saw virtue in the "commons." Aristotle spelled out virtues of character in *The Ethics.* One of his lasting contributions was the "doctrine of the mean." This principle holds that people can achieve the good life by developing virtues of moderation. Aristotle gave us many ideas, including his arguments for private property in *The Politics.* Aristotle observed that, "what is common to the greatest number has the least care bestowed upon it." Thus, Aristotle rejected Plato's ideas of the virtues of the "commons." Aristotle argued that there is virtue in things that are private. Plato had argued for a form of communal living where community property was shared, which included sharing wives and children. Aristotle rejected the whole concept, and his ideas have persevered in the western world. His idea is the basis for the property rights theorists, who argue that public ownership dilutes responsibility and rights. This argument has been incorporated into the dominant values of the American system by providing the theoretical basis for private ownership and personal property. Today, we take for granted that private ownership of personal property is normal. This is a value that is a part of our ethical principles.[16] The *Stoic school of ethics* includes the belief that virtue is found only within oneself and should be valued for its own sake. That is, virtue is a greater reward than external wealth. In the world of organizations, the legacy of the Greeks remains as a conviction that values like honesty, charity, obedience to the law, loyalty, good citizenship, courage, and the correct use of power are important.

- *Christianity.* Moral philosophy was greatly influenced by theologians. Two of the most influential were St. Augustine (354–430) and Thomas Aquinas (1226–1274). Both advocated the need for the individual to have the right relationship with God and believed that the primary purpose of life was to prepare the soul for Heaven. One should behave ethically in this world, as defined in the Bible and the ten commandments, to help one get into the next world. Theologians have emphasized the distinction between religion and philosophy. Religion requires faith and a belief in God, whereas the principles and morals associated with philosophies do not. The impact of Christian-based morals on American society has been significant.

- *The Enlightenment.* Many secular thinkers who have influenced ethics and modern society characterize this era. Philosophers like Baruch Spinoza (1634–1677), who sought to make ethical conduct rational or intellectual rather than religious-based, and Immanuel Kant (1724–1804), who sought to find universal and objective rules in logic, dominated this period. Jeremy Bentham (1748–1832) developed the basic utilitarian principle. He maintained the necessity of sacrificing smaller interests for the greater interest. John Stuart Mill (1808–1873) added to the utilitarian ideas.[17] The utilitarian principle was interpreted to mean that whatever brings the most good to the most people is good and just. This principle was also used to justify economic expansion because the majority benefited. John Locke (1632–1704) added the idea of human rights and freedoms, which included the principle that people were born free and have inalienable rights. These rights are well known to Americans; they include the right to pursue life, liberty, and happiness. The realists' schools believed that a mixture of good and evil dominates nature, and therefore the same marks human behavior. Machiavelli's (1467–1526) writings suggest that achieving an important end justifies the means, while Herbert Spencer argued the evolutionary position that what is good survives and what is bad fails. Friedrich Nietzsche (1844–1900) rejected most Christian ideas and earlier ethics. His position was that the ethical ideas of the past were recipes for timidity. Nietzsche saw a conflict between what he called a "master morality" of great individuals and a "slave morality" of the masses. He felt that the "slave morality" of the masses shackled the potential of great individuals with the rules and morals imposed by Christianity and philosophy. At the beginning of the 20th century, G. E. Moore founded a new school (called the emotivists), which advocated the idea that ethical judgments are nothing but expressions of personal preference and cannot be objectively proven as right or wrong, or shown to be contrary to divine will.

Secular values also have influenced western thought and contribute to the amoral orientation of organizations. For example, most Americans believe that government and religion should be separate. This allows individuals to practice whatever faith they choose while maintaining a neutral or benign orientation for institutions and organizations. However, it also contributes to the idea that two acceptable codes of ethical conduct exist in society.

THE LEGAL SYSTEM

The law is a codification of customs, ideas, beliefs, and ethical standards. Written law typically echoes the basic belief system of a society, but laws cannot cover all of the ethics in society. Thus, the legal system represents a partial codification of the ethics of society. Major aspects of the law generally reinforce our value systems. For example, we are taught to obey the law because we are a nation that believes in a society governed by written law. This idea, which is also a societal value, dates back to the founding period. Having a nation governed by law is more desirable than being governed by the whims of kings and dictators.

But the law also echoes many parts of our basic belief system (e.g., murder, stealing, and the like are not only unethical but also illegal and punishable by the state).

Our legal system in the United States is also a part of the principles of our democracy. John Rohr, in *Ethics for Bureaucrats,* advanced the idea that the Constitution could serve as a basis of administrative ethics. He argued that the Constitution coupled with the courts' interpretations encompass "regime values" that are binding on public administrators and public officials.[18] Thus, ethical behavior is imposed on public administration by the courts and laws. Although public administrators must abide by the law and implement it, theologians and philosophers have dealt with the idea of *higher law* for centuries.[19] That is, they have claimed that some laws may be legal but unethical because they conflict with *higher law.* For example, for many years, the law in southern states mandated racial segregation. Even the ASPA's Code of Ethics advocates the idea that public administrators should work to change laws that are counterproductive or obsolete. This does not sanction disobedience, but it does look kindly on those who strive in an appropriate manner to get "bad" laws changed.

CODES OF CONDUCT

Most professions (and even students at a university) have a written code of conduct that is supposed to be followed. Corporations and public organizations also have codes of conduct. These are usually contained in manuals that specify what is expected. Some codes of conduct are lengthy and detailed. For example, International Business Machines (IBM) has been considered a model for others to follow for many years. Public agencies have codes of conduct, but they also fall under a variety of laws passed by legislatures. For example, in most areas of government, accepting gifts is monitored or forbidden, often by law. The American Society for Public Administration (ASPA) developed a code of ethics specifically for public administrators, which is discussed later in this chapter. As people enter professions, they are further socialized by codes of conduct written specifically for particular professions. However, most professional codes of ethics echo the same values that are generally accepted in society; they are just tailored to a given profession and the types of situations faced by practitioners in areas such as medicine and law.

MAJOR ETHICAL PRINCIPLES

Public administrators have many standards that can be used when faced with ethical dilemmas. Since the subject of ethics dates back many centuries, a number of principles have been developed. This section contains a sample of some of the major models with brief descriptions.[20]

The Categorical Imperative This principle refers to a command that has no exceptions. German philosopher Immanuel Kant developed the concept, which is similar to the absolute or prescriptive ethical standards discussed earlier. Using this guideline, managers faced with making a moral choice will act in a way that they believe is right and just for any other person in a similar situation. Each action should be judged by asking: "Could this action be turned into a universal code of behavior?" Kant believed that a principle should not be adopted unless everyone else could adopt it, without inconsistency. The idea is that universal principles exist to guide our conduct when we are faced with the same situation. The idea also suggests that there are *universal principles.*

The Conventionalist Ethic This view holds that it is fine for individuals to further their own self-interest *as long as they do not break any laws.* Albert Carr's book, *Business as a Game,*[21] popularized this position, which can be summed up in the saying, "Business is business, and when in business, do as the others do or risk defeat." This position also justifies the amoral orientation discussed earlier. Another way of thinking about this concept is, "when in Rome, do as the Romans do." Decision makers are allowed to bluff and take advantage of all legal opportunities, widespread practices, and customs. It is believed that the rules and practices used in business and government are different from those that we adopt in our personal life. This is simply the way the world works. To try to apply one's personal moral standards in the world of business or government will not work. It will result in humiliation and failure because the real world does not play by our personal standards.

The Disclosure Rule This rule is often included in corporations' codes of ethics. The IBM rule states, "Ask yourself: If the full glare of examination by associates, friends, even family, were to focus on your decision, would you remain comfortable with it? If you think you would, it probably is the right decision." When faced with an ethical dilemma, managers can ask themselves how they would feel if the details of the decision (e.g., the logic, rationale, and the like) were disclosed to a wide audience.

The Doctrine of the Mean This model comes from Aristotle in *The Nicomachean Ethics.* It holds that virtue comes through moderation. In this view, right actions are located between extreme behaviors. When faced with a problem, the manager first identifies the ethical virtue involved, such as truthfulness, and then seeks the mean or moderate course of action between an excess of that virtue (boastfulness) and a deficiency of it (understatement). Likewise, according to Aristotle, modesty is the mean between shyness and shamelessness. Today, the doctrine of the mean is little recognized and is mostly of historical interest.

The Golden Rule The golden rule represents a universal idea found in every major world religion. It has been a popular guide to moral decisions for centuries. Simply put, it says, "Do unto others as you would have them do unto you." This includes not knowingly doing harm to others. Decision makers who are trying to solve a moral problem place themselves in the position of another party who will be affected by their decision and try to determine what action is most fair to that person.

The Intuition Ethic The intuition ethic says that what is good is indefinable and simply understood. People are endowed with a kind of moral sense with which they can comprehend right and wrong. The solution to moral problems lies simply in what one "feels" to be right for a given situation. In a managerial situation, this ethic would have managers rely heavily on their intuition to make the right decision.

The Market Ethic Adam Smith introduced the market ethic in his book *The Wealth of Nations* (1776). Implicit in Smith's market economy is the idea that selfish actions in the marketplace are virtuous because they contribute to the efficient operation of the economy. This efficient operation is, in turn, responsible for the higher goods of prosperity and optimum use of resources. Applied to organizational settings, decision makers may take selfish actions and be motivated by personal gain in their business dealings. They should ask whether their actions in the market further financial self-interest. If so, the actions are ethical. This principle is what public choice theorists use to illustrate how public managers, pursuing their self-interest, can create problems, such as empire building and proliferation of the bureaucracy. This is because public administrators are supposed to "maximize" the public interest rather than their own self-interest. This created a theoretical problem for economists. They concluded that public managers are no different from private sector managers and cannot maximize the public interest. Thus, applied to public organizations, the market ethic causes problems. It is hard to argue that public managers pursue the public interest while at work and then pursue their self-interest once they leave the office and become citizens and consumers. This principle is often dismissed by critics who argue that the theory is too simplistic and parsimonious, and not applicable to government organizations.

The Means-Ends Ethic (The Ends Justify the Means) This principle is associated with Machiavelli, who is most famous for writing an analysis of statesmanship and power, *The Prince*.[22] He believed that worthwhile ends justify efficient means, and that when the ends are of overriding importance or virtue, unscrupulous means may be employed to reach them. When confronted with a decision involving a potentially unethical course of action, the decision maker should ask whether some overall good (e.g., the survival of a country or organization) justifies any moral transgression. This principle, however, has been misused and misunderstood. Machiavelli did not argue that one could use this principle to justify the means needed to attain any goal. Contemporary uses in the business world have included the belief that undertaking unethical and illegal means to save a company may be acceptable. This can be illustrated in the case of DeLorean Motor Company (DMC). John DeLorean was a successful

General Motors executive who quit his job at GM and founded DMC. By the early 1980s, DMC was in financial trouble. To raise cash for his company, DeLorean got involved in drug-trafficking ventures that turned out to be a Drug Enforcement Agency (DEA) sting operation. DeLorean was arrested in 1982. His career was ruined, and his famous sports car company was shut down in 1983. However, at his trial, DeLorean argued that the government had entrapped him. The court agreed, and he was acquitted. But is saving a company a laudable enough goal to justify using unethical (or illegal) means?

The Might-Equals-Right Ethic This model defines justice as the interest of the stronger. It is represented by Nietzsche's "master-morality." What is ethical refers to what an individual has the strength and power to accomplish. When faced with a moral decision, individuals using this principle seize what advantages they are strong enough to take without respect to ordinary social conventions and laws. This ethic is often used in organized crime.

The Organization Ethic This is an old principle for resolving ethical questions with an increased application in modern times. We live in an age of large-scale organizations. Simply put, this principle states: "Be loyal to the organization." Many people have a deep sense of loyalty to the organization that transcends self-interest. People have jeopardized their health and worked excessively long hours without pay because of their loyalty to their task and/or the organization. Individuals may have similar loyalties to subordinates or supervisors. In practice, the organization ethic implies that the wills and needs of individuals should be subordinated to the greater good of the organization, whether it is a church, state, business, the military, or even a university. An individual using this ethic will ask whether the actions are consistent with organizational goals and will do what is good for the organization. In short, the needs of the organization overshadow the needs of the individual.

The Practical Imperative Immanuel Kant developed a practical, as well as categorical, imperative. The practical imperative holds that one should treat humanity *as an end and never as a means*. Simply stated, it admonishes a manager to treat people as ends in themselves, and not as means to ends or objects of manipulation. Each person, by his or her existence as a rational being, is entitled to be treated as a human, with all the respect of common decency. No person should be manipulated for the selfish ends of others. Managers can comply with this by using the "reversibility test"—that is, by asking themselves if they would be willing to change places with the people who will be affected by the contemplated policy or action.

The Principle of Equal Freedom Herbert Spencer developed this principle, which holds that a person has the right to freedom of action unless that action deprives another person of a proper freedom. Spencer believed that individual freedom was the most laudable goal in society, and he sought to protect it from infringement by others. In application, managers ask themselves whether a planned action will restrict others from actions they have a legiti-mate right to undertake. This principle is still popular today. Other versions of it are: "Your right to swing your fist ends where my nose begins," and "I am free to do whatever I please as long as it doesn't hurt someone else." Herbert Spencer used this principle to justify the accumulation of enormous wealth by robber barons during the 19th century. Today, the principle is also consistent with libertarian political views that place individual freedoms as the most laud-able goal and right of people. Examples can be found in the work of economist Milton Friedman, *Free to Choose*.[23]

The Proportionality Ethic This ethic was developed by medieval Catholic theology. It was designed to justify actions that had both good and evil conse-quences. In cases where a manager's action results in an important good effect but also will cause an inevitable bad effect, the concept of proportionality may be employed. Thomas Garrett popularized this principle in the mid-1960s.[24] He laid out five considerations to assist people when they are weighing actions and their consequences:

1. The type of good or evil involved
2. The probability of good and evil effects
3. The urgency of the situation
4. The intensity of one's influence over the effects
5. The availability of alternative means not involving bad results

The combination of these factors may provide a proportionate reason for tak-ing an action even if bad consequences will result.

The Professional Ethic In an age of specialization and education in complex skills, this ethic has gained importance and popularity. In simple form, it holds that *you should do only that which could be explained before a committee of your peers.* This ethic is applied to physicians, engineers, architects, professors, lawyers, and business executives. Professionals have strongly internalized ethical codes that guide their actions. Many of these standards are deep-seated and reflect unbending convictions. Standards of conduct exist in all major professions. For example, one expects an engineer designing an automobile or an architect designing a skyscraper to design a high-quality product. The safety of thousands of people is at stake. The same kind of expectation is held of doctors, attorneys, and virtually all of the traditional professions. In professions, this is one of the most powerful sources of ethical standards. Professions tend to socialize their members during the educational and training process (law school, medical school, and doctoral programs).

The Rights Ethic This ethic encompasses the notion that people have fun-damental rights. Rights are entitlements to something. Ethical persons recog-nize the duty to protect the rights of others. Fundamental human rights may be abridged only for compelling reasons that benefit society. These rights generally include freedoms, such as freedom of speech, the right to be honestly informed, the right to own property, and freedom of conscience. Such rights are founded in the writings of John Locke, which provide the basis for the American Bill of Rights. The decision maker evaluates actions based on whether they deprive a person of a right that must be respected. For example, a private company should not allow the operation of an unsafe machine because workers would be deprived of the right to a safe workplace. Public agencies should not put employees in situations where their health and safety are at unreasonable risk. Even in agencies where risk is a real factor, employees should be properly trained and demonstrate the necessary skills to perform the job. For example, a municipal fire department should properly train firefighters. Rights may be expanded by government action using laws. This is exactly what has occurred with government intervention into many areas of safety, such as the Occupational Safety and Health Administration (OSHA) and other regulatory agencies that are involved with public health.

The Theory of Justice Ethical theories of justice define the nature of fairness in organizations and society. Justice requires that benefits and burdens be distributed based on impartial criteria; that rewards and punishments be meted out evenhandedly; that laws, rules, and administrative procedures apply equally to all. A contemporary philosopher, John Rawls, developed a widely discussed set of principles. In *A Theory of Justice,*[25] Rawls speculates that rational persons situated behind a hypothetical veil of ignorance, and not knowing their place in society (e.g., social class position and status, economic fortune, intelligence, appearance, etc.) but knowing general facts about human society (e.g., political, sociological, economic, and psychological theory) would choose two rules to ensure fairness in any society they created. First, each person is to have an equal right to the most extensive basic liberty that is compatible with a similar liberty for others. The second rule is that social and economic inequalities are to be arranged so they are both reasonably expected to be to everyone's advantage and attached to positions and offices that are open to all. The lofty generalizations of Rawls are used in the analysis of broad social questions that pertain to business and large organizations. His book was very much in vogue during the 1970s and falls into the category of critical theory in political science and philosophy. The theory is best applied to broad social analysis.

The Utilitarian Ethic This principle remains popular. It holds that actions that bring the "greatest good for the greatest number" are ethical. Jeremy Bentham and John Stuart Mill popularized this principle. In making a decision with this principle in mind, one must determine whether the harm in an action is outweighed by the good that is produced. If the action maximizes benefit, then it is the optimum course to take among alternatives that provide less benefit. Individuals and decision makers should try to maximize pleasure and reduce pain, not only for themselves but also for every party affected by their decisions. This principle is popular and widely used. Cost-benefit and risk-benefit studies embody the spirit of this principle.

Considering the many principles that can be used to guide decisions, which does a manager use? Unfortunately, there is no agreement on which of these (and other) principles is the best approach. Some of the principles are not very applicable to public agencies, and the use of some requires a leap of faith. Some of the ethical guidelines are inappropriate for certain individuals. For example, a highly religious person might have problems adhering to the market ethic, which justifies selfish actions. Many of the ideas overlap with each other. But all offer some basis and justification for their use. Also, these principles do not completely define an ethical code of conduct, but they do provide a basis on which to build a professional code for various types of organizations and for individuals. Ethical principles are important because they allow us to *justify* our actions and decisions with some rationale that is consistent with our ethical standards and our consciences. Because ethical decisions can be grounded in many different principles, no one can prescribe which is the best principle to use in public administration or in our personal lives. Determining to use these or some other principles is an individual choice.

INDIVIDUAL ETHICS
AND ORGANIZATIONS:
WHERE VALUES CAN COLLIDE

It is clear that our society has a conflict regarding two sets of ethics: one for organizations, and one for individuals. Chester Barnard recognized many years ago that the values of the individual and the authority of the organization can conflict.[26] Barnard was dealing with organizational communication and authority, but values and ethics are important factors. It is not hard to imagine how such conflicts can occur. Some people are highly religious, and some of the activities of an agency or a business might conflict with their religious convictions. For example, performing sanitation inspections at abortion clinics might be troublesome for a person whose religion teaches that abortion is wrong. If such a person were a health inspection officer, ethics would be involved in forcing him or her to perform inspections at abortion clinics for several reasons. First, such inspectors might place their personal code of ethics ahead of professional ethics in conducting these inspections. These inspectors also might be too harsh and impose a higher standard on abortion clinics than that used at other health care facilities because of their personal feelings. This would be wrong and unfair. At the same time, it might be problematic for a supervisor to have people who are opposed to abortion conducting sanitation inspections of abortion facilities. It would probably be more prudent to have them inspect hospitals, doctors' offices, and dental offices rather than abortion clinics. This would end the whole ethical dilemma for everyone.

Barnard developed a concept called the "zone of indifference" to illustrate the demands and orders that an employee will accept or reject. This model also illustrates the relationship between personal values and organizational values. Figure 9.2 contains a diagram of the model. In the "zone of indifference," employees have no problem accepting the tasks assigned to them as being legitimate. For example, if a professor asks a student teaching assistant to grade examinations, the teaching assistant is likely to comply without giving the request much thought. This type of request meets all the criteria described by Barnard. Four conditions must be met before employees will comply with employer demands:[27]

- The person must understand the communication.
- At the time of the decision, the person must believe that what is to be done is consistent with the purpose of the organization.
- At the time of the decision, the person must believe that what is to be done is compatible with his or her personal interests. (Note that this involves values and ethics. *If the request goes beyond the zone of indifference into the person's zone of personal values, problems will arise because the values of the organization or supervisor will conflict with the individual's personal values.*)
- The person must be mentally and physically able to comply with the request in the communication.

Asking a teaching assistant to grade examinations or to administer an examination is consistent with the activities that are associated with the job and organization. But if the professor asks a teaching assistant to come to his or her house and wash the family car, this request would be inconsistent with the purpose of the university and would be unethical. Such a request would break through the zone of indifference into the student's zone of personal values. As long as the requests remain in the zone of indifference, most of us will comply because there is no conflict between the authority of the supervisor, the organizational values, and our personal value system or ethics.

WHAT DOES IT MEAN TO BE
AN ETHICAL ADMINISTRATOR?
ASPA'S CODE OF ETHICS

Discussions about ethics and codes of conduct, guiding principles, and what it means to be "moral" have puzzled philosophers and theologians for centuries. But the important question for public administration is: What does it mean to be an ethical administrator? Clearly, this brief overview of principles, values, and culture illustrates that developing a code of ethical conduct is difficult because there are plenty of standards to use. The American Society for Public Administration (ASPA) is the main professional association for the discipline and practice of public administration. The code of conduct shown in Box 9.3 represents the work of the leading professionals in public management. The

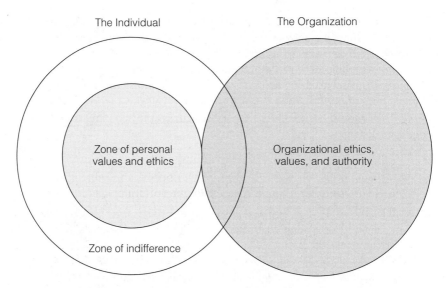

The Individual   The Organization

Zone of personal values and ethics

Organizational ethics, values, and authority

Zone of indifference

FIGURE 9.2 The Zone of Indifference

SOURCE: The "Zone of Indifference" was developed by Chester Barnard, *The Functions of the Executive* (Cambridge, MA: Harvard University Press, 1968). The diagram is adapted from David Schumann and Dick Olufs, III, *Public Administration in the United States,* 2nd ed. (Lexington, MA: D. C. Heath, 1993), p. 188.

ASPA Code of Ethics contains values that the profession believes are important if one is to be an ethical administrator. ASPA's code is not much different from other professional codes. Most ethical codes generally say the same thing: (1) Do not lie, cheat, steal, or break laws; (2) be nice, and be fair; and (3) make sure that you uphold the professional standards of your profession. In the case of ASPA, that also means to remember that you are to serve the *public interest.*[28]

ASPA's code contains five important sections. *Serve the Public Interest:* The first section of the code reminds us that the first duty of public administrators is to serve the public interest, which includes opposing discrimination, supporting public disclosure of information (the public's right to know the public's business), maintaining a service-oriented posture (helping citizens), including citizen participation in policy decision making, and being responsive to citizens. *Respect the Constitution and the Law:* The second section reminds us that public administration is rooted in public law and that public administrators must maintain respect for the Constitution and public law. *Demonstrate Personal Integrity:* This section emphasizes the need to maintain high standards to help build trust and confidence in public service. Personal integrity involves maintaining the high standards of personal conduct, as indicated in the specifics of the ASPA's code. *Promote Ethical Organizations:* This section advocates the need to strengthen the capabilities of public organizations to apply a variety of values that include ethics and accountability. *Strive for Professional Excellence:* The last section promotes the need to develop and maintain a high sense of professionalism in public service. By and large, the ASPA Code of Ethics exists to remind public administrators of their responsibility to serve the public while maintain-

BOX 9.3   ASPA's Code of Ethics

I. Serve the Public Interest
Serve the public, beyond serving oneself. ASPA members are committed to:

1. Exercise discretionary authority to promote the public interest.
2. Oppose all forms of discrimination and harassment, and promote affirmative action.
3. Recognize and support the public's right to know the public's business.
4. Involve citizens in policy decision making.
5. Exercise compassion, benevolence, fairness, and optimism.
6. Respond to the public in ways that are complete, clear, and easy to understand.
7. Assist citizens in their dealings with government.
8. Be prepared to make decisions that may not be popular.

II. Respect the Constitution and the Law
Respect, support, and study government constitutions and laws that define responsibilities of public agencies, employees, and all citizens. ASPA members are committed to:

1. Understand and apply legislation and regulations relevant to their professional role.
2. Work to improve and change laws and policies that are counterproductive or obsolete.
3. Eliminate unlawful discrimination.
4. Prevent all forms of mismanagement of public funds by establishing and maintaining strong fiscal and management controls, and by supporting audits and investigative activities.
5. Respect and protect privileged information.
6. Encourage and facilitate legitimate dissent activities in government and protect the whistleblowing rights of public employees.
7. Promote constitutional principles of equality, fairness, representativeness, responsiveness and due process in protecting citizens' rights.

III. Demonstrate Personal Integrity
Demonstrate the highest standards in all activities to inspire public confidence and trust in public service. ASPA members are committed to:

1. Maintain truthfulness and honesty and to not compromise them for advancement, honor, or personal gain.
2. Ensure that others receive credit for their work and contributions.
3. Zealously guard against conflict of interest or its appearance (e.g., nepotism, improper outside employment, misuse of public resources, or the acceptance of gifts).
4. Respect superiors, subordinates, colleagues, and the public.
5. Take responsibility for their own errors.
6. Conduct official acts without partisanship.

IV. Promote Ethical Organizations
Strengthen organizational capabilities to apply ethics, efficiency, and effectiveness in serving the public. ASPA members are committed to:

1. Enhance organizational capacity for open communication, creativity, and dedication.
2. Subordinate institutional loyalties to the public good.
3. Establish procedures that promote ethical behavior and hold individuals and organizations accountable for their conduct.
4. Provide organization members with an administrative means for dissent, assurance of due process, and safeguards against reprisal.
5. Promote merit principles that protect against arbitrary and capricious actions.

(continued)

BOX 9.3 *continued*

6. Promote organizational accountability through appropriate controls and procedures.
7. Encourage organizations to adopt, distribute, and periodically review a code of ethics as a living document.

V. Strive for Professional Excellence
Strengthen individual capabilities and encourage the professional development of others. ASPA members are committed to:

1. Provide support and encouragement to upgrade competence.
2. Accept as a personal duty the responsibility to keep up-to-date on emerging issues and potential problems.
3. Encourage others, throughout their careers, to participate in professional activities and associations.
4. Allocate time to meet with students and provide a bridge between classroom studies and the realities of public service.

SOURCE: American Society for Public Administration. ASPA's Code of Ethics usually appears on the back cover of *Public Administration Review,* the leading professional journal for the discipline and the practice of public administration. ASPA's Code of Ethics can also be found on their Web site at http://www.aspanet.org.

---

ing respect for the law and constantly promoting a strong sense of excellence in everything that public administrators do. Professionals need to have a sense of pride in and respect for their work. Public service is a high calling because the nature of the activities performed is intended to help make a better society possible. The ASPA code essentially says all of the things that one would expect to hear said about public service values and ideals.

Being an ethical public administrator, however, probably takes more than simply following the guidelines developed by the ASPA or any other code aimed at describing the responsibilities of public service.[29] In fact, some may not agree with every point included in the code; some of the points are very reflective of the times (these are often referred to as "regime values"). The code does not have the power of law; it is only intended to serve as a guideline to help promote excellence and professionalism in public service. This sort of guidance is needed in all professions. Being an ethical manager may be the same as being a *good* public manager (if being ethical is considered to be one of the qualities, along with managerial skills, needed to be defined as *good*). This requires performing one's duty, maintaining consistent and fair standards, promoting excellence, setting and promoting high standards, managing by example, following the law, implementing the law properly, and maintaining a proper sense of perspective about fulfilling the responsibilities of being a public manager.

Management implies that one has position, power, and authority over others, and this position must be used wisely; it should never be abused. Managers are responsible for ensuring that both the internal work environment and external relations with the public are professional. But ethics involve both personal and professional moral standards. Sometimes, whether we like to admit it or not, these standards are inconsistent, confusing, and conflicting.[30] Public administrators are people, not machines. They bring with them to public service a set of life experiences and values that affects the way they deal with ethical issues and choices.[31] A national survey of public administrators found that more than three-quarters of the respondents agreed that moral standards are ultimately the responsibility of the individual, but that organizations define and control the situations in which decisions are made.[32] This suggests that although society places an emphasis on personal conscience, organizations are major agencies of social control. A manager's personal ethics are often secondary to organizational ethics and standards. Public managers must work in an environment where ethical conduct consists of a combination of ethics and values imposed by the organization coupled with their personal values. This is the reality of organizational life. The great task involves balancing the ethics imposed by organizations and law that may conflict with personal ethical standards.

ETHICS AND THE PUBLIC INTEREST

One of the most enduring problems in public administration is the concept of the *public interest*.[33] The core of what government does is presumed to be serving the public interest, and this concept has ethical implications. It is the first point included in ASPA's Code of Ethics, which makes it very clear that one of the ethical requirements of public administrators is to serve the public interest. Yet, even after centuries of debate, we still have trouble defining this critical concept. Pendleton Herring once argued that the public interest is as important to public administration as the concept of due process is to law.[34] Public administrators, public officials, and politicians often speak about how their actions serve the public interest, but when pressed for a definition, they offer multiple definitions, and the waters become murky. The corporate world of private business does not have a comparable problem defining its purpose, since the pursuit of profit is very clear.

The public interest means different things to different people. Public interest is a fuzzy concept that can be defined in a number ways. Recall that public choice theory rejected the idea that public administrators can maximize the public's interest rather than their own self-interest. Are public choice theorists correct? Can we put aside our personal ambitions and self-interest and look after the public's interest? Public choice theorists say that we cannot. But exactly what is the *public interest?* It would help if we had a clear definition of the term. Scholars and philosophers have debated the meaning of *public interest* for centuries, and no clear consensus has ever been established, only categories of definitions. The public interest can be synonymous with majoritarian politics (whatever the majority of people want is viewed as the public interest). It can take on a utilitarian definition, meaning whatever brings the most good to the most people. The public interest also can refer to whatever is in the *best interest* of the people or the state; that is, decisions and actions sometimes have to be taken that are in the *best interest* of citizens, even if citizens do not agree with them at the time. Examples include public health and safety matters that people and groups may oppose because they do not understand the dangers of certain types of pollution or because the actions of government will harm their vested interests in some type of industry. In addition, the public interest can refer to the many interests that exist in society being combined together to form one (i.e., the public interest). In this view, there exists an amalgamation of interests that often are conflicting, but at some point among these many interests, there is a compromise area or "middle ground" that might represent the public interest.

Some argue that the public interest is a vacuous concept that has no real meaning whatsoever. In this vein of thought, the concept of a public interest is merely political dogma used by politicians. Public interest also can refer to an *ideal,* meaning the greatest good that can be achieved for society through politics—something that is not achievable but serves as an aspiration or goal in trying to improve the quality of life in society. And to many, the concept simply means taking some action that serves some public good (meaning something that brings about something desirable for society or the community). The definition of *public interest* is a "slippery" concept that cannot be settled here.[35]

In the case of public administration, the public interest could be defined as enforcing and advocating regime values for the good of society. Regime values are defined in the political process, and public administrators are bound to implement and follow the law. For example, a regime value of the contemporary era is affirmative action. Public administrators may agree or disagree with this idea, but they are bound to uphold the law, and currently, affirmative action is federal law. Recall that the first section of ASPA's Code of Ethics requires public administrators to "serve the public interest." Although defining this concept is difficult, the public interest probably refers to action that serves some greater public good. For example, promoting public education for everyone is desirable and benefits society as a whole. Most people agree that education is good and beneficial, but opinions are more diverse on most other issues. Defining what "a greater public good" means is rather subjective. The concept of the public interest affects ethics if one considers serving the public interest to be an ethical value. To take actions that are not in the public interest would be, by definition, unethical.

Public administrators are faced with a dilemma. Ethics come in many forms, and the standards used in public service are often vague and contradictory. Administrators are left with a variety of conflicting standards. They must obey and implement the law that is mandated by the political process, even though laws are often vague and contradictory. They must deal with the value of neutrality in organizational hierarchies. Neutrality implies that public administrators can be neutral—that is, that they can use bureaucratic discretion without personal responsibility, since mandates have come from legislative action. They are only implementing what was ordered from higher authorities in the political process. They are asked to serve the public interest, yet government cannot articulate precisely what the public interest means. At the same time, every public administrator has his or her own set of personal ethics that may conflict with organizational ethics. Organizations vary between the amoral and moral unity orientations, and every person has a personal moral code that is developed while growing up that affects his or her ethical standards. These conflicting and confusing standards do not add clarity to what it means to be an ethical public administrator.

Ultimately, it is left to individual public administrators to synthesize the ethical puzzle and do the best they can at being ethical. Life comes in shades of gray; it is not black and white. The world of public administration, just like the rest of the social world, also comes in shades of gray. Morality is often painted in black and white, but it, too, comes in shades of grey. There are exceptions, mitigating circumstances, and the like that affect moral reasoning when people face ethical choices. Administrators must deal with ethical situations on a regular basis. It is ultimately the job of public administrators to implement public law and policy whether or not they agree with it. People in organizations have jobs and tasks to perform, whether these involve implementing public policy in a governmental agency or working at a bank. A value that has been taught for a long time is that when we get to work we are supposed to do our jobs and leave our personal problems and lives outside the workplace. This is virtually impossible to accomplish; personal problems often affect our performance on the job in negative or positive ways. Just as it is impossible to separate our personal lives from our jobs, neither can we leave personal values and ethics at home. Our personal ethics influence how we react and handle ethical issues in the public agencies. Thus, public administration has limitations with respect to ethics and morality. Granted, penalties and punishments can be imposed for misconduct, but values are formed long before people enter public service. Ultimately, the responsibility to be "ethical" resides in the individual.

SUMMARY

This chapter has provided a general overview of how ethics affect public administration and society. High standards of ethical conduct are expected in public organizations and in public service. Laws dictate much of the ethical guidelines in public agencies; public agencies are obligated to follow the law. Sometimes, we expect a higher standard from public officials than from private citizens.

Ethics are derived from values, and American society has long had a tension between competition, materialism, and success, and the conflicting morals that are usually based in religion. Values are formed as we grow up. Our values are influenced by many sources, such as families, friends, religion, and our educational experience. There are two major orientations about ethics and organizations. The idea that organizations must be amoral holds that the realities of the world require that a different, more permissive set of ethics be used. The theory of moral unity holds that only one code of ethics is needed and that the same code we use in our personal lives should be the standard used in organizations. In reality, personal ethics and organizational ethics can conflict. The secular nature of our public (and economic) institutions contributes to the existence of two sets of ethical codes for most Americans. The great task lies in trying to sort out the differences in order to bring these two ethical standards closer together.

Over the centuries, many principles have been developed to help us with ethical decisions. Philosophers and theologians have provided a variety of principles, ranging from absolute rules of moral conduct that have no exceptions to subjective ethics that are highly individualized. Professions also have developed codes of ethics that can be used as guidelines. But applying a set of professional codes is difficult because morality is defined for the individual from sources other than a professional code of ethics. Personalities, backgrounds, and personal convictions vary. Being an ethical administrator entails applying a variety of conflicting and subjective concepts. When dealing with ethical choices related to their jobs, public administrators must sort through the maze of ethics that learned while growing up and through their additional socialization into the world of public service, and do the best they can in dealing with ethics imposed by the legal system, society, and the profession. Ultimately, the use of good judgment depends largely on the quality of character of the individual public administrator. The professionalism that is now associated with the practice of public administration helps attract qualified and dedicated people into public service who possess the capacity to deal with the ethical dilemmas found in public agencies, public policy, and the political arena. The great task lies in trying to maintain one's personal standard of ethics while working within the often conflicting realities of government and business, which play by a different set of rules.

CONCLUDING COMMENTS

This book has introduced you to a variety of the subject areas and issues involved in the world of public administration. Public agencies are responsible for administering many important tasks that are necessary in modern society, including implementing public policy and regulating important activities. Public administration exists in the political arena along with the other institutions of government. They help shape society, and they are influenced by society. This brief journey has included most of the major areas associated with public administration: the environment in which public administration exists, the history of the discipline, the dynamics of bureaucratic structure, organizational theory and behavior, the complexities of personnel systems, public budgeting, public policy, and ethics. Many other issues have been interwoven in our discussion of each of these areas, such as ways to improve government performance. Government does not lend itself to any measure of performance comparable to profit-and-loss statements found in business. Moreover, government is a monopoly. Competition in the same sense as it exists in the marketplace is absent. This poses many challenges to managers in making sure that public agencies perform their work effectively.

The quality of public agencies is reflected in the quality of the people who serve in public service. The *static element* of organizations is found in the structure or framework. People provide the *dynamic element,* and people are what make public agencies work. Granted, public administration is a complex and often conflicting environment, but this is the nature of democracy, which is a system that irons out compromises between competing interests. Laws dictate much of what public administration does, but the system allows, in many cases, bureaucratic discretion to make laws work better. The competing goals in public agencies, such as efficiency, effectiveness, and equity, must be balanced. Public administration is a necessary part of our society that helps to build a better society for all of us.

NOTES

1. Laurence Urdang, Ed., *The Oxford Desk Dictionary: American Edition* (New York: Oxford University Press, 1995).

2. Dennis F. Thompson, "The Possibility of Administrative Ethics," *Public Administration Review 45* (September/October 1985), pp. 555–561.

3. See Peter Madsen and Jay Shafritz, Eds., *Essentials of Government Ethics* (New York: Meridian, 1992). Section 4 contains a variety of articles about corruption in government.

4. Peter Madsen and Jay Shafritz, Eds., *Essentials of Government Ethics,* p. 1. Also see Dennis Thompson, *Political Ethics and Public Office* (Cambridge, MA: Harvard University Press, 1987).

5. The phases begin at birth as children are imprinted with values from their parents and other sources. The first phase is called *imprint* because as very young children we "take in" values rather than interpret or react to them. This phase is important because the basic personality is formed early in life. The modeling phase occurs when we begin to imitate or *model* ourselves after our heroes, such as movie stars, celebrities, sports stars, and so on. In the final phase, called *socialization* in Figure 9.1, young people truly react to the inputs in a different way; they accept, reject, rebel, and synthesize the inputs. It is believed that by the time we reach our early twenties, the gut-level values are formed, and we will continue to turn to these values for the rest of our lives. This model relies heavily on behavioral theory and the influence of environmental factors. It is generally accepted that the environment

greatly shapes our belief system and therefore our values. In short, this process teaches us about society, about norms, and about life.

6. The conscience is very important for ethical conduct because it serves as an internal force of parental authority with the power to hand out psychological rewards and punishments. Also, research suggests that our ability to use moral reasoning develops in stages that vary among individuals. Lawrence Kohlberg studied 75 American boys and found that our moral reasoning ability is largely acquired during the first 20 years of life. Kohlberg believed that there are six sequential stages of moral development. The six stages begin with the child being completely reliant on external rules and standards and progress to states in which the person increasingly relies on internal controls. The stages are: (1) avoidance of breaking rules in order to avoid punishment; (2) obedience to ethical standards to satisfy self-centered needs and to get reciprocity from others; (3) subordination of self-interest to group interests to please others and gain their approval; (4) respect for the law and authority as necessary to preserve the social order; (5) flexible interpretation of legal authority as balanced with the rights of individuals; and (6) principled reason with ethical concepts of personal choices. In the study, most individuals reached four of the stages by adulthood, but only a few progressed to the sixth phase. If this theory is correct, then managers respond differently to moral decisions based on their level of moral development. See Lawrence Kohlberg,

Moral Stages: A Current Formulation and a Response to Critics (New York: Karger, 1983). Also see Lawrence Kohlberg, *The Philosophy of Moral Development: Moral Stages and the Idea of Justice* (San Francisco: Harper & Row, 1981).

7. For example, the most senior generation in our society grew up during the Great Depression and World War II, which contributed to some of the unique characteristics associated with that generation. This generation remembers what it was like to live during the worst of economic times and what it was like to be involved in a global war. The changes this generation experienced changed American society forever because many of the operating values were changed by the experiences of the era. Men (and many women) were catapulted across the globe to fight the war. They were sent from the cornfields of Iowa and rural mountains of North Carolina to places like London, Paris, and Italy, and they experienced things that they otherwise would never have experienced, both good and bad. Women went to work, and the majority of women never really returned home to be housewives. "Rosie the Riveter" (the symbol of American women working in factories during the war) joined the workforce along with millions of other American women. After World War II, America became a mobile society and experienced a remarkable economic boom. This generation was exposed to events that altered their value systems and changed society. Their children, the baby boomers, grew up during the Cold War with the Soviet Union, the Vietnam War, Watergate, the sexual revolution, television, rock music, the civil rights movement, and civil unrest on college campuses and in society. They have been called the rejectionist generation because they rebelled against traditional values of the older generation on a scale unheard of up until that time. They also grew up with more affluence and tended to be from the suburbs. Society was more dynamic and mobile. Technology was rapidly changing, which also altered their values. Like their parents, they were affected by the characteristics of the times in which they were raised, which altered many of the operational values in society. The same is true for every generation.

8. The value-programming model was derived from Morris E. Massey, *People Puzzle: Understanding Yourself and Others* (Englewood Cliffs, NJ: Prentice-Hall, 1980). The three phases are distinct stages. The imprint period is the very early years when the child is looking out at the world and being bombarded by all types of values. By the age of 10 or 12, children synthesize the inputs and begin to model their heroes. This is considered to be perfectly normal. The last phase is when young people begin to learn about becoming young adults. They are exposed to work and different types of relationships. Their world continues to expand, and by the time they reach their early twenties, they have formed their basic set of values. These values will continue to modified and expanded for several more years, but the basic set is in place, and they will use these values to make decisions about what is right and wrong for the rest of their lives.

9. Gabriel Almond, *The American People and Foreign Policy* (New York: Praeger, 1960), pp. 48–53.

10. Gabriel Almond's points are illustrated in the example of young urban professionals (yuppies), although they are not the first generation to seek material success. This group of baby boomers wants successful jobs and success in the organizations where they work. Among their desires is to own condominiums or homes with the right furniture, to have a BMW in the driveway, to own the latest stereo equipment and hot tubs, and to indulge in whatever is faddish at the time, such as health clubs, country clubs, hiking, and the right clothes. Moreover, they want instant gratification and can have the material goods they want, thanks to credit cards, loans, and professional jobs that pay incomes large enough to pay the bills. (Yuppies are used here just to illustrate a point, and the description is somewhat facetious.) At the same time, this group is tempered to some degree by religious moral codes that run completely counter to the idea of worldly, material goods. These are ignored as much as possible,

though they may cause guilt. At a minimum, this trend is a contradiction in our society. The quest for material goods and success has been a part of the American social landscape for several generations, and the amount of material wealth one acquires says something about people and their place in the system of social stratification. Failure is not accepted very well in our society. This was Almond's point. Families and individuals are highly competitive throughout the social stratification system. Of course, this is a very broad generalization that does not apply to every individual, and some will disagree that this is an accurate characterization of American society. It can be argued that America is a very broad and diverse nation and that the pursuit of material success is not the guiding virtue. But for several generations, the American dream has been defined as the pursuit of the "country club life." This suggests that a person works hard and retires to an easier life.

11. George Steiner and John Steiner, *Business, Government, and Society: A Managerial Perspective,* pp. 322–324.

12. Donald Klingner, *Public Administration: A Managerial Approach* (Boston: Houghton Mifflin, 1983), p. 314.

13. Some believe that genetics affects our values. Sociobiology provides a basis for arguing that evolutionary forces operating to promote the survival of groups have an important influence on the development of traits such as cooperation, mercy, altruism, and other traits such as competitiveness. The theory is based on the idea that gene frequency in populations evolve when the average fitness of all individuals within groups displaying a trait is greater than the average fitness of all individuals in otherwise comparable groups. This view is controversial and leads to arguments over the influence of heredity versus environment on human behavior.

14. Aristotle, *Politics,* translated by Benjamin Jowett (London: Oxford University Press, 1931), Book II, p. 57.

15. In the contemporary era, the term *tragedy of the commons* is associated with Garrett Hardin's article "The Tragedy of the Commons," *Science 162* (1968), pp. 1243–1248. Environmentalists use the

concept to justify government regulation of pollution and land use. The contemporary definition involves the undesired result of exploitation of others: a phenomenon in which individuals attempt to exploit the resources of a group, but only harm themselves because everyone adopts the same strategy and resources are uniformly depleted. The theory of the tragedy of the commons states that when a resource is collectively owned by a group of people, each will exploit the resource, overuse it, and thus ultimately destroy it. In other words, everyone acts as a free rider, ignoring the group's collective interests in favor of one's own. The concept dates back to Aristotle, but the term *tragedy of the commons* is credited to William Forster Lloyd (1794–1852), a professor at Oxford. He noticed that in a common pasture owned by all of the villagers, each villager overgrazed the pasture, ruining it for everyone. The original citation is William Forster Lloyd, *Two Lectures on the Checks to Population* (Oxford: Oxford University Press, 1833).

16. Environmental groups coupled private property rights with the "tragedy of the commons" theme and argued that private property has negative spillover effects, such as pollution, that damage society and, therefore, both public and private property should be regulated.

17. Utilitarianism is also included in the work of theologian William Paley. Paley combined utilitarianism with individualistic hedonism and theological authoritarianism. He defined virtue as doing good for mankind, in obedience to the will of God, and for the sake of everlasting happiness.

18. John Rohr, *Ethics for Bureaucrats* (New York: Marcel Dekker, 1978). This idea was expanded upon by David Rosenbloom in "The Constitution as a Basis for Public Administration Ethics," in Peter Madsen and Jay Shafritz, Eds., *Essentials of Government Ethics* (New York: Oxford University Press, 1992), pp. 48–64.

19. For an excellent discussion of the concept of higher law as it relates to the U.S. Constitution, see Edward Samuel Corwin, *The "Higher Law" Background of American Constitutional Law* (Ithaca, NY:

Cornell University Press, 1929). Corwin opposed the idea of applying higher law to the Constitution.

20. This section relies heavily on the work of George Steiner and John Steiner, *Business, Government, and Society: A Managerial Perspective,* Chapter 12. The authors go into much greater detail than what is provided here, and their focus is on how these principles apply to business managers.

21. Albert Carr, *Business as a Game* (New York: New American Library, 1969).

22. Niccolo Machiavelli, *The Prince,* translated by Luigi Ricci with an introduction by Christian Gauss (New York: Mentor Books, 1980).

23. Milton Friedman and Rose Friedman, *Free to Choose: A Personal Statement* (New York: Avon Books, 1979).

24. Thomas Garrett, *Business Ethics* (New York: Appleton-Century-Crofts, 1966).

25. John Rawls, *A Theory of Justice* (Cambridge, MA: Harvard University Press, 1971).

26. Chester Barnard, *The Functions of the Executive* (Cambridge, MA: Harvard University Press, 1939).

27. Cited in David Schumann and Dick Olufs, III, *Public Administration in the United States,* 2nd ed. (Lexington, MA: D. C. Heath, 1993), p. 117.

28. David Shuman and Dick Olufs, III, *Public Administration in the United States,* p. 72.

29. Other ethical codes for public service also exist, such as the International City/County Association's Code of Ethics.

30. See John Rohr, "The Problem of Professional Ethics," *The Bureaucrat* (Summer 1982), pp. 47–50.

31. David Shuman and Dick Olufs, III, *Public Administration in the United States,* p. 72.

32. James Bowman, "Ethics in Government: A National Survey of Public Administrators," *Public Administration Review 50* (May/June 1990), pp. 345–353. This is an excellent article that contains a wealth of information about how public administrators view ethics and morals in their agencies. For example, most of the respondents (90 percent) did not feel that morality in government was lower than in the business world. They did not feel that business sets the moral standards for public life. The survey involved a random sample of 750 public administrators who were members of ASPA.

33. Anthony Downs, "The Public Interest: Its Meaning in a Democracy," *Social Research 29* (Spring 1962), pp. 1–36.

34. Pendleton Herring, *Public Administration and the Public Interest* (New York: McGraw-Hill, 1936).

35. Discussions about the public interest go well beyond the purpose of this book. Each definition used has its own set of inherent problems. For example, the idea that whatever the majority wants is the public interest (which comes from Rousseau) does nothing to protect minority rights. The idea that the public interest refers to whatever is in the best interest of the people or society can clash with democratic principles. If experts in the bureaucracy make the decisions, citizens' freedoms may be compromised. This problematic debate is discussed in Chapter 7 (expertise versus democracy).

Index